Crusades
Volume 6, 2007

Crusades

Edited by
Benjamin Z. Kedar and Jonathan S.C. Riley-Smith
with Jonathan Phillips

Crusades is published annually for the Society for the Study of the Crusades and the Latin East by Ashgate. A statement of the aims of the Society and details of membership can be found following the Bulletin at the end of the volume.

Manuscripts should be sent to either of the Editors in accordance with the guidelines for submission of papers on p. 305.

Subscriptions: Crusades (ISSN 1476–5276) is published annually.

Subscriptions are available on an annual basis and are £65 for institutions and non-members, and £22 for members of the Society. Prices include postage by surface mail. Enquiries concerning members' subscriptions should be addressed to the Treasurer, Professor James D. Ryan (see p. 236). All orders and enquiries should be addressed to: Subscription Department, Ashgate Publishing Ltd, Gower House, Croft Road, Aldershot, Hants GU11 3HR, U.K.; tel.: +44 (0)1252 331551; fax: +44 (0) 1252 344405; email: journals@ashgatepublishing.com

Requests for Permissions and Copying: requests should be addressed to the Publishers: Permissions Department, Ashgate Publishing Ltd, Gower House, Croft Road, Aldershot, Hants GU11 3HR, U.K.; tel.: +44 (0)1252 331551; fax: +44 (0)1252 344405; email: journals@ashgatepublishing.com. The journal is also registered in the U.S.A. with the Copyright Clearance Center, 222 Rosewood Drive, Danvers MA 01923, U.S.A.; tel.: +1 (978) 750 8400; fax: +1 (978) 750 4470; email: rreader@copyright.com and in the U.K. with the Copyright Licensing Agency, 90 Tottenham Court Road, London, W1P 9HE; tel.: +44 (0)207 436 5931; fax: +44 (0)207 631 5500.

Crusades

Volume 6, 2007

Published by ASHGATE *for the*
Society for the Study of the Crusades
and the Latin East

Published by
Ashgate Publishing Limited
Gower House
Croft Road
Aldershot
Hampshire GU11 3HR
Great Britain

Ashgate Publishing Company
Suite 420
101 Cherry Street
Burlington, VT 05401–4405
USA

Ashgate website: http://www.ashgate.com

ISBN: 978-0-7546-6070-5

ISSN 1476–5276

Typeset by N²productions

Printed in Great Britain by MPG Books Ltd, Bodmin, Cornwall.

CONTENTS

Abbreviations   ix

ARTICLES

Motivating Listeners in the *Kitab al-Jihad* of ʿAli ibn Tahir al-Sulami
   (d. 1106)   1
   Niall Christie

"There Is None Like You Among the Mute": The Theology of *Ein
   Kamokha Ba-Illemim* in Context, with a New Edition and Translation   15
   Laura Lieber

Rescuing Syria from the Infidels: The Contribution of Ibn ʿAsakir of
   Damascus to the *Jihad* Campaign of Sultan Nur al-Din   37
   Suleiman A. Mourad and *James E. Lindsay*

Infidel Dogs: Hunting Crusaders with Usama ibn Munqidh   57
   Paul M. Cobb

The French Translation of William of Tyre's *Historia*: the Manuscript
   Tradition   69
   Peter Edbury

Muslim Chroniclers and the Fourth Crusade   107
   Taef El-Azhari

Paris Masters and the Justification of the Albigensian Crusade   117
   Jessalynn Bird

Genuas angebliche Allianz mit den Kreuzfahrerstaaten von 1233   157
   Hans Eberhard Mayer

The Social Context of Gravestones: Two Portraits   167
   Anna-Maria Kasdagli and Yanna Katsou

The articles by Christie, Lieber, Mourad and Lindsay, Cobb and Bird are based upon papers given at the conference: *Crusading and Against Whom? Holy Violence in the Middle Ages*, held at Middlebury College, Vermont in October 2004.

REVIEWS

Adrian J. Boas, *Archaeology of the Military Orders. A Survey of the
Urban Centres, Rural Settlements and Castles of the Military Orders
in the Latin East (c. 1120–1291)* (John Rosser)   181
Damien Carraz, *L'Ordre du Temple dans la basse valée du Rhône
(1124–1312). Ordres militaires, croisades et société méridionales*
(Jochen G. Schenk)   183
Nicole Chareyron, *Pilgrims to Jerusalem in the Middle Ages*, trans.
W. Donald Wilson (Susan B. Edgington)   185
Eastward Bound: Travel and Travellers, 1050–1550, ed. Rosamund Allen
(Susan B. Edgington)   185
*La Croisade Albigeoise. Actes du Colloque du Centre d'Études Cathares,
Carcassonne, 4, 5 et 6 octobre 2002*, ed. Michel Roquebert (Jessalynn
Bird)   188
Erica Cruikshank Dodd, *Medieval Painting in the Lebanon* (Lucy-Anne
Hunt)   191
Crusading in the Fifteenth Century. Message and Impact, ed. Norman
Housley (Christoph T. Maier)   193
Alain Demurger, *Les Templiers. Une chevalerie chrétienne au moyen âge*
(William Chester Jordan)   195
The Gesta Tancredi *of Ralph of Caen: A History of the Normans on the
First Crusade*, trans. with an introduction by Bernard S. Bachrach and
David S. Bachrach (Susan B. Edgington)   197
Henricus Lettus, *The Chronicle of Henry of Livonia*, trans. with new
introduction by James A. Brundage (Alan V. Murray)   199
The Livonian Rhymed Chronicle, trans. Jerry C. Smith and William L.
Urban (Alan V. Murray)   199
*Identités croisées en un milieu méditerranéen. Le case de Chypre
(Antiquité – Moyen Âge)*, ed. Sabine Fourrier and Gilles Grivaud
(Peter Edbury)   202
Michael Lower, *The Barons' Crusade. A Call to Arms and Its
Consequences* (Deborah Gerish)   203
Anthony Luttrell, *The Town of Rhodes: 1306–1356* (Chris Schabel)   205
Λεόντιου Μαχαιρά *Χρονικό της Κύπρου*, Παράλληλη διπλωματική
έκδοση των χειρογράφων. [Leontios Machairas, *The Chronicle of
Cyprus, Parallel Diplomatic Edition of the Manuscripts*], ed. and
with introduction by Michael Pieres and Angel Nikolaou-Konnari
(Aphrodite Papayianni)   207
Klaus Militzer, *Die Geschichte des Deutschen Ordens* (Karl Borchardt)   209
Piers D. Mitchell, *Medicine in the Crusades. Warfare, Wounds and the
Medieval Surgeon* (Jonathan Riley-Smith)   210

Colin Morris, *The Sepulchre of Christ and the Medieval West. From the Beginning to 1600* (Andrew Jotischiky) 212

Robert the Monk's History of the First Crusade: Historia Iherosolimitana, trans. Carol Sweetenham (Susan B. Edgington) 214

Steven Runciman, *The First Crusade* (Jonathan Riley-Smith) 216

Sylvia Schein, *Gateway to the Heavenly City. Crusader Jerusalem and the Catholic West (1099–1187)* (Colin Morris) 218

Caroline Smith, *Crusading in the Age of Joinville* (William Chester Jordan) 220

Damian J. Smith, *Innocent III and the Crown of Aragon: The Limits of Papal Authority* (James M. Powell) 221

Kristjan Toomaspoeg, *Les Teutoniques en Sicile (1197–1492)* (Marie-Luise Favreau-Lilie) 223

Annemarie Weyl Carr, *Cyprus and the Devotional Art of Byzantium in the Era of the Crusades* (Jaroslav Folda) 226

Dorothea Weltecke, *Die "Beschreibung der Zeiten" von Mor Michael dem Großen (1126–1199). Eine Studie zu ihrem historischen und historiographiegeschichtlichen Kontext* (Ralph-Johannes Lilie) 228

SHORT NOTICES

Chemins d'outre-mer. Études sur la Méditerranée médiévale offerts à Michel Balard, ed. Damien Coulon, Catherine Otten-Froux, Paule Pagès and Dominique Valérian 230

The Experience of Crusading. Volume One: Western Approaches, ed. Marcus Bull and Norman Housley 232

The Experience of Crusading. Volume Two: Defining the Crusader Kingdom, ed. Peter Edbury and Jonathan Phillips 232

Bulletin No. 27 of the SSCLE 235

Guidelines for the Submission of Papers 305

Membership Information 306

Abbreviations

AOL	*Archives de l'Orient latin*
Autour	*Autour de la Première Croisade. Actes du colloque de la Society for the Study of the Crusades and the Latin East: Clermont-Ferrand, 22–25 juin 1995*, ed. Michel Balard. Paris, 1996
Cart Hosp	*Cartulaire général de l'ordre des Hospitaliers de Saint-Jean de Jérusalem, 1100–1310*, ed. Joseph Delaville Le Roulx. 4 vols. Paris, 1884–1906
Cart St Sép	*Le Cartulaire du chapitre du Saint-Sépulcre de Jérusalem*, ed. Geneviève Bresc-Bautier, Documents relatifs à l'histoire des croisades 15. Paris, 1984
Cart Tem	*Cartulaire général de l'ordre du Temple 1119?–1150. Recueil des chartes et des bulles relatives à l'ordre du Temple*, ed. Guigue A. M. J. A., (marquis) d'Albon. Paris, 1913
CCCM	Corpus Christianorum. Continuatio Mediaevalis
Chartes Josaphat	*Chartes de la Terre Sainte provenant de l'abbaye de Notre-Dame de Josaphat*, ed. Henri F. Delaborde, Bibliothèque des Écoles françaises d'Athènes et de Rome 19. Paris, 1880
Clermont	*From Clermont to Jerusalem: The Crusades and Crusader Societies 1095–1500. Selected Proceedings of the International Medieval Congress, University of Leeds, 10–13 July 1995*, ed. Alan V. Murray. International Medieval Research 3. Turnhout, 1998
Crusade Sources	*The Crusades and their Sources: Essays Presented to Bernard Hamilton*, ed. John France and William G. Zajac. Aldershot, 1998
CS	*Crusade and Settlement: Papers read at the First Conference of the Society for the Study of the Crusades and the Latin East and Presented to R.C. Smail*, ed. Peter W. Edbury. Cardiff, 1985
CSEL	Corpus Scriptorum Ecclesiasticorum Latinorum
EC, 1	*The Experience of Crusading 1: Western Approaches*, ed. Marcus G. Bull and Norman J. Housley. Cambridge, 2003
EC, 2	*The Experience of Crusading 2: Defining the Crusader Kingdom*, ed. Peter W. Edbury and Jonathan P. Phillips. Cambridge, 2003
FC	Fulcher of Chartres, *Historia Hierosolymitana (1095–1127)*, ed. Heinrich Hagenmeyer. Heidelberg, 1913

GF	*Gesta Francorum et aliorum Hierosolimitanorum*, ed. and trans. Rosalind M. T. Hill and Roger Mynors. London, 1962
GN	Guibert of Nogent, *Dei gesta per Francos*, ed. Robert B. C. Huygens CCCM 127A. Turnhout, 1996
Horns	*The Horns of Hattin*, ed. Benjamin Z. Kedar. Jerusalem and London, 1992
Kreuzfahrerstaaten	*Die Kreuzfahrerstaaten als multikulturelle Gesellschaft. Einwanderer und Minderheiten im 12. und 13. Jahrhundert*, ed. Hans Eberhard Mayer with Elisabeth Müller-Luckner. Schriften des Historischen Kollegs, Kolloquien 37. Munich, 1997
Mansi. *Concilia*	Giovanni D. Mansi, *Sacrorum conciliorum nova et amplissima collectio*
MGH	Monumenta Germaniae Historica
MO, 1	*The Military Orders: Fighting for the Faith and Caring for the Sick*, ed. Malcolm Barber. Aldershot, 1994
MO, 2	*The Military Orders*, vol. 2: *Welfare and Warfare*, ed. Helen Nicholson. Aldershot, 1998
MO, 3	*The Military Orders*, vol. 3: *Their History and Heritage*, ed. William G. Zajac. Aldershot, 2006
Montjoie	*Montjoie: Studies in Crusade History in Honour of Hans Eberhard Mayer*, ed. Benjamin Z. Kedar, Jonathan Riley-Smith and Rudolf Hiestand. Aldershot, 1997
Outremer	*Outremer. Studies in the History of the Crusading Kingdom of Jerusalem Presented to Joshua Prawer*, ed. Benjamin Z. Kedar, Hans E. Mayer and Raymond C. Smail. Jerusalem, 1982
PG	Patrologia Graeca
PL	Patrologia Latina
PPTS	Palestine Pilgrims' Text Society Library
RHC	*Recueil des Historiens des Croisades*
Darm	*Documents arméniens*
Lois	*Les assises de Jérusalem*
Oc	*Historiens occidentaux*
Or	*Historiens orientaux*
RHGF	*Recueil des Historiens des Gaules et de la France*
RIS	Rerum Italicarum Scriptores
NS	New Series
ROL	*Revue de l'Orient latin*
RRH	Reinhold Röhricht, comp., *Regesta regni hierosolymitani*. Innsbruck, 1893
RRH Add	Reinhold Röhricht, comp., *Additamentum*. Innsbruck, 1904
RS	Rolls Series

Setton, *Crusades*   *A History of the Crusades*, general editor Kenneth M. Setton, 2nd edn., 6 vols. Madison, 1969–89

SRG   Scriptores Rerum Germanicarum

WT   William of Tyre, *Chronicon*, ed. Robert B. C. Huygens, with Hans E. Mayer and Gerhard Rösch, CCCM 63–63A. Turnhout, 1986

Motivating Listeners in the *Kitab al-Jihad* of 'Ali ibn Tahir al-Sulami (d. 1106)

Niall Christie

University of British Columbia and Corpus Christi College, Vancouver, Canada[1]

Introduction

In April 1097, Christian troops from western Europe crossed the Bosphorus from Constantinople and began an assault on Muslim lands, a campaign that would go on to capture Jerusalem and later be referred to as the First Crusade. Eight years later, in 1105, a Muslim jurisprudent from Damascus named 'Ali ibn Tahir al-Sulami (d. 1106) preached a sermon urging his listeners to take up arms against the crusaders. Al-Sulami was a teacher of philology at the Great Umayyad Mosque who also took an interest in Shafi'i jurisprudence. He dictated his call in a number of parts in the Mosque of Bayt Lahiya in the suburbs of Damascus over the course of the year 1105 – the manuscript was, after all, at least twelve sections long – while the crusaders were still expanding their holdings in the Levant. He also repeated the dictation of the second part of his work at the Great Mosque in July and August, 1105.[2] His treatise, the *Kitab al-Jihad* (Book of the Holy War), exhorted all Muslims in the region to unite in opposition to the Christian invaders, but his call seems to have been mostly ignored, at least by the political authorities who could initiate a military response to the situation.[3] The full text of al-Sulami's call has not survived; only a partial manuscript remains, currently kept in the Asad National Library in Damascus.[4] It is unfortunate that the manuscript is incomplete, for it is a remarkable document, containing both the text of al-Sulami's dictation and

---

[1] I would like to thank the participants in the conference on *Crusading & Against Whom? Holy Violence in the Middle Ages*, held at Middlebury College in October 2004, for their comments on the earliest incarnation of this article. Suleiman Mourad and Deborah Gerish, in particular, gave invaluable advice and suggestions, for which I am extremely grateful.

[2] Emmanuel Sivan, "La génèse de la contre-croisade: un traité damasquin du début du XIIe siècle," *Journal Asiatique* 254 (1966), 204–5, and Nikita Elisséeff, "The Reaction of the Syrian Muslims after the Foundation of the First Latin Kingdom of Jerusalem," in *Crusaders and Muslims in Twelfth Century Syria*, ed. Maya Shatzmiller, The Medieval Mediterranean 1 (Leiden, 1993), pp. 162–72, here p. 163.

[3] For more information on the impact of al-Sulami and those who followed him, see Sivan, "Génèse," pp. 204–6, and Carole Hillenbrand, *The Crusades: Islamic Perspectives* (Edinburgh, 1999), pp. 108–16.

[4] Al-Sulami, *Kitab al-Jihad*, unpublished manuscript, Asad Library, Damascus (no cataloguing information available), formerly kept at the Zahiriyya in Damascus under the numbers 3796 and 4511. I would like to acknowledge gratefully the contributions of Professor Carole Hillenbrand of the University of Edinburgh and Dr 'Ammar Amin of the Juma' al-Majid Center for Culture and Heritage in Dubai, who provided me with copies of the original manuscripts.

marginal notes by the author or scribe. The manuscript has been partially edited by Emmanuel Sivan.[5]

This article will explore the methods by which al-Sulami attempted to provoke his listeners into action, examining in particular how far he attempted to base his work on original ideas and how far he drew on pre-existing Islamic traditions. The first part of al-Sulami's manuscript has not survived; what fragments remain begin with the second part. Hence it is impossible to determine what his opening gambit may have been; however, one can make an educated guess. In later parts of his work, al-Sulami adopted the method of including in the beginning of his discussion of any particular topic quotations from the *Qur'an* that supported his point.[6] One can also see this method in use in the earliest known treatise on the topic of the *jihad*, the *Kitab al-Jihad* (Book of the Holy War) of the famous jurisprudent and *jihad* fighter, ʿAbd Allah ibn al-Mubarak (d. 797). In opening his treatise, Ibn al-Mubarak presented multiple quotations from the *Qur'an*, including in particular numerous verses that urge the Prophet's listeners to go out to fight for the cause of God.[7] Thus, for Ibn al-Mubarak, the first reason for Muslims to go out to fight the *jihad* was because they were commanded to do so by God. Given that the *Qur'an*, as the word of God, is the first source for all Islamic laws and practices, it would not be unreasonable to expect al-Sulami to have taken a similar view and opened his own treatise with similar Qur'anic exhortations.

In the absence of evidence, this proposed beginning to al-Sulami's work must remain speculation; however, in what remains of his text it is possible to see three major motivational threads running through the narrative. Al-Sulami attempted to provoke his listeners into action through playing on feelings of guilt or shame, frightening them with the probable consequences of inaction, and tempting them with earthly and heavenly rewards.

Neglected Duties

Al-Sulami sought to provoke his listeners by presenting the *jihad* as a duty that they had neglected. Drawing on the *hadith*, the accounts of the sayings and actions of the Prophet and his Companions used by Muslims scholars to explain and elaborate on the pronouncements made in the *Qur'an*, he pointed out that the *jihad* was a concern of all Muslims, and would remain so until the Day of Resurrection.[8]

---

[5] Extracts from the *Kitab al-Jihad* are translated and edited in Sivan, "Génèse," pp. 197–222. The author of this article is currently in the process of producing a full text, translation and study of al-Sulami's manuscript. References below to al-Sulami's work refer to the manuscript, and folio page numbers indicate either the right-hand page (a) or the left-hand page (b).

[6] See, for example, Sulami, *Jihad*, fol. 193a and fol. 222b.

[7] Ibn al-Mubarak, *Kitab al-Jihad*, ed. Nazih Hammad (Beirut, 1971), pp. 27–29.

[8] Sulami, *Jihad*, fol. 174a. It will not be the function of this article to trace the textual origins of the

He demonstrated that the early caliphs were unstinting in their prosecution of the *jihad* and that it was only the weakness and negligence of later caliphs that led to it eventually being abandoned.[9] This abandonment was something that al-Sulami regarded as shameful. In one *hadith* in particular he gave a description of an *amir* of Mecca who harangued the people of the city for devoting themselves to building up and worshipping at the Kaʿba but neglecting the *jihad* against evil.[10] The implication is that the Muslims were content to stay at home and conduct religious observances there, but in doing so they were neglecting other equally important duties. Quoting the *Qurʾan*, al-Sulami reminded his listeners that only those who undertook the *jihad* were true believers.[11]

In addition to its use of *hadith*, al-Sulami's exhortation may show the influence of an important figure in the history of *jihad* preaching. During the tenth century, the Hamdanid dynasty of northern Syria and north-western Mesopotamia became so famous for its prosecution of the *jihad* on the Muslim–Byzantine border that thousands of volunteers from Central Asia traveled west to join the effort. The most famous of these Hamdanid rulers was Sayf al-Dawla, who ruled from 944 to 967; it was during his reign that a preacher named Ibn Nubata al-Fariqi (d. 984 or 985), of Mayyafariqin in Asia Minor, delivered a number of sermons to the people of both his home town and Aleppo. These sermons, the first of which was given in 959, became models for later *jihad* preaching and some of Ibn Nubata's themes and oratory techniques echo perceptibly through the work of al-Sulami.[12] Among these is criticism of the audience for shirking their duties. In his first sermon, Ibn Nubata also harangued his listeners for their neglect:

> O you people! How many times do you hear speech and not remember? How many times are you rebuked and not torn out [from your complacency? It is] as if your ears vomit back the remembrance of admonitions, or as if your hearts are too proud to preserve them. Your enemies conduct their operations in your countries, and as a result of your staying away from the *jihad* against them they achieve their hopes. Satan called them to his falsehood and they answered him, and the Merciful entrusted you with His truth, but you stayed away. ... You flee like camels from your enemies, and for them you wear the armour of weakness and failure.[13]

In this way Ibn Nubata, almost 150 years before al-Sulami, also attempted to shame his listeners into action by focusing on their neglect of the *jihad*. Naturally, such rhetorical techniques were not original to Ibn Nubata, as he himself drew on a rich

---

hadiths that al-Sulami cited. For the purposes of the argument presented here, it is more important to note that he chose to use the *hadith* material as support for his exhortations.

[9] Ibid., fol. 174b.

[10] Ibid.

[11] Ibid., fol. 190b. The quotation is from *Qurʾan* 49.15.

[12] On the *jihad* in the tenth century and Ibn Nubata, see Hillenbrand, *Crusades*, pp. 101–2.

[13] *Recueil de textes relatifs à l'émir Sayf al-Daula le Hamdanide*, ed. M. Canard (Algiers, 1934), p. 130.

tradition dating back to the earliest days of Islam, but, given the earlier preacher's importance, it is possible that al-Sulami had him in mind when he used similar devices in his work.

Al-Sulami's message was aimed primarily at the politico-military classes, those he described as "you community of *sultans* of this country, and those prominent persons, soldiers and others who are considered prominent from the young men, stalwart supporters and lords recently acquired from wealth and passed as inheritance among intimates, families and close friends, who follow them."[14] In his view, God had appointed these to watch over and defend from enemies the people under their care, the territories that they ruled and the faith itself.[15] Thus he was utterly astonished at those rulers who did not take action, even when they were in a position where they themselves might have been attacked by the enemy,[16] and exhorted them and their subordinates to "drive away insignificant things and sluggishness and go to fight the *jihad* with your wealth and yourselves,"[17] a turn of phrase the latter half of which recalls a commandment given in many places in the *Qur'an*.[18]

Al-Sulami's text does not include a source for this view of the defensive responsibilities of rulers, but his comments were clearly based on ideas that were circulating at the time. Probably the most influential political thinker of the period was the eleventh-century judge, Abu'l-Hasan al-Mawardi (d. 1058). In his *Ahkam al-Sultaniyya* (Rules of Government), al-Mawardi argued that conduct of the *jihad* was incumbent upon both the caliph and those whom he had appointed as provincial rulers. He listed the following among the ten public duties of the caliph:

> 3. He must protect the territory of Islam and defend the sanctuaries so that people may earn their sustenance and journey safe from any threat to their persons or belongings; …
> 5. He must fortify the border posts against attack and defend them with force against an enemy which might appear unexpectedly and violate what is sacred or shed the blood of Muslims or *dhimmis* protected by a pact;
> 6. He must make *jihad* against those who resist Islam after having been called to it until they submit or accept to live as a protected *dhimmi*-community – so that Allah's rights, may He be exalted, "be made uppermost above all [other] religion." (*Qur'an* 9.33)[19]

---

[14] Sulami, *Jihad*, fol. 177b. "Lords recently acquired from wealth and passed as inheritance among intimates, families and close friends, who follow them" refers to the *mamluks*, essentially soldiers who were bought as slaves, educated in Islam and the arts of war, then freed upon reaching adulthood. By this period many *mamluks* had risen to important positions in Muslim governments, though it would be almost 150 years before the *mamluks* would stage a takeover and become rulers of the region.

[15] Ibid., fol. 177a.

[16] Ibid., fol. 177b.

[17] Ibid.

[18] *Qur'an* 4.95, 9.81, 9.88 and 9.111.

[19] Abu'l-Hasan al-Mawardi, *Kitab al-Ahkam al-Sultaniyya wa'l-Wilayat al-Diniyya*, ed. Ahmad Mubarak al-Baghdadi (Kuwait and al-Mansura, 1989), pp. 22–23; and *Al-Ahkam as-Sultaniyyah*, trans. Asadullah Yate (London, 1996), p. 28.

No less than three of the ten public duties of the caliph found in al-Mawardi's work concern pursuit of the *jihad* and defense of his subjects. By the same token, al-Mawardi stated that provincial governors who were stationed in provinces that bordered hostile territory were obliged to conduct the *jihad* against the enemy.[20] Most importantly for al-Sulami, he also stated that the provincial rulers did not require the caliph's permission to wage defensive war against enemies,[21] a ruling that had clear relevance for the Damascene preacher to the current state of affairs in the Levant, in that it meant that there was no need for lack of caliphal permission to prevent the local rulers from taking action against the Franks. Thus these rulers were even more culpable for their neglect of their obligations.

The rest of the Muslims were not exempted from the obligation to go out and fight to defend Muslim lands. Drawing heavily on the writings of the founder of his legal school, Muhammad ibn Idris al-Shafiʿi (d. 820), al-Sulami demonstrated that, while rulers were meant to lead both the offensive and defensive *jihad*, the obligation of defensive *jihad* was imposed on all Muslims, provided that they were free, adult, male and sane.[22] Thus the duty was not imposed on women or slaves; in fact, in another part of his work, al-Sulami, citing a Shafiʿite prayer-leader, specifically prohibited women from taking part in the fighting.[23] This is not to say that al-Sulami expected all qualified Muslims to fight in the defensive *jihad* all the time. The Muslims were only expected to take action as far as was needed to ensure the fulfillment of the obligation: in this case the successful defense of Muslim territory. By way of explanation he quoted his contemporary, the great Shafiʿite theologian, Abu Hamid Muhammad ibn Muhammad al-Ghazali (d. 1111):

> Whenever a year passed without an expedition taking place in it, every Muslim who was free, responsible and capable of taking part in an expedition betook himself to it, it being sought by to exalt the word of God, who is praised, to demonstrate His religion, to suppress by it His enemies, the polytheists, to achieve the reward that God, who is praised, and His Prophet promised to whomever fought the *jihad* in His cause and to gain their enemies' wealth, women and lands, until there might be, of those who came to face the enemy, enough to fight them in the expedition.[24]

Citing another unnamed Shafiʿite scholar, al-Sulami went on to explain this passage:

---

[20] Mawardi, *Kitab*, pp. 40–41, and *Ahkam*, p. 48.

[21] Mawardi, *Kitab,* p. 44, and *Ahkam*, pp. 52–53. Al-Mawardi actually devoted an entire chapter to laying out in detail the regulations affecting the conduct of an *amir* charged with waging the *jihad*. See Mawardi, *Kitab*, pp. 47–73, and *Ahkam*, pp. 57–82.

[22] Sulami, *Jihad*, fol. 175a and fol. 188a.

[23] Ibid., fol. 210a.

[24] Ibid., fol. 175b. Sivan suggests that al-Sulami attended the lectures given by al-Ghazali during his visit to Damascus in 1095–96, but it is also possible that he instead (or also) met the eminent scholar on another occasion during the latter's time in the city; see Sivan, "Génèse," p. 223.

That is to say that the *jihad*, however, is a duty of sufficiency. If the group that was facing the enemy had enough people in it, then it would be possible for the group to fight the *jihad* on its own, and evil was defeated while they were isolated from others. Yet if the group was weak and was not able to be sufficient to face the enemy and defeat its evil, then the duty to help was imposed on the people of the nearby countries, such as *al-Sham*,[25] for example. If the enemy made for one of its cities and there were not enough people in it to fight and defeat them, it was obligatory for all the cities of *al-Sham* to send people to it to fight until there were sufficient numbers to oppose the enemy. At that time the duty would fall from the others.[26]

It should be noted that both of al-Sulami's sources were merely quoting standard *jihad* theory, rather than formulating new doctrine as a response to the Frankish attacks. Al-Ghazali in particular is not known to have made any specific response to the crusaders' arrival in the Levant, so it may be that al-Sulami was essentially "name-dropping" here, seeking to strengthen his case by using the famous theologian as his authority. Al-Sulami further supported these statements with opinions of other scholars both from his own, Shafi'ite, school and from the school of Malik ibn Anas (d. 795), who was one of al-Shafi'i's teachers.

As should by now be clear, al-Sulami described the *jihad* as both a collective and an individual obligation. In Islamic law, an individual religious duty (*fard 'ayn*) is one that each person should seek to fulfill on their own, not requiring authorization from any higher earthly authority. Meanwhile, a collective religious duty (*fard kifaya*) is one that is incumbent on all members of the community, but if enough people undertake it to complete it successfully (the Arabic term actually means "*jihad* of sufficiency"), then the remainder are neither still obliged to do so nor blamed if they do not.[27] As al-Sulami indicated, the defensive *jihad*, being both a *fard 'ayn* and a *fard kifaya*, is incumbent upon every individual, but only until there are adequate numbers to provide an effective defense of Muslim lands.[28] The leaders of the realm are meant to take the lead in this duty, but if they do not then the people themselves may take action, without the permission of their political superiors, to ensure that it is fulfilled and that the lands of the Muslim world are kept secure.

It is clear that al-Sulami saw a need for unity among Muslims, and most particularly among the rulers of the Muslim lands. He presented the current disunity in the Muslim ranks as the result of their impiety and failure to fulfill their obligations, in that their abandonment of the *jihad*, combined with other sins, had led God to disperse their unity and tempt their enemies to attack Muslim lands.

---

[25] The term used by mediaeval Muslim writers to refer to the region roughly corresponding to the modern states of Syria, Lebanon, Jordan, Israel, the Palestinian autonomous areas and the edge of south-east Turkey.

[26] Sulami, *Jihad*, fol. 175b.

[27] The first jurist to formalize the doctrine of *fard kifaya* was al-Shafi'i, the founder of al-Sulami's legal school. On this see Michael Bonner, *Aristocratic Violence and Holy War* (New Haven, CT, 1996), p. 40.

[28] Sulami, *Jihad*, fols. 175b–177a.

It is in this context that he saw both the Christian conquest of Muslim territories in Iberia between the ninth and eleventh centuries and the Norman conquest of Sicily in 1061–91:

> A number of the enemy pounced on the island of Sicily while the Muslims disputed and competed, and they conquered in the same way one city after another in al-Andalus [Muslim Spain]. When the reports confirmed for them that this country suffered from the disagreement of its masters and its rulers' meddling, with its consequent disorder and disarray, they confirmed their resolution to set out for it, and Jerusalem was their dearest wish.[29]

In this way al-Sulami presented the crusaders' arrival in the Levant as part of a grander scheme of conquest directed against Muslim lands, making the crusaders seem considerably more aware and systematic in their aggression against the Muslims than they actually were and linking the Christian expansions together in a way that no one in Europe did. It is not clear how al-Sulami learned that the ultimate goal of the crusade was Jerusalem. A few lines later he also commented that the crusaders were fighting a *jihad*, a holy war, against the Muslims. In both cases he showed much greater perceptiveness, or perhaps honesty, than his contemporaries, who presented the crusaders as being motivated by mere greed or malice; it was over a century before another Muslim writer, in this case the Mosuli historian Ibn al-Athir (d. 1233), noted that the crusaders were fighting a *jihad*.[30] Al-Sulami then observed that the lack of Muslim opposition to the crusaders had encouraged them to continue in their efforts, seeking to conquer more of the country and kill and imprison more of the inhabitants than they had originally intended.[31] Thus, by presenting the crusaders as more systematic and opportunistic than they actually were, al-Sulami increased the magnitude of the threat, with the intention of effectively frightening his listeners into action.

We have seen that in al-Sulami's view the Muslims' misbehavior had led God to punish them with disunity and the loss of some of their territories to a systematic campaign of aggression waged by the crusaders.[32] Al-Sulami saw this Muslim disunity, which was still continuing in the wake of the crusaders' arrival, as all the more shameful because, even in the time before the first revelation of the *Qurʾan*, people had recognized the value of unity. As examples, he cited the Arabs of

---

[29] Ibid., fol. 174b.

[30] For a full discussion of this issue, see Niall Christie, "Religious Campaign or War of Conquest? Muslim Views of the Motives of the First Crusade," in *Noble Ideals and Bloody Realities: Warfare in the Middle Ages*, ed. Niall Christie and Maya Yazigi (Leiden: E. J. Brill, 2006), pp. 57–72.

[31] Sulami, *Jihad*, fol. 175a.

[32] It is interesting to note that the Spanish scholar, Ibn al-ʿArabi (d. 1148), who traveled in the Muslim east between about 1092 and 1100, perceived Muslim disunity as having facilitated the Frankish conquest of Jerusalem, although he did not specifically read any divine plan into this. On Ibn al-ʿArabi see Joseph Drory, "Some Observations During a Visit to Palestine by Ibn al-ʿArabi of Seville in 1092–1095," *Crusades* 3 (2004), 101–24, here p. 120.

pre-Islamic Arabia, who would join together to fight against external enemies, and the kings of Persia, who would unite to drive away their enemies and then take the opportunity to remain on good terms with each other afterwards.[33] Al-Sulami did not cite his sources in either case, but to support his point he paraphrased a *hadith* from the Prophet, saying, "Do not snub each other, oppose each other or envy each other. Be worshippers of God in a brotherhood as God, who is exalted, ordered you."[34] It seems that al-Sulami was distressed that non-Muslims could see the value of unity, but his fellow Muslims could not.

Fearful Consequences

We have already alluded to the dire consequences of inaction with which al-Sulami threatened his listeners: divine displeasure and conquest by the crusaders. With regard to the former, in al-Sulami's view the punishments that the Muslims had endured so far were as nothing compared to the possible consequences of continued failure to react. In responding to the crusader threat, al-Sulami exhorted his listeners to "Beware with all watchfulness that you avoid disgracing yourselves or you will arrive at a fire with its flames, which God, who is exalted, has made an evil place and worst final destiny."[35] Thus he threatened his listeners with the fires of hell if they did not take up arms and fight hard in the *jihad*. In his use of these warnings al-Sulami again echoed the earlier preaching of Ibn Nubata al-Fariqi, for the latter also threatened his listeners with the fires of hell in a number of his sermons.[36]

At the same time, al-Sulami described the more immediate, worldly consequences of inaction as "conquest by these blasphemers, expulsion from the country by force and subjugation, or staying with them in degradation and servility, with the killing, capture, imprisonment and torture by night and day that that exposes one to."[37] "If only you would desist from sin!" al-Sulami exclaimed, "otherwise God will make you fall into the hands of your enemy as a matter of serious vengeance, extirpation and removal."[38] In this way al-Sulami threatened his listeners with the consequences of God's wrath in both this world and the next.

---

[33] Sulami, *Jihad*, fol. 189a–b.
[34] Ibid., fol. 189b.
[35] Ibid., fol. 177a.
[36] Canard, *Recueil*, pp. 131–32, 159 and 164.
[37] Sulami, *Jihad*, fol. 177b.
[38] Ibid., fol. 181a.

Earthly and Heavenly Rewards

Not all the methods used by al-Sulami to motivate his listeners were negative in tone; he also provided numerous incentives for them. He offered his contemporaries a number of rewards in both this life and the next, the most prosaic of which was the opportunity to gain plunder from their enemies. As noted earlier, al-Ghazali stated that one of the reasons people undertook the *jihad* was to gain the enemies' wealth, women and lands.[39] Quoting a follower of the Hanbali school of legal thought, al-Sulami asserted that it was not merely permitted but actually obligatory for Muslims to raid enemies for plunder if the opportunity arose.[40] Plunder was always regarded as one of the benefits of conducting warfare against the enemy, and numerous regulations existed governing its distribution and use. Al-Sulami himself quoted over 25 pages of *hadith* on this topic, covering the treatment of both inanimate plunder and prisoners.[41]

However, al-Sulami clearly gave precedence to less materialistic rewards. In his text the regulations concerning plunder only follow descriptions of benefits that are rather less worldly in origin, even if their manifestations might be said to be rather more earthly in character. He offered his listeners the opportunity to fulfil a great prophecy, saying that the Prophet had predicted that a group of Muslims would conquer their enemies and fight for the truth until the Day of Judgment. He went on to reveal that this group was drawn from *al-Sham*, and in particular from Jerusalem and the territory surrounding it, with specific mention being made of Damascus, the city in which he was preaching.[42] He then introduced another prophecy, this time stating that the Muslims were fated to conquer Rome and Constantinople, with Constantinople being the first to fall.[43] Al-Sulami then drew the two prophecies together in a grand exhortation, suggesting to his listeners that they were the ones to whom the prophecies referred:

> We have heard in what we have heard of a sufficiently documented *hadith* stating that the Byzantines will conquer Jerusalem for a set period of time, and the Muslims will gather against them, drive them out of it, kill all except a few of them, then pursue their scattered remnants to Constantinople, descend on it and conquer it. ... If this situation is occurring during that time, and if those who fight the *jihad* are from this conquering group [the group who will fight until the Day of Judgment], among them are those who will succeed in driving them out of Jerusalem and other parts of this country. They are the ones who will conquer Constantinople ... with success granted by God, who is praised, and the holding of His aid. Fight hard, God have mercy on you, in this *jihad*. You may be the ones who will gain the merit of this great conquest, having been kept for this noble rank.[44]

---

[39] Ibid., fol. 175b.
[40] Ibid., fol. 176b.
[41] Ibid., fols. 222b–237a.
[42] Ibid., fols. 178a–179b.
[43] Ibid., fol. 180a.
[44] Ibid., fol. 180a–b.

In this fashion al-Sulami presented the current situation in the Levant as the precursor to the fulfillment of this prophecy. If his listeners, who, after all, may have been the ones fated to fight the *jihad* until the end of time, took up arms now and drove the enemy out of Jerusalem, they might gain the opportunity to go on to conquer Constantinople, as was promised, with Rome presumably following in due course. Constantinople and Rome were both seen by the Muslims as centres of Christian power and, of the two, Constantinople was both the more immediately important and geographically the more proximate. When the first Muslim armies surged out of the Arabian Peninsula in the seventh century, Constantinople was the capital of the first major Christian power that they encountered. Several attempts were made to conquer the city, the last being in 716–17, and this failure marked the beginning of the recession of Muslim borders. Thus Constantinople came to be seen as a bulwark of Christian power that was yet to be overcome, and so gained a significant position in Muslim eschatology.[45]

So what relevance does this have to the activities of the crusaders? While the prophecy stated that the Byzantines, rather than the western European crusaders, would take control of Jerusalem, contemporary Muslim writers often confused or conflated the Byzantines and the Europeans, particularly as the two groups were both Christian;[46] thus al-Sulami would still have seen the prophecy as being applicable in this instance. In this way he offered his listeners the opportunity to fulfill a divinely ordained prophecy, gaining a sacred status in this life.

Al-Sulami's prediction of the fate of his listeners was based upon a number of *hadiths*, and he went to great lengths to prove the authenticity of his claims. He gave multiple citations of *hadiths*, to emphasize their validity,[47] and was careful to comment repeatedly on the fact that these are sufficiently documented *hadiths*, indicating that they were to be trusted.[48] In the rest of his work he was not normally this exacting; it is clear that he saw this prediction as vital in his attempts to motivate his listeners, and so did his best to ensure that it would be taken seriously.

Another reward that al-Sulami offered his listeners was a chance to reconcile themselves with God. By the twelfth century, Muslim jurists, particularly those with a mystical focus, had elaborated a two-part theory of *jihad*. The military *jihad* against external enemies was, in fact, regarded as the less meritorious of two *jihads*, known as the *jihad al-asghar* ("lesser *jihad*") or *jihad* of the sword. Of greater merit, in fact, was an internal moral and spiritual *jihad* fought against evil, the *jihad al-akbar* ("greater *jihad*"), also known as the *jihad* of the tongue or *jihad* of the pen.

---

[45] On Muslim views of the Byzantine Empire and Constantinople, see also Nadia Maria El Cheikh, *Byzantium Viewed by the Arabs* (Cambridge, MA, 2004).

[46] See Niall Christie, "Levantine Attitudes towards the Franks during the Early Crusades (490/1096–564/1169)" (unpublished Ph.D. thesis, University of St. Andrews, June 1999), pp. 17–20 and 64.

[47] For example, on the identity of the ones who will fight until the Day of Judgment, see one *hadith* in Sulami, *Jihad*, fols. 178a–b, and three *hadiths* in ibid., fols. 179a–b.

[48] For examples, see ibid., fols. 179a and 180a.

This took two major forms: speaking out against evil wherever one perceived it (in speech or writing, thus *jihad* of the tongue or pen) and struggling against the evil in one's own soul, which would also enable one to be a moral exemplar for others.[49] Al-Sulami made this last struggle a prerequisite for taking part in the lesser *jihad*:

> Give precedence to *jihad* of yourselves [or "your souls"] over *jihad* of your enemies, for if yourselves are among your enemies prevent them from being disobedient to their Creator, who is praised. You will succeed in your hopes of victory over them. Make right what is between you and your Creator, and what is wrong with your current state of being will be made right for you, and your enmity will be reconciled. Tear out your disobedience to God, who is praised, and follow your tearing it out with doing what is right in what you start afresh. It may be that your Lord will destroy your enemy and make you rulers over the world. He may observe how you act and how you arrange that which God, who is praised, ordered your Prophet, may God bless him, and his companions regarding giving Him priority by carrying out the *jihad*. The most important priority is seriousness in obedience to Him and being sincere in fighting hard in the *jihad*. Among His words, and He is exalted, are: "O you who believe! Bow and prostrate yourselves in prayer, worship your Lord and do good. Perhaps you will prosper."[50] Then He said after that, "Strive for God to fulfill the due of *jihad*."[51]

Al-Sulami clearly prioritized the internal struggle against one's own wickedness over the struggle against external enemies, suggesting that waging this internal struggle would lead to reconciliation with God and, if God approved of one's internal efforts, this might lead to success against the enemy. In this way he simultaneously offered his listeners a chance to achieve moral harmony with God and implied that this might be followed by earthly success against the enemy.

Al-Sulami regarded the timing of the crusaders' invasion as, in some ways, a golden opportunity for his listeners. As noted above, he stated that the arrival of the crusaders gave the Muslims the chance to reconcile their sinful natures with God. For al-Sulami, it was a particularly good time for the Muslims to attempt to regain divine favor, for God Himself was giving them a chance to do so. He stated, "Know that God, who is praised, only sent this enemy to you as a trial, to test your steadfastness with it. He, who blesses and is exalted, said, 'We will test you so that We will know those of you who fight hard and are steadfast, and We will test your experiences.'"[52] In this manner al-Sulami, using the *Qurʾan* as his authority, presented the crusaders as instruments used by God to test His followers, with the promise that, if they turned back to Him, God would give them victory over their enemies. Even better for al-Sulami's listeners, the enemy were, as he perceptively noted, few in number, with their sources of potential reinforcements being far

---

[49] On the development of the greater *jihad*, see Alfred Morabia, *Le Gihad dans l'Islam Médiéval* (Paris, 1993), pp. 256–57 and 293–336.

[50] *Qurʾan* 22.77.

[51] Sulami, *Jihad*, fol. 180b. See also *Qurʾan* 22.78.

[52] Ibid., fol. 177b. See also *Qurʾan* 47.31.

away.[53] Thus al-Sulami was exhorting his contemporaries into action by saying that this was an ideal moment for the Muslims to attract divine goodwill. It is interesting that al-Sulami presented the crusaders as being both powerful and weak in his work, in that when he wanted to frighten his listeners into action, the crusaders were depicted as well-organized and intimidating, but when he wanted to present those around him with an easy opportunity to gain divine favor, they were weak and vulnerable. In this way, he presented contradictory views of the enemy within the same work, and actually within a few pages of each other, subordinating narrative consistency to the means by which he attempted to provoke a response in his listeners.

It was not only in this life that rewards were to be found. Again working from *hadith* material, al-Sulami also presented some images of the joys that awaited those who were killed fighting in the *jihad*. He cited a number of *hadiths* in which an individual was granted a vision of what awaited them in the Afterlife. In one example, a pious Muslim named Saʿid ibn al-Harith, who was taking part in an expedition against the Byzantines in the Muslim year 88 (706–7 CE), was granted a vision of his eventual fate in a dream. Having seen the dead risen from their graves, and met two handsome beings, probably angels, who led him to a massive silver castle, apparently his, filled with beautiful servants, Saʿid was finally admitted into a chamber filled with bejewelled, golden thrones. Saʿid described the inhabitants of the chamber thus:

> Upon every throne was a servant girl whom none of those created by God, who is mighty and exalted, could ever adequately describe, and in the middle of them was a woman who exceeded them in her height, haughtiness, beauty and perfection. The two men said, "This is an honour for you, and these are your people. Here is your reward and the favour your Lord has for you, so increase your efforts in the *jihad*!" They departed from me, and the servant girls rushed towards me with greetings, salutations and the seeking of counsel as if they were members of the family of an absentee when he returns to them. They led me forth and sat me upon the central throne beside that more beautiful servant girl, and they said, "This is your wife, and there are others like her with her. We have been waiting for you a long time." She spoke to me, and I spoke to her, and I asked, "Where am I?" She answered, "In the Paradise of Rest." I inquired, "Who are you?" and she responded, "I am your eternal wife." I asked, "Where are the others?" and she answered, "In your other castle." I said, "I will remain with you today, then I will go away to those others tomorrow." Then I extended my hand towards her, but she fended it off gently and said, "As for today, it is not going to happen thus, because you are returning at once to the world." I replied, "I do not want to return." She said, "That is inevitable. You will remain there three days, then you will break your fast from the third night with us, if God wills." I asked, "That night is the night that I will come?" and she said that it was a fore-ordained matter. Then she got up from her seat, hastening to stand, and there I was, having woken up.[54]

53 Sulami, *Jihad*, fol. 176b–177a. This is again a recognition of realities in the region by al-Sulami that was apparently not shared by other writers from the period.
54 Ibid., fol. 220a.

Over the next three days Saʿid exerted himself greatly in the *jihad* against the Byzantines, and on the third night he was mortally wounded and died praising God.[55] Al-Sulami presented three more *hadiths* in similar vein, one of which he cited as being transmitted by Ibn al-Mubarak and can indeed be found, with minor variations, in the latter's *Kitab al-Jihad*.[56] In all cases, the potential martyr met his heavenly wife but was returned to this world before his extended hand could reach her. In this way al-Sulami dangled a vision of heavenly joys before his listeners, which was made conditional upon their going out to die fighting in the *jihad*.

It is important to note, however, that fighting purely in the hope of gaining these sensual rewards was not enough to gain one a place in heaven. As noted above, al-Sulami made the reconciliation of one's own will with that of God a necessary step before taking part in any military action. Citing *hadith* again, he made it absolutely clear that a *jihad*-fighter whose intentions were impure would be damned to hell-fire, regardless of his efforts. In a *hadith* recounted by the Prophet's Companion, Abu Hurayra, on the authority of the Prophet, the speaker described the fate of three hypocrites on the Day of Judgment:[57]

> Abu Hurayra said, "The first ones to be called to God will be a man who memorised the *Qurʾan*, a man who was killed for the cause of God and a rich man. [The man who memorised the *Qurʾan* is shown only to have done so for the reputation that it would bring him, while the rich man is shown to have donated liberally to charity only so that people would say that he was generous.] The man who was killed for the cause of God, who is mighty and exalted, will be brought forward, and it will be said to him, 'For what were you killed?' The man will say, 'You ordered us to fight the *jihad* for Your cause, and I fought until I was killed.' God will say, 'You have lied,' and the angels will say, 'You have lied,' and God will say, 'On the contrary, you desired that it would be said about you, "So and so is a courageous man," and that was indeed said.' Then the Messenger of God, may God bless him, struck my knee and said, 'O Abu Hurayra, those are the first three members of God's creation who will be judged, but the fire will be kindled with them on the Day of Resurrection.'"[58]

In this manner al-Sulami emphasized the importance of undertaking the *jihad* out of piety, rather than for other reasons; indeed, Saʿid ibn al-Harith, the joyful martyr, was presented as almost obsessive in his piety. Both the heavenly and earthly joys that al-Sulami presented were merely fringe benefits.

---

[55] Ibid., fol. 220b.
[56] Ibid., fols. 221a–222b. See also Ibn al-Mubarak, *Jihad*, pp. 118–20.
[57] Ibid., fols. 182a–b.
[58] Ibid., fol. 182b.

Conclusion

It is clear that al-Sulami made use of a range of strategies in his efforts to provoke his listeners into action. He attempted to shame his audience into responding; he threatened them with the dire consequences of failure to respond; and he offered his listeners a variety of rewards in both this world and the next, including earthly wealth, reconciliation with God, heavenly joys and a place in Muslim eschatology. To support his exhortations he used a variety of sources, including both deliberate use of evidence from the *Qur'an*, the *hadith* and the works and opinions of other earlier and contemporary scholars from both his own and other legal schools, and unacknowledged, possibly unconscious, use of opinions and rhetorical techniques of other writers. In this he seems to have shown very little originality in his writing; however, this was definitely not his purpose. If anything, the last thing al-Sulami wished to be accused of was presenting a text that took an original approach to the *jihad*. In a legal tradition in which legitimacy rests, for the most part, on the precedents set by earlier authorities, al-Sulami had a vested interest in his preaching being seen as legitimized by earlier rulings, and it is for this reason that he relied so much on his chosen sources.

Nevertheless, it would be hasty to claim that al-Sulami's work is in no way original. Al-Sulami faced the formidable task of adapting existing Islamic teachings on the *jihad* to a new situation and a new enemy. An invasion of Muslim territory of this magnitude was something that was unprecedented in Islamic history, at least in the Levant, and so the onus was on al-Sulami to prove that the extant doctrine regarding the defensive aspect of *jihad* was as valid in this situation as it was in the case of smaller conflicts. He was helped in this by the Muslims' apparent confusion concerning the relationship of the western Europeans to the Byzantines – an error that he may or may not have shared – in that it enabled him to incorporate the westerners into the prophecies regarding the Byzantine conquest of Jerusalem, the Muslim retaliation, and the eventual capture of Constantinople and Rome. The fact that most of the literature on *jihad* did not specify the ethnic origins of the enemy was also useful for his arguments. Thus, for al-Sulami the *jihad* doctrine and the rewards that accompanied its prosecution remained valid, despite the circumstantial differences, and the society that he was addressing was still obliged to respond.

"There Is None Like You Among the Mute": The Theology of *Ein Kamokha Ba-Illemim* in Context, with a New Edition and Translation

Laura Lieber

Middlebury College, Vermont

"*Ein Kamokha Ba-Illemim!*" From this first line, Isaac bar Shalom (twelfth-century Rhineland) exploits pun and allusion to devastating effect.[1] The poet accuses God: "There is none like You among the mute!" At first, we may think he is going to quote Psalm 86.8, "There is none like You, O Lord, among the gods." Through a simple pun in the line's last word, however, the poet undermines our expectations. By changing the psalm's word, *elim* (gods), to a different but similar-sounding word, *illemim* (mute), the divine is silenced. With this shift, a biblical hymn of praise is turned into an exclamation of dismay.

In the following essay, I will present a reading of the poem that acknowledges not only Isaac bar Shalom's originality, but his conventionality. Through a careful reading, we will see how one minor poem generates meaning through the creative and selective use of literary conventions, exegetical traditions, liturgical station, historical allusion, and scriptural quotations.[2]

Background: Form and Liturgical Station

Isaac bar Shalom was neither a great nor a prolific writer.[3] He lived in the twelfth century in the Rhineland, a centre of Jewish learning. The poem refers to events that happened on a specific date: 20 Nisan (30 March) in 1147. But from the moment the

---

[1] The Hebrew text follows the critical edition which forms an appendix to this essay. A translation of the full poem is also provided.

[2] The poetry of Ashkenazic (primarily German, and later Eastern European) Jewry has been neglected as literature mainly because it has been considered less beautiful than the lyrics of the great poets of Andalusian Jewry, such as Solomon ibn Gabirol and Judah Halevi. Because it was not seen as sophisticated literature, it was not studied as art. Furthermore, the language of the poems can be dense and obscure, drawing on rabbinic idiom, which was seen as less pure than biblical Hebrew. If these poems were not attractive as poems, then they were to be used in a more utilitarian fashion. They served the needs of history rather than those of art.

[3] Isaac bar Shalom was a contemporary of Rabbi Qalonymous b. Judah (the Younger) and grandfather of Rabbi Isaac Or Zaru'a. See Avraham Habermann, *Sefer Gezerot Ashkenaz ve-Tsarefat* (Jerusalem, 1945), p. 113. Leopold Zunz mentions Isaac in his discussions of Qalonymous the Younger and the commemorations of the Second Crusade; see his *Die synagogale Poesie des Mittelalters*, 2nd ed. (Frankfurt am Main, 1920), pp. 16 and 196; and also *Literaturgeschichte der synagogalen Poesie* (Berlin, 1865), pp. 164–66.

poem was accepted into the liturgy of the Central and Eastern European Jewish communities, Isaac bar Shalom's work was placed into the wider context of post-crusade German-Jewish martyrology and lore.

Formally, *Ein Kamokha Ba-Illemim* consists of rhymed quatrains with a refrain built upon an alphabetic acrostic, which is then followed by an acrostic of the poet's name and the poetic exhortation, "Be strong!"[4] In terms of genre, the poem is a "*Zulat*," a poem inserted in the Sabbath morning liturgy after the central, creedal prayer, the *Shemaʿ*, which begins: "Hear [Hebrew, *Shemaʿ*], O Israel, the Lord is our God, the Lord is One" (Deut. 6.4). Though this poem is not preserved in most modern printings of the Ashkenazic prayer book, in older versions of the rite it was recited on the first Sabbath after Passover; modern Jewish liturgists have selected it for creative Holocaust Remembrance Day liturgies as well.[5] In old Ashkenazic tradition, the weeks between Passover and Shavuot (Pentecost) were devoted to commemoration of the Jewish communities of the Rhineland that had been devastated by the crusades.

The blessings which framed this poem emphasized the theme of redemption, particularly the Exodus from Egypt. Specifically, *Ein Kamokha Ba-Illemim* was inserted between the proclamation, *Ein Elohim Zulatekha* ("There is no God but You") and the affirmation, *Ezrat Avoteinu Atah Hu Me-Olam* ("The help of our fathers You have always been"). The opening line of the poem, *Ein Kamokhah Ba-Illemim*, plays on the phrase it follows – *Ein Elohim Zulatekha* – as well as the familiar biblical text that follows it, from Exodus 15, the Song at the Sea, *Mi Kamokha Ba-Elim* ("Who is like You among the gods?"). Isaac bar Shalom's content and context, however, adapt, reinforce, and undermine the traditional texts that frame it. The poem complains to a God who has *not* redeemed, in the context of a prayer that celebrates redemption. This ironic juxtaposition adds a particular note of bitterness to the poem's opening exclamation.

Interpretation, Allusion, and Quotation

Literary and liturgical contexts established, let us turn and briefly consider a few examples of this poem's use of allusion to biblical and post-biblical Jewish tradition. The explication follows the poem's order. In all manuscript editions, the poem has a refrain concluding each stanza: "Do not be silent!" The refrain, though it seems bold, comes from the opening verse of Psalm 83.2–5:

---

[4] All extant manuscripts include the refrain, although the version published in *Sefer Ha-Demaʿot*, vol. 1 (Berlin, 1924), pp. 217–21, does not.

[5] See *Nightwords: a Liturgy on the Holocaust*, ed. David Roskies (New York, 2000). This anthology of texts opens with the motif of *Ein Kamokhah Ba-Illemim*, terming it "sacred parody" (p. 2), one that "borders on blasphemy" (p. 3).

O God, do not be silent, do not hold aloof.
Do not be quiet, O God!
For, lo, Your enemies rage,
Those who hate You arrogantly raise their heads.
Against Your people they plot secrets,
Take counsel against Your treasured ones.
They say, "Come, let us wipe them out as a nation;
Israel's name will be mentioned no more."[6]

From the beginning, both in the opening words of the poem and the refrain that follows every verse, the poet's choice of text and allusion tells us that his personal tale of woe is not new, but a reiteration of a traditional theme. To phrase it differently, freshness of grief is not his complaint; its antiquity is.

The refrain is not original; neither is the aggressive opening line. The accusation, "There is none like You among the mute!" can be traced back to a second-century CE source, a midrash (homily on a scriptural passage) called the *Mekhilta of Rabbi Ishmael*, the earliest rabbinic interpretation of the book of Exodus.[7] In a discussion of the phrase from Exodus 15, "Who is like You among the gods (*elim*)," we find it written:

"Who is like You among the gods (*elim*)?" [Rather, understand it as] 'Who is like You among the mute (*illemim*).' Who is like You, seeing the grief of Your children and keeping silent?[8]

This tradition also appears in the Talmud as part of an exposition of Psalm 89.9:

Abba Hanan said: [It is written in the psalm:] "Who is mighty like You, O Lord?" – [That is,] Who is like You, mighty in self-restraint, that You can hear the blaspheming and insults of the wicked and keep silent? In the school of Rabbi Ishmael it was taught: "Who is like You among the gods (*elim*)?" – Who is like You among the mute (*illemim*)?[9]

The subtle shift of sound results in a theological accusation that might sound blasphemous to some ears, for all that the poem was written for the liturgy. The attention-getting incipit of Isaac bar Shalom's medieval liturgical poem, however,

---

[6] Translations are the author's unless otherwise noted.

[7] Several potentially unfamiliar terms should be defined at this point. Midrash, including the *Mekhilta*, refers to rabbinic explications of biblical texts. The Mishnah is an anthology of rabbinic legal traditions (probably compiled around 210 CE). The Tosefta is similar to the Mishnah and contemporary with it but of a secondary status. The Talmud is a commentary on the Mishnah. There are, in fact, two Talmuds: the Babylonian Talmud (henceforth BT) sealed, according to tradition, by Rav Ashi in 427 CE (in reality it was open for several generations more) is the primary; the Palestinian Talmud (henceforth PT) (closed around 500 CE) is of lesser prominence.

[8] *Mekhilta de-Rabbi Ismael*, ed. H. S. Horowitz and I. A. Rabin, Jerusalem, 1960, p. 142.

[9] BT *Git.* 56b. Notice that this passage refers to "the school of Rabbi Ishmael," the same school associated with the midrash known as the *Mekhilta of Rabbi Ishmael*.

predates both the poet and the Crusades by centuries. Isaac bar Shalom's question comes not from compatriots on the verge of despair but from the rabbinic sages of old.

The opening line tells the audience that this poem will not be one of comfort or cheap consolation; it demands divine attention. The bold refrain, "Do not be silent," hammers insistently on God's door, daring the mute deity to speak or act. The poet's means of gaining attention, however, are sacred words from traditional texts. If any words have power, these do. The poet creates his complaint against God by quoting from God's own book.

In the poem's distinctive Jewish–Christian dialogue, which occurs in the first four stanzas of the poem, both parties speak quotations from Scripture.[10] The Jews speak with the voice of the Torah and biblical prophets, while the Christian mob has the words of ancient enemies (Samaritans and Shechemites) placed in their mouths. In the first line, the gentiles mock the Jews: "Where is your King?" (l. 3).[11] This taunt echoes the anxiety expressed in Joel 2.14: "Let not the nations say, 'Where is your God?'" The prophet begged God, "Let not …" but in Isaac bar Shalom's poem, these fears materialize verbatim. Of course, this is not how Jews – let alone Christians – of the medieval period actually spoke.[12] This entire dialogue, with all its pathos and wit, is pure poetic artifice. By drawing the dialogue from biblical sources, Scripture is brought to life while the contemporary quarrel is rendered timeless. It is as if the Jews, the nations, and God are rehearsing a pastiche of familiar episodes.

In the second stanza, through a reworking of the difficult phrase *gerushim min gev* ("Those cast out from the community") (l. 5) from Job 30.5, the poet may acknowledge the origins of Christianity within Judaism. If this interpretation is correct, irony suffuses the Christian invitation for the Jews to "unite" with the Church (ll. 9–12): those who left the community of Israel invite the faithful to join them in spiritual exile; a divided, warlike Christian mob speaks to the Jews of unity and overcoming strife! Isaac bar Shalom's wording implies profound distaste. While he acknowledges that, from the Christian perspective, the Jews are the losers, the poet's anger is rooted in his rejection of their supercessionist claims. His use of the prophetic texts – including his acid allusion to Isa. 14.19, when he refers to Jesus as "the filthy Nazarene," punning on the word for "carrion" (l. 11) – and the rabbinic traditions in these opening lines emphasize and legitimize the poet's rejection of Christianity and its teachings about Judaism but also articulate his grief and rage against God. These texts and traditions do not justify the actions or

---

[10]   Susan Einbinder is the only scholar to discuss that the debate is presented as a dialogue; see Susan Einbinder, *Beautiful Death* (Princeton, 2002), p. 35.

[11]   All line numbers refer to the translation and critical edition of the poem at the end of this essay.

[12]   Christians certainly did not refer to their God as "the filthy Nazarene/carrion" [*netzer nit'av*, with both meanings probably intended], despite its basis in Isa. 14.19; later versions of the poem censor this line. See discussion below.

words attributed to the mob any more than they justify the inaction and silence of the deity.

Perhaps most graphically, the terminology of Leviticus permeates the description of the slaughter that follows the rejection of the Christians' overtures. Through this conceit, the poet transforms the trauma into something sacred – perhaps into an effort to influence God. If, after all, the sacrifice of an animal pleased God, then perhaps the willing sacrifice of His most treasured creatures will gain His attention. Anxiety over martyrdom, however, also existed. In a tradition that values life above all else, is there a danger that this slaughter, suicide and murder, could be sinful? The poet hints at this fear when he quotes Leviticus 10.6, "All the house of Israel wept at the burning" (l. 26). In its biblical context, the burning to which this verse refers is the immolation of Nadav and Avihu, the sons of Aaron, who brought "alien fire" before the Lord and were themselves consumed. All Israel wept at the pointlessness of their death, which was rooted (perhaps) in heady over-zealousness.[13] Their father, Aaron, however, kept silent. The offering of Nadav and Avihu was not proper worship; they were fools to die for pride and vanity. Does Isaac bar Shalom hint that this suicide, while true to martyrological ideals of Ashkenaz, was not necessarily the right choice? It is difficult to read that much into the allusion, but the possibility is there.

In several instances within this section, biblical quotations are overt and intended to be understood as such.[14] In the fifth stanza (ll. 18–19), the key verse of the *Shema*ᶜ is recited by the dying Jews: "Hear [*shema*ᑫ], O Israel, the Lord is our God, the Lord is One!" (Deut. 6.4). Since Talmudic times, if not earlier, this verse has been associated with martyrdom, and that is no doubt how it functions in this poem.[15] In the medieval world, the assertion that "God is One" served as a pointed rejection of Christian Trinitarian claims. But the poet is subtle, as well; the liturgical context of this poem is, after all, the blessings surrounding the *Shema*ᶜ. The *Shema*ᶜ of martyrdom is embedded within the *Shema*ᶜ of praise.

---

[13] This positive understanding of the sacrifice of Nadav and Avihu can be traced back to Philo. See Philo's *Legum Allegoria* 2.57–58; and *De Somnis* 2.67. For rabbinic sources – more likely to have been known by our poet – see *Sifra Shemini* 3.32 and *Leviticus Rabba* 12.2. For a modern exploration of Nadav and Avihu's sacrifice, see Michael Fishbane, *The Kiss of God* (Seattle, 1994), esp. p. 21.

[14] The Bible enriches the poem in more subtle ways. Scripture provides a wellspring of poetic epithets in order to designate commonplace figures. God is depicted as "bright and ruddy" and "coming from Seir" (a conflation of Song 5.10 and Isa. 63.1–3). Israel is called "the apple of God's eye" (quoting Deut. 32.10); or "the smitten ones" (based on rabbinic Hebrew); or simply, "Your people." Christendom is invoked through the image of "the beast that roots like a boar" – taken from Psa. 80.3; and "that dainty one who sits there" (Isa. 47.8). The epithet of "boar" in Psa. 80 was understood by ancient exegetes to refer to Amalek/Rome, but it was also an insult based on what Christians ate.

[15] The earliest mention of this use of the *Shema*ᶜ is in the *Testament of Dan* 5.3. See also the teaching of Rabbi Meir, the teacher of Rabbi Akiva, in *Sifre Deuteronomy* 32. The fullest forms of Akiva's martyrdom occur in BT *Berakhot* 61b and PT *Sota* 5.20c. On the early history of Jewish martyrology, see Michael Fishbane, *The Kiss of God*; and also Daniel Boyarin, *Dying for God: Martyrdom and the Making of Christianity and Judaism* (Stanford, 1999).

The poet relies upon rabbinic texts and traditions as well as biblical ones. Comparing the devastated community to "an oven neither covered nor swept" (l. 25), Isaac bar Shalom draws on an image from Sabbath law discussed in a second-century legal text, the Tosefta.[16] The reference to Hannaniah, Azariah, and Mishael assumes knowledge of the traditional interpretation of the book of Daniel. These characters from the biblical text were regarded by later generations to be prototypical martyrs – despite the fact that they survived their ordeal.

The striking image of the letters of the Torah ascending to heaven as the scrolls are burned (l. 31) alludes to the legend of the martyrdom of Rabbi Haninah ben Teradyon as described in the Talmud.[17] According to rabbinic tradition, Rabbi Haninah, convicted of the crime of teaching Torah, was burned alive while wrapped in a Torah scroll. When his disciples asked him, "What do you see?" he replied, "The parchments are being burnt, but the letters are flying upwards." In Isaac bar Shalom's poem, the text itself is a victim; the letters – like human souls – ascend to Heaven. The text is not the only casualty, however. Martyred scholars are described in terms of text study in lines 39–40: they are "seekers of the major and minor" (categories in legal exegesis) and "employers of analogy," referring to their use of logical reasoning in traditions of interpretation.

The poet repeatedly invokes the desecration of sacred books and the murder of the scholars who studied them. Perhaps this sacrifice, if not the blood of pious commoners, will gain the attention of the divine. The poet pleads: "Almighty! Be jealous of Your Torah" (l. 41) – if human suffering won't move You to pity, then perhaps Your Torah, physically desecrated by those who willfully misread it, will? But the divine silence remains. The holy letters, each rich with meaning to the scholars who studied them, fly up to heaven, but fail to move God.[18]

Up to this point, the very "conventional" nature of the poet's language and imagery prevents a reader from knowing if the author had any specific event in mind when he composed. Lest the reader think the poet generalizes, however, he specifies the exact date of the events that brought him to such grief: 20 Nisan 4907 AM, or 30 March 1147 CE.[19] He is specific about not only the date, but its meaning; before telling us explicitly that the events transpired on 20 Nisan, he tells us "The end came when Nahshon hallowed God" (l. 37). Presumably the medieval Jewish audience was familiar with the tradition that while all the other Israelites stood on the shore of

---

[16]   Tos. *Shabb.* 3.1 (Zuckermandel p. 112).

[17]   BT *Avodah Zarah* 18b.

[18]   See *LamR* Pet. 24, where each of the letters of the Torah testifies before God on behalf of Israel; in this instance, too, the letters fail to sway God.

[19]   The calculation of this date depends on a hint embedded through *gematria* (numerology, reading the Hebrew letters in terms of numeric equivalents) in the only extremely difficult line of the text (l. 35). According to Eliezer Landshuth, *Amudei Ha-Avodah* (Berlin, 1857–62), p. 127, the word *va-areshet* – literally, "and a clue" (translated as "in 4907 AM") – is, in fact, a clue to the year of the poem. The numerical value of *va-areshet* is 4907, which would convert to 1147 CE. Subsequent scholars have accepted this explanation.

the Red Sea at the time of the Exodus, Nahshon son of Amminadab trusted in God and jumped in first, his faith sanctifying God's name. This terrible leap towards death was transformed, through a miracle, into a leap towards life and freedom.[20] It is the leap of one ready to die for his trust in God's promises. By adducing this legend, the poet invokes the trust the martyrs had in God, and then juxtaposes it against the deaths of the scholars. This contrast – human fidelity, divine absence – sharpens the tone of anger and brings the poem's bitterness to a head.

Throughout the poem, people act (for good and ill) while the deity sits on the sidelines, and the poet cannot fathom His thoughts. The Christians are certainly guilty of crimes, but it is God whose behavior baffles the poet, and the tension increases as the poem continues. At the end of the poem, the poet beseeches a wrathful God to act: "Garb Yourself in vengeance and rage!" he writes (l. 41); "Rebuke the beast … / … with destruction and havoc and shattering – / Him and all his people, with plague!" he envisions (ll. 43–44); "[C]rush [the enemy's] skull with a hammer!" he pleads (l. 45). Isaac bar Shalom does not want silence; he wants the warlike noise of justice followed by the tranquility of peace. When he contemplates retribution, he is fully capable of dreaming in the terms of his own day, although again, he does so in terms of familiar imagery.[21]

In the end, it is not human deeds that are troubling in this poem but the failure of these deeds to move God to action. The poem ends with a plea for divine movement: a public display of God's redemptive powers, an answer to all the questions that have been posed, but most importantly the question of the first stanza: Where is your God? Any action, it seems, would be preferable to silence.

Theology, Textuality, and Cultural Context

Where was God? This question forms the theological, not historical, basis of the poem. I say "not historical" precisely because, as the poet's own language and use of sources illustrates, there is something fundamentally *old* about the suffering he has witnessed.

---

[20] On the "sanctification of God's name" undertaken by Nahshon son of Amminadav, see *Mekhilta* BeShallah 5 (H-R, p. 107).

[21] On the importance of liturgical poetry in creating a yearning for a "redemption of vengeance" in medieval Ashkenaz, see Israel Yuval, "Vengeance and Damnation, Blood and Defamation: From Jewish Martyrdom to Blood-Libel Accusations," *Zion* 58 (1993), 33–90 [Hebrew]. In *Zion* 59 (1994), the reactions of – and Yuval's responses to – Ezra Fleischer, Jeremy Cohen, Mordecai Breuer, and Abraham Grossman can be found. Yuval's monograph, *Two Nations in Your Womb* (Tel Aviv, 2000) is now available in English (Berkeley, 2007). Isaac bar Shalom particularly favors the paradigm of the destruction of the Egyptians in Exodus. While these violent fantasies may disturb modern readers, such discomfort is, of course, anachronistic. The final lines of Psa. 137 would be a classic example from the biblical text of such gleeful, violent imaginings.

Isaac bar Shalom takes the motif of "There is none like You among the mute," attested in the scholarly sources, and invokes it in the public square, harshly and unapologetically. Grounded in the tradition of *hutzpah kelapei shemaya* – "indignation against Heaven" – the poet has taken his argument with God into the open.[22] He gets no answer from the whirlwind, yet he chooses God's silence over any answer he could offer himself. The divine voice, so clearly heard in the past, does not respond.

The dismaying assertion that God's most amazing power may be His ability to remain unmoved in the face of direct and indirect attacks has deep roots in Jewish history. To be sure, in every era, some would search for an answer and find one. In medieval Jewish thought – building on the theology of rabbinic Judaism – Jews typically blamed themselves for their fate. Indeed, the idea that punishment results from sin, individual or communal, is a major motif posited and refined throughout the Hebrew Bible.[23] Despite the eloquent protest of Job, mainstream Jewish theology assumes a cause-and-effect structure: if we are punished, we (or our ancestors) must have sinned: by our own lack of piety, by our own weakness, by building the Golden Calf ("the sin" par excellence), or by selling Joseph into Egyptian slavery.[24] Affliction is understood as justice, and suffering redefined as purifying divine attentiveness.

Not every Jewish theodicy focuses on human culpability. Isaac bar Shalom's poem reflects the tradition of theology that rejects an explanation for the problem of evil. The poet depicts Jews who are saints; their suffering cannot be their fault. No ancestral sins are mentioned. Even the Christian mobs merely play out their assigned role. Our poem, like others of this bent, confronts God directly, with bewilderment and dismay. It does not try to clean up history with tidy explanations. It refuses to put the guilt on the victim. Suffering alone should move God, regardless of suffering's cause. The relationship between God and Israel is assumed; it is the neglected responsibilities of that covenant that Isaac bar Shalom invokes. The

---

[22] The Rabbis would trace this tradition back to Abraham's argument with God on behalf of Sodom in Gen. 18.

[23] See, for example, the tension over the idea of transgenerational guilt (Exod. 34.7 being a famous example) vs. individual guilt (Jer. 31, Ezek. 18).

[24] The Byzantine-era martyrological poem, "These will I remember" (*Eleh Ezkarah*), recited as part of the Yom Kippur liturgy, includes the motif of the ongoing punishment of the Jews – particularly their leaders – on account of the sin of selling Joseph for a pair of sandals. All variants of this particular text have been gathered and published in a critical edition by Gottfried Reeg, *Die Geschichte von den zehn Märtyrern* (Tübingen, 1985). The sandal-motif itself can be traced back to a poem by Pinhas HaKohen (eighth-century Galilee?), "You sold a brother for your pair of sandals" (*Ah Be-Na'aleikhem Mekhartem*). See T. Carmi, *Penguin Anthology of Hebrew Verse* (New York, 1981), pp. 233–34 [hereafter, "Carmi"] for the HaKohen poem in both Hebrew and English (a prose translation). For a critical edition of the Hebrew, see Ezra Fleischer, *The Yotzer: Its Emergence and Development* (Jerusalem, 1984), pp. 139–41; Hebrew. The motif can be traced in prose sources to the midrashic text, *Pirke deRabbi Eliezer* 38 (itself dating perhaps as late as the eighth century CE, although it may contain earlier traditions).

question is not Israel's status as "chosen," but God's baffling failure to act His part. Isaac bar Shalom is not interested in blame but accountability.

An important example of the tradition in which Isaac bar Shalom is rooted can be found in the Babylonian Talmud. In the Talmud, the Rabbis note a strange discrepancy among the divine attributes as stated by Moses, Jeremiah, Daniel and Nehemiah. Bracketing biblical history, Moses the Torah-giver and Ezra the Scribe both refer to God as "great, mighty, and awesome." The prophet Jeremiah, however, only called God "great and mighty" – not awesome; the wise hero Daniel described the deity as "great and awesome" – but not mighty. Could there be theological disagreement among four such important men? The rabbis discuss this problem and imagine the following scenario:

> Why were Ezra and his men called "the Great Synod"? Because they restored the crown of God's [three] attributes to its ancient completeness. Moses had come and said: The great God, mighty and awesome. But Jeremiah [at the time when the first Temple was destroyed] came and said: Foreigners are destroying His Temple; where are His awesome deeds? Hence Jeremiah omitted the attribute "awesome." Daniel [in the time of the Babylonian Exile] came and said: Foreigners are enslaving His children; where are His mighty deeds? Hence he omitted the word "mighty." ... How could [Jeremiah and Daniel] abolish something established by Moses? Rabbi Eleazar said: Since they knew that the Holy One, blessed be He, insists on truth, they would not ascribe false things to Him.[25]

God respects truth, not flattery. From the bold opening line, our poet, Isaac bar Shalom, is clear: like Jeremiah and Daniel, witnesses to incomprehensible tragedy, he will not flatter his God. Like Jeremiah and Daniel, he will ask questions: Where are Your mighty deeds? How can You stay silent? The events of the sixth century BCE, as read by the Rabbis, provide the language, images, and basis for descriptions of all later devastations, including that of 1147 CE.[26]

Isaac bar Shalom joins himself to this "timeless" tradition both by drawing from it and by de-emphasizing his own historical context. He embeds his date, 1147, in a code. His antagonists are anonymous – simply "the enemy." Only the author's biography, his location in the Rhineland during the Second Crusade, and other subtle cues permit us to understand that the events are in some way connected to the crusades or the social upheaval they engendered. It is not even clear that the poet was an eyewitness to the events, although the subtle switch to the first person in the ninth stanza implies that he was. Medieval Hebrew aesthetics, however, emphasize the cyclical nature of events – bad as well as good. Old sufferings provide the language of fresh grief, while ancient redemptions remain the paradigm for

---

[25] BT *Yoma* 69b; this talmudic parallel is adduced by Jakob Petuchowski, *Theology and Poetry*, p. 72, and is used subsequently by Roskies, *Nightwords* (see n. 5 above), pp. 2–3.

[26] For this nullification of historical consciousness in favor of a personalized memory model, see Yosef Hayim Yerushalmi, *Zakhor* (Washington, 1982) and subsequent writings based on his approach to historiography.

future hopes. The very creation of tropes – of patterns of literary imagery, allusion, and rhetoric – undermines our ability to treat poems such as this as historical sources. The importance of convention and tradition significantly complicate historiographical analyses of such works.

Of particular interest here, however, are not the historic events underlying this poem's creation but rather the poet's choice of a daring, anguished theological tradition that had not been widely employed outside the rabbinic sources already cited. Isaac bar Shalom offers us a reaction, a *sense* of events, if not actual records. To understand this poem, we should understand its context, liturgical and literary. We must consider how the poet uses old words to shape his new work, how creativity functions in a form heavily steeped in tradition. With this established, it will be more likely that we can understand what the poet has achieved in writing this powerful and painful poetry.

First, we turn to the poetic tradition in which Isaac bar Shalom wrote. Jewish poetry written in the wake of the First and Second Crusades contains some of the most vivid and disturbing images written in the Hebrew language since the book of Lamentations. A world of martyrdom embraced over apostasy, of mothers killing sons, fathers killing daughters, husbands killing wives. The goriness and graphic violence of these poems may startle modern readers or strike them as distasteful, but it reflects medieval communal religious and aesthetic ideals if not the reality of the Jews' daily existence.

Reflecting an aesthetic and theology similar to that of Isaac bar Shalom, his contemporary Ephraim of Bonn writes:

> Woe is me if I speak and cast doubt upon my Maker.
> But woe is me if I do not speak, venting my sorrow …
> I am stoned, I am struck down, I am crucified
> Is the Lord's arm so short that He cannot change my lot?[27]

Similarly, Baruch of Mainz, another twelfth-century Ashkenazic poet, accuses God with blunt words:

> Remember this and abandon hope:
> They were given away and devoured,
> Though they sang Your praises daily in their multitudes.
> Did You, their helper and their shield, think this just? …
> You forbade the uncircumcised to offer you even rams.
> Why, then, did You hide Your face when they ravaged the holy people,
> The feeble Jews who put their trust in You?[28]

---

[27] Text and translation from: Carmi, pp. 384–85.
[28] Text and translation from: Carmi, p. 387.

Poet after poet expresses dismay and awe. An anonymous poet exclaims:

O Unique One, O Lofty One,
We are pierced and murdered for Your sake,
For refusing to bow our heads before the child of wantonness [Jesus] …
Has the like of this ever been seen or heard?
Could anyone believe such a stupefying sight?
They lead their children to the slaughter
As if to a beautiful bridal canopy.
After this, O exalted and triumphant Lord,
Will you hold back?[29]

Isaac bar Shalom, for all his anger, is keeping august company. Indeed, his despair over God's passivity is not as bold as Ephraim of Bonn's questioning of God's actual potency. Isaac bar Shalom writes from within a distinctive Ashkenazic tradition.

The powerful, even violent, imagery of these poems is so intense that these works have often been treated as if they are eyewitness accounts rather than literature. Contemporary historians, however, have done remarkable work uncovering the rich, diverse, and surprisingly fruitful intellectual, social, and religious lives of the Jews of medieval Ashkenaz.[30] At the same time that the idea of Andalusian Jewish *convivencia* is being critiqued, the so-called "lachrymose" theory of Ashkenazic Jewish history is being discarded. Scholars have uncovered a reality dramatically more complex and rich than the picture presented in these poems on their own. Nevertheless, if the poems often focus on the valiant actions of mothers and wives, they are not simply giving us demographic information but are telling us about – and, in turn, shaping – ideals of femininity, perhaps in contrast to the Holy Family of Christianity.[31] Martyrological texts and traditions, going back to classical antiquity, have shaped these later works, both their hagiographical depictions and their theological outbursts. Ideals and ideology, text and tradition, all intersect in these works. Scholarship is now approaching these texts with much greater nuance,

---

[29] Text and translation from: Carmi, pp. 374–75.

[30] For some outstanding examples of the complex, and occasionally controversial, historiography undertaken in recent years, see: Ivan Marcus, "History, Story, and Collective Memory," *Prooftexts* 10 (1990), 365–88; "Jews and Christians Imagining the Other in Medieval Europe," *Prooftexts* 15 (1995), 209–26; "The Jewish–Christian Symbiosis," in *Cultures of the Jews*, ed. Davud Biale (New York, 2002), pp. 448–503; Jeremy Cohen, "Between Martyrdom and Apostasy," *Journal of Medieval and Early Modern Studies* 29 (1999), 431–71; Shmuel Shepkaru, "Death Twice Over," *Jewish Quarterly Review* 93 (2002), 217–56; and, "Scholarship as Lamentation: Shalom Spiegel on 'The Binding of Isaac,'" *Jewish Social Studies* 5 (1998/99), 80–91. The most important single monograph on the complex relationship of history and literature in the martyrological poems of northern France is Einbinder, *Beautiful Death*. More generally, see Boyarin, *Dying for God* and Fishbane, *The Kiss of God*.

[31] On the depictions of women – real, ideal, and polemical – in medieval Hebrew texts (not exclusively poetic), see Ivan Marcus, "Mothers, Martyrs, and Moneymakers," *Conservative Judaism* 38 (1986), 34–45.

borrowing from the advances in the study of hagiography, in particular, but also from innovations in Jewish text-study.

Indeed, the overarching context of these medieval poems is broad, well beyond their moment of origin and deeply into the long tradition of Jewish sources. The language of these poems is dense with allusions: to the biblical book of Lamentations, with its graphic and emotional depictions of Jerusalem's destruction at the hands of the Babylonians – itself partaking of literary conventions of the ancient world; to Leviticus, where we find sacrificial laws inverted by the medievals through acts of martyrdom; to the binding of Isaac, and Daniel's friends in the furnace – literary traditions shaping historical acts. And the medieval poetry draws upon post-biblical Jewish traditions, as well: midrashic collections, the Talmud, and other ancient works. It is not just a matter of what the poets say, but how they say it; not just the existence of exegetical traditions but the poet's decision to use a specific tradition after centuries of latency.

Most modern readers lack a basic literacy the medieval writers assumed. Tradition colored how they spoke of what they saw, and helped them find understanding. Sometimes tradition let them speak ideas too bold to invent; and sometimes it let the poet conceal complexity within simple, familiar words. In other words, these medieval poems are deeply traditional, and to focus primarily on their historicity or their superficial narratives, as has often been done, is to discount their very profound and significant conventionality.[32] The images of parents slaughtering their children in these texts is horrifying, but no more horrifying than the passage in Lamentations where women dying of starvation are said to eat their young. Even the bursts of rage against God that we see in the medieval works are rooted in the biblical lament's accusations: "When I cry and plead, [God] shuts out my prayer … You have slain without pity! You have screened Yourself off with a cloud that no prayer may pass through" (Lam. 3.8, 43–44). The enemy has changed, but the experience has not. And Isaac bar Shalom, like those before and after him, took up the ancient burden of lamentations.

This is not to say that the poems are devoid of historical detail, any more than their biblical and rabbinic precedents are. Some medieval Jewish poems make explicit reference to crusaders. An anonymous text opens with this vivid description, among the most explicit of crusaders in medieval Jewish poetry:

"Come with us, You of the smitten cheeks,"
Say the uncircumcised and unclean,

---

[32] The assumption that these poems are simple historical records is no longer commonplace in serious medieval academic histories, thanks to the works noted above. On the issue of using these texts solely as sources of historical information, however – still commonly found in oversimplified form in primary sources readers aimed at undergraduates and non-specialists – see the careful and significant work of Susan Einbinder in *Beautiful Death*, esp. pp. 10–11. Regarding poems such as this only in light of their potential historical information overlooks the ancient and medieval traditions in which they operated, as well as the conscious constructive-theological role such works played among Ashkenazic Jewry.

The smooth-tongued enemies.
"We are on our way to the land of the lovely diadem,
The radiant land.
We shall attack and plunder
The spoil of the fortified cities.
There we shall take our shares,
To each man two lengths of dyed cloth!"[33]

Other texts refer to "straying vagabonds" [*to'im*]; still others speak more generally of Christian mobs that sought to compel the Jews to abandon their faith and turn to Christianity: "We have been abandoned, alone and suffering, because we refused to bow our heads before the crucified one, a corpse trampled underfoot; let all who put their trust in him be put to shame!"[34] The poets have many colorful names for their persecutors, which show that Jews were just as capable of vitriol as their medieval Christian counterparts. Ephraim of Regensburg (twelfth century), for example, writes: "The men of deceit and sham rejoice in houses full of ease, while those who revere You are stoned and strangled. Only those who cling to the Lord are scourged ... They urge me to betray You, those who fall down before an image hanging on a rack, who worship a block of wood. But I did not join its ranks."[35] The language is one turn shy of explicit – the "men of deceit and sham" alludes to Ezekiel 13, where it refers to false prophets; the "child of wantonness" refers to an old Jewish polemic that Jesus was a not divine, but a bastard (the Jewish "counter text" to the Virgin birth). In other texts, commonplace epithets such as "the boar" or "Esau" allude to the Church and Christendom. These codes, in Hebrew, were perhaps safer than openly anti-Christian language, but they were far from opaque, and these texts were often censored. In the end, these poems have value as both literature and history, but neither category fully contains them.

The significance of context for understanding *Ein Kamokha Ba-Illemim* ("Who is Like You among the Mute") does not stop at the level of *literary* context, however. This poem was written for the liturgy. It was not only read but prayed. Anger, rage, and dismay were not hidden away from the public view but were given an unmistakable voice in the house of prayer. Such words were not spoken by blasphemers or outcasts; they were written by sages and performed in full public view. It is likely that the refrain – the plea, "Do not keep silent!" – was recited by the community as a whole. Setting, performance, and repetition are of crucial importance for understanding the power of the poem: they imbue it with the power not only to express belief but to shape it. Recited not once but annually, century after century, anguished laments such as these played an ongoing role in constructing both the theology and world-view of the Jews who heard them.

---

[33] Carmi, p. 368.
[34] Carmi, p. 373.
[35] Carmi, p. 378.

Conclusions

What can we learn from this poem, which draws on ancient texts and tropes as much as contemporary sources and events? On the one hand, *Ein Kamokha Ba-Illemim* is profoundly conventional, both as a medieval Hebrew poem in the wake of the Second Crusade and as a vehicle for conveying traditions of interpretation going back a thousand years. Its traditionalism makes the history beneath the surface difficult to detect. At the same time, this reliance on traditions not previously associated with poetry or with synagogue performance grounds the poet's angry accusation against God in Jewish history. He does not suffer alone; the martyrs did not die alone. The community does not – shall not, must not – grieve alone. Suffering is part of a pattern that takes on its own meaning. What did our poet witness and what did he invent? We will never know. But his bold accusation against the God who is mute has behind it the strength of tradition, the support of convention, the silent assent of poetic wrath of generations past.

"There is None Like you Among the Mute" – critical edition

The six MSS of the poem consulted for this edition are remarkably similar and are all relatively early witnesses. They were copied in Ashkenaz, that is, in geographic proximity to the poem's setting. They are all written in clear hand, with vocalization and occasional corrections included. The majority of differences among them consist of variations in spelling, as well as the occasional addition or deletion of a conjunction.

I use the following sigla:

M   Munich, Cod. Heb 88 (F 1673)[36]
M2 Munich, Cod. Heb. 21 (F 1173)
L   Haifa, Lifshitz 1 (F 39522)
N   Nuremberg Mahzor
O   Oxford, Bodl. MS Opp. 668 (F22612)
W   Wroclaw (Breslau) II Ort. 577 (F 16586)

The Nuremberg Mahzor, which served the basis for the previous critical edition by Avraham Habermann,[37] dates from 1331. None of the other MSS has a colophon allowing precise dating. Based on script and context, the Institute of Microfilmed Hebrew Manuscripts catalogue estimates that the two Munich MSS were copied around 1200 in Ashkenaz. The Oxford MS is tentatively dated to around 1200 but,

---

[36] F = film number, referring to the catalogue system of the Institute of Microfilmed Hebrew Manuscripts at the Jewish National and University Library, Jerusalem.

[37] *Sefer Gezerot Ashkenaz ve-Tsarefat* (Jerusalem, 1945), pp. 113–14.

unlike the roughly contemporary Munich MSS, it consistently favors defective spellings. The Haifa and Wroclaw MSS are dated to the thirteenth century, with the latter – which served as the cover or binding for a later codex – containing only one-third of the poem.

The following edition follows Munich Cod. Heb. 88, chosen because of its clarity in consonants and vowels as well as its early date, except in places where the other MSS appear to give a better reading. Differences in vocalization not reflected in spelling differences that change the meaning (for example, the use of pausal forms) are not noted in the apparatus. The printed edition of Simon Bernfeld[38] will be cited in the apparatus as B.

My thanks to Mr. Avraham Fraenkel for his assistance.

Printed editions

This poem is listed in Israel Davidson's *Thesaurus*.[39] Previously published scholarly versions of this poem can be found in Bernfeld and Habermann, noted above. A more popular version, which includes an English translation and a limited commentary, can be found in Jakob Petuchowski, "The Silent God," *Theology and Poetry: Studies in Medieval Piyyut* (Cincinnati, 1978; repr. 2000), pp. 74–77. Israel Davidson also cites other printed rites, including *Otzar Ha-Tefillot*, 2 vols (Vilna, 1914), 2:256, noted as "OT" in the apparatus; *Seder Avodah ba-Lev*, 2 vols (Leipzig, 1840), 2:223; and *Siddur ve-Machzor Kol Bo*, 4 vols. (Vilna, 1905), 4:307.

---

[38] *Sefer Ha-Dema`ot*, vol. 1 (Berlin, 1924), pp. 217–21.
[39] Israel Davidson, *Thesaurus of Medieval Hebrew Poetry*, 4 vols (New York, 1924), 1:142, no. 3027.

"There is None Like You Among the Mute"

Translation of *Ein Kamokha Ba-Illemim*

There is none like You among the mute,
Silent and still before those who cause us grief.
    Our enemies, rising up, are many.
When they assemble together to mock us,
    "Where is Your King?" they taunted us.
    We have not forgotten You; we have not lied.
Do not be silent![1]

Those cast out from the community were haughty;
    Your people with violence they crushed.
    Your haters carried high their heads,
They sought sooth from ghosts and godlings.
    Our enemies, judges, said:
    "How wretched are these Jews!"[2]
    Do not be silent!

"Let us give you some good advice,
    Lest you come to shame –
    Indeed, to quarrelling and violent strife!
If you will be like us
    And turn to the filthy Nazarene[3]
    'And one people shall we become.'[4]"
    Do not be silent!

The smitten cried out their reply:
    "We shall neither turn to him nor worship him;
    'You shall detest him utterly, completely abhor him!'[5]
The One who lives and endures is our Redeemer,
    Him we worship and Him entreat.
    'At the time of affliction, He is our salvation.'[6]"
    Do not be silent!

---

[1] Psa. 83.2
[2] Neh. 3.34
[3] Or "carrion" – see Isa. 14.19
[4] Gen. 34.16
[5] Deut. 7.26
[6] Isa. 33.2

יצחק ברבי שלום

אֵין כָּמוֹךָ בָּאִילְּמִים

אֵין כָּמוֹךָ בָּאִילְּמִים   דּוֹמֵם וְשׁוֹתֵק לְמַעֲגִימִים
צָרֵינוּ רַבִּים קָמִים

בְּהִוָּסְדָם יַחַד לְנָדְפֵנוּ   אַיֵּה מַלְכְּכֶם חֵרְפוּנוּ
וְלֹא שְׁכַחֲנוּךָ וְלֹא שִׁקַּרְנוּ   אַל דֳּמִי לָךְ

גֵּרוּשִׁים מִן גֵּיו גָּאוּ   וְעַמְּךָ בְּפֶרֶךְ דִּכְּאוּ   5
מְשַׂנְאֶיךָ רֹאשׁ נָשָׂאוּ

דָּרְשׁוּ לְאוֹבוֹת וֶאֱלִילִים   דִּבְּרוּ אוֹיְבֵינוּ פְּלִילִים
מָה הַיְּהוּדִים הָאֻמְלָלִים   אַל דֳּמִי לָךְ

הָבוּ לָכֶם עֵצָה   פֶּן תִּהְיוּ לְשִׁמְצָה
הֵן לְרִיב וּמַצָּה   10

וְאִם תִּהְיוּ כָּמוֹנוּ   לְנֵצֶר נִתְעָב תִּפְנוּ
לְעַם אֶחָד הָיִינוּ   אַל דֳּמִי לָךְ

זָעֲקוּ לוֹקִים וַיַּעֲנוּ   לֹא נָשׁוּב וְלֹא נַעַבְדֶנּוּ
שַׁקֵּץ תְּשַׁקְּצֶנּוּ וְתַעֵב תְּתַעֲבֶנּוּ

חַי וְקַיָּם גּוֹאֲלֵנוּ   אוֹתוֹ נַעֲבוֹד וּנְחַטְּבֶנּוּ   15
בְּעֵת צָרָה יְשׁוּעָתֵינוּ   אַל דֳּמִי לָךְ

כתבי היד: מ — מינכן M   י — מינכן M2   א — אוקספורד O   ו — וורוצלב W
נ — מחזור נירנברג N   ל — ליפשיץ 1 דף 117 ע״ב L   ב — ברנפלד B

כותרת: זולת לשבת אחרת מ
רפריין אחרי כל שתי סטרופות **אוילמ** רפריין נוסף גם אחרי סטרופות 1, 3, ...5 י
| 4 לא שכחנוך א לא שכחנו ב | שיקנו מ[1] שיקרנו מ[2]   5 גרושים: גרשוני מ |
מן גיו ו | עמך ו | עמך נ | בְּפֶרֶךְ למ | 7 דורשי אובות ב | דְּרְשׁוּ י | לאובות
חס׳ מ | ואלילים: לאלילים מ | דברו: יאמרו ב   12 והיינו **אבוי**[2]ל[2]נ
13 ויענו: חס׳ מ[1] הושלם מ[2] | לא: ולא מ[1] לא מ[2] | נשוב חס׳ ו | ולא: חס׳ מ[1] ו הושלם
מ[2] | נעבדינו חס׳ מ[1]   14 נשקצנו נ | נתעבנו נ   15 נחטבנו מ[1] וְנַחְטְּבֶנּוּ ל

To slaughter children we readied ourselves.   The blessing over sacrifice we practiced.
    " 'Hear, O Israel, the Lord is our God,
The Lord is One,'[7] – Let us proclaim His unity.   To sanctify His name, we have been slain.
    Let our wives and babes fall upon the sword."   *Do not be silent!*

Priests, to slaughter their burnt offerings,   Bound both mother and child;
    In fire, they burned their skins.
Sprinkling the blood of sisters and brothers,   Offering as incense those lambs of pleasing scent,
    Both the head and the severed parts.   *Do not be silent!*

A row of scorched heaps,   Like an oven neither covered nor swept.
    "All the house of Israel wept at the burning."[8]
Those who fall into the flames of the fire of God   Are fated for fellowship with Heaven's own sons:[9]
    Hannaniah, Mishael, and Azariah.   *Do not be silent!*

Like rubbish they treated the Torah of Moses,   And the Talmud of Ravina and Rav Ashi.
    How can You remain restrained and silent, with this?
Pages and scrolls, put to the slaughter,   While holy letters fly up in flame.
    The writing of God engraved upon tablets.   *Do not be silent!*

The enemy strutted with his sword,   My good ones he destroyed, made like nothing.
    He slew every delight of my eye.
A specific indication: in the year 4907 AM[10]   Affliction followed on affliction's heel.
    For my feet, they set a snare.   *Do not be silent!*

The end came when Nahshon hallowed God: The enemy smote the apple of (His) eye.
    On the 20th day of the first month[11]
They were dashed to bits, the seekers of the major   And the minor in Torah law, employers of analogy,
    In statutes and ordinances and commandments.   *Do not be silent!*

---

[7] Deut. 6.4
[8] Lev. 10.6
[9] See BT Sukkah 45b and BT Sanhedrin 97b
[10] That is, 1147 CE
[11] Nisan

בְּרַכַּת הַזֶּבַח כִּנּוּ   טָבוֹחַ יְלָדִים הֵכִינוּ

שְׁמַע יִשְׂרָאֵל יי אֱלֹהֵינוּ

עַל קִידּוּשׁ שְׁמוֹ הוֹרַגְנוּ   יי אֶחָד וּנְיַחֲדֶנּוּ

לִנְפּוֹל בַּחֶרֶב נָשֵׁינוּ וְטַפֵּינוּ   אַל דֳּמִי לָךְ   20

עָקְדוּ יְלָדִים וְאִמּוֹתָם   כֹּהֲנִים לְזֶבַח עוֹלָתָם

וְשָׂרְפוּ בָאֵשׁ אֶת עוֹרוֹתָם

וּלְהַקְטִיר אֵימוּרֵי נִיחוֹחִים   לִזְרוֹק דְּמֵי אַחֲיוֹת וְאַחִים

אֶת הָרֹאשׁ וְאֶת הַנְּתָחִים   אַל דֳּמִי לָךְ

כְּכִירָה לֹא קְטוּמָה וּגְרוּפָה   מַעֲרָכָה גְּדוֹשָׁה שְׂזוּפָה   25

וְכָל בֵּית יִשְׂרָאֵל יִבְכּוּ אֶת הַשְּׂרֵפָה

נוֹעָדִים לְמִחֲצַת בָּנֵי עָלֶיהָ   נוֹפְלִים לְרִשְׁפֵּי שַׁלְהֶבֶת יָהּ

חֲנַנְיָה מִישָׁאֵל וַעֲזַרְיָה   אַל דֳּמִי לָךְ

וְתַלְמוּד רָבִינָא וְרַב אַשֵׁי   סָחִי שָׁמוּ תּוֹרַת מֹשֶׁה

הַעַל אֵלֶּה תִּתְאַפַּק וְתֶחֱשֶׁה   30

וְאוֹתִיּוֹת קְדוֹשׁוֹת פּוֹרְחוֹת   עַמּוּדִים וּגְוִילִים לַאֲבָחוֹת

מִכְתַּב אֱלֹהִים חָרוּת עַל הַלּוּחוֹת   אַל דֳּמִי לָךְ

וְאִיבֵּד טוֹבַי וְשָׁם לְאַיִן   פָּסַע אוֹיֵב בְּזַיִן

וַיַּהֲרֹג כֹּל מַחֲמַדֵּי עַיִן

צָרָה אֶל אֲחוֹתָהּ נִגְּשֶׁת   צִיּוֹן לִפְרָט וַ'אַ'רְ'שׁ'ת'   35

הֵכִינוּ לְפַעֲמֵי רֶשֶׁת   אַל דֳּמִי לָךְ

נָגַע צַר בָּאִישׁוֹן   קֵץ קִידּוּשׁ נַחְשׁוֹן

בְּעֶשְׂרִים לַחוֹדֶשׁ הָרִאשׁוֹן

וְקַלּוֹת וְשָׁווֹת גְּזֵרוֹת   רוֹטְשׁוּ דוֹרְשֵׁי חֲמוּרוֹת

הַחֻקִּים וְהַמִּשְׁפָּטִים וְהַתּוֹרוֹת   אַל דֳּמִי לָךְ   40

17 כינו: בֵּרַכְנוּ **ל** כּוּנוּ **ב**   19 ועל **ב** | שמו: שמך **ול**   20 בנפול **ו**
21 לְזֶבַח עוֹלָתָם **מ** | עולותם **או**   22 ועקדו **לם**   23 ואחיות אחים **ל¹**
אחיות ואחים **ל²**   25 שזופה **ל¹** גרושה **ל²** ושזופה **ן** | בכירה קטומה ולא גרופה **ל**
27 למחיצה **ל**   28 וחנניה **ל** כחנניה **ן** | וחנניה ומישאל ועזריה **מ**   31 לַאֲבָחוֹת **מין**
33 טובַי **אמנ** טוֹבִי **ב**   35 א'ר'שׁ'ת' **ל**   36 לִפְעָמֵי **בל**   39 שוות וגזירות **ל**

Almighty! Be jealous of Your Torah!

    Wake up Your mighty power,

Rebuke the beast that roots like a boar

    Him, and all his people, with plague.

Once Your right hand split Rahab;

    That one, so dainty, who just sits there!

Bright and ruddy from Seir,

    You will stir up fury like a man of war![12]

Take back, once again, our remnant;

    Prepare peace for us,[13]

Pity, O Holy One of ours, those You scattered.

    Arise, O our Help, and save us!

Garb Yourself in vengeance and rage,

With destruction and havoc and shattering –

Do not be silent!

Now crush her skull with a hammer –

You will rebuke her princes with destruction

Do not be silent!

In public, show us Your wonders.

Let a noble spirit sustain us.

Do not be silent!

---

[12] Isa. 42.13

[13] Isa. 26.12

שַׁדַּי קַנֵּא לְתוֹרָתֶךְ   לְבוֹשׁ נִקְמָתֶךָ וְקִנְאָתֶךְ
וְעוֹרְרָה אֶת גְּבוּרָתֶךְ

תִּגְעַר חַיַּת נוֹבֵר   בְּכִלָּיוֹן וְשׁוֹד וְשֶׁבֶר
אוֹתוֹ וְאֶת עַמּוֹ בַּדְּבֶר   אַל דֳּמִי לָךְ

יְמִינְךָ רַהַב מַחֲצֶבֶת   הָרֵץ גֻּלְגּוֹלֶת בְּמַקֶּבֶת   45
זֹאת עֲדִינָה הַיּוֹשֶׁבֶת

צֹח וְאָדוֹם מִשֵּׂעִיר   נְסִיכֶיהָ בְּכִלָּיוֹן תַּגְעִיר
כְּאִישׁ מִלְחָמוֹת קִנְאָה תָּעִיר   אַל דֳּמִי לָךְ

קַנֵּה שֵׁנִית שְׂרִידֵנוּ   בְּרָבִּים נִסֶּיךָ תַּרְאֵינוּ
שָׁלוֹם תִּשְׁפֹּת לָנוּ   50

חֲמוֹל זְרוּיֶיךָ קְדוֹשֵׁינוּ   וְרוּחַ נְדִיבָה תִּסְמְכֵינוּ
קוּמָה עֶזְרָתָה לָּנוּ וּפְדֵינוּ   אַל דֳּמִי לָךְ

---

41 לְבַשׁ **ב** | קנאתך ונקמתך **אנ**[1] נקמתך וקנאתך **נ**[2]   43 נ'ו'ב'ר' **נ** | שוד **א**   45 גולגלתו **יל**
46 יושבת **ל**   47 נסיכה **בל** | תסעיר **בנ**   48 יעיר **א** תגעיר **ל**[1] תעיר **ל**[2]   49 שרידנו
קדושינו **א**

Rescuing Syria from the Infidels: The Contribution of Ibn ʿAsakir of Damascus to the *Jihad* Campaign of Sultan Nur al-Din

Suleiman A. Mourad (Smith College)
and
James E. Lindsay (Colorado State University)

The arrival of the crusaders in the Near East and their invasion of coastal Syria in 1098–99 exposed a major area of the Islamic heartland to non-Islamic rule for the first time since the Arabian Islamic conquests four and one half centuries earlier. The rapid success with which the crusaders established themselves there alarmed the local religious establishment and created a realization among the religious scholars that the Muslims and their military leaders had failed in their duty, as prescribed by God and his prophet Muhammad, to defend the lands of Islam against the infidels. ʿAli ibn Tahir al-Sulami (d. 1106) was the first to author a treatise calling on his fellow Muslims to respond militarily to the crusader threat. Composed shortly after the sack of Jerusalem in 1099, al-Sulami's *Kitab al-Jihad* (Book of the Holy War) denounces his fellow Muslims for their weakness and division, and calls upon them to unite in religious purification – which he called *al-jihad al-akbar* (the greater *jihad*) – so that they might better wage *al-jihad al-asghar* (the lesser *jihad*) and defeat the invaders.[1]

Since Ibn ʿAsakir of Damascus (1105–76) entered this world one year before al-Sulami entered the next and six years after the crusaders conquered Jerusalem, he had no recollection of a Syria devoid of the Frankish presence. It should come as no surprise then that he, like al-Sulami before him, was preoccupied with the crusader threat and the Muslims' internal divisions and rivalries. Consequently, he eagerly placed himself in the service of sultan Nur al-Din (d. 1174), whom he saw as the ideal leader to unite the Muslims and rally them to *jihad* in the path of God (*jihad fi sabil Allah*) to uproot all types of heresies and disbelief from Syria and Egypt. To that end and at the request of his patron, Ibn ʿAsakir authored a treatise entitled *al-Arbaʿin fi al-ijtihad fi iqamat al-jihad* (The Forty *Hadiths* on the Obligation to Wage *Jihad*), in which he presents forty *hadiths* that praise *jihad* as a religious duty, lay out the conditions to be met by the individuals who are waging *jihad*, promise rewards for *jihad* fighters and punishment for deserters, and establish the many ways one can contribute to *jihad* without actually fighting.

---

[1] On the text of al-Sulami, see Niall Christie, "Motivating Listeners in the *Kitab al-Jihad* of ʿAli ibn Tahir al-Sulami (d. 1106)," above pp. 1–14.

The Concept of *Jihad*

The meaning of the term *jihad* has become a controversial issue in recent years. In the search to explain its persistence in Islamic scholarship, apologists and revivalists have disagreed on the meaning of *jihad*.[2] The lexicographical meaning is to exert one's effort toward an objective; in a religious context in particular, *jihad* has one meaning: to exert one's effort in fighting the enemies of God by acts or by words.[3] Several Qur'anic verses extol the virtues of *jihad*, and often associate conducting the duty with either one's self (*nafs*) or one's personal wealth (*mal*).[4] The most important material is in the ninth chapter (*Repentance*) – the only chapter of the Qur'an's 114 that does not begin with the phrase, "In the name of God the Merciful, the Compassionate." Whatever the reason for its unique opening, it is the content of the chapter that concerns us here. Since it is far too long to reproduce, we have selected four passages that convey the basic principles of military *jihad* and its rewards. There are, of course, relevant passages elsewhere in the chapter and throughout the Qur'an as well.[5]

The first two passages speak of *jihad* as offensive warfare against idolaters, polytheists, and infidels. Note that Jews and Christians are placed in this category despite many other passages in the Qur'an that speak favorably of those among the Jews and Christians who shall see paradise.[6]

> When the sacred months are over slay (*qtulu*) the idolaters wherever you find them. Arrest them, besiege them, and lie in ambush everywhere for them. If they repent and take to prayer and render the alms levy, allow them to go their way. God is forgiving and merciful. (Qur'an 9.5)[7]

> Fight against (*qatilu*) such of those to whom the Scriptures were given and believe neither in God nor the Last Day, who do not forbid what God and His apostle have forbidden, and do not embrace the true Faith, until they pay tribute out of hand and are utterly subdued. The Jews say that Ezra is the son of God, while the Christians say the Messiah is the son of God. Such are their assertions, by which they imitate the infidels of old. God confound them! How perverse they are! (Qur'an 9.29–30)

---

[2] A range of these views are discussed in Reuven Firestone, *Jihad: The Origin of Holy War in Islam* (New York, 1999), pp. 3–4. See also David Cook, *Understanding Jihad* (Berkeley, CA, 2005); idem, "Muslim Apocalyptic and *Jihad*," *Jerusalem Studies in Arabic and Islam* 20 (1996), 66–104; Rudolph Peters, *Jihad in Classical and Modern Islam* (Princeton, 1996); and Emmanuel Sivan, *Radical Islam: Medieval Theology and Modern Politics* (New Haven, CT, 1985).

[3] See Ibn Manzur (d. 1311), *Lisan al-ʿArab*, 15 vols. (Beirut, 1990), 3:135 (*j-h-d*).

[4] See, for instance, verses 4.95, 8.72, 9.20, 9.41, and 9.88.

[5] See Ella Landau Tasseron, "Jihad," in *Encyclopaedia of the Qur'an*, ed. Jane Dammen McAuliffe (Leiden, 2001–2006), 3:35–43.

[6] Fred M. Donner examines the relevant Qur'anic passages on Jews and Christians in "From Believers to Muslims: Confessional Self-identity in the Early Islamic Community," *Al-Abhath* 50–51 (2002–3), 9–53.

[7] All Qur'anic citations are from N. J. Dawood, *The Koran*, 5th rev. ed. (New York, 1999).

Jihad is not only to be conducted offensively against the idolaters, polytheists, and infidels, but also defensively against those who fight against Muhammad, his followers, and right religion in general:

> Will you not fight (*tuqatilun*) against those who have broken their oaths and conspired to banish the Apostle? They were the first to attack you. Do you fear them? Surely God is more deserving of your fear, if you are true believers. Make war on them (*qatiluhum*): God will chastise them at your hands and humble them. He will grant you victory over them and heal the spirit of the faithful. He will take away all rancour from their hearts: God shows mercy to whom He pleases. God is all-knowing and wise. (Qurʾan 9.13–14)

The rewards awaiting those who strive in the path of God include gardens watered by running streams, in which they shall abide forever:

> But the Apostle and the men who shared his faith fought (*jahadu*) with their goods and with their persons. These shall be rewarded with good things. These shall surely prosper. God has prepared for them gardens watered by running streams, in which they shall abide forever. That is the supreme triumph. (Qurʾan 9.88)

In addition to these and other Qurʾanic passages, Muslim scholars also appealed to a host of *hadiths* that extolled the merits of *jihad* against the enemies of right religion, however defined, and the rewards that awaited those engaged in it. According to one such *hadith*, Muhammad said:

> If anyone is pleased with God as Lord, with Islam as religion and with Muhammad as messenger, paradise will be assured to him. ... There is also something else for which God will raise a servant in paradise a hundred degrees between each two of which there is a distance like that between heaven and earth. ... [That is,] "*Jihad* in God's path; *jihad* in God's path; *jihad* in God's path".[8]

Since Muhammad found himself at war with the Meccans and others after his *hijra* (migration) to Medina in 622, it is easy to see the relevance of such statements to his immediate situation. After his death, his followers used these and many others like them to form the basis for the ideology of *jihad* in the medieval Islamic world. They inspired many of the faithful during the first century of conquests even as others were undoubtedly inspired merely by booty and glory in battle. Once the frontiers of the new Islamic empire were more or less stabilized, the caliphs maintained an expansionist *jihad* ideology by leading or ordering raids along the Syrian–Byzantine frontier. Many a caliph strengthened his own religious and political credentials by leading the raids himself, like the ʿAbbasids Harun al-Rashid

---

[8] Al-Tibrizi (fl. 1337), *Mishkat al-Masabih*, trans. James Robson, 3 vols. (Lahore, 1963–65), 3:817. Ibn ʿAsakir includes a variant of this *hadith* in his *Forty Hadiths*, no. 12.

(r. 786–809) and his son, al-Ma'mun (r. 812–833), who actually died in Tarsus, in Asia Minor, while conducting a *jihad* campaign against the Byzantines.[9]

But it was left to the scholars of Islam to define *jihad* as a religious duty. In fact, most medieval and early modern legal treatises, including the *Hadith* collections, contain a chapter on *jihad* that incorporates the standard material from the Qur'an and *Hadith*. The earliest treatises specifically on the topic of *jihad* were compiled by scholars who themselves were *jihad* fighters, such as the *Kitab al-Jihad* (Book of the Holy War) by Ibn al-Mubarak (d. 797) and the *Kitab al-Siyar* (Book of Proper Comportment) by Abu Ishaq al-Fazari (d. in or after 802).[10] Their interest in *jihad* was not merely personal. They understood it as a religious duty to campaign, especially along the Byzantine frontiers, because, in their view, the caliphs were neglecting their duty to wage the yearly *jihad* campaign, or at least not doing enough towards it. These scholars were transformed by their followers into saints, which in return empowered their militant vision of *jihad* and established it as mainstream dogma in medieval Islamic religious thought.

Most of the treatises and chapters on *jihad* argue that it is as obligatory on all able-bodied Muslims as are the obligations to perform the ritual prayer (*salat*), the pilgrimage (*hajj*), and to give alms (*zakat*). According to the jurist al-Shafi'i (d. 820), after whom a Sunni school of law (*madhhab*) was named and who himself was influenced by *jihad* scholars like al-Fazari, the Qur'anic statements on *jihad*

> mean that the *jihad*, and rising up in arms in particular, is obligatory for all able-bodied [believers], exempting no one, just as prayer, pilgrimage and [payment of] alms are performed, and no person is permitted to perform the duty for another, since performance by one will not fulfill the duty for another.[11]

As Muslim scholars honed their understanding of right religion, they divided the world into two broad spheres – the Abode of Islam (*dar al-Islam*; lit., the Abode of Surrender or the Abode of Submission to God) and the Abode of War (*dar al-harb*) – in an effort to clarify the role of *jihad* and warfare in Islam. The Abode of Islam was comprised of those territories under Islamic political domination. The Abode of War was everywhere else. This division of the world into two spheres did not mean that all Muslims were at all times engaged in a state of open warfare against the Abode of War. Formal truces did exist. Moreover, for purely practical

---

[9] On the involvement of 'Abbasid caliphs in *jihad* against the Byzantines, see Michael Bonner, *Aristocratic Violence and Holy War: Studies in the Jihad and the Arab–Byzantine Frontier* (New Haven, 1996); and Hugh Kennedy, *The Early Abbasid Caliphate* (London, 1981). On the caliph al-Ma'mun, see Tayyeb El-Hibri, *Reinterpreting Islamic Historiography: Harun al-Rashid and the Narrative of the 'Abbasid Caliphate* (New York, 1999), pp. 95–142; Michael Cooperson, *Classical Arabic Biography: The Heirs of the Prophets in the Age of al-Ma'mun* (Cambridge, 2000), pp. 24–69; and idem, *al-Ma'mun* (Oxford, 2005).

[10] See Bonner, *Aristocratic Violence*, pp. 107–34.

[11] On al-Shafi'i's discussion of *jihad* see Majid Khadduri (trans.), *Al-Shafi'i's Risala: Treatise on the Foundations of Islamic Jurisprudence* (Cambridge, 1987), pp. 81–87.

reasons of inertia, military capability, and political calculation, expansion of the borders of Islam waxed and waned over time. As the central authority of the ʿAbbasid caliphs waned in the late ninth century, petty states and principalities on the frontiers took up the ideology of expansionist *jihad* in India, Central Asia, Anatolia, Africa, and Spain.

At other times we find Muslim armies fighting against other Muslim armies within the Islamic world in order to restore a particular vision of proper Islamic religion and government. We see this in the civil wars that plagued the early Muslim community during the Rashidun (632–661) and the Umayyad caliphates (661–750).[12] We see this also in the ʿAbbasid Revolution in the late 740s that established the ʿAbbasid caliphate, which endured until the Mongols sacked Baghdad in 1258.[13] The Almoravids (1062–1147) and the Almohads (1130–1269) represent two major revivalist movements that employed the ideology of *jihad* against what they viewed as corrupt Muslim regimes in North Africa and Spain, and against the Christian kings and princes in Iberia as well.

Whether the motivation for the *jihads* fought throughout the medieval Islamic world met the standards for religious purity in every instance is beyond our concern. We do know, however, that some of those ostensibly engaged in *jihad* against the external enemies of Islam and internal schismatics and heretics, however defined, were little more than bandits, thugs, and soldiers of fortune – at least, they are portrayed as such by many of the Muslim scholars and historians who wrote our sources.

During the 1060s, Muslim pastoral nomadic Turkomans legitimated their raiding and pillaging along the Byzantine frontier with the ideology of *jihad* as well. Like the Ottomans some two centuries later, they argued that they were merely striving in the path of God against the Byzantines – the preferred infidel enemy of Islam since the days of the early Islamic conquests.[14] Not surprisingly, the Byzantines viewed these Turkomans as nothing more than barbarian raiders. Matters came to a head in 1071 as the Byzantine emperor Romanus Diogenes led several Byzantine columns eastward to deal with this Turkish menace once and for all. Already on campaign in Syria, the Seljukid sultan, Alp Arslan, turned his forces north to come to the aid of his fellow Turkomans. A pitched battle between the two sides took place at Manzikert, near Lake Van, in the summer of 1071. Alp Arslan's forces were victorious and Romanus Diogenes was taken captive. He was ultimately ransomed and deposed. A disastrous defeat for the Byzantines, the Battle of Manzikert marks the beginnings of the process by which Anatolia became Turkey.

---

[12] On these civil wars, see Wilferd Madelung, *The Succession to Muhammad: A Study of the Early Caliphate* (Cambridge, 1997); and Mahmoud Ayoub, *The Crisis of Muslim History: Religion and Politics in Early Islam* (Oxford, 2003).

[13] On the ʿAbbasid revolution, see Jacob Lassner, *The Shaping of ʿAbbasid Rule* (Princeton, 1980); and Paul M. Cobb, *White Banners: Contention in ʿAbbasid Syria, 750–880* (Albany, 2001).

[14] On the Muslims' view of the Byzantines, see Nadia Maria El Cheikh, *Byzantium Viewed by the Arabs* (Cambridge, MA, 2004).

In 1095, Pope Urban II preached a sermon in Clermont, southern France, in which he called on the interminably feuding nobility of Western Europe to turn their energies to the cause of Christ and his Church. Urban was by no means the first to call on them to use their military skills in aid of their Byzantine Christian brothers who, since the Battle of Manzikert, were increasingly threatened by Muslim Turkish marauders in eastern and central Anatolia. In fact, Pope Gregory VII had proposed that he himself lead a force of some 50,000 men to liberate their Eastern brethren in 1074. More importantly, however, Urban called on the Frankish nobility to take up the cross of Christ and make an armed pilgrimage to Jerusalem in order to redeem their Lord's patrimony which had been stolen by the infidel Saracens some four centuries earlier.[15] By the summer of 1099, Jerusalem was in the hands of the crusaders. Unfortunately for Pope Urban II, he died shortly after the holy city was taken, but before word reached Western Europe.[16]

So far we have spoken of *jihad* as offensive and defensive warfare. It should be noted that some Muslims, especially followers of mystical Sufi traditions and other more pious-minded scholars, argued that there were in fact two types of *jihad*. For them, the greater *jihad* was that internal struggle within oneself against temptation and evil. This greater *jihad* is also referred to as the *jihad* of the tongue or the *jihad* of the pen; that is, the *jihad* of piety and persuasion. According to this position, military *jihad* was the lesser *jihad*, also known as the *jihad* of the sword.[17]

Ibn ʿAsakir

Abu al-Qasim ʿAli ibn al-Hasan was the most notable figure of the ʿAsakir family, whose members occupied prestigious positions as judges and scholars of the Shafiʿi school of Sunni law in Damascus for almost two centuries (1077–1261).[18] Ibn ʿAsakir was born in 1105, six years after the crusaders captured Jerusalem, and died in 1176, two years after Salah al-Din (Saladin) succeeded Nur al-Din as leader of Syria and Egypt.[19] He started his pursuit of religious education at the age

---

[15] Five versions of Pope Urban II's speech at Clermont are translated in Edward Peters, *The First Crusade: The Chronicle of Fulcher of Chartres & Other Source Materials* (Philadelphia, 1998), pp. 25–37.

[16] On the Crusades in Europe and the Near East, see Jonathan Riley-Smith, *The Crusades: A History*, 2nd ed. (London and New York, 2005); idem, *The Oxford Illustrated History of the Crusades* (Oxford, 1995); and Carole Hillenbrand, *The Crusades: Islamic Perspectives* (Edinburgh, 1999).

[17] Al-Sulami develops this view of the greater *jihad* and the lesser *jihad* in his *Kitab al-Jihad*: see Christie, "Motivating Listeners." See also Cook, *Understanding Jihad*, pp. 32–48.

[18] Nikita Elisséeff, *La description de Damas d'Ibn ʿAsakir* (Damascus, 1959), xviii. (The date 1077 is given there as 1177, clearly a typo.)

[19] It took some time before Saladin could establish himself as the legitimate and uncontested successor of Nur al-Din. On Saladin, see Malcolm Lyons and D. E. P. Jackson, *Saladin: The Politics of Holy War* (Cambridge, 1997); and Yaacov Lev, *Saladin in Egypt* (Leiden, 1999).

of six,[20] accompanying his father al-Hasan (d. 1125) and elder brother Hibat Allah (d. 1167) to the teaching circles of several renowned Damascene scholars at the Umayyad mosque and the Aminiyya school of Shafiʿi law.[21] His maternal lineage – his mother was from the prestigious al-Qurashi family which traced its genealogy back to the Umayyad dynasty – was fundamental in allowing him easy access to the high scholarly community of Damascus at that time.[22]

The political instability in Damascus, and Syria in general, in the early twelfth century as a result of the crusaders' invasion and intra-Muslim rivalry and animosity certainly compelled the young scholar to seek higher religious education elsewhere in the Muslim world. Between 1126 and 1141, Ibn ʿAsakir embarked on two ambitious educational journeys that took him to the most prestigious centers of Islamic learning in his day: Baghdad (where he studied at the famous Nizamiyya *madrasa*), the Hijaz (Mecca and Medina), Kufa, and Islamic lands further East – Isfahan, Khurasan, Transoxiana, Merv, Nishapur, and Herat.[23] Ibn ʿAsakir's distant travels in search of religious knowledge during his twenties and thirties place him firmly in the established educational tradition that is illustrated eloquently by a *hadith* in which Muhammad is reported to have told his followers that they should seek religious knowledge (*talab al-ʿilm*) even unto China; that is, to the ends of the earth.[24] He composed a three-volume work, entitled, *Muʿjam al-shuyukh*, in which he names some 1,600 teachers whom he met and studied with, including around 80 women.[25] The enormous knowledge that Ibn ʿAsakir acquired, especially of *Hadith* and scriptural exegesis (*tafsir*), earned him the title of *Hafiz* (great memorizer), and he became the most learned and renowned scholar of his day.

Ibn ʿAsakir's service to sultan Nur al-Din began shortly after the latter occupied Damascus in 1154.[26] Nur al-Din's political and religious ambitions attracted a large number of Sunni scholars, who saw him as the ideal candidate to liberate Syria from the Frankish menace and reunite it after centuries of intra-Muslim division and hostility. Nur al-Din came from a Kurdish background. His father, Zangi (murdered in 1146) had a successful career fighting the Franks in northern Syria and south-eastern Anatolia, and is celebrated for capturing the county of

---

[20] Ibn ʿAsakir attended a class in 1111 with Abu al-Wahsh Subayʿ ibn al-Muslim ibn ʿAli (d. 1115), and read parts of al-Khatib al-Baghdadi's *Taʾrikh Baghdad* with Abu Turab Haydara ibn Ahmad ibn al-Husayn al-Ansari (d. 1112): Ibn ʿAsakir, *Taʾrikh madinat Dimashq*, ed. ʿUmar ibn Gharam al-ʿUmrawi and ʿAli Shiri (Beirut, 1995–2001), 13:466–67.

[21] Elisséeff, *La description de Damas*, xix–xx.

[22] Ibid., xviii.

[23] His first trip lasted from 1126 to 1131, and his second lasted from 1134 to 1141. Ibid., xx–xxii.

[24] See Sam Gellens, "The Search for Knowledge in Medieval Muslim Societies: A Comparative Approach," in Dale F. Eickelman and James Piscatory, *Muslim Travellers: Pilgrimage, Migration, and the Religious Imagination* (Berkeley, 1990), pp. 50–68.

[25] See Ibn ʿAsakir, *Muʿjam al-shuyukh*, ed. Wafaʾ Taqiy al-Din, 3 vols. (Damascus, 2000).

[26] Elisséeff, *La Description de Damas*, xxii.

Edessa in 1144.[27] Nur al-Din inherited part of his father's territories and spent his career fighting other Kurdish and Turkish princes in north and central Syria and Mesopotamia (*al-Jazira*), and, with the help of his lieutenant Saladin, toppled the Fatimid dynasty in Egypt. As a pragmatic politician, he negotiated several truces with the Franks, a reality that reflects how crucial the reunification of Syria and Egypt was to his overall political and religious aspirations, and the priority he gave it. It was as a result of Nur al-Din's efforts that the alliance between Muslim politicians and religious scholars was cemented around the ideology of *jihad* and the revival of Sunni Islam in Syria and Egypt.[28]

To that end, Nur al-Din employed in his army a host of religious scholars and preachers whose sole function was to indoctrinate and stimulate the troops.[29] Moreover, he ordered a huge network of religious and secular institutions and monuments (mosques, minarets, schools, hospitals, city walls, fortifications, and so on) to be built throughout his reign. The purpose of these buildings and monuments was to further enhance the sultan's religious and public image, which gained him tremendous support from the scholars and the Syrian masses.[30] They are also extraordinary testimonies of his use of propaganda to advance his political and religious ambitions, as most dedicatory inscriptions on these buildings and monuments celebrate him as the great *jihad* warrior.[31]

Nur al-Din found in Ibn 'Asakir a particularly ardent defender of Sunni Islam and ordered that a school – known as *Dar al-Hadith* (House of the Study of *Hadith*) or *Dar al-Sunna* (House of the Study of *Sunna*) – be built for his new scholarly ally.[32] This school, constructed in 1170, later became known as *Dar al-Hadith al-Nuriyya*, after Nur al-Din, and served as the intellectual epicenter of Nur al-Din's *jihad* in Syria and Egypt. The building is still standing in old Damascus in what is known as the 'Asruniyya market area.[33]

Under Nur al-Din's patronage, Ibn 'Asakir composed several books, among them the largest work of history ever produced by a medieval Muslim scholar: *Ta'rikh madinat Dimashq* (The History of Damascus), which he had started in 1134. The *History of Damascus* is primarily a biographical dictionary now published in a

---

[27] On the career of Zangi, see Carole Hillenbrand, "'Abominable Acts': The Career of Zengi," in *The Second Crusade: Scope and Consequences*, ed. Jonathan Phillips and Martin Hoch (Manchester, 2001), pp. 111–32.

[28] On the career of Nur al-Din, see Nikita Elisséeff, *Nur ad-Din: Un grand prince musulman de Syrie au temps des croisades (511–569 H./1118–1174)*, 3 vols. (Damascus, 1967); and Carole Hillenbrand, *The Crusades: Islamic Perspectives* (Edinburgh, 1999), pp. 117–70.

[29] See Elisséeff, *Nur ad-Din*, 3:735; and Hillenbrand, *The Crusades*, pp. 119–22.

[30] On the function of these buildings and monuments, see Hillenbrand, *The Crusades*, pp. 122–31; and Yasser Tabbaa, *The Transformation of Islamic Art during the Sunni Revival* (Seattle, 2001).

[31] See Yasser Tabbaa, "Monuments with a Message: Propagation of Jihad under Nur al-Din," in *The Meeting of Two Worlds: Cultural Exchange between East and West during the Period of the Crusades*, ed. Vladimir P. Goss and Christine Verzár Bornstein (Kalamazoo, 1986), pp. 223–40.

[32] Elisséeff, *La description de Damas*, xxii–xxiii.

[33] See Qutayba al-Shihabi, *Mu'jam Dimashq al-tarikhi*, 3 vols. (Damascus, 1999), 1:274.

partially complete edition in 74 volumes plus indices. It celebrates the holiness of Syria, with Damascus as its center, by documenting the lives and achievements of the notable men and women (religious figures, politicians, scholars, poets, and so forth) who lived in it or merely passed through it, and the many anecdotes they reported on its sanctity. He also devotes considerable attention to a large number of pre-Islamic sacred figures, including Abraham, Sarah, Hagar, David, Jesus, Mary, and John the Baptist, to name but a few. This is the only Muslim biographical dictionary that features substantial biographical notices for pre-Islamic sacred figures outside the Tales of the Prophets (*qisas al-anbiya*) literature.[34] The first two chapters of Ibn ʿAsakir's *History of Damascus* are devoted to the sanctity of Damascus and Syria, and list the sites and events that make the region holy. It is one of the treasures of medieval Islamic historiography in that it preserves extensive excerpts from hundreds of now-lost works authored by Muslim historians and religious scholars before Ibn ʿAsakir's day.[35]

A theme that emerges quite clearly in Ibn ʿAsakir's *History of Damascus* is that his choice of subjects and the narrative structure of his biographies – reaching from Adam, to his recently deceased contemporaries – reflect a chronological, thematic, and even moralistic continuity in his understanding of Syria's history. We see this clearly in one of the explicit ways he articulates his vision of Syria's past for his time. That is, the great figures of Syria's past did not simply bless it by living in it or passing through it, they also stood up to defend it when necessary. Ibn ʿAsakir's unique depiction of Jesus provides us some clues to this grand scheme in the presentation of his subjects. Ibn ʿAsakir's Jesus will return before the Day of Judgment as the *Mahdi* – the Messiah figure of Islamic eschatology – to kill the Antichrist (*al-Dajjal*) at the gates of Jerusalem, lead the Muslims to victory over their enemies, and re-establish the triumph of Islam.[36] In his biography of Jesus, Ibn ʿAsakir records a particularly interesting prophecy that speaks directly to the troubling circumstances of his time and, together with other traditions about the End of Times, highlights Jesus as waging *jihad* in the path of God:

Son of the sheep-bearing (*Ibn Haml al-Daʾn*), a Byzantine, one of whose parents is a demon, is about to come out against the Muslims leading 500,000 [soldiers] by land and [another] 500,000 by sea and disembarking between Acre and Tyre. Then he will say:

---

[34] On the *Tales of the Prophets*, see *The Tales of the Prophets of al-Kisaʾi*, trans. Wheeler M. Thackston (Boston, 1978) and *ʿAraʾis al-majalis fi qisas al-anbiyaʾ* or *"Lives of the Prophets"* as Recounted by Abu Ishaq Ahmad ibn Muhammad ibn Ibrahim al-Thaʿlabi, trans. William Brinner (Leiden, 2002). See also James E. Lindsay, "ʿAli Ibn ʿAsakir as a Preserver of *Qisas al-Anbiyaʾ*: The Case of David Son of Jesse," *Studia Islamica* 82 (1995), 45–82.

[35] On Ibn ʿAsakir's *Taʾrikh*, see James E. Lindsay, ed., *Ibn ʿAsakir and Early Islamic History* (Princeton, 2001); and Elisseéff, *La description de Damas*, xxix–liii.

[36] On Ibn ʿAsakir's treatment of Jesus, see Suleiman A. Mourad, "Jesus According to Ibn ʿAsakir", in *Ibn ʿAsakir and Early Islamic History*, ed. James Lindsay (Princeton, 2001), pp. 24–43. For a range of traditions on the Second Coming of Jesus, see Suleiman Mourad, *Sirat al-sayid al-masih li-Ibn ʿAsakir* (Amman, 1996), pp. 234–82.

"People of the ships, come out from them," and he will order them (the ships) to be burnt. The Muslims will seek each other's help. Then they will fight for a month, and [the Muslims] will find no people to stand between them and Constantinople and Rome. While they (the Muslims) are in that [situation], they will [hear] that the Antichrist (al-Dajjal) has taken over among their families. They will drop what is in their hands and return. A famine will fall upon the people (the Muslims), and while they are in this [situation], they will hear a voice from Heaven [saying]: "Rejoice, help is coming to you." They will say: "Jesus son of Mary has descended." They will rejoice in him, and he will rejoice in them, and they will say [to him]: "[Lead us in] prayer, O Spirit of God," and he will say [to them]: "God has honored this [Muslim] community; therefore, no one should lead their prayers except [one] of them." … After Jesus finishes [his prayer], he will take his lance, go toward the Antichrist and kill him. …[37]

This prophecy, which Ibn ʿAsakir attributes to the companion ʿAbd Allah ibn ʿAmr ibn al-ʿAs (d. 684), is meant to explain the well-known *hadith* regarding the coming of a revivifier of Islam at the beginning of every century: "God will send this community a person who will renew its faith at the beginning of every hundred years."[38]

Interestingly, the prophecy has several themes that are peculiar to the Frankish presence in the Near East. First, they came by sea and overland, and their two most prestigious centers were Acre and Tyre.[39] Second, the Frankish challenge widened the divisions among Muslim leaders, especially in Syria and Egypt, which created some sort of an eschatological hope for a Muslim leader to emerge, reunite the Muslims, and defeat the Christians. Jesus is not that leader, for his role in Islamic eschatology is clear: He will return to kill the Antichrist. But it is the Muslims' responsibility to prepare the conditions for his return. Hence, in Ibn ʿAsakir's opinion, it was incumbent upon the Muslims to unite, obviously under the leadership of his patron Nur al-Din.[40] This eschatological expectation is reminiscent of Guibert of Nogent's version of Pope Urban II's speech at Clermont, which raised similar, although in an opposite way, eschatological hopes regarding the need to liberate Jerusalem (Mother of Churches) to prepare the way for the return of Christ.[41]

Beside the Frankish challenge, Ibn ʿAsakir was very much concerned with preserving what he considered the proper Sunni character of Islam, and he did so as

---

[37] Mourad, *Sirat al-sayid al-masih*, pp. 257–61.

[38] Abu Dawud, *Sunan Abu Dawud*, ed. Muhammad M. ʿAbd al-Hamid, 4 vols. (Cairo, 1951), 4:156 (no. 4291).

[39] It was Tyre's resistance to the attempts of Saladin to capture it in 1187 that allowed the Franks to regroup and launch a counter-offensive with the Third Crusade, and consequently remain in the Near East for an additional 105 years, until 1291 when the Mamluk sultan al-Malik al-Ashraf brought an end to the Frankish military presence.

[40] For a discussion of this prophecy, see Mourad, "Jesus According to Ibn ʿAsakir," pp. 31–35.

[41] On the version of Guibert of Nogent, see Peters, *The First Crusade*, pp. 33–37. We are not suggesting a connection between Guibert and Ibn ʿAsakir, for there was none. We are only pointing to the similarity between Christian and Muslim religious literature at the time of the crusades.

an eager and effective advocate of Nur al-Din's *jihad* against Sunni Islam's internal enemies, primarily the Ismaʿili Shiʿi Fatimids. In this respect, one clearly notices his eagerness to highlight the morality and religiosity of his figures, even the most problematic ones, such as the second Umayyad caliph Yazid, under whose rule Imam al-Husayn, the grandson of the prophet Muhammad and the most important religious figure for the Shiʿis, was slain in 680. Yazid, in Ibn ʿAsakir's *History of Damascus*, is a righteous and pious ruler who, beside his eagerness to protect the lands of Islam from the Byzantines, was involved in the transmission of certain *hadiths* from the prophet of Islam.[42] In short, Ibn ʿAsakir's intent was to demonstrate the pivotal role which Syria has played in his understanding of the past in which God has intervened and acted at times to reward the righteous and punish the wicked. Such a vision of the past is certainly not unique, and parallels that of his many contemporaries and predecessors and successors – whether Muslim, Christian, or Jewish.[43]

In addition to his *History of Damascus*, Ibn ʿAsakir authored several other religiously and politically motivated works. With respect to theology, he authored two books in defense of the Sunni theologian al-Ashʿari and his school, which was under attack by rival Sunni groups in Damascus, especially the Hanbalis. The two works are: *Manaqib Ashʿariya* (Ashʿari's Virtues) and *Tabyin kadhib al-muftari ʿala Abi al-Hasan al-Ashʿari* (Exposing the Slanderer's Mendacity against Abu al-Hasan al-Ashʿari).[44] Ibn ʿAsakir also composed two other works on the virtues of *jihad*. The first is *Fadl ʿAsqalan* (The Merits of Ascalon), a celebration of Ascalon's holiness to Islam which was written in reaction to the fall of the city to the Franks in 1153 and served as an appeal for the Muslims to recapture it.[45] The second is the aforementioned *al-Arbaʿin fi al-ijtihad fi iqamat al-jihad*, a collection of forty *hadiths* attributed to the prophet Muhammad, which emphasize the duty and obligation to wage *jihad*. It is the subject of our discussion below.

As a scholar, it is fair to say that Ibn ʿAsakir very much embraced the *jihad* of the pen, though certainly not at the expense of the more common vision of the *jihad* of the sword. While we do not have any information regarding his involvement in the latter form of *jihad* or that he preached directly to the army, Ibn ʿAsakir's role among

---

[42] On Ibn ʿAsakir's presentation of the Umayyad caliph Yazid, see James E. Lindsay, "Caliphal and Moral Exemplar? ʿAli Ibn ʿAsakir's Portrait of Yazid b. Muʿawiya," *Der Islam* 74 (1997), 250–78.

[43] For other discussions of the way Ibn ʿAsakir treats his subjects, see the studies in Lindsay, *Ibn ʿAsakir and Early Islamic History*. On Muslim literature on the holiness of Syria, see Paul M. Cobb, "Virtual Sacrality: Making Muslim Syria Sacred Before the Crusades," *Medieval Encounters* 8.1 (2002), 35–55.

[44] For studies on these works by Ibn ʿAsakir, see August Ferdinand Mehren, *Exposé de la réforme de l'islamisme commencée au IIIème siècle de l'Hégire par Abou-ʾl-Hasan Ali el-Ashʿari et continuée par son école avec des extraits du texte arabe d'Ibn Asâkir* (Leiden, 1878); and Justin MacCarthy, *The Theology of al-Ashʿari* (Beirut, 1953).

[45] *Fadl ʿAsqalan* is unfortunately lost; but a few excerpts from it have survived in Ibn ʿAsakir's *History of Damascus*.

the scholarly elite was fundamental to Nur al-Din's success, especially because, under Ibn ʿAsakir's direction, *Dar al-Hadith* became the institutional center for Nur al-Din's *jihad* propaganda against the internal and external enemies of Sunni Islam throughout his realm.[46] Hence, Ibn ʿAsakir's *Forty Hadiths* should be seen as one of many texts he produced as part of his personal mission to assure the propagation of right religion and the success of *jihad* under the leadership of his patron, Nur al-Din. As we will see below, this treatise includes praises not only for those who fight, but also for those who contribute in many ways to the success of *jihad*.

The Forty *Hadiths* Genre

The forty *hadiths* genre was very popular in medieval Islamic scholarship. This was especially the case among the lower classes of religious scholars and the educated masses precisely because the conciseness of such works made them easy to copy and to memorize. The religious foundation of the forty *hadiths* collections is in fact a *hadith*, likely a forged one, which enjoins Muslims to memorize forty *hadiths* that help sustain either one's own faith or that of the community.[47] As was customary within the genre, Ibn ʿAsakir cites this *hadith* at the beginning of his forty *hadiths* collection:

> The Prophet said: "He who memorizes forty *hadiths* that helps sustain the religious beliefs of the Muslims will be resurrected on the Day of Judgment as a scholar. The scholar is ranked seventy ranks above the average worshiper; only God knows what is between each two ranks."[48]

It was not uncommon for notable scholars to compile a forty *hadith* collection that addressed a particular theme, such as asceticism, mysticism, or *jihad*. In addition to Ibn ʿAsakir's work, notable examples of the genre include *Kitab al-Arbaʿin hadithan* (The Forty *Hadiths*) by Abu Bakr Muhammad ibn al-Husayn al-Ajurri (d. 970); *Kitab al-Arbaʿin min masanid al-mashayikh al-ʿishrin ʿan al-ashab al-arbaʿin* (The Forty *Hadiths* from Forty Companions of the Prophet Muhammad Extracted from the Twenty Authoritative *Hadith* Collections) by Abu Saʿd ʿAbd Allah ibn ʿUmar al-Qushayri (d. 1204); *Kitab al-Arbaʿin fi al-jihad wa-l-mujahidin* (The Forty *Hadiths* on *Jihad* and *Jihad* Fighters) by Abu al-Faraj Muhammad ibn ʿAbd al-Rahman al-Muqriʾ al-Wasiti (d. 1221); and the *Kitab*

---

[46] Elisséeff, *La description de Damas*, xxii–xxiii; and Hillenbrand, *The Crusades*, p. 127.

[47] On the authenticity of this *hadith*, see *An-Nawawi's Forty Hadith*, trans. Ezzedin Ibrahim and Denys Johnson-Davies (Jakarta, n.d.), p. 21.

[48] See Ibn ʿAsakir, *Forty Hadiths*, Damascus, Zahiriyya Library, MS *Majmuʿ Lugha* No. 40, fol. 68a. See also al-Badr, *Kitab al-Arbaʿin fi al-jihad wa-l-mujahidin*, p. 19; *An-Nawawi's Forty Hadith*, trans. Ibrahim and Johnson-Davies, pp. 19–21.

al-Arbaʿin al-ʿushariyya (The Forty *Hadiths* Each with a Chain of Authorities that Include Ten Generations of Transmitters) by Abu al-Fadl ʿAbd al-Rahim ibn al-Husayn al-ʿIraqi al-Misri (d. 1403).[49] The most famous of the forty *hadiths* genre is undoubtedly *al-Arbaʿin al-Nawawiyya* (al-Nawawi's Forty *Hadiths*) by Muhyi al-Din al-Nawawi (d. 1277).[50]

Ibn ʿAsakir's *Forty Hadiths On the Obligation to Wage Jihad*

In the short introduction to his *Forty Hadiths*, Ibn ʿAsakir states that Nur al-Din had asked him to compose this collection so that it could be used "to stimulate the strong and valiant fighters (*mujahidin*) … and stir them up in the battlefield to uproot those who spread disbelief and tyranny."[51] While "those who spread disbelief and tyranny" are most obviously the Franks, Ibn ʿAsakir also had in mind those Muslim military leaders who refused to submit to Nur al-Din's leadership and were, therefore, responsible for keeping Muslim Syria and Egypt in a state of disunity, turmoil, and weakness. These leaders included the Ismaʿili Shiʿi Fatimids of Egypt as well as the anti-Nur al-Din Turkish and Kurdish Sunni principalities in northern and eastern Syria and south-eastern Anatolia.

Unlike al-Sulami's lengthy *Kitab al-Jihad* or the work by Ibn al-Mubarak (d. 797) bearing the same title, Ibn ʿAsakir's *Forty Hadiths* is a brief collection of forty *hadiths*. He does not incorporate the Qurʾanic material that one usually finds at the beginning of works on *jihad*. Nor does he provide commentary on these *hadiths* other than the short note at the end of nearly every *hadith* regarding its authenticity. In this respect, Ibn ʿAsakir seems not to have been concerned with producing a comprehensive work on *jihad*.

As an authority on *Hadith* and head of the *Dar al-Hadith* in Damascus, Ibn ʿAsakir simply and dutifully fulfilled the request of his sultan and patron Nur al-Din. In addition, his *Forty Hadiths* can be viewed as an assertion of his scholarly superiority vis-à-vis his Syrian contemporaries. Ibn ʿAsakir's *Forty Hadiths* is an explicit testimony to the vast knowledge he had acquired as a result of his travels. In fact, one can detect a subtly disguised self-praise in the manner by which he cites his authorities for each of the forty *hadiths*. In other words, the *Forty Hadiths* constitutes a kind of a *curriculum vitae* in which Ibn ʿAsakir displays the names of his most distinguished teachers, who were also notable scholars of *Hadith*. Understandably, most of the *hadiths* in Ibn ʿAsakir's collection are found in the

---

[49] On these authors and their forty *hadiths* collections, see Abu Bakr al-Ajurri, *Kitab al-Arbaʿin hadithan wa-yalih Kitab al-Arbaʿin min masanid al-mashayikh al-ʿishrin ʿan al-ashab al-arbaʿin*, ed. Badr ibn ʿAbd Allah al-Badr (Kuwait, 1987); and Abu al-Faraj al-Wasiti, *Kitab al-Arbaʿin fi al-jihad wa-l-mujahidin wa-yalih Kitab al-Arbaʿin al-ʿushariyya*, ed. Badr ibn ʿAbd Allah al-Badr (Beirut, 1992).

[50] See *An-Nawawi's Forty Hadith*, trans. Ibrahim and Johnson-Davies.

[51] Ibn ʿAsakir, *Forty Hadiths*, fol. 67b.

major *Hadith* compilations: such as the *Muwatta'* of Malik ibn Anas (d. 796), the *Sahih* of al-Bukhari (d. 870), the *Sahih* of Muslim (d. 875), and the *Musnad* of Ahmad ibn Hanbal (d. 855).

While Ibn 'Asakir readily admits that the forty *hadiths* in his collection can be found in the major *Hadith* collections, it would have been a great embarrassment to him had he simply copied the *hadiths* from these texts; after all, anyone could copy from books in a library. As a respected *Hafiz*, Ibn 'Asakir is keen to present his personal license to transmit each of these *hadiths*, which he received from the notable scholars he had met on his sojourns in Iraq, Iran and Central Asia (Baghdad, Isfahan, Nishapur, Samarqand, and Herat). By showcasing that he had studied with pious and prestigious scholars in the leading centers of religious scholarship of his day, Ibn 'Asakir extends a powerful message to the sultan as well as to his peers regarding his command of, and qualifications in, the discipline of *Hadith*.

The *Forty Hadiths* has survived in a manuscript at the Zahiriyya Library in Damascus (now in the possession of the Asad Library in that city). The manuscript is a *majmu'* (assembled loose folios in a single volume), and contains a number of works; Ibn 'Asakir's text is the third, covering folios 67a–81b. We know from the colophons at the end of the text that it was read out to large crowds in several locations in and around Damascus. Since the first reading session was dictated in Ibn 'Asakir's presence by his son al-Qasim in a garden in the town of Mazza – now a suburb of Damascus – in the year 1170, we know that Ibn 'Asakir compiled the work sometime between 1154 (Nur al-Din's occupation of Damascus) and 1170. Four years later, in 1174, it was read out at the Umayyad mosque, and again in 1221. It was also read out at the Khatuniyya school and at the *Zawiya* (Sufi retreat) of Nasr al-Maqdisi in 1227,[52] at the Umayyad mosque in 1227 and 1229, and at *Dar al-Sunna* (that is, *Dar al-Hadith*) in 1230.[53] The manuscript was finally copied by Yusuf ibn al-Hasan ibn Badr ibn al-Hasan ibn al-Nabulsi on Friday, 28 June 1236 in the al-Kallasa school, adjacent to the Umayyad mosque from the western side.[54] The ownership of the copy later passed to Muhammad ibn 'Abd Allah ibn Ahmad Ibn al-Muhibb (1313–87), who registered his own reading on the cover page in 1318, nearly three decades after the last Frankish outpost in Syria had been removed in 1291.[55]

---

[52] The Khatuniyya school was built by the widow of Nur al-Din, al-Khatun 'Ismat al-Din, in 1175, and is located inside old Damascus; it should be distinguished from another Khatuniyya school outside the city: see al-Shihabi, *Mu'jam Dimashq al-tarikhi*, 2:180–81. As for the *Zawiya* of Nasr al-Maqdisi, it is located, according to the colophon, to the west of the Umayyad mosque.

[53] See Ibn 'Asakir, *Forty Hadiths*, fols. 79b–81a.

[54] On the Kallasa school built in the reign of Nur al-Din in 1160, see al-Shihabi, *Mu'jam Dimashq al-tarikhi*, 2:206.

[55] Ibn al-Muhibb was brought by his father to study the *Forty Hadiths* with al-Qasim ibn al-Muzaffar ibn Mahmud Ibn 'Asakir, a descendant of Ibn 'Asakir's elder brother Hibat Allah. On Ibn al-Muhibb, see Ibn Hajar al-'Asqalani, *al-Durar al-kamina fi a'yan al-ma'a al-thamina*, 4 vols. (Beirut, 1993), 3:465. On al-Qasim Ibn 'Asakir (d. 1323), see ibid., 3:239–40.

These instances demonstrate that Ibn ʿAsakir's *Forty Hadiths* received tremendous attention from the Damascene scholarly community, during his lifetime and for more than a century after his death. Some of the colophons even mention children (including a two-year-old girl) who were brought by their fathers to receive the right – *ijaza* or license – to transmit the text when they grew up and became scholars.[56] Although we do not know whether the *Forty Hadiths* was available in other parts of Syria and the Muslim world, the wide interest in the text demonstrated by Damascene scholars confirms the role it played in promoting the mentality of *jihad* in the final century of the Frankish presence.

Four major themes characterize Ibn ʿAsakir's *Forty Hadiths*: (1) the importance of *jihad* in comparison to other religious duties; (2) the punishments that await those who neglect the duty of *jihad*; (3) the rewards that await those who undertake *jihad*; and (4) the requirements that the *jihad* fighters must fulfill before waging *jihad*.

1. Importance of jihad *in Comparison to Other Religious Duties*

The first theme that Ibn ʿAsakir highlights is the significance of *jihad* in comparison to Islam's other religious duties. Such examples include:

(H1)   Abu Hurayra said: "The Messenger of God was asked: 'Which category of belief is the best?' He replied: 'The belief in God.' He was asked again: 'And what comes next?' He replied: 'Next is fighting (*al-jihad*) in the path of God.'"

(H2)   Abu Dharr said: "I asked the Messenger of God: 'Which of the religious practices is the best?' He replied: 'Believing in God and fighting (*jihad*) in His path.'"

(H3)   ʿAbd Allah ibn Masʿud said: "I asked the Messenger of God: Which of the religious practices is most dear to God? He replied: 'To pray the prayers in their time.'" Ibn Masʿud asked again: "And then?" The Prophet replied: "Taking care of one's parents." Ibn Masʿud asked again: "And then?" The Prophet replied: "fighting (*al-jihad*) in the path of God."

Ibn ʿAsakir's intent with these *hadiths* is not to create confusion as to which religious duties are more important than others. Rather, it is to emphasize the crucial importance of the duty of *jihad*, which according to these *hadiths* is very dear to God and to His messenger, Muhammad.

The virtues of *jihad* are further clarified by Ibn ʿAsakir with other *hadiths*, which appear to make *jihad* surpass all other religious obligations:

---

[56] On the trend of bringing children, especially to attend seminars by aging scholars, in order to receive *ijazas*, see Jonathan Berkey, *The Transmission of Knowledge in Medieval Cairo: A Social History of Islamic Education* (Princeton, 1992).

(H8)   Abu Hurayra said: "A man came to the prophet and asked him: 'O Messenger of God, teach me something that equals *jihad* in the path of God?' The Prophet replied: 'I cannot find any. Can you when the warrior goes out to fight in the path of God enter the mosque, pray ceaselessly and fast continuously?' The man replied: 'That I can never do.'"

(H13)   ʿImran ibn Husayn said: "The Prophet said: 'Lining up for a battle in the path of God is worthier than 60 years of worship.'"

Obviously, Ibn ʿAsakir's intent is not to argue that no religious duty is the equal of *jihad*; he was far too astute a scholar and theologian to make such an argument. But these *hadiths* should be understood in the context of stressing the virtues of *jihad* (however hyperbolically), rather than actually establishing it as the most noble religious duty.

2.   Punishment

The second theme in Ibn ʿAsakir's *Forty Hadiths* is the punishment for neglecting the obligation to wage *jihad* against Islam's enemies. Clearly, Ibn ʿAsakir is here referring to those Muslims who ignored it entirely or argued against it. Seemingly as a way to answer these groups, he included the following *hadith*:

(H16)   Anas ibn Malik said: "The Prophet said: 'At the end of days, there will appear a group of people who do not believe in *jihad*. God took an oath upon Himself that every one who says that will be tortured like no other sinful human being.'"

The theme of the end of days occurs frequently in Ibn ʿAsakir's writings, especially in the biography of Jesus in the *History of Damascus*, as noted earlier. Given the imminent threat posed by the Franks and the Muslims' division and discord, one is left to ponder whether Ibn ʿAsakir was identifying the situation of Syria as approximating the conditions that would lead to the second coming of Jesus and the End of Days. Why else would he be interested in such a *hadith* unless he intended to use it against those Muslims who were neglecting the duty of *jihad*, and thus endangering Muslim Syria and making it easy for the Christians to occupy and control?

3.   Rewards

The third theme is the rewards that are amassed by waging *jihad*. According to the following *hadith*, the work of a *jihad* fighter, unlike that of other believers, multiplies over the years, as if it accrues a kind of interest rate from the time of his death until the Day of Judgment when he appears before the Lord.

(H22)   ʿUqba said: "the Messenger of God said: 'The deed of the dead person is placed in a closed book [and will be opened on the Day of Judgment] except that of the garrisoned warrior in the path of God whose work accumulates rewards from the time of his death until the Day of Resurrection.'"

Yet, the rewards from *jihad* are not limited to the fighters. In certain respects, the entire society can benefit from *jihad*, provided they contribute to it in some way or other. According to the following *hadith*, every arrow used in the battlefield admits not only the *jihad* fighter to heaven, but also the laborer who manufactured the arrow and the individual who paid for its workmanship:

(H29)   The Messenger of God was heard saying: "Every arrow thrown in a fight in the path of God, God will admit into Heaven its maker, the person who donates it to the army, and the warrior who shoots it."

Here, Ibn 'Asakir is obviously rallying the entire society to gather around the *jihad* fighters and help meet the conditions for a successful *jihad* in whatever way they could. According to this *hadith*, the artisans and the benevolent individuals were also waging a de facto *jihad*. In some ways, Ibn 'Asakir realizes the importance of maintaining a supportive society around the fighters. In this respect, the following *hadith* shows the significance of social endorsement and sponsorship of those individuals who leave their families and communities behind in order to fulfill their duty to engage in *jihad*.

(H20)   Abu Umama [al-Bahili] said: "The Messenger of God said: 'He who does not participate in raiding [the enemy], sponsor a raider, or take care of a raider's family, God will strike him with the calamity of the Day of Judgment.'"

Whereas H29 opens the positive rewards of *jihad* to those who contribute in some way to the cause of *jihad*, H20 emphasizes the negative punishments that await those who neither engage in *jihad* nor contribute in kind whether by sponsoring the expenses of a soldier or pledging to look after his family. These *hadiths* remind us of similar patterns in Europe during the later crusades, where redemption of vows for cash to sponsor certain expeditions was encouraged by the papacy.[57]

These particular *hadiths* raise the question of the role of scholars in the service of *jihad*. Theoretically, they are neither artisans who manufacture weapons or other items needed by the troops, nor are they wealthy merchants who are in a position to donate money to the army or subsidize their families. Do scholars, then, have a role in *jihad* other than joining the ranks and fighting? Here, one expects Ibn 'Asakir, who was never involved in physical *jihad*, to find a *hadith* that celebrates the scholars' input in this process. As if on cue, he quotes the following *hadith*:

---

[57]   See Simon Lloyd, "The Crusading Movement, 1096–1274," in *The Oxford Illustrated History of the Crusades*, ed. Jonathan Riley-Smith (Oxford, 1995), pp. 49–50.

(**H31**)   Anas [ibn Malik] said: "The Messenger of God said: 'Fight the infidels with your wealth, with your souls, or with your tongues.'"

It is the *jihad* of the tongue, or, to put it more accurately, the *jihad* of the pen that Ibn ʿAsakir was engaged in. As a scholar, his contribution is to produce literature that can be used to spread the culture of *jihad*. By so doing, even the scholar who stays behind in his school and mosque receives the rewards of *jihad*.

4.   Requirements jihad *fighters must fulfill before waging* jihad

The fourth theme in Ibn ʿAsakir's *Forty Hadiths* is the personal requirements that a fighter must fulfill before he can wage *jihad* and receive its rewards.

(**H40**)   The martyrs are of three kinds. First is a believer who exerts his life and wealth fighting in the path of God, and battles the enemy until he is killed. He is a tested martyr. His abode will be the tent of God underneath His throne; nothing separates him from prophets except the title. Second is a believer with some sins and transgressions to his record who exerts his life and wealth fighting in the path of God, and battles the enemy until he is killed. He is cleansed from his sins and transgressions because the sword purifies the person from sins. He will be admitted to Heaven from whichever gate he chooses, for Heaven has eight gates, and Hell has seven gates. And third is a hypocrite who exerts his life and wealth fighting in the path of God, and battles the enemy until he is killed. He is in Hell, because the sword does not cleanse the person from hypocrisy.

The three categories in this *hadith* clearly reflect the Muslim society of Syria and Egypt in Ibn ʿAsakir's day: pious, semi-pious and hypocrites. *Jihad* is a salvation for the first two groups, but never for the last. Clearly, this *hadith* echoes Ibn ʿAsakir's endorsement and justification for pious and semi-pious Muslims to cleanse their society from the hypocrites. It also reminds us of the two types of *jihad* addressed by al-Sulami: *al-jihad al-akbar* (the greater *jihad*) against one's desires, and *al-jihad al-asghar* (the lesser *jihad*) against one's enemies. If the individual does not undergo the *jihad* of piety first, he does not have a chance of receiving the rewards of the *jihad* of the sword. His efforts are in vain. This emphasis is obviously not limited to the fulfillment of the religious duty of *jihad*. Ibn ʿAsakir means here that the fighter has to be a good Muslim. In other words, he cannot be a heretic, an Ismaʿili Shiʿi Fatimid caliph in Egypt for example, he can only be a Sunni.

Conclusion

In conclusion, it is fair to say that, as a scholar, Ibn ʿAsakir very much embraced the *jihad* of the tongue, or of the pen, though certainly not at the expense of the more common vision of the *jihad* of the sword. His *Forty Hadiths*, written at the request of sultan Nur al-Din, exemplifies the type of scholarship he produced as his contribution to the *jihad* campaign of his patron. The *hadiths* upon which Ibn ʿAsakir drew to explain the vision of Islam's prophet regarding the duty of *jihad* also speak to the conditions of his own time. He used them to underscore its importance vis-à-vis other religious duties, the religious purification required of the individual *jihad* fighters, the promises they will receive, the punishments that will befall the deserters or those who argue against *jihad*, and finally society's responsibility to support the endeavors and to assure the success of the fighters.

Ibn ʿAsakir clearly used religion to serve the political agenda of his patron Nur al-Din, and used politics to promote his own religious conviction. Exalting the holiness of Syria (for example, Damascus, Jerusalem, Ascalon) and urging the Muslims to wage *jihad* against the internal and external enemies are, therefore, to be seen as his scholarly contribution to the success of Nur al-Din's campaign, and subsequently to the triumph of Sunni Islam in Syria and Egypt.

Infidel Dogs:
Hunting Crusaders with Usama ibn Munqidh[1]

Paul M. Cobb

University of Notre Dame

Introduction

Few works of medieval Arabic literature are as valuable to the student of Islamic perspectives on the Crusades as the *Kitab al-I'tibar* or *Book of Learning by Example* by the Syrian warrior and man-of-letters Usama ibn Munqidh (1095–1188). The work was intended to provide, as its title suggests, lessons based upon real-life experiences that demonstrate the inevitability of God's will. Happily, most of those lessons are drawn from its author Usama's own life. So frank a portrait of Usama's world and his world-view does the *Book of Learning* permit us that the work is almost universally, though erroneously, called his "memoirs," most notably in the title of its well-known English translation by Philip Hitti, *An Arab-Syrian Gentleman and Warrior in the Period of the Crusades*.[2] The text is famously filled with the minutiae of daily life at Usama's family home of Shayzar in northern Syria, and in the various courts and royal patrons with whom Usama consorted after his exile from Shayzar in 1138, including the Fatimids of Egypt, the atabeg Zangi of Mosul and Aleppo, his son Nur al-Din, and even the near-legendary Saladin, under whom Usama completed the *Book of Learning* and many other works besides. And, in addition to the details of daily life, *The Book of Learning* is filled with its author's thoughts, hopes, and fears. Few medieval Muslim minds are as open to us as Usama's, even if they are mediated through his desire to provide instructive lessons and to tell a good story.[3]

---

[1] Versions of this paper were presented at the conference "Crusading, and Against Whom?" held at Middlebury College on 4 October 2004, and at the Notre Dame History Faculty Colloquium in September 2004. I would like to thank the panelists and audience members at both venues for their feedback and criticisms, in particular this journal's anonymous reviewer, who supplied some valuable references. The faults that remain are entirely my own. Some of the ideas expressed here appear in other forms in Paul M. Cobb, *Usama ibn Munqidh: Warrior-Poet of the Age of Crusades* (Oxford, 2006).

[2] Usama ibn Munqidh, *Kitab al-I'tibar*, ed. Philip K. Hitti (Princeton, 1930). Translated by Philip K. Hitti as *An Arab-Syrian Gentleman and Warrior in the Period of the Crusades: Memoirs of Usamah Ibn-Munqidh* (New York, 1929). References in this article are to this edition (hereafter referred to as "KI"), followed by Hitti's translation separated by a slash "/".

[3] On Usama's life and works, see Cobb, *Usama*. The classic biography of Usama is Hartwig Derenbourg, *Ousâma ibn Mounkidh. Un emir syrien au premier siècle de croisades (1095–1188). Tome Premier: Vie d'Ousâma.* (Paris, 1889), although many of Usama's surviving works were unknown to Derenbourg.

But for all that the *Book of Learning* contains, it is strangely lacking in the one thing that a document of Muslim mentalities from the age of the Crusades would be expected to contain: holy war. The word *jihad* itself occurs but once in the *Book of Learning*, and the participle derived from it, *mujahid* (one who fights in holy war), also only once. Usama also presents various Prophetic traditions (sing. *hadith*) about *jihad* in the section on courage in his manual of ideal conduct, his *Lubab al-Adab* or *Kernels of Refinement*.[4] And both there and in the *Book of Learning* he refers on occasion euphemistically to holy war as fighting "in the path of God" (*fi sabil allah*). But if this sparse evidence certainly shows that Usama was no stranger to the concept of holy war (one could hardly assume otherwise), it underscores the fact that in his own descriptions of his own fighting, he never once uses the term, and otherwise utterly shuns the discourse of holy war. This tendency is striking given the fact that Usama lived and wrote in an atmosphere that is supposed to have seen the florescence of a revived understanding of the concept of *jihad*, an understanding fostered and manipulated by the leaders of the counter-crusade: Zangi, Nur al-Din, and Saladin. The low incidence of *jihad* in Usama's writings is doubly striking when we recall that it was under precisely these three almost totemic patrons of *jihad* – what P. M. Holt has called the counter-crusade's "apostolic succession" – that Usama served and worked both as warrior and as a courtier.[5] Usama, the most famous "gentleman and warrior in the period of the Crusades," servant of the most famous Muslim holy warriors, seems not to have paid much attention to the counter-crusade. How can we account for this?

Usama and Holy War

Grateful as we are for what little scraps our sources tell us, historians of the Crusades and of medieval Islam have not been keen to note what the sources leave out, and so few have noted Usama's blind-spot with regard to *jihad*. Only Robert Irwin seems to have tried to make sense of it, noting that Usama's book "is singularly free [*sic*] of any reference to jihad." Irwin suggests that this may be due to Usama's embarrassment at the fact that he spent many years involved in diplomatic negotiations with the Franks, and even called a few of them his friends, and to the fact "that Usamah was ... a Shi'ite Muslim, and therefore he had no belief in the special religious validity of a *jihad* waged under the leadership of a usurping warlord

---

[4] Usama ibn Munqidh, *Lubab al-Adab*, ed. A. M. Shakir (Cairo, 1935). For samples of traditions on holy war, see pp. 160 ff. On the *Kernels*, see now Paul M. Cobb, "Usama ibn Munqidh's *Kernels of Refinement (Lubab al-Adab)*: Autobiographical and Historical Excerpts," *Al-Masaq: Islam and the Medieval Mediterranean* 18 (2006), 67–78.

[5] P. M. Holt, *The Age of the Crusades. The Near East from the Eleventh Century to 1517* (London, 1986), p. 38.

like Saladin."[6] In another article on Usama, Irwin offers the same explanation, but this time he notes that "according to Shi'ite doctrine, this duty [of *jihad*] is in abeyance until the Last Days, when the Hidden Imam will emerge from occultation and bring justice and victory to the true Muslims."[7]

Neither of these explanations (Usama's embarrassment at his diplomatic past and his Shi'ite beliefs) is really a satisfactory explanation of why Usama avoids describing warfare against the Franks as *jihad*. First, the embarrassment theory. This is plainly illogical, and ignores the very obvious negative statements about the Franks that Usama does make. If his past diplomatic relations with Crusaders discouraged him from using the language of *jihad* in describing warfare against them in his work in later life, then surely it would also have discouraged him from describing Franks as comic, uncivilized boors. But it does not; indeed, as is well-known, he routinely and famously lampoons Frankish manners and customs throughout the *Book of Learning*. For Usama, his diplomatic missions with Crusaders and his campaigns against them were all part of the same service he rendered to patrons. Truces and diplomacy were all perfectly acceptable components of protracted wars, even holy wars. And one could still befriend individual Franks but loathe them as a group. Usama's past relations with Franks then, are unlikely to be the factor that made him shy of *jihad*-speak.[8]

As for Irwin's theory about Shi'ism, its biggest flaw is the fact that Usama was not a Shi'ite. I am fairly certain that Usama was a Sunni Muslim, despite the prevailing assumption in the field and one piece of pretty explicit evidence that he was Shi'ite (see below). It is a complicated matter, made more complicated by Usama's unwillingness to reveal much about his own religious life, but most of the evidence for his Shi'ism is rather circumstantial. Presumably Usama can pass for a Shi'ite because in his writings he admires 'Ali, the cousin of the Prophet Muhammad and the first of the legitimate religious leaders (*imams*) recognized by Shi'ites as having succeeded the Prophet at his death.[9] Moreover, the Banu Munqidh, Usama's clan, have a history of cooperation with Shi'ite dynasties in the area, and Usama himself served in the court of the Fatimid dynasty of Egypt. Usama's service to Shi'ite states, according to this theory, would be in keeping with his Shi'ite beliefs.[10]

---

[6] Robert Irwin, "Islam and the Crusades, 1096–1699," in Jonathan Riley-Smith, ed., *The Oxford Illustrated History of the Crusades* (Oxford and New York, 1997), p. 233.

[7] Robert Irwin, "Usamah ibn Munqidh: An Arab-Syrian Gentleman at the Time of the Crusades Reconsidered," in *Crusade Sources*, pp. 78–79.

[8] On truces between Franks and Muslims, see M. A. Köhler, *Allianzen und Verträge zwischen frankischen und islamischen Herrschern im Vorderen Orient* (Berlin, 1991).

[9] KI, pp. 173/205; 177–178/208–09.

[10] Irwin, "Usamah," p. 78, n. 36, notes that "It seems possible that the Banu Munqidh, like their allies, the Banu 'Ammar clan of Apamea, were all Shi'ites." The Banu 'Ammar were the rulers of Tripoli, not Apamea. And their assumed Shi'ism seems only attributed to them by association, since they were governors for the Fatimids. Moreover, even if the Banu 'Ammar were Shi'ites, it is not a contagious condition. And the Banu 'Ammar did not shy from alliances with Sunnis. Indeed, while Usama's

But none of this is very good evidence for one man's religious convictions.[11] On the one hand, admiration for ʿAli, a beloved relative and companion of the Prophet, was hardly incompatible with Sunnism. On the other, the Fatimids employed many non-Shiʿites. Indeed, it is safe to say that the majority of people working for the caliphs in Cairo, including military men like Usama, were Sunni Muslims. His actual religious practice as he reports it in the *Book of Learning* and his other works is at best ambiguous with regard to his religious identity. He fasts, he prays, he goes on pilgrimage, he reads the Qurʾan. This is hardly sectarian behavior of any specific kind. But there is some other evidence about Usama's religious beliefs, and, for champions of Usama's Sunni identity, it is, one has to admit, a bit embarrassing. This is a reference to a now lost biographical dictionary of Shiʿites by the thirteenth-century historian Ibn Abi Tayyiʾ cited in an even later work by the historian al-Dhahabi (d. 1348 or 1352). In this passage, Ibn Abi Tayyiʾ says unequivocally that Usama was a Shiʿite, and that he practiced *taqiyya*, the dissimulation of one's religious beliefs that Shiʿites employed as a matter of survival:[12]

> Yahya ibn Abi Tayyiʾ mentions [Usama] in his *History of the Shiʿites*, saying: "My father related to me the following: 'I met him a number of times. He was an Imami Shiʿite, sound in his beliefs except that he used to conceal his orientation and exhibit *taqiyya*. He had abundant wealth and he used to help out the Shiʿites, being kind to the poor and giving to the notables.'"

It is difficult to know what to do with Ibn Abi Tayyi's evidence. If Usama was a dissimulating Shiʿite, that could certainly account for his apparent nondescript Sunnism, and we would be obliged to agree that Usama was as Shiʿite as they come. However, there is still one last piece of evidence about Usama's religious beliefs that is as unambiguous as the claims of Ibn Abi Tayyiʾ and it argues for Usama being a Sunni Muslim. For, although it would be a very rare thing for a Shiʿite, even a Shiʿite pretending to be Sunni, to cite in his works, as Usama does, the authority of Sunni figures such as the early caliphs Abu Bakr and ʿUthman, men reviled by the Shiʿite community as usurpers, it was not impossible.[13] But it is certainly peculiar, even for

---

grandfather did serve in the court at Tripoli, the leader of the Banu ʿAmmar refused the Banu Munqidh's invitation to stay at Shayzar after Tripoli was taken by the Crusaders, but instead took service in the court of the (Sunni) Burid rulers of Damascus and, ultimately, in the court of the (Sunni) Abbasid caliphs in Baghdad. Irwin also says that, in Egypt, all of Usama's enemies were Sunni. In fact, with the exception of the Fatimid ruling family, the religious elite and select officials (Shiʿites, who were hardly all friends of Usama), almost everyone in Fatimid Egypt, friend or foe, was Sunni.

[11] On the religious world of Usama, see Cobb, *Usama*, ch. 4.

[12] Cited in Derenbourg, *Ousâma*, p. 602.

[13] For example, Usama, *Lubab*, pp. 13, 14, 21 (where Abu Bakr dictates his succession-document to ʿUthman), 143 175, 179, 185, 303. This would be very unlikely in a Shiʿite, but not unheard of. One Shiʿite author, for example, for reasons of *taqiyya*, was obliged to write in defense of ʿAʾisha, the Prophet's wife and normally a focus of Shiʿite antipathy. See Wilferd Madelung, "Imamism and Muʿtazilite Theology," in *Le Shīʿisme imâmite. Colloque de Strasbourg (6–9 mai, 1968)* (Paris, 1970), p. 21.

a dissimulating Shiʿite, to sit down and compose, as Usama did, a work devoted to the merits of the caliph ʿUmar ibn al-Khattab, a caliph whom Shiʿites especially loathe, the work itself being an abridgement of a longer work by the famous Sunni scholar Ibn al-Jawzi (d. 1200).[14] In the face of this direct documentary evidence of Usama engaging in Sunni devotional writing, it seems safer to assume that Usama was a Sunni Muslim, who was at most, like many Sunnis of his day, an adherent of what was called "laudable Shiʿite tendencies" by having a more than passing association with Shiʿite regimes and possibly more than passing admiration for ʿAli and his kin. If this is so, then Ibn Abi Tayyiʾ may merely be guilty of claiming a distinguished member to include in his biographical dictionary of Shiʿites, a common activity for authors of such works.[15]

But as it turns out, Usama's religious beliefs do not really matter in respect to *jihad*. Shiʿite or Sunni, Usama's religious orientation cannot be used to explain the relative absence of *jihad* in his work. Now, Irwin is quite right that Shiʿite religious law puts (or rather, used to put) the duty of *jihad* in abeyance until the return of the Hidden Imam. That is, it did in the ninth and tenth centuries. But by the time Usama was living and writing, Shiʿite doctrine on *jihad* had changed to reflect contemporary realities. By Usama's day, the first major modification had taken place to the classical Shiʿite doctrine on *jihad*, making it perfectly allowable for Shiʿites to engage in holy war without waiting for the Hidden Imam's say-so. The great Shiʿite theorist al-Tusi (d. 1067), for example, stressed that a defensive *jihad* can still be carried out in the absence of the Imam, and it was a meritorious deed to guard the frontiers of the *dar al-Islam*, the "abode of Islam," a phrase beloved by the Shiʿite jurists to denote, in this case, any Shiʿite territory. Thus, Irwin's Shiʿite theory is not quite convincing here, either, even assuming Usama was a Shiʿite. Not only were Shiʿites allowed to engage in *jihad* without the Imam; but if, like Usama at Shayzar, they did so in a frontier zone, they were to be rewarded for it.[16]

So what can explain the rarity of *jihad* in Usama's *Book of Learning*? It may help if we consider the instances when holy war *does* make an appearance. There are (*pace* Irwin) only four cases. The first two are oblique references, since Usama does not use the actual term *jihad* or its derivates in these passages, though the indication of holy war is unambiguous. In one, he refers to the death of his brother, ʿIzz al-Dawla ʿAli, who died in 1152 fighting the Franks at Gaza, and calls him a "martyr" (*shahid*) who "fought for religion, not for this world," a clear reference to

---

[14] Usama's treatise is entitled *Manaqib ʿUmar ibn al-Khattab wa-manaqib ʿUmar ibn ʿAbd al-ʿAziz* and remains in manuscript (Cairo, Dar al-Kutub: MS *taʾrikh* Taymur #1513 [11147]).

[15] For a study that involves this practice at an earlier period in Islamic history, see Michael Cooperson, *Classical Arabic Biography. The Heirs of the Prophets in the Age of al-Maʾmun* (Cambridge, UK, 2000).

[16] On the history of Imami Shiʿite concepts of *jihad*, see Etan Kohlberg, "The Development of the Imami Shiʿi Doctrine of Jihad," *Zeitschrift der Deutschen Morgenländischen Gesellschaft* 126 (1976), 64–86. My thanks to Robert Gleave for points of clarification.

the doctrine of *jihad* and its reward of martyrdom.[17] In the other, he lauds the martyrdom of the Damascene scholar al-Findalawi and his companion who died fighting the Franks during the Second Crusade, holding them up as examples of men "who battle, just as the Companions of the Prophet used to battle, for the hope of Paradise and not in order to satisfy a desire or win a reputation."[18] The second pair of references are direct references to *jihad*. In the first, Usama simply notes that for his father, a renowned sportsman, hunting "was his only distraction; he had no other business but combat and holy war [*jihad*] against the Franks, and copying the Book of God [the Qur'an]."[19] There is nothing especially remarkable about this instance, save that Irwin, had he seen it, would have had a hard time calling the Banu Munqidh Shi'ites according to his own theory. But, as we have seen, by Usama's day fondness for *jihad* was no indicator of religious affiliation. Usama's father is simply praised for his devotion to *jihad* as a pious duty, here mentioned alongside transcribing the Qur'an.

The second instance is far more telling. In the account in question, Usama describes the fate of a vaunted Crusader foe:[20]

> In the church of Hunak was a window forty cubits high. Every day at noontime a leopard would come and jump to the window, where it would sleep until the end of the day, at which time it would jump down and go away. At that time Hunak was held as a fief by a Frankish knight named Sir Adam, one of the devils of the Franks. Sir Adam was told the story of the leopard and he said, "As soon as you see it, let me know."
>
> The leopard came as it was wont to do and jumped into the window. One of the peasants came and told Sir Adam about it. The latter put on his coat of mail, mounted his horse, took his shield and lance and came to the church, which was all in ruins with the exception of one wall which was standing and in which the window was. As soon as the leopard saw him, it jumped from the window upon him while he was on his horse, broke his back and killed him. It then went away. The peasants of Hunak used to call that leopard, "the leopard that takes part in the holy war" (*al-namir al-mujahid*).

There are at least two observations to make about this remarkable story. First, one cannot miss Usama's sense of humor here. On the one hand, Usama may well have wished to show how stupid or canny or just quaint the peasants of Hunak were in so naming the leopard that haunted the Byzantine ruins of their village or perhaps he just wanted to mock the Frankish knight that was so easily overcome. On the other hand, he may also have found it amusing that an animal should be, as it were, lionized for possessing the very human spirit of the age. And this brings us to our second observation: throughout his entire *Book of Learning*, it is clear that, for Usama, the violence of men and the violence of animals were closely intertwined.

---

[17] *yuqatil li'l-din la li'l-dunya.* KI, pp. 16–17/41–42.

[18] KI, pp. 124/94–95.

[19] KI, pp. 192/222.

[20] KI, pp. 110–11/140–41.

As we shall see, it is in fact utterly appropriate that, in one of the few direct references to *jihad* in his writings, Usama should attribute it not to himself or to Saladin, but to an animal.

For, as I shall show below, Usama did not leave *jihad* out of his discussion of warfare against the Crusaders because of some social or religious scruple, but because other metaphors of warfare were more important and more immediate, and, to his mind, more appropriate for his milieu. For Usama was not waging holy war against the Crusaders. He was hunting them.

Crusader Bestiality

As is well known, the peoples of medieval Christian Europe rather underwhelmed their Muslim observers in the Middle East. From an early date, the Franks left a reputation in the Islamic world as rough and stupid barbarians famous, as Carole Hillenbrand has demonstrated, for their moral (especially sexual) laxity and their impurity, both real and metaphorical.[21] When one speaks of the location of Franks in the medieval Islamic imaginary before the Crusades, when one spoke of Franks at all, it was in the realm of cosmography and descriptive geography, the *National Geographic* of the age, in which early Islamic scientists and travelers reported on dark corners of the known world and the bizarre customs of the peoples who lived there, as in this famous account by al-Mas'udi (d. 956):

> As regards the people of the northern quadrant, they are the ones for whom the sun is distant from the zenith, … such as the Slavs, the Franks, and those nations who neighbor them. The power of the sun is weak among them because of their distance from it; cold and damp prevail in their regions, and snow and ice follow one another in endless succession. The warm humor is lacking among them; their bodies are large, their natures gross, their manners harsh, their understanding dull, and their tongues heavy. Their color is so excessively white that it passes from white to blue; their skin is thin and their flesh thick. Their eyes are also blue, matching the character of their coloring; their hair is lank and reddish because of the prevalence of damp mists. Their religious beliefs lack solidity …[22]

Other geographers had similar tales to tell of the inhabitants of the northern climes, noting their bravery but also their moral laxity, their innocence of the basics of personal hygiene, and their low intelligence. A tenth-century physician named Ibn al-Ash'ath, for example, composed a *Book of Animals* which also features a classification of human races. The Franks, like other northerners, lack wisdom, and,

---

[21] Carole Hillenbrand, *The Crusades: Islamic Perspectives* (London, 1999), pp. 274 ff.

[22] Cited in Hillenbrand, *Islamic Perspectives*, p. 272. On the limited interest of Muslim geographers in the European sub-continent, see Eliyahu Ashtor, "La geografia dell'Europa nelle opere di Persiani e Arabi nell'undicesimo secolo," in *Popoli e paesi nella cultura altomedievale. Spoleto: Centro italiano di studi sull'alto Medioevo, 23–29 aprile 1981* (Spoleto, 1983), pp. 647–99; 701–8.

like animals, they have only generic characteristics and lack all individuality. Ibn al-Ash'ath also says that the Franks shed their hair annually as do other beasts.[23]

This, then, is something of the pool of ethnographic ideas about the Franks that Usama inherited by the time he was writing, and, although he at least is able to rise slightly above it through his own personal relationships with Franks in Syria and Palestine, most of the familiar themes can still be found in his writings. Foremost among such themes is that of Frankish bestiality. For Usama, the Franks, though human, flirted dangerously with the qualities of the animal kingdom:

> Mysterious are the works of the Creator, the author of all things! When one comes to recount cases regarding the Franks … he sees them as animals possessing the virtues of courage and fighting, but nothing else; just as animals have only the virtues of strength and carrying loads.[24]

The Franks are both possessed of animal qualities and devoid of civilized human traits. Like animals, the Franks have neither jealousy nor zeal, but great courage.[25] Just as Usama and his household raced hounds to pass the time, the Franks amuse themselves, in one instance noted by Usama, by making old women race for the coveted prize of a live hog.[26] They are variously described as devils[27] and dogs,[28] and Usama's contemporaries extended the metaphors to other animals, notably pigs. The Franks that inhabit Usama's environment have set ways, and Usama, like a naturalist, made a practice of observing their ways and noting their habits and favored ambuscades, just as he did with the lions, cheetahs, gazelles and geese that he hunted. Like ducks and partridges, the Franks in Usama's world have specific places near Shayzar where they tend to congregate.[29] When killed in battle, their heads were occasionally cut off and sent back to Shayzar to be counted or displayed on the saddles of Turkish horsemen as trophies, precisely as was done with lions killed on the hunt.[30]

But if the Franks shared many qualities with animals, they almost failed to rank as human, given their shortcomings in certain distinct areas. These strange and violent newcomers to Usama's world are said to have a "curious mentality," and to speak words "which would never come out of the head of a sensible man."[31] They are stupid, unlettered and do not control their women. They do not cover themselves in the bath. They have no law worthy of the name,[32] and their medicine has only

---

[23] Cited in Hillenbrand, *Islamic Perspectives*, p. 271.

[24] KI, p. 132/161.

[25] KI, p. 137/166.

[26] KI, p. 138/167.

[27] KI, p. 134/163.

[28] KI, p. 91/121.

[29] KI, pp. 43/71; 85/114.

[30] KI, pp. 2/25; 149/178–79; 116/146.

[31] KI, p. 132/161.

[32] KI, pp. 84–85/167–68.

little to recommend it.[33] They lack all sense of social order: "The Franks ... possess none of the virtues of men except courage, consider no precedence or high rank except that of knights, and have nobody that counts except knights."[34] They are paradigmatic barbarians, innocent of the capability to speak any noble tongue. Usama complains, "These people speak nothing but Frankish; we do not understand what they say."[35] Finally, they are an accursed race and do not assimilate except with members of their own kin,[36] although, Usama admits, it is the newcomers you have to watch out for; once the Franks get acclimated to the Near East, some of them can be perfectly decent people.[37]

Hunting and Warfare at Shayzar

So, in Usama's mind, the Crusaders that he knew were humans, but imperfect specimens. And wherever they seemed to have shortfalls of humanity, they made up for it by exhibiting bestial behavior in equal measure. Crusaders and animals shared much of the same mental territory for Usama, and the implications of that awkward condominium do not stop there. For, if Crusaders and animals were hard to distinguish, violence against Crusaders – what we call warfare – often seemed as delightfully distracting as violence against animals – a practice we call in euphemism, hunting. Just as Usama allowed the Franks to slip into the realm of the bestial unopposed, so too did warfare often intrude upon the hunt, and vice versa.

For Usama, hunting is clearly analogous to warfare. He betrays the analogical relationship between these two activities in the very way he organizes his thoughts about them. For example, of the dangers in life that his father did not forbid him Usama provides two examples: combat against the Franks and, as a child, killing a serpent bare-handed. Serpent-killing and Frank-slaying: these are two dangerous activities of the same order.[38] Indeed, Usama explicitly divides the anecdotes in his *Book of Learning* into a section on "battles, fights and adventures" and one on "the field of hunting, be it the chase or falconry."[39] In thus attempting to organize these activities in different compartments, he nevertheless highlights their similarity in his mind. But it is not an organizational scheme he can maintain for very long, in any case, and his section on battles is in fact filled with anecdotes about hunting.

Warfare was an ever-present danger at Shayzar, and was likely to intrude upon hunting at any moment. This intrusion could be physical, as in two instances when

---

[33] KI, pp. 132–33/162. On Usama's evaluation of Frankish law and medicine, see Cobb, *Usama*, ch. 5.

[34] KI, p. 74/93.

[35] KI, p. 66/95.

[36] KI, p. 130/159.

[37] KI, p. 134/163.

[38] KI, pp. 103–4/133–34.

[39] KI, p. 191/221.

a sudden Frankish foray against Shayzar caught the men of the Banu Munqidh household unawares while they were out hunting.[40] Or, more commonly, the intrusion of warfare into hunting was implied. Usama tells us his father "used to go out to the chase, with us, his four children, accompanying him, and taking with us our attendants, our extra horses led by our side and our weapons. For we never felt secure on account of the Franks, whose territory was adjacent to ours."[41] The Franks, like lions and bandits, were at Shayzar a serious security risk.[42]

It is no accident, then, that Usama's descriptions of hunting sound rather like military campaigns. Take this account, for example, which, even in the original Arabic, sounds as bellicose as Hitti's English translation:

> I have seen lions do many things which I never expected them to do. Nor did I ever before believe that lions, like men, have among their number the courageous and the cowardly. This is the way it happened.
>
> One day [a servant] came to us running and said. "There are three lions in the thicket of Tall al-Tulul." So we mounted and rode out to them and lo, there was a lioness with two lions behind it. We reconnoitered the thicket, but the lioness came out to attack us, and then stopped. My brother charged the lioness and gave it a blow with his lance which killed it. … On our return to the thicket, one of the two remaining lions came out to attack us … As we stood in its way, we had the backs of our horses turned towards it and held our lances backward, pointed in its direction, believing that it would attack us, upon which we would stab it with our lances and kill it. [They kill it] … We then turned back to the last lion with about twenty footmen of Armenian troops who were good archers … The Armenians covered its route with a shower of arrows … but it kept straight on.[43]

Usama's father was an insatiable hunter, who certainly treated his campaigns against the animals of Shayzar as very serious business. "My father," Usama mentions, "had a way of organizing the hunting party as though it were a battle array or a very grave matter. No one was supposed to engage in conversation with his companion, and everybody was expected to have one concern only, scanning the ground to spy out a hare in its form or a bird in its nest."[44] The hunting parties that Usama described at Shayzar and elsewhere often included a detachment of horsemen, some of them drawn from the *mamluk* troops of the castle,[45] footmen, tents, strategy, tactics, formations, and even drums.[46] That war could be brought to the hunt and that hunting bled into warfare was an appealing situation for Usama, who occasionally made use of the phenomenon in a poem: "My whole ambition was to engage in combat with my rivals, whom I always took for prey."[47]

---

[40] KI, pp. 55/84, 213/243.
[41] KI, p. 201/230.
[42] KI, p. 84/113.
[43] KI, p. 106/136.
[44] KI, p. 202/231.
[45] KI, pp. 125–26/154–55.
[46] KI, pp. 192–93/222–24.
[47] KI, p. 161/191.

Conclusions

Do the facts that Usama saw Franks to be similar to animals and warfare to be a close cousin of hunting explain his reluctance to conceive of warfare against Crusaders as *jihad*? I think yes, at least partly so. My point is not that he *actually* thought he was hunting animals when he fought the Franks. Rather, for Usama, fighting Franks fit the mold of the aristocratic pastimes of hunting and run-of-the-mill fighting better than it did holy war or any other activity. That Usama liked to think of Franks not as a serious religious or political threat, but instead as marauding, thick-fingered brutes surely assisted this act of analogy. If there could be Crusading Franks, then Mujahideen leopards are not too far away. Fighting Muslims, hunting cheetahs, fighting lions, hunting Crusaders, these were all activities that shared qualities as encounters with outsiders, and encounters with danger. Usama touts all such activities in his writings as anecdotes to showcase his or his family's commitment to manliness and civilization, at least Islamic civilization, by demonstrating their prowess over nature and over the forces of chaos embodied in native enemies and foreign-born infidels. For Usama's own self-representation in his writings, *jihad* was undeniably a laudable activity, and he praised those who engaged in it, such as his father and brother. But Usama, who fancied himself a living embodiment of the fate-struck warrior-poets of old, did not need *jihad* to explain his delight at fighting the Franks; for him, fighting people of that kind was simply an extension of the bloody deeds that noble men were expected to perform.[48]

We may compare this attitude to groups who *did* cast fighting the Franks as *jihad*, namely the ruling elites of Syria and Iraq in Usama's day, those famous symbols of the counter-crusade whom I have already mentioned: Zangi, Nur al-Din, Saladin, and the other Turkish warlords and atabegs who came before them, like Tughtakin of Damascus or his successor Unur – men who are not as famous today as Saladin, but who nonetheless matched him in their fondness for *jihad*. What makes them different from Usama? By Usama's own testimony, Zangi and Unur and Saladin all enjoyed the hunt as much as he did, and they were as likely to share his preconceived ideas about Frankish bestiality as anyone else. If this is so, why didn't the counter-crusade fall prey to hunting analogies with these men and become a grand royal pastime, instead of a religious duty as *jihad*?

The answer, I think, lies in culture. For the leaders of the *jihad* against the Franks were, unlike Usama, Turks or Kurds. And all of them were, compared to the Banu Munqidh, recent arrivals in Syria. The Saljuq warlords and atabegs in Syria were in many ways a foreign, conquering elite. They lived in citadels within cities, protected by garrisons of fellow Turks, in some cases speaking only Turkish, a language that local elites like Usama did not deign to learn. They were a social stratum seeking to acquire a greater local profile through urban alliances and patronage, and also

---

[48] On Usama's self-representation, see Cobb, *Usama*, ch. 6.

one which was desperately seeking legitimacy. To achieve that legitimacy, as other historians of Islam have extensively documented, the warlords and atabegs allied themselves with Islamic elites, with scholars, mystics, and preachers. They built mosques, religious colleges, and Sufi meeting-houses. They eliminated Shi'ites in their midst and, lastly, embraced *jihad* as a distinctive plank in their foreign-policy platform.[49]

It is thus entirely in keeping with the needs of the Turkish elite of medieval Syria that it was they, and not the local Arab princes like Usama, who heeded the challenges of preachers like the Damascene al-Sulami and embraced it with such gusto.[50] But not *everyone* heeded this appeal to *jihad* so zealously. Usama did not take to it like his Turkish masters not because he was not a good Muslim, but because he did not need to prove he was a good Muslim and because concepts of ennobling aristocratic violence, not religious duty, best accounted for his own pursuit of Frankish game. Usama's reticence about *jihad* is thus a reminder that holy war was *not* the default response for Muslims confronting Franks in the Crusader era, but rather one response adopted by specific segments of Syrian society for specific purposes. And it is a further reminder that, in order for us to assess "Islamic perspectives" of the Crusades, we should not limit ourselves to chasing our prey in the discourse of *jihad* manipulated by the ruling elite, but be prepared to pursue our quarry into the deeper and more difficult reaches of the cultural history of the medieval Middle East.

---

[49] The literature on the interdependence of the 'ulama and the ruling strata in the medieval Near East is comparatively vast. Ira M. Lapidus, *Muslim Cities in the Later Middle Ages* (Cambridge, MA: 1967) is the starting-point. See also Michael Chamberlain, *Knowledge and Social Practice in Medieval Damascus, 1190–1350* (Cambridge: 1994).

[50] On al-Sulami, see the essay by Niall Christie in this volume.

The French Translation of William of Tyre's *Historia*: the Manuscript Tradition[1]

Peter Edbury

Cardiff University

Archbishop William of Tyre wrote his history of the crusades and the Latin East between the late 1160s and 1184, and Robert Huygens' definitive edition of William's Latin text, based on a critical analysis of seven manuscripts (plus one fragment), appeared in 1986.[2] At some point between the end of the Third Crusade and the early 1230s someone translated the work into French,[3] and 51 manuscripts of the translation dating from before 1500 survive in public collections. These are listed below in Appendix 1.[4] The French version, usually referred to as *L'estoire de Eracles* or, more simply, *Eracles* (thanks to the mention of the seventh-century Byzantine emperor Heraklios in the first sentence), was published in 1844 in the *Recueil des historiens des croisades: historiens occidentaux*, volume 1, where the text occupies the lower half of the same page as William's Latin text, and again, in 1879–80, by Paulin Paris.[5] All modern scholars who have had occasion to refer to the translation have used one or other of these editions. Most of the *Eracles* manuscripts have continuations which take the narrative well into the thirteenth century, and these continuations were published in 1859 in *Recueil des historiens des croisades: historiens occidentaux*, volume 2. The only sections from the continuations to have been re-edited since then are those covering the years 1184–97 from the Lyon, Bibliothèque de la Ville, ms. 828 (F72)[6] and 1191–97 from the Florence, Biblioteca Medicea-Laurenziana, ms. Plu. LXI.10 (F70) which Ruth Morgan published in 1982.[7]

[1]   Research for this paper has been facilitated by a grant from the British Academy. I thank Professor Jaroslav Folda for reading and commenting on an earlier draft.

[2]   *Willelmi Tyrensis Archiepiscopi Chronicon*, ed. Robert B. C. Huygens, 2 vols., CCCM 63 (Turnhout, 1986). (Henceforth: WT)

[3]   John H. Pryor, "The *Eracles* and William of Tyre: an Interim Report", in *Horns*, pp. 270–93 at pp. 288–89 (arguing for a date after 1204 and before 1234).

[4]   I have seen all except the fire-damaged Turin Biblioteca Nazionale, ms. L. II. 17 .

[5]   *L'estoire de Eracles empereur et la conqueste de la terre d'Outremer*, RHC Oc., 1 (1844); *Guillaume de Tyr et ses continuateurs: text français du XIIIe siècle*, ed. Paulin Paris, 2 vols. (Paris, 1879–80).

[6]   To simplify referring to the manuscripts I have followed the numbering in Jaroslav Folda, "Manuscripts of the *History of Outremer* by William of Tyre: a Handlist", *Scriptorium* 27 (1973), 90–95. "F72" is thus Folda no. 72. Book and chapter numbers are given thus: 15.12.

[7]   *La continuation de Guillaume de Tyr (1184–1197)*, ed. Margaret Ruth Morgan, Documents relatifs à l'histoire des croisades 14 (Paris, 1982).

Historical enquiry into the French William of Tyre has tended to concentrate on two distinct areas: the manuscript illuminations and the continuations. Between them Hugo Buchthal and Jaroslav Folda established that some of the most notable illuminated manuscripts of *Eracles* were produced in the Latin East in the second half of the thirteenth century, and their discoveries have shed considerable light on the artistic *milieu* there in the decades before the fall of Acre in 1291.[8] The French continuations are a major source for our knowledge of the history of the Latin East after 1184 – there was no historian there writing in Latin of the stature of William of Tyre to describe later events – and so, with the late Ruth Morgan leading the way, it is not surprising that they should have come under critical scrutiny.[9] The text of the translation itself, however, has received less attention, even though historians have been aware of significant differences between it and the original Latin version. A group of scholars met at the Institute for Advanced Studies of the Hebrew University of Jerusalem in 1987 to investigate the relationship between the *Eracles* text and William's Latin chronicle, and their report, composed by John Pryor, began by explaining that they realized from the outset that "the attainment of [their] objectives would, at the very least, be severely hampered by the unsatisfactory nature of the current edition of the *Eracles*."[10] The discussions on that occasion were fruitful, but, as the participants would doubtless be the first to admit, many problems remain. More recently, Bernard Hamilton, a member of the 1987 group, has published a detailed analysis comparing the Latin and French texts of books 21–23 which cover the reign of Baldwin IV from 1174 until the point early in 1184 at which William ceased writing.[11] This is an important article with many pertinent comments, designed to show how, and to what extent, the translator modified what was before him. However, Hamilton's analysis does require a confidence in the printed text of the translation – in this instance the Paulin Paris edition – which, sadly, is not entirely warranted. Even so, it is much to be hoped that other scholars will repeat this exercise for different periods in William's narrative.

The present paper aims to lay the groundwork for establishing a stemma of the extant manuscripts. Such an exercise has to be seen as a pre-requisite for a critical

---

[8] Hugo Buchthal, *Miniature Painting in the Latin Kingdom of Jerusalem* (Oxford, 1957); Jaroslav Folda, *Crusader Manuscript Illumination at Saint-Jean d'Acre, 1275–1291* (Princeton, 1976). For recent work, see for example Bianca Kühnel, "The Perception of History in Thirteenth-Century Crusader Art," in *France and the Holy Land: Frankish Culture at the End of the Crusades*, ed. Daniel H. Weiss and Lisa Mahoney (Baltimore, 2004), pp. 161–86, at pp. 173–78; Jaroslav Folda, *Crusader Art in the Holy Land, From the Third Crusade to the Fall of Acre, 1187–1291* (Cambridge, 2005), pp. 217–18, 235–36, 345–50, 401–8, 424–27, 495–97, 525–26.

[9] Margaret Ruth Morgan, *The Chronicle of Ernoul and the Continuations of William of Tyre* (Oxford, 1973); eadem, "The Rothelin Continuation of William of Tyre," in *Outremer*, pp. 244–57; Peter W. Edbury, "The Lyon *Eracles* and the Old French Continuations of William of Tyre," in *Montjoie*, pp. 139–53 (critical of Morgan's 1973 monograph).

[10] Pryor, "The *Eracles* and William of Tyre," p. 270.

[11] Bernard Hamilton, "The Old French translation of William of Tyre as an historical source," in *EC*, 2, pp. 93–112.

edition. By consulting those manuscripts identified as most closely preserving the text of the original translation, the sort of exercise that Hamilton embarked upon would be made more secure. In addition, an enquiry into the way in which the text developed should shed light on where and how it circulated and also on the practices followed in individual workshops. It might also be of interest to know if, and to what extent, textual affiliations run parallel to artistic linkages.

One major problem with vernacular texts from this period is that copyists did not regard the exemplars they were using as sacrosanct. That meant they would modify the text by improving or modernizing the word-order and the vocabulary. They might also change the structure of the text by dividing or amalgamating chapters, by interpolating fresh material, or by making omissions. Deliberate changes are one thing; inadvertent mistakes quite another, but both would be transmitted to posterity by a copyist utilizing a particular manuscript as his exemplar. Textual variations and changes to the structure of the books and chapters along with the presence or otherwise of rubrics provide the raw material for investigating the relationships between the manuscripts.

The procedure adopted for the analysis that follows in this paper has been to take a microfilm or microfiche of each manuscript in turn and note the first six and the last six words of each chapter; the information thus gathered provides a sample of variant readings and allows for the identification of merged, split and missing chapters. It must be stressed, however, that this analysis is not comprehensive; the conclusions are therefore not final but should be regarded as the fruits of "work in progress". In particular, it has not proved possible to construct a tidy "family tree" on which each manuscript can be assigned a place that would denote its relationship to all the other manuscripts; rather in most instances the best that can be done is to establish which manuscripts have textual affinities with which others. Part of the difficulty is that anomalies abound, and it is demonstrable that some copyists used more than one exemplar in preparing a new codex, with the result that we have hybrid texts that cannot be fitted neatly into a stemma. The thinking behind this approach perhaps needs a little more explanation. If a manuscript has a particular variant reading, or divides a chapter at a particular place, or merges two chapters and does not share this feature with any other manuscript, all that can be said for certain is that no other manuscript has been derived directly from it; indeed the feature could well have been introduced by the copyist of the manuscript in question. On the other hand, when several manuscripts share the same reading, division or amalgamation, that could indicate a common ancestor, and the textual affinity would be confirmed if the same group of manuscripts have several other similar features in common. It has, however, to be remembered that such features might arise independently: after all, if a scribe wanted to split a chapter into two there are only so many possible places he could do so sensibly. As will become clear later, one of the problems faced in undertaking this project results from the lack of consistency within each manuscript which means that particular copies may have features in common for a limited section of the text, only to lose this common ground thereafter.

Neither of the nineteenth-century editions is satisfactory. The *Recueil* edition was based on readings supplied by a selection of manuscripts chosen primarily, so it would seem, because they happened to be in Paris. Apparently the editors used the fifteenth-century Paris, BN, ms. fr. 2627 (F02) as their base manuscript which they compared with three other Paris manuscripts: BN, ms. fr. 2825 (F58), BN, ms. fr. 2827 (F48), and BN, ms. fr. 9082 (F77).[12] They seem to have been rather arbitrary in deciding which readings to prefer. They also adopted a policy of altering the structure of the French translation to bring the chapter divisions into conformity with the divisions in the Latin text. This approach meant that some chapters were made to begin and end where the Latin begins and ends and not where they do in the manuscripts. It also led to a number of chapters in the French version being split in two and those in the rest of the book in question being renumbered accordingly. (For details see below, Appendix 2.) The *Recueil* edition comes with a complete set of rubrics, pieced together from those contained in F58 and F77 – F02, the Paris, BN, ms. fr. 2627, lacks rubrics. Paulin Paris chose a manuscript datable to ca. 1300 – and so by no means the earliest – as his base: it is now the Baltimore, Walters Art Gallery, ms. 142 (F52). Had he simply transcribed this manuscript and modernized the punctuation, we should, as will become clear presently, possess an edition that would be reasonably dependable. What he did was to create a pastiche by introducing readings from the *Recueil* edition into his text, and he also appears to have made some use of the manuscript that is now the Baltimore, Walters Art Gallery, ms. 137 (F31); moreover, he followed the *Recueil* by imposing many of the same unwarranted chapter divisions, and he added the rubrics from the *Recueil*, although here again there were none in his base manuscript.

In the nineteenth century, Louis de Mas Latrie and Paul Riant listed the manuscripts then known, sorting them into groups depending on whether they contained a version of the continuation to William's text, and, if so, where they ended.[13] In 1973, Folda published a handlist, essentially an up-dated version of Riant's work, in which he noted new discoveries and current shelf marks, and it is on this guide to the manuscripts that I have relied.[14] Following his nineteenth-century models, Folda divided the *Eracles* manuscripts into four groups:

- Those with no continuation (F01–F06)
- Those with a continuation that is virtually identical to the text known as the *Chronique d'Ernoul et de Bernard le Trésorier* for the period beginning in

---

[12] *RHC Oc.*, 1, p. xxvi. For the modern shelf marks, see Paul Riant, "Inventaire sommaire des manuscrits de *l'Eracles*," *AOL*, 1 (1881), 247–52 at pp. 248 (nos. 1, 3), 250 (no. 32), 251 (no. 67). The editors claimed that what is now the ms. fr. 2627 is a thirteenth-century manuscript when in reality it dates to the fifteenth.

[13] Louis de Mas Latrie, "Essai de classification des continuations de l'historie des croisades de Guillaume de Tyr," in *Chronique d'Ernoul et de Bernard le Trésorier* (Paris, 1871), pp. 473–565 at pp. 480–88; Riant, "Inventaire sommaire," pp. 247–52, cf. pp. 716–17.

[14] Folda, see above note 6.

the mid-1180s and ending with events in Latin Greece datable to 1232 (F30–F51)[15]

- Those with the further continuation for the period 1232–61 known as the "Rothelin Continuation" (F52–F66)[16]
- Those with a completely different continuation for the period 1232 onwards, in several instances going on to the 1260s or 1270s, and which is known as either the "Acre Continuation" or the "Noailles Continuation" (F67–F78).[17]

For scholars more interested in the continuations than the text of the translation itself, this categorization was sensible, but it is of limited value in an analysis of the translation. A number of manuscripts lack their concluding folios, usually breaking off in mid-sentence at the end of a page, and so we can never know for certain where they originally finished. Thus three of the six manuscripts of the first group (F01, F03 and F04) are truncated, while the same is true of eight out of the 22 manuscripts in the second group (F30, F32, F34, F35, F41, F43, F49, F51). On the other hand, some manuscripts had continuations added later. A good case in point is the Walters Art Gallery, ms. 142 (F52) which provided Paulin Paris with his base. Here the text originally finished at fol. 263r where the Latin text ends with the events of 1184; fol. 263v is blank, and then the continuations, which conclude with the Rothelin text, follow in a different hand starting at fol. 264r. Folda has suggested that the text of the translation was copied ca. 1300 and the continuations added ca. 1340.[18] There is therefore a good case for considering this manuscript in conjunction with the other manuscripts with no continuation rather than with the Rothelin group. Similarly the Brussels, Bibliothèque Royale, ms. 9492–3 (F54) originally ended in 1232 at fol. 380r, and the Rothelin continuation, beginning at fol. 381r, was clearly added subsequently. Arguably it belongs with the other 1232 manuscripts, and features of the text of the translation in this manuscript support that view.

The Original Translation

William's Latin text broke off with the events of early 1184 and the appointment of Count Raymond III of Tripoli as regent of the kingdom of Jerusalem. Three of the *Eracles* manuscripts (Paris, BN, ms. fr. 2627 (F02), Paris, BN, ms. fr. 9081 (F05), and Rome, Biblioteca Apostolica Vaticana, ms. Pal. lat. 1963 (F06)) plus a fourth, the Baltimore, Walters Art Gallery, ms. 142 (F52) where the continuation was added subsequently, end at the same place as the Latin text. The existence of this group is sufficient to show that the French translation was in circulation before someone decided to bring the narrative closer to the present – in fact to 1232 – by adapting

---

[15] *Chronique d'Ernoul et de Bernard le Trésorier*, ed. Louis de Mas Latrie (Paris, 1871).

[16] *RHC Oc.*, 2: 483–639.

[17] *RHC Oc.*, 2: 380–481.

[18] Folda, *Crusader Manuscript Illumination*, p. 212. See also the catalogue description at pp. 212–13.

the so-called *Chronique d'Ernoul et de Bernard Le Trésorier* and pasting it on at the end. The Paris, BN, ms. fr. 9081 (F05) is the earliest *Eracles* manuscript with illustrations; it was executed in Paris in the years 1245–48, in other words on the eve of Louis IX's crusade.[19] Folda has argued that the Biblioteca Apostolica Vaticana, ms. Pal. lat. 1963 (F06) originated in Antioch, and he has recently proposed that it is to be dated to between ca. 1260 and the city's destruction in 1268.[20] Although the Paris, BN, ms. fr. 2627 (F02) was made in the fifteenth century, it is clear from an analysis of the variant readings that it was a faithful copy of an early version of the text, and so the editors of the *Recueil* had justification for choosing it as their base manuscript. The Baltimore, Walters Art Gallery, ms. 142 (F52), which dates from ca. 1300 and which was used by Paris for his edition, would also seem to provide a text that comes close to the original form of the translation.

Whilst the original translation did not follow William's text slavishly, it did at least follow his chapter divisions to a considerable extent. So when we are faced with a manuscript that contains a number of examples of William's chapters having been divided or amalgamated, we can conclude that such a feature indicates a move away from the original structure of the translation. In other words, the fewer examples there are of divisions or amalgamations, the closer we might appear to be to the original. Of the four manuscripts mentioned as ending in 1184, F02 has just one example of a chapter split into two, and one example of two chapters run together; for F05 the totals are again one and one; F06 by contrast has four chapters split into two, one split into three and 15 examples of chapters run together, while F52 lacks 8.23 but has no examples of divided chapters and only one instance, at 13.24–25, of an amalgamation.[21] F05, which dates from the mid-1240s, is among the earliest surviving manuscripts, but three other manuscripts, which have been dated to about the same period or slightly later, show no clear pattern. The mid-thirteenth-century London, BL, Henry Yates Thompson ms. 12 (F38), perhaps the oldest extant manuscript to have a continuation, contains just one split chapter and one example of two chapters run together in the text of the translation. Similarly the Paris, BN, ms. fr. 2826 (F04), which, so it is claimed, dates to the first half of the thirteenth century, has no split chapters and 11 amalgamations, yet another early manuscript, the Paris, BN, ms. fr. 2632 (F03), has 149 split chapters but just one amalgamation. The rather later Paris, BN, ms. fr. 67 (F41), another manuscript with the 1232 continuation, has just two amalgamated chapters and no examples of

---

[19] Ibid., p. 31 and n. 27; *Crusader Art in the Holy Land*, pp. 217, 235–36 and n. 44 (p. 614).

[20] Jaroslav Folda, "A Crusader Manuscript from Antioch," *Atti della Pontificia Accademia Romana di Archeologia*, Ser. 3, *Rendiconti*, 42 (1969–70), 283–98; *Crusader Art in the Holy Land*, pp. 218 n. 614 (p. 611), 347–50 and n. 877 (pp. 641–42).

[21] It is possible that this apparent amalgamation in fact preserves an original feature of the translation as there is no chapter division in the Latin text at this point. Four other manuscripts, F36, F43, F44, F73, none of which is particularly close to the original, also run 13.24–25 together, but all the other seemingly "primitive" versions of the text have a division here.

chapters that have been divided. Apart from F03, these figures are very low, as the table listing these divisions and amalgamations in Appendix 4 makes clear. Anyone wishing to find manuscripts with a text of the translation that most closely reflects the original version might well begin with an examination of F02, F04, F05, F38, F41 and F52, all of which come near to preserving the chapter divisions found in William's Latin text.[22]

Unfortunately things are by no means so simple. By far the most frequently occurring amalgamation is at 22.24–25. Of the 50 manuscripts under consideration, 38 run these chapters together, while 11 retain the division as found in the Latin text, and one (F01) lacks this section of the narrative. But of those 11 manuscripts, only one (F52) is among those identified at the end of the last paragraph as preserving an early version of the text. F06, the manuscript attributed to Antioch that ends where William's Latin does, is another, but the remaining 9 are problematic. Two, F03 and F46, have numerous divided chapters, and it could be that a copyist, who was evidently prone to split chapters had, perhaps without knowing, restored the division at the original point in what had now become a rather lengthy chapter. However, such a coincidence seems less likely in respect of F70 or F74 or the closely interrelated group of manuscripts with the Rothelin continuation, F60, F61, F62, F63 and F65. These manuscripts have somehow managed to preserve a feature that could well have been present in the original version of the translation even though, in other respects, they are further removed from that original than several others in which these two chapters are merged.

Two Distinct Manuscript Traditions

At an early stage in my investigation it became clear that a major bifurcation exists in the manuscript tradition. A significant group of manuscripts all have the same features in common: 1.2 follows 1.1 without a break, and then 1.2 itself is divided into three; moving on we find that the following chapters are merged: 3.24–25, 5.4–5, 8.21–22, 12.24–25, 19.9–10, 21.17–18, 21.20–21 and 22.25–26. It is a pattern that is shared by 24 manuscripts:[23]

F06   Rome, Biblioteca Apostolica Vaticana, ms. Pal. lat. 1963 (Antioch: 1260s)
F30   Arras, Bibliothèque Municipale, ms. 651 (N. France: early 14th century)
F32   Bern, Bürgerbibliothek, ms. 112 (N. France: ca. 1270)
F33   Bern, Bürgerbibliothek, ms. 163 (N. France: 3rd quarter of 13th century)
F37   London, BL, Royal ms. 15. E. I (Flanders: late 15th century)

---

[22]   The translator evidently used a Latin manuscript which lacked William's autobiographical chapter (19.12) and which probably resembled most closely those in Huygens's β group (though without the reference to Pontigny at 12.7). See the introduction to the Latin edition, pp. 3–19.

[23]   Allowing for the fact that F54, F55 and F65 are damaged and in each case lack the first element.

F39 Paris, Bibliothèque de l'Arsenal, ms. 5220 (N. France: 3rd quarter of 13th century)
F40 Paris, Bibliothèque du Ministère des Affaires Etrangères, Mémoires et Documents 230*bis* (S. France: 3rd quarter of 13th century)
F42 Paris, BN, ms. fr. 68 (Flanders: ca. 1450)
F43 Paris, BN, ms. fr. 779 (N. France: ca. 1275)
F44 Paris, BN, ms. fr. 2629 (Flanders: ca. 1460)
F45 Paris, BN, ms. fr. 2630 (N. France: 3rd quarter of 13th century)
F47 Paris, BN, ms. fr. 2824 (N. France: ca. 1300)
F48 Paris, BN, ms. fr. 2827 (N. France: 3rd quarter of 13th century)
F51 Paris, BN, ms. fr. 24208 (N. France: 3rd quarter of 13th century)
F53 Brussels, Bibliothèque Royale, ms. 9045 (Flanders: ca. 1460)
F54 Brussels, Bibliothèque Royale, ms. 9492–3 (Paris: ca. 1291–95)
F55 Lyon, Bibliothèque de la Ville, ms. Palais des Arts 29 (Paris: ca. 1295–96)
F58 Paris, BN, ms. fr. 2825 (Paris: early 14th century)
F60 Paris, BN, ms. fr. 9083 (Ile de France: 2nd quarter of 14th century)
F61 Paris, BN, ms. fr. 22495 (Paris: 1337)
F62 Paris, BN, ms. fr. 22496–7 (Paris: ca. 1350)
F63 Paris, BN, ms. fr. 24209 (Ile de France: 3rd quarter of 14th century)
F64 Rome, Biblioteca Apostolica Vaticana, ms. Reg. Suec. lat. 737 (Paris: early 14th century)
F65 Turin, Biblioteca Nazionale, ms. L I. 5 (France: 15th century)

Three further manuscripts should be associated with this group. The Besançon, Bibliothèque Municipale, ms. 856 (F34 – N. France: ca. 1300) has all the listed features bar two (no amalgamation at 8.21–22, and 12.24–25), and the Geneva, Bibliothèque Publique et Universitaire, ms. 85 (F36 – Artois: 3rd quarter of the 15th century) has the last five amalgamations but not the others. In both cases it may be wondered whether there had been a change of exemplars at some previous point in the transmission of the text.[24] The Paris, BN, ms. fr. 2754 (F46 – N. France: ca. 1300), which only begins at 16.1, has two out of the four amalgamated chapters in the extant portion of the text, and should perhaps therefore be considered as belonging with this group.[25] Variant readings confirm this division in the manuscript tradition. A clear example is provided by the concluding phrase of 13.7 where none of the manuscripts included in the list given above (including F34 and F36) contains the word "onques" in the phrase "onques fait devant," whereas all the others do.[26]

---

[24] The idea that the central section of F34 may be derived from a manuscript from a different tradition is perhaps confirmed by the fact that in four instances chapters are divided in the same place as the β manuscripts, F31 and F35: 7.25, 7.19, 9.13, 16.21.

[25] A feature of F46 is the large number of divided chapters, and it is possible that the copyist responsible for most of these divisions reintroduced divisions at 21.17–18 and 22.25–26.

[26] The only exceptions are F45 and F46 (and also F77) where the folios with this passage are missing.

It is highly significant that the Antioch manuscript, F06, falls into this category, as it is sufficient to prove that manuscripts with these diagnostic features – nine amalgamated chapters and one chapter split into three – were already in circulation before it became normal to attach a continuation to the text. F06 is also the only manuscript out of the total of 28 that has been attributed to the Latin East. None of the manuscripts from Acre (F49, F50, F69–F73, F78) and none of the manuscripts with the so-called "Acre" or "Noailles" continuation (F67–78) appears in this group. What is striking is that, with the exception of F06 and also F40 (which, it is suggested, was copied in southern France),[27] all the manuscripts datable to the latter part of the thirteenth century or the very beginning of the fourteenth – F30, F32, F33, F34, F39, F43, F45, F47, F48, F51, F54, F55, F58 – are from northern France. This list includes a distinctive group of seven manuscripts – F32, F33, F39, F43, F45, F48, F51 – which, as Jaroslav Folda has kindly informed me, contain related cycles of miniatures.[28] Of the manuscripts with the fewest merged or divided chapters, and hence *prima facie* those closest to the original, mention should be made of the Paris, Bibliothèque de l'Arsenal, ms. 5220 (F39) with, apart from the merged and divided chapters that identify this group, no divided chapters and seven amalgamated chapters; the Paris, BN, ms. fr. 2825 (F58) with four and five; the Rome, Biblioteca Apostolica Vaticana, ms. Pal. lat. 1963 (F06) with four and six; the Paris, Bibliothèque du Ministère des Affaires Etrangères, Mémoires et Documents 230*bis* (F40) with three and nine; the Rome, Biblioteca Apostolica Vaticana, ms. Reg. Suec. lat. 737 (F64) with five and seven; and the mutilated Lyon, Bibliothèque de la Ville, ms. Palais des Arts 29 (F55) with three and five.

Henceforth I shall refer to the manuscripts which do not share the characteristics of the group discussed here as the "alpha (α) group", and the manuscripts listed above as the "beta (β) group."

The α group

Having already listed the manuscripts which together make up the β group, it will be helpful now to provide a similar list of those 23 manuscripts which comprise the α group:

F01 Cambridge, Sidney Sussex College, ms. 93 (England: late 13th century)
F02 Paris, BN, ms. fr. 2627 (N. France: 15th century)
F03 Paris, BN, ms. fr. 2632 (Latin East or France: 1st half of 13th century)
F04 Paris, BN, ms. fr. 2826 (Latin East or France: 1st half of 13th century)
F05 Paris, BN, ms. fr. 9081 (Paris: ca. 1245–48)
F31 Baltimore, Walters Art Gallery, ms. 137 (Paris: ca. 1295–1300)

---

[27] Folda, 'Manuscripts', p. 94; cf *Crusader Manuscript Illumination*, p. 146 n. 129.
[28] Private communication.

F35 Epinal, Bibliothèque Municipale, ms. 45 (Paris: ca. 1295–1300)

F38 London, BL, Henry Yates Thompson ms. 12 (England: mid-13th century)

F41 Paris, BN, ms. fr. 67 (N. France: 2nd half of 13th century)

F49 Paris, BN, ms. fr. 9085 (Acre: ca. 1277–80)

F50 Paris, BN, ms. fr. 9086 (Acre: ca. 1255–60)

F52 Baltimore, Walters Art Gallery, ms. 142 (Paris: ca. 1300 and ca. 1340)

F57 Paris, BN, ms. fr. 2634 (Ile de France: 1st quarter of 14th century)

F67 Amiens, Bibliothèque Municipale, ms. 483 (Flanders: mid-15th century)

F68 Bern, Bürgerbibliothek, ms. 25 (N. France: 1st half of 15th century)

F69 Boulogne-sur-Mer, Bibliothèque Municipale, ms. 142 (Acre: ca. 1287)

F70 Florence, Biblioteca Medicea-Laurenziana, ms. Plu. LXI. 10 (Acre: ca. 1290, and Italy: 1st half of 14th century)

F71 St Petersburg, National Library of Russia / Российская Национальная Библиотека, ms. fr. f° v. IV.5 (Acre: ca. 1280)

F72 Lyon, Bibliothèque de la Ville, ms. 828 (Acre: ca. 1280)

F73 Paris, BN, ms. fr. 2628 (Acre: late 1250s/early 1260s and late 1270s)

F74 Paris, BN, ms. fr. 2631 (Lombardy: ca. 1291–95)

F77 Paris, BN, ms. fr. 9082 (Rome: 1295)

F78 Paris, BN, ms. fr. 9084 (Acre: ca. 1286)

Taken together, the features that distinguish the β group are unmistakable, but it is nonetheless true that a few of the α manuscripts share some of them. Thus four – F04, F70, F72 and F77 – all begin with 1.2 following 1.1 without a break and then dividing 1.2 into three;[29] F04, F70 and F72 and also F73 then merge 3.24–25, and F04 and F72 also merge 5.4–5. Several others – F67, F68, F69, F74 and F78 – merge 8.21–22. When we turn to examine the variant readings, we find instances of F04, F70 and F72 sharing characteristic readings with the β group, as for example in the final phrase in 4.18, and, in the case of F70 and F72, at the end of 4.20.[30] It would therefore appear either that somewhere in their ancestry, a copyist had begun by copying a manuscript from the β group before switching to one from the α group, or that some of the characteristic features in the β group appeared in the manuscript tradition before others, and that these manuscripts preserve part of this transitional stage. But apart from this handful of exceptions, the α manuscripts have none of the other group's distinctive merged chapters in common.

The manuscripts which earlier were identified as preserving the most primitive form of the translation – F02, F04, F05, F38, F41 and F52 – require further consideration. In F02, F04, F05, F41 and F52 the chapters are numbered, a feature not shared by most of the manuscripts in either the α group or the β group. It seems clear that numbering chapters was characteristic of earliest versions, and that this

---

[29] It is not entirely clear whether F04 has the two chapter divisions in 1.2, as the folio is largely illegible.

[30] 4.18: "bobans" or "bouban" for "feste;" 4.21: "ou que .iiii." for "ou que .iii. ."

practice was jettisoned as the manuscript tradition developed. In F04 and also in F03 the chapters are provided with numbers, but not where a chapter has been divided with the result that the numbers assigned to chapters later in the same book remain unchanged. An echo of the practice of numbering chapters is preserved in some of the later α manuscripts which were either copied in Acre or which are derived from those that were. At the end of 19.23 we are told that Muslim losses amounted to 1,500 men,[31] and this figure is repeated in almost all the manuscripts. However, F49, F70, F72, F77 give the figure as 1,524. It is apparent that what has happened is that the copyist of the ancestor of this group, working from a manuscript in which the chapters were numbered, conflated the figure in the text with the chapter number that followed in his exemplar.

The British Library, Henry Yates Thompson ms. 12 (F38) is of particular interest. As mentioned already, it may well be the oldest surviving manuscript to contain the continuation to 1232 adapted from the *Chronique d'Ernoul et de Bernard le Trésorier*. The text of the translation appears to be very close to F05 except in one important respect: there are three places – at 19.21, 19.30 and 22.29 – where other passages from the *Chronique d'Ernoul* have been interpolated.[32] This is the only manuscript with these interpolations, and so it stands alone in the manuscript tradition. What they show is that an editor, evidently working at some point between 1232, which is when the continuation concludes, and around 1250 when the manuscript was produced, was not content simply to attach the portion of the *Chronique d'Ernoul* relating to the period 1184–1232 to the end of the translation, but attempted to integrate the two texts. As Folda has pointed out, the illustrations too represent a unique, independent cycle. One, at the beginning of book 21, showing schoolboys pinching the future leper king Baldwin IV, and William of Tyre himself examining the royal prince, is particularly striking. (It was this incident as recorded by William in the first chapter of book 21 that provided the first inkling that the young Baldwin was afflicted with leprosy.)[33]

The rather later Paris, BN, ms. fr. 67 (F41) similarly has a text that is close to F05 and F38, although in this case there are no miniatures. This manuscript too has a unique feature in that it alone of all the *Eracles* manuscripts is prefaced by an annal in French, covering the period from the time of Julius Caesar to 1095, which fills the first 81 folios. According to the catalogue in the reading room of the Bibliothèque Nationale, this annal is from the world history by Guillaume de Nangis. I have not yet been able to investigate this text further, but its presence here is suggestive. In Acre in the second half of the thirteenth century a substantial number of French William of Tyre manuscripts were produced – eight survive, and no doubt many

---

[31] Cf WT, p. 901.

[32] Respectively *Chronique d'Ernoul*, pp. 25–31, 35–41, 114.

[33] Folda, *Crusader Manuscript Illumination*, p. 32 n. 33. The miniature is reproduced in Bernard Hamilton, *The Leper King and his Heirs: Baldwin IV and the Crusader Kingdom of Jerusalem* (Cambridge, 2000), p. 251.

more have not. At the same period the other principal historical text that was being copied in Acre was the compendium of biblical and classical knowledge known as the *Histoire Universelle*. This work ends with the rule of Julius Caesar, and so it may be wondered whether someone sought to fill the gap between the two works by introducing this extended annal. F41 was not copied in the Latin East, but it could well be that whoever commissioned its production was attuned to the intellectual world which accorded prominence to these two texts, the French William of Tyre and the French *Histoire Universelle*.

The Paris, BN, ms. fr. 2632 (F03) is a manuscript which is thought to date from the first half of the thirteenth century, but unlike the other earliest manuscripts it has many examples of chapters that have been split into two or more parts. In common with the other early copies, the chapters are numbered, but, as mentioned previously, the new chapters formed from dividing the longer chapters are not normally assigned numbers of their own. There are no miniatures, although at fol. 16r there is a rather splendid mermaid in the margin and later, at fol. 37r, more marginalia with a cross of Jerusalem and what may well be intended as a Lusignan lion. The importance of this manuscript lies in the clear affinity its text has with that to be found in two others of an appreciably later date – the Baltimore, Walters Art Gallery, ms. 137 (F31) and the Epinal, Bibliothèque Municipale, ms. 45 (F35), both of which are believed to be of Parisian provenance from the very end of the thirteenth century. Folda has discussed the evident relationship between the miniatures in F31 and F35 and the extent to which they were influenced by those executed in Acre.[34] Textually F31 and F35 are very close. They have a large number of chapter divisions in common, many of which, at least until 16.18, they share with F03; thereafter the distinguishing characteristics do not cease entirely but become appreciably less frequent. Clearly they are derived from a text that in many respects resembled F03. An important feature of F31 and F35 (but not F03) is that they contain as an interpolation a prose version of the text known as the *Ordene de la Chevalrie*, which is inserted after 21.27. At the end of 21.27 (21.28 in the Latin text) William recorded the capture of Hugh of Tiberias in 1179. The *Ordene* then follows with its fictional account of how Saladin persuaded Hugh to instruct him in the ways of western chivalry and dub him knight.[35]

Two other manuscripts that have recognizable affinity are the Baltimore, Walters Art Gallery, ms. 142 (F52) copied in Paris ca. 1300 (with the continuations from 1184–1261 added ca. 1340) and the Cambridge, Sidney Sussex College, ms. 93 (F01) which would seem to be of late thirteenth-century English provenance. The Cambridge manuscript ends part-way through 16.15, and several of the earlier folios are missing. Unlike F52, which seems to have preserved the chapter-structure of

---

[34] Folda, *Crusader Manuscript Illumination*, pp. 146–51. See also the catalogue descriptions at pp. 205–11.

[35] WT, p. 1002. In F35 the latter part of the interpolation is lost due to a missing folio.

the original, F01 has several examples of chapters that have been split in two, or, in one instance (1.5), into three. What seems to have happened is that there were two distinct elements in its make-up. At the beginning and at least until 2.19 it shares a number of features in common with a group of Acre or Acre-related manuscripts: F50, F73 (and the associated F57), F69 (and the associated F67 and F68), F74 and F78. There are ten examples between the start of the manuscript and 2.19 where F01 has chapter divisions found in all or most of these others. It might be added that, although F01 was not illustrated, the decorated capitals at the start of each book appear to be rather basic adaptations of characteristic Acre initials. After book 2, however, this textual affinity with the Acre manuscripts ceases, and the similarities with F52 come to the fore. The most obvious point in common is that both F01 and F52, alone of all the *Eracles* manuscripts, lack 8.23. I have also noted several instances in which F01 and F52 share readings which set them apart from those found in the other manuscripts with "primitive" versions of the text: F02, F05, F38, and F41. Thus, for example, at the start of 4.24, F01 and F52 read "autres grans princes des mescreanz" whilst the others (and also F03, F04, F31 and F35) have "autres mescreans princes." William's Latin reads "ceteros infidelium principes,"[36] and so here at least the readings in F01 and F52 would seem preferable. Another example is provided at the end of 12.24 where F01 and F52 read "... l'en asserroit icele cite [Tyre] sanz demeure" while all the others lack the final two words. Here again, F01 and F52 would seem to be preferable, preserving a rendering of William's phrase "sine questione."[37] At the end of 5.21 (5.22 in the Latin text), speaking of the dead bodies lying in the streets of Antioch, the other manuscripts, but not F01 and F52, include the words "tuit nu" in the phrase "gisoient tuit nu parmi les rues." There is no warrant for "tuit nu" in William's Latin. Here the other manuscripts divide over whether to read "rues" (F02, F03, F31, F35 plus F01 and F52) or "voies" (F04, F05, F38, F41). On the other hand, at the start of 12.1 the French translation, although not the Latin text, made mention of the ancient Persian ruler Xerxes, but here these manuscripts divide quite differently: F02, F03, F05, F38 and F41 call him "Xerses," while F04, F31, F35 plus F01 and F52 call him "Perses;" F01 alone of the manuscripts under discussion here introduces the word "mult" into the phrase "Perses fu .i. mult puissanz rois."[38]

The other α manuscripts were all either products of the Acre scriptorium from the second half of the thirteenth century (F49, F50, F69–F73, F78) or in some way derived from them. Two fifteenth-century manuscripts with a version of the so-called "Acre continuation" ending in 1275 (the Amiens, Bibliothèque Municipale, ms. 483 (F67) and the Bern, Bürgerbibliothek, ms. 25 (F68)) have as their direct ancestor the Boulogne-sur-Mer, Bibliothèque Municipale, ms. 142 (F69) which was

---

[36] WT, p. 267.
[37] Ibid., p. 577 at line 49. The chapter divisions in the Latin and French versions do not coincide here.
[38] F01 shares this reading with F78 and F36.

produced in Acre ca. 1287.[39] This can be shown not just from the fact that F67 and F68 replicate the chapter divisions and amalgamations found in F69, but also because they lack a passage that is missing from F69 as the result of a lost bifolium from the middle of the signature.[40] The missing section extends from part-way through 22.19 to part-way through 22.22, and the copyists of F67 and F68 simply wrote down what was in front of them, seemingly ignoring the evident disjuncture in the text.

The Paris, BN, ms. fr. 2628 (F73), which was produced in Acre in the late 1250s or early 1260s and was completed there in the late 1270s, and the Paris, BN, ms. fr. 2634 (F57), an early fourteenth-century manuscript from the Ile de France, are the only two manuscripts to preserve the so-called Colbert-Fontainebleau text of the continuation for the period 1184–1232.[41] Not surprisingly, these two manuscripts also have many features in common in their text of the translation. Indeed, until the beginning of book 15 they share almost every merged or divided chapter; after that point their unanimity wavers somewhat, and the differences are sufficient to indicate that F57 was not derived from F73 itself but from a manuscript containing a similar, if not totally identical, version.[42]

Eight manuscripts dating to the second half of the thirteenth century survive from Acre. Following the work of Folda, who has made a special study of them, we can divide them on the basis of date and artistic considerations into three groups:

1   The Paris, BN, ms. fr. 9086 (ca. 1255–60) (F50 = *RHC Oc.*, ms "C") is a high-quality manuscript but has no miniatures.[43] Unlike the others it concludes with the events of 1232. Of approximately the same date is the Paris, BN, ms. fr. 2628 (F73 = *RHC Oc.*, ms "B") which does have a series of miniatures, and which, as mentioned in the previous paragraph, contains the "Colbert-Fontainebleau" continuation.[44]

2   Two manuscripts from the late 1270s or early 1280s have miniatures that are the work of the same artist: the St. Petersburg, National Library of Russia, ms. fr. f° v. IV.5 (F71) and the Lyon, Bibliothèque de la Ville, ms. 828 (F72 = *RHC Oc.*, ms "D"). Folda has argued that F71 slightly pre-dates F72.[45] From the same

---

[39]   F68 and F69 end with the events of 1275. F67 seems to have lost the last folio or folios and breaks off in 1274.

[40]   Between fol. 276v and fol. 277r. This loss explains the aberrant six-folio signature (no. 35) noted by Folda in his catalogue description of this manuscript. See Folda, *Crusader Manuscript Illumination*, p. 185.

[41]   This version of the continuation is published as the principal version of the continuation in *RHC Oc.* 2, pp. 1–379 with the text adapted from the *Chronique d'Ernoul* noted as variants or provided in small print at the foot of the page. It would appear to have been a product of the 1230s or 1240s.

[42]   For the unique nature of the continuation in F57 (= ms. A), see Morgan, "The Rothelin Continuation," pp. 245, 252–53.

[43]   Catalogue description in Folda, *Crusader Manuscript Illumination*, p. 175.

[44]   Description in Folda, *Crusader Art in the Holy Land*, pp. 639–40.

[45]   Catalogue description in Folda, *Crusader Manuscript Illumination*, pp. 176–78.

workshop and approximate date is the Paris, BN, ms. fr. 9085 (F49).[46] This manuscript is been extensively mutilated and all the miniatures it once possessed cut out. The text ends in the middle of the description of the events of 1187; whether it originally ended in 1232 or, like the others, included the "Acre" continuation cannot be known.

3   The final three manuscripts were produced in the last few years of Christian rule in Acre and contain miniatures that are the work of the "Paris-Acre Master."[47] In order of production, they are the Paris, BN, ms. fr. 9084 dated to ca. 1286 (F78),[48] the Boulogne-sur-Mer, Bibliothèque Municipale, ms. 142 of ca. 1287 (F69),[49] and the Florence, Biblioteca Medicea-Laurenziana, ms. Plu. LXI. 10 of ca. 1290 (F70).[50]

Associated with these Acre manuscripts are two of Italian provenance dating from shortly after the end of Christian rule in the Levant: the Paris, BN, ms. fr. 2631 (F74) which has been ascribed to Lombardy ca. 1291–95,[51] and the Paris, BN, ms. fr. 9082 (F77 = *RHC Oc.*, ms "G") which, as its colophon informs us, was produced in Rome in 1295.[52] It would seem likely that these manuscripts were copied from manuscripts from the Acre scriptorium.

When we turn from an art-historical analysis to a textual analysis, we find that the Acre manuscripts no longer slot neatly into these same three groups. Indeed, taken together they lack common defining textual characteristics and show a surprising absence of consistency. For example, F70 and F72 frequently share features that set them apart from the others, but equally, on occasion, they have distinctive readings in common with some of them. Table 1 shows the chapters that are run together without a break. What this illustrates is that no two manuscripts keep in step throughout, although, like F70 and F72, F50 and F73 usually do. The Paris-Acre Master manuscripts, F78 and F69, frequently merge the same chapters, but they have few examples in common with F70, the third manuscript he illustrated. F49, F50, F71, F73, and the Italian F77 have three proximate instances in common – 6.10–11, 6.20–21 and 7.12–13 – but none elsewhere. Similarly, F50, F73, F74 and F77 share the same five examples in book 8, but again this pattern is not repeated in other parts of the work.

This lack of a consistent pattern is, at first sight, bewildering. On reflection, however, it does suggest an important possibility about the way in which the workshops in Acre operated. If a client wanted to commission a copy of the French

---

[46]   Ibid., pp. 175–76; *Crusader Art in the Holy Land*, p. 407 and note 370 (p. 657).

[47]   Otherwise known as the "Hospitaller Master." He is known to have accepted a commission from the Hospitaller Guillielmo di S. Stephano.

[48]   Catalogue description in Folda, *Crusader Manuscript Illumination*, pp. 182–84.

[49]   Ibid., pp. 184–87.

[50]   Description in Folda, *Crusader Art in the Holy Land*, pp. 663–64.

[51]   Catalogue description in Folda, *Crusader Manuscript Illumination*, pp. 199–200.

[52]   Ibid., pp. 200–204.

Table 1: Amalgamated chapters in the Acre and related manuscripts[a]

	50	73	70	72	49	71	78	69	74	77
1.1–2			X	X	–	–				X
1.12–13			X	X	–	–				
3.24–25		X	X	X						
5.11–12	X	X			X					
5.20–21	X	X	X		X					
6.10–11	X	X			X	X				X
6.20–21	X	X			X	X				X
6.22–23					–	X				X
7.12–13	X	X			X	X				X
7.18–19	X	X				–				X
7.20–21	X	X				–				X
8.1–2	X	X			–	–	X	X	X	X
8.4–5	X	X				–			X	X
8.6–7	X	X				–			X	X
8.13–14	X	X				–			X	X
8.15–16	X	X				–			X	
8.19–20	X	X	X	X		–			X	X
8.21–22						–	X	X	X	
9.14–15	X	X	X	X						X
9.19–20		X	X							
10.8–9	X	X	X	X						X
10.17–18							X			X
11.20–21								X	X	
12.5–6		X	X	X						X
12.11–12	X	X		X			X	X	X	
12.19–20	X	X	X							
13.2–3	X	X								–
13.7–8			X	X						–
15.19–20			X	X						
16.1–2					–	X	X	X	X	
16.18–19			X	X	X	–				
17.11–12	X	X								X
18.6–7					–		X	X		
18.25–26			X	X	X					
19.12–13			X				X			
20.27–28		X							X	X
21.2–3			X	X	X	X	X	X		
21.14–15			X	X	X	X	X	X	X	
21.26–27			X	X						
22.2–3			X	X						
22.11–12							X		X	
22.24–25	X	X			X	X	X	X		X

[a] This table only gives instances where two or more manuscripts amalgamate the same chapter. A dash indicates that the chapters are missing from the manuscript.

William of Tyre, he did not borrow a manuscript from an acquaintance and tell the staff to copy it. If that were so, then each manuscript would preserve the same amalgamations as its exemplar, perhaps adding some more depending on the copyist's whim, and it would be fairly easy to prepare a stemma on the basis of data of this sort. Certainly the information tabulated above would show a clearer lineal development. What instead seems to have happened was that when a client commissioned a manuscript, the scribes would use their own workshop copies, often switching between those manuscripts they had to hand. For practical reasons it would have been easier for scribes to work from texts kept in unbound signatures rather than from fully bound codices, and, if that surmise is correct, then swapping between versions would almost certainly have occurred. If this theory is right, that at least could explain the feature mentioned at the end of the previous paragraph: that it is possible to identify patterns common to several manuscripts which only continue for a limited extent. Perhaps we can go further. If we imagine a situation in which the atelier owned several copies, and hence several versions, of a popular text, then it could well be that manuscripts were being produced commercially for sale to the public "off the shelf," and not just in response to a client's order. Thus a wealthy collector, visiting Acre from western Europe, could purchase a ready-made manuscript rather than have to wait for one to be copied, illuminated and bound – a process which might well take far longer than his proposed stay in the East. Folda has drawn attention to evidence which shows that one of the Acre manuscripts was not taken to the West as soon as it was made, but remained in the East for several years before being completed.[53] But it may be that that was an exception. The very fact that these manuscripts as well as manuscripts of other works from the Acre scriptorium survive at all stems from their having been removed from Latin Syria within a few years of their production.

The hypothesis that these manuscripts were derived from several different exemplars can be tested by broadening the enquiry to look at some examples of variant readings and at those chapters that were divided into two or more parts. It is clear from Table 1 that the two earliest Acre manuscripts, F50 and F73, have many merged chapters in common. When we add in those instances of merged chapters that are unique to individual Acre manuscripts and so do not appear on the table, we find that in total F73 has seven examples not in F50, and F50 has just three examples not in F73. It may be that most of these represent the vagaries of the individual scribes responsible for the execution of the actual manuscripts, rather than merged chapters that had already found their way into the manuscript tradition. But it is striking that there is a cluster of examples from near the beginning: F73 but not F50 has merged chapters at 2.3–4, 2.17–18, 3.17–18, and 3.24–25, while F50 but not F73 has merged chapters at 4.15. When we turn to the examples of chapters split into two or more parts, we find a similar picture. Before the end of book 4 there are six

---

[53] Folda, *Crusader Art in the Holy Land*, p. 403.

examples of F50 and F73 sharing the same divisions, but F73 has six instances of divided chapters not shared with F50, and F50 has four examples not shared with F73. After book 4 there are just two examples of F50 having divided chapters not in F73, none at all of F73 with split chapters absent from F50, and fourteen that are common to both manuscripts. All this points to the conclusion that these two manuscripts or their antecedents had different exemplars for the early books, but for the later portions of the text depend on a common source. This conclusion is amply confirmed by an examination of a sample of variant readings. F73 has, it will be recalled, an associated fourteenth-century manuscript, F57 (= *RHC Oc.*, ms "A"). At 2.22 and at 4.21 the name of the Greek commander ("Tatinus" in the Latin text) is given uniquely in F73 and F57 as "Stacins" or "Statins," while F50 and most of the other manuscripts read "Tatins" or "Tantins." At the end of 4.18, F50 uniquely adds the phrase "por ceste merveilleuse chose;" at the end of 4.20, F57 and F73 alone read "eschapa mie .ii. ." But after the start of book 5, F50 and F73 come into harmony. So for example, at the start of 12.23, F50, F73 and F57 alone of all the manuscripts begin with the words, "En la noise ...," and the same three, once again uniquely, begin 12.25 with the words, "Tuit li baron et li prelat ..."

These last two examples help locate another *Eracles* text. In addition to the manuscripts under discussion in this paper, there is a substantial fragment of the French William of Tyre copied into the version of the report from the mid-1240s by the Venetian *bailo* Marsilio Zorzi preserved in the Venice Biblioteca Querini-Stampalia Cod. IV.3 (1064). This fragment comprises 12.22–13.14 and describes the siege and capture of Tyre in 1124.[54] The copy employed by Marsilio was closely related to F50 and F73. His version of the text shares the distinctive readings at 12.23 and 12.25 mentioned at the end of the last paragraph, as well as the phrase "quil eussent la vile prise" which ends 13.11 in F50, F57 and F73, and is not found in any other manuscript. In common with these three manuscripts, the Marsilio text also merges 13.2–3 and divides 13.7.[55] What this means is that Marsilio, who was in Acre in the mid-1240s, had access to an *Eracles* text that would seem to have closely resembled these two manuscripts of Acre provenance which date from around 1260.

Moving on, we turn to F72 and F70. Probably about ten years separate the production of these two manuscripts. F70 could well be the last surviving illustrated manuscript to have been produced in the Acre scriptorium before the destruction of the city in 1291; alone of the Acre manuscripts, it has a complete (and unique) set of rubrics, and, alone of all the *Eracles* manuscripts, it is prefaced by a version of the *Annales de Terre Sainte*. F72 (the so-called "Lyons *Eracles*") has a unique continuation for the period 1184–97, and F70 has a related version of this continuation for the period 1191–97.[56] These two manuscripts share fifteen

---

[54] *Der Bericht des Marsilio Zorzi: Codex Querini-Stampalia IV3 (1064)*, ed. Oliver Berggötz (Frankfurt am Main, 1991), pp. 102–8, 116–34.

[55] *Der Bericht des Marsilio Zorzi*, pp. 103, 107, 119 note u, 125, 133.

[56] Edited by Ruth Morgan. See above note 7:

examples of merged chapters; in addition, F72 has five not in F70, and F70 has twelve not in F72. There are only three instances of F70 and F72 sharing merged chapters with F50 and F73; it is perhaps significant that these come fairly close together – 8.19–20, 9.14–15, 10.8–9 – and that in each case they share this feature with F77, one of the manuscripts of Italian provenance. The statistics for split chapters are not too dissimilar: F72 and F70 have twelve in common; F72 has six more not in F70, and F70 has seventeen not in F72. In only two instances do F72 and F70 share a divided chapter with F50 and F73 – at 10.5 and 15.1 – and there is just one instance in which F70 but not F72 shares one with F50 and F73. The divisions at 10.5 and 15.1 are also shared with F77 as well as with F03 and F31.[57] F72 and F70 also have readings in common that set them apart from the other Acre manuscripts. Two examples will suffice: at the start of 5.11 they (and the Italian F77) have "bone cite" instead of "saint cite," and at the end of 11.14 they alone of the all the *Eracles* manuscripts wrongly give the date as 12 May instead of 19 December.

Before considering the implications of this data, we need to examine two other related manuscripts, F78 and F69, both of which were illustrated by the Paris-Acre master and date to ca. 1286–87. As they come from the same scriptorium and were produced in quick succession, we might assume that their texts would be closely related. F78 and F69 have eight merged chapters in common; F78 has four more not in F69, and F69 three not in F78. They share two of the merged chapters they have in common with F72 and F70 and three others with F50 and F73. Far more impressive are the figures for divided chapters. Here I have counted 34 instances of chapters divided in both manuscripts in the same place against just two instances of a division in F78 not found in F69 and four in F69 not in F78. With one exception these extra divisions are unique to these manuscripts, and so we can perhaps assume that they were probably introduced by the copyists and were not transmitted as part of the manuscript tradition. Table 2 shows which other manuscripts share the divided chapters found in both F78 and F69. Early on F01 and F73 feature strongly. As argued already, it would appear that both these manuscripts switched to different exemplars thereafter, respectively akin to F52 and F50. While this table shows that F78 and F69 have noticeably little similarity with F72 and F70 or, after the first two books, with F50 and F73, there is a clear connection between F78 and F69 and, on the one hand, the earlier, defective F71 and, on the other, the later Italian F74.[58]

F71 is the manuscript illustrated by the same artist as F72, but textually they have few distinctive features in common. It is much closer to F49, another defective manuscript from the same workshop and of about the same date. But an analysis of their relationship to the other manuscripts shows two quite distinct patterns. As mentioned earlier (and as shown in Table 1), F49 and F71 merge chapters 6.10–11, 6.20–21 and 7.12–13 in common with F50, F73 and F77; and perhaps associated

---

[57] F35, the other manuscript associated with F03 and F31 shares the division at 10.5 but not 15.1.

[58] For example, F74 is the only manuscript to omit the first sentence in 2.1 in common with F69 (plus the derivative F67 and F68) and F78.

Table 2: Split chapters common to F78 and F69 that are also to be found in other Acre and related manuscripts.[a]

	69/78	01	03/31/35	50	73	49	71	72	70	74	77
1.2	X	X		X	X	–	–			X	
1.5	X	X		X	X	–	–			X	
1.5	X	X			X	–	–			X	
1.6	X		X			–					
1.7	X	X		X	X	–	–		X	X	
1.9	X		X			–					
1.9	X	X		X	X	–	–			X	
1.10	X					–					
1.14	X	X			X	–	–			X	
1.15	X	X			X	–	–			X	X
1.20	X	X			X	–	–			X	
2.2	X	X	X		X	–	X			X	X
2.2	X		X			–	X			X	
2.7	X		X			–	X			X	
2.19	X	X	X	X		–	X			X	
3.6	X		X			–	X			X	
4.2	X		X			–	X				X
4.11	X		X								X
4.21	X		X			X	X			X	X
7.13	X									X	
7.21	X		X				–			X	
8.3	X		X				–			X	
9.22	X	–				–	–				
10.15	X		X				X			X	
12.12	X[b]		X				X			X	
13.27	X	–	X	X	X		X			X	
14.5	X		X			–	X			X	
15.7	X		X				X	X	X	X	
15.12	X		X				X			X	X
15.13	X		X				X			X	
15.23	X					X	X			X	
16.16	X	–	X				X			X	
20.18	X	–	X				X	X	X		
20.24	X	–	X			X	X				
21.9	X	–								X	

[a] A dash indicates that the chapter is missing from the manuscript.
[b] In F69 only.

with this cluster are 5.11–12, merged in F49, F50 and F73, and 5.20–21, merged in F49, F50, F70 and F77. But when F49 reappears later, its affinity is clearly with F72 and F70. F49, F72 and F70 are the only manuscripts to merge 16.18–19 and 18.25–26, and then these same three manuscripts, along with F71, F78, and F69, merge 21.2–3 and 21.14–15.[59] These combinations also appear when we turn to the divided chapters. F49, F50, F71, F73 and F77 all divide chapters 6.11 and 6.21. F49, F50 and F73 also share a division at 5.12, at 8.16 (together with F74) and at 8.18 (with F74 and F77). But towards the end of work, we find that F49 shares a division in common with F72 and F70 at 16.12, and then at 20.18 the same manuscripts that merge 21.2–3 and 21.14–15 (F49, F72, F70, F71, F78 and F69) also split 20.18.[60] Similarly, as noted in a different part of this discussion, F49, F72, F70 and also F77 share the error at the end of 19.23 which, by adding on a chapter number, changed the number of Muslim casualties from 1,500 to 1,524. So if F71 has much in common with F78 and F69 throughout, F49 seems to move from having an affinity with F50 and F73 in the early books to an affinity with F72 and F70 later on. There is just one instance – interestingly poised in the middle of the text at 10.5 – where F49 divides a chapter in the same place as both F50 and F73 *and* F72 and F70, and also F77.

What this rather laborious discussion has shown is that it is possible to identify clusters of instances where particular groups of manuscripts seem to run in parallel before diverging. All the Acre manuscripts plus the two Italian manuscripts from the 1290s have enough in common to show that they belong in the same tradition, but within that tradition there are various re-alignments which would seem to confirm the hypothesis that copyists had more than one exemplar from which to work. I have noted one instance in which a copyist has apparently conflated readings from different versions. It was observed above that at the end of 5.21 some of the early *Eracles* manuscripts read "parmi les rues" while others have "parmi les voies;" F72, F70 and F77 read "parmi les rues et par les voies" – perhaps evidence that the scribe of the common ancestor of these manuscripts had two copies to hand from which he was working. Indeed, such is the nature of the textual affinity between the Acre manuscripts, that, for the second half of the thirteenth century, we can be reasonably confident in speaking of "scriptorium" in the singular rather than "scriptoria."

The question remains of how the texts in these manuscripts relate to the early versions of the text as preserved in F02, F03 (and the associated F31 and F35), F04, F05, F38, F41 and F52. With the exception of F03, F31 and F35, these manuscripts have few merged or divided chapters, and those that they do have shed no light on possible connections with the Acre group. F03, F31 and F35 share a large number of divided chapters – far more than in any of the Acre group manuscripts – but on a number of occasions where a chapter division is common to several of the Acre-group manuscripts, these three manuscripts have it as well. A sample of

---

[59] 21.14–15 is also merged in F74.
[60] Similarly F49, F71, F78 and F69 all split 20.24.

variant readings points in differing directions. To start with the examples identified previously in which F52 and F01 differ from the others: at the start of 4.24, F50, F69, F71, F73, F74 and F77 all follow the lead given by F52 and F01, while only F70 and F72 follow F02, F03, F04, F38 and F41; at 12.24 all the Acre manuscripts follow F51 and F01 in preference to the readings found in the others;[61] at 5.21 the Acre manuscripts all follow F52 and F01 in preference to the readings found in the others except for F70, F72 and F77 – which, as mentioned in the previous paragraph, have their own distinctive variant. At the start of 5.20 the Acre group follow F52 and F01, except for F70, F72 and F77 which follow the readings found in the other early versions. At the end of 11.14 where the date in the Latin text is given as 19 December,[62] we find the following alignment: all the early versions and F49, F71, and F78 have 19 December; the two later manuscripts associated with F03, F31 and F35, and most of the rest of the Acre manuscripts have 10 December; F72 and F70 go their own way with 12 May. At the start of 12.1, F02, F03, F05, F38, F41, F50, F70, F71, F72, F73, F77 all give the ancient Persian ruler as "Xerses" or "Xerces," while F01, F04, F31, F35, F52, F69, F74 and F78 have "Perses" or "Perces."

It is all rather confusing, but some points do seem to emerge. Clearly the Acre group and F52 (and the associated F01) have antecedents in common, but so too do they have common antecedents with F03 (and the associated F31 and F35). Some of the Acre manuscripts share the β-group features found in F04. While none of the Acre group have the interpolations found in F38, there are common readings with F05, F41 or the late F02. In other words, the distinctive features of F38 apart, there is nothing in the early group of manuscripts which cannot be found in those from the Acre scriptorium.

The β Group

Their defining characteristics aside, the β group show only a limited degree of homogeneity. A few manuscripts have large numbers of chapters that are split or merged. Thus the fifteenth-century Geneva, Bibliothèque Publique et Universitaire, ms. 85 (F36) has 97 divided chapters and 101 instances of chapters that are merged, while another fifteenth-century manuscript, the Paris, BN, ms. fr. 2629 (F44), has a staggering 214 instances where two chapters have been run together. Two earlier manuscripts, the Brussels, Bibliothèque Royale, ms. 9492–3 (F54), which has been attributed to a Parisian workshop from ca. 1291–95, and another northern French manuscript, the Paris, BN, ms. fr. 2754 (F46), which is apparently slightly later, have striking numbers of divided chapters. In the case of F54, a change of hand at fol. 144r (= 11.24) signals a major change: up to this point just two chapters have

---

[61] F49 and F77 lack the folios containing this chapter. The same pattern is discernible at the end of 13.28 where all the Acre manuscripts plus F01 and F52 lack the word "clers" in the final phrase.
[62] WT, p. 519.

been split;[63] subsequently there are no less than 363 instances of divisions. F46 only comprises books 16 to the end, but even in these surviving seven books we find 64 instances of divided chapters. These are extreme examples, but what is even more striking are the comparatively few instances where particular chapter divisions are shared by two or more manuscripts. F54 has 43, or, in other words, 322 instances of divided chapters which are unique among β group manuscripts. F46 has 24 split chapters shared with one or more other manuscripts in the β group and 40 that are unique. So the fact that F54 and F46 have 18 divided chapters in common can scarcely be used as an argument for any particular textual affinity between them. The high incidence of unique divisions is not simply a feature of the manuscripts with an abnormally large number of split chapters. At one extreme F33 has 30 unique divisions out of a total of 32, while several others – F06, F30, F32, F40 and F47 – have around two-thirds of their divided chapters all to themselves. On the other hand, every instance of a divided chapter in F55 and F65 is to be found elsewhere. Turning to the merged chapters, we discover that here the proportion of instances that are unique to a single β manuscript is on the whole lower, usually totalling between a third and a half. F44 has 125 cases of merged chapters not found elsewhere out of a total of 214, and F06 with 11 unique examples of merged chapters out of 15, F48 with 10 out of 14, F55 with 6 out of 9, and F58 with 9 out of 14 are others with a high proportion.

With these features in mind, identifying discrete groups of manuscripts with enough merged or divided chapters in common to indicate a clear textual affinity requires the establishment of a clear recurrent pattern and needs to be approached in conjunction with a search for distinctive variant readings. The most obviously related group of manuscripts, all of which contain the Rothelin continuation, are F60, F61, F62, F63 and F65. All date to the fourteenth century – F61 bears the date 1337 – or, in the case of F65, to the fifteenth. F65 is a fire-damaged manuscript in Turin; the others all have the same additional materials prefaced to the *Eracles* text, but whether F65 also once had these additional texts is not clear. These manuscripts have 27 instances of merged chapters and 3 examples of divided chapters in common. There are several more instances in which two of more share merged or divided chapters. They also have similar rubrics and lack a section of the text at 12.15–12.17. Not surprisingly they share some variant readings, as for example at the end of 11.13 giving the date wrongly as 8 April.[64] Two other Rothelin manuscripts, F58 and F64, both of which contain the French text of the *De Excidio Urbis Acconis*, also have features in common with each other: 5 merged chapters and 4 divided chapters, and the same distinctive readings at the end of 15.27, 19.23

---

[63] These figures ignore the two divisions in 1.2 which are a defining characteristic of the β group.

[64] The only other manuscripts to share this reading (*recte* 27 April) are the α group F31 and F35. Morgan ("The Rothelin Continuation," p. 246) identified four of these five manuscripts as having a closely related text of the Rothelin continuation, and her research showed that the Rothelin text appended to F52 also belongs with this group. The exception is F62.

and 19.24. Another pair of late manuscripts, the fifteenth-century London, BL, Royal ms. 15. E. I (F37) and the Paris, BN, ms. fr. 68 (F42), similarly have 10 divided chapters and 10 merged chapters in common and share a number of distinctive readings; for example, in the final phrases of 4.18, 4.20, 13.18 and 21.8. F43, F45 and F51 have 3 divided chapters and 18 merged chapters in common; in several instances these features are shared with F47 and F53; all five assert that the Templars had nineteen brothers at the time of the council of Troyes in 1129, whereas all the other manuscripts put the figure at nine.

The only β group manuscript attributed to the Latin East is the Rome, Biblioteca Apostolica Vaticana, ms. Pal. lat. 1963 (F06). Alone of all the β group manuscripts it has no continuation but ends where William's Latin finished, and Folda has argued that it is from Antioch and dates to the 1260s. Its importance is therefore beyond doubt, but when compared with the other manuscripts in this group, or indeed with the α group manuscripts, what is striking is its unique quality. It shares divided chapters with F37 and 42 at 15.23 and with F36, F44, F51 and F53 at 19.10, but otherwise has none in common with other β manuscripts. It is therefore to be assumed that these divisions are coincidental and not attributable to any common original. An analysis of the merged chapters reveals a similar lack of any discernable pattern: at 5.15–16 it has merged chapters in common with F30, F36 and F44; at 18.1–2 with F43, F45 and F54; and at 22.23–24 with F33, F34, F36, F40, F43, F44, F45 and F51. Moreover, F06 has a number of unique variant readings. At the start of 4.21 it alone reads "Tandis com cil desleaux Grex ...," while most of the other manuscripts have (with a wide variety of spellings) "Tatins cil desloiaus Griex ...;" at the end of 7.19, alone of all the *Eracles* manuscripts, it gives the date as the "sisieme jor davrill;" at the end of 10.8 it alone speaks of "li roiaume de Jerusalem" instead of "le roiaumes de Surie;" at the end of 11.14 it alone has the date as 17 December instead of 19 December. Most of these variants should probably be regarded as the result of careless copying, but at the beginning of 12.16, where the manuscripts that are closest to the original form of the translation and most of the β group read "Un voisin avoit li rois d'outremer ...," and F06 has "rois de Surie," it is clear that a scribe has made a deliberate alteration. The "rois d'outremer" in this context is Baldwin II of Jerusalem, but because for someone working in the East Jerusalem is "deca mer,"[65] it is understandable why such a change should have been introduced.[66]

If F06 preserves a number of unique features that isolate it from the rest of the β manuscripts, it is also true that the western manuscripts in this group that can be dated to the thirteenth century or the early years of the fourteenth century – F30, F32, F33, F34, F39, F40, F43, F45, F46, F47, F48, F51, F54, F55, F58 – show little consistency in dividing or amalgamating chapters, although, as noted above, F43,

---

[65] For the use of "deca mer," there contrasted with "la terre de crestiens," see 12.7.

[66] The Acre group of α manuscripts also suppress the word "outremer," though without using the phrase employed in F06.

F45 and F51, and to a lesser extent F47 and the fifteenth-century F53, have a number of divisions and amalgamations in common. On the other hand, none of these fifteen manuscripts has distinctive readings that set it apart to the extent that F06 does. The conclusion has to be that F43, F45, F47, F51 and F53 have a common ancestor which itself was closely derived from the β group archetype, and that all the others listed above were either derived directly from that archetype, or, if they were derived from it indirectly, that no other manuscript with the same immediate ancestor has survived. So, whereas the Acre manuscripts and the others associated with that group seem to have had at least three source-texts and reveal some hybridization, these manuscripts come from a single source which gave the copyists no clear lead as to which chapters they should merge or divide. On the other hand, the copyists do seem to have kept reasonably close to the text. What may have happened is that all or most of the manuscripts mentioned in this paragraph were produced at the same workshop in Paris over the course of some thirty to forty years from exemplars kept in that workshop. That conclusion would also be consistent with the fact that several of these manuscripts have a related cycle of illustrations.

Although it has not yet been possible to construct a stemma, it is now possible to sort the manuscripts into groups based on an analysis of the text of the translation rather than on the contents of the continuations.

- Those manuscripts with texts closest to the original translation are F02, F04, F05, F38, F41 and F52. Although it has many more divided chapters, F03 also seems to preserve a primitive version of the text itself and so should be included with these others. Associated with F03 are F31 and F35, and associated with F52 is F01.
- The eight manuscripts copied in Acre in the second half of the thirteenth century (F49, F50, F69, F70, F71, F72, F73, F78) have, despite their differences, features that link them into a definite group, and to this group should be added two manuscripts from Italy, F74 and F77. Associated with F73 is F57; associated with F50 and F73 is the fragment preserved by Marsilio Zorzi; derived from F69 are F67 and F68.
- The manuscript attributed to Antioch, F06, shares the characteristics of the β group but otherwise stands alone.
- A large group of β manuscripts that were produced in France in the latter part of the thirteenth century or the very beginning of the fourteenth (F30, F32, F33, F34, F39, F40, F43, F45, F46, F47, F48, F51, F54, F55, F58) all seem to derive directly or indirectly from the same exemplar. F43, F45, F47 and F51, together with the fifteenth-century F53, comprise a recognizable sub-group; as do F58 and F64.
- Of the later β manuscripts, F60, F61, F62, F63, and F65 share a common source, as do F37 and F42.

This just leaves two other fifteenth-century β group manuscripts: F36 (the Geneva, Bibliothèque Publique et Universitaire, ms. 85) and F44 (the Paris, BN, ms. fr. 2629), both of which extensively rephrase and, in places, abbreviate the text.

Along the way there have been a number of important discoveries, but this analysis cannot be seen as either complete or final; there are unanswered questions, both about the precise relationship between the surviving manuscripts, and about the process of production and circulation. It would seem that in Acre, and probably in Paris too in the later years of the thirteenth century, copies were being produced commercially and not only in response to specific commissions. An examination of the manuscripts may reveal more about their owners, although few seem to give any clues from before the seventeenth century. There is, for example, no conclusive evidence that any were owned by members of the Latin Syrian or Cypriot royal family or nobility. As for the stemma, a closer examination of variant readings than has been attempted here is needed to test and refine my findings: one way forward will be to collate all the manuscripts, and so produce a critical edition, of one or more sample chapters.[67]

One final question that should be addressed is when and where the major developments in the text took place. It is assumed that the translation was made in the West for a Western audience by a cleric who had at some point visited the East,[68] and this would seem to be supported, for example, by the readings of the earliest manuscripts at the beginning of 12.16 which speak of Baldwin II as the "rois d'outremer." This opening phrase does not find a counterpart in the Latin text.[69] But if the translation was made in the West, all the continuations appear to have been written in the East, and so where and how they were added also needs more thought. The fact that the earliest surviving manuscripts with the *Chronique d'Ernoul* continuation to 1232 were produced in the West does not necessarily mean that adding this continuation began there. The Rothelin continuation is only found in manuscripts copied in the West; it too appears to have been composed in the East, but, unlike the *Chronique d'Ernoul*, so far as is known it seems not to have circulated as an independent work. With the Acre continuation we are on safer ground. Composed in the East and found primarily in manuscripts copied in the East, there is no doubting its provenance. But this work too, and the related versions of the *Annales de Terre Sainte* and associated texts, would repay further enquiry.

---

[67] Since completing the present paper I have edited two sample chapters (12:7 and 20:30): "The Old French William of Tyre and the Origins of the Templars," in *Knighthoods of Christ: Essays on the History of the Crusades and the Knights Templar presented to Malcolm Barber*, ed. Norman Housley (Aldershot, 2007), pp. 151–64; "The Old French William of Tyre, the Templars and the Assassin Envoy," in *The Hospitallers, the Mediterranean and Europe from the Crusades to the Ottomans*, ed. Karl Borchardt, Nikolas Jaspert and Helen Nicholson (Aldershot, 2007), pp. 25–37.

[68] Pryor, "The *Eracles* and William of Tyre," pp. 276–77, 284, 288, 293 *et passim*; Hamilton, "The Old French translation of William of Tyre," pp. 93–94.

[69] WT, p. 565.

Appendix 1: The Manuscripts

This list is based on the guide published by Jaroslav Folda in *Scriptorium* 27 (1973),[1] which in turn followed the pattern established in the nineteenth century by Louis de Mas Latrie and Paul Riant.[2] These scholars sorted the manuscripts into groups depending on whether they contained a version of the continuation to William's text, and, if so, where they ended. F7–15 comprise manuscript fragments from the French William of Tyre, and these have not been analysed in this discussion. F16–29 (Section II) are not manuscripts of William of Tyre at all but of the *Chronique d'Ernoul et de Bernard le Trésorier* or of the text known as the *Estoires d'Outremer et de la naissance Saladin*. Four other items in Folda's list have also been disregarded: F56 is an abbreviated version of the French William of Tyre; F59 is an eighteenth-century copy of F60; F75 is an eighteenth-century copy of F77; and F76 is an eighteenth-century copy of the continuation as published by the Maurists in 1729.[3]

Section I: No Continuation

F01 Cambridge, Sidney Sussex College, ms. 93 (England:[4] late 13th century)
F02 Paris, BN, ms. fr. 2627 (N. France: 15th century)
F03 Paris, BN, ms. fr 2632 (Latin East or France: 1st half of 13th century)
F04 Paris, BN, ms. fr. 2826 (Latin East or France: 1st half of 13th century)
F05 Paris, BN, ms. fr. 9081 (Paris: ca. 1245–48)[5]
F06 Rome, Biblioteca Apostolica Vaticana, ms. Pal. lat. 1963 (Antioch: ca. 1260–68)[6]

Section III: Continuations to 1232

F30 Arras, Bibliothèque Municipale, ms. 651 (N. France: early 14th century)
F31 Baltimore, Walters Art Gallery, ms. 137 (Paris: ca. 1295–1300)[7]
F32 Bern, Bürgerbibliothek, ms. 112 (N. France: ca. 1270)[8]
F33 Bern, Bürgerbibliothek, ms. 163 (N. France: 3rd quarter of 13th century)

---

[1] Folda, "Manuscripts", pp. 90–95.
[2] Mas Latrie, "Essai de classification", pp. 480–88; Riant, "Inventaire sommaire", pp. 247–52, 716–17.
[3] *Veterum Scriptorum et Monumentorum ... Amplissima Collectio*, ed. Edmond Martène and Ursin Durand, 5 (Paris, 1729), 581–752.
[4] Folda says southern France, but the writing is clearly an example of English Court or Business Hand of the period.
[5] For the date, see Folda, *Crusader Art in the Holy Land*, pp. 217, 235–36.
[6] For the date, ibid., pp. 218, 347–50.
[7] For the place of production and the date, see Folda, *Crusader Manuscript Illumination*, p. 208.
[8] For the date, see ibid., p. 33 n. 38.

F34 Besançon, Bibliothèque Municipale, ms. 856 (N. France: ca. 1300)

F35 Epinal, Bibliothèque Municipale, ms. 45 (Paris: ca. 1295–1300)[9]

F36 Geneva, Bibliothèque Publique et Universitaire, ms. 85 (Artois: 3rd quarter of 15th century)

F37 London, BL, Royal ms. 15. E. I (Flanders: late 15th century)[10]

F38 London, BL, Henry Yates Thompson ms. 12 (England: mid-13th century)

F39 Paris, Bibliothèque de l'Arsenal, ms. 5220 (N. France: 3rd quarter of 13th century)

F40 Paris, Bibliothèque du Ministère des Affaires Etrangères, Memoires et Documents 230*bis* (S. France: 3rd quarter of 13th century)

F41 Paris, BN, ms. fr. 67 (N. France: 2nd half of 13th century)

F42 Paris, BN, ms. fr. 68 (Flanders: ca. 1450)

F43 Paris, BN, ms. fr. 779 (N. France: ca. 1275)

F44 Paris, BN, ms. fr. 2629 (Flanders: ca. 1460)

F45 Paris, BN, ms. fr. 2630 (N. France: ca. 1250–75)[11]

F46 Paris, BN, ms. fr. 2754 (N. France: ca. 1300)

F47 Paris, BN, ms. fr. 2824 (N. France: ca. 1300)

F48 Paris, BN, ms. fr. 2827 (N. France: ca. 1250–75)[12]

F49 Paris, BN, ms. fr. 9085 (Acre: ca. 1277–80)[13]

F50 Paris, BN, ms. fr. 9086 (Acre: ca. 1255–60)[14] (= *RHC Oc.*, 2, ms. C)

F51 Paris, BN, ms. fr. 24208 (N. France: ca. 1250–75)[15]

Section IV: The "Rothelin" Continuation to 1261

F52 Baltimore, Walters Art Gallery, ms. 142 (Paris: ca. 1300 and ca. 1340)[16]

F53 Brussels, Bibliothèque Royale, ms. 9045 (Flanders, ca. 1460)

F54 Brussels, Bibliothèque Royale, ms. 9492–3 (Paris: ca. 1291–95)[17]

F55 Lyon, Bibliothèque de la Ville, ms. Palais des Arts 29 (Paris: ca. 1295–96)[18] (= *RHC Oc.*, 2, ms. E)

F57 Paris, BN, ms. fr. 2634 (Ile de France: 1st quarter of 14th century) (= *RHC Oc.*, 2, ms. A)

F58 Paris, BN, ms. fr. 2825 (Paris: early 14th century)[19] (= *RHC Oc.*, 2, ms. F)

---

[9] For the place of production and the date, see ibid., p. 205.

[10] Folda says ca. 1475, but the Tudor rose incorporated into the design of fol. 1r might suggest a post-1485 date.

[11] For the date, see Folda, *Crusader Manuscript Illumination*, p. 33 n.36.

[12] Ibid.

[13] For the date, ibid., p. 175.

[14] Ibid.

[15] For the date, ibid., p. 33 n.36.

[16] For the place of production and the date, ibid., p. 212.

[17] Ibid., p. 198.

[18] Ibid., p. 204.

[19] Ibid., p. 213.

F60 Paris, BN, ms. fr. 9083 (Ile de France: 2nd quarter of 14th century) (= *RHC Oc.*, 2, ms. H)

F61 Paris, BN, ms. fr. 22495 (Paris: 1337) (= *RHC Oc.*, 2, ms. I)

F62 Paris, BN, ms. fr. 22496–7 (Paris: ca. 1350)

F63 Paris, BN, ms. fr. 24209 (Ile de France: 3rd quarter of 14th century) (= *RHC Oc.*, 2, ms K)

F64 Rome, Biblioteca Apostolica Vaticana, ms. Reg. Suec. lat. 737 (Paris: early 14th century)[20]

F65 Turin, Biblioteca Nazionale, ms. L I. 5 (N. France: 15th century)

F66 Turin, Biblioteca Nazionale, ms. L. II. 17 (Ile de France: 1st quarter of 14th century) – not seen

Section V: The "Acre" Continuation, beyond 1232

F67 Amiens, Bibliothèque Municipale, ms. 483 (Flanders: mid-15th century)

F68 Bern, Bürgerbibliothek, ms. 25 (N. France: 1st half of 15th century)

F69 Boulogne-sur-Mer, Bibliothèque Municipale, ms. 142 (Acre: ca. 1287)[21]

F70 Florence, Biblioteca Medicea-Laurenziana, ms. Plu. LXI. 10 (Acre: ca. 1290, and Italy: 1st half of 14th century)

F71 St. Petersburg, National Library of Russia / Российская Национальная Библиотека (formerly M. E. Saltykov-Schchedrin State Public Library), ms. fr. f° v. IV.5 (Acre: ca. 1280)

F72 Lyon, Bibliothèque de la Ville, ms. 828 (Acre: ca.1280) (= *RHC Oc.*, 2, ms. D)

F73 Paris, BN, ms. fr. 2628 (Acre: late 1250s/early 1260s and late 1270s)[22] (= *RHC Oc.*, 2, ms B)

F74 Paris, BN, ms. fr. 2631 (Lombardy: ca. 1291–95)[23]

F77 Paris, BN, ms. fr. 9082 (Rome: 1295) (= *RHC Oc.*, 2, ms. G)

F78 Paris, BN, ms. fr. 9084 (Acre: ca. 1286)[24]

---

[20] Ibid.

[21] For the date, see ibid., p. 184.

[22] For the date, see Folda, *Crusader Art in the Holy Land*, pp. 218 n. 608, 403–5.

[23] For the date, see Folda, *Crusader Manuscript Illumination*, p. 199.

[24] Ibid., p. 182.

Appendix 2: Numbering the Books and Chapters

In its original form the French William of Tyre was divided into twenty-two books
and followed the divisions in William's Latin text. The only exception relates to
William's final book, book 23, which in the Latin version comprises an extended
prologue and a single chapter. None of the French manuscripts has the prologue, and
it is safe to assume that it was omitted by the original translator. The one chapter,
however, was included in the translation and followed the last chapter of book 22.
So what in the Latin text is 23.1, becomes in the French text 22.30. Otherwise
most manuscripts preserve all or most of William's book divisions. Many have
illuminations and/or decorated capitals to signify the start of a new book. Several,
especially some of the later copies, have further illuminations elsewhere: these
include F31, F35, F36, F37, F40, F42, F57 and the group of related manuscripts –
F60, F61, F62, F63, F65; while others (for example, F31 and F35 at 10.1, 11.1 and
17.1, and F67, F68, F69, F74, F78 at 12.1 and 13.1) have instances where no new
book is signalled where it might be expected.

It is when we turn to the question of numbering the chapters that the situation
becomes much more complicated. As explained above, in both nineteenth-century
editions the normal policy was to alter the structure of the French translation to make
the chapter divisions coincide with the divisions in the Latin text, even though there
was no warrant for this in the manuscripts themselves. Thus in a few instances
chapters were made to begin and end where the Latin begins and ends and not where
they do in the manuscripts.[25] It also led to a number of chapters in the French version
being split in two,[26] and those in the remainder of that book being renumbered
accordingly. The situation is made more complicated by the fact that Huygens'
edition of the Latin text has a number of cases where the chapter divisions in the
Latin and the subsequent numbering of the chapters in the book concerned differ
from the *Recueil* edition.[27] There is thus considerable scope for confusion, as the
same chapter could have different numbers in the French text and each of the Latin
editions. The guiding principle throughout this article is to refer to the chapters by
number as they appear in the earliest versions of the translation, and the following
table is intended to help identify them. Books 4, 6, 8, 12, 16 and 17 present no
problems – all the chapters coincide in both the Latin and the French versions. The
left-hand column gives the numbers as referred to here, and then, reading from left
to right, the other columns give the numbers as they appear in the Paris edition, the
Recueil and the Huygens' editions. It has not been thought necessary to list every
chapter, but simply indicate the numbering for first and last chapter in each book and
where in the book the numbering ceases to be synchronized.

---

[25] In the *Recueil* edition this is true of 10.17–18, 11.28–31, 12.5–6, 12.24–25, 13.9–10, 16.7–8 and
21.9–10, and in the Paris edition of all these except 10.17–18 plus 14.11–12.

[26] 1.14, 2.9, 5.19, 7.16, 9.22, 11.27, 13.3, 15.14, 18.32, 20.9.

[27] But note that in two instances, at 3.1–2 and 10.8, Huygens' division of chapters in his Latin edition
coincides with those in the French version and differs from the *Recueil*.

Eracles	Paris	Recueil	Huygens
1.1	1.1	1.1	1.1
1.14	1.14–15	1.14–15	1.14–15
1.15	1.16	1.16	1.16
1.29	1.30	1.30	1.30
2.1	2.1	2.1	2.1
2.9	2.9–10	2.9–10	2.9–10
2.10	2.11	2.11	2.11
2.19	2.20	2.20	2.20–21
2.20	2.21	2.21	2.22
2.22	2.23	2.23	2.24
3.1	3.1	3.1	3.1
3.2	3.2	3.1 cont.	3.2
3.3	3.3	3.2	3.3
3.26	3.26	3.25	3.26
5.1	5.1	5.1	5.1
5.19	5.19–20	5.19–20	5.19–20
5.20	5.21	5.21	5.21
5.22	5.23	5.23	5.23
7.1	7.1	7.1	7.1
7.15	7.15–16	7.15–16	7.15–16
7.16	7.17	7.17	7.17
7.24	7.25	7.25	7.25
9.1	9.1	9.1	9.1
9.22	9.22–23	9.22–23	9.22–23
10.1	10.1	10.1	10.1
10.3	10.3	10.3–4	10.3–4
10.4	10.4	10.5	10.5
10.8	10.8	10.9–10	10.9
10.9	10.9	10.11	10.10
10.28	10.28	10.30	10.29
11.1	11.1	11.1	11.1
11.27	11.27–28	11.27–28	11.27–28[28]
13.1	13.1	13.1	13.1
13.2	13.2	13.2–3	13.2–3

---

[28] For the remainder of book 11, the chapter divisions in the French and Latin texts diverge.

Eracles	Paris	Recueil	Huygens
13.3	13.3–4	13.4–5	13.4–5
13.4	13.5	13.6	13.6
13.24	13.25	13.26	13.26
13.25	13.25 cont.	13.26 cont.	13.26 cont.
13.26	13.26	13.27	13.27
13.27	13.27	13.27 cont.	13.27 cont.
13.28	13.28	13.28	13.28
14.1	14.1	14.1	14.1
14.11	14.11	14.11–12	14.11–12
14.12	14.12	14.13–15	14.13–15
14.13	14.13	14.16	14.16
14.27	14.27	14.30	14.30
15.1	15.1	15.1	15.1
15.5	15.5	15.5	15.5
15.6	15.5 cont.	15.5 cont.	15.15 cont.
15.7	15.6	15.6	15.6
15.14	15.13–14	15.13–14	15.13–14
15.15	15.15	15.15	15.15
15.27	15.27	15.27	15.27
18.1	18.1	18.1	18.1
18.32	18.32–33	18.32–33	18.32–33
18.33	18.34	18.34	18.34
19.1	19.1	19.1	19.1
19.6	19.6	19.6–7	19.6–7
19.7	19.7	19.8	19.8
19.10	19.10	19.11	19.11
–	–	19.12	19.12
19.11	19.11	19.13	19.13
19.30	19.30	19.32	19.32
20.1	20.1	20.1–2	20.1–2
20.2	20.2	20.3	20.3
20.9	20.9–10	20.10–11	20.10–11
20.10	20.11	20.12	20.12
20.20	20.21	20.22	20.22
20.21	20.22	20.22 cont.	20.22 cont.
20.22	20.23	20.23	20.23

Eracles	Paris	*Recueil*	Huygens
20.30	20.31	20.31[29]	20.31
21.1	21.1	21.1	21.1
21.2	21.2	21.2–3	21.2–3
21.3	21.3	21.4	21.4
21.7	21.7	21.8	21.8
21.8	21.8	21.9–10	21.8 cont., 21.9
21.9	21.9	21.11	21.10
21.28	21.28	21.30	21.29
22.1	22.2	22.1	22.1
22.2	22.2	22.2–3	22.2–3
22.3	22.3	22.4	22.4
22.7	22.7	22.8	22.8–9
22.8	22.8	22.9	22.10
22.29	22.29	22.30	22.31
22.30	23.1	23.1	23.1

[29] A series of misprints in *RHC Oc* (pp. 995–1000) wrongly numbers the chapters 20.29–20.31 as 20.31–20.33.

Appendix 3: Incomplete Manuscripts

A number of manuscripts – most notably F30, F49, F55 and F71 – have missing or mutilated folios. In several instances it would appear that someone has cut out pages containing illuminations. In two cases, F01 (which ends at 16.15) and F46 (which begins at 16.1), it is possible that the manuscript was once bound in two volumes, one of which has subsequently been lost. (F62 and F71 are bound in two volumes with both parts surviving.) The fire-damaged F65 is substantially complete and legible from 1.12 onwards, although the conservators did not re-assemble all the folios in the correct order. These defects in the manuscripts mean that it is not always possible to check particular features which might help establish their interrelationship.

In some cases material is missing not because a folio is lacking or damaged, but either because of haplography or because the exemplar itself was defective. Some omissions would appear to have been deliberate, as for example in F53 book 16 where the copyist of this manuscript or its direct ancestor ended a number of chapters several sentences early. Absences from the text not resulting from missing or mutilated folios are indicated by an asterisk in the following list of chapters or parts of chapters missing from the manuscripts ("3.5pt" means that part of book 3 chapter 5 is lacking).

F01   5.22–6.1pt; 8.23*; 9.21pt–10.5pt; 12.25pt–13.4pt; 13.8pt–13.27pt; 16.15pt–
      end

F03   22.30pt

F04   22.26pt–end

F05   3.25pt–4.2pt; 5.22pt–6.1pt; 15.27pt–16.3pt; 16.23pt–16.24pt; 17.30pt

F06   2.21–22

F30   1.8pt–1.10pt; 1.12.pt–1.16pt; 1.18pt–2.4pt; 2.5pt–2.6pt; 2.7pt–3.8pt; 3.9pt–
      3.10pt; 3.12pt–3.13pt; 4.8pt–4.11pt; 4.24pt–5.2; 5.16pt–5.17; 7.6pt–7.7pt;
      8.4pt–8.6pt; 9.3pt–9.7pt; 9.10pt–9.13pt; 10.14pt–10.15pt; 11.11pt–11.13pt;
      11.22–12.20pt; 12.25pt; 13.20pt–13.23pt; 13.28pt–14.1pt; 14.17pt–14.19pt;
      14.23pt–14.27pt; 16.20pt–17.7pt; 17.8pt–17.12pt; 17.28–17.29; 18.8pt;
      18.15pt–18.17pt; 18.32pt–18.33pt; 19.1pt–19.3pt; 19.16pt–19.18pt; 19.26pt;
      19.29pt; 20.1pt; 20.22pt–21.5pt; 21.9pt–21.11pt*; 22.10pt–22.12pt; 22.17pt–
      22.20pt

F31   21.10*

F32   16.25pt–17.1pt

F33   6.1–2; 10.27pt–11.1pt; 11.28pt–12.1pt; 12.23pt–13.1pt; 18.22pt–18.31pt

F35   1.1–1.3pt; 12.1pt–12.3pt; 14.26pt–15.1pt; 17.20pt–17.23pt; 18.33pt–19.2pt;
      21.10*; interpolation (pt) and 21.28–22.1pt

F36   12.15pt–12.17pt

F37   6.9*

F38   1.1pt; 1.3pt–1.4pt

F40   10.13pt–10.15pt; 11.16pt–11.19pt; 14.11pt–15.20pt

F41   12.10–12.15*; 19.6–20.24*; 22.2pt–22.8

F43   12.20pt–12.21pt

F44   4.21*; 12.1–12.2*; 16.1–16.2pt

F45   13.5pt–13.27pt

F46   1.1–15.27

F49   1.1–3.9; 3.12pt–3.17pt; 4.2pt–4.5pt; 4.22pt–4.24; 6.1–6.3pt; 6.22pt–7.1pt; 7.24pt–8.2pt; 8.22pt–9.1pt; 9.21pt–10.1pt; 10.28pt–11.1pt; 11.22pt–11.23pt; 11.31pt–12.2pt; 12.24pt–13.1pt; 13.28pt–15.4pt; 15.27pt–16.3pt; 16.28pt–17.1pt; 17.30pt–18.13pt; 18.33pt–19.2pt; 19.29pt–20.1pt; 20.30pt–21.2pt; 21.28pt–22.1

F52   8.23*

F53   3.22*; 15.21–23*; 15.25*; 16.5pt–16.6*; 16.9pt*; 16.13pt*; 16.15pt*; 16.16pt–16.17*; 16.19*; 16.21pt*; 16.23pt*; 16.26pt*; 16.28pt*

F54   1.1–1.2pt

F55   1.1–5.7pt; 6.23pt–7.1pt; 7.24pt–8.1pt; 8.23pt–9.1pt; 9.23pt–10.1pt; 11.1pt; 11.31pt–12.1pt; 12.25pt–13.1pt; 13.28pt–14.6pt; 15.1pt; 15.17pt–15.21pt; 15.27pt–16.1pt; 16.28pt–17.1pt; 17.30pt–18.1pt; 18.33pt–19.2pt; 19.30pt–20.1pt; 20.17pt–20.22pt; 20.25pt–20.28pt; 20.30pt–21.1pt; 21.28pt–22.1pt; 22.21pt–22.23pt

F58   8.3*

F60   12.15pt–12.17pt*

F61   12.15pt–12.17pt*

F62   12.15pt–12.17pt*

F63   11.8*; 11.11pt*; 11.14pt*; 11.15pt; 12.15pt–12.17pt*; 20.23pt–20.30pt*

F65   12.15pt–12.17pt*

F67   22.19pt–22.22pt*

F68   1.1–1.2pt; 22.19pt–22.22pt*

F69   17.26pt–17.27pt; 22.19pt–22.22pt

F71   1.1–1.29; 7.15pt–9.1pt; 9.21pt–10.1pt; 16.5pt–16.8pt; 16.18pt–16.19pt; 19.9pt–19.12pt; 20.28–20.30

F77   12.20pt–13.23pt; 16.23pt–16.26pt; 17.14pt–17.17pt

Appendix 4: Chapter Divisions and Amalgamations

The statistics set out in the following table give the number of instances in which chapters have been split or run together. There are many cases of chapters having been divided into three or more parts, and also a number of examples of more than two chapters being amalgamated to form just one. These figures go some way to show how far the chapter structure of the manuscript in question has moved away from the Latin original, although the figures for incomplete or badly mutilated manuscripts (marked with an asterisk) are of course too low.

	Split	Amalgamated
*F01	11	0
F02	1	1
F03	149	1
F04	0	11
F05	1	1
F06	6	15
*F30	44	40
F31	281	5
F32	8	21
F33	32	22
F34	13	17
F35	281	5
F36	97	101
F37	13	23
F38	1	1
F39	2	16
F40	5	18
F41	0	2
F42	12	21
F43	7	38
F44	24	214
F45	8	33
*F46	64	11
F47	9	19
F48	15	14
*F49	15	12
F50	25	24
F51	7	40
F52	0	1
F53	18	24

	Split	Amalgamated
F54	365	19
*F55	3	9
F57	37	26
F58	6	14
F60	11	38
F61	9	37
F62	7	39
F63	5	41
F64	7	16
*F65	6	38
F66	–	–[30]
F67	38	11
F68	53	16
F69	38	11
F70	31	27
*F71	22	10
F72	18	22
F73	26	28
F74	40	18
F77	25	22
F78	36	12

[30] Not seen.

Muslim Chroniclers and the Fourth Crusade[1]

Taef El-Azhari

University of Helwan

Constantinople was built by one of the Byzantine kings, and was named after him. The stories about its greatness and glory are countless. The city is engulfed by the sea on two sides, east and north, while the west and south are inland. The thickness of its greater wall is almost 21 cubits in width. It had been mentioned that Constantinople had nearly 100 gates. One of them is the Golden Gate. Today the city is under the Franks, who defeated the Byzantines and seized it.

These lines were written by the famous Iraqi geographer Yaqut (d. 1228), a Muslim of Greek ancestry who lived in the Levant during the Fourth Crusade. His description of Constantinople as an august city is one that is commonly employed in all contemporary Muslim accounts.[2] Following the invitation of Carole Hillenbrand to examine and translate the Muslim sources,[3] the aim of this paper is to explore how the Muslim chroniclers saw the fall of Constantinople, especially since neither of the existing translations of Ibn al-Athir[4] has focused on that topic. One should add that most studies of the Fourth Crusade have concentrated on the evidence in Latin and Greek chronicles. What do the Arabic sources tell us about this event?

This study will discuss the Muslim accounts of the capture of Constantinople, and the mentality of their authors; it will also ask whether the Ayyubids knew of the intentions of the crusaders before the spring of 1204 and how they reacted to the news.

Muslim Accounts of the Fall of Constantinople

Only one contemporary Muslim historian, the Iraqi Ibn al-Athir (1160–1232), provided a detailed report of the capture of Constantinople. Most other historians repeated what he had written. Ibn al-Athir is considered by almost all scholars of medieval history to be the second most important (Arab-Muslim) chronicler after al-Tabari (d. 923). His fame comes from his voluminous work *al-Kamil fi al-Tarikh* (*The Universal History*), which is a mine of information that has still to be fully

---

[1] My thanks go to my colleague Professor Paul M. Cobb of Notre Dame University for his valuable comments.

[2] Yaqut al-Hamawi, *Mujam al-Buldan*, ed. Ihsan ʿAbbas, 7 vols., 4 (Beirut 1984), 347, 348.

[3] Carole Hillenbrand, *The Crusades. Islamic Perspectives* (Edinburgh, 1999), pp. 2–4.

[4] William MacGuckin de Slane and Charles A. C. Barbier de Meynard in *RHC Or* 2; Johannes E. Ostrup, *Arabiske Kroniker, til Korstogenes periode 1098–1193* (Copenhagen, 1906).

exploited.[5] No historian who came after him could afford to ignore his writings. The importance of his chronicle lies in the fact that his life coincided with much of the crusader period and he had his own firsthand information from various sources, including his brother Diya al-Din, a vizier in Ayyubid Damascus. Moreover, although he compiled his chronicle in the first decade of the thirteenth century, he did not actually publish it until after 1222, as he preferred to revise it thoroughly.[6] He may well also have been influenced by European or Byzantine accounts of the Fourth Crusade; his account goes as follows.

The Seizure of Constantinople from the Byzantines (Rum)[7]

This year, in Shabaan 600 [April 1204], the Franks seized the city of Constantinople from the Byzantines and uprooted their rule from it. The reason for this was that the king of the Byzantines [Isaac II] married a sister of the French king who was the greatest among all Frankish kings. He had a son by her. A brother of the king [Alexius III] overthrew him and seized the realm, gouged out his eyes and put him in prison.

The young prince [the future Alexius IV] escaped, seeking assistance from his uncle, against [Alexius III]. That coincided with a huge gathering of the Franks who were preparing to journey to Syria to rescue Jerusalem from the Muslims. The Franks took the king's son with them, and conducted their crusade by way of Constantinople seeking to reconcile the boy with his uncle. The boy did not have any other wish.

When they arrived at Constantinople, his uncle [Alexius III] came out with a Byzantine army to confront them. The assault took place in Rajab 599 [July 1203] and the Byzantines were defeated and retired back inside the city. The Franks entered with them, so the king [Alexius III] fled to a remote area of the empire. It had been said that the king of Byzantium did not engage in battle with the Franks outside the city wall but that they besieged him inside.

Within the walls, there was a group of Byzantines who supported the prince. They started fires in the city, which distracted the people. At that, these supporters opened a gate to the city by which the Franks entered and the king fled. The Franks now made the boy king, but in name only, and they released his father from prison. The Franks were the *de facto* rulers of the city. They harassed the inhabitants and demanded money and taxes they could not afford to supply. They confiscated the wealth of the monasteries, and what they contained, such as gold and other precious items. Even materials decorating the crosses and icons of Jesus, peace be upon him, and the Apostles, and materials decorating the New Testaments as well.

The people were greatly angered, and set upon the boy-king and killed him. They then drove the Franks outside the city and closed the gates. That took place in Jumada I 600 [February 1204]. As a result, the Frankish forces camped outside, besieging the Byzantines who were fighting them. They persevered, fighting day and night.

---

[5] Ibn al-Athir, *Kitab al-Kamil fi al-Tarikh*, ed. Carl J. Tornberg, 14 vols. (Uppsala 1851–53).

[6] Franz Rosenthal, "Ibn al-Athir," *Encyclopaedia of Islam*, 2nd ed. 10 vols. and supplement (Leiden and London, 1954–); M. Hammad, "Latin and Muslim historiography of the Crusades: A comparative study of William of Tyre and Izz ad-Din b. al-Athir," unpublished Ph.D. dissertation (University of Pennsylvania, 1987), p. 122.

[7] Ibn al-Athir, *al-Kamil*, 12:190–92.

The Byzantines became extremely debilitated, and they wrote to the sultan Rukn al-Din Sulayman Ibn Qilij Arslan, lord of Konya and other domains, urging him to send help. But he was not able to.

A large contingent of nearly 30,000 Franks was then living in Constantinople, but due to the vast size of the city, their numbers had no influence. They conspired with the Franks outside and revolted, starting a fire that burned nearly one-quarter of the city. They opened the gates to the Frankish forces, who made their way in, putting the Byzantines to the sword for three days. The Franks ravaged the Byzantines, killing and looting them until all of them were either murdered or destitute.

A group of Byzantine notables took refuge in the great cathedral called Sophia and the Franks followed them. A group of priests, bishops and monks, marched out of the cathedral, carrying the cross and the New Testament, pleading with the Franks to spare them, but they paid no attention to them and massacred them all. Then they ransacked the cathedral.

The leaders of the Franks were three. Dux of the Venetians [Doge Enrico Dandolo] owned the fleet and they sailed to Constantinople in his ships. He was blind and used to be led about when he rode upon his horse. The second was called the Marquis, and he was the lord of the French [Boniface of Montferrat]. The third was called Kand Ifland [Count Baldwin IX of Flanders], who commanded the largest forces. When they captured Constantinople, they held an election for the rulership. The outcome was in favour of Kand Ifland. They repeated the ballot a second and a third time, and still he won. So they crowned him. God grant His power to whom He, the Almighty, wishes; He removes it also as He wishes.

They crowned him ruler over Constantinople and its dominions. The Dux was to hold the islands, such as Crete, Rhodes and others. The Marquis was to hold the lands to the east of the [Bosphoros] like Iznik [Nicaea] and Ladhik [Lentiana]. None of them achieved anything, apart from the one who took Constantinople, because the rest of the territories were not surrendered by the Byzantines. In regard to the dominions east of the Bosphoros that used to belong to the king of Constantinople, which were adjacent to the territories of Rukn al-Din Sulayman ibn-Qilij Arslan and included Iznik and Ladhik, these were seized by one of the leading Byzantine princes, named Lashkari [Lascaris] and he still governs them today.

Of the other Muslim historians, the following accounts survive.

The Account of Abu Shama (d.1268)[8]

In the last months of 601 [1204] a group of the Franks, known as the Venetians, captured Constantinople, and ousted the Byzantines from the rule after a period of siege and assault. The Franks took possession of the kingdom, looted its treasures and all the fixtures and marbles in its churches. They then brought them to the lands of Egypt and Syria, where they were sold. Damascus has seen plenty of that marble.

---

[8] Abu Shama, *al-Dhayl ala al-Rawdartain*, ed. A al-Husaini (Beirut, 1965), p. 52. Ibn Aybak (*Kanz al-Durar*, ed. Said Ashur (Cairo, 1972), 7:158) mentioned the same story but reported the looted treasures appearing in Alexandria.

The Account of Ibn Wasil (d. 1298)[9]

In the year 600 [1204] the city of Constantinople had been under the Byzantines from ancient times until this year, when the Franks came out from their countries in their colossal forces. They besieged it until it was captured, removing Byzantine rule from it. Constantinople remained under the Franks until 660 [1261] when the Byzantines managed to recover it.

The Account of Ibn Kathir (d. 1372)[10]

In the year 600 [1204], the Franks had gathered a large army to restore Jerusalem from the Muslims, but Almighty God had them preoccupied by the assault on the Byzantines. As they were heading for the Levant through Constantinople they found its rulers in conflict among themselves. As a result they besieged the city, then captured it, putting it to the sword for three days. [After a short account of the sacking, he wrote:] And thank God the most merciful.

Ibn al-Athir considered the Fourth Crusade to be just another campaign to the Levant, a campaign that was less important than the continental effort made by the crusaders, including those in Iberia, which had started the whole movement in 490 (1097).[11] He was confused about the relationship of the Byzantine emperor with the Germans, presenting Isaac II as having married a sister of the French king and fathered a son by her, and stating that when Alexius III seized power, the young prince escaped to his mother's brother. In fact, the future Alexius IV took refuge with his brother-in-law Philip of Swabia.[12] Ibn al-Athir believed that he had provided the Fourth Crusade with a cause, a European power acting in defence of a relation by marriage, and he seems to have believed also that the intention was to reconcile the Byzantine leaders – an aim of Alexius IV – and not to attack Constantinople.

One wonders where he collected his material. His account agrees in certain respects with that of Geoffrey of Villehardouin, particularly with respect to the assault of July 1203. That is, after the emperor had sallied out, he retired to the city, where he was besieged; he then fled, the boy Alexius IV was crowned and his father (Isaac II) released from prison.[13] Ibn al-Athir's opinion that the Franks were at this stage the *de facto* masters of the city agrees with the Christian narratives.

His account also exhibits some parallels with the version of Nicetas Choniates with regard to the plunder and looting of different monasteries, in addition to Hagia Sophia.[14] Although Ibn al-Athir gave details of the massacres committed by the

---

[9] Ibn Wasil, *Mufarrij al-Kurub*, ed. Jamal al-Din al-Shayyal, Said A. F. Ashur and Hasanayn al-Rabiʿ, 6 vols. so far (Cairo, 1963–77), 3:160.

[10] Ibn Kathir, *al-Bedaya wa al-Nehaya*, ed. Ali Atowi, 14 vols. (Beirut, 1982), 13:40.

[11] Ibn al-Athir, *al-Kamil*, 10:272, 273.

[12] Joan Hussey, "Byzantium and the Crusades 1081–1204," in Setton, *Crusades*, 2:149.

[13] Ibn al-Athir, *al-Kamil* 12:190; Geoffrey of Villehardouin, *La conquête de Constantinople*, ed. Edmond Faral, 2 vols. (Paris, 1961), 1:178–84.

[14] Nicetas Choniates, "Historia," *RHC Grecs* 1:397.

crusaders, he offers not a single word of rejoicing or gloating at the loss of this grand Christian city as other Muslim sources do.[15] And he never followed the word "Franks" with his usual phrase, "may they be doomed by the Almighty," probably because he viewed this as an internal Christian feud. Indeed, he showed some sympathy when reporting the exhaustion of the Byzantine side and their appeal for help to the Muslim Sultan Rukn al-Din Sulayman. He probably had some Byzantine sources translated for him or he met with Muslims leaving Constantinople at that time in order to supply us with this unique piece of evidence.

Its context is provided by the situation in the Saljuqid sultanate of Anatolia. The Sultan Qilij Arslan had divided his realm into *iqta*'s for his eight sons in 587 (1191), in accordance with the Turkmen tradition of the Saljuqs. After his death in the following year the sultanate suffered from a long civil war generated by the ambition of Rukn al-Din b. Qilij Arslan, lord of Duqat.[16] Until the fall of Constantinople, Rukn al-Din was preoccupied with stripping his brothers of their dominions. In 588 (1192), he seized Konya from Ghyath al-Din Kaykhisraw, who took refuge in Constantinople some years before the arrival of the crusaders and married a daughter of a leading Byzantine named Maurozomes.[17] Suspicious of the Greeks who had agreed to help another of his brothers, Masud,[18] who held Ankara, Rukn al-Din launched a campaign against him. He was besieging Ankara until August 1204,[19] which explains why he could not offer the Byzantines military assistance.

Ibn al-Athir furnishes us with details about the three leaders of the crusade, Enrico Dandolo, Boniface of Montferrat and Baldwin of Flanders. He seems to have imagined Enrico Dandolo sharing power with the others. He gives us a glimpse of how the crusaders solved their power struggle and his description of the distribution of the conquered territories was partially correct with respect to Venice, which was interested more in commercial naval bases, as was his account of the crusaders' failure to expand eastwards into lands dominated by the Greeks and the Saljuqs.

Abu Shama, Ibn Wasil, and Ibn Kathir extracted material from Ibn al-Athir's *al-Kamil*. Abu Shama, the Damascene historian, whose book *al-Rawdatain* contains more than 200 documents on the Ayyubid period, is considered a particularly valuable source, as it incorporates other lost chronicles.[20] With regard to the Fourth Crusade, he also took material from another Damascene historian, al-Izz b. Taj al-Umana (d. 643/1245), from the famous house of Ibn Asakir. Abu Shama had the opportunity to enlarge on his account of these events, especially as he compiled

[15] See below.

[16] Ibn al-Athir, *al-Kamil*, 12:88, 169, 195, 200.

[17] Ibn al-Athir, *al-Kamil*, 12:200; Claude Cahen, *Pre-Ottoman Turkey* (London, 1968), p. 116.

[18] Cahen, *Pre-Ottoman Turkey*, p. 117.

[19] Ibn al-Athir, *al-Kamil*, 12:200.

[20] M. Hilmy and M. Ahmad, "Some notes on Arabic historiography during the Zangid and Ayyubid periods," *Historians of the Middle East*, ed. Bernard Lewis and Peter M. Holt (London, 1962), pp. 79–97, at p. 84.

this volume near the end of his life, thereby following the tradition of writing a continuation (*Dhayl*) to his previous chronicles; but instead, he simply narrated how a Frankish faction, the Venetians, looted Constantinople. His short narrative of the sack of the city matches the account of Nicetas Choniates.[21] The fact was that, for Abu Shama, Ibn Wasil and Ibn Kathir, the fall of Constantinople was not a major event; Ibn Kathir expressed his joy on the sack and capture of the city.[22] This approach influenced later historians, like Ibn Khaldun (d. 1406) and al-Maqrizi (d. 1441). No source criticized the diversion of the Fourth Crusade from Jerusalem and Muslim lands. The Muslim sources recorded this fact without surprise or criticism; they seem to have understood the pragmatism of the crusaders.

Turning to a non-Muslim source from the Levant, Bar Hebraeus (Ibn al-Ibri, d. 1286), we find that he merely copied Ibn al-Athir, and extracted from his account the final assault, the sack of Hagia Sophia, the election of the emperor and the division of the Byzantine dominions.[23] This Christian and Jacobite Monophysite archbishop appears not to have used Greek sources. He did not express his horror at the fall of Constantinople. He even used the Muslim calendar in his chronicle in addition to the Greek one.

Knowledge of Events in the West

Muslim sources do not refer to the emissaries reported as being sent to the West during the preparations for the Fourth Crusade,[24] although they narrate the story of al-Kamil of Egypt's envoy to the emperor Frederick II and the commission of his crusade in the 1220s.[25] But evidence for Ayyubid knowledge of Western planning is to be found in the history of the prominent Syrian historian Ibn Wasil (d. 1298) who wrote the most comprehensive work on the Ayyubids. This contains hundreds of documents and pieces of correspondence between the Ayyubid rulers, many from original sources and not found elsewhere.[26] With reference to the year 599 (1203), Ibn Wasil included a dialogue that took place some time around June–July 1203 between an envoy from the Templars in Syria to the Ayyubid lord of Hamah, al-Mansur, as well as correspondence between al-Adil, and al-Mansur, written some time after July 1203. Ibn al-Athir also provides us with precious information.

---

[21] Nicetas Choniates, p. 397. See R. Stephen Humphreys, *Islamic History* (Princeton, 1991), p. 131.

[22] Ibn Kathir, 13:41.

[23] Ibn al-Ibri (Bar Hebraeus), *Tarikh Mukhtasar al-Duwal*, ed. A. Salhan (Beirut, 1958), p. 285.

[24] See Robert de Cléry, *La conquête de Constantinople*, ed. Philippe Lauer (Paris, 1956), p. 7; Gunther of Paris, *Hystoria Constantinopolitana*, ed. Peter Orth (Hildesheim and Zürich, 1994), pp. 121, 122–23, 130, 140; "L'Estoire de Eracles," *RHC Oc.* 2:250–52.

[25] al-Ayni, *Iqd al-Jaman* 4 (Cairo, 1984), 156; al-Maqrizi, *al-Suluk*, ed. Muhammad M. Zeyada, 4 vols. (Cairo, 1934–72), 1:221–23.

[26] Jamal al-Din al-Shayyal, "Ibn. Wasil," *Encyclopaedia of Islam*, 2nd ed.; Ibn Wasil, *Mufarrij* 3:34–35.

The Dialogue between the Templars' Envoy and al-Mansur

This dialogue is said to have taken place around Ramadan 599 [June–July 1203].[27]

> An envoy from the Templars arrived at the court of al-Mansur, saying that the Franks were journeying to Acre from overseas amidst a host of about 60,000 men, both turcopoles between turcopoliers, and infantries. Their intention was to head to Jabala and Latakia.
>
> The envoy also reported that the leader of the Hospitallers, the Templars and King Aimery were travelling to Ibn Lawon [Leon] king of the Armenians to reconcile him with the prince of Antioch [Bohemond IV]. They will seek the help of Leon to unite with the Franks, and they will all gather together to fight the Muslims.
>
> He also reported that Marquis [Boniface of Montferrat] and kund Qaland [Baldwin IX of Flanders], who were the commanders of the armies proceeding to Syrian lands, had engaged in a huge battle against the king of Hungary. They seized a large city [Zara] from him, and massacred a large number.
>
> [He also reported] that a galley arrived from their side, with news that they were reconciled, and that they will advance out to Syria during the celebration of the Cross [Easter].
>
> Al-Mansur replied: "We neither fear nor pay attention. Even if they were many times as much, I will encounter them. We realized their intention toward us, and knew of that. There is no chance of reconciliation with the Hospitallers."
>
> Then the messenger entreated him to grant the Templars the peace they came for, and apologized for their previous words. al-Mansur granted the envoy his wish. The envoy was pleased by that.

The context for this discussion is provided by the actions of the Hospitallers, who had tried several times to attack the dominions of Ayyubid Hamah (by way of Barin) from their bases at Crac des Chevaliers and al-Marqab. When al-Mansur overwhelmed them, they asked the Templars to mediate for them and they accepted what Hardwicke has called an "unfavorable peace."[28] It is clear that this detailed account was taken from the Ayyubid archive. Although the size of the Frankish army coming from overseas was exaggerated and the references to turcopoles are not clear, the leaders of the expedition were known, as was the fact that Zara had been captured. In addition, news had reached the Latin East that they were preparing to come to Syria soon.

---

[27] Ibn Wasil, *Muffarij*, 3:145, 146, 147. al-Maqrizi (*al-Suluk* 1:161) very largely repeated these details, although the army had grown to 70,000.

[28] Mary N. Hardwicke, "The Crusader States, 1192–1243," Setton *Crusades* 2:535; Ibn Wasil, *Muffarij*, 3:146.

The Correspondence between al-Adil and al-Mansur

This information caused alarm to the Ayyubids and to al-Adil I in particular. He had only recently become sultan of Egypt, and was at that moment fighting to assert his supremacy over his domains, especially Syria. As a result, he wrote two messages to al-Mansur, both referred to by Ibn Wasil. The first was a note of caution, in which al-Adil informed al-Mansur about the Franks who were coming from overseas and reported that their intention was to advance to Latakia and other territories. The second was a letter included with the warning; after he had defeated the Hospitallers, al-Mansur wrote to al-Adil and sought his advice in dealing with them. Since al-Adil, as Ayyubid sultan, resided in nearby Damascus throughout this particular year, this was a sound gesture on al-Mansur's part. Al-Adil replied: "Whatever [action] your council considers advantageous should be taken regarding the Franks – may the Almighty confound them! Their supplies are scarce, their support is delayed and messages come from every corner carrying the news of their weakness." The only more recent news was their advance to Antioch to reconcile the prince with Ibn Lawon (Leon).[29]

al-Adil was obviously following matters closely, monitoring the movements of the Franks and fearing their hidden intention. Although he saw them to be weak, he chose to be reconciled with them, instead of initiating an offensive, because he was concerned what might come from overseas. For that reason, among others, he strengthened the fortifications of Damascus, circled the city with a stone wall and deepened the citadel's moat, running water into it.[30] He knew from previous experience of crusades how rapidly targets changed and alliances shifted.

It is possible that, during the period the crusaders were encamped outside Constantinople, news had reached the Ayyubids about their strength, either from the Muslims living in Constantinople or from the Byzantines, especially when we consider the fact that, in 1195, Alexius III had sent messages to al-Aziz of Egypt with the intention of improving relations between the two powers.[31] Furthermore, those members of the crusade, who had not participated on the attack of Constantinople and who had arrived in Acre in 1202 and 1203, must have brought some information about the main force.

---

[29] Ibn Wasil, *Mufarrij*, 3:147, 152; the same letter was reported by Ibn al-Furat, *Tarikh al-Duwal wa al-Muluk*, 4, ed. Hassan al-Shamma' (Beirut, 1967), p. 255. Ibn al-Furat (3:135) reported that the news reached Acre that the Franks in Sicily were planning to invade Egypt. See also al-Maqrizi, *al-Suluk*, 1:160.

[30] Ibn Wasil, *Mufarrij*, 3:141.

[31] al-Maqrizi, *al-Suluk*, 1:129.

Ibn al-Athir

Ibn al-Athir provides most information. With respect to the year 600 (1204), when reporting the consequences for the Levant of the capture of Constantinople, he commented as follows:[32]

> In this year, a large crowd of the Franks came out from overseas to Syria. Their mission was facilitated by their seizure of Constantinople. They arrived at Acre and intended to invade Jerusalem (may the Almighty protect it) and to save it from the Muslims. After their halt in Acre, they marched and looted several Muslim areas in the vicinity of Jordan. They ravished the region, putting Muslims to the sword.
>
> King al-Adil was in Damascus. He ordered forces to muster in Syrian and Egyptian lands. He marched and camped at al-Tur near Acre, in order to deter the Franks from targeting the land of Islam.
>
> The Franks came out to meadows beyond Acre and raided Kafr Kanna near Nazareth, They took all the inhabitants captive and confiscated their wealth. The amirs were urging al-Adil to raid and plunder their dominions, but he did not. They remained in their positions till the end of this year, when he made a truce with the Franks. He would keep Damascus and its dominions, and all the Syrian territories under his authority. He conceded to them Nazareth and others (Jaffa), and surrendered the halves of Sidon, Ramla, and others (Lydda). Then he headed for Egypt. As a result, the Franks marched to the city of Hamah. Its lord, al-Mansur, went out to confront them, He had a small force and was defeated. The Franks pursued him to the city. The locals went out to fight them. The Franks killed a few of them and then retreated.

None of the Muslim sources reported the duration of this truce (which was six years) or tried to explain why al-Adil had conceded more territories than he had given up in the accord of July 1198 with Aimery of Jerusalem, which had been supposed to last until the spring of 600 (1204).[33] Neither did they give the reasons why he turned down the desire of his commanders to fight, although according to Abu Shama many locals in Syria, particularly in Damascus, were calling for a *jihad*.[34] Ibn Kathir, who copied a few lines from Ibn al-Athir, seems to have added some invented details in which al-Adil's armies fought a fierce battle against the Franks near Acre and siege warfare that lasted a long time between the two sides. He expressed his disappointment at the negotiated peace, in spite of presenting al-Adil as a powerful lord.[35]

---

[32] Ibn al-Athir, *al-Kamil*, 12:194–95.

[33] R. Stephen Humphreys, *From Saladin to the Mongols: the Ayyubids of Damascus 1193–1260* (Albany, NY, 1977), 108; Hardwicke, "Crusader States," p. 532.

[34] Abu Shama, *Dhayl*, p. 79.

[35] Ibn Kathir, 13:42.

In fact, al-Adil was in a difficult situation. His control over some Ayyubid lords in central and northern Syria was weak; other Salahi commanders were disloyal. In May 1204, the Ayyubid forces were also fighting the Zangids at Mosul, where a siege of the city continued until October. al-Adil had no additional forces with which to confront the Franks near Acre. He could not venture against the Christians, fearing the arrival of more Western armies, particularly after a daring attack by a fleet from Acre on the Nile Delta in May 1204 and the helplessness of the Egyptians when confronted by it.[36]

Moreover, al-Adil's financial and military resources had also been weakened by famine in Egypt, which had damaged the country for four years up to 1200 and had lasting effects: al-Maqrizi mentioned that after the truce al-Adil went to Cairo and began putting Egypt's affairs in order. The earthquake which had struck the whole of the Levant in 1202 had wrecked Ayyubid fortified defences that had already suffered from an earlier tremor in 1200. This was why al-Adil focused on the refortification of Damascus and other Syrian cities.[37]

Another part of the Ayyubid realm had been disordered since 1201. There was chaos in Yemen following the assumption of power in 1201 of al-Nasir b. Tughtakin, al-Adil's nephew.[38] Different Mamluk commanders followed one another in taking control. al-Nasir was assassinated and his mother kept sending to al-Adil urging him to send a capable candidate to take over. al-Adil was alarmed by these events and fought to keep Yemen within the Ayyubid orbit, an aim he did not achieve until 1214.[39] Yemen lay on a major commercial route from the Indian Ocean to Egypt and the Levant, and he could not afford to lose it, especially because any disorder in the Yemeni markets directly affected the prices in Egypt.[40] Moreover, the Saljuq sultan Kaykhisraw was acting against al-Adil's interests early in 1205 by welcoming his rebellious nephew al-Afdal to his court and asserting his lordship over the Turkmen Artukids in Khartpert.[41] With his limited forces spread thinly in Syria, Egypt, Iraq, al-Jazir, and Yemen, and a hostile relationship with the Saljuqs of Anatolia, al-Adil opted for a sensible *modus vivendi* with the crusaders.

---

[36]   Abu Shama, *Dhayl*, p. 50; Ibn al-Athir, *al-Kamil*, 12:198; al-Maqrizi, *Suluk*, 1:163–64.

[37]   Ibn al-Athir, *al-Kamil*, 12:170, 198; Ibn Wasil, *Mufarrij*, 3:161; al-Maqrizi, *Suluk*, 1:164. From the eleventh century onwards the name Misr is usually applied to Cairo in many places, but in this instance al-Maqrizi used it of both Cairo and Egypt in the same sentence.

[38]   Ibn Aybak, *Kanz al-Durar*, 7:177.

[39]   Ibid.; Ibn Wasil, *Mufarrij*, 3:136–39.

[40]   Sibt ibn al-Jawzī, *Mirat al-zaman fi tarikh al-aʿ yan*, 8, ed. Ali Sevim (Hyderabad, 1951–52), pp. 522–53; S. Uthman, *Tejarat al-Muhit al-Hindi fi Asr al-Seyada al-Islamiyya. 904–1498* (Kuwait, 1990), p. 176.

[41]   Ibn al-Athir, *al-Kamil*, 12:202.

Paris Masters
and the Justification of the Albigensian Crusade[1]

Jessalynn Bird

Independent Scholar

Despite recent extensive explorations of the contributions of the Cistercian and mendicant orders to preaching against heresy and the justification of anti-heretical crusades, comparatively speaking, much less attention has been given to the influence of Paris masters in these arenas.[2] Yet throughout the late twelfth and early thirteenth centuries, networks of Paris-trained reformers collaborated with individuals from the Praemonstratensian, Cistercian and Victorine orders, local prelates and noblemen in the legal and pastoral fight against heresy in northern Europe and the promotion of the anti-heretical crusade. This paper will examine how Paris masters joined their regular religious colleagues and canonists in providing guidance to prelates, secular rulers and noblemen on the conduct and conditions essential for a just war. Their advice influenced debates conducted between the Paris-educated Pope Innocent III, his legates, prelates and secular rulers over the sanctioning, *modus operandi* and goals of the Albigensian Crusade.

As early as the late twelfth century, Paris masters including Peter the Chanter, Prevostin of Cremona, Peter of Blois, Ralph Niger, and Alan of Lille were either keenly aware of, or had become directly involved in, the struggle against heresy in northern Europe, England and the Midi. By the early thirteenth century, some Paris masters (Stephen Langton and James of Vitry among them) were credited with debating against heresiarchs in Italy. Others – such as James of Vitry, Oliver of Paderborn, Conrad of Speyer, John of Xanten, Robert Courson and William,

---

Much of the research for this article was done with the generous support of the Fulbright and Thouron foundations and the Visiting Scholar program at Northwestern University.

[1] I would like to thank Christoph Maier and Nicole Bériou for generously lending me critical transcriptions of the sermons of Philip the Chancellor and Odo of Châteauroux delivered during Louis VIII's crusade, soon to be published in the Classiques de l'histoire de France series under the title *Le sources de la croisade Albigeoisie de 1226*. I will cite these sermons by their author, title or incipit, and number as listed in Johannes Baptiste Schneyer, *Repertorium der lateinischen Sermones des Mittelalters, für die Zeit von 1150–1350*, 11 vols. (Münster, 1969–89) (hereafter Schneyer). The suggestions of the *Crusades'* anonymous readers also proved most helpful in revising this article; all errors remain mine alone.

[2] For example, Martha G. Newman, *The Boundaries of Charity: Cistercian Culture and Ecclesiastical Reform, 1098–1180* (Stanford, CA, 1996), esp. pp. 223–32; Christine Thouzellier, *Catharisme et valdéisme en Languedoc à la fin du XIIe et au début du XIIIe siècle*, 2nd ed. (Paris, 1969; repr. Marseille, 1982); Marie-Humbert Vicaire, *Saint Dominic and his Times*, trans. Kathleen Pond (New York, 1964); Beverly Mayne Kienzle, *Cistercians, Heresy and Crusade in Occitania, 1145–1229* (Rochester, NY, 2001); Christoph T. Maier, *Preaching the Crusades: Mendicant Friars and the Cross in the Thirteenth Century* (Cambridge, 1994). See also the works cited below.

archdeacon of Paris – collaborated with Cistercians including Guy, abbot of Vaux-de-Cernay, Arnaud Amaury and Fulk, bishop of Toulouse, in promoting the crusade in northern Europe. Some accompanied and advised their recruits in the Midi. Moreover, bishops who had relied on Paris masters as expert witnesses and judge delegates for the suppression of heresy in northern Europe, including Odo of Sully (1197–1208) and Peter Nemours (1208–19), bishops of Paris, the bishops of Nevers, Auxerre and the former Paris masters Alberic, archbishop of Reims and Peter Corbeil, archbishop of Sens (1200–22), dominated the early stages of the crusade's organization in northern France or participated in the campaign itself. As archbishop of Canterbury, Stephen Langton was said to have opposed John of England's favorable reception and support of his brother-in-law, Raymond VI of Toulouse, in the winter of 1213–14. Stephen's brother Walter served in the anti-heretical crusade from ca. 1211 to 1218, while Stephen's archiepiscopal *familia* included an archdeacon from Narbonne and the Paris-educated Alexander of Stavensby. Alexander would instruct the early Dominicans in Toulouse before, as bishop of Coventry and Lichfield, he also supported the anti-heretical crusade in England. A considerable proportion of the noblemen who played key roles in the anti-heretical crusade – including Robert, count of Dreux, Hervé IV, count of Nevers, Peter Courtenay, count of Auxerre, Odo III, duke of Burgundy, Simon de Montfort, Robert Mauvoisin and Enguerrand de Boves – possessed ties to Paris masters and their Cistercian and Victorine co-workers. These noblemen's support for the Albigensian crusade seems to have stemmed from their previous and contemporaneous collaboration with local bishops and these Parisian and monastic reformers in various legal cases, the suppression of heresy (both in their own lands and in the Midi), and the foundation or support of religious houses and the eastern crusades.[3]

---

[3] I am writing articles on the involvement of Paris masters in recruiting for the initial stages of the Albigensian Crusade and in early inquisitions against heresy. See Peter Biller, "William of Newburgh and the Cathar Mission to England," in *Life and Thought in the Northern Church, c.1100–c.1700. Essays in Honour of Claire Cross*, ed. Diane Wood, Studies in Church History, Subsidia 12 (Rochester, NY, 1999), pp. 11–30; Jessalynn Bird, "The Construction of Orthodoxy and the (De)construction of Heretical Attacks on the Eucharist in *Pastoralia* from Peter the Chanter's Circle in Paris," in *Texts and the Repression of Medieval Heresy*, ed. Caterina Bruschi and Peter Biller (York, 2003), pp. 45–62; Nicholas Vincent, "England and the Albigensian Crusade," in *England and Europe in the reign of Henry III (1216–1272)*, ed. Björn K. U. Weiler and Ifor Rowlands (Aldershot, 2002), pp. 67–97, here pp. 67–75; G. B. Flahiff, "Ralph Niger: An Introduction to his Life and Works," *Mediaeval Studies* 2 (1940), 104–26; idem, "*Deus non Vult*: A critic of the Third Crusade," *Mediaeval Studies* 9 (1947), 162–88; Ralph Niger, *De re militari et triplici via peregrinationis Ierosolimitane (1187/88)* 66, ed. Ludwig Schmugge (New York, 1977), pp. 187–88; Jessalynn Bird, "Heresy, Crusade and Reform in the Circle of Peter the Chanter, c.1187–c.1240" (D.Phil. thesis, University of Oxford, 2001), pp. 86–119.

The Legal Justification of the Albigensian Crusade

In an era when canon law and theology remained deeply entwined, Paris-trained masters drew on contemporary practice, scriptural and patristic writings, recent decretals and Gratian's *Decretum* when discussing the concept of just war in their theological *summae*, biblical commentaries, sermons and pastoral manuals. They adopted and popularized canonists' definition of just war as a defensive action motivated by necessity, including the punishment of obstinate sinners or rebels who refused legal settlements or those who unjustly seized lands, possessions or rights.[4] Members of Peter the Chanter's circle, responsible for training future prelates and shaping the policies of lay and ecclesiastical magnates through reform campaigns, preaching, teaching, confession and ecclesiastical sanctions, urged rulers and their subjects to weigh the justness of particular campaigns and to potentially withhold their support for iniquitous enterprises despite the serious consequences this might entail.[5] Their insistence on the scrupulous examination of one's own conduct and conscience and the proper authorization and motives for a war impacted upon the baronial revolt in England,[6] and both generated and colored intense debates amongst the leaders and participants of the Fourth Crusade.[7]

Many of those involved in the Fourth Crusade looked to the Paris-educated legate Peter Capuano, German and French prelates, and Cistercian abbots, including Guy

---

[4] Canonists contemporary to or cited by Peter the Chanter's circle in Paris include the anonymous *Summa Parisiensis*, Sicard of Cremona (who participated in the Fourth Crusade), Stephen of Tournai (an associate of Peter the Chanter and Guy of Vaux-de-Cernay) and Huguccio. See note 7 below; Frederick H. Russell, *The Just War in the Middle Ages* (Cambridge, 1975), pp. 88–99, 137–38, 213–15, 221–22; Robert Courson, *Summa* 15.2–3 and 26.10, Paris, Bibliothèque Nationale, MS Latin 14524, fols. 63vb–64vb, 92rb–va, edited in John W. Baldwin, *Masters, Princes and Merchants: The Social Views of Peter the Chanter and His Circle*, 2 vols. (Princeton, 1970), 1:208 and 2:146–47, notes 23–24 (hereafter MPM).

[5] When citing the unpublished works of various Paris masters, I will refer when possible to excerpts published in MPM and other secondary works. See MPM, 1:209–11, notes 32–39; Russell, *Just War*, pp. 218, 221, 225–28, 230, 233–34, 244–45; Thomas of Chobham, *Summa confessorum* 7.4.6a.10, ed. F. Broomfield, Analecta mediaevalia Namurcensia 25 (Louvain, 1968), pp. 432–33; Peter the Chanter, *Summa de sacramentis et animae consiliis*, ed. Jean-Albert Dugauquier, Analecta mediaevalia Namurcensia 4, 7, 11, 16, 21 (Louvain, 1954–67), §§155, 15, II:383, 465, and §270, IIa:290; Stephen Langton, *Questiones*, Cambridge, St. John's College, MS 57, fols. 204rb, 334vb–335ra and MPM, 2:112, note 33 and 2:147–48, notes 33, 35; Robert Courson, *Summa* 26.10, 15 and 30.9, BN Lat. 14524, fols. 50va–vb, 92rb–va, 107ra and MPM, 2:146–48, notes 23, 26, 32, 37.

[6] For Stephen Langton's pivotal role in both the Canterbury electorial dispute and the conflict between John and his barons, see W. L. Warren, *King John* (Berkeley, 1978), pp. 157–89, 202–51, 265–77; Ralph V. Turner, *King John* (Harlow, 1994), pp. 155–252; Christopher R. Cheney, *Pope Innocent III and England*, Päpste und Papsttum 9 (Stuttgart, 1976), pp. 147–78, 298–400; Frederick M. Powicke, *Stephen Langton* (Oxford, 1965), pp. 75–141.

[7] See Raymond H. Schmandt, "The Fourth Crusade and the Just-War Theory," *Catholic Historical Review* 61 (1975), 191–221; Donald E. Queller and Thomas F. Madden, *The Fourth Crusade: The Conquest of Constantinople*, 2nd edn. (Philadelphia, 1997), pp. 58–67, 73–95, 97–99, 101–2, 112, 133, 141, 143, 154–56, 165, 168, 171–75, 179–81; *Contemporary Sources for the Fourth Crusade*, ed. and trans. Alfred J. Andrea (Leiden, 2000).

of Vaux-de-Cernay, for guidance over the appropriate goals of the expedition and the proper conduct of its participants, among whom were Simon de Montfort and other noblemen who later formed the vanguard of the anti-heretical crusade.[8] In fact, some ecclesiastics on the Fourth Crusade believed themselves better informed than the pope to decide whether the diversion of the crusade to Zara and Constantinople was justified by necessity, utility, the Greeks' schismatic state and "treachery" or the Zarans' "rebellion" against the Venetians. They pointed to canonical authorities which sanctioned bishops, ecclesiastical judges, and church councils to call upon princes and ordinary Christians to attack heretics, evil Christians and anyone else molesting the Christian faith, the peace of the church or one's homeland. Their decision to suppress what they perceived as ill-informed papal instructions was decried by Innocent III and others in the crusading army, such as Guy of Vaux-de-Cernay, who believed that papal authorization was essential for both declaring and defining the parameters of a just war. Ironically, Innocent III's reluctant acceptance of the conquest of the former Byzantine empire after the fact confirmed in the minds of some prelates, Cistercians and Paris masters the assumption that those with local knowledge of the situation were best equipped to decide crusading policy. Yet the diversion of the Fourth Crusade meant that Innocent III would attempt to control the authorization and conduct of the Albigensian crusade much more closely.[9] His legates would defy him by redefining the scope and goals of the crusade and ignoring papal mandates to rehabilitate Raymond of Toulouse and other noblemen whom they regarded as completely untrustworthy.

During the long and tortured course of the anti-heretical crusade, dialogues concerning its justness were dominated by references to several key authorities. One was *causa* 23 of Gratian's *Decretum*, which described a hypothetical scenario where a heretical bishop used physical force and persuasion to compel his flock to convert. Local orthodox bishops possessing temporal power were ordered by the pope to defend the orthodox and constrain the heretics to convert. After mustering an army, they killed, despoiled or imprisoned many of the heretics. Gratian concluded that the

---

[8] See note 7 above; Monique Zerner-Chardavoine, "L'abbé Gui des Vaux-de-Cernay prédicateur de croisade," in *Les cisterciens de Languedox (XIIIe–XIVe s.)*, ed. Edouard Privat, Cahiers de Fanjeaux 21 (Toulouse, 1986), pp. 183–204; Monique Zerner-Chardavoine and Hélène Piéchon-Palloc, "La croisade albigeoise, une revanche. Des rapports entre la quatrième croisade et la croisade albigeoise," *Revue historique* 267 (1982), 3–18; Werner Maleczek, *Petrus Capuanus: Kardinal, Legat am vierten Kreuzzug, Theologe (†1214)* (Vienna, 1988); Jean Longnon, *Les compagnons de Villehardouin: recherches sur les croisés de la quatrième croisade* (Geneva, 1978).

[9] See notes 7–8 above; Russell, *Just War*, pp. 115–18 (including Stephen of Tournai, Sicard of Cremona, the *Summa Parisiensis* and Huguccio); PL 215:103–10; PL 216:11–12; *Contemporary Sources*, ed. Andrea, pp. 115–76. For an interpretation of Innocent's policy in the context of recent research stressing that the image of a particular region as heresy-ridden was largely manufactured by ecclesiastical and secular princes in the service of their own interests, see Monique Zerner, "Le déclenchment de la croisade Albigeoise retour sur l'affaire de paix et de foi," in *La croisade Albigeoise*, ed. Michel Roquebert (Balma, 2004), pp. 127–42 and Pilar Jiménez-Sanchez, "Le Catharisme fut-il le véritable enjeu religieux de la croisade?" in ibid., pp. 143–55.

campaign was just because its participants obtained proper authorization and did not seek their own profit but rather the restoration of peace and the defensive avenging of injuries to persons or possessions through the coercion of the Church's enemies. Just war could also be invoked on princes who failed to punish their subjects for misdeeds or refused to restitute unjustly acquired property.[10]

The second authority was a decree of the Third Lateran Council (1179) which excommunicated heretics and mercenaries who had committed depredations and atrocities against the unarmed and the church in the south of France. Their defenders or employers shared in this excommunication, while the vassals of stubbornly unrepentant excommunicates could be absolved from any obligations owed to the anathematized. Prelates were urged to call upon secular princes to confiscate the lands of recalcitrant excommunicates in return for crusading privileges and an indulgence to be set at local bishops' discretion.[11] This authority was invoked by Innocent III and Stephen Langton during their negotiations with King John, excommunicated for his despoliation of the ecclesiastical supporters of both the papal interdict imposed on his lands and the exiled archbishop-elect of Canterbury, Stephen Langton.

As legate for the crusade in France, Robert Courson also adapted Third Lateran's decrees to local circumstances at the council of Bordeaux in 1214. Nicholas Vincent has recently posited that Robert reduced the indulgence offered for the anti-heretical effort from the plenary to a mere sixty days at Bordeaux in obedience to specific papal instructions. By the time that the council met, however, the plenary indulgence for the Albigensian crusade temporarily suspended by Innocent III had been reinstituted and recruitment was again in full swing. It would seem that, in his anxiety to preserve the legal rights of John of England, who had placed himself under papal and legatine protection and pledged to suppress heresy in his lands, Robert offered a sixty-day indulgence to all who resisted heretics, *routiers* and their supporters as an added incentive for local authorities (including John) to suppress heresy by force in the archdiocese of Bordeaux; this was an alternative to the extension of the existing anti-heretical crusade led by Simon de Montfort into this region. If they made no move to seek absolution, those excommunicated as abettors of heretics would forfeit the support of their vassals after a mere forty days. After consultation with the incorrigible's overlords, the secular rulers, prelates and communes of the province were urged to punish the recalcitrant by confiscating their lands and making satisfaction to those churches which had suffered injury.

---

[10] Russell, *Just War*, pp. 56–83; James A. Brundage, "Holy War and the Medieval Lawyers," in *The Holy War*, ed. Thomas P. Murphy (Columbus, OH, 1976), pp. 99–140, here pp. 106–9; Gratian, *Decretum, causa* 23, in Emil Friedberg, ed., *Corpus iuris canonici*, 2 vols. (Leipzig, 1879–81; repr. Graz, 1955), 1:889–965 (hereafter CIC).

[11] CIC 2:779–80; Third Lateran Council (1179), c.27, in Joseph Alberigo et al., eds., *Conciliorum oecumenicorum decreta*, 3rd ed. (Bologna, 1973), pp. 224–25 (hereafter COD); Alan of Lille, *Liber Poenitentialis* 3.29, 31, ed. Jean Longère, Analecta mediaevalia Namurcensia 17–18 (Louvain, 1965), 2:144–46; Thouzellier, *Catharisme*, pp. 23–24; and the discussion below.

Many of Robert's modifications would be incorporated into the Fourth Lateran Council's definitive *Excommunicamus*, although the period for repentance would be lengthened to one year.[12]

Both Robert's decree and *Excommunicamus* were indebted to two final major sources for the anti-heretical debate. The papal decretals *Ad abolendam* (1184) and *Vergentis in Senium* (1199) added to the authorities outlined above by subjecting those excommunicated as suspect of heresy who failed to clear themselves within a year to various penalties: their possessions could be confiscated and they were banned from public office, giving testimony in court, making a will or inheriting. Those convicted of heresy could incur the same penalty as traitors: death. Secular rulers were to swear to repress heresy in their lands and aid the church in doing so or face excommunication and its attendant penalties, including the confiscation of property by one's overlord.[13] Innocent III would use the canonical authorities outlined above to instruct his legates and prelates in the south of France to uproot error through preaching and to exhort local authorities to wield the material sword against heretics from 1198 onwards. They would continue to influence crucial deliberations and decisions concerning the excommunication or reconciliation of lords in the Midi and the disposition of their lands during the first stages of the anti-heretical crusade (1207–15), the Fourth Lateran Council (1215), the crusade of Louis VIII (1226), and the final reconciliation of Raymond VII of Toulouse (1229).[14]

---

[12] Robert's legation included the Albigensian crusade and was meant to help prepare for the impending business of the Fourth Lateran Council: the reform of the Church and a proposed eastern crusade. The council of Avignon (1209) had previously reiterated the Third Lateran decree. See Vincent, "England," p. 76; PL 216:741–44, 817–22; Peter of Vaux-de-Cernay, *Hystoria albigensis* 399, 401–11, 422, 438–32, 440–41, ed. P. Guébin and E. Lyon, 3 vols. (Paris, 1926–39), 2:97–105, 114–15, 128–35 (hereafter VDC); Marcel and Christine Dickson, "Le Cardinal Robert de Courson: sa vie," *Archives d'histoire doctrinale et littéraire du moyen âge* 9 (1934), 53–142; Thomas Rymer et al., eds., *Foedera, conventiones, litterae, et cuiuscunque generis acta publica inter reges Angliae et alios quosvis imperatores, reges, pontifices, principes vel communitates, 1101–1564*, 4 vols. in 7 pts. (London, 1816–69), 1.1:121–22; Fourth Lateran Council (1215), c.3, in COD, pp. 233–35; Avignon (1209), 1.10, 1.16, in Mansi, *Concilia*, 22:789, 790.

[13] See CIC, 2:780–83; Robert Courson, *Summa* 30.1–2, 5, BN Lat. 14524, fols. 104vb–105ra, 106ra–rb; and MPM, 2:216, notes 60–61; and note 14 below.

[14] For the impact of these decrees on the fight against heresy, see note 9 above; Fourth Lateran Council (1215), c.3, in COD, pp. 233–35; MPM, 2:321–32; Thouzellier, *Catharisme*, pp. 45–48, 139–212; Edward Peters, *Inquisition* (New York, 1988), esp. pp. 45–48; idem, "Wounded Names: The Medieval Doctrine of Infamy," in *Law in Medieval Life and Thought*, ed. Edward B. King and Susan J. Ridyard, Sewanee Medieval Studies 5 (1990), pp. 43–89, esp. pp. 53, 65, 69, 76–79, 81–85; Raoul Manselli, "De la 'Persuasio' a la 'coercitio,'" in *Le credo, la morale et l'inquisition*, Cahiers de Fanjeaux 6 (Toulouse, 1971), pp. 175–97; Newman, *Boundaries*, pp. 181, 185–88, 192–93; Peter Diehl, "'Ad abolendam' (X.5.7.9) and Imperial Legislation against Heresy," *Bulletin of Medieval Canon Law* 19 (1989), 1–11; Henri Maissoneuve, *Études sur les origines de l'Inquisition*, 2nd ed. (Paris, 1960), pp. 133–37, 151–57, 281–84, 339–57; Kenneth Pennington, "'Pro peccatis patrum puniri': A Moral and Legal Problem of the Inquisition," *Church History* 47 (1978), 137–54; H. G. Walther, "Häresie und päpstliche Politik: Ketzerbegriff und Ketzergessetzgebung in de Übergangsphase von der Dekretistik zur

In fact, the early stages of the Albigensian crusade were marked by a nigh-dominating legal tone and limited goals. Trained in canon law and in theology at Paris, Innocent invoked the theory of the two swords to remind, first, Philip Augustus of France, and then his leading barons, of their duty as princes to protect the church and uproot heresy by forcibly confiscating the possessions and lands of those who refused to cooperate with his legates in the repression of heresy in the Midi, particularly Raymond VI, count of Toulouse.[15] After consulting with the bishop of Paris and other prelates, Philip acknowledged that Raymond had proven himself an unfaithful vassal, and offered to send money and men to aid Innocent's legates in the Midi if his barons and clergy provided adequate assistance and a truce was secured with his enemy, John of England. However, Philip retained reservations concerning the legality of Innocent's exhortations for military intervention in the south of France. As he had on previous occasions, he appears to have turned to learned men in Paris for legal advice. They assured him that, according to canon law, Raymond's lands could not be declared open to occupation until he was formally condemned for heresy. Even then, proof of his guilt and a formal request should be sent to Philip, Raymond's overlord, who alone possessed the authority to declare the count's lands open to seizure.[16]

For, acting on information from his legates in the south of France, Innocent had refined the case against Raymond: excommunicated for breaking his oaths to keep the peace and expel heretics from his lands, he was also implicated in the assassination of the papal legate Peter of Castelnau. When appeals for intervention

---

Dekretalistik," in *The Concept of Heresy in the Middle Ages (11th–13th centuries)*, ed. Willem Lourdaux and Daniël Verhelst (Louvain, 1983), pp. 104–43; Othmar Hageneder, "Der Häresiebegriff bei den Juristen des 12. und 13. Jahrhunderts," in ibid., pp. 42–103; idem, "Studien zur Dekretale 'Vergentis' (X.5.7.10). Ein Beitrag zu Häretikergesetzebung Innocenz III," *Zeitschrift der Savigny-Stiftung für Rechtsgeschichte 80, Kanonistische Abteilung* 49 (1963), 138–73; Walter Ullmann, "The Significance of Innocent III's Decretal *Vergentis*," in *Études d'histoire du droit canonique. Festschrift dediées à Gabriel Le Bras*, 2 vols. (Paris, 1965), 2:729–44. For anti-heretical decrees and the negotiations with Raymond, see the works cited above and Mansi, *Concilia*, 22:789–90; 815–16, 855–64, 931–34, 935–54, 1087–90, 1206–10; 1214–20, 23:21, 22–23, 161–76, 185–88, 195; VDC 37–39, 162–64, 212, 368, 542–47, 1:140–45, 165–69, 210–11, 2:66–96, 236–40; Richard Kay, *The Council of Bourges, 1225: A Documentary History* (Aldershot, 2002); Gerard Sivéry, *Louis VIII: le lion* (Paris, 1995); and the discussion below.

[15] For the development of Innocent III's presentation of the crusade, see PL 214:537–39; PL 215:176–80, 358–62, 501–3, 525–28, 1246–48, 1358–59; Thouzellier, *Catharisme*, pp. 188–89; Maissonneuve, *Études*, pp. 196–97, 199–209; Raymonde Foreville, "Innocent III et la croisade des Albigeois," in *Paix de Dieu et guerre sainte en Languedoc au XIIIe siecle*, ed. Edouard Privat, Cahiers de Fanjeaux 4 (Toulouse, 1969), pp. 182–217; Helmut Roscher, *Papst Innocenz III und die Kreuzzüge*, Forschungen zur Kirchen-und Dogmengeschichte 21 (Göttingen, 1969), pp. 222–31; compare Alan of Lille, *Sermo ad milites*, PL 210:185–87.

[16]   John W. Baldwin, *The Government of Philip Augustus: Foundations of French Royal Power in the Middle Ages* (Berkeley, 1986), pp. 41, 122; Claude de Vic, Joseph Vaissete et al., eds., *Histoire générale de Languedoc avec des notes et les pièces justificatives*, 16 vols. in 18 (Paris, 1872–1904), 8:557–58 (December 1207), 8:558–59 (April 1208) (hereafter HGL); PL 215:1246–48; Roscher, *Papst Innocenz III*, p. 223.

to Philip Augustus, Raymond's immediate overlord, had failed, Innocent III called upon the penalties outlined in canon law for excommunicates to absolve Raymond's vassals of their obligations and declare his lands open to *anyone* who would occupy them and extirpate heresy as Raymond had failed to do, saving the feudal rights of Philip Augustus. Those who did so would enjoy the full privileges and indulgences granted to crusaders to the Holy Land. Raymond's only hope of retaining his lands lay in fulfilling his promises to undertake the penance imposed upon him, repress heresy and make restitution. If he failed to do so, the *militia Christi* were urged to abolish heresy, which was presented as more harmful than the attacks of Saracens, and reinstitute peace by confiscating the lands of those who fostered heresy and installing catholic rulers who would serve God and preserve the orthodox faith.[17]

Innocent's arguments correlate with opinions voiced by his former fellow students in Paris and contemporary canonists. Simply speaking, as wicked Christians whose attacks on the faith transgressed the law, offended God and persecuted the Church, heretics forfeited their legal rights to property and rule. For unlike Saracens and pagans, who could not be compelled to convert and ought to be resisted only if they attacked the Church, schismatics and heretics who verbally assailed the faith or sinful men who physically attacked the Church could be compelled to re-enter it through excommunication, and, if necessary, force. Moreover, following Old Testament authorities cited by Gratian, reformers and canonists concluded that princes, if their motives were just and they were acting on ecclesiastical authority, could justly dispossess legitimate heirs and grant out their conquered lands in fiefs.[18] For example, prior to his appointment as legate for the crusade in France, Robert Courson taught that, if an excommunicated prince attacked ecclesiastics or their possessions, defended his crimes or engaged in a unjust war, his vassals were absolved from military service and taxation; this conclusion was formally applied by Innocent III to the contumacious Raymond of Toulouse.[19] Yet many inhabitants

---

[17] VDC 27–46, 62–64, 1:30–41, 62–65; PL 215:1354–60; and note 15 above. Compare Philip the Chancellor, *Sermo scolaribus ... tempore quo rex Ludovicus assumpsit crucem in Albigenses*, Schneyer, no. 269, 4:837.

[18] See X.5.7.8–10, 13, in CIC, 2:779–83, 787–89; Russell, *Just War*, pp. 112–15, 196–97, 221–22, 252–53; Robert Courson, *Summa* 15.2–4 and 26.10, BN Lat. 14524, fols. 63vb–64vb, 92rb–va; MPM, 1:208–9 and 2:146–47, notes 23–25; Thomas of Chobham, *Summa de arte predicandi* 3, ed. Franco Morenzoni, CCCM 82 (Turnhout, 1988), pp. 76–77; James of Vitry, *Sermo ad fratres ordinis militaris insignitos charactere militiae Christi*, no. 37, and *Sermo ad fratres ordinis militaris*, no. 38, in Johannes-Baptiste Pitra, ed., *Analecta novissima spicilegii Solesmensis: altera continuatio*, 2 vols. (Paris, 1885–88), 2:405–21 (partial edition), esp. pp. 405, 416–20.

[19] The threat of a similar application loomed over other excommunicated rulers, in particular John of England, a conclusion not lost on Robert Courson's colleague, the reformer Stephen Langton, with whom Robert was in communication. See Russell, *Just War*, pp. 104, 231–32; MPM, 1:211–13; Robert Courson, *Summa* 4.4, 4.12, and 26.9, BN Lat. 14524, fols. 27rb–vb, 29ra–va, 92ra–rb and MPM, 2:151–52, notes 53, 55–56; compare Peter the Chanter, *Summa* §24, III2b:740 and §317, III2a:370–71; Thomas of Chobham, *Summa de arte predicandi* 3, pp. 78–79. For England, see Kathleen Major, ed., *Acta Stephani Langton Cantuariensis archiepiscopi, AD 1207–1228*, Canterbury and York Society 50 (Oxford, 1950), 1:5, no. 2; Cheney, *Innocent III*, pp. 261, 320–21, 327, 338–41, 358, 391; Turner, *King*

of southern France would disregard papal menaces or canonistic arguments and would resist the invading crusaders in order to protect their lords and the lands they held from them.[20]

Nonetheless, many of leaders of the early phases of the Albigensian crusade were associated with the prelates, Cistercians and Paris masters recruiting for it, and they attempted to fulfill Innocent's commission to the letter through the election of Simon de Montfort as an impeccably orthodox overlord of the newly conquered lands in 1209. Perhaps his electors hoped that Simon's history of obedience to papal commands, manifested in his refusal to embrace a dubious campaign against fellow Christians during the Fourth Crusade at the expense of the Holy Land, would extend to his tenure in the Midi. For, with Simon's election and the temporary reconciliation of Raymond of Toulouse, Innocent III appears to also have considered the goal of the crusade accomplished and to have contemplated shifting resources to the organization of a crusade to recover Jerusalem, a project he had long cherished.[21]

Within a short time, however, the anti-heretical crusade took on broader goals. Raymond soon fell foul of the papal legates in charge of the crusade and his lands were seized by force.[22] Philip Augustus' qualms regarding the unproven nature of the claims against Raymond and the count's own appeals to Rome led a stern Innocent III to order his legates to provide the count of Toulouse with opportunities to clear himself of the serious accusations leveled against him through canonical purgation. Even when Raymond failed to comply with the severe penances and conditions the legates set for compurgation and absolution and broke his oaths, Innocent insisted that final judgment be reserved to Rome and that the door should remain open to reconciliation.[23] Innocent appears to have been motivated partly by a concern that his own, his legates', and the local church's comportment be perceived as just. Although he initially did not challenge Arnaud Amaury's summary dispossession and imprisonment of the viscount of Béziers and Carcassonne as a supporter of heresy and the assignment of his lands to Simon de Montfort, both his

---

John, pp. 163–68; Warren, *King John*, pp. 174–75, 202–3, 248; Powicke, *Stephen Langton*, pp. 90, 104–5.

[20]   See the discussion below.

[21]   VDC 75–80, 101–2, 108, 110–15, 1:75–80, 101–2, 112–13, 115–19; PL 216:152–53; Roscher, *Papst Innocenz III*, pp. 234–40; Raymonde Foreville, *Le Pape Innocent III et la France*, Päpste und Papsttum 26 (Stuttgart, 1992), pp. 249, 268. Peter of Vaux-de-Cernay was careful to counter insinuations that Simon was a land-grabber who attacked Christians in order to obtain their land by highlighting Simon's refusal to do this during the Fourth Crusade (VDC 105–6, 1:105, 107–11).

[22]   Maissoneuve, *Études*, pp. 156–58; Foreville, "Innocent III et la croisade," pp. 184–217; Thouzellier, *Catharisme*, pp. 136, 146, 155–56; Lothar Kolmer, Ad capiendas vulpes: *die Ketzerbekämpfung in Südfrankreich in der ersten Hälfte des 13. Jahrhunderts und die Ausbildung des Inquisitionsverfahrens* (Bonn, 1982), pp. 35–41.

[23]   *The History of the Albigensian Crusade: Peter of les Vaux-de-Cernay's* Historia Albigensis, trans. W. A. and M. D. Sibly (Rochester, NY, 1998), pp. 317–20; Foreville, "Innocent III et la croisade," pp. 205–7, 209–11; PL 216:171–74, 183–84, 524–25, 613–14, 739–44, 959–60. On Raymond's appeals, see note 14 above; Foreville, *Innocent III et la France*, pp. 225, 228–33, 264–65, 266–67.

legates and Simon felt his ire in 1213 when rumors of the viscount's assassination by the crusading army further threatened the fragile reputation of the Church in the region. For Innocent had previously urged his legates to shun even the appearance of evil and continued to insist upon complete proof before the confiscation of Raymond's lands. Although the pope hailed Simon's election as an opportunity for fulfilling the goals of the *negotium pacis et fidei*, he maintained that the lands conquered from Raymond could not be permanently transferred to another person until his formal condemnation. By 1213, Innocent was urging his legates to defer the decision of Raymond's guilt and the disposition of the conquered lands to the ecumenical council which would meet in 1215.[24]

However, Innocent's legates clearly believed that they and councils composed of prelates local to the Midi (many of whom were recently appointed reformers) were competent to excommunicate Raymond and other lords and to impose the specific conditions required for their absolution and resumption of rulership.[25] Unlike Innocent, who was notoriously ready to forgive whomever unconditionally acknowledged papal authority,[26] his legates appear to have shared the views of Paris reformers connected to the anti-heretical crusade that nothing other than complete repentance, manifested in spurning every trace of one's former crimes and the willingness to fulfill whatever penance was imposed, could permit the rehabilitation of a former excommunicate such as Raymond. They refused to lift the excommunication laid upon Raymond and halt the confiscation of his lands until he had performed the onerous conditions laid upon him, just as Stephen Langton would attempt to insist that King John complete the restitution of damages done to ecclesiastics and regular religious in England before the interdict was lifted.[27]

---

[24] See note 23 above; Elaine Graham-Leigh, "Morts Suspectes et Justice Papale. Innocent III, les Trencavel et la réputation de l'église," in *La croisade albigeoise*, pp. 219–33, here pp. 222–32; Foreville, "Innocent III et la croisade," pp. 205–11; PL 216:151–54, 158–60; Karl Joseph von Hefele, *Histoire des conciles d'après les documents originaux*, trans. H. Leclerq, 22 parts in 11 vols. (Paris, 1907–73), 5.2:1316–98 and 1722–33; VDC 522–23, 2:215–17 and notes; William of Puylaurens, *Chronica* 34, ed. and trans. Jean Duvernoy (Paris, 1976), pp. 92–93; Stephan Kuttner and Antonio García y García, "A New Eyewitness Account of the Fourth Lateran Council," *Traditio* 20 (1964), 115–78, here pp. 124–25 and 138–43; Cheney, *Innocent III and England*, pp. 395–96; Foreville, "Innocent III et la croisade," pp. 213–16; Foreville, *Innocent III et la France*, pp. 328–30.

[25] For Raymond, see notes 14 and 23–24 above. For the insertion of reformers, see Thouzellier, *Catharisme*, pp. 243–44; Foreville, *Innocent III et la France*, pp. 174–80.

[26] For example, when John of England swore fealty to Innocent III and adopted the crusader's cross, Innocent accepted his *volte face* without hesitation. See Cheney, *Innocent III*, pp. 332–36, 338, 365–66, 374–75; Turner, *King John*, pp. 168–71, 233; Powicke, *Stephen Langton*, pp. 126–32; Warren, *King John*, pp. 209, 244–45.

[27] See notes 14, 23–24 and 26 above, and notes 28 and 61 below; James of Vitry, *Sermones in epistolas et evangelia dominicalia totius anni*, ed. Damianus a Ligno (Antwerp, 1575), pp. 703–5; Jessalynn Bird, "Reform or Crusade? Anti-Usury and Crusade Preaching during the Pontificate of Innocent III," in *Pope Innocent III and His World*, ed. John C. Moore (Aldershot, 1999), pp. 165–85, esp. pp. 169, 174, 177–81 (emphasis on restitution and penance before absolution); Turner, *King John*, pp. 166–72; Powicke, *Stephen Langton*, pp. 90, 104–5; Warren, *King John*, pp. 207–13; Cheney, *Innocent III*, pp. 330, 343–55, 368–69.

The Impact of Reformers' Image of the Just Ruler

Another important factor affecting the fate of those accused of fostering heresy in the Midi and those who wished to replace them was the image of the just ruler popularized by Paris reformers and their collaborators. Innocent III, his legates and Paris reformers considered the creation of peace and just secular government, the protection of ecclesiastical rights and property, and the cessation of inequitable taxes and tolls, internecine wars and fostering of mercenaries, heretics, usurers and Jews as essential both for the repression of heresy in the Midi and for the promotion and ultimate success of the crusade to the Holy Land. The Midi's ecclesiastics and noblemen must aid the Church in implementing this program.[28] Innocent's legates soon constructed a case against Raymond of Toulouse and other lords that was composed of charges calculated to incur the penalties laid out in the canonical authorities: failure to keep the oaths they swore to suppress heresy, keep the peace, give justice to their adversaries when requested, make restitution for past injuries and accomplish the conditions imposed for absolution from the excommunication they had incurred, including oaths to obey the Church's commands in all matters concerning the "business of the peace and of the faith."[29]

These charges were informed by the image of the ideal ruler presented by Innocent III, his legates, and Paris reformers promoting the Albigensian Crusade. In private conversations, court cases, letters, sermons, the confessional, and church councils, reformers reminded powerful men and knights (*milites*) of their duty to restrain evil, do justice and protect the Church and the poor, widows and orphans.[30] They ought to consult men learned in God's law (that is, canon lawyers and theologians) to exercise justice and punish their enemies with proper motives rather than indulging in vengeance, hatred or cruelty.[31] For evil rulers and knights broke the peace by fighting amongst themselves or rebelling against their superiors.

---

[28] On the *negotium fidei et pacis*, see note 9 above; VDC 6–7, 27–28, 55–66, 74–81, and *passim*, 1:5–7, 30–32, 51–65, 74–81, etc.; Marie-Humbert Vicaire, "'L'affaire de paix et de foi' du midi de la France," in *Paix de Dieu et Guerre Sainte en Languedoc au XIIIe siècle*, Cahiers de Fanjeaux 4 (Toulouse, 1969), pp. 102–27; Vicaire, *Saint Dominic*, pp. 62, 149, 298, 320–25, 334, 369–70, 375, 378–80, 462–63; Thouzellier, *Catharisme*, pp. 183–212; Catharine Thouzellier, "La légation en Lombardie du cardinal Hugolin (1221): un épisode de la cinquième croisade," *Revue d'histoire ecclésiastique* 45 (1990), 508–42; James M. Powell, *Anatomy of a Crusade, 1213–1221* (Philadelphia, 1986), pp. 33–50; Augustine Thompson, *Revival Preachers and Politics in Thirteenth-century Italy* (Oxford, 1992), pp. 83–135.

[29] See notes 14, 23–24 and 28 above, and notes 40 and 51 below; PL 214:537–39; PL 215:1166–68; PL 216:89–98; VDC 77, 137–39, 164, 195–96, 370–411, 1:77–78, 140–45, 167–69, 196–99, 2:69–105; Mansi, *Concilia*, 22:793–94, 815–16, 865–94; William of Tudela, *Chanson de la croisade*, laisses 58–61, 143–52, trans. Janet Shirley (Aldershot, 1996), pp. 37–39, 72–82 (hereafter Tudela).

[30] James of Vitry, *Sermo ad potentes et milites*, no. 51, in Douai, Bibliothèque Municipale, MS 503, fols. 374r–376v, here fol. 374r–v; idem, *Sermo ad potentes et milites*, no. 52, in Douai 503, 376v–379v, here fols. 377v–378r; Alan of Lille, *Sermo ad milites*, PL 210:186.

[31] James of Vitry, *Sermo ad potentes et milites*, no. 51, in Douai 503, fols. 374r–375v.

Dissatisfied with lawful and time-honored revenues, they persecuted the poor by levying additional new taxes, tolls and exactions. They fostered brigands, Jews, and usurers and perverted the course of justice by oppressing the poor and accepting bribes. They attacked God by detaining tithes, offerings and other possessions of the Church, infringing upon ecclesiastical immunities and liberties, harassing or assaulting clergymen, ignoring sanctuary and committing sacrilegious theft.[32] In contrast, the ideal knight provided a refuge for the poor and powerless and humbly obeyed the prelates and doctors of the Church, defending it against the wolves of tyrants, heretics, pagans, schismatics and other enemies of the faith of Christ while expelling usurers and other harmful or criminal men from his lands.[33] Just and god-fearing, he devoted himself to confession, penance and the sacraments, made reparation to anyone he had wronged and gave additional alms for his sins to the poor, widows, orphans and religious houses. When death threatened, he sought out the body and blood of Christ and arranged for alms and prayers to lighten his penance and speed him through purgatory, as purportedly had a knight who fought under Charlemagne in Spain, who deeded his horse and arms to the poor.[34]

Dependent upon renewed papal authorization of the crusade indulgence and the financial support and recruits provided by the Cistercian order and prelates and masters from northern France who often accompanied him in his campaigns, Simon de Montfort appears to have done his best to live up to their image of the ideal ruler. The historian Peter of Vaux-de-Cernay carefully contrasted Simon's devotion to the eucharist, confession and prayer to the anticlericalism and sacrilege of the *routiers* associated with Raymond of Toulouse and the count of Foix. Similarly, he depicted a victorious Simon donating his horse and weapons to the poor after the battle of Muret.[35] In a series of statutes composed at Pamiers (1212), Simon sought to reassure legates, reformers and the local populace that he would adhere to the very stipulations which Raymond had not. He would subject his new lands to the authority of the Church, suppress heresy and keep the peace. He and his knights would live from their rents and stipends rather than imposing immoderate exactions on their subjects in the form of rapine, unjust tallages and tolls. They would preserve churches, their tithes and privileges, protect clergymen, the poor, widows and orphans and provide due justice. They would abolish Sunday markets, impose an inheritance tax on merchants and usurers, mandate church attendance, and expel

---

[32] James of Vitry, ibid., fol. 375v; idem, *Sermo ad potentes et milites*, no. 52, in Douai 503, fols. 378r–379r; idem, *Sermo ad potentes et milites*, no. 53, in Douai 503, fol. 381r–v; Alan of Lille, *Sermo ad milites*, PL 210:186.

[33] James of Vitry, *Sermo ad dolentes*, no. 46, in Douai 503, fols. 360v–363v, here fol. 361v; idem, *Sermo ad potentes*, no. 52, in Douai 503, fol. 378r; idem, *Sermo ad potentes*, no. 53, Douai 503, fol. 380r–v; Philippe Buc, *L'Ambiguïté du livre: prince, pouvoir et peuple dans les commentaires de la Bible au moyen-âge* (Paris, 1994), pp. 213–24; Philip the Chancellor, Schneyer, no. 269, 4:837; Alan of Lille, *Sermo ad milites*, PL 210:186; and note 107 below.

[34] James of Vitry, *Sermo ad dolentes*, no. 45, Douai 503, fols. 357v–360v, here fols. 359v–360r.

[35] VDC 466, 2:157–58. For *routiers*, see notes 71 and 98 and discussion below.

prostitutes from towns. Many of these decrees appear to have been inspired by Paris-trained reformers attending the council: one measure requiring laypersons to return churches and tithes they were detaining was promptly enforced, partly because reformers believed that the material impoverishment of local churches directly affected their ability to provide the orthodox pastoral care deemed essential for combating heresy.[36]

In fact, it was under the aegis of his duty to keep the peace that Simon extended his campaigns into areas not originally targeted by the crusade. He infiltrated the Agenais, Périgord, Quercy and diocese of Rodez with the aid of local bishops who, as they had in other regions, invited him to invade their dioceses in order to establish peace and eliminate "traitors" and harborers of *routiers* and heretics who attacked the Church.[37] These lands included possessions of subjects of John of England and Peter of Aragon. Peter soon charged Simon with unjustly shedding innocent blood and usurping possessions by attacking the lands of his vassals who were free from heresy, thereby injuring him and impeding his ability to fight the Saracens in Spain. Simon ought to restore the lands lest he seem to be working more for personal advantage than the defense of the Catholic faith.[38] Innocent swiftly rebuked Simon and his legate Arnaud Amaury for exceeding their papal authorization and sullying the crusade by stretching avaricious hands towards lands untainted by heresy. Moreover, he ordered Simon to make restitution to Peter's vassals, whom he had unjustly attacked.[39] At the council of Lavaur, however, local prelates, papal legates and Paris-trained and Cistercian reformers drafted a dossier of charges against Peter and his vassals which they sent to Rome, stressing the scandal which would arise if the pope canceled the crusade in the Midi and returned the land bought with so much Christian blood to "tyrants" or their heirs. Under Simon, heretics and *routiers* were being suppressed and the Church of God restored, but evil men harbored by the count of Foix and other southern noblemen were planning an alliance with Otto in Germany and Muslims in Spain, which threatened the downfall of all Christendom. In response to the legation, which included William, archdeacon of Paris, Innocent gave his permission for new indulgences to be promulgated should the counts of Foix and Toulouse prove obstinate to legal or penitential reconciliation.[40]

Yet the king of Aragon was not the only person to turn the canon law arguments and sermons of recruiters and legates against them. Guillaume le Clerc used a

---

[36] See note 96 below; Pamiers (1212), in Mansi, *Concilia*, 22:855–64; Jean-Louis Biget, "La dépossession des seigneurs méridionaux: modalités limites, portée," in *La croisade albigeoise*, pp. 261–99, here p. 269. Compare Avignon (1209), in Mansi, *Concilia*, 22:783–94; PL 216:89–98, 151–53, 690–94.

[37] VDC 246–47, 487–89, 509–10, 516, 519, 528, 532–34, 537, 541, 1:245–47, 2:179–83, 205–6, 212–15, 222–23, 227–29, 230–32, 235–36.

[38] Peter and his advisors were here invoking the concept that just motives rather than ambition or greed must mark the conduct of a just war. See PL 216:739–43; Russell, *Just War*, pp. 196–97.

[39] PL 216:739–40.

[40] VDC 367–418, 2:65–95, 110; PL 216:833–52; Foreville, *Innocent III et la France*, pp. 235–37.

sermon on the parable of the wheat and the tares of a noted patron of reformers from Peter the Chanter's circle – Maurice of Sully, bishop of Paris – to argue that the Albigensian Crusade was no just war. The pope ought to use exhortation and spiritual sanctions to rehabilitate penitents such as Raymond of Toulouse rather than branding them as heretics and declaring their lands open to invasion; a criticism echoed by William of Tudela's continuator. Moreover, the crusaders' conduct was worse than that of their "heretical" opponents.[41] Guilhem de Mur similarly contrasted the pure motives of crusaders who sought to free the Holy Land with the anti-heretical crusaders' dispossession of fellow-Christians, which he claimed could not lead to salvation.[42] For William of Tudela's continuator, the unjust seizure of another man's lands under the pretence of a crusade debased the law.[43] He depicts a "master Robert," a citizen of Toulouse, warning Simon de Montfort that, as the papally appointed leader of the crusade, he ought to remain bound by reason and the law. He ought not to sack the city of Toulouse unless the accusation of treason he had brought against it was first proven by legal means.[44] The continuator also criticized the Albigensian Crusade for undermining the *paratge* system, and made one of Simon's former supporters lament that he wished that he had followed his own path to salvation and honestly saved his soul rather than believing clergymen's lies that driving out his own lord was good service to his spiritual lord, Christ.[45] On the other hand, the poetess Gormonda used terms from papal letters and recruiting sermons to

---

[41]   Charles A. Robson, *Maurice of Sully and the Medieval Vernacular Homily* (Oxford, 1952), p. 45; Guillaume le Clerc, *Le Besant de Dieu* vv. 1584–776, 2387–99, 2485–90, 2501–7, ed. Pierre Ruelle (Brussels, 1973), pp. 110–16, 131–33. The parable of the wheat and the tares (Matt. 13.24–30) was a key authority in arguments for and against the prosecution of heretics. Some argued that, as in the parable, the tares ought to be allowed to grow with the wheat until the final judgment. While clergymen ought to advise secular leaders to wield the sword against evildoers, they ought only to excommunicate (not execute) individuals after they had been condemned by due process (that is, by full proof of their guilt or their legal confession) and given an opportunity to repent, lest the innocent be unjustly condemned. Others argued against this position. For example, Caesarius of Heisterbach and Robert of Auxerre claimed that anti-heretical preaching had failed and the tares were taking over the wheat to such an extent that all Europe would have been corrupted if not for intervention with the material sword. See PL 214:695, 788–89, 793–95; PL 215:358–59, 526; PL 216:1210; Robert Courson, *Summa* 30.1, 4, 7–8, BN Lat. 14524, fols. 105rb–106rb, 107ra–rb; Caesarius of Heisterbach, *Dialogus Miraculorum* 5.21, ed. Joseph Strange, 2 vols. (Cologne, 1851), 1:300–302 (hereafter DM); Robert of Auxerre, *Chronicon*, RHGF 18:279; VDC 5, 1:5; James of Vitry, *Sermo ad fratres ordinis militaris*, no. 38, ed. Pitra, 2:419; James of Vitry, *Sermones in epistolas*, pp. 179–83; Kienzle, *Cistercians*, pp. 95, 100–101, 104–5, 166; Beryl Smalley, *The Gospels in the Schools, c.1100–c.1280* (London, 1985), pp. 109–10; Beryl Smalley, "The Gospels in the Paris Schools in the Late Twelfth and Early Thirteenth Centuries: Peter the Chanter, Hugh of Saint Cher, Alexander of Hales, John of La Rochelle," *Franciscan Studies* 39 (1979), 230–54 and 40 (1980), 298–369, here pp. 240–41; note 14 above and note 120 below. For William of Tudela, see Tudela, laisses 208, 212, pp. 176, 188 and discussion below.

[42]   Guilhem de Mur, "D'un sirventes far," ed. Carl Appel, in *Provenzalische inedita aus Pariser Handschriften*, Altfranzösische Bibliothek 13 (Leipzig, 1892), pp. 144–46.

[43]   See notes 44 and 51 below; Tudela, laisses 142–53, 191, 202, 208–9, pp. 72–83, 143, 165–66, 176, 179.

[44]   Tudela, laisses 132–34, 169, 170, 172, pp. 66–67, 102, 105, 107.

[45]   Tudela, laisses 137, 154, 161, pp. 68, 85, 92–93.

defend the anti-heretical crusade against assorted naysayers. Raymond and the citizens of Toulouse had forfeited their lands by refusing to suppress heretics who posed a greater threat to Christendom than the geographically distant Saracens. The defeat of the Fifth Crusade before Damietta and Louis VIII's death were not divine judgment upon the greed of pseudo-crusaders, as some had insinuated. Rather, the anti-heretical crusade was a valid form of martyrdom and penance, and those who came to the Midi to combat heresy earned a true indulgence.[46]

Innocent's legates also proved stubborn regarding the disposition of the lands conquered by anti-heretical crusaders. While still teaching in Paris, and almost certainly mindful of events during the recent Fourth Crusade, Robert Courson had argued that the papal ability to judge the justness of a war could be impaired by Rome's distance from the events in question. In this case, a legate or local prelate could delay the implementation of a papal order or respect the intent rather than the written word of instructions from Rome because the pope would inevitably change his mind once he was better informed of the situation.[47] As his colleague and fellow teacher Stephen Langton did during various crises in England, Robert followed his own advice. As legate for the crusade in France, he ignored Innocent III's command to postpone any disposition of the lands in question until the Fourth Lateran Council met in 1215. In 1214, he formally granted to Simon de Montfort and his heirs all the lands conquered in the south of France. A council at Montpellier (1215) composed of local prelates soon seconded Robert's decision by electing Simon lord over the disputed territory. However, Peter Beneventano, the papal legate and famed lawyer overseeing the council, stuck to papal instructions and maintained that he could not grant the lands to Simon without the pope's express permission and the sanction of the upcoming ecumenical council. The prelates therefore sent a delegation to Rome seeking papal confirmation of their selection.[48] Explaining his decision at Livrade (1214) in terms derived from *Ad abolendam*, Robert argued that the disputed lands

---

[46] Elizabeth Siberry, *Criticism of Crusading, 1095–1274* (Oxford, 1985), p. 167; Palmer A. Throop, *Criticism of the Crusade: A Study of Public Opinion and Crusade Propaganda* (Amsterdam, 1940; repr. Philadelphia, 1975), p. 45; Gormonda de Montpellier, "Greu m'es a durar," 7.67–8.88, 10.100–11.121, 14.145–15.165, 17.177–87, ed. Vincenzo de Bartholomaeis, in *Poesie provenzali storiche relative all'Italia*, 2 vols. (Rome, 1931), 2:108–11; notes 42 above and 85 below. For alternative editions and translations of this poem, see Matilda T. Bruckner, Laurie Shepard and Sarah White, eds. and trans., *Songs of the Women Troubadours* (New York, 1995), pp. 106–19; Katharina Städtler, "The *Sirventes* by Gormonda de Montpellier," in *The Voice of the Trobairitz: Perspectives on Women Troubadours*, ed. W. D. Paden (Philadelphia, 1989), pp. 129–55, here pp. 130–37.

[47] Robert Courson, *Summa* 26.10, BN Lat. 14524, fols. 92rb–93ra; Powicke, *Stephen Langton*, pp. 131–32, 138–41; Cheney, *Innocent III*, pp. 371–81.

[48] Innocent retained his previous position that suspect individuals ought to be reconciled to the Church if possible and a final decision reserved for the ecumenical council. See the discussion and note 12 above; PL 216:958–60; Alexandre Teulet et al., eds., *Layettes de trésor des chartes*, 5 vols. (Paris, 1863–66; repr. Nendeln, 1977), 1:409–10, no. 1099; MPM, 1:214, note 57; VDC 542–48, 2:236–41; Mansi, *Concilia*, 22:935–54; Austin P. Evans, "The Albigensian Crusade," in *Crusades*, 2:227–324, here pp. 304–5, 306–7; Foreville, *Innocent III et la France*, p. 269. For Peter Beneventano's decisive intervention in military and diplomatic matters, see, for example, VDC 503, 550–67, 2:196–98, 242–58.

had been possessed by heretics and their defenders who had been faithless in their promises of obedience to the Church and Simon, had used mercenaries, and had fostered heresy and usury. After Innocent III had declared the lands of such men open to invasion, Simon had occupied them at the express command of papal legates (including Robert himself) and had restored order like a dutiful and catholic prince.[49]

Robert had previously taken steps at the council of Bordeaux (1214) to stem John of England's resistance to the anti-heretical crusade's expansion to the Agenais and Périgord, an opposition which threatened to prolong the Albigensian Crusade and thereby endangered the crusade for the Holy Land which Robert was responsible for organizing. In order to strengthen Simon's military position before the final disposition of lands at the Fourth Lateran Council, Robert appears to have supported Simon's annexation of further territory in these regions, perhaps justifying his decision by the fact that, like his son-in-law Raymond VI, John had been excommunicated for his depredations upon the Church and had faced the prospect of the papal revocation of his vassals' oaths of fidelity before taking the crusader's cross to earn legal protection and credence with Innocent III. Certainly, John's support for his son-in-law damaged his reputation as ruler in England and led many of his vassals to boycott a royal muster intended to aid Raymond in 1213. Hostile English chroniclers seized upon John's association with heretics to portray him as allied with the Moors in Spain; the Dunstaple annalist claimed that some English barons even contemplated deposing John and replacing him with the impeccably orthodox Simon de Montfort. Aware of his precarious situation, the king negotiated extensively with Robert in person and through representatives and letters. He stressed his willingness to obey papal and legatine commands, offered to place royal possessions in Agen, Cahors, the Toulousain and other regions under papal and legatine custody, and to lend whatever assistance required to drive heretics from those regions and bring them before the legate for judgment. In return, he asked that nothing be done to prejudice the rights of himself or his vassals in these regions, a request whose grant Robert reserved for Innocent III himself. Perhaps at Robert's suggestion, John also arranged for money to be secretly sent to Simon de Montfort, conceivably as a form of reparation for his former support for Raymond. John's offer to play the role of the orthodox ruler dutifully aiding the Church in suppressing heresy not only successfully prevented the crusaders from extending their campaigns into the Aquitaine and Gascony, but, in the aftermath of the battle of Bouvines (1214), ensured Robert's crucial mediation in securing a truce between John and Philip Augustus under terms relatively favorable to the vanquished king of England.[50]

---

[49] HGL 8:653–56, no. 177.

[50] See Vincent, "England and the Albigensian Crusade," pp. 74–77, 96–97; Claire Taylor, "Pope Innocent III, John of England and the Albigensian Crusade (1209–1216)," in *Pope Innocent III and his World*, ed. Moore, pp. 205–28, esp. pp. 208–14, 219–21; Powell, *Anatomy*, pp. 33–38; MPM, 1:21–22;

Similarly, Innocent III's desire to promote the peace and stability essential for a crusade to the Holy Land and to enable the suppression of heresy through a strong orthodox ruler shaped the final ruling of the Fourth Lateran Council, which many reformers and Paris masters attended. Although John of England's chancellor presented a strong legal case that the Agenais, as the dowry of Raymond VII's mother, was his to inherit even if he could not inherit his father's lands, bishops from the Languedoc may have cornered Innocent in the Lateran gardens and threatened to revolt if he did not uphold their decision at Montpellier to grant the lands appropriated by crusaders to Simon. In the end, Innocent ceded the majority of the territory seized by the crusaders to Simon as a fief held from Philip Augustus.[51]

Propaganda and the Popular Justification of the Albigensian Crusade

In common with their predecessors during the Fourth Crusade, Paris reformers and their prelatial and Cistercian colleagues played key roles not only in justifying the new anti-heretical crusade in newsletters, councils, courts, and Rome itself, but in sermons delivered to potential recruits and actual participants. Worries about the moral purity of the crusading army, and the fact that its goal was the suppression of heresy, removed any lingering doubts concerning the participation of clergy; their presence was considered essential to define and combat heresy while preserving the army from contamination. Preachers and prelates accompanying the anti-heretical armies participated in military councils and strove to convince their recruits of the justness of their enterprise through preaching, liturgy and battlefield exhortations.[52]

The Paris circle's influence was felt from the very outset of the anti-heretical crusade, partly as a result of their involvement in the preceding Fourth Crusade. For the abbot of Saint-Victor (a canonry with numerous ties to Paris masters) had joined Guy of Vaux-de-Cernay, Nivelon, bishop of Soissons, and Odo of Sully, bishop of Paris, as part of a papal commission charged with aiding the Paris-educated legate Peter Capuano in co-ordinating recruitment for the Fourth Crusade in northern France, collecting the clerical income tax instituted for it, and commuting the penance of persons desiring to aid the Holy Land to alms. For the latter task, the commission was urged to consult prudent men, presumably the canons of Saint-Victor and Paris-trained moral theologians who specialized in thorny penitential

---

Dickson and Dickson, "Cardinal Robert de Courson," pp. 92–93, 105–8; VDC 522, 2:215–16, and note 4. For the Council of Bordeaux (1214), see Mansi, *Concilia*, 22:931–34; Rymer, *Foedera*, 1.1:121–22; VDC 522, 2:216–17 and notes; MPM, 1:20; Dickson and Dickson, "Cardinal Robert de Courson," pp. 100, 141; and note 12 above.

[51] See note 24 above; Taylor, "Pope Innocent III," pp. 225–27; Tudela, laisses 142–53, pp. 72–83, VDC 522–23, 555–58, 2:215–17, 248–52; William of Puylaurens, *Chronica*, pp. 92–93; Anonymous, *Histoire de la Guerre des Albigeois* 31 in RHGF 19:156–60; Kuttner and García y García, "Eyewitness," pp. 124–25 and 138–43.

[52] See note 7 above; Tudela, laisses 13, 21, pp. 17, 21; and the discussion below.

cases. The commission had also supported the revivalist preaching of various Paris masters (including Fulk of Neuilly and perhaps Robert Courson) and their monastic colleagues for the crusade. Instructed by Innocent III to set an indulgence for the new anti-heretical crusade and to organize recruitment and taxation for it, Odo of Sully almost certainly consulted the theologians of Paris before he offered the plenary indulgence associated with the eastern crusade in return for forty days' service in the Midi and mobilizing his diocesan priests to publicize the crusade.[53] Odo's successor Peter, the brother of the Paris master and recruiter William, archdeacon of Paris, soon reaffirmed this grant through liturgical prayers and masses meant to earn divine favor for the crusade through creating an atmosphere of moral renewal in the home front.[54] By the final crusade of Louis VIII, the liturgy had broadened to daily prayers during the mass and processions were held in Paris to beseech the divine aid of Christ, the Virgin Mary and the saints.[55] The language of just war and pre-battle liturgies involving penitential fasts, confession, masses and the use of standards incorporating the cross or saint as a reminder that heavenly patrons were fighting on behalf of one's just cause were never confined strictly to the crusades alone.[56] These rituals aided enormously in reaffirming the

---

[53] Jessalynn Bird, "The Victorines, Peter the Chanter's Circle, and the Crusade: Two Unpublished Crusading Appeals in Paris, Bibliothèque Nationale, MS Latin 14470," *Medieval Sermon Studies* 48 (2004), 5–28; Alberic of Troisfontaines, *Chronicon*, ed. P. Scheffer-Boichorst, MGH SS 23:631–950, here pp. 877–78; Robert of Auxerre, *Chronicon*, ed. Othmar Holder-Egger, MGH SS 26:216–87, here pp. 257, 272–73; PL 215:1361–62; Odette Pontal, ed., *Les statuts synodaux français du XIIIe siècle. Vol. I. Les statuts de Paris et le synodal de l'ouest (XIIIe siècle)*, Collections de documents inédits sur l'histoire de France 9 (Paris, 1971), 1:45, 81, 88–89 (hereafter Pontal). For other surviving sermons from this period, see Nicole Bériou, *L'Avènement des maîtres de la parole. La prédication à Paris au XIIIe siècle*, 2 vols., Études Augustiniennes 31–32 (Paris, 1998), 1:58–63, 67–69, 95–96, 143–45, 2:681–86. For the development of the indulgence in the letters of Innocent III for the Albigensian crusade, from initial offers of an indulgence equivalent to the pilgrimage to Rome or Compostella to the plenary indulgence originally reserved for the eastern crusades, see Roscher, *Papst Innocenz III*, pp. 222–31, 233; Foreville, *Innocent III et la France*, pp. 251–59.

[54] Pontal, 1:96–97. For sermons from this period, see note 53 above.

[55] Both Christoph Maier and Nicole Bériou have argued that a liturgy for the crusade was instituted only during the crusade of Louis VIII. However, there is some evidence that prayers and diocesan recruiting were instituted in the diocese of Paris at an earlier date. See notes 53–54 above; Nicole Bériou, "Le prédication de croisade de Philippe le Chancelier et d'Eudes de Châteauroux en 1226," in *Le prédication en Pays d'Oc (XIIe–début XVe siècle)*, Cahiers de Fanjeaux 32 (Toulouse, 1997), pp. 85–109, here pp. 93–95; Christoph T. Maier, "Crisis, Liturgy and the Crusade in the Twelfth and Thirteenth Centuries," *Journal of Ecclesiastical History* 48 (1997), 628–57, here pp. 640–41, 644–46, 650, 656; Philip the Chancellor, Schneyer, no. 269, 4:837; idem, *Sermo de eodem*, Schneyer, no. 271, 4:837; idem, *Sermo ... apud Sanctum Victorem in processione pro rege Ludovico quando erat ante Avinionem*, Schneyer, no. 328, 4:842; Odo of Châteauroux, *Sermo contra hereticos de Albigensibus partibus*, Schneyer, no. 863, 4:464.

[56] Michael McCormick, *Eternal Victory: Triumphal Rulership in Late Antiquity, Byzantium and the Early Medieval West* (Cambridge, 1986); "Militia Christi" e crociata nei secoli XI–XIII. Atti della undecima settimana internazionale di studio, Mendola, 28 agosto–1 settembre, 1989, Miscellanea del Centro di studi medioevali, 13 (Milan, 1992); D. S. Bachrach, *Religion and the Conduct of War, c. 300–1215* (Rochester, 2003); Baldwin, *Government of Philip Augustus*, pp. 215–16; Georges Duby,

religious identity and unity of the crusaders while depicting the "otherness" of their opponents, whether they were evil Christians, schismatics, infidels, pagans, or heretics.[57]

Prior to the Battle of Muret in 1213, for example, a mass to the Virgin Mary was used to create a cohesive identity between Simon and his men as members of the body of Christ even as the counts of Toulouse, Foix and Comminges and their allies (including by implication Peter of Aragon) were solemnly excommunicated to illustrate their complete excision from Christendom and God's favor. During the offertory, Simon dramatically offered himself and his weapons to God in reciprocation of Christ's redemptive work on the cross recapitulated in the mass. After confession and prayer, the army was ordered into three battle lines, a reminder of their commission to protect the concept of the Trinity from heretical assault. The bishop of Comminges signed the host with a crucifix and assured them that he would act as their guarantor on the Day of Judgment that all who died that day would escape purgatory and fly straight to heaven as martyrs, provided that they had or intended to confess their sins.[58] Knights and clergymen alike reminded the army on other occasions of the fame and indulgences awaiting those who emulated Christ's salvific sacrifice in defense of the faith, recounting tales of individuals meeting with glorious martyrdom in battle, the stock-in-trade of chivalric literature and recruiters for various crusades.[59] Critics of the anti-heretical crusade were familiar with these arguments and claimed in their turn that the indulgence offered to the anti-heretical warriors was null and void because their actions were unjust, and their motives were avarice and the disinheritance of others by any means. Those who died in battle were not glorified martyrs, but rather unrepentant and unshriven sinners bound for hellfire. Guilhem Figueira went so far as to accuse preachers who offered "false pardons" for the Albigensian Crusade of luring Louis VIII and many barons to their deaths in the Midi.[60]

The Legend of Bouvines: War, Religion and Culture in the Middle Ages, trans. Catherine Tihanyi (Cambridge, 1990), pp. 113–15, 119–21, 130–34; William the Breton, Philippidos 10.759–90, 12.190–344, in Henri-François Delaborde, ed., Oeuvres de Rigord et de Guillaume le Breton, 2 vols. (Paris, 1885), 2:305–8, 313–14, 359.

[57] See notes 7 and 56 above; VDC 297, 1:291.

[58] See note 59 below; VDC 453–54, 457–58, 461–62, 2:144–71, 149, 151–53; James of Vitry, Historia Occidentalis, ed. John F. Hinnebusch, Spicilegium Friburgense 17 (Fribourg, 1972), p. 177. For a similar scenario, see VDC 606–9, 2:308–13.

[59] Tudela, laisses 33, 95, 1:26, 52; VDC 272, 284, 1:268–69, 280; Anonymous, Brevis ordinacio de predicacione crucis, in Reinhold Röhricht, ed., Quinti belli sacri scriptores minores (Geneva, 1879), pp. 3–26, here pp. 24–26; compare Itinerarium Peregrinorum et gesta regis Ricardi, in William Stubbs, ed., Chronicles and memorials of the reign of Richard I, 2 vols., RS 38 (London, 1864), 1:97–109; Christoph T. Maier, ed., Crusade Propaganda and Ideology: Model Sermons for the Preaching of the Cross (Cambridge, 2000), pp. 60–61, 112–18; DM 10.12, 2:226–27; and note 71 below.

[60] Tudela, laisses 8, 30, 158–62, 169–70, 189–93, 206, 208, pp. 14–15, 25, 89–95, 102, 105, 134–37, 145, 173, 176; "I saw the World." Sixty Poems from Walther von Vogelweide (1170–1228), trans. Ian G. Colvin (London, 1938), no. 56, pp. 95–96; Guilhem Figueira, "D'un sirventes far," ed. Bartholomaeis, 2:98–104; Throop, Criticism, pp. 33–37, 41–43; Siberry, Criticism, pp. 158–68.

Faced with preventing the army's crusader identity from being eroded by the fact that their opponents were technically fellow Christians, clergymen focused on the heretics' attacks on orthodox beliefs, including Christ's incarnation, his redemptive work and its dissemination through the sacraments, the doctrine of purgatory, and indulgences. They used detailed explanations and graspable images to defend and popularize the doctrine of purgatory, the salvific nature of confession, penance and the aid available through the eucharist and the suffrages of the Church. These were linked to the crusade, which they portrayed as an act of the utmost Christianity and orthodoxy in imitation of Christ's own sacrifice.[61] Preachers were thus able to simultaneously portray the anti-heretical crusade as an attractive route to redemption while painting heretics as the worst kind of threat to Christendom and the Church, body and soul. The crusader's cross delivered him from the ravages of sin; it was the sign of the elect that differentiated the orthodox crusader from sinners and heretics, and a talisman which not only symbolized the spiritual and temporal privileges granted to him, but protected him from spiritual and physical harm. The point was driven home in numerous *exempla* featuring crusaders preserved by their cloth crosses from natural disasters, the assaults of demons or their heretical opponents.[62]

Preachers also stressed that attempts to convert pious-seeming heretics through preaching had failed. Similar to leprosy, cancer or gangrene, heretics threatened to contaminate all of Christendom by striking at the head of the Church – Christ and the faith. It was the duty of the faithful to save the remaining members of the Church by using force to amputate the source of corruption from the body politic. Co-existence was impossible; if the sheeplike populace wanted to end their war with the heretical wolves by ignoring their guardian sheepdogs (the prelates), the wolves would

---

[61] Paris, Bibliothèque Nationale, MS Latin 14859, fols. 233r–234r; Newman, *Boundaries*, pp. 187–89; Bird, "Victorines," 5–28; Bird, "Construction of Orthodoxy," pp. 45–62; James of Vitry, *Sermones feriales et communes*, in Université de Liège, Bibliothèque Générale, MS 347, fols. 138va–145vb, 146rb–148vb; *Brevis ordinacio*, pp. 3–12; Tudela, laisse 34, p. 26; J. Longère, *Oeuvres oratoires de maîtres parisiens au XIIe siècle*, 2 vols. (Paris, 1975), 1:423 and 2:326, notes 124–25; Alan of Lille, *De fide catholica contra hereticos* 1.1–76, in PL 210:305–78; James of Vitry, *Sermones in epistolas*, pp. 117–18; James of Vitry, *Vita Mariae Oigniacensis*, ed. Damien van Papenbroeck, AA SS June 23, vol. 5 (Antwerp, 1707), pp. 636–66; VDC 5, 12–54, 1:5, 12–49; DM 3.15–17, 21, 1:130–34, 136–37; A. Hilka, *Die Wundergeschichten des Caesarius von Heisterbach*, 3 vols. (Bonn, 1933–37), 3:91–93; Maier, *Propaganda*, pp. 84–88, 102–12. On miraculous hosts used by recruiters, see DM 9.2–3, 2:167–69; Hilka, *Wundergeschichte*, 3:20–21. For anecdotes on the power of confession and the priestly keys, see Stephen of Bourbon, *Tractatus de diversis materiis praedicabilis*, in *Anécdotes historiques, légends et apologues tirés du recueil inédit d'Étienne de Bourbon, Dominicain du XIIIe siècle*, ed. Albert Lecoy de la Marche (Paris, 1877), §174, pp. 153–54; DM 3.14–17, 1:130–34.

[62] See note 61 above and note 71 below; Robert of Auxerre, *Chronicon*, MGH SS 26:275; VDC 144, 1:150; Gervase of Prémontré, *Epistolae* 42–43, ed. C. L. Hugo, in *Sacrae antiquitatis monumenta historica, dogmatica, diplomatica*, 2 vols. (Étival, 1725), 1:41–43; Bird, "Victorines," pp. 23–25; Odo of Châteauroux, *Sermo de cruce et de invitatione ad crucem*, Schneyer, no. 604, 4:443; idem, *Sermo ad invitandum ad crucem*, Schneyer, no. 700=909, 4:451, 468; Philip the Chancellor, *Dicit Dominus ad Moysen*, Schneyer, no. 298, 4:839; compare *Itinerarium peregrinorum*, ed. Stubbs, p. 107.

devour them.[63] In a crusading bull of 1208, Innocent III similarly welded the image of the little foxes ruining the vineyard of the Church to that of the parable of the ungrateful tenants. Papal legates and preachers were the workers sent to trap the foxes and had been beaten, despoiled and finally killed by the evil inhabitants of the region. Peter of Castelnau assumed the christological overtones of the last messenger, martyred by that most ungrateful tenant of all, the count of Toulouse, whose crimes and failure to reconcile himself to the Church were rehearsed in detail. Those kindled with zeal for avenging just blood which cried out to heaven and a desire to stop those who attacked the peace and truth, body and soul, would earn a full remission of sins.[64] Similarly, when the Paris master Odo of Châteauroux was preaching the anti-heretical crusade ca. 1226, he alluded to an episode frequently cited in discussions of just wars: the defeat of the tribes of Israel in a divinely mandated war against the Benjamites, who had harbored the murderers of a Levite's defiled and butchered spouse. Like a faithless wife, the Albigensian church had deserted Christ her spouse and refused to return to him despite years of attempts to woo her back. It was because the Albigensians were already bad Christians that they had fallen prey to the heretics' teachings; they were not innocent victims.[65] Chronicle evidence confirms that these themes were particularly effective in persuading audiences to participate in the anti-heretical crusade.[66]

Traditionally, preachers for the eastern crusades had also exploited the massacre of eastern Christians and the desecration of the Holy Land or the relic of the True Cross to conjure up feelings of anger, shame and vengeance and to exhort their audiences to act as Christ's loyal vassals by avenging his injuries and recovering his unjustly seized patrimony.[67] Similarly, recruiters for the anti-heretical crusade borrowed from Holy Land propaganda techniques in using biblical images of desecration and defilement to incite their audiences to follow the example of various Old Testament warriors in not resting until all the pagan inhabitants polluting the chosen land (in this case, Christendom) had been slain.[68] These exemplars were also meant to reaffirm the identity of the crusaders as God's chosen people, the

---

[63] PL 215:1246–48; James of Vitry, *Sermones communes et feriales*, Liège 347, fols. 147ra–148va–b; DM 5.21, 1:300–302; VDC 5, 12, 20–26, 47–51, 1:5, 12–13, 21–29, 41–46; Philip the Chancellor, Schneyer, nos. 269, 271, 328, 4:837; idem, *Sermo de eodem*, Scheyer no. 270, 4:837; Maier, *Propaganda*, p. 90; Bird, "Construction of Orthodoxy," pp. 46–47.

[64] This bull was known to Robert Courson and other Paris masters. See PL 215:1354–60, 1545–46; VDC 55–65, 1:51–65; note 112 below.

[65] Odo of Châteauroux, Schneyer, no. 863, 4:464.

[66] VDC 81, 1:80–81 and *passim*; Odo Rigord, *Gesta Philippi Augusti*, ed. Delaborde, *Oeuvres*, 1:1–167, here p. 167; Renier of Liège, *Annales Sancti Jacobi Leodiensis, 1066–1230*, ed. L. C. Bethmann, MGH SS 16:651–80, here pp. 663–64.

[67] See Penny Cole, *The Preaching of the Crusades to the Holy Land, 1095–1270* (Cambridge, MA, 1991); Maier, *Propaganda*, pp. 88, 90–94, 96–98.

[68] Mansi, *Concilia*, 22:1203–6; Gervase of Prémontré, *Epistolae*, no. 129, ed. Hugo, 1:115; Odo of Châteauroux, Schneyer, no. 863, 4:464; Philip the Chancellor, Schneyer, no. 269, 4:837; compare Maier, *Propaganda*, pp. 55–56, 94.

militia of Christ (*militia Christi*), an image familiar from the oldest conceptions of holy war.[69] Recruiters also utilized contemporary *exempla* confirming the refusal of heretics to convert[70] and bloodcurdling tales of atrocities committed by heretics and *routiers* sheltered by southern noblemen. Assaults upon Christ's ministers or fellow-Christians graphically manifested heretics' hatred for Christendom and Christ himself, re-crucified through verbal and physical attacks on the Virgin Mary, pilgrims, the consecrated host, crucifixes, relics, communion vessels, priests, monks, church ornaments and buildings.[71] Heretics' intellectual and physical attacks upon Christ's salvific work and the sacraments through which that work was administered to his people were the equivalent of the infidels' physical attacks upon the holy places; in fact they were worse. While the infidel killed Christians' bodies; heretics murdered both body and soul.[72] Many of these *exempla* also circulated among the crusading army, and some tales sought to reaffirm the efficacy of these orthodox symbols and the practices or persons they stood for by demonstrating their ability to avert or avenge assaults.[73]

Yet as the crusade dragged on, recruiters and advisors were forced to explain why such a just cause did not meet with immediate victory. Like Bernard of Clairvaux before them, they claimed that failure resulted from the sins of Christendom or the crusaders and that God was providing an extended opportunity for sinners to earn pardon by vindicating Christ's injuries.[74] Aware of contemporaries' criticism of the motives of the anti-heretical crusade, Paris-trained recruiters warned their audiences to take the cross for proper reasons, not from pride, fear of a superior, during a moment of danger, from desire for revenge and bloodshed, or an attempt to avoid paying debts or tithes. The cross should be taken in a state of contrition, of one's own free will, and in a spirit of compassion for the correction of sinners. One ought also to show an example of longsuffering and humility to others who would hasten to take

---

[69] Notes 56 and 68 above; VDC 276, 431, 1:271–72, 2:123, 3:xxxii–xxxiii and note 21; Roscher, *Papst Innocenz III*, p. 245; Gervase of Prémontré, *Epistolae*, no. 129, ed. Hugo, 1:115; Odo of Châteauroux, Schneyer, no. 863, 4:464; Philip the Chancellor, Schneyer, nos. 269–71, 328, 4:837, 842.

[70] E.g., VDC 22, 26, 51–54, 1:24–26, 28–29, 46–49; DM 5.18–25, 1:296–309.

[71] VDC 5, 10–19, 35, 40, 47, 52–53, 85–86, 89–91, 198–201, 203–7, 218–19, 223, 360–61, 382, 606–9, 1:5, 9–20, 34, 37–38, 46–47, 87–88, 90–92, 199–202, 203–4, 205–7, 217–19, 223, 2:59–61, 78–80, 308–13, 3:xxxvi–xxxvii, xciii; J. Berlioz, "*Exemplum* et histoire: Césaire de Heisterbach (v.1180–v.1240) et la croisade albigeoise," *Bibliothèque de l'École des chartes* 147 (1989), 49–86, here pp. 56–69; DM 5.21 and 7.21, 1:302–3, 2:31–33; Tudela, laisses 69–70, p. 42; James of Vitry, *Vita Mariae Oigniacensis*, p. 658; Robert of Auxerre, *Chronicon*, RHGF 18:279.

[72] See notes 62, 68 and 71 above. Compare DM 5.21, 1:303; *Itinerarium peregrinorum*, ed. Stubbs, p. 107; and VDC 40, 1:37–38; James of Vitry, *Sermones feriales*, Liège 347, fol. 146rb–vb; Carolyn Muessig, "Les sermons de Jacques de Vitry sur les cathares," in *La prédication en Pays d'Oc (XIIe–début XVe siècle)*, Cahiers de Fanjeaux 32 (Toulouse, 1997), pp. 69–83, esp. p. 72.

[73] See note 71 above; VDC 159, 223, 266–67, 499–500, 1:162–63, 223, 226–28, 2:190–92; Stephen of Bourbon, *Tractatus*, ed. Lecoy de la Marche, §328, pp. 277–78.

[74] PL 215:1545–46; VDC 109, 1:113–14; Philip the Chancellor, Schneyer, nos. 269–70, 4:837; Maier, *Propaganda*, pp. 96–98, 116; Cole, *Preaching*, pp. 47–61.

the cross if a powerful or learned or religious man does.[75] The powerful who were the target of crusading sermons ought to repent from their pride, pursuit of pleasure and depredation upon the poor and innocent, for God abhorred men of blood and those who refused to live up to the reformers' image of the ideal ruler and knight.[76]

After the failure of the Fifth Crusade, preachers were also forced to address criticisms that the anti-heretical crusade was siphoning off men and money needed for the Holy Land. Phillip the Chancellor grasped the bull by the horns and explained that recent crusades to the Holy Land had failed because of the West's sins. In order for the East to be re-won, heresy must first be eradicated to purify the West. Moreover, unlike the infidel, the heretics sought the spiritual corruption of the faithful; heresy was a peril graver than Islam itself. Although the East was sanctified as the place where Christ died, the faith which was the fruit of his passion ought to be defended at the expense of all else; the limbs must be risked to preserve the head of the faith, the Church.[77] Other Parisian and Cistercian recruiters also conflated or likened the danger of heresy to the Church and the faith to the threats posed by schismatics, pagans, the infidel and internecine wars. For example, the legate Arnaud Amaury and other members of the Cistercian order publicized the image that the Moors in Spain were colluding with the heretics in the Midi to overthrow all of Christendom.[78]

Paris Masters and the Financing of the Albigensian Crusade

Paris masters and their supporters also influenced the terms for debates regarding and the actual institution of the financial basis of the Albigensian crusade. Although they generally believed that the centralization and expansion of papal and royal

---

[75] Philip the Chancellor, Schneyer, no. 271, 4:837.

[76] Philip the Chancellor specifically mentions seeking gain, giving bad advice, anticlericalism, tithe-retention, taking bribes, and cheating poor and orphans rather than doing justice (Schneyer, nos. 298, 328, 4:839, 842).

[77] Philip the Chancellor, Schneyer, nos. 269–70, 4:837.

[78] See notes 3, 18 and 41 above; Joachim of Fiore, *Expositio in Apocalypsim* (Venice, 1527; repr. Frankfurt, 1964), fols. 134rb–135ra, 145va–vb; James of Vitry, *Historia Occidentalis*, pp. 73–74; James of Vitry, *Sermones de sanctis*, Douai 503, fols. 133r–134v (sermon on saints Simon and Jude, incipit: *Stelle manentes in ordine et cursu suo*, Schneyer, no. 269, 3:203); DM 5.21, 1:303; PL 215:453–61; PL 216:699–703; *Annals of Margam*, in Henry R. Luard, ed., *Annales Monastici*, 5 vols., RS 36 (London, 1857–69), 1:32; VDC 395–97, 440, 2:92–95, 132; *Annales Coloniensis maximi ab O.C. – 1237*, ed. Karl Pertz, MGH SS 17:723–847, here p. 826; Oliver of Paderborn, *Historia regum terrae sancte* 114, ed. Hermann Hoogeweg, in *Die Schriften des Kölner Domscholasters, späteren Bischofs von Paderborn und Kardinalbischofs von S. Sabina Oliverus*, Bibliothek des literarischen Vereins 202 (Tübingen, 1894), pp. 80–158, here pp. 157–58; RHGF 19:250–54; Jessalynn Bird, "Crusade and Conversion after the Fourth Lateran Council (1215): Oliver of Paderborn's and James of Vitry's Missions to Muslims Reconsidered," *Essays in Medieval Studies: Proceedings of the Illinois Medieval Association* 21 (2005), 23–47; Daniel Baloup, "La croisade albigeoise dans les chroniques léonaises et castillanes du XIIIe siècle," in *La croisade albigeoise*, pp. 91–107.

power at the expense of intermediary jurisdictions ought to be curbed, Peter the Chanter's circle and their Victorine associates invoked the just war against pagans and heretics as an exceptional case which allowed secular and ecclesiastical rulers to demand of their subjects what they otherwise could not in the name of the defense of the faith, public necessity and the common good.[79] If the kingdom or the Church were threatened by the attacks of pagans or heretics, both Robert Courson and Stephen Langton justified prelates paying taxes to secular rulers from both regalian possessions and non-regalian resources (which were intended to be devoted to the Church and the poor) in extraordinary cases, provided that ecclesiastics' consent was obtained. Their conclusions reflected the social reality of previous levies for the Third Crusade and the ransom of Richard I, which had met with considerable resistance and caused earlier masters, including Gerald of Wales, Stephen of Tournai and Peter of Blois to protest that crusade taxes were ruining the Church. However, by the time Robert Courson was writing his *summa* (ca. 1208–13), what had been first cautiously justified as an emergency exception reliant on the consent of the taxed had become common practice. Paris masters' justification of taxation for the crusades also reflected their involvement, together with various prelates and colleagues from the Victorine and Cistercian orders, in the collection and/or disbursement of taxes and other monies for the Fourth, Albigensian and Fifth Crusades and the expedition of Frederick II.[80]

Acting on the precedent of the Saladin tithe and the clerical income tax for the Fourth Crusade (which he had attempted to present as a non-precedenting voluntary aid before its mandatory imposition), Innocent III exhorted his legates to urge the inhabitants of the lands of noblemen who took the cross for the Midi to pay one-tenth of their revenues for one year. However, he also warned his legates to proceed cautiously, after they met with stiff resistance. Although the clergy could be forced to pay the new tax through the threat of ecclesiastical censures, grave scandal ought to be avoided at all costs, and the laity could and should not be coerced to pay without the consent of their secular rulers. Educated in Paris, Innocent was familiar with the arguments he must invoke to justify the new imposition. Those who defended the public good ought to be publicly funded. All the faithful were obliged to aid their neighbors, particularly ecclesiastics who lived from the patrimony of the

---

[79] MPM, 1:215–24; Buc, *Ambiguïté du livre*, pp. 239–60, 263–70, 283, 287–98, 340–49; Russell, *Just War*, pp. 236–38; Turner, *King John*, pp. 90–113, 147–53, 196–98; note 80 below.

[80] I am writing an article on the involvement of Paris-trained reformers and their colleagues in the regular religious orders in the financing of the crusades in the late twelfth and early thirteenth centuries. See notes 53 and 79 above; MPM, 1:215–20 and notes 74–77, 79, 82, 90–97; Robert Courson, *Summa* 10.11–12, 16 and 15.6–7, 13–16, BN Lat. 14524, fols. 49ra–va, 50vb–51ra, 65rb–va, 66va–67ra in MPM, 2:154, 156–57, notes 74–75, 77, 79, 88, 95–97; Stephen Langton, *Questiones*, Cambridge, Saint John's College, MS 57, fols. 195va–vb in MPM, 2:155, note 85; Buc, *Ambiguïté du livre*, pp. 287–98; Powicke, *Stephen Langton*, pp. 91–94; Turner, *King John*, pp. 112–13; Cheney, *Innocent III*, pp. 240–48, 267–68, 296–98; Giuseppe Martini, "Innocenzo III ed il finanziamento delle crociate," *Archivio della R. Società Romana di Storia Patria* 67 (1944), 309–35; Bird, "Victorines," pp. 9–11.

crucified Christ. Just as the possessions of the Church had been used in the past to ransom captives (for example, Richard I), so now they ought to be used to ransom souls imprisoned in heretical error.[81]

The exigencies of the Albigensian Crusade were soon also used to divert taxes originally imposed and collected for the crusade to the Holy Land. When the death of Simon de Montfort imperiled the anti-heretical effort in 1218, Honorius III again sought to secure royal participation in the crusade. He not only reiterated the rationale employed by Innocent III (including a ruler's duty to restrain evil men and heretics as well as those rebelling against his vassals), but promised Philip Augustus and his son Louis half of the clerical income tax collected for the Fifth Crusade in France. Amaury de Montfort was granted the entire tax from the Languedoc region.[82] In 1221, Honorius again turned to the reasoning which had served Innocent so well to instruct the new legates he had appointed for the crusade (the archbishops of Reims, Sens and Bourges) to raise a subsidy for Amaury to hire mercenaries, retain knights and ransom captives. Just as Innocent III had ostensibly bowed to the theoretical claim that tacit consent must be obtained from those who would pay newly imposed taxes, by waiting for the Fourth Lateran council to impose a heavy clerical income tax for the Fifth Crusade, so too the archbishops (who included Innocent III's former master Peter Corbeil) summoned local councils which reluctantly "consented" to a triennial clerical income tax of one-twentieth. Certain cathedral chapters still complained that the tax had been imposed without consulting them in council as canon law required. Some cut a deal with the legates to pay lump sums rather than annual installments, with papal approval; others evaded it entirely.[83]

Similarly, despite reformers' vehement excoriation of ecclesiastics who alienated Church lands or rights through taking out interest-bearing loans or mortgages on them, the necessity of wars against the infidel, pagans and heretics had been widely invoked to permit clergymen to mortgage their revenues for several years to fund their personal participation in various crusades. Further exemptions were soon permitted for the anti-heretical crusade; some Languedocian prelates mortgaged their lands or offered themselves as hostages to raise funds for Amaury de Montfort. Other prelates who took the cross were not only exempted from the crusade tax, but were allowed to use the taxes gathered from their dioceses to fund their participation

---

[81]   See note 79 above; VDC 60, 1:60–61; PL 215:361, 1469–70; PL 216:97–100, 158–60; Foreville, "Innocent III et la Croisade," pp. 200–203; Roscher, *Papst Innocenz III*, pp. 232–33; Foreville, *Innocent III et la France*, pp. 228–29, 260–62.

[82]   See notes 79–80 above; Evans, "Albigensian Crusade," in *Crusades*, 2, p. 315; Roscher, *Papst Innocenz III*, pp. 241–48; Richard Kay, "The Albigensian Twentieth of 1221-3: An Early Chapter in the History of Papal Taxation," *Journal of Medieval History* 6 (1980): 307–15, here pp. 308–9; Kay, *Council of Bourges*, pp. 6–8, 13–14; Pietro Pressutti, ed., *Regesta Honorii papae III*, 2 vols. (Rome, 1888–95), nos. 1577–78, 1614–17, 1987, 1995, 3948, 3950, 4620, 4698 (hereafter Pressutti); RHGF 19:666, 669, 671–72, 681–82.

[83]   Kay, "Albigensian Twentieth," pp. 309–12; Kay, *Council of Bourges*, pp. 12–13; Tudela, laisse 192, pp. 142–43; RHGF 19:715–17, 721–23.

in the anti-heretical crusade and were urged to use these monies to bring hired soldiers. Impoverished by his participation in the crusade, the bishop of Maguelonne was even permitted to extract an additional moderate subsidy from the churches of his diocese.[84]

Nonetheless, after the failure of the Fifth Crusade, the diversion of recruits and monies from the Holy Land to a "false" crusade which attacked Christians in France led to a storm of protest, not only among troubadours,[85] but also among clergymen, including one Master Adam, canon of Aix, and his accomplices, who refused to pay the twentieth, claiming that the pope could not spend a Holy Land tax on the Albigensian Crusade.[86] Yet the legate Romanus would later persuade the French episcopate to reluctantly consent to an enormous aid and a five-year, ten-percent income tax at the Council of Bourges (1225) as the price for Louis VIII's involvement in the anti-heretical crusade.[87] In a series of sermons delivered at key councils, and shortly after the commissioning of preachers for the renewed crusade, the Paris masters Philip the Chancellor and Odo of Châteauroux sought to sell the new tax to the clergy of France. Their sermons attacked avaricious and worldly clergymen and urged ecclesiastics to end contention with princes and set an example by contributing to the crusade through intercessions and alms (that is, taxation).[88] Nonetheless, the staggering sum which had to be raised quickly for the aid met with wide protest, as did the new income tax. Some episcopal chapters refused outright to pay; even the canons of Nôtre Dame in Paris provided only half of the sum due in the year of Louis's death.[89]

Other moral quandaries were attached to alternative means of funding the anti-heretical effort. Simon de Montfort resorted to loans from Cahorsin usurers later repaid from booty acquired in battle,[90] while due to the prolonged collection of

---

[84] PL 215:1469–71 (1208); Sivéry, *Louis VIII*, pp. 373–75; Kay, "Albigensian Twentieth," pp. 307–15; Roscher, *Papst Innocenz III*, pp. 242–48; Pressutti, nos. 3374, 3625, 3639, 3644, 3698, 3779, 3783, 3860, 3925, 3947, 4607, 4613, 4621, 4630, 4959, 5337, 4959; RHGF 19:720.

[85] *"I saw the World,"* no. 28, pp. 66–67; Guilhem Figueira, "D'un sirventes far," 1.1–23.184, ed. Bartholomaeis, 2:98–104; Huon of Saint Quentin, "Rome, Jérusalem se plaint" 7.79–84, 22.253–64, ed. Arié Serper (Madrid, 1983), pp. 89–107, here pp. 94, 104; Tomier and Palazi, "De chantar farai," 1.1–9.72, ed. Bartholomaeis, 2:54–57; Throop, *Criticism*, pp. 33–37, 41–43; Siberry, *Criticism*, pp. 158–68.

[86] As early as 1219, the legate for the Fifth Crusade also complained that the anti-heretical crusade was diverting aid from the crusaders in Egypt. Honorius justified the diversion by saying that the heretics were a worse threat than the Saracens (Pressutti, nos. 2195, 3658, 3698; RHGF 19:690–91).

[87] Sivéry, *Louis VIII*, pp. 369–70; Kay, *Council of Bourges*, pp. 17–18, 20–21, 72–104, 130–31, 135–46, 303–5, 385–91, 401–55.

[88] Bériou, "Prédication," pp. 93–95; Maier, "Crisis," pp. 640–41, 643–66, 650, 656; Sivéry, *Louis VIII*, pp. 267–68, 322–23, 364–72; Evans, "Albigensian Crusade," in *Crusades*, 2:316; Mansi 23:9–12; Philip the Chancellor, Schneyer, nos. 269–70, 328, 4:837, 842.

[89] Sivéry, *Louis VIII*, pp. 371; Evans, "Albigensian Crusade," in *Crusades*, 2:316–19; Kay, *Council of Bourges*, pp. 147–73.

[90] Tudela, laisses 72, 84–85, pp. 43, 48; Bird, "Reform or Crusade?," p. 170 and note 23; Biget, "Dépossession," pp. 268–69.

the twentieth, legates for the crusade in France were urged to borrow money to pay stipendiary warriors and to stump up emergency cash for Amaury de Montfort by taking out loans based on the projected proceeds of the tax.[91] While Robert Courson and other Paris reformers had vigorously combined the prosecution of usurers with the promotion of various crusades, they may well have viewed Simon's actions as permissible in the context of the *negotium fidei et pacis*. In his *summa*, Robert had argued that, even though the prince's coronation oath to punish evildoers and reward the good could be interpreted as meaning that he was required to force usurers in his lands to restitute the interest they charged, the pressing necessity of aiding the Holy Land or using the material sword to defend the Church against heretics who ignored excommunication enabled princes to impose *tailles* on towns (a practice normally condemned by the Chanter's circle as an unjust imposition), despite the risk of confiscating money derived from usury or rapine and thereby preventing restitution to criminals' victims. Similar to the individual crusader who, after exploring all other options, resorted to a usurer to fund his pilgrimage, the prince who lacked other sources of licit funding could accept illicitly acquired money through taking out interest-bearing loans, imposing *tailles*, confiscating the possessions of Christian or Jewish usurers or accepting gifts from them. However, he ought to restitute the funds as soon as possible after the war's successful conclusion – an opinion which perhaps influenced Simon de Montfort's prompt repayment of his creditors with war spoils.[92]

Similarly, although reformers, citizens and prelates inveighed against princes, including Raymond of Toulouse, who violently imposed new taxes and tolls, the moralists of Peter the Chanter's circle allowed that princes could do so in a state of emergency if they lacked other funds, obtained the consent of the taxed, and used the monies earned to protect citizens from brigands and keep the peace.[93] In the statutes formulated at Pamiers (1212) with the consent of his new southern subjects and sealed by attending reformers, Simon pledged to uphold justice and the peace, to abolish recently instituted tolls, and to seek to prevent the exaction of unjust *tailles* in his new lands while instituting a new papal *census* and ordering all church tithes to be paid.[94] The continuator of William of Tudela, however, painted Simon in terms reminiscent of the complaints of unjust tallages imposed without consulting their subjects and extorted by force or threats of violence levied against Raymond of Toulouse and John of England by their ecclesiastical and secular subjects. He

---

[91]   Pressutti, nos. 3969, 4613–15, 4618, 4643.

[92]   Bird, "Reform or Crusade?," pp. 165–85; Bird, "Heresy, Crusade and Reform," pp. 236–82 (fuller treatment); Robert Courson, *Summa* 10.11–12, 16, and 15.13, 16, BN Lat. 14524, fols. 49ra–vb, 50vb–51ra, 66va–67ra and MPM, 2:154 and 157, notes 75–77, 79, 95–97; Tudela, laisses 84–85, p. 48.

[93]   See notes 14, 23–24, 29, and 40 above; MPM, 1:235–41; Robert Courson, *Summa* 1.37 and 15.1, 4, 12–13, BN Lat. 14524, fols. 13rb–va, 63vb, 64va, 65ra–rb, 66rb–va; James of Vitry, *Sermo ad potentes et milites*, no. 52, in Douai 503, fols. 376v–379v, here fol. 379r–v; James of Vitry, *Sermo ad potentes et milites*, no. 53, in Douai 503, fols. 379v–385r, here fol. 381r.

[94]   Pamiers (1212), cs. 4, 6–8, 11–13, 16, 26–34, 40, in Mansi, *Concilia*, 22:855–64.

claimed that Simon and his army arrived before Toulouse with the connivance of the city's bishop, Fulk, a known associate of many Paris-trained moralists. Simon demanded a heavy *taille* from its citizens and yet was still determined to raze their city because he was in debt, had mortgaged all his rents and revenues, and was in need of money to regain Provence, which they had robbed him of by supporting Raymond of Toulouse and other *faidits*. Although Simon appears to have presented his case in terms of the rationale accepted by reformers for the imposition of a *taille*, the poet complained that Simon ought to have submitted his grievance to a court and treated the citizens with respect, accepting whatever they felt free to give rather than extorting taxes and levies through violence, perhaps recalling Simon's pledges at Pamiers (1212).[95]

Necessity was also invoked to permit compromise in the matter of church tithes. For although reformers and papal legates inveighed against secular rulers such as Raymond of Toulouse who detained Church tithes and possessions, at the Council of Bordeaux (1214), Robert Courson followed the consensus of his scholastic contemporaries in permitting laymen participating in a crusade to temporarily retain the use of tithes they should normally pay, with their prelates' permission, provided that on their death the tithes reverted to the Church.[96] Similarly, as seen above, although Paris-trained reformers abhorred the alienation of Church property and tithes, they also rationalized permitting clergymen to mortgage tithes and other Church revenues in genuine emergencies, a right exploited by Innocent III to expand clerical participation in the Holy Land and anti-heretical crusades.[97]

The use of mercenaries by crusaders was another potentially problematic issue. Although canon law's attempt to ban their deployment in Europe was ubiquitously ignored, from the late twelfth century onwards the *negotium pacis et fidei* sought to link the suppression of heresy to the tradition of papally and episcopally sanctioned regional peace associations and militias used to combat roving bands of mercenaries and private wars facilitated by the lack of a central authority in the Midi. One of the primary charges used to excommunicate and dispossess Raymond of Toulouse and other southern nobleman was their employment of mercenaries who committed sacrilegious depredations upon the poor, ecclesiastics and Church property, groups traditionally sheltered under the Peace and Truce of God. The expulsion of all such hirelings from their territories was one of the conditions for their rehabilitation.[98]

---

[95] See notes 92–94 above; Turner, *King John*, pp. 108–9, 172; Cheney, *Innocent III*, p. 309; Tudela, laisses 171–213, pp. 106–89.

[96] See note 97 below and note 36 above; MPM, 1:233; Rymer, *Foedera*, 1.1:122.

[97] MPM, 1:229–35, 276; Buc, *L'Ambiguïté du livre,* pp. 263–70.

[98] In general, see Matthew Strickland, *War and Chivalry: the Conduct and Perception of War in England and Normandy, 1066–1217* (Cambridge, 1996), pp. 34–35, 71–72, 297–300, 320–26; Thomas Head and Richard Landes, *The Peace of God: Social Violence and Religious Response in France around the Year 1000* (London, 1992); *Paix de Dieu et guerre sainte en Languedoc au XIIIe siècle*, ed. Edouard Privat, Cahiers de Fanjeaux 4 (Toulouse, 1969); Thouzellier, *Catharisme*; Vicaire, *Saint Dominic*; VDC 27, 55, and *passim*, 1:30–31, 51, etc. For the charges against Raymond, see notes 14, 23–24 and 27–29 above, and note 99 below; Tudela, laisses 2–4, p. 13. For the atrocities of *routiers*, see note 71 above and

Ironically, in order to restore the peace felt to be essential for the reform of the Church and the extirpation of heresy, Simon de Montfort supplemented the vast majority of crusaders who served for only forty days with mercenaries, stipendiary knights, foot soldiers and engineers funded by war spoils, loans from notorious usurers, donations from prelates and noblemen participating in the crusade and crusade taxes.[99] Yet the crusading army both depicted and treated their opponents' mercenaries in a manner similar to heretics. For example, during the siege of Moissac, Simon permitted its defenders to go free with the exception of the mercenaries they had retained, whom the crusaders lynched, as did Louis VIII with the Flemish and Brabançon *routiers* he captured at Avignon.[100]

This dualistic treatment of mercenaries may be explained by the fact that, even as Paris reformers and their Cistercian colleagues enthusiastically adopted the Third Lateran's condemnation of *routiers* and their employers, they used motives to distinguish between men of this ilk, who fought in order to obtain loot, and salaried knights and foot soldiers, who, unlike *routiers*, could theoretically be safely employed in just wars.[101] Moreover, although the use of crossbowmen against Christians had been banned by Church councils and they possessed a reputation akin to that of the despised *routiers*, Paris moralists maintained that defensive wars against the infidel and heretics justified their employment.[102] Similarly, while reformers urged employers of salaried soldiers to pay them properly in order to prevent them from looting, and exhorted fighters to be content with their pay rather than fighting for the sake of plunder and to refuse to sack churches and oppress the poor, the problem remained that much of these troops' wages were customarily derived from the spoils of war. Although Robert Courson retained serious reservations about using plunder for wages, many of his contemporaries claimed that it could be used provided it was not taken from, and prevented the looting of, the

---

VDC 198–200, 218–19, 341, 353, 359, 361, 382, 1:199–202, 218–19, 2:40, 50, 57, 60–61, 78–80; Strickland, *War and Chivalry*, pp. 81–84, 291–304, 311–20.

[99] Sibly, *History*, pp. 299–301; VDC 273, 1:270; C. H. Haskins, "The Heresy of Echard the Baker of Rheims," in idem, ed., *Studies in Mediaeval Culture* (Oxford, 1929), pp. 245–55, here note 2, p. 249; Tudela, laisses 86, 88–89, 93, 95, 98, 103, 115–16, 123, 127, 159, 201–2, pp. 48–49, 50, 51–53, 54, 59, 61, 63, 91, 159–62.

[100] Despised for their low status and the depredations they committed, an opponent's captured *routiers* were commonly summarily executed, even by lords who employed mercenaries themselves. See VDC 353, 2:49–50; Tudela, laisse 123, p. 61; Sivéry, *Louis VIII*, pp. 369–70; Strickland, *War and Chivalry*, pp. 179–81, 301, 322.

[101] MPM, 1:220–24; Russell, *Just War*, pp. 241–43; Duby, *The Legend of Bouvines*, pp. 82–83; Third Lateran, c. 27, in COD, pp. 224–25; Alan of Lille, *Liber Poenitentialis* 2.22, 2:145–46; Robert Courson, *Summa* 4.13 and 10.15, BN Lat. 14524, fols. 29vb–30ra, 50ra and MPM 2:158, note 104; James of Vitry, *Sermo ad potentes et milites*, no. 52, Douai 503, fols. 376v–79v, here 376v, 377v; Philippe Contamine, *War in the Middle Ages*, trans. Michael Jones (New York, 1984), pp. 90–101, 243–47.

[102] The restriction of the use of crossbows against fellow Christians was widely flouted. See Strickland, *War and Chivalry*, pp. 72, 180–81; Russell, *Just War*, pp. 243–44; Contamine, *War in the Middle Ages*, pp. 71–72; MPM, 1:223–24, 2:160, notes 125, 128; Robert Courson, *Summa* 10.10, 12, 15, BN Lat. 14524, fols. 48vb, 49va–50va and MPM, 2:159–60, notes 116–17, 127.

poor, widows and orphans (a category which included ecclesiastics and regular religious).[103] As had happened during the campaign of the Fourth and other eastern crusades, some clergymen and leaders in the anti-heretical army also attempted to use the spiritual censure of excommunication to restrain the violence of crusaders towards non-combatants and to ensure that spoils be put into a common pool for fair division or reservation for the new leader which the crusading army would elect to replace the "unjust" rulers they were dispossessing. These more orderly dispositions characterized situations such as the siege of Carcassonne, which was taken as the result of a negotiated surrender, rather than sieges ended by storm.[104]

Conducting a Just War: Theory and Practice

Reformers realized that even a just or holy war entailed activities which, at best, occupied a morally grey area: the taking and ransoming of prisoners, executions and mutilations, pillaging and foraging, the destruction or confiscation of an unjust opponent's property. They taught that all of these actions could be tolerated if they were unavoidable, not excessive, and undertaken with pure motives. If tainted by sinful motives such as greed, the offender ought to be forced to make restitution.[105] Peter of Vaux-de-Cernay was responding to these arguments when he portrayed Simon de Montfort's resort to mutilations after the capture of Bram by storm as done, not from delight in inflicting torment, but as a just retaliation for similar atrocities committed by his traitorous opponents, claiming that he was a "prince slow to punish and quick to reward, who grieved when driven to be hard." Mutilation of captured opponents was commonly employed as a form of revenge, humiliating punishment, or intimidation, particularly in the case of armed rebellion or treason, or in instances where opponents were perceived as barbarian, pagan, infidel or heretical. Yet such actions potentially undermined the crusaders' claim to be exercising a just war and had to be rationalized. Chroniclers supporting the crusaders stressed that their opponents had in many instances feigned allegiance to

---

[103]   See notes 101–2 above; MPM, 1:220–24; Peter the Chanter, *Summa*, §155, II:383 and §270, III2a:290 and MPM, 2:158–59, notes 109, 116–17; Robert Courson, *Summa* 4.13, 10.15, 15.4, BN Lat. 14524, fols. 29vb–30ra, 49va–50va, 64vb, in MPM 2:158–59, notes 104, 116–17; Russell, *Just War*, pp. 241–46; Robert of Flamborough, *Liber Poentientialis* 4.6.206–7, 209, ed. J. J. Francis Firth (Toronto, 1971), pp. 184–86; Thomas of Chobham, *Summa confessorum* 7.6.9a, p. 502. In a sermon to the powerful, James of Vitry warned that to harm the poor was to attack Christ, and savaged those who despoiled clergymen and the poor, including those who stole peasants' livestock or their scanty harvest. See James of Vitry, *Sermo ad potentes et milites*, no. 52, Douai 503, fols. 376v–379v, here fols. 377r, 378v–379r; idem, *Sermo ad potentes et milites*, no. 53, Douai 503, fols. 379v–385r, here fols. 381r–382r.

[104]   VDC 97–98, 1:98–99; William of Puylaurens, *Chronica* 14, ed. Duvernoy, pp. 62–63; Tudela, laisses 33–35, 113, pp. 26–27, 57; Robert of Auxerre, *Chronicon*, MGH SS 26:273; Alberic of Troisfontaines, *Chronicon*, MGH SS 23:890; Queller and Madden, *Fourth Crusade*, pp. 179–81; Maurice Keen, *The Laws of War in the Late Middle Ages* (London, 1965), pp. 137–55.

[105]   See note 97 above; Russell, *Just War*, pp. 105, 160–69, 179.

the crusading cause only to betray their allies and embark upon guerilla warfare characterized by atrocities and ambushes which spared none. The association of heresy with treason in papal decretals including *Vergentis in senium* meant that these relapsed heretics were viewed as doubly traitorous; they had not only broken solemn oaths of vassalage but their return to the vomit of heresy had betrayed the very Church to which they had speciously reconciled themselves.[106] For example, when Fulk of Toulouse was preaching in the Languedoc on the theme of heretics as wolves in sheep's clothing, a verse traditionally used to justify secular rulers' defense of the Church with the sword, a heretic mutilated and blinded by Simon de Montfort rose up and cried out: 'You heard what the bishop said: we are wolves and you are sheep, but have you ever seen a sheep which bit a wolf in this way?' Fulk quickly responded that just as shepherds used dogs to defend their sheep from the wolves, so the Church appointed a strong dog in Simon, who savaged this wolf because he was eating the Church's Christian flock.[107]

Although raids and the destruction of Church property, the countryside and its cultivators in order to prevent one's opponents living from the land were a commonly employed tactic both in wars in Europe and in various crusades,[108] these attacks were typically deplored by ecclesiastics even while they were viewed as necessary evil by the warrior class. Similar atrocities and attacks on the unarmed and clergy had formed part of the charges levied against Raymond of Toulouse and other supporters of mercenaries and heretics. Soon they also formed part of the accusations leveled at Simon and his allies in poems and letters meant to undermine papal and popular support for the anti-heretical crusade. For example, in a direct appeal to the tradition of the Peace of God, the citizens of Toulouse complained to Peter of Aragon that the legate, their bishop and crusaders had killed unarmed

---

[106] The translation is taken from Peter of Vaux-de-Cernay, *History of the Albigensian Crusade* 142, trans. Sibly and Sibly, p. 79; VDC 127, 142, 1:131–32, 148. For atrocities, see Jim Bradbury, *The Medieval Siege* (Rochester, NY, 1999), pp. 312–13, 329–31; Malcolm Barber, "The Albigensian Crusades: Wars like any Other?," in *Dei gesta per Francos: études sur les croisades dédiées a Jean Richard. Crusade studies in honour of Jean Richard*, ed. Michel Balard, Benjamin Z. Kedar and Jonathan Riley-Smith (Aldershot, 2001), pp. 45–55; Laurence W. Marvin, "War in the South: A first look at Siege Warfare in the Albigensian Crusade, 1209–1218," *War in History* 8.4 (2002), 373–95; Robert of Auxerre, *Chronicon*, MGH SS 26:274–75; Strickland, *War and Chivalry*, pp. 52–53, 201–3, 240–49, 309–10.

[107] See notes 33 and 63 above; Matt. 7.15; John 10.12; Stephen of Bourbon, *Tractatus*, ed. Lecoy de la Marche, pp. 23–24, note 3. See also Caesarius of Heisterbach, *Homiliae festivae*, ed. J. A. Coppenstein, 1 vol. in 3 pts. (Cologne, 1615), no. 37, 3:57–61; Hilka, *Wundergeschichten*, 1:147–49; James of Vitry, *Sermones feriales*, Liège 347, fol. 148va–vb; idem, *Sermones in epistolas*, pp. 699–700; idem, *Sermo ad potentes et milites*, no. 53, Douai 503, fols. 379v–385r, here fol. 378r; Philip the Chancellor, Schneyer no. 269, 4:837; Alan of Lille, *Contra hereticos*, PL 210:377–78; Kienzle, *Cistercians*, pp. 87, 93, 96–97, 104, 124, 166.

[108] Laurent Macé, "*Homes senes armas*: les paysans face à la guerre," in *La croisade albigeoise*, pp. 245–57; Strickland, *War and Chivalry*, pp. 71, 75–97, 259–90; Keen, *Laws of War*, pp. 189–97; Bradbury, *Medieval Siege*, p. 299; VDC 144, 147, 245, 327, 423, 434, 447, 1:150, 151–52, 244–45 and 2:27–28, 115–17, 125–26, 138–39; William of Puylaurens, *Chronica* 36, pp. 128–30.

persons working in the fields and were destroying agriculture in the Toulousain.[109] Accused by his opponents of complicity in these and similar atrocities because he accompanied Simon de Montfort's and Louis VIII's forces, Fulk of Toulouse was later credited by his supporter William of Puylaurens with attempting to save the women and children of Labécède from the customary slaughter when Louis VIII took the town by storm.[110]

Certainly, canonists and theologians also worried about the proper role of the clergy during times of war. Although, as a general principle, churchmen were barred from shedding blood, the extent of this prohibition remained contested.[111] However, Robert Courson and some of his contemporaries approved of ecclesiastics' supporting role in the crusades. Referring explicitly to Innocent III's anti-heretical crusading bull of 1208, Robert noted that the pope commissioned legates and bishops precisely to recruit men to slay infidels and heretics in the defense of the Church and the faith. However, other reformers argued that even these causes did not justify ecclesiastics killing, or ordering specific individuals to be killed or mutilated, although clergymen could and should instruct princes in general terms concerning what kinds of sentences ought to be inflicted upon certain categories of criminals or heretics. Similarly, while crusading prelates or ecclesiastics with military obligations could lead troops into battle, they ought not to directly participate in the fray but provide counsel and prayers for the warriors they led or employed.[112]

These guidelines appear to have been generally followed by Innocent III and other preachers who exhorted men to fight against heretics in the Midi. In addition to those who recruited for the crusade, reformers including the Cistercians Guy of Vaux-de-Cernay and Fulk of Toulouse, along with the Paris-educated William, archdeacon of Paris, and Alberic, archbishop of Reims, labored to keep up the morale and religious solidarity of the army through daily harangues. Alberic also "preached" by his personal demonstration of patience and magnanimity after the mangled corpse of his much-beloved nephew was catapulted into the crusader army. Other prelates set living examples by braving enemy fire to rally crusaders engaged in dangerous or critical tasks.[113] As would the Paris-educated Oliver of Paderborn

---

[109] VDC 27, 42 and *passim*, 1:30–31, 38–40, etc; HGL 8:612–19, esp. cols. 612–13; Tudela, laisses 80, 131, pp. 46, 65; Strickland, *War and Chivalry*, pp. 283–90; and notes 103 and 108 above, and 110 below.

[110] William of Puylaurens, *Chronica* 35–36, pp. 124–30; Tudela, laisses 171–213, pp. 106–89 (contrast idem, laisses 68, 71, pp. 41–43) and note 122 below.

[111] Russell, *Just War*, pp. 88–99; Brundage, "Holy War," 111–12.

[112] See note 118 below; PL 214:647–50; Russell, *Just War*, pp. 75–81, 106–11, 116–17, 207–9 (decretalists), 251; Brundage, "Holy War," pp. 109–12; Robert Courson, *Summa* 30.1, 5, BN Lat. 14524, fols. 104rb–va and MPM, 2:216, note 60 and 2:125, note 87; Thomas of Chobham, *Summa confessorum* 5.1.16a, 7.4.6a.3, 7.4.6a.6–13, 7.4.7a.1–6, 7.4.8a.1, pp. 228, 423, 426–45; Alan of Lille, *Liber Poenitentialis* 2.58, 3.22, 2:77, 146; Robert Flamborough, *Liber Poentientialis* 3.3.103–7 and 5.2.247, 250, pp. 119–23, 214, 216.

[113] VDC 128, 342–43, 346–47, 351, 1:133, 2:41–42, 44–45, 47–48; Tudela, laisses 118, 121–22, pp. 60–61.

during the Fifth Crusade, William archdeacon of Paris also formed a confraternity which financed siege engines and other expensive projects by drumming up collections and advised the craftsmen building them. Both William and Guy of Vaux-de-Cernay led foot soldiers and unarmed crusaders on expeditions to forage timber from surrounding forests.[114] Other prelates came from noble families and arrived with their relations and salaried troops, as well as providing liberal financial assistance to the army.[115] As the soldiers went out to do battle, the army's clergymen arrayed themselves as a spiritual army, which in vestments and bare feet, brandished liturgical crosses and relics, invoking divine and saintly aid through prayers and hymns.[116] All of these functions were known and familiar to Paris masters arguing the theory of ecclesiastical involvement in crusading from the fresh experiences of clergymen and crusaders involved in the recent campaigns of the Third and Fourth Crusades.[117]

Yet clergymen's presence in the anti-heretical crusading army subjected them to intense pressures. During the siege and sack of Béziers (1209), many crusaders were present who were known to and probably recruited by Parisian reformers. These included Innocent III's former teacher, master Peter Corbeil, archbishop of Sens, and the duke of Burgundy and the count of Nevers, who had and would continue to avidly suppress heresy in their own domains with the aid of Paris masters and the bishops of Auxerre and Paris.[118] The writings of individuals in communication with the Chanter's circle and returning crusaders may reveal some of the justifications circulated by those who took part in the siege. Alberic of Troisfontaines, Caesarius of Heisterbach, Robert of Auxerre and Peter of Vaux-de-Cernay took pains to depict the inhabitants of Béziers as guilty of the worst acts of sacrilege and treason. The citizens' desecration of the gospels, violent mugging of a priest carrying the consecrated host, and treacherous slaughter of their lord and wounding of their bishop in the city's main cathedral graphically demonstrated their utter disregard for the Church and the body of Christ. Both the citizens and their current lord were

---

[114] Their roles appear to have been modeled after the behavior of clergymen on the Third and Fourth Crusades. Similar roles were played by two recruiters for the Albigensian crusade who later participated in the Fifth Crusade – Oliver of Paderborn and James of Vitry. See note 7 above; *Itinerarium peregrinorum*, ed. Stubbs, pp. 218–19; Oliver of Paderborn, *Historia Damiatina* 12–13, ed. Hoogeweg, in *Schriften des Kölner Domscholasters,* pp. 181–86; James of Vitry, *Lettres* 4, ed. Robert B. C. Huygens (Leiden, 1960), p. 106; VDC 175, 180, 1:178–79, 183.

[115] VDC 342–43, 422–23, 434–35, 2:41–42, 114–16, 125–26.

[116] VDC 95, 351, 520, 524, 526, 1:96, 2:47–48, 214–15, 218–21; Tudela, laisses 114, 139, pp. 57, 70.

[117] For example, see the descriptions of the spiritual, financial and military influence of Baldwin of Canterbury and other clergymen in the army of the Third Crusade in *Itinerarium peregrinorum*, ed. Stubbs, pp. 93, 111, 116, 119–24, 133–35, 218–19, 245, 253–54. For clergymen and the Fourth Crusade, see note 7 above.

[118] Robert Courson intervened in several legal cases on behalf of Hervé of Nevers during the course of the Albigensian crusade and was later appointed spiritual legate for a contingent of French participants in the Fifth Crusade at Hervé's request. See note 3 above; VDC 82, 1:81–84; Tudela, laisses 12–13, pp. 16–17; Robert of Auxerre, *Chronicon*, MGH SS 26:273; Alberic of Troisfontaines, *Chronicon*, MGH SS 23:889–90.

guilty of harboring heretics after their refusal to comply with the demands of the crusaders' leaders that they hand over the heretics in their midst or leave the city to avoid perishing with them. Their violent attack on the crusading camp during negotiations justified, in these writers' eyes, the common folk of the army assailing the city, taking it by storm, and pillaging and massacring its inhabitants. The more sympathetic William of Tudela claimed that the commoners' actions, particularly the burning of large portions of the city, angered the military leaders of the army, who were thereby deprived of the spoils and operational base deemed essential for their campaign. William also suggested that the clergymen and barons from northern France who dominated the crusading host had previously decided that every city which refused to surrender should be put to the sword in order to lessen resistance, a plan perhaps manifested in the ultimatum previously delivered to the citizens of Béziers: deliver the heretics and their possessions to the crusaders, or if this were not possible abandon them, lest their own blood be on their heads for opposing the crusading army. To many northern chroniclers and to the legate Arnaud Amaury, who reported the incident to Innocent III, the massacre of the inhabitants remained the just vengeance of Christ or of his saints, wronged by the citizens' evil actions.[119]

Some contemporary theologians explicitly joined these sources in concluding that crusaders did not incur guilt when Christians who were indistinguishable from the heterodox, or had been given sufficient warning to escape, were killed in campaigns against heretics or the infidel. Written 1215–17, probably with Béziers in mind, Johannes Teutonicus' widely read gloss to Gratian's *Decretum* went so far as to declare that if heretics were present, an entire city might be lawfully burnt.[120] Certainly, Paris reformers and canon lawyers alike had cited the general principle that those who consented to sin through failing to restrain others from evil deserved to share in their punishment. This axiom was used to justify laying an interdict upon an entire region or city, as well as the punishment of the offspring of usurers and

---

[119] See note 118 above; Peter of Vaux-de-Cernay, *History*, trans. Sibly and Sibly, pp. 289–93 (analysis of sources); VDC 84–90, 1:86–91; Tudela, laisses 16–23, pp. 19–22; PL 216:137–41; DM 5.21, 1:302; Berlioz, "*Exemplum*," pp. 75–85; Marco Meschini, "*Diabolus ... illos ad mutuas inimicitias acuebat*: divisions et dissensions dans le camp des croisés au cours de la première croisade albigeoise (1207–1215)," in *La croisade albigeoise*, pp. 171–96, here pp. 177–78; Elaine Graham-Leigh, "Justifying Deaths: The Chronicler Pierre des Vaux-de-Cernay and the Massacre of Béziers," *Mediaeval Studies* 63 (2001), 283–303.

[120] Alan of Lille had suggested a merciful penance for those who inadvertently slew Christians indistinguishable from pagan adversaries, while an anonymous commentary on Exodus, probably written in the 1230s or 1240s in Oxford, came to a similar conclusion. Those who killed Christians who had been warned to leave lest they be confused with the heretics among whom they lived incurred no guilt. Modern opinions regarding the nature of the massacre at Béziers range from viewing it as "remarkably savage" even for its day to an event all too typical of a city taken by storm. See Beryl Smalley, *The Study of the Bible in the Middle Ages*, 2nd ed. (Blackwell, 1983), pp. 277–78, note 2; Alan of Lille, *Liber Poenitentialis* 2.59, 2:77; Russell, *Just War*, p. 256; Brundage, "Holy War," p. 123 and note 167, p. 139; Marvin, "War in the South," p. 381 and note 4.

heretics through the confiscation of their property. Moreover, in an anti-heretical treatise dedicated to one of the most zealous prosecutors of heretics in the region, William of Montpellier, Alan of Lille had justified the use of the death penalty not only as the just temporal punishment for sins against God and one's neighbors, but as a correction and deterrent to other potential criminals.[121]

These theories would be again put into practice at the *castrum* of Lavaur, which surrendered only after its wall had been breached in the spring of 1211. As traitors to the crusader side and protectors of the heretics jammed within Lavaur's walls, Aimeric, lord of Montréal and his garrison were summarily executed by the sword and gallows. His sister Giralda, characterized by hostile chroniclers as a notorious heretic and adulteress who had committed incest with either her brother or her son was, in an Old Testament twist, thrown into a well and stoned to death. Although the common folk were spared, several hundred heretics who had sought refuge in Lavaur were burned. Robert of Auxerre alone stressed that they had been given the choice of conversion beforehand, a detail which may have been furnished to him by colleagues of Paris reformers including James of Vitry and Robert Courson who were present at the siege: the count of Auxerre, Peter, bishop of Paris, William, archdeacon of Paris, and Fulk, bishop of Toulouse. In fact, the army was packed with recruits from Germany, Frisia, and the Île-de-France region where Paris masters including James of Vitry, Oliver of Paderborn, Conrad of Speyer, and William, archdeacon of Paris are known to have recruited. Fulk had also provided much-needed reinforcements to the crusaders by leading the armed anti-heretical confraternity he had organized in Toulouse to the siege. It is difficult to know what the precise role that, in the absence of the legate Arnaud Amaury, the clergy played in the executions. The severity of the punishments meted out were probably due to several factors: a long and frustrating siege which ended in taking the *castrum* by force, determination to extirpate the heretics who had taken refuge there and make an example of their traitorous defenders, and revenge for the "massacre" of crusader reinforcements at Montgey by Aimery's ally, the notorious count of Foix. Those killed at Montgey at the hands of "heretics" and mercenaries were quickly labeled as martyrs by recruiters and clergymen in the crusading army, who soon circulated miracle stories meant to reassure their surviving compatriots of the salvation potentially gained via the anti-heretical crusade.[122]

---

[121] Peter Clarke, "Peter the Chanter, Innocent III, and Theological Views on Collective Guilt and Punishment," *Journal of Ecclesiastical History* 52.1 (2001), 1–20; idem, "Innocent III, the Interdict and Medieval Theories of Popular Resistance," in *Pope, Church and City: Essays in honour of Brenda M. Bolton*, ed. Frances Andrews, Christoph Egger and Constance M. Rousseau (Leiden, 2004), pp. 77–97; idem, "A Question of Collective Guilt: Popes, Canonists and the Interdict, c. 1140–c. 1250," *Zeitschrift der Savigny-Stiftung für Rechtsgeschichte* 85 (1999), 104–46; Alan of Lille, *De fide catholicorum contra hereticos* 4.22, PL 210:397–98; Thouzellier, *Catharisme*, pp. 81–106.

[122] Robert of Auxerre, *Chronicon*, MGH SS 26:276; Alberic of Troisfontaines, *Chronicon*, MGH SS 23:892; VDC 213, 215–29, 1:211–12, 214–29; Tudela, laisses 63, 67–71, pp. 41–43; HGL 8:612–19; William of Puylaurens, *Chronica* 15–16, pp. 64–66, 68–70; Marvin, "War in the South," p. 392.

As had happened during the Fourth Crusade, crusaders actively sought guidance from legates and clergymen present in the army when engaging in potentially morally dubious behavior. Caesarius of Heisterbach claimed that some crusaders asked Arnaud Amaury what to do with the citizens of Béziers, since they could not distinguish the innocuous from the heretical. Fearing that heretics would act the orthodox part to escape execution only to later corrupt the region, Arnaud reportedly proclaimed, "Kill them all: God will recognize his own!"[123] Whether this episode was apocryphal or not, the crusaders' supposed qualms correlate to analogous episodes recounted by Peter of Vaux-de-Cernay. The quotation attributed to Arnaud referred to biblical authorities which were commonly cited in contemporary anti-heretical writings and were traditionally glossed as meaning that it was impossible for humans to discern who was heretical and who was orthodox when judging by appearances. The truth would be known only at the Last Judgment.[124] Moreover, many of the Cistercians and Paris masters recruiting or overseeing the crusaders often referred to the parables of the wheat and the tares and the wolves disguised as sheep to stress the hypocrisy and deceit of pious-seeming heretics. Their exhortations may have been interpreted by their audiences as meaning that the conversion of heretics was not to be trusted and may explain the crusaders' propensity to condemn the innocent rather than spare the potentially contaminating guilty, particularly when towns or castles were taken by storm.[125]

Similarly, after the negotiated surrender of Minerve in 1210, Arnaud Amaury followed Paris reformers' advice in declaring to Simon de Montfort that, although he longed for the death of heretics, as a monk, priest and papal legate, he could not sentence them to death outright, but must promise those reconciled to the Church their lives. However, the nobleman Robert Mauvoisin, a close associate of many Parisian and Cistercian reformers, insisted that the crusaders would not tolerate heretics being freed to corrupt others after faking conversion until he was reassured that very few would in fact recant. In this instance, the heretics were given a period of time to convert. Those who openly continued to cling to their heresy were burned, while those who renounced heresy were spared, including three women snatched from the flames and reconciled to the Church.[126] In a comparable case at Lombers, Simon de Montfort wanted to burn the disciple of a Cathar perfect despite his willing

---

[123] DM 5.21, 1:302.

[124] Berlioz, "*Exemplum*," pp. 82–85; 2 Tim. 2.19; Num. 16.5.

[125] According to the conventions of contemporary warfare, fortifications and settlements taken by storm were subject to sack and often the massacre of their inhabitants. See Strickland, *War and Chivalry*, p. 36; Bradbury, *Medieval Siege*, pp. 296, 301–2, 317–33; notes 33, 41, 63, 107 and 120 above.

[126] See VDC 154–56, 1:157–61; Robert of Auxerre, *Chronicon*, MGH SS 26:275. For Mauvoisin, see Bird, "Victorines," p. 10; Tudela, laisses 51–52, p. 34. For clergymen and the death penalty, see note 97 above; MPM, 1:185–91, 318–32; Peter the Chanter, *Summa*, 323–25, 327–28, 332, III2a:383–88, 389–93, 401–2; Thomas of Chobham, *Summa confessorum* 5.4.11a, 7.4.6a.6, 7.4.6a.9–11, pp. 305, 426–27, 429–35; Robert Courson, *Summa* 30.1–2, BN Lat. 14524, fols. 104ra–105rb and MPM 2:124, 128–29, notes 84, 104–7; Fourth Lateran Council (1215), c.18, in COD, p. 244.

abjuration of heresy and avowal of obedience to the Roman Church in all matters. Some clamored for his pardon, while others claimed that as a manifest heretic he ought to be burned for simulating repentance to escape death. Simon decided to burn the "penitent" with the intent that the fire would serve as an earthly purgation for his genuinely repented sins or the due penalty for his perfidy. Happily for the former *credens*, the fire spared him.[127] This episode suggests audiences' refractive reception of *exempla* traded by Paris masters and Cistercian abbots who had recruited for the Albigensian and other crusades. Meant to defend the efficacy of a genuine confession in sparing the penitent from purgatory, and in some cases, earthly punishment, these tales featured heretics and criminals who had passed judicial ordeals or survived the stake after making genuine private confessions, although one featured a heretic who relapsed after a confession saved him from being sentenced to death. It would appear that Simon and Robert Mauvoisin gave their own personal interpretations to similar *exempla*, which together with sermons instructing rulers on their duties to suppress heresy, made them wish to err on the side of condemning the innocent rather than sparing the guilty.[128]

As these examples illustrate, although crusading leaders often chose to ignore the advice of particular clergymen in their army and occasionally deeply resented their intrusion into what they perceived as feudal or strategic matters, clergy did often take part in war councils and frequently influenced the conduct of a campaign. In fact, many chroniclers and poets blamed a clerical stranglehold, or the influence of a specific prelate or legate upon the crusading armies, for the failure of the Fifth and Albigensian Crusades. Popes and clergymen ought to cease meddling in political affairs, declaring crusades against Christians or involving themselves in the military leadership of the campaigns and instead devote themselves to the reform of the Church and spiritual intercessions.[129] Many poets had in mind the papal legate Romanus who, with other French clergymen present in Louis VIII's army, persuaded the young king to lay siege to the city of Avignon in 1226. In return for

---

[127] VDC 113, 1:117–18.

[128] The *exempla* were traded by Conrad of Speyer and Walter, abbot of Villers. Walter was well-acquainted with James of Vitry (who, similar to the Paris-educated Conrad, had recruited for the anti-heretical crusade). All three men were associates of Conrad of Porto, previously abbot of Villers, who served as legate for the Albigensian crusade in the early 1220s. See James of Vitry, *Lettres* 1–2, 4, 6–7, ed. Robert B. C. Huygens (Leiden, 1969), pp. 71–97, 101–11, 123–55; Paul B. Pixton, "Konrad von Reifenberg, eine talentierte Persönlichkeit der deutschen Kirche des 13. Jahrhunderts," *Archiv für Mittelrheinische Kirchengeschichte* 34 (1982), 43–81; Falko Neininger, *Konrad von Urach (1227): Zähringer, Zisterzienser, Kardinallegat* (Paderborn, 1994); note 61 above.

[129] The poet William of Tudela claimed that French prelates and noblemen dictated the crusading army's decisions. One of Philip Augustus' most trusted counsellors, the former Hospitaller Guérin, bishop of Senlis, had similarly dominated Louis VIII's two earlier expeditions to the Midi. See note 52 and discussion above; Throop, *Criticism*, pp. 32–33, 43; Baldwin, *Government*, pp. 115–18, 123–25, 340–41; Sivéry, *Louis VIII*, pp. 208–9; *"I saw the World,"* pp. 51–53, 55, 64–67, 102; Guillaume le Clerc, *Le Besant de Dieu*, vv. 2387–99, 2547–64, ed. Ruelle, pp. 131, 134–35; Huon of Saint-Quentin, "Rome, Jérusalem se plaint," 1.1–26.312, ed. Serper, pp. 89–107.

absolution from excommunication and the safety of their persons and possessions, the Avignonese had previously promised Louis free passage and to attempt to deliver key *castra* to him. Yet in an open letter vindicating the siege, Romanus and other ecclesiastics portrayed Avignon's citizens in terms corresponding to those used to criminalize Raymond VII of Toulouse and cited the Fourth Lateran's recent decrees concerning the suppression of heresy. Excommunicated as aiders and abettors of heretics for over ten years, they had sworn to obey all Romanus' commands as the price for their absolution. However, they had broken their oaths by failing to make adequate satisfaction for their crimes and to deliver the *castra*, sending unsuitable hostages, denying Louis's army transit and supplies, and killing some crusaders. Because the Avignonese had refused to make amends, the siege of the city was justified as necessary vengeance for these affronts and for the injury inflicted upon the name of Christ by the citizens' aiding and abetting of heresy. The same clergymen were also faced with justifying the assault to the town's overlord Frederick II, who, as an individual who had taken the cross for the Holy Land crusade, ought to have been immune from attack from fellow Christians. They painted the Avignonese as traitors who had plotted to capture Louis VIII and had imprisoned or slain some of the crusaders whom he had sent in his place, to whom they had granted a safe conduct.[130] In persistently citing the Avignonese's denial of free passage to the crusading troops, Romanus and the prelates in the army, who included the former Paris master Walter Cornut, archbishop of Sens (1223–41),[131] may well have been arguing from Gratian's *Decretum*, which cited the case of the Israelites going to war against the Amorites, who had denied them free passage. This authority had been previously cited by Robert of Courson and others to conclude that princes could justly dispossess legitimate heirs and confiscate lands if their motives were righteous and they were acting on ecclesiastical authority.[132] In contrast, Guérin, bishop of Senlis, one of Philip Augustus' former chief advisors, urged Louis not to attack, probably for fear of violating the non-aggression pact which Louis had signed with Frederick II in 1225.[133]

In conclusion, while historians have traditionally focused on papal initiatives or the role of the Cistercians or mendicants when discussing the promotion of the Albigensian Crusade, Paris masters also played a crucial part in shaping the terms and outcome of the debate over the justification, conduct and prolongation of the anti-heretical crusade through their teaching, sermons, recruiting, and

---

[130] Sivéry, *Louis VIII*, pp. 379–80, 382–84; *Layettes de trésor*, nos. 1787–89, 2:85–88.

[131] *Layettes de trésor*, 2:89, note 2; Baldwin, *Government*, p. 441.

[132] See note 10 above; Gratian, *Decretum* 23.2.3, CIC 1:895; Russell, *Just War*, pp. 64, 221–22, 252–53; MPM, 1:206–9; Robert Courson, *Summa* 15.2–3 and 26.9–10, BN Lat. 14524, fols. 63vb–64vb, 92ra–93ra and MPM, 2:146–47, notes 23–25.

[133] Note 129 above; Sivéry, *Louis VIII*, pp. 367–68.

correspondence with popes and kings. As recruiters, they adapted liturgies, techniques and propaganda from crusades to the Holy Land to persuade others to join the anti-heretical effort and to galvanize the home front. Moreover, their personal involvement in organizing the financing of various crusades and their teaching concerning the parameters of clerical taxation helped to define the terms of the struggle between the papacy and clergy over the imposition, collection, and transferral of subsidies and taxes imposed for the crusades. As spiritual mentors and advisors, reformers' and ecclesiastics' guidance was valued by crusaders seeking to navigate the moral quagmires which characterised the campaigns of the Albigensian Crusade. Their activities testify to the exchange of ideas and practices between crusade campaigns and to the way in which the very concept and implementation of the crusade was shaped and reshaped via a continual dialogue between canon lawyers and theologians, clergy and laity, popes and legates, reformers and prelates.

Genuas angebliche Allianz mit den Kreuzfahrerstaaten von 1233

Hans Eberhard Mayer

Christian Albrechts Universität, Kiel

Es gilt als gesicherte Erkenntnis der Forschung, daß Genua 1233 eine Allianz mit den Baronen des Königreichs Jerusalem und dem Königreich Zypern schloß, die sich nach Lage der Dinge nur gegen den genuesischen Erzfeind Pisa und gegen Kaiser Friedrich II. und seinen Regenten im Osten, den Reichsmarschall Richard Filangieri, richten konnte. Alle führenden einschlägigen Werke vertreten diese Meinung.[1] Eine Allianz zwischen Genua einerseits und Zypern und den Baronen des Königreichs Jerusalem andererseits war für beide Seiten von Interesse. Seit Herbst 1231, als Filangieri als der Statthalter des Kaisers ins Hl. Land kam, wo er auftragsgemäß sofort die Baronie Beirut zugunsten der Krone einzog, wehrten sich die Barone gegen ein Vorgehen, das sie als Verfassungsbruch ansahen und das die Sicherheit ihrer Besitzungen bedrohte, wenn das Beiruter Beispiel Schule machen sollte.[2] Das Instrument ihres Widerstandes war die Kommune von Akkon, zu deren Führer 1232 Johann von Ibelin wurde, bekannt als der Alte Herr von Beirut. Die bewaffneten Auseinandersetzungen, ein wirklicher Krieg, tobten im Königreich Jerusalem ebenso wie im Königreich Zypern, wo der König Heinrich I. erst 1232 volljährig wurde.

Die Barone mußten Truppen von einem zum anderen Kriegsschauplatz bewegen, was nur ging, wenn man Flottenhilfe bekam. Pisa fiel hierfür wegen seiner notorischen Kaisertreue aus. Genua war dagegen dazu bereit, denn es stand zu

---

[1] Louis de Mas Latrie, *Histoire de l'île de Chypre sous le règne des princes de la maison de Lusignan*, 1 (Paris, 1861), S. 302 f.; Wilhelm Heyd, *Histoire du commerce du Levant au moyen-âge*, 1 (Leipzig, 1885), S. 341; Hans Müller, *Der Longobardenkrieg auf Cypern 1229–1233* (Halle an der Saale, 1890), S. 62; Reinhold Röhricht, *Geschichte des Königreichs Jerusalem (1100–1291)* (Innsbruck, 1898), S. 824 f.; Eugene H. Byrne, "The Genoese Colonies in Syria," in *The Crusades and Other Historical Essays Presented to Dana C. Munro*, ed. Louis J. Paetow (New York, 1928), S. 177 f.; John L. La Monte, *Feudal Monarchy in the Latin Kingdom of Jerusalem 1100 to 1291*, Monographs of the Mediaeval Academy of America 4 (Cambridge, Mass., 1932), S. 268; Sir George Hill, *A History of Cyprus*, 2 (Cambridge, England, 1948), S. 127 f.; Joshua Prawer, *Histoire du royaume latin de Jérusalem*, 2 (Paris, 1970), S. 250 f.; Peter W. Edbury, "Cyprus and Genoa: the Origins of the War of 1373–4," *Praktika tou Deuterou Diethnous Kypriologikou Synedriou*, 2 (Nicosia, 1986; seitengleicher Nachdruck in Edbury, *Kingdoms of the Crusaders. From Jerusalem to Cyprus*, Variorum Collected Studies Series 653 [Aldershot, 1999]), S. 110; Edbury, *The Kingdom of Cyprus and the Crusades, 1191–1374* (Cambridge, England, 1991), S. 65, 67

[2] Jonathan Riley-Smith, *The Feudal Nobility and the Kingdom of Jerusalem, 1174–1277* (London, 1973), S. 175 tritt dafür ein, daß die Konfiskation Beiruts eine Eigenmächtigkeit der Anführer von Filangieris Truppen war, doch berief sich dieser später auf einen kaiserlichen Befehl; *Estoire de Eracles Empereur*, RHC Oc (Paris, 1859), S. 391.

Anfang der dreißiger Jahre mit Kaiser Friedrich II. sehr schlecht. Genua hatte sich
Friedrich II. schon 1220 entfremdet, als er zwar die auf das Kaiserreich bezüglichen
Teile der Privilegien seiner Vorgänger bestätigte, nicht aber, was darin über Genuas
Rechte in Sizilien gestanden hatte. Daraufhin weigerten sich die Genuesen,
Friedrich nach Rom zur Kaiserkrönung zu begleiten.[3] Der Kaiser bemühte sich zwar
1224, die genuesische Position in Akkon zu verbessern,[4] doch hielt das nicht lange
vor. Endgültig waren die Beziehungen vergiftet, als der Kaiser im Februar 1231
seinen Bailli im Osten, damals Balian von Sidon, anwies, von den Genuesen einen
Einfuhrzoll von 10 Prozent zu erheben.[5] Zwar scheiterte dies, aber im folgenden
Jahr ging der Kaiser gegen Genua in Italien vor. Er verkündete im Januar 1232
den sehr weitgehenden Rechtsspruch, keine kaisertreue Stadt dürfe einen Podestà
wählen oder behalten, der aus einer der Städte des mit Friedrich II. verfeindeten
zweiten lombardischen Bundes stamme.[6] Das traf Genua schwer, denn schon im
September 1231 hatte sich die ligurische Metropole einen Podestà aus der gegen den
Kaiser rebellierenden Stadt Mailand gewählt und mit diesem den üblichen Vertrag
geschlossen. Er sollte sein Amt Anfang Februar 1232 antreten. Genua wollte sich
zwar künftig an den Rechtsspruch halten, bat aber ohne Erfolg, jetzt auf dessen
Exekution zu verzichten, weil die Wahl ja erfolgt sei, ehe das neue Gesetz überhaupt
erlassen wurde. Als der Kaiser auf sofortiger Exekution bestand, obsiegte im
Stadtrat von Genua jene Fraktion, die darauf beharrte, an dem gewählten Podestà
festzuhalten und ihn aufzunehmen.

Friedrich II. reagierte darauf mit der Verhaftung aller Genuesen im Königreich
Sizilien und mit Einziehung ihres Besitzes.[7] Sowohl in Genua wie auch bei den
Genuesen in Tunis, wo Genua seit spätestens 1223 ein Quartier mit Fondaco, Ofen
und Bad hatte,[8] lief jetzt das Gerücht um, der Kaiser habe seinen Bailli Filangieri
angewiesen, alle Genuesen aus dem Königreich Jerusalem auszuweisen.[9] Genua
sandte zum Schutz seiner überseeischen Besitzungen zunächst 5 Galeeren und zwei
Segelschiffe in den Osten, danach am 11. August 1232 nochmals 10 Galeeren und
zwei Segelschiffe.[10]

---

[3]   Johann Friedrich Böhmer, *Die Regesten des Kaiserreiches unter Philipp, Otto IV, Friedrich II,
Heinrich (VII), Conrad IV, Heinrich Raspe, Wilhelm und Richard 1198–1272*, neu bearbeitet von Julius
Ficker, 1 (Innsbruck, 1881), no. 1179; *Annali Genovesi di Caffaro e de' suoi continuatori*, 2, ed. Luigi
Tommaso Belgrano und Cesare Imperiale di Sant'Angelo, Fonti per la storia d'Italia (Rom, 1901), S.
168 f.

[4]   Böhmer – Ficker, *Regesta imperii*, 1, no. 1526.

[5]   *Annali Genovesi*, 3 (Rom, 1923), S. 55.

[6]   Ibid., 3, S. 60 f.

[7]   Ibid., 3, S. 60–63.

[8]   Ibid., 3, S. 192.

[9]   Ibid., 3, S. 63: *omnes Ianuenses, qui erant in partibus Tunesi*. Schon Eduard Winkelmann, *Kaiser
Friedrich II.*, 2 (Leipzig, 1897), S. 391, Anm. 1, hat dies richtig korrigiert zu *in partibus Syrie*. Philipp
von Novara, *Guerra di Federico II in Oriente (1223–1242)*, ed. Silvio Melani (Neapel, 1994), S. 166
§ 170.

[10]   *Annali Genovesi*, 3, S. 63.

Filangieri siegte zunächst gegen die rebellischen Barone auf dem Festland in der Schlacht bei Caselimbert (3. Mai 1232), trug den Krieg aber dann nach Zypern, wo Johann von Beirut 1229/1230 ein von Friedrich II. eingesetztes Konsortium von fünf Baillis entmachtet hatte. Auch die Barone brachten ihre Truppen nunmehr dorthin, unterstützt von genuesischen Schiffen.[11] Ende Mai 1232 segelten die Truppen der Barone von Akkon nach Famagusta. Der gerade volljährig gewordene König Heinrich I. gab den Genuesen am 10. Juni 1232 ihr grundlegendes Privileg für Zypern RRH no. 1037. Am 15. Juni 1232 erfochten die Barone bei Agridi einen entscheidenden Sieg über die kaiserlichen Truppen. Diese hielten auf der Insel aber noch die starke Burg Kyrenia an der zyprischen Nordküste. Sie konnte erst bezwungen werden, als das zweite genuesische Geschwader eintraf, das im August Genua verlassen hatte.[12] Die Burg fiel kurz nach Ostern (3. April) 1233.[13] Damit war der antistaufische Kampf auf der Insel zuende, während es auf dem Festland zu einer fast zehnjährigen praktischen Teilung des Landes kam: Die staufische Administration unter Richard Filangieri herrschte in Tyrus, die Barone und die Kommune von Akkon regierten dort. Es kam zu mancherlei Versuchen des Kaisers, um zu einem Ausgleich mit den Baronen zu kommen, doch blieben sie alle erfolglos, und 1242 wurde die kaiserliche Verwaltung aus Tyrus und überhaupt aus dem Land vertrieben.

Rückblickend hatte es also für die Genuesen wie auch für die Barone genug Konfliktstoff mit dem Kaiser gegeben, so daß eine Allianz zwischen den beiden für die Zukunft durchaus Sinn machte. Es gibt zwei original erhaltene Notariatsinstrumente, die sich damit befassen, vom 24. Oktober 1233 und vom 2. Dezember 1233.[14] Ich beginne mit dem zweiten.[15] Aus dem Stück geht hervor, daß die genuesischen Konsuln und Vizegrafen für Syrien, Petrus de Mari und Piccamiglio, als Beauftragten Castellanus de Savignono[16] nach Nikosia geschickt hatten, wo er mit König Heinrich I. von Zypern und 50 zum Teil führenden Baronen Jerusalems und Zyperns den Vertrag aushandelte. Man versprach, die Kommune Genua und die Genuesen einschließlich der als Genuesen Bezeichneten, d. h. derer, die unter genuesischer Flagge Handel trieben, in beiden Reichen zu Wasser und zu Lande zu schützen und zu verteidigen (*defendere*), ebenso die gegenwärtigen und früheren genuesischen Rechte und Besitzungen, jedoch *salvo tamen iure dominii regni Iherusalem*. Die Abmachung sollte gelten von sofort an bis zum 1. Juni 1234 und ab dann auf fünf Jahre, insgesamt also bis 1. Juni 1239. Sollte ein Bailli im Königreich Zypern, wo es im Moment keinen gab, oder im Königreich Jerusalem, wo in Tyrus der kaiserliche Bailli Richard Filangieri amtierte, etwas gegen diese

---

[11] Philipp von Novara, *Guerra di Federico II*, S. 166 § 170. *Estoire de Eracles Empereur*, S. 396.

[12] Philipp von Novara, *Guerra di Federico II*, S. 196 § 199.

[13] *Estoire de Eracles Empereur*, S. 402.

[14] Staatsarchiv Genua, Sezione Governo, Archivio Segreto 2723 no. 41 und 43.

[15] RRH no. 1049; gedruckt bei Louis de Mas Latrie, *Histoire de Chypre*, 2 (Paris, 1852), S. 56–58 nach dem Original, das sich damals als eine Spätfolge der napoleonischen Wirren in Turin befand.

[16] Er wurde 1248 in Genua *consul de placitis; Annali Genovesi*, 3, S. 178.

Abmachung unternehmen, so verpflichteten sich die Aussteller gegenüber Genua, die Genuesen gegen den oder die Baillis oder deren Beauftragte zu unterstützen. Umgekehrt versprach Castellanus, Genua werde während der Laufzeit des Vertrages die Aussteller und ihren Besitz in beiden Reichen zu Wasser und zu Lande durch jene Genuesen verteidigen lassen, die sich vorübergehend in Zypern aufhielten (*qui pro tempore in Cypro fuerint*). Danach heißt es, was ich vorerst unerörtert lasse: *et quod omnes Ianuenses, qui citra mare sunt et quos volueritis nominare, hanc conventionem iurabunt attendere et observare*. Beide Seiten beschworen die Abmachungen auf die Evangelien (RRH no. 1049). Das Dokument wurde verfaßt und ausgefertigt von *Iacobus Petri Rufi sacri imperii notarius*. Mas Latrie, gefolgt von Byrne, nannte das Stück in der Überschrift zu seiner Edition eine Offensiv- und Defensivallianz.[17] Aber der Vertrag war nur defensiv angelegt. Griff Richard Filangieri die Barone an, so mußte Genua helfen. Griffen diese aber Filangieri an, war Genua zu nichts verpflichtet. Umgekehrt war es ebenso, die Barone waren Genua nur dann zur Hilfe verpflichtet, wenn es angegriffen wurde, nicht wenn es selbst angriff. Genua hatte einen Vorteil, den die Barone nicht hatten: Trat der casus foederis auf dem Festland ein, so waren nur die in Zypern befindlichen Genuesen von dem Vertrag erfaßt und gehalten, die Barone zu unterstützen. Die Genuesen in Akkon konnten sich dagegen aus der Sache heraushalten.

Vorausgegangen war dieser Übereinkunft die andere vom 24. Oktober 1233. Sie betraf aber nur das für Genua besonders wichtige Verhältnis zu Pisa. Sechs führende Barone des Königreichs Jerusalem verpflichteten sich, bis zum 1. Juni 1234 und darüber hinaus auf fünf Jahre keinerlei Allianz mit den Pisanern einzugehen, weder persönlich noch durch eigene Parteigänger, und überhaupt nichts ohne Wissen und Zustimmung der beiden syrischen Konsuln Genuas oder ihrer Nachfolger geschehen zu lassen (RRH no. 1047).

Im Gegensatz zu RRH no. 1049 vom 2. Dezember ist RRH no. 1047 wesentlich schwieriger zu benutzen. Es wurde deshalb in der Forschung auch weniger herangezogen, und soweit dies geschah, dürfte man sich der Inhaltsangaben bei Mas Latrie oder Röhricht bedient haben.[18] Alles andere führt in die Irre, und schon Heyd referierte den Inhalt des von ihm als unediert bezeichneten Stückes insofern verkehrt, als er meinte, RRH no. 1049, das sich mit Pisa aber überhaupt nicht befaßt, habe RRH no. 1047 bestätigt.[19] Außerdem erklärte er drei seigneuriale Gunsterweise von 1221, 1223 und 1234 zu Teilen von RRH no. 1047, in dem sie aber überhaupt nicht erwähnt werden. Heyd hatte hier die Urkunden im Auge, die Johann von Ibelin, Herr von Beirut, und Rohard von Haifa den Genuesen

---

[17]   Aber in dem später erschienen Band 1 seiner *Histoire de Chypre*, S. 302 sprach er nur noch von einer Defensivallianz.

[18]   Mas Latrie, *Histoire de Chypre*, 2, S. 58 Anm. 1; RRH no. 1047.

[19]   Heyd, *Histoire du commerce*, 1, S. 341 mit Anm. 5.

gewährten.[20] Diese Ausweitung "verdankte" Heyd dem völlig falschen Regest von RRH no. 1047 bei Olivieri, wo als Ausstelldatum auch noch 1253 statt 1233 angegeben wird.[21] Heyd kannte auch den Auszug aus RRH no. 1047 bei Canale, mit dem aber nicht viel anzufangen ist, weil Canale *facientes* statt *faventes* und *aliquos nostrum* statt *aliquis nostrum* druckte.[22] Olivieri und Canale entfernten sich so weit vom Inhalt von RRH no. 1047, daß Heyd den einzigen bisherigen Volldruck von RRH no. 1047 durch Grasso für eine ganz andere Urkunde hielt. Grassos Druck war der Forschung außerhalb Italiens nur schwer greifbar,[23] aber demnächst wird RRH no. 1047 in meiner Edition der Königsurkunden von Jerusalem als Regentenurkunde D. 786 neu ediert werden.

Hätte man Grassos Druck benutzt, so wäre das Urteil über die Allianz von 1233 vielleicht anders ausgefallen, erst recht wenn man die äußeren Aspekte des Originals beizieht. Dieses in Akkon ausgestellte Stück der sechs Barone des Hl. Landes nennt als Empfänger für die Komune Genua den Petrus de Mari, genuesischen Konsul und Vizegrafen für Syrien, und seinen Amtkollegen Piccamiglio, von dem gesagt wird, er sei im Moment abwesend. Diktiert und geschrieben wurde es von *Petrus Petri Rufi notarius ... iussu predictorum baronum*. Die Initiative ging also von den Baronen aus, nicht von Genua. Der Notar war der Bruder jenes *Iacobus Petri Rufi notarius*, der RRH no. 1049 schrieb (siehe oben). Die beiden gehörten klar zum genuesischen Notariatsmilieu, denn schon der Vater Petrus Rufi war Notar in Genua gewesen und tritt als solcher 1225–27 dort auf.[24] Jakob erscheint in Genua 1225.[25] Auch der jüngere Petrus war 1225 noch in Genua.[26] Er hatte ein sehr charakteristisches Diktat, das gekennzeichnet ist durch die Häufung von Synonymen, in RRH no. 1047 unter anderem *in qua conventione pacto federe societate aut collegio*, ferner durch die Wendung *promitto et convenio* und durch den Zusatz *per me (nos)* zu dispositiven Verben wie *dono (donamus)* oder ähnlich. Nach dem Diktat zu urteilen, verfaßte der jüngere Petrus im Osten neben RRH no. 1047 sehr wahrscheinlich auch das grundlegende Diplom Heinrichs I. von Zypern für Genua vom 10. Juni 1232 (RRH no. 1037), mindestens einen Entwurf dazu, ferner eine Urkunde der Königin Alice von Zypern für die Johanniter vom 30.

---

[20] RRH no. 950, 963, 1050; neu ediert in Dino Puncuh, *I Libri iurium della Repubblica di Genova*, 1/2, Fonti per la storia della Liguria 4 (Genua, 1996), S. 174 no. 349, S. 176 no. 350; Sabina Della Casa, *Libri iurium di Genova*, 1/4, Fonti per la storia della Liguria 11 (Genua, 1998), S. 49 no. 674.

[21] Agostino Olivieri, *Carte e cronache manoscritte per la storia genovese esistenti nella biblioteca della R. Università Ligure* (Genua, 1855), S. 59 f.

[22] Michelle G. Canale, *Nuova istoria della repubblica di Genova*, 2 (Florenz, 1858), S. 291.

[23] G. Grasso, "Lega tra Genova e vari signori feudali di Siria," *Giornale ligustico di archeologia, storia e belle arti*, 4 (1877), S. 22.

[24] *Notai liguri del secolo XII e del XIII*, 6: *Lanfranco (1202–1226)*, ed. H. C. Krueger und R. L. Reynolds, 2 (Genua, 1952), S. 283 no. 1599; Sandra Macchiavello und Maria Traino, *Carte del monastero di S. Siro di Genova*, 2, Fonti per la storia della Liguria 6 (Genua, 1997), S. 7 no. 354, 17 no. 363, 19 no. 364, 22 no. 367, 23 no. 368; vgl. *Lanfranco*, 1 (Genua, 1951), S. 124 no. 272 von 1203.

[25] *Lanfranco*, 2, S. 225 no. 1454, 313 no. 1673.

[26] Ibid., 2, S. 224 no. 1452.

September 1232 (RRH No. 1038) und schließlich am 12. Januar 1234 eine Urkunde Rohards von Haifa für Genua (RRH no. 1050), in der er sich nennt wie in RRH no. 1047: *Ego Petrus Petri Rufi notarius iussu predicti domini Rohardi scripsi*. Auch in RRH no. 1049, verfaßt von seinem Bruder Jakob, schimmert sein Diktat so deutlich durch, daß RRH no. 1047 als Formularbehelf gedient haben dürfte.

Sieht man sich das Original von RRH no. 1047 an, so fällt ins Auge, daß unterhalb der Unterfertigung des Notars nicht weniger als sieben Leerzeilen folgen. Das parallel zur längeren Seite beschriebene Pergament mißt rechts und links 15 cm in der Höhe, doch nur 9, 5 davon sind beschrieben. Es werden sechs Siegel der ausstellenden Barone angekündigt, doch finden sich keine Spuren einer Besiegelung, nicht einmal Löcher für die Siegelschnüre oder eine Plica, obwohl wirklich genügend Platz gewesen wäre. Am rechten Rand ist in der unteren Hälfte der Urkunde ein großer, den Text nicht tangierender Ausriß, dessen Symmetrie verrät, daß er am gefalteten Pergament ausgeführt wurde. Das könnte auf eine seitliche Besiegelung deuten, wie sie bei *litterae clausae* üblich war.[27] Im Osten war RRH no. 598a, das aber Balduin III. zuzuordnen ist, vermutlich so besiegelt, ebenso mit Sicherheit RRH no. 623, 1140.[28] Aber bei RRH no. 1047 spricht nichts für eine *littera clausa* mit seitlicher Besiegelung. Die Schnüre für die sechs angekündigten Siegel wären in dem Ausriß nicht unterzubringen gewesen, und auf der Rückseite fehlt eine Adresse, wie sie bei *litterae clausae* üblich war. Das Stück wurde also unbesiegelt nach Genua geschickt. Damit fehlte ihm die wesentliche Beglaubigung. Natürlich bedurfte ein Notariatsinstrument an sich keiner Besiegelung, um öffentlich glaubwürdig zu sein. Wurden jedoch Siegel angekündigt, dann aber nicht angebracht, so trat natürlich keine Wirksamkeit ein; man kann RRH no. 1047 als unvollzogen bezeichnen. Tatsächlich war eine Besiegelung bei der Ausstellung durch den Notar Petrus gar nicht beabsichtigt gewesen, denn im Text heißt es im Futur I, und das ist bisher nur dem Druck von Grasso zu entnehmen: *Et ut presens scriptura firmum robur obtineat, quisque nostrum* (scil. jeder der sechs Aussteller) *suo sigillo proprio eam roborabit et roborare promittit et in publicam formam eam redigi precipimus*. In der Zukunft erst sollte ein RRH no. 1047 vergleichbarer Text über die Ausgrenzung der Pisaner im Königreich Jerusalem irgendwann besiegelt werden. Ein ähnlicher Befund findet sich in RRH no. 1049. Obwohl der König, der

---

[27] Siehe generell Léopold Delisle, "Notes sur les sceaux des lettres closes," Appendix zu Delisle, "Mémoire sur une lettre inédite adressée à la Reine Blanche par un habitant de La Rochelle," *Bibliothèque de l'Ecole des Chartes*, 17 (= 4. Serie 2, 1856), S. 533–537; Georges Tessier, *Diplomatique royale française* (Paris, 1962), S. 300 f.; Hans E. Mayer, "Abu ʿAlis Spuren am Berliner Tiergarten. Ein diplomatisches Unikat aus dem Kreuzfahrerkönigreich Jerusalem," *Archiv für Diplomatik*, 38 (1992), S. 128 Anm. 35; vgl. ebd. 122–127.

[28] Abbildung von RRH no. 598a bei Mayer, *Abu Alis Spuren,* nach S. 122. RRH no. 623: Bayerisches Hauptstaatsarchiv München, Scheyern Urk. 10, siehe dazu Hans Eberhard Mayer, *Das Siegelwesen in den Kreuzfahrerstaaten*, Abhandlungen der philosophisch-historischen Klasse der Bayerischen Akademie der Wissenschaften, Neue Folge 83 (München, 1978), S. 34 Anm. 112; RRH no. 1140: Pamplona, Archivo Real y General de Navarra, Archivo de la Caméra dos Comptos, cájon II no. 11.

im Juni RRH no. 1037 für Genua in der üblichen Weise hatte besiegeln lassen, hier der wichtigste Aussteller war, wird kein Königssiegel angekündigt, sondern die Parteien beschworen lediglich die Abmachung. Es wird auf Seiten der Zyprioten auch keine künftige Besiegelung in Aussicht genommen, wohl aber *quod omnes Ianuenses, qui citra mare sunt et quos volueritis* (scil. die Zyprioten) *nominare, hanc conventionem iurabunt attendere et observare*. Auch hier ein Futur I.

Sowohl RRH no. 1047 wie RRH no. 1049 fehlt je ein angekündigtes Beglaubigungsmittel, das (gegebenenfalls) erst künftig nachgereicht werden sollte. Der Grund ist leicht zu erkennen. Sowohl RRH no. 1047 wie RRH no. 1049 waren zwar ausgehandelt worden zwischen den Baronen und König Heinrich I. von Zypern einerseits und den genuesischen Vertretern im Osten andererseits, waren aber de facto nur Vorverträge, nur ein Angebot der Jerusalemitaner und Zyprioten an Genua, das dort erst noch akzeptiert werden mußte. Man muß davon ausgehen, daß die Barone mit dem Projekt einer Allianz an die genuesischen Konsuln in Akkon herangetreten waren, wie es in RRH no. 1047 ausdrücklich heißt (*de iussu predictorum baronum scripsi*). Die Konsuln, die natürlich verpflichtet waren, solche Angebote nach Genua weiterzureichen, hatten sich der Zustimmung ihrer Landsleute im Osten versichert, denn die genuesischen Konzessionen in RRH no. 1049 erfolgten *de voluntate Ianuensium, qui sunt citra mare*.

Das war natürlich nicht einmalig, die Konsuln waren ja nicht befugt, die heimische Kommune ohne deren Zustimmung langfristig politisch zu binden. Der genuesische Podestà ratifizierte am 8. Juli 1267 mittels der Anbringung des Stadtsiegels eine Übereinkunft, die ein genuesischer Funktionär im Osten mit den Templern im Februar geschlossen hatte (RRH no. 1353). Andere Seestädte hielten es nicht anders. Vor dem Bailli des Königreichs Jerusalem schlossen Marseille einerseits und die Templer und Johanniter andererseits am 3. Oktober 1233 in Akkon einen Vertrag über die Schiffahrtsrechte der beiden Ritterorden für die Levantefahrt von Marseille aus. Am 17. April 1234 wurde der Vertrag in Marseille förmlich ratifiziert (RRH no. 1046, 1052). RRH no. 1046 trug einst die Siegel der beiden Ordensmeister und zweier marseillaisischer Gesandter sowie des Bailli von Jerusalem, war aber inhaltlich nur ein Vorvertrag, der ausdrücklich vorsah, daß er vom Grafen von Toulouse als Stadtherren und von der Kommune Marseille ratifiziert werden müsse. Erst die Ratifikationsurkunde RRH no. 1052 trug dann das kommunale Siegel Marseilles. Ohne RRH no. 1052 wäre der Vertrag RRH no. 1046 lettre morte geblieben. Der Doge von Venedig ratifizierte in gesonderter Urkunde einen Vertrag, den der Pleban von San Marco in Akkon und der venezianische Bailli daselbst, Giovanni Dandolo, am 19. Januar 1261 mit dem Bischof von Akkon geschlossen hatten.[29] Der Vertrag selbst genügte nicht, denn er hatte ausdrücklich

---

[29] Marco Pozza, "Venezia e il regno di Gerusalemme dagli Svevi agli Angioini," *I comuni italiani nel regno crociato di Gerusalemme*, Atti del Colloquio "The Italian Communes in the Crusading Kingdom of Jerusalem" (Jerusalem, May 24 – May 28, 1984), ed. Gabriella Airaldi und Benjamin Z. Kedar, Collana storica di fonti e studi (Genua, 1986), S. 385 no. 3. Datum des Vertrages ebd. S. 392.

die Ratifikation mittels einer goldbullierten Dogenurkunde bis September 1261 vorgesehen und stipuliert, daß bei Ausbleiben der Ratifikation der Vertrag ex tunc unwirksam sei.[30]

Der genuesische Admiral Benedetto Zaccaria schloß am 21. September 1288 einen Vertrag mit König Heinrich II. von Zypern. Der Vertrag erregte Anstoß in Genua, *maxime quia in dicta conventione exceptati non erant reges et principes, cum quibus conventiones antea habebamus.* Der König hatte den Bischof von Famagusta nach Genua geschickt, um dort die Ratifikation zu erwirken, aber Genua verweigerte die Ratifikation, obwohl man Benedetto ursprünglich sogar *potestas plenaria* gegeben hatte, im Osten verbindlich für Genua zu kontrahieren.[31] Ja mehr noch, Genua erbat und erhielt am 17. Mai 1292 die förmliche Aufhebung des Vertrags von 1288 durch Heinrich II. von Zypern. Bezeichnenderweise liegt die Revokation von 1292 noch im Staatsarchiv Genua und wurde auch in den Liber iurium II aufgenommen,[32] während der Text des revozierten Vertrags von 1288 nicht mehr erhalten ist.

Vergleichbar ist der Befund bei RRH no. 1047, 1049. Das Diplom Heinrichs I. von Zypern für Genua von 1232 Juni 10 (RRH no. 1037) steht im Liber iurium I.[33] Dagegen hat man RRH no. 1047, 1049, obwohl man die beiden Notariatsinstrumente in Genua vorliegen hatte, wo sie ja noch heute liegen, nicht in die Libri iurium aufgenommen, eben weil die Allianz zwar ausgehandelt worden, letztendlich aber nicht zustandegekommen war. Die Stadtannalen von Genua schweigen ebenfalls darüber. Auch hört man nicht das Geringste über irgendeine politische oder militärische Zusammenarbeit zwischen Genua und den Baronen Zyperns und des Hl. Landes während der projektierten Laufzeit des Vertrages. Erst 1242 bei der Vertreibung der staufischen Administration aus dem Land war Genua wieder behilflich, aber da wäre die Allianz, wäre sie denn zustandegekommen, bereits seit drei Jahren ausgelaufen gewesen. Die angebliche Allianz Genuas mit den Baronen im Osten wurde projektiert, von beiden Seiten wurde darüber verhandelt, zwei Entwürfe wurden nach Genua gebracht, aber abgeschlossen hat man sie offenkundig nicht. Hätte man das getan, dann wären neue Vertragsinstrumente oder mindestens eine Urkunde über die Ratifikation der beiden in Genua erhaltenen Entwürfe ausgefertigt worden, die dann wirklich von den sechs Baronen besiegelt

---

Dementsprechend ist RRH no. 1285, das andere, vom Bischof von Akkon ausgestellte Vertragsexemplar, umzudatieren zu 1261 Januar 17 (*a. inc. 1260, ind. 4* [statt 14], *decima septima* [statt *septima*] *die mensis Ianuarii*).

[30] RRH no. 1285; siehe den Text bei G. L. F. Tafel und G. M. Thomas, *Urkunden zur älteren Handels- und Staatsgeschichte der Republik Venedig mit besonderer Beziehung auf Byzanz und die Levante*, Fontes rerum Austriacarum, 2. Abteilung, Band 14/3 (Wien, 1857), S. 36 f.

[31] *Annali Genovesi*, 5 (Rom, 1929), S. 89–91.

[32] Pasquale Lisciandrelli, *Trattati e negoziazioni politiche della Repubblica di Genova*, Atti della Società Ligure di Storia patria 75 (Genua, 1960), no. 457; Ercole Ricotti, *Liber iurium reipublicae Genuensis*, 2, Historiae patriae monumenta 9 (Turin, 1857), S. 275 f.

[33] Dino Puncuh, *I libri iurium della Repubblica di Genova*, 1/2, Fonti per la storia della Liguria 4, (Genua, 1996), S. 179 no. 351.

worden wären, und die Genuesen im Osten wären aufgefordert worden, den Vertrag zu beschwören. Die Allianz ist, wie man auf Englisch sagt, ein Non-event, nicht mehr als ein politisches Planspiel.

Edbury scheint empfunden zu haben, wie mißlich es ist, daß die Allianz von 1233 so gar kein Echo in den Ereignissen fand. Er hat jedenfalls versucht, RRH no. 1049 auf Dezember 1232 zu legen, was dann auch Rückwirkungen hätte auf RRH no. 1047.[34] Zwar nenne die Urkunde das Inkarnationsjahr 1233, aber auch die sechste Indiktion (Herbst 1232 – Herbst 1233), was auf 1232 deute. Edbury kann so RRH no. 1049 in die Zeit des Endkampfes um Zypern und der Belagerung Kyrenias (kurz nach 15. Juni 1232 – nach Ostern 1233) verlegen, als die Genuesen nachweislich auf Seiten der Barone gegen die Kaiserlichen halfen. Das ist scharfsinnig beobachtet, aber nicht mehr haltbar, wenn man erkannt hat, daß sowohl RRH no. 1047 wie RRH no. 1049 von genuesischen Notaren geschrieben wurden, die erst kurz im Osten waren und daher präzis, aber nach genuesischen Usancen datierten. Genua hatte einen Jahresanfang vom 25. Dezember und setzte die Indiktion am 24. September um. Aber man numerierte die Jahre der Indiktion in Genua durchweg um eine Einheit niedriger als anderswo, wovon die genuesischen Annalen ständiges Zeugnis ablegen. Der 24. Oktober und der 2. Dezember 1233, Indiktion 6 ist daher für Genuesen eindeutig Oktober und Dezember 1233, nicht 1232.

Die Ursache für das Nichtzustandekommen der Allianz dürfte in Genua liegen. Die Beziehungen zu Kaiser Friedrich II. hatten sich 1232 gebessert. Als am 24. Oktober 1233 RRH no. 1047 über die Ausgrenzung der Pisaner im Königreich Jerusalem erging, wurden als Konsuln und Vizegrafen für Syrien Petrus de Mari und Piccomiglio genannt. Letzterer hatte, zusammen mit dem in RRH no. 1047 genannten Zeugen Montanarius de Marino, 1232 die Freilassung der in Sizilien inhaftierten Genuesen ausgehandelt.[35] Als die Angebote der Jerusalemitaner und Zyprer von Oktober und Dezember 1233 wegen des winterlichen Ruhens der Schiffahrt wohl eher im Frühjahr oder Sommer 1234 in Genua eintrafen, kann dies nicht mehr auf nachhaltiges genuesisches Interesse gestoßen sein. Die akute Bedrohung von 1231 und 1232 war vorüber, Genua, das sich dem zweiten Lombardenbund nicht anschloß, steuerte in Italien einen Kurs vorsichtiger Neutralität, den es erst 1237/1238 aufgeben mußte.[36] Bis dahin machte es keinen Sinn, den Kaiser, dessen langem Arm man sich in Italien zu entziehen trachtete, im Osten zu provozieren durch eine Allianz mit den gegen Friedrich rebellierenden Baronen der Königreiche Jerusalem und Zypern.

---

[34] Edbury, *Cyprus and Genoa*, S. 110 Anm. 9; Edbury, *Kingdom of Cyprus*, S. 65 Anm. 88, 67.

[35] *Annali Genovesi*, 3, S. 65.

[36] *Annali Genovesi*, 3, S. 81 f., 86–88; Böhmer – Ficker, *Regesta imperii,* 1, no. 2324. 2375.

The Social Context of Gravestones: Two Portraits

Anna-Maria Kasdagli and Yanna Katsou

Greek Ministry of Culture

The "unidentified church on Kisthiniou Street" is incorporated in the eastern part of the Hospitaller enceinte of Rhodes, near the Acandia Gate. It is a single-aisled, barrel-vaulted building whose apse is part of the city wall (Fig. 1). It was already shown as a ruin in an 1828 engraving when Rottiers, a Belgian traveller, identified it with Santa Maria della Vittoria, a church built by Grand Master Pierre d'Aubusson to honour the Virgin for her assistance in repulsing the Turks in the 1480 siege of Rhodes.[1] This identification was more or less forgotten by scholars when Albert Gabriel, in his monumental architectural study of medieval Rhodes, adopted another ruined church in the neighbourhood as Aubusson's dedication.[2] However, recent re-examination of the problem in the light of new discoveries, including several fragments from an early fifteenth-century gravestone on the site favoured by Gabriel, tips the argument against his choice: if in the early fifteenth century this church was already in existence, it cannot have been built by Aubusson.[3]

In contrast, the Rottiers church is definitely later in date: a marble slab with the arms of Grand Master Fluvian (d. 1437) and the Order, once mounted on the fortifications, was used as the top of a table-like altar in its sanctuary. Moreover, excavation by the 4th Ephorate of Byzantine Antiquities in 1995, has brought to light a burial chapel to the north of the church (Fig. 2). The evidence unearthed so far by the excavator, Ms. Yanna Katsou, indicates that north of the chapel stood another, larger church, which may well have been Aubusson's main construction; in this case, the vault incorporated in the city wall must have belonged to the nearby Greek Orthodox church of St. Panteleemon, built to honour the saint upon whose feast day the besieged won their decisive victory in 1480. Unhappily, investigation on the site has halted pending expropriation of the land, and many questions remain unanswered. However, the floor of the chapel, laid with clay tiles, preserves *in situ* two marble gravestones of the late Hospitaller period, whose presence agrees with other evidence that this was a new construction, dated to the late fifteenth century.

The first gravestone is dated to 1493. It was found broken in several pieces and lying over the skeleton of an elderly woman who suffered from arthritis. Reassembled in the conservation laboratory, it was entered in the internal Catalogue

---

[1] Bernard Rottiers, *Description des monuments de Rhodes* (Brussels, 1830), pl. LVII.

[2] Albert Gabriel, *La cité de Rhodes II, Architecture civile et religieuse* (Paris, 1923), p.180.

[3] For a more detailed exposition of the problem see Elias Kollias, "Αναζητώντας τα χαμένα μνημεία της μεσαιωνικής πόλης της Ρόδου," *15 Χρόνια έργων αποκατάστασης στη Μεσαιωνική Πόλη της Ρόδου*, Vol. A (Athens, 2007), pp. 283–297.

Fig. 1   View of the "unidentified church on Kisthiniou Street" from the north-west.

of Hospitaller Sculptures as No. F213. It measures 1.85 × 0.46–0.52 metres and is slightly trapezoidal (Fig. 3). Apart from a banner at the top, carved in two-plane relief, the slab is incised. The banner is borne on the upper part of a lance and bears the following arms: Quarterly; 1st and 4th quarter: a chief; 2nd and 3rd quarter: five *billets* in *saltire* (Fig. 4).

Most of the slab is covered with a Latin inscription arranged in twenty lines, with letters 4.5 cm high. Below it are rendered, rather clumsily, scattered human bones: a skull, a lower jaw, a scapula, a femur, and a rib (?). The layout belongs to a type frequently encountered at Rhodes from the fourteenth century onwards, with the owner's arms accompanied by an incised inscription.[4] The bones at the bottom of the slab, recalling the transient nature of worldly affairs, are an innovation for Rhodes; the same idea, in the form of a skull and crossbones, is encountered in two other, slightly later gravestones of Rhodes.[5] The provenance of this element of

---

[4] A. M. Kasdagli, "Τα ταφικά μνημεία της Ιπποτοκρατίας στη Ρόδο," *Δελτίον Εραλδικής και Γενεαλογικής Εταιρίας Ελλάδος* 11 (Athens, 2001), p. 122.

[5] Gravestone of Thomas Newport (†1502, inv. no. F10), with skull and crossbones on the lower part, Gregorios Konstantinopoulos, *Museums of Rhodes I, Archaeological Museum* (Athens, 1977), p. 16, fig. 7, and upper part of gravestone of medical doctor Thomaseus Liberalis (after 1510), inv. no. F40, ibid., p. 16, fig. 6, with skull on the corner of a decorative border.

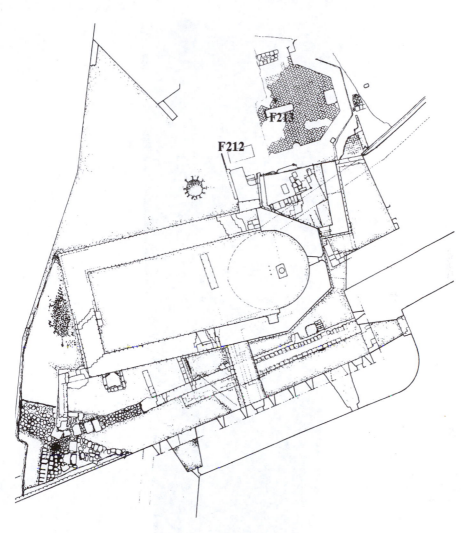

Fig. 2   Rhodes, unidentified church on Kisthiniou Street, excavation plan 1995

the macabre was apparently north-western Europe, where it is expressed in its most extreme form, the *transi* tomb, in the fourteenth and fifteenth centuries.[6]

The inscription is as follows:

+HIC SITA EST NO / BILIS FEMINA BA / RONV(M) BRITAN(N)IE / EX CLARA
FAMI / LIA DE PERIER IO / HA(N)NA D(OMI)NA DE / QVER ET COVER / DAINT
QVE SVP(RA) / SEXVM ANIMO / ET PRVDENCIA / PREDITA ITERA / TO A

---

[6] Cf. Paul Binski, *Medieval Death* (London, 1996), pp. 139–52.

Fig. 3   Tomb slab of Joanna de Perier, inv. no. F213

Fig. 4   Tomb slab of Joanna de Perier, detail

IEROSOLI / MIS REDIENS / XVI K(ALENDARVM) SEPTEM / BRIS DIEM CLAV /
SIT EXTREMV(M) / M CCCC / LXXXXIII / REQVIESCAT / IN PACE

Here is laid a noblewoman of the barons of Brittany, the glorious Perier family, Johanna,
lady of Quer and Couerdaint who, given spirit and prudence above her sex, having toured
Jerusalem, on her return, on the 16th of the calends of September ended her last day. 1493.
May she rest in peace.

Thus, we have Joanna de Perier, a Breton noblewoman who died on Rhodes on
the return leg of a pilgrimage to the Holy Land. The forceful personality of the lady
is evident in every detail: from the banner, seldom used by women since it was the
mark of a feudal lord who led his own men into battle,[7] to her attitude on worldly
things, graphically expressed by the scattered bones on the lower part of the slab.
How much of this impression is directly due to Joanna herself is hard to say. It is
likely that, knowing her end to be near, she left instructions about her grave to a
dependant or companion. It is also possible that he was so strongly influenced by her
personality that he endeavoured to leave a record of it on the stone for posterity.

---

[7] Instead of the lozenge women usually bore in this period. On Rhodes there are two examples of
lozenge shields: a stray find (inv. no. F82, Anna-Maria Kasdagli, "Κατάλογος των Θυρεών της Ρόδου,"
Αρχ.Δελτ. 48–49 (1994–95), Μελέτες, p. 228, no. 58) and another *in situ* in the rural chapel of St. Luke,
Soroni (Kasdagli, op. cit., p. 236, no. 125).

However, if the banner was included at the express wish of Joanna, the formulation *supra sexum animo* ... does not show much appreciation for women in general; it seems rather an expression of clerical ideas about feminine nature at a time when noblewomen would control the property and relations of husbands and sons too often absent on campaign or crusade. Would Joanna, "lady of Quer and Couerdaint", broadcast such contempt for her own sex?

The inscription is in Roman capitals distinguished by a freedom of line closely related to the inscription preserved on the stone of Knight Hospitaller Pedro Fernandez de Heredia, head of the Tongue of Aragon, who also died in 1493, just a month before Joanna de Perier.[8] Besides, the two works share the same, rather austere aspect (Fig. 5). Of course, the Heredia slab is inlaid with lead, a more expensive technique consonant with the temporal gap between a passing pilgrim and a Hospitaller officer of the first rank. Nevertheless, both epitaphs seem to have shared the same calligrapher.[9] This is matched by the epitaphs themselves, which have much in common: a preference for the word CLARA, the mention of "calends," the comment on the personality of the deceased just after the reference to social status, and the elaborate exposition of the time of death at the end. It is possible that the same scribe, in collaboration with the same marbler, was responsible for the composition of both epitaphs commissioned by the people who took care of the burial in each case.

If the banner ever bore coloured inlays, they do not survive. We can, however, recover the tinctures from armorials of the Breton nobility.[10] The Periers bore *billets or* on a field *azure*. Normally, according to the strict rules of heraldry, the Perier arms should occupy the first and fourth quartering of the shield, the "male" side in a marriage of arms. The irregularity encountered on the banner needs explaining. Investigation into the arms of those who married into the Perier family locates, in the early fifteenth century, Plézau, heiress of the house of Quintin, who bore *argent*, a chief *gules*. She had married Geoffroy IV de Perier,[11] to whom she passed the land of Quintin (Fig. 6). Normally, his children should have borne the Perier arms in the 1st and 4th quarter of the shield, and those of Quintin in the 2nd and 3rd. However, the Perier family history includes an event which explains the irregularity seen in the slab of Joanna.

---

[8] Inv. no. F13. Konstantinopoulos, *Museums of Rhodes* I, p. 20, fig. 10.

[9] Features in common: strong contrast between broad and narrow letters, with identical D, P, R, E, F, I (with dot above), N, Q and K; the difference in the serifs of M and A is explained by the inlay technique employed in the Heredia slab. There is also a decorative dot in the middle of the stem of T; there are also dots between words.

[10] Pierre le Baud, *Histoire de Bretagne avec les Chroniques des Maisons de Vitré et de Laval* (Paris 1538), Johannes B. Rietstap, *Armorial Général*, 2nd edn. (London, 1887); Henri Jougla de Morenas, *Grand Armorial de France, Catalogue général des armoiries des familles nobles de France* V (Paris, 1948).

[11] Benjamin Jolivet, *Les Côtes-du-Nord, histoire et géographie de toutes les villes et communes du Département* (Guincamp, 1856); Jean-Marie Rigaud, *Géographie historique des Côtes-du-Nord* (Saint-Brieuc, 1890).

Fig. 5   Tomb slab of Pedro Fernandez de Heredia, inv. no. F13

Jean IV, the son of Geoffroy IV, married twice. Under the influence of his second wife, Constance Gaudin, he tried to withhold the Quintin heritage from his firstborn son, another Geoffroy (Geoffroy V), to the benefit of Jean, a younger son he had had from Constance. In fact, it was not unusual for a younger son to succeed to property descended from the distaff side; however, Quentin was too important to let slip from Geoffroy's hands, and he reacted. A family quarrel ensued. In the end, not only did Geoffroy win his case, becoming count of Quintin in 1437, but his recalcitrant father, Jean IV, was obliged to go on pilgrimage to the Holy Land in 1445, "in penance for the discord he had brought into the family." In essence, he had been

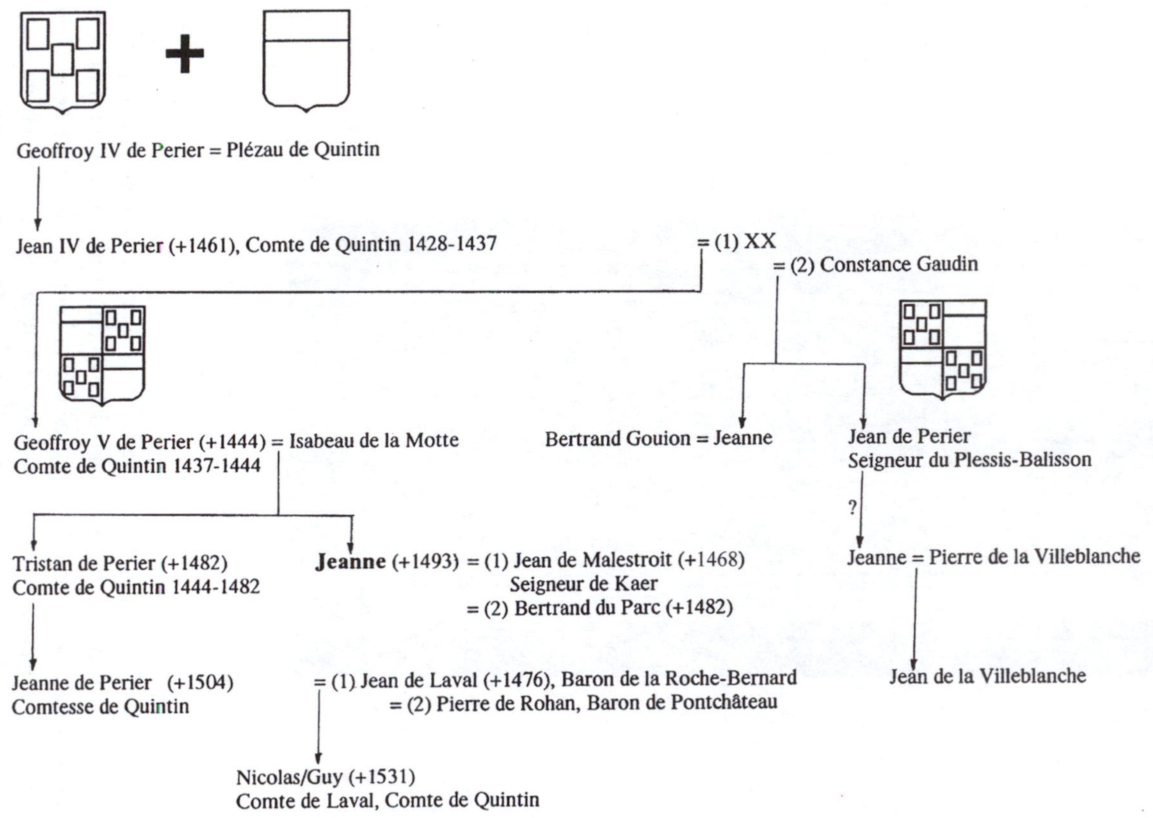

Fig. 6 The Perier family tree

forced to remove himself when Geoffroy V died, so that his grandson, Tristan de Perier, son of Geoffroy, could come into his inheritance without hindrance. It seems that Constance Gaudin and her son, then apparently aged around twenty, were still claiming their rights to the property.

Joanna, who was buried in Rhodes, was the daughter of Geoffroy V de Perier and his wife, Isabeau de la Motte, and sister to Tristan de Perier.[12] She had first married Jean de Malestroit, who is known to have held the property of Quer or Kaer. After Jean de Malestroit's death in 1468, Joanna married Bertrand du Parc, who died in 1482, as did her brother, Tristan. A year later, according to a written source,[13] Joanna was departing on pilgrimage to the Holy Land and ten years later she was dying on Rhodes. One further detail: above her banner two crosslets potent have been incised – and a cross potent usually represents Jerusalem. Perhaps the crosslets imply two visits to the Holy City? A first one begun in 1483 and mentioned in the archives of Brittany, and a second one which concluded prematurely in 1493? We will probably never know, but it is not unlikely: stalwart widows have been known to turn to the wandering life.

As her gravestone indicates, Joanna may have abjured the flesh but was still very much a member of the landed nobility. On her banner the arms of Quintin took pride of place; a change which must have occurred in her father's lifetime to mark his successful claim to the honour. The Perier arms, handed down by an unnatural father too much under the influence of a strange woman, were thus demoted to a secondary position on the shield. It is worth mentioning that the descendants of this unappreciated ancestor through the seductive Constance – who should recall to an impartial observer the tribulations of medieval widows and orphans – retained the original form of the arms: Perier in the 1st and 4th quarter, Quintin in the 2nd and 3rd.[14]

---

[12] This is certain, although there were three more Joannas in the family. The first was the heiress of Tristan de Perier; she died in 1504. The second was the heiress of Jean de Perier, lord of Plessis-Balisson, son of Constance Gaudin and Jean IV de Perier; this Joanna was much younger that the one who died on Rhodes. The third Joanna was the daughter of Constance Gaudin and Jean IV de Perier, but apparently she married Bertrand Gouion and had nothing to do with the land of Quer or Kaer. In contrast, the sister of Tristan de Perier is the only one of the four immediately connected to this property, was sufficiently well-to-do and of the right age – Geoffroy V de Perier was much older than his half-siblings – and she had had her sights on the Holy Land since 1483. Finally, only she and her niece could display the Quintin arms in the 1st and 4th quarters of their device as their side of the family had had the upper hand in the quarrel over that honour. A. de la Borderie, "La ceinture de la Sainte Vierge conservée à Quintin. Documents inédits, xii, Nouvelle généalogie des seigneurs de Quintin du XIIIe au XVIe siècle," *Mémoires de la Société archéologique et historique des cotes-du-nord*, série 3 (1889), pp. 235–84; Abbé Auguste Lemasson, *Un coin du Poudouvre. La Châtellenie du Plessis-Balisson*, 2nd edn. (Rennes, 1927); Augustin du Paz, *Histoire généalogique de plusieurs maisons illustres de Bretagne* (Paris, 1620), 1b, pp. 92, 160; Gwyn Meirion-Jones and Michael Jones, "Le Plessis-Kaer en Crac'h, Morbihan," *Mémoires de la société archéologique et historique de Bretagne* 78 (2000), p. 538. The analysis of the Perier family tree and the relevant bibliography are the generous contribution of Professor M. C. E. Jones.

[13] Du Paz, *Histoire généalogique*, Ia 180, 1b 193–94.

[14] Martine Fabre, *Héraldique médiévale bretonne. Images personnelles (vers 1350–1500). Armoriaux, scéaux, tombeaux*, I (Lille, 1993), p. 262 no. 1103.

Fig. 7   Tomb slab of Martinus de Rossca, inv. no. F212

The second gravestone discovered in the burial chapel (inventoried as F212) dates
from 1505 and measures 1.49 × 0.75 metres (Fig. 7). It was found intact, and has
yet to be removed from the floor to allow examination of the human remains
underneath. It is an attractive example of the restrained but elegant Renaissance
slabs of early sixteenth-century Rhodes. The arms of the deceased, five linden

leaves placed *in saltire*, occupy the centre, framed by a wreath of bay leaves decorated with symmetrically curving ribbons; the whole competently carved in rather low relief. The epitaph, in inlaid Roman capitals 5 cm high, is disposed around the slightly raised edge of the slab. It reads:

MARTINVS DE ROSS / CA BISSCAINVS MAHUMETTHANORVM AC / ERRIMVS PERSECVT / OR HIC IACET AN(N)O D(OMI)NI M(ILLESIM)O CCCCCV

Martinus de Rossca from Biscay, keenest persecutor of the followers of Mahomet, lies here in the year of our Lord 1505

Rossca is a version of Rosa, a rather common family name in the lands united under the crown of Aragon in the northern part of the Iberian peninsula.

The Catalans, able mariners and mercenaries and, above all, dreaded corsairs, were particularly active in the eastern Mediterranean from the thirteenth century onwards. Under licence by the Order of St. John, which used them as a weapon against Ottoman expansion, they plied the waters of the Aegean Sea in the fifteenth century and only towards 1500 does their presence appear somewhat less marked. They left the ports of Catalonia, often arming their vessels in Sicily, an intermediate stage on the way to the East, and after a period of action in the Aegean or the eastern Mediterranean went to Rhodes, where they could dispose of their booty and captives. Such ventures were often licensed by the master of the Hospital, but they could cause diplomatic problems. In the fifteenth century, Catalan corsairs seem to have been a major preoccupation for the Turks: they are specifically mentioned in the peace treaty of 1451 with the Hospital, although they are absent from that of 1481.[15]

We do not know whether Rossca belonged to this class of privateer or whether he was a sailor of Atlantic waters, one of those who facilitated Hospitaller communications with the Order's properties in the British Isles via the Bay of Biscay. There was nothing to stop an enterprising seaman from grasping the chance to profit from his presence in the East with a stout ship; to the crusading *mores* of the period this would, indeed, appear meritorious. A serious investigation in the archives of northern Spain might, perhaps, discover the traces of our "corsair" in the land of his birth; until then, his burial slab will remain just another relic of the stressful times between the two great sieges of Rhodes in 1480 and 1522.

The earliest laurel wreath on a Rhodian slab had appeared sometime earlier, in 1476, and belonged to a lay member of one of the great Venetian clans.[16] On that

---

[15] Zacharias Tsirpanlis, *Η Ρόδος και οι Νότιες Σποράδες στα χρόνια των Ιωαννιτών Ιπποτών (14ος–16ος αι.)* (Rhodes, 1991), pp. 51, 77, 266; idem, *Ανέκδοτα έγγραφα για τη Ρόδο και τις Νότιες Σποράδες από το αρχείο των Ιωαννιτών Ιπποτών, 1421–1453* (Rhodes, 1995), pp. 51, 58, 368.

[16] Iacobus de Prioli, son of patrician Pietro Prioli. The slab, inv. no. F207, was found *in situ* in 1998 at the Holy Apostles, and is displayed in the chapel surviving on the site.

slab, the artistic influence of the Renaissance is present,[17] but is less well served by the lapidary. Then we have the slab of Italian Knight Hospitaller Tommaso Provana,[18] dated to 1499; this is the immediate precursor of the Rossca slab (Fig. 8). The similarities are such that it may easily be supposed that we are dealing with the same workshop, if not with the evolving style of a single capable *tombier*. The arrangement of the various features on both works is particularly telling.

Besides stylistic similarities, however, there is also the characteristic form of the Roman lettering: it is a conscious imitation of classical models, elaborated by the inclusion of some letters within others, employed as a space-saving device. This feature is shared with three other works: the gravestones of knights Rainier Pot[19] and Nicolas de Montmirel,[20] who both held the office of Hospitaller and died in 1498 and 1511 respectively; and the Greek tomb slab of 1508, unfortunately preserved only in fragmentary state.[21] If these five works are considered the products of a single workshop, active at least between 1498 and 1511, its capabilities are impressive. It had at least one calligrapher able to create Latin and Greek lettering of high aesthetic quality, a sculptor skilled in the rendering of the naturalistic low relief required by burial slabs, and offered its clients the option of inlay, a technique visible on the slabs of Rossca and Montmirel but also known to have been selected to grace the tomb of Grand Master Fabrizio del Carretto in 1521.[22] Of course, in this prosperous period of Rhodian history, the existence of more workshops served for certain lengths of time by particular able craftsmen in various fields – calligraphers, engravers and sculptors – is equally possible.

That there was more than one calligrapher employed in the supposed workshop may be inferred from the examination of another slab sharing certain features with that of Rossca. It belonged to an English knight,[23] turcopolier Thomas Newport,[24] who was buried in Rhodes in 1502. Here, also, the arms are set within a laurel wreath rendered in shallow relief executed by a competent sculptor, accompanied by a skull and crossbones carved on the lower part of the slab. However, the engraving of the epitaph in this example is much inferior to the others in the group. It therefore seems reasonable to suppose that, if this slab came from the same workshop as the others,

---

[17] Inscription in Roman capitals on a spread scroll, Renaissance shield form; attempt at naturalistic rendering of the wreath.

[18] Inv. no. F 12. Konstantinopoulos, *Museums of Rhodes* I, pp. 19–20, fig. 9.

[19] Inv. no. F 22. Ibid., p. 29, fig. 21.

[20] Inv. no. F 11. From 1993 at the Grand Masters' Palace. Ibid., pp. 18–19, fig. 8.

[21] Inv. no. F202. Grand Masters' Palace. *Αρχ.Δελτ.* 39 (1984), Β, Χρονικά, p. 340.

[22] Rottiers, *Description*, pl. XLI.

[23] Inv. No. F10. On display at the Archaeological Museum of Rhodes. Konstantinopoulos, *Museums of Rhodes* I, pp. 16–18, fig. 7.

[24] Neil Clarke, "On the Trail of a Shropshire Knight Hospitaller," part 3, *Telford Historical and Archaeological Society Journal* 5 (2001), p. 4, and Jürgen Sarnowsky, *Macht und Herrschaft im Johanniterorden des 15. Jahrhunderts: Verfassung und Verwaltung der Johanniter auf Rhodos (1421–1552)*, (Münster, 2001), p. 657.

Fig. 8   Tomb slab of Thomas Provana, inv. no. F12

a different calligrapher – and engraver – were used. It is possible that the Rossca slab was commissioned by one of the Knights Hospitaller who, as we have seen, patronized such workshops. Finally, it may be added as a postscript that another Thomas Newport – very probably a relative of the turcopolier commemorated in the surviving tomb slab – and conceivably the man actually responsible for the commission of the slab, was drowned in the Bay of Biscay on his way to succour the final endeavour of the Knights to defend Rhodes in January 1523;[25] a journey rendered twice futile because by then the town had surrendered: Newport was sacrificing his life for a cause already lost.

Medieval gravestones form a corpus of inscriptional evidence which sculpture has served incidentally and, on Rhodes, often indifferently. They reflect the financial and social status of the people commemorated by the epitaphs, and the broader attitudes of a period. It is for this reason that this aspect of the artifacts presented here was examined in such detail. The history of art is another way to study the past in depth, if it is not limited to its most outstanding expressions. It is rather striking that, on Rhodes, funerary inscriptions are not penitential in character – as though, by ending their lives in the forefront of Christendom and under the shadow of Islam, people believed that they ensured a place in the company of the Blessed. Be that as it may, Brittany and the Iberian coastline produced some of the most exceptional seafarers of Europe, as well as some of its most notorious marauders. Naturally, the call of distant lands also marked the lives of some who sank into oblivion, only to re-emerge in our day like Jonah from the belly of the whale. Those who commissioned their memorials recorded aspects of their personality, exposing powerful historic trends whose influence has yet to fade. It is, perhaps, a twist of fate that the confrontation of major religions, and the independence of women, are issues still very much alive.

---

[25] Clarke, "On the Trail."

REVIEWS

Adrian J. Boas, *Archaeology of the Military Orders. A Survey of the Urban Centres, Rural Settlements and Castles of the Military Orders in the Latin East (c. 1120–1291)*. Abingdon and New York: Routledge, 2006. Pp. xviii, 318. ISBN 0 415 29980 2.

As with the author's previous book, *Crusader Archaeology: The Material Culture of the Latin East* (1999), the chief utility of this book lies in the fact that much of this information would otherwise remain in diverse archaeological journals, which are sometimes not readily available. However, despite its general similarity, this book has a narrower focus, concentrating on recent archaeological research of the Military Orders, with an emphasis on architecture. The author justifies the emphasis by pointing out that not only were the most important crusader urban institutions constructed by the Military Orders, but the chief examples of Frankish military architecture were also built by the Military Orders as well. "Almost all the major castles in the Latin East, and many of the lesser ones, were built or rebuilt by them. This was above all due to the fact that they alone had the financial resources necessary to construct these enormous and complex constructions" (p. 100). Put simply, the king of Jerusalem did not have the resources to build Belvoir castle, but the Hospitallers did. Despite the emphasis on architecture, the book does not neglect the small finds from archaeological excavations, since these clearly illustrate the daily life of the Military Orders.

The book is organized into several parts. "Background" offers a dozen pages of basic information about each of the various Military Orders (for example, their origins, contemporary sources, expansion), including the Hospitallers, the Templars, the Teutonic Knights, the Leper Knights of St. Lazarus, and the Order of St. Thomas of Canterbury. Part I, "Urban Administrative Centres" has major sections on the urban quarters of each of these Military Orders. Part II, "The Rural Activity of the Countryside," discusses Hospitaller, Templar, Teutonic, and Order of St. Thomas rural possessions. Part III, "The Defence of the Latin East," includes sections on the differing defensive role of the Military Orders; the factors influencing the choice of plan; castle typology (tower keeps, large enclosure castles, *quadriburgia*, hilltop and island castles); the non-defensive components of a castle; the chief elements of fortification (for example, gates, posterns, portcullises, ditch); stone masonry; weapons and armor. Part IV, "Additional Archaeological Evidence," includes an interesting section on the daily life of the Military Orders, including sleeping quarters, tableware and utensils, bathing and hygiene, games and other recreation, seals and bullae, and horse equipment, sculpture, frescoes and reliquaries. Some of the small finds demonstrate the use of luxury ceramic and glass wares, and, despite prohibitions, indulgence in games of dice. There is a brief conclusion of just over two pages, followed by two appendices, including a

"Chronology of Castles" (Appendix I) and a "Gazetteer of Sites of the Military Orders" (Appendix II). Finally, there are extensive notes, as well as an extensive bibliography.

In addition to providing an overview of recent research, Boas has opinions on scholarly issues. For example, he agrees with a consensus of opinion that there was no pre-planned defensive system, including no overall conception of border defense. Nevertheless, the Military Orders played a key role in defending frontier regions, including the Armenian kingdom in Cilicia. He agrees with Kennedy and other scholars that the type of castle built at a site depended on site-topography, on the availability of water and building stone (often including ancient ruins with *spolia*), and on intended function. As for T. E. Lawrence's argument that the Templars had a different building style than the Hospitallers, Boas argues that it is impossible to generalize on the subject (p. 101). Nevertheless, the Military Orders preferred the enclosure castle, built around a courtyard, since it allowed space for the spiritual and military needs of the garrison. Boas disagrees with H. Kennedy (p. 122) that quadrangular enclosure castles with projecting towers (*quadraburgia*) lost their relevance following Hattin in 1187. He points out that Belvoir withstood Saladin's forces for a year and a half. All scholars seem to agree that Belvoir castle, the chief seat of the Hospitallers, was an epitome of a certain type of castle development whose design greatly enhanced its effectiveness under siege (p. 123). Boas describes Belvoir castle as "a superbly compact design with two enclosure castles, one within the other, unique in the Latin East except for the smaller and later castle of Saranda Kolones in Paphos, western Cyprus" (p. 13).

Saranda Kolones castle (which I excavated with A. H. S. Megaw) is, according to Boas, "remarkably similar in form to Belvoir" (p. 123), which "leaves no room for doubt that it was designed in imitation of the latter" (p. 124). Nevertheless, Boas reverses his previous opinion (in his 1999 book, p. 109) that this impressive castle was possibly built by the Hospitallers. He now believes that it could not have been because "no mention is made of it in Hospitaller sources" (p. 124). Hence, Saranda Kolones does not appear as a site "of known location" (p. 222) of the Military Orders in Appendix II, despite the fact that some structures listed in the Gazetteer (for example, the tower at Bait Jubr at-Tahtani and Casale Doc) also have no direct literary texts to support an attribution to the Military Orders. Nevertheless, in my view there is credible circumstantial evidence that the Hospitallers built Saranda Kolones. Aimery of Lusignan, ruler of Cyprus when Saranda Kolones was built (ca. 1200), was too poor to defend Cyprus. Doubtless for this reason, in 1198, Pope Innocent III requested that the Military Orders defend Cyprus. Considering the poverty of Aimery, who else but one of the Military Orders could have built Saranda Kolones? To quote Boas again: "Almost all the major castles in the Latin East, and many of the lesser ones, were built or rebuilt by them. This was above all due to the fact that they alone had the financial resources necessary to construct these enormous and complex constructions" (p. 100). It is precisely for this reason that Saranda Kolones should be assigned to one of the Military

Orders. The unique similarity of its design to Belvoir argues for its construction by the Hospitallers.

However, the 1210 grant of Hugh I of Cyprus to the Hospitallers makes no mention of a Paphos castle in their possession. This could be explained by the following circumstantial evidence. Saranda Kolones was constructed ca. 1200, presumably to defend Paphos against the threat of a Byzantine attempt to retake Cyprus. That threat disappeared in 1204 when Constantinople was conquered by the Fourth Crusade. The numerous blocked-up (or never completed) sallyports, and the unfinished quarrying in the west ditch of Saranda Kolones point to a full-stop in the castle's construction, perhaps in 1204 as news of the Fourth Crusade's conquest reached Cyprus. In 1205, Hospitaller garrisons were withdrawn from Cyprus, so it is reasonable to speculate that the Hospitallers may have begun construction on this castle in response to the appeal of Pope Innocent III, but stopped construction by 1205. Thereafter, the unfinished castle could have been given to a baron of Hugh I to administer. Such, in brief outline, is the fuller argument I would make for the Hospitallers having begun construction on a castle they never completed, and never really possessed. For those who find this too speculative, I return to the core of my argument, which is founded on an assertion made in the book under review, namely that crusader castles the size and complexity of Saranda Kolones were typically constructed by one of the Military Orders. Since the design of Saranda Kolones is so similar to that of Hospitaller Belvoir, it seems reasonable to conclude that the Military Order that constructed Saranda Kolones was the Order of the Hospital of St John.

JOHN ROSSER
BOSTON COLLEGE

Damien Carraz, *L'Ordre du Temple dans la basse valée du Rhône (1124–1312). Ordres militaires, croisades et société méridionales* (Collection d'histoire et d'archéologie médiévales, 17). Lyon: Presses Universitaires de Lyon, 2005. Pp. 662. ISBN 2 7297 0781 6 (paperback).

Historians have used up enough ink contemplating the Templars' wheeling and dealing as economic power brokers in narrowly-defined geographical areas for one to be forgiven for not expecting too many new contributions in yet another regional study about the order. Therefore, while its scope and perspective offer little comparison to other regional monographs about the Temple, it does come as a pleasant surprise that this book is loaded with new discoveries. Using the lower Rhone valley as a reference point, with its rich archives and well-documented religious and social history, Damien Carraz has launched an erudite and complex investigation into the social and religious circumstances that once allowed military orders like the Temple to become, and prosper as, integral elements of the social and religious landscape of medieval western Europe. The number and variety of sources consulted by Carraz is vast (in addition to the Vatican Archive and the Bibliothèque Nationale in Paris, he has ploughed through no fewer than nine departmental and municipal archives, examining many thousands of documents) and the questions he applied to them are for the most part original.

Divided into three parts and nine chapters, the book covers, chronologically and thematically, a variety of topics relating to the Order of the Temple's inner development and outward perception as a religious institution with a distinctively military function. The role of Provence in the early crusading period and the impact of interreligious warfare (at home, in Spain and in the Holy Land) on the collective memory of society in southern France are discussed first, followed by an assessment of the Templars' entanglements with, and gradual inclusion into, the wide-spun networks of kinship and loyalty that governed medieval society. The first part ends with an interesting discussion of how and to what end both church and laity in Provence responded to the two movements which, in the author's opinion, together defined the *contexte favorable* for the advent of the military orders: the religious reform movement and the crusades. Not all of the author's assessments are easy to swallow and some observations – for example, that families disposed of younger sons (Carraz calls them "adventurers") by putting them in charge of possessions in the county of Tripoli or that knights engaged with the military orders to help protect their own overseas possessions – are intriguing and certainly still open to debate. The overall argument that families who supported the military orders were often also heavily involved in the crusading movement, however, is convincing and solidly supported by the evidence. Equally well founded is the author's interesting observation that reform bishops and their social networks often played major roles in the creation and development of Templar communities, which seems to have been part of a strategy to implement the parishes with ideas of reform.

The book's second part examines the topographical setting of Templar communities and the economic efforts of the Templars (and other military communities) to establish, enhance and consolidate their local presence. It discusses various forms of association with the Order and the origin of Templar postulants, before illustrating, albeit briefly, how the Templars conducted their liturgy and involved themselves in parish work. Next the author examines the Templars' functions and influence as feudal lords, their attitude towards (and employment of) secular laws and justice, and their close relations with the lay establishment, the *élites laïques*. In all this Carraz proves a great talent for synthesis, which he couples with his strong sense of curiosity to introduce new potential fields of inquiry. The role and outlay of urban commanderies, the attachment of families from the rural "*intelligentsia*" to Templar communities, as lawyers and notaries, the comparison of the Templars with the early mendicants, and the long-term association of particular kin-groups with individual communities are only a few topics worthy of further investigation.

The third part of the book discusses the political dynamics underlying the military orders' conflicting alliances in the struggle over lordship, church control and *spiritualia*, fields in which the Templars were active contestants. Carraz's analysis illustrates very clearly the many paradoxes that still characterize the conduct of international institutions in local political theatres (pro-Catalan in the on-going conflict between Barcelona and Toulouse, the Templars seem to have sided with Simon de Montfort and the French crusaders in the Albigensian crusades, yet offered refuge to individuals in conflict with Catholic doctrine; directly subordinate to the pope, they responded positively to imperial approaches until well into the thirteenth century, before, like the Hospitallers, shifting their alliance to Charles of Anjou). This, of course, demonstrates just how flexible and adaptable to circumstances the individual units of these orders often were. Provided next is an account of the military orders' increasingly futile efforts in the late thirteenth and early fourteenth centuries to engage society in crusading campaigns and thus to maintain their image as crusader institutions. The book concludes with a brief summary of the arrest of the Templars in Provence, their trial and the destiny of their possessions.

The book is a tour de force. It sparkles with new ideas, which, although not always fully elaborated, compel further research. (The commitment of the Templars to *cura animarum* is one of many topics raised in this book that is deserving of a more detailed study.) At the very least, Carraz deserves praise for demonstrating (in a skillful manner) the urgent need for a discourse that acknowledges the military orders not simply as integral elements of crusading history but, perhaps first and foremost, as powerful expressions of the spiritual, religious and social developments in Catholic Europe at the time of the crusades. He has produced a long-awaited and well-placed signpost as to how a holistic understanding of the military orders' social and religious functions can be achieved. With its extraordinary catalogue of primary sources (consisting mainly of hitherto unpublished charters) this book will undoubtedly become an important reference work for any scholar interested in the social history of medieval southern France and the military orders.

JOCHEN G. SCHENK
PONTIFICAL INSTITUTE OF MEDIAEVAL STUDIES, TORONTO

Nicole Chareyron, *Pilgrims to Jerusalem in the Middle Ages*, trans. W. Donald Wilson. New York: Columbia University Press, 2005. Pp. xvi, 287. ISBN 0 231 13230 1.

Eastward Bound: Travel and Travellers, 1050–1550, ed. Rosamund Allen. Manchester: Manchester University Press, 2004. Pp. xv, 270. ISBN 0 7190 6690 5 (hardback), 0 7190 6691 3 (paperback).

Nicole Chareyron's handsome volume, which was published in French in 2000, is both smaller and greater in scope than the title suggests. It confines its attention only to Christian pilgrims and the later Middle Ages (fourteenth to sixteenth centuries), but for those travellers and that period it is rich in both detail and analysis, based on the study of more than one hundred firsthand accounts. The first chapter gives a necessarily, but rather brutally, brief history of the Latin occupation of the Holy Land to 1291, and also discusses questions of genre and language in the pilgrims' accounts, and of motivation among the pilgrims themselves. Alongside pious motives, and possible espionage and fact-finding missions, Chareyron discerns in the pilgrims' accounts the growth of curiosity: a conventional view of the late medieval period, but open to challenge from historians of earlier centuries.

Once these preliminaries are disposed of, the narrative gets into its stride with fifteen chapters which follow the pilgrims on their journeys, from their departure out of Venice to their eventual return to western Europe. These chapters are a rattling good read, incorporating many anecdotes and long quotations from the pilgrims' accounts, and covering diverse aspects of medieval tourism. Thus, in Venice we are told of the fascination of its relics, but also about arrangements for exchanging money; the hardships of the five-week voyage are described, and also the delights of the ports of call; the excitement of arriving in the Holy Land is tempered by putting in at "Jaffa the desolate." Naturally there is much on Jerusalem and the Holy Places (including the miserable lodgings), and a whole chapter is devoted to the Church of the Holy Sepulchre where – then as now – the rivalries of the different churches were much in evidence. Many pilgrims then ranged more widely: popular sites around Jerusalem included Bethlehem, the River Jordan, the Dead Sea and Galilee. In these areas the travellers encountered the native peoples – Saracens, Arabs, Jews, Bedouin – and their recorded reactions are examined, with some attention to their attitudes to Islam. Many pilgrims extended their tours into Egypt, travelling via Hebron to visit St. Catherine's monastery and Mount Sinai, then on to Cairo and "Pharaoh's Granaries" – notably, some observers were sceptical about the idea that the pyramids were ever used for storing grain. In fact, as many chapters are devoted to Egypt and its wonders, and exotic fauna, as to the Holy Land itself. After Egypt, the pilgrims would take ship home again from Alexandria. A final chapter looks at the "alchemy of memory" and the construction of the pilgrims' narratives, ending with a reference to the "brilliant future" of travel writing.

The text is supported by copious endnotes, a time chart and maps. There is a comprehensive bibliography; however, although this was updated to accompany the translation of the book, it does not generally include English translations of primary sources, where these exist, but only French ones. In the translated text, too, which generally reads very well, names are left in their French versions, which are less familiar to an anglophone audience: for example, Godefroy, Jean de Mandeville. The index is not as helpful as it might be, having long and undifferentiated entries for individual pilgrims, but, with rather endearing eccentricity, listing individual animals under "Fauna, exotic." (How many people want to look up crocodiles, and would think of looking under the letter "f"?) A useful prosopographical appendix of "Pilgrims' Profiles" is also included. Overall, *Pilgrims to Jerusalem in the Middle Ages* is both authoritative and immensely enjoyable.

Eastward Bound, a collection of essays, also contains much of interest. Its editor, Rosamund Allen, has brought together eleven contributors and she herself provides an excellent overview in the introduction. The essays are loosely but logically arranged to proceed from the general to the particular and from the earlier to the later. Jewish and Muslim travellers are included, and not all journeys were made to Jerusalem. Thus there is some overlap with the Chareyron book, but also much different material. Bernard Hamilton sets the scene with "The impact of the crusades on western geographical knowledge," a *tour de force* which deploys encyclopaedic knowledge of a vast number of sources, and of medieval and modern geography. Two case studies follow. Elka Weber writes on Jewish travellers to the Land of Israel: this is particularly interesting on the relations between Muslims, Jews and Christians at sites holy to the three religions. The referencing is rather cavalier, though, and I should have liked to be able to source the "presumption" that Jews were not allowed to live in Jerusalem, and the "relatively wide circulation" in the tenth century of Josephus in a Hebrew paraphrase. The importance of patronage for Muslim travellers is the theme of Shawkat M. Toorawa's contribution, which focuses on the career, as writer and physician, of ʿAbd al-Latif (1162–1231CE), whose patrons included Saladin and his sons. Staying in the Islamic world, Niall Christie's essay on women in the "memoirs" of Usamah Ibn Munqidh rather strains the framework of travel "eastward bound," but nevertheless provides additional material to the usual well-worn anecdotes.

Closer to the book's theme, Andrew Jotischky's discussion of "The Mendicants as missionaries and travellers in the Near East in the thirteenth and fourteenth centuries" has some overlap with the Chareyron volume, but, as a study-in-depth, it adds significant details: as a minor example the expense of taxes, tolls and entry fees which were a real burden to the friars, and more importantly their attitudes to the different groups of eastern Christians. The following essay, by Catherine Delano-Smith on the use of maps for the Jerusalem pilgrimage, is a comprehensive survey of the maps available in the late medieval period, but it failed to engage me because of the writer's device of "an imaginary, timeless, placeless, learned and pious pilgrim as our hero." This was not a bad idea in itself, but its execution involved sustained use of convoluted conditional constructions (for example, "our pilgrim would have had to" – why not "could" or "might"?) which became unduly distracting. The next essay, by Evelyn Edson, looks at the work of Sanudo and Vesconte to revive the crusade, and is more successful with respect to its smaller canvas. Finally, four contributions deal with specific travellers in the late medieval period. John Mandeville's book (Suzanne Conklin Akbari) is perhaps more revealing of inner worlds than real journeyings. Margery Kempe (Rosalynn Voaden) and two German pilgrims, Ludolf von Sudheim and Hans Tucher (Anne Simon), offer case studies which overlap with the Chareyron book, but are used differently, as individual studies-in-depth rather than as part of a synthesized account. Sudheim's observations about the ruins of crusader castles are particularly interesting. The final essay, by Barry Taylor, considers four Spanish travellers from the fifteenth and sixteenth centuries and examines themes in their written accounts (including fauna). A general and comprehensive bibliography is included of primary and secondary sources (Chareyron is not in it). The index is rather hit-and-miss: I looked up Antioch to find only two references, whereas there are several rather important passages in different essays which are not indexed. There is, however, a long and differentiated entry for animal(s)!

Leaving aside their shared fascination with exotic fauna, there is significant common ground between these two books, but as their perspectives are quite distinct, both may be enjoyed for their complementary strengths.

Susan B. Edgington

Queen Mary, University of London

La Croisade Albigeoise. Actes du Colloque du Centre d'Études Cathares, Carcassonne, 4, 5 et 6 octobre 2002, ed. Michel Roquebert. Carcassonne: Le Centre d'Études Cathares, 2004. Pp. 409. ISBN 2 9521024 0 6 (paperback).

This conference volume provides a thorough re-examination of extant sources on the Albigensian crusade and also a re-evaluation of the anti-heretical campaigns' origins, evolution, and impact upon Occitania. Articles by Martin Aurell, Karin Cavozzocca Mazzanti, Kay Wagner, Robert Moore, Daniel Baloup, and Anne-Marie Lamarrigue provide solid surveys of past literature on the three major sources for the crusade (Peter of Vaux-de-Cernay, William of Puylaurens and the *Chanson de la croisade*), while highlighting neglected evidence including Robert of Auxerre, source material from England and the Iberian peninsula, and the histories of the Limousin inquisitor Bernard Gui. Aurell rightly urges research within regional archives and on specific families to better map the social background of Occitania and explain individuals' choice of allegiances during the struggle against heresy. These articles also reveal a lively debate over the nature of the charter of Niquinta (1167). If authentic, the document potentially testifies to the wide diffusion and formal ecclesiastical structure of Catharism within Occitania by the mid-twelfth century. If inauthentic, it may nonetheless disclose the motives of various parties interested in intervening in the region, the subject of recent studies by Peter Biller, Robert Moore and Nicholas Vincent on the conception and presentation of heresy in England. Motivated by hostility toward Raymond V, count of Toulouse, the Plantagenets and chroniclers associated with them formulated the image of heresy in the Toulousain as a virulent contagion which threatened all Christendom. Although, with the marriage of Richard I's sister Jeanne to Raymond VI (1191), Plantagenet policy would dramatically reverse to one of mutual alliance against the threatened Capetian domination of Occitania, the image would be powerfully invoked in later anti-heretical campaigns.

Yet these fresh insights and Aurell's call for the utilization of often overlooked evidence such as iconography, archaeology, hagiography and some homiletic sources – including a previously unnoted collection of *exempla* and the *Brevis ordinacio* (mistakenly described as a sermon collection rather than a preaching treatise) – only highlight this volume's omission of fresh and important work on previously neglected sermon literature. This despite the fact that major articles, monographs and upcoming editions by Beverly Kienzle, Carolyn Muessig, Nicole Bériou, and Christoph Maier, among others, have illuminated the importance of the Cistercian homiletic tradition and the recruiting sermons of Paris-trained masters including James of Vitry, Philip the Chancellor, and Odo of Châteauroux in transmitting images of heterodoxy and legal justifications of the anti-heretical crusade to lay audiences.

However, a recent resurgence of interest in the history of the Iberian peninsula is reflected in Baloup's treatment of Iberian chroniclers' unique views of the Albigensian crusade. Damian Smith provides crucial insight into papal relations with Aragon and Catalonia, while Philippe Contamine and Martín Cabrer analyze the historical importance and traditional presentations of the battle of Muret (1213), which resulted in the death of Peter of Aragon, the orthodox papal champion of the battle of Las Navas de Tolosa (1212). While Contamine tackles the question of whether Muret proved a crucial turning point in the creation of "France," Cabrer argues that Peter's demise merely contributed to a very glacial erosion of a "hispano-occitan" culture which united the Midi and Aragon.

Michel Roquebert, Monique Zerner and Pilar Jiménez-Sanchez likewise rescrutinize the roles played by concepts of just war, peace and heresy in shaping the legal background of the Albigensian crusade. Contravening much of the historiographical tradition, both Zerner and Jiménez-Sanchez conclude that the crusade was begun for political, not religious reasons; accusations of heresy were constructed and wielded by the papacy, ecclesiastics and princes to combat their enemies and to impose peace and a political theocracy upon Occitania and the papal patrimony. Elaine Graham-Leigh illustrates how the anti-heretical crusade's early campaigns were defined by the "spin" placed upon two suspect deaths: the assassination of the legate Peter Castelnau, which provided a convenient pretext for fresh appeals to military action, and the demise of the Trencavel viscount Raymond-Roger, which spawned persistent rumors that he had been murdered by Simon de Montfort. Marco Meschini deftly traces the impact of regional politics and rivalries and the troubled relationships between the pope, his legates, and Simon de Montfort upon the nature and success of the *negotio pacis et fidei*. For beneath the veneer of unity manufactured by propagandists such as Peter of Vaux-de-Cernay, the crusader army seethed with disagreements over the financing of the crusade, its military course and ultimate goals, the partition of conquests, and the treatment of heretics.

Some of this volume's most important contributions come in its reassessment of the effects of the Albigensian crusades upon Occitania, including Claudie Amado's innovative use of sociological models to gauge the crusade's influence upon the material framework and very values of noble Occitan society, including *paratge*. Despite modern agendas and macrohistorical models which portray the crusade as one manifestation of a growing royal power consolidating itself at the expense of the regional nobility, both Christine Keck and Jean-Louis Biget carefully segregate the intentions of early crusaders from the Capetians' eventual use of the crusade to intrude political control into Occitania. Both also argue for a lack of systematic "northern" colonization and profound transformation of the native aristocratic hierarchy in Occitania. For, although the "treachery" of southern castral lords led Simon de Montfort to directly invest some of his most loyal followers and local prelates and religious houses with newly confiscated lands, his actions primarily affected the lower nobility. Many towns were also rewarded for their support with greater autonomy from previous obligations to local lords. Yet after Simon's death in 1218, many of his adherents abandoned their new lands, allowing southern lords to recover much of their inheritances, although urban settlements and churches largely managed to retain their newly acquired privileges and possessions. Similarly, although some northerners returned with Louis VIII's army, reclaiming "their" lands and forming the core of a new royal administration in Occitania, they tended to gradually assimilate with the local nobility, who dominated the lower ranks of the new bureaucracy. The impact of property seizures stemming from royally-supported inquisitions against heresy and the rebellion of *faidits* in the 1240s likewise varied according to region and social class. In some areas, powerful lords conserved most of their domains, while castellans and knights suffered dispossession, although the obverse scenario prevailed in other regions. And while destruction or the massive transferral of resources followed the capture of some important cities, towns and *castra*, others escaped relatively unscathed.

In fact, the general consensus of this conference is that the immediate impact of the crusade upon Occitania remains difficult to distinguish from that of larger, often pre-existing, historical trends and processes, as illustrated by the effect which the Cistercians' support for the crusade had upon the order's houses in this region. For while noting that the climate of insecurity contributed to isolated acts of violence and usurpation and that some houses (notably Fontfroide and Villelongue) benefited from the receipt of possessions confiscated from "heretics," Mireille Mousnier argues that the long-term evolution and economic health of Cistercian houses was far more influenced by individual houses' roles in the local economy and alliances with regional powers. Similarly, Laurent Macé notes that, while the anti-heretical crusades did in fact embroil the peasantry in warfare and resulted in depredation of the countryside, the region appears to have rebounded rapidly. Archeologists Jean-Paul Cazes, David Maso, Nicolas Portet, Marie-Élise Gardel, Dominique Baudreu, Jean-Loupe Abbé, and Charles Peytavie paint similarly complex portraits of the crusades' impact upon the seigneurial fortresses of Termes, Fenouillet, Montaillou, the *castrum* of Cabaret, and the town of Limoux, concluding that it is difficult to draw conclusions applicable to Occitania as a whole from the varying fates of individual sites.

Given the impressive contributions of this volume's many articles, one can only hope that the conference roundtable's proposition to utilize the combined resources of the SSCLE and Centre d'Études Cathares to organize a conference commemorating the initiation of the Albigensian crusade in 2009 will be realized. Their proposal for a comprehensive international bibliography on the same subject is also most welcome. Certainly this reader would have profited from the inclusion of a bibliography within the conference proceedings themselves, although they remain an invaluable resource for scholars of the anti-heretical crusades and French history.

JESSALYNN BIRD
INDEPENDENT SCHOLAR

Erica Cruikshank Dodd, *Medieval Painting in the Lebanon* (Sprachen und Kulturen des Christlichen Orients, 8). Wiesbaden: Reichert Verlag, 2004. Pp. x, 450. ISBN 3 89500 208 9.

This beautifully produced book represents a major contribution to the growing body of work on the Christian visual arts of the medieval Mediterranean during the period of the crusades.

Twenty-six monuments in four main areas in the Lebanon are included, located in or near the Koura – the plain near Tripoli; the Qadisha valley, high in the mountains; the foothills behind Batroun, below Tripoli; and the area of Jbeil (Byblos) and Beirut. The paintings are described in the catalogue, with their inscriptions and a bibliography, with proposed dating. There are numerous black-and-white and colour plates, a map, plans, bibliography, and index.

Chapter I treats the "History and Documentation of the Paintings." The author considers the surviving evidence and remarks that their survival can be attributed to the remoteness of churches in many cases. Most of the churches are within the Latin county of Tripoli, now North Lebanon. Tripoli was taken in 1109 and continued in crusader hands after Jerusalem fell to the Muslims, until its own fall in 1289, shortly before Acre in 1291. Cyprus after 1192 is brought into the historical equation, as are the various Christian groups, and Tripoli as a centre of learning and commerce. The impact of Byzantium, either directly or via Cyprus, as well as Coptic, Jerusalemite and European traditions, is considered. Amongst the sources Cruikshank Dodd refers to are inscriptions in Syriac, Greek, and Latin.

Chapter II deals with the architecture of the churches. These have a single or a double nave, some with side aisles. Cruikshank Dodd relates the construction, which she describes as "provincial" to that of Palestine and Cappadocia. While she considers the possible funerary function of the double nave, she comes down on the side of a liturgical purpose, to serve two communities. This is followed by a statement on the "Problems of Restoration and Authenticity" by Jean Yasmine, the architect responsible for many of the plans in the book.

Chapter III is concerned with the iconography of the wall paintings. Again "provincial" is the word used to describe them. The fall of Constantinople during the

Fourth Crusade in 1204 is adduced to explain the prevalence of Byzantine influence before that date and the Syrian after it. Much of the work is attributed to mixed workshops. Only one programme, that of the church of Mar Tadros at Bahdeidat, is seen as "unified and cohesive." The themes found in the various parts of the churches, the main apse, side apses, the bema, and the walls, are surveyed, with reference to wall painting elsewhere, as well as icons, and noting where losses have occurred.

Imagery reflecting cultural life during the crusades includes military saints, and an image of a crusader knight named Philip at the feet of his eponymous saint near the apse in Mar Phokas, Amioun. The cave-church of Mart Shmuni is dedicated to St. Salome, the mother of the Macabees, who was worshipped in the Qadish valley. The image of Zacchaeus, or a dendrite saint, at Mar Marina, now totally destroyed, has bearing on the famous illustration from a model book in the Augustinermuseum in Freiburg. On one of the piers in the Church of Mar Phokas at Amioun is a standing saint tempted by a devil, which is related to crusader work in the Holy Land. Donors are depicted, including those at Mar Charbel in Ma'ad, Mar Tadros at Bahdeidat (below St. George), at Mar Saba in Eddé and at Amioun (Philip already mentioned). Two female donors kneeling at the feet of the Virgin in the wall painting from Mart Barbara, Beirut, are now in the National Museum of Antiquities there.

Chapter IV discusses the style of the paintings, noting the eclecticism overall. Cruikshank Dodd divides these according to their sources as she perceives them: A. Cappadocia, (an example being the crucifixion scenes at Deir es-Salib); B. Cyprus and Byzantium (including the relationship between the Koura paintings with Cyprus, especially in the twelfth century); C. Syrian Orthodox (Bahdeidat and Ma'ad); D. European painters; and E. The Dormition, Mar Saba, Eddé, Batroun, which she regards as a special case.

Cruikshank Dodd concludes that "the remains of medieval painting in the Lebanon are not rich or profuse." The "perpetuation of Early Christian themes" includes the iconography of Christ in Majesty, which she relates to the non-Chalcedonian liturgy of St. James, as in Cappadocia. No distinct iconographical types are associated with any of the different churches in the Lebanon. She associates stylistic groupings with historical and cultural circumstances, including location. An outcome of the First Crusade, it is suggested, was to introduce local Christians to Byzantine painting in Cyprus, with the paintings at Amioun and Deir es-Salib particularly displaying Comnene influence. After the fall of Constantinople in 1204, the Greek Orthodox community was weakened in northern Lebanon, to the advantage of the Syrian Orthodox. Enhanced Eastern contacts, including with Iraq, are identified at Ma'ad and Bahdeidat, which displays parallels with Mar Musa Habashi in Syria. Links with the Copts, icons at Sinai, and Cypriot art at the church at Moutoullas are mentioned, as, finally, Jerusalem. A local style in Palestine is assumed to have existed. While she admits "Some … relationships are still unclear" she postulates connections with the West, through French or Italian artists. However, she concludes that "on the whole, this study has discovered the Crusader impact to be relatively weak and that it did not endure." Rather, she perceives influence as going from east to west, with, for example, the plan of the double-naved church as having originated in the Levant. But she admits that "future studies should determine how significant was the role played by East Christians in the transmission of artistic ideas into Europe."

This is the first book to bring so much material of this subject together and the issues it raises will be discussed for a long time to come. One may quibble with the organization of the book in places. It might, for example, be easier for the reader with an interest in the crusades, but lacking background knowledge of the wall paintings, to start by reading the catalogue first, with its useful thumbnail sketch to be found there under each descriptive section, and then work backwards to the more interpretative chapters. There is some rather hectic writing in places, especially in the catalogue, and again Cruikshank Dodd concedes this in admitting "the relationships between monuments in Lebanon and monuments outside Lebanon, (and) the reasons for dating them, may not always be obvious," and briskly recommends the use of the chapter index. Some errors have inevitably escaped proofreading, such as the ambiguity of the caption to Plate C9 and the error of date when the caption is repeated on p. 433. There will doubtless be further discussion of "older, traditional motifs" and the role of Jerusalem, which, while raised as an issue, is unresolved. Amongst the other issues that need further exploration in the future are the Western/crusader connections, as well as the relationship of the wall paintings to the major centres, including Tripoli and Acre, and also Sinai and Egypt and elsewhere, and other works of art beyond painting. Some of Cruikshank Dodd's datings and interpretations may be queried and revised by future work. There will surely be further study of the architecture of the churches. But Cruikshank Dodd acknowledges this in saying that some of her assumptions are provisional. This does not detract from the overall importance of the work. The illustrations are also particularly useful.

The future work invited by this study has already begun. Continuing restoration work draws attention to the state of Lebanese frescoes. New discoveries have been, and are continuing to be, made. Given recent, tragic events in Lebanon, this task has become ever more urgent.

LUCY-ANNE HUNT
MANCHESTER METROPOLITAN UNIVERSITY

Crusading in the Fifteenth Century. Message and Impact, ed. Norman Housley. Basingstoke and New York: Palgrave Macmillan, 2004. Pp. x, 251. ISBN 1 4039 0283 6.

The crusades of the later Middle Ages have by now stepped out of the shadow previously cast by a bulwark of traditional crusade scholarship which for a long time had upheld the year 1291 as the date when "serious" crusading stopped. No one has done more to place the period between 1300 and 1600 firmly on the map of crusader studies than Norman Housley, the editor of this collection which presents eleven essays on different aspects of crusading in the fifteenth century. During this period crusading received new impulses and was promoted with perhaps greater urgency than during the previous century due to developments on the peripheries of Christendom. Most significant among these developments were the steady push of the Ottoman Empire towards Europe, which became a matter of grave concern throughout Europe even before the fall of Constantinople in 1453, and the final stages of the Reconquista, which came to an end with the conquest of Córdoba in 1492. In accordance with the subtitle of this collection, its contributions can be divided into two groups, those concentrating on the message and those focusing on the impact of the crusade in the fifteenth century.

The first group starts off with an essay by Margaret Meserve ("Italian Humanists and the Problem of the Crusade"), who investigates the humanist response to the renewed Turkish threat and the promotion of crusade projects, which in typical humanist fashion was built on a strong historical foundation and dressed with a good deal of keen theological reasoning and sharp political observation. Nancy Bisaha ("Pope Pius II and the Crusade") covers similar ground, taking a closer look at how Pope Pius II tried to translate his humanist convictions into political action and observing an increasing emphasis on the religious aspect of crusading in the course of Pius's career. Strangely both authors fail to discuss Ludwig Schmugge's ground-breaking work on humanist historians and the crusade (*Die Kreuzzüge aus der Sicht humanistischer Geschichtsschreiber*, 1987). Johannes Helmrath ("The German *Reichstage* and the Crusade") treats orations advocating measures against the Turkish threat delivered at the Imperial diets during the fifteenth century. Helmrath stresses the forcefulness of the messages channelled through these assemblies which became one of the main forms for broadcasting propaganda during the periods when the Turkish threat was perceived to be most imminent. Jaques Paviot ("Burgundy and the Crusade") explores the enthusiastic support of the crusade in the fifteenth century by the dukes of Burgundy. He explains that the dukes and their noble entourage adhered to a chivalric idea of the crusade very much linked to the traditional aspect of the liberation of Jerusalem. Concluding this first batch of essays is what might arguably be considered the most innovative piece within this collection. Claudius Sieber-Lehmann ("An Obscure but Powerful Pattern: Crusading, Nationalism and the Swiss Confederation in the Late Middle Ages") investigates the impact the crusade – and more specifically crusade rhetoric – had upon the conduct of conflicts in and surrounding the emerging Swiss confederation of the fifteenth century. The Swiss, for example, did not only label Charles the Bald the "Turk in the West," they were themselves equated by their own opponents with the Ottomans attacking the Holy Roman Empire. This kind of transfer of crusading ideas upon secular conflicts deserves a closer look elsewhere.

Norman Housley's essay on John of Capistrano ("Giovanni da Capistrano and the Crusade of 1256") links the first group of essays to the second, as it investigates the campaign of this extraordinary crusade leader both in terms of his propagandist and military achievements. János M. Bak ("Hungary and Crusading in the Fifteenth Century") portrays the role of Hungary as an *antemurale Christianitatis* and the complicated political conditions which governed the military response to the Turkish threat in Hungary. On a much smaller scale, Natalia Nowakowska ("Poland and the Crusade in the Reign of King Jan Olbracht, 1492–1501") sketches out crusading activities in Poland around 1500. The collection is concluded by two essays on crusading at opposite ends of the Mediterranean by Nicolas Vatin ("The Hospitallers at Rhodes and the Ottoman Turks, 1480–1522") on the Knights of St. John's fight against the Turks and by John Edwards ("*Reconquista* and Crusade in Fifteenth-Century Spain"), who describes the vitality of the institution of the *cruzada* in the final phase of the Reconquista on the Iberian Peninsula.

These essays do not follow a set of common questions. In their diversity, however, they show fifteenth-century crusade studies to be developing vigorously. Within the wider field of crusade history these essays highlight areas that have moved into the main focus over the past years: propaganda, crusading in Eastern Europe, and the influence crusading ideology had on other aspects of life and thought in later medieval Europe. This collection is another significant step towards intensifying the very important area of later medieval crusade studies.

CHRISTOPH T. MAIER
UNIVERSITÄT ZÜRICH

Alain Demurger, *Les Templiers. Une chevalerie chrétienne au moyen âge*. Paris: Éditions du Seuil, 2005. Pp. 669. ISBN 2 02 066941 2.

A version of this book appeared in 1985 under the title *Vie et mort de l'ordre du Temple* from the same publisher. Given the state of research at the time and the generally agreed upon conclusions, it was rapidly regarded as a fundamental synthesis, especially of the material relevant to the experience of the Templars in France over nearly two hundred years and their tribulations in the last decade of their existence. But the various fields from which the author had to draw were themselves producing scholarship by leaps and bounds. Crusade studies, already flourishing in the mid-1980s, started what still looks like an unstoppable *essor*. Investigations into the settlement and occupation of the Holy Land took off at roughly the same time, and more and more work has appeared either as dissertations or published studies on the political, social, economic and military relations of the constituent groups of crusader society. Rich new studies continue to appear on the art of the Crusader States and (not quite the same thing, though it overlaps strongly) crusader art. Increasing numbers of researchers are exploring European archives outside of already well-explored France to recover the history of the international military orders in other regions. A number of scholars (Jonathan Riley-Smith, Barbara Frale, and Sophia Menache come to mind) have also looked penetratingly and provocatively at the swirl of suspicions around, and the trial of, the Templars, the role of Pope Clement V, and the vexing question of whether there is any truth to be got from their confessions of strange ritual practices.

With all this new material, and especially the controversy about the extent, if any, of the Templars' guilt, Alain Demurger decided to produce a revised edition of *Vie et mort*. In doing so, he discovered that he nearly had to write a different book (hence, the new title). It is every bit as good, indeed even better, than the earlier one. With a mastery of the original sources that is close to being unequalled among publishing scholars, and a panoramic though selective view of the scholarship for all the relevant countries, he takes readers through the long history of the Templars and at every stage – in a firm but judicious manner – explodes the myths and the misinterpretations that have arisen in the course of the centuries. What makes his revisions so good and so persuasive is that he really seems to be trying hard to discover the basis and even to make the case for the contrary opinions of other scholars. In the end, he often dismantles their opinions, but he always does so with grace. (Lawrence of Arabia was not a scholar, and his observations receive a more vitriolic and dismissive treatment.)

The book is a model of historical reasoning. The author has a keen sense of what documents are intended to convey. Their slant often explains, if considered apart from other evidence, why the Templars or the military orders in general have sometimes got a bad reputation. Of course, he acknowledges, there were rivalries among the orders, but to conclude from the most vituperative reports and denunciations of individual arguments, without carefully sifting through other evidence, leads to the fallacious conclusion that the whole history of the orders in the Holy Land was one of everlasting contention. He also explodes the easy identification of the Templars and the Hospitallers with stable oppositional parties, either royal or baronial, in the East or stable factions that favored or opposed alliances with any or select Muslim powers. And all this is achieved in a prose so readable and vigorous that it sweeps one along. This is just a brilliant book.

Les Templiers ends on a sombre note, an evaluation of the truth value of the confessions. I think it would be fair to say that there has been a recent tendency to give some truth value to the confessions about anti-Christian gestures in Templar initiation rites. Largely, though not exclusively, in a series of public lectures, Riley-Smith has taken the lead on this, although it is sometimes difficult to pin him down as to the degree of truth in the confessions and the geographical extent of the alleged practices. Nor has there yet appeared a sophisticated investigation drawing on the extraordinary and also extraordinarily sophisticated body of research on modern torture and fear of torture and the truth content of confessions to try to assess the Templar data. Demurger does not draw on these psychological studies of modern victims and victims' statements either, but he analyzes the same evidence as Riley-Smith and others and reaches an almost minimalist's conclusion: whatever a deviant here or there in the order did (and every organization has those who deviate from its ideal), the Templars were innocent of the serious charges against them. Pope

Clement V determined this to be the case and thus suppressed but did not condemn the order; yet, he still allowed the leadership to be executed. According to Demurger, this was a trade-off. Clement feared that the trial of his predecessor Boniface VIII would undermine the authority of the Universal Church. It could not destroy it. It was God's Church. But it could render it terribly weak for who knew how long. In a sense, then, the pope bought Philip IV off. There would be no trial for the dead Boniface. The ultimate price was the burning of Jacques de Molay and any number of other innocent men. Christ gave up his life to establish his Church; the Templar victims, unwillingly to be sure, were compelled by the head of Christ's Church to die so that that Church might avert the wrath of the king of France.

WILLIAM CHESTER JORDAN
PRINCETON UNIVERSITY

The Gesta Tancredi *of Ralph of Caen: A History of the Normans on the First Crusade*, trans. with an introduction by Bernard S. Bachrach and David S. Bachrach (Crusade Texts in Translation, 12). Aldershot and Burlington, VT: Ashgate, 2005. Pp. xii, 183. ISBN 0 7546 3710 7.

The appearance of the *Gesta Tancredi* in English translation is very welcome: Ralph of Caen is one of a small group of authors – which also includes Caffaro and Albert of Aachen – who did not participate in the First Crusade, but wrote soon afterwards and, crucially, without apparent knowledge of those eyewitness accounts which are better known and highly regarded today. Thus one looks to the *Gesta Tancredi* for unique information and insights, which, however, have hitherto been shrouded in Ralph's convoluted Latin style. I, at least, have used the text in the past, cited from it and referred to it, but have never been able to read it from beginning to end as narrative history. Bernard and David Bachrach have made this possible.

Such a reading confirms the value of the *Gesta Tancredi* as a source, though not for details of events of the First Crusade, which were reconstructed and written down at least a decade later. The subtitle, provided by the translators, indicates the partiality of the narrative, and Ralph begins with eulogies of Tancred and Bohemond, while his account of the crusade plunges straight into hostile relations with the Byzantines. Thereafter, the narrative of events is from the point of view of Tancred, Ralph's chief informant, which means an interesting new perspective on certain episodes, including Tarsus, the capture of Antioch, and the sack of Jerusalem. It also gives the Normans of South Italy a voice in the debates and disputes of the leadership: not necessarily a voice that can be trusted, but it is one that can now be heard.

Ralph's account becomes particularly interesting after the capture of Jerusalem, the point at which most other histories of the First Crusade end. Here he is drawing on much more recent memories, since he arrived in Outremer with Bohemond, whose service he had entered in 1106. (It is unfortunate that the *Gesta Tancredi* breaks off in 1107–8, before it describes any events of which Ralph had firsthand experience.) Ralph's is a very individual voice for the short period 1099–1107, starting by dismissing the battle of Ascalon in a few sentences, and spending more space on the iniquities of Raymond of Saint-Gilles (ch. 138). The focus is fixed on Tancred in the ensuing period, and well worth comparing with the accounts of Fulcher of Chartres, Matthew of Edessa, Albert of Aachen, and ibn al-Qalanisi.

Ralph also merits attention where he provides information from his own knowledge, rather than hearsay. Cases in point are his descriptions of Antioch (ch. 48), Beit She'an (ch. 139) and Latakia (ch. 144). His descriptions of people are biased, of course, but there is an intriguing vignette of Patriarch Bernard of Valence of Antioch, whom he knew well, in the retreat from Harran (1104, ch. 150), and an extraordinary and ambivalent description of a confrontation after the capture of Jerusalem between Arnulf, Ralph's teacher and the dedicatee of the *Gesta*, and Tancred, his patron in Outremer (chs. 135–37). Even though he was present on neither occasion, Ralph appears to be well informed and to be recounting incidents which accord with his knowledge of the personalities concerned.

The translators have earned our gratitude for providing access to this wealth of material. This is not to say that the *Gesta Tancredi* has become an easy read. The high-flown language of both prose and poetry (the work is about 80:20) is very difficult to render in readable English. The translators have usually chosen to stay close to the original rather than resorting to paraphrase. This is often awkward and confusing, and occasionally unintentionally amusing. In chapter 5, when Bohemond's army has to cross a river, "Fluuium alii tranant, pars remigare docta cymbas traducunt." Surely "some who knew how to row" would be clearer than "others, having been taught to row," which summons up a vision of lessons on the riverbank? Yet elsewhere a departure from over-literal translation says the crusaders "moaned with joy," where the Latin, "unde gemuerant gaudent," must mean "whence they had groaned, they now rejoiced" (ch. 120). Sometimes the Latin is comparatively clear, but the translation has introduced complication: in a note to chapter 121, commenting on the translation of "Ipse non secus turmas ac tubas quam patriam et tibiam perhorrescens," it is commented, "The horns in this sentence probably refer to the composite bows of the Muslims, which were constructed from horn." But the "tibia" (flute or pipe) in the comparison means it must be musical instruments to which "tubas" refers – war-trumpets. These examples are a few where the translation jarred sufficiently to drive me back to the Latin. They may not be representative, but they are enough to undermine complete confidence.

There is a short introduction which largely reproduces the one in the *Recueil* edition. This is not surprising, since little is known about Ralph other than what he tells us in the *Gesta Tancredi*. The translators have worked from the *Recueil* edition and not consulted the original manuscript, which is a pity, as it is known that in the nineteenth century there were illegible passages, which might be readable now via ultraviolet or digital enhancement techniques. (Rather alarmingly, the *Recueil* editors used the services of "un chimiste illustre" to try to restore the lost words.)

The translation also has notes which usefully identify people and places, and elucidate some of the more obscure passages. With a few exceptions, there is no attempt to cross-reference with parallel sources for the crusade, so this is a job still to be done. A focused bibliography and a helpful index complete the volume. To be used with a certain amount of caution, yet it is a valuable addition to the translated sources for the First Crusade.

SUSAN B. EDGINGTON
QUEEN MARY, UNIVERSITY OF LONDON

Henricus Lettus, *The Chronicle of Henry of Livonia*, trans. with new introduction by James A. Brundage (Records of Western Civilization). New York: Columbia University Press, 2003. Pp. xliii, 262. ISBN 0 231 12888 6 (hardback); 0 231 12889 4 (paperback).

The Livonian Rhymed Chronicle, trans. Jerry C. Smith and William L. Urban, 2nd edn. Chicago: Lithuanian Research and Studies Center, 2001. Pp. xl, 134. ISBN 0 92970 034 1 (paperback).

The Latin chronicle of the German priest Henry of Livonia and the anonymous Middle High German *Livonian Rhymed Chronicle* are the two principal extant narrative sources for the crusades to Livonia in the thirteenth century and the history of the areas occupied by modern Estonia, Latvia and Lithuania during that period. Translations of these two works into English – first published in 1961 and 1977 respectively – have now again been made available with new apparatus and, in the case of the *Rhymed Chronicle*, a revised version of the original translated text.

The chronicle of Henry of Livonia is a delightful source which covers the first forty or so years of the Christian settlement and conversion of Livonia. It also gives a wealth of circumstantial information on topography, economics, native customs and languages, warfare, and of course church organization and the mechanics of Christianization, ranging from baptisms to terrifying re-enactments of Old Testament history staged for the benefit of apprehensive neophytes. While Brundage provides a completely new introduction (printed along with the original one), and an updated bibliography, together with four maps, the English text given is that of the 1961 edition. Although it shows its age in the odd archaic spelling such as "Esthonians" or "Wisby," and some Germanisms such as "Wierland" for "Vironia," this translation has stood the test of time, although there are a few cases where Brundage's renderings are open to question. In connection with an episode in which some Livonians renounce Christianity, Brundage interprets the phrase *fidem susceptam exfestucantes* as referring to "beating with a rod (*festuca*), as is done when washing out dirty clothes" (p. 34), although he concedes that the wording is strange. Admittedly, the previous sentence describes the Livonians pouring water from the River Dvina over themselves in an evident attempt to reverse the ceremony of baptism. Yet it is difficult to reconcile the term *exfestucantes* as relating to washing; beating clothing with sticks is not an efficient way of removing dirt, even in primitive societies. It is more likely that this ritual is something akin to the feudal ritual of *exfestucatio*, in which rods were broken as a public sign of breaking of fidelity or alliance, and which is well attested in twelfth-century Europe. A more serious matter is the misleading translation of the words *ballista* and *ballistarius*. Brundage glosses *ballista* as a "large, wheeled cross-bow, which was sometimes provided with a pouch and a double string and could thus be used for throwing stones" (p. 27 n. 9). This is certainly *one* of the valid meanings of the term in medieval (as opposed to classical) Latin, but it is not convincing when one considers the frequency and range of occurrences that figure in the chronicle. The *ballistarii* figure as a regular component of crusader military forces in the Baltic lands, used offensively as well as in defence; they are described as climbing up onto ramparts (pp. 62–63) and siege towers (p. 153), attacking the enemy up mountain slopes (p. 112) and running on the field of battle (p. 98) – presumably carrying their weapons in all cases – and in the last case their effects are contrasted with those wrought by stone-throwing machines. These examples do not accord with men servicing large, wheeled, and therefore unwieldy, weapons, and it is much more likely that the terms simply refer to the normal, portable crossbow or arbalest and its operator. Despite these instances, the translation is highly literate and readable, copiously annotated, and with an index both detailed and well-organized.

Historians who wish to produce English translations of medieval Latin sources can avail themselves of a long tradition of scholarly translation as well as numerous *instruments de travail*. Translating from Middle High German is a quite different matter. The *Rhymed Chronicle* is a particularly difficult text, given the circumstance that it is written in rhyming couplets, derives much of its vocabulary and imagery from heroic poetry, and includes a large amount of phrasing simply to provide appropriate rhymes or metre. Jerry Smith and William Urban are two of the few who have attempted this task, having to date translated four works from the time of the Baltic Crusades. Their translation of the *Rhymed Chronicle* is based on the edition by Leo Meyer (*Livländische Reimchronik* [Paderborn, 1876]), which remains an immensely valuable research tool, particularly as one of the two known manuscripts used by him, R, has disappeared in the meantime.

The chronicle covers most of the thirteenth century, and is mainly concerned with the history of the Sword Brethren and the Teutonic Knights and their wars against the heathens and Russians. The new edition is preceded by a detailed, updated introduction and bibliography, and is accompanied by 17 maps. It also contains two appendices: an independent primary account of the end of the Sword Brethren by Brother Hartmann von Heldrungen, and a short survey of the role of castles in Livonia. The two translators state that they intended to produce an edition which is "more accurate and more readable" than their original attempt, as well as making use of the secondary literature which has appeared since 1977 (p. v). It is a pity that they do not discuss the language of the chronicle or address the problems this creates in greater detail, as such a discussion would have been a help to the reader.

The main changes in this edition are a tightening up of the accuracy of the translation, which is mirrored by a significant increase in the number of footnotes, as well as a more detailed level of commentary within them. An example can be seen in the account of the murder of Mindaugas, king of Lithuania, of whom the MHG text says: *ein ander Lettowe der trûc nît / ûf in heimelîche; / der was ouch alsô rîche / und der vrûnde alsô grôz* (Meyer, lines 7124–27). The original translation rendered this as "there was another Lithuanian who bore him great hatred and who was powerful and had many noble friends"; the individual concerned is named in a footnote as one Trianate, without further identification. The new edition gives the same four lines as "there was another Lithuanian who *secretly* bore him great hatred and who was powerful and had many *allies*" (p. 73; my emphasis, AVM). Significantly, it now translates the crucial word *heimelîche* ("secretly"), whose force had previously been omitted, and also renders *vrûnde* more accurately as "allies" rather than the literal meaning "friends," so that the entire sentence gives a much more plausible statement of a political situation; the Lithuanian is now identified as Daumantas (Dovmont) of Pskov, who is accorded five further lines of commentary. In other cases the new translation could probably still be improved upon. In the description of a defeat of the Sword Brethren at Saule in 1236, the lines *ir genûc sach man sô verzagen, / daz sie zû lande vluhen wider* (lines 1936–37) are rendered as "there was a sizeable number who were so cowardly that they fled homewards" (p. 24); however, *verzagen* more readily implies a case of loss of heart than cowardice. The inhabitants of Pskov are described as *lûte harte sûr* (line 2103); to translate this as "extremely evil" (p. 26) probably imputes a theological dimension to the language that was not intended at this point, even though the anonymous author is happy to demonize the enemy on other occasions. There are also instances where the translation is misleading. On one occasion Mindaugas leads his troops against a castle held by the Teutonic Order. The MHG text reads *Myndowe hiez zû sturme gân. / dâ sach man manchen heiden stân / von den pferden ûf daz gras* (lines 2511–13). The translation reads "Mindaugas ordered the attack on the castle, and many heathens fell from their horses onto the grass" (p. 31). In fact the idiom *von den pferden stân* must mean "dismount" rather than "fall from a horse"; the action is taken so that the Lithuanians, who have arrived on horseback, can assault the castle on foot, as was only practical. However, the following lines indicate that the Teutonic Knights are still concealed in ambush, so battle has not yet been joined, but the translation suggests that the Lithuanians were somehow already suffering casualties while still mounted.

These examples should demonstrate that the translators have succeeded in their aim of producing a translation which is more readable and largely more accurate, but some of the individual renderings are open to debate, and for absolute accuracy the English version needs to be read alongside Meyer's edition. The main weakness is the index, which does not give the impression of having been compiled by the translators themselves. The battle mentioned above is listed, as one might expect, under "Saule River," but another is listed under "Battle of Durben" rather than "Durben." The seventeen references to Reval should also have incorporated the single one to "Tallinn," rather than giving the impression that these were different places. Numerous matters are indexed so sketchily as to be useless: it is surprising that a text describing some ninety years of unremitting warfare should have only one page reference each for topics such as "crusades" or "death," or two for "siege machines." As far as proper names are concerned, anyone wishing to work with the *Rhymed Chronicle* would be well advised to ignore this index and start from that given with Meyer's edition.

The reissues of these two works are a welcome addition to the literature on the Baltic Crusades, and will be particularly useful for teaching the subject. One hopes that their publication will encourage the production of translations of some of the other sources, particularly the vernacular ones, connected with the Teutonic Order.

ALAN V. MURRAY
INSTITUTE FOR MEDIEVAL STUDIES
UNIVERSITY OF LEEDS

Identités croisées en un milieu méditerranéen. Le case de Chypre (Antiquité – Moyen Âge), ed. Sabine Fourrier and Gilles Grivaud. Mont-Saint-Aignan: Publications des Universités de Rouen et du Havre, 2006. Pp. 436. ISBN-10: 2 87775 407 3. ISBN-13: 978 2 87775 407 1.

This collection of nineteen papers is the product of a colloquium held at the University of Rouen in 2004. Almost half relate to the island of Cyprus in the period of the crusades, and their range and quality provide ample testimony to the current vitality of this field of study. Three papers focus on the possibilities of archaeological and architectural survivals for understanding the interplay of different ethnic groups: Tassos Papacostas considers the pre-1191 evidence and another rising star, James Schryver, the evidence from the Lusignan centuries; Thierry Soulard concentrates on two Orthodox churches built in the Gothic style and the light they may shed on relations between the Greeks and the Franks. (Although Soulard includes a discussion the clear architectural affinity between the cathedral of St. George in Famagusta and the nearby church of St. Peter and St. Paul, it would have been helpful if he had ventured an opinion on the rite employed in the latter.) Also on the theme of archaeology is Nolwenn Lécuyer's report on the Potamia-Agios Sozomenos landscape survey. Chris Schabel, in a characteristically incisive and persuasive paper, disposes of the mythology surrounding the supposed role of Queen Alice in subjugating the Orthodox and shows how historians have compounded previous ill-founded assumptions and inferences. Another leading historian of Latin Cyprus, Catherine Otten-Froux, provides a masterly survey of the place of the various Italian nations in Cyprus under the Lusignans. Alexander Beihammer has a useful discussion of the Vatican MS Palatinus Graecus 367, the single most important source for the Greek population of Cyprus under the Latins in the period before 1320, and Daniele Baglioni examines the "plurilinguisme" demonstrated by fifteenth-century material from Cyprus. Finally, Angèle Nicolaou-Konnari traces the lives and works of Pierre and Georges de Nores, the seventeenth-century descendants of a family of Frankish nobles present in the island from the early thirteenth century until the Ottoman conquest. All this, not to mention ten more papers on the pre-medieval epochs of Cypriot history, make this collection one that should not be allowed to pass unnoticed.

PETER EDBURY
CARDIFF UNIVERSITY

Michael Lower, *The Barons' Crusade. A Call to Arms and Its Consequences* (Middle Age Series). Philadelphia: University of Pennsylvania Press, 2005. Pp. xi, 256. ISBN 0 8122 3873 7.

Michael Lower sets himself an ambitious goal in exploring an understudied, obscure crusade of the thirteenth century. The end result – part narrative history, part comparative history, part keen analysis – demonstrates how multifaceted and revealing local history can be, especially when the scholar compares several local histories. Buttressed by substantial exploration of primary sources and an expansive knowledge of secondary research, Lower's book argues that the Barons' Crusade (1232–41) shatters several crusading stereotypes. First, although Roman Catholics did share a common identity as Christians, there was no concomitant unity of belief or action among them either before or during the crusade. Although Gregory IX tried to consolidate his position as pope using this crusade, responses varied from place to place, and crusaders generally pursued their own interests rather than papal goals. Furthermore, Christians did not view non-Christians as a unified Other; crusaders treated Muslims, Jews, and Cumans in varying ways across Europe and in Syria. Lower concludes that, although medieval Christians saw the world in binaries, these dichotomies did not consistently determine behavior. Instead, Catholics might employ such categories differently based on context. Lower proves his thesis through a complex and remarkably clear discussion of the lengthy preparations for a relatively brief crusade. His findings and method illuminate not only the Barons' Crusade but also historiographical issues that are simultaneously simple, profound, and pervasive.

Lower opens by exploring papal plans for a crusade. Pope Gregory IX began calling for a campaign to Syria using heretofore unavailable resources such as vow redemption and the mendicant orders. Gregory was the first to emphasize vow redemption as a way of including every Catholic in Europe: those deemed unsuitable for combat could still "participate" by paying the monetary worth of their vows. Thus the pope was able to mobilize women, the old, the sick, and the poor – or at least their financial resources. He reached this audience by deploying mendicant preachers, for the Dominicans and Franciscans were now established enough to become viable messengers. The initial response was encouraging, at least among the crowned heads of Europe. Although they didn't take the cross themselves, they allowed their nobles to do so.

Yet things never seemed to turn out the way Gregory planned. Crusading fever caught on readily in Hungary, Brittany, Champagne, and England, but nowhere else. Those who took the cross generally resisted Gregory's attempts to divert the crusade to Constantinople after he had called for a campaign in Jerusalem. Treatment of non-Christians in Europe ran the gamut from violence to financial extortion to (surprisingly) improved conditions. Lower notes that these varying responses to European non-Christians did not align with papal interests. Here, as elsewhere, local barons pursued their own agendas, whatever Gregory IX intended.

Once the crusaders left Europe, the situation did not noticeably improve. Crusaders failed to unite behind their common purpose, pursuing personal vendettas and alliances up to the end. The Constantinople expedition got nowhere because crusaders overwhelmingly preferred to crusade in the Holy Land; Gregory's diversion efforts failed to raise enough money or manpower. All but one of the major barons who took the cross headed for Outremer. Yet even a shared interest in Jerusalem could not smooth over fragmentation within the campaign. They squabbled over leadership of the expedition, pursued individual alliances or treaties with different Muslim leaders in the now-fragmented Ayyubid states, and generally preferred diplomacy to fighting even when they could agree on a suitable target. This crusade, Lower indicates, did not contain any of the elements scholars expect to see in a successful expedition, and yet it did significantly strengthen the Kingdom of Jerusalem. He credits these accomplishments to crusade leaders' awareness of Muslim disunity; they neither viewed nor treated non-Christians as an undifferentiated Other. Christian identity did not lead to Christian unity in thought, word, or deed. Indeed, he argues throughout the book that the Barons' Crusade demonstrates diversity in Christian responses driven by particular circumstances.

Lower's conclusions are useful in and of themselves, and they raise important questions about methodology and historiography within crusades studies. At first glance, Lower seems to set up straw men: a new, shared Christian unity based on crusading fever; Christendom unified under papal direction; consistent hostility toward non-Christians, who were seen as a collective. Any crusades historian might frown or even scoff at these oversimplifications. Lower skilfully deflects such criticism in his introduction. These are not, he argues, mere medieval textbook generalizations, but views fundamental to post-1950s scholarship on crusading. Pious individuals did not take the cross *only* because they identified themselves with institutionalized forms of piety or because they recognized the pope as leader of the institutional Church. Nor did everyone involved in crusading view non-Catholics as a similarly unified mass. Lower sees such formulae, based on the idea that crusaders' religious beliefs or identity led to consistent actions, as overly simplistic. He contends that numerous other considerations might lead someone to take the cross or not. Lower suggests that certain generalizations have insidiously become assumptions underpinning current research. Thus he calls for local and comparative studies that will establish a more realistic and complex framework for medieval crusading. Lower perceptively and persuasively illuminates holes in the models he explores. And he does so by examining failures of papal initiatives. Lower's emphasis on local and comparative history determines his method.

Here we see a fundamental issue in historiography that warrants ongoing discussion. Those who look for models in history use a vertical approach, as early modernists have labelled it. This perspective concentrates on similarities, categories, and classification systems – the big picture – and in so doing becomes almost Whiggish in its emphasis on what endures and succeeds. A horizontal approach, in contrast, "gives the contingent, the idea which withered and perished, … equal importance in recapturing the particularity of the past" (John Morrill, *The Nature of the English Revolution*, 1983, p. 443). Morrill notes that scholars sympathetic to this attitude can, however, easily lose sight of the forest for the trees. Lower's book shows how useful horizontal history can be. Yet a full swing of the pendulum might not prove any more fruitful. A balance between models and particulars, forests and trees, would be the most desirable end of all.

DEBORAH GERISH
EMPORIA STATE UNIVERSITY

Anthony Luttrell, *The Town of Rhodes: 1306–1356*. Rhodes: City of Rhodes Office for the Medieval Town, 2003. Pp. xxiv, 304. ISBN 960 214 208 1.

Currently crusader cities attract great interest, as studies of Jerusalem, Acre, Nicosia, and other towns demonstrate. After the fall of Acre in 1291, the Knights of St. John of Jerusalem, or Hospitallers, moved their headquarters to Limassol, Cyprus, only establishing a new *raison d'être* with their conquest of Byzantine Rhodes starting in 1306. They used the island as a base against the Turks for over two centuries, and when the capital fell to the Ottomans in 1522 and the Order relocated to Malta, the knights left behind a splendid later-medieval city. Early archaeology and reconstruction caused irreparable damage to our potential knowledge of Rhodes' history and topography. Recent investigations in archaeology, art history, and other disciplines have been much more professional, providing new data. The city of Rhodes and the regional antiquities authorities wisely decided to enlist a historian to elucidate these findings based on the written evidence. In particular, the earlier phase – arbitrarily the first 50 years – was chosen "so that later developments should not be mistakenly projected backwards" (p. v), to quote the local director of Byzantine antiquities, Maria Michaelidou. As Mayor George Yannopoulos relates with understatement, "Dr Luttrell is one of the leading specialists in the history of the Order of the Knights Hospitaller" (p. iii), and so he was the logical choice for the task.

This task is both more fruitful and more difficult than it would be for a place like the Order's previous home, Limassol. While Mamluks and Turks eliminated the Crusader States in Syria-Palestine, Cyprus, and Frankish Greece, and the Templars were suppressed, the Hospitallers' survival and move to Malta entailed the preservation of a much greater quantity of documentary material. Only a veteran like Luttrell could control this mass of archival evidence, and only his enthusiasm and diligence could collate this research with the architectural and artistic remains and extensive bibliography, and the "Heraldic Evidence," "Tombs and Inscriptions," "Pictorial Representations," and "Monies and Measures," which are the subtitles of divisions of the first section of the book.

Probably given *carte blanche*, Luttrell was free to do the book he wanted. From many possible organizations, Luttrell chose to begin with a section (I) on "Problems and Sources," and follow it with (II) a "Historical Survey," (III) a "Chronological Register," (IV) "Selected Texts," (V) "Magistral Bulls," and (VI) "Topographical and Other Materials." He is candid in the preface about the respective roles and limitations of "art historians, numismatists, archaeologists, and others" in the "creation of history." This frank approach to his interdisciplinary project (for example, p. 6, n. 13: "Permission to consult unpublished materials from Rhodes in the Scuola Archeologica Italiana in Athens was refused") continues in the first section, an interesting and critical presentation of the historiography, a list of Hospitaller officers, an analysis of the types of evidence, and a cautious evaluation of our ability to achieve certitude about Rhodes in the first half-century of Hospitaller rule.

Although there is a glossary in section I, the "more general reader" is advised "simply to read the relatively uncluttered chronological narrative in Section II" (p. xvii). Here the criticism of previous works (his own included) is mostly in the notes, and Luttrell describes Byzantine Rhodes, the need for the Hospitallers to escape from their "Cypriot captivity" and establish their own state, the conquest itself, the development of the town, the fortifications, the buildings – where Luttrell's love for art and architectural history shines through – and districts, the government, and the local and foreign population. His treatment of the controversial topics of ecclesiastical history and the Greeks (pp. 100–103, 124–34, 148–50, 164–70) is especially balanced and useful, concluding that the Hospitallers' "institutions had been formed not in the West but in Syria and Cyprus, where they had been accustomed to governing non-Latin subjects. There was no open rebellion and no known sign of protest" (p. 170).

Most scholars of the crusades and the Latin East will be able to use this book, often in comparative studies, since Luttrell has dealt with so many aspects of history with skill and care. This is certainly true for the remaining sections: section III summarizes and comments on important sources for the narrative history of the period, many of them unpublished, while section IV gives key documents in the original languages (French, the *langue d'Oc*, Greek, Latin, and Italian) with English summaries and comments. Most have been published, but among those that have not is a crucial papal letter of 1322 delineating the property, income, and jurisdiction of the Latin archbishop of Rhodes (pp. 199–202, although the MSS's repetition of ten lines requires explanation). Section V prints, with brief English summaries, unpublished magistral bulls of 1347–58 concerning the city. Section VI contains further analysis of the walls, important buildings, the visit of a famous traveller (Martoni), and other things that could perhaps have been distributed earlier in the book, but presumably did not fit comfortably.

Experts will likely have some disagreements, he admits: "Uncertainties, errors and omissions undoubtedly remain for future amendment, especially since few historians possess the expertise to deal with all the varying technical problems presented by this book's subject" (p. xvii). For example, the builders of the Conventual Church (pp. 94–99) need not have looked directly to mendicant models in Italy (p. 153), since the exact plan was already used in the Morea (Dominican St. Sophia, Andreville), and similar designs can be seen in Crete and elsewhere in Frankish Greece. My only quibbles concern formatting: the bibliographical system is not accessible, especially considering the somewhat limited index; typographical errors are few, but something has gone wrong with the footnotes on pp. 105 and 108–10; and, although the book is well illustrated with black-and-white photos, plans, and maps, the main maps could have been more conveniently placed for frequent reference.

I applaud the City of Rhodes for its initiative, and Anthony Luttrell is to be congratulated for producing an enjoyable and yet scholarly interdisciplinary study that few individuals are in a position to contemplate, let alone execute successfully.

CHRIS SCHABEL
UNIVERSITY OF CYPRUS

Λεόντιου Μαχαιρά, *Χρονικό της Κύπρου*, Παράλληλη διπλωματική έκδοση των χειρογράφων. [Leontios Machairas, *The Chronicle of Cyprus, Parallel Diplomatic Edition of the Manuscripts*] (Peges kai Meletes tes Kypriakes Istorias, 48). Introduction, edition by Michael Pieres and Angel Nikolaou-Konnari. Nicosia: Kentro Epistemonikon Erevnon, 2003. Pp. 489. ISBN 9963 0 8085 5.

The Chronicle of Cyprus by Leontios Machairas (ca. 1360–ca. 1432) is an important historical source for the period when Cyprus was ruled by the Lusignan dynasty (thirteenth–fifteenth centuries). It survives in three manuscripts in the Biblioteca Markiana, Venice, the Bodleian Library, Oxford, and the Biblioteca Apostolica, the Vatican. Machairas begins *The Chronicle* with an introduction to the story of the Holy Cross and the history of Cyprus up to the accession of Peter I Lusignan; it then examines in detail the reign of four kings of the Lusignan dynasty (Peter I, Peter II,

James I and Janus); and concludes with the reign of King John II and the death of his daughter, Queen Charlotte. *The Chronicle* is also important from a linguistic point of view, with one of its surviving manuscripts (the Venetian manuscript) written in a rather scholarly language, and the other two (the Oxford and the Ravenna manuscripts) written either in the fifteenth or in the sixteenth century in a language that is closer to the vernacular, with the inclusion of many foreign loan-words, mainly Venetian and French.

This is the first time that the entire text of *The Chronicle* from the Oxford and Ravenna manuscripts has been published. Previous editions cited the text of one manuscript (Sathas, Cervellin-Chevalier: the Venice manuscript) or offered a critical edition combining two of the manuscripts (Miller-Sathas, Dawkins, Paulides: the Venice and Oxford manuscripts). In Pieres and Nikolaou-Konnari's edition the text of the three manuscripts is reproduced in parallel format in three columns in chronological order (the first column is the oldest surviving manuscript from Venice, followed by the Oxford and Ravenna manuscripts), thus allowing the easy identification of differences in names, dates and numbers, as well as in the context, style and vocabulary.

The structure of the volume is good. The book includes a useful introduction in which the principles of the edition are fully discussed (pp. 60–62) and a detailed description of the physical condition, the scripture, the content and the history of the three manuscripts is offered (pp. 27–39), together with the citation of all the notes written on the three manuscripts which either refer to the text of *The Chronicle* or concern their owners or readers (pp. 43–58).

The carefully edited text is presented in almost four hundred pages (pp. 65–462) followed by twelve colour photographs of selected folios from the three manuscripts. The book is supplemented by a comprehensive bibliography, which includes all the editions and translations of *The Chronicle of Cyprus* as well as studies of *The Chronicle* (pp. 13–18).

The edition, the preparatory work for which took more than fifteen years, meets all the requirements of a serious scholarly work with one important exception: it does not include an index, the inclusion of which is made even more necessary because of the absence of a summary of the content of *The Chronicle*. According to the two editors, it was impossible to compile an index "because of the nature and the aims of the current edition" and they promise (p. 62) that they will address the lacuna in the forthcoming electronic edition of *The Chronicle*. That means, however, that if someone wants to find an extract from the text, he has to refer to Dawkins' edition (where, in the margin of the Greek text, reference to the folio of the Oxford manuscript is given) in order to find it in Pieres and Nikolaou-Konnari's edition. Undoubtedly, the compiling of an index is a very difficult and laborious task. It does bring long-term rewards, however, for it ensures that the book can be used effectively and that its content is easily accessible to a broad range of readers.

This consideration apart, the two editors are to be congratulated on the completion of an onerous task that would have daunted others. High praise is due to them for having offered scholars a book that adheres so strictly to the rules of a diplomatic edition. And the scholarly community can look forward to the new critical edition of *The Chronicle* which Pieres promises (p. 40).

APHRODITE PAPAYIANNI
UNIVERSITY OF LONDON

Klaus Militzer, *Die Geschichte des Deutschen Ordens*, Kohlhammer: Stuttgart, 2005. Pp. 225. ISBN 3 17 018069 X.

Together with Udo Arnold, Klaus Militzer is one of the most important German-speaking scholars who has been studying the Teutonic Order during the past few decades. At least three of his many publications in this field can be called really outstanding: *Die Entstehung der Deutschordensballeien im Deutschen Reich*, (2nd edn., 1981); with Lutz Fenske, *Ritterbrüder im livländischen Zweig des Deutschen Ordens* (1993); and *Von Akkon zur Marienburg: Verfassung, Verwaltung und Sozialstruktur des Deutschen Ordens 1190–1309* (1999). In his present book Klaus Militzer, now retired, sums up his academic teaching on the Teutonic Order. In three long chapters he deals with the formative period, the thirteenth century in the Latin East, in Prussia and Livonia (pp. 12–94); the heyday ("Blütezeit"), that is, the fourteenth century in Marienburg / Prussia, in Livonia and in Germany (pp. 95–142); and finally with the decline during the fifteenth century (pp. 143–83). It is remarkable, however, to write a book of 225 pages entitled *Die Geschichte des Deutschen Ordens* and to devote only six pages of text to the five centuries after 1500. The reader is provided with reliable facts about the administrative structures, the brethren in the Order and the places where the Order founded commanderies. Although there are only a few short notes, the book is useful for finding the important sources and literature. For the sake of shortness, sometimes imprecision is unavoidable, for example when it is stated that the commandery of Rothenburg was founded in 1237. The Neumark was not sold, but pawned to the Order in 1402 (p. 114) and redeemed in 1455. The Lithuanian prince is called Olg(i)erd, Algirdas, not Olgier (pp. 116 and 219). There are other small inconsistencies; such as when a publication by Heinz von zur Mühlen on Livonia is recommended on p. 10 but missing in the bibliography (that is, in *Deutsche Geschichte im Osten Europas, Baltische Länder*, ed. Gert von Pistohlkors, 2002, pp. 26–172). Every scholar will have similar flaws in his own books and one should not be too severe on things that may easily be amended in a second edition.

The concept of rise and fall could be refined and complemented with the idea of transformations, of adaptations to new religious, social and political challenges. There was no heyday of the Teutonic Order in Germany during the fourteenth century, as the author rightly stresses: Donations ceased, purchases were hindered by statutes against the *manus mortua*, and a financial crisis – the background of which needs further research but which affected the Hospitallers in the same way –

forced the knights to sell many possessions and reduce the numbers of brethren in the commanderies. Even in Prussia, where the Order's territories reached their maximum extent during the fourteenth century, the situation was desperate enough, as the *Litauerreisen* came to be criticized for their cruelty, their lack of success and their inappropriateness after the baptism of the Lithuanian prince in 1386. Klaus Militzer is well aware of all these problems and puts the phrase "Blütezeit" in quotation marks. On many broader issues one would wish, however, to be offered a few more general explanations: Why did the Order receive no possessions in certain German regions compared with others (p. 61)? Were the religious instructions by Highmaster Luther von Braunschweig and the visitations carried out by Highmaster Winrich von Kniprode reactions to abuses (pp. 101–3)?

The Latin East does not figure prominently in this book. The possessions around the Mediterranean are discussed very briefly, including Armenia, Cyprus, Greece, Apulia, Sicily, Spain, Rome, and Lombardy (Venice). These paragraphs are mainly based on Militzer's 1999 book. With reference to Favreau-Lilie, it is stated that there was no connection between the Order's hospital at Acre and older German hospices in Jerusalem before 1187. The close cooperation of Highmaster Hermann von Salza with Emperor Frederick II is described. As a consequence, as Militzer notes, the Order could not establish itself properly on Cyprus; therefore the Order left Acre in 1291 for Venice, whereas both Hospitallers and Templars went to Cyprus. Between 1252 and 1290 the highmasters are said to have stubbornly supported the Holy Land, whereas a majority of brethren saw the future in the Baltic. Disappointed about the meagre echo for his appeals, Highmaster Burchard von Schwanden resigned in 1290 and became a Hospitaller. In 1303, the brethren in Prussia persuaded Highmaster Gottfried von Hohenlohe to resign, so that his successor Siegfried von Feuchtwangen finally moved from Venice to Marienburg. An English translation of this short but generally reliable story of the medieval Teutonic Order would be welcome. If some illustrations were added, one would have a counterpart to Helen Nicholson's (*The Knights Hospitaller*, 2001; reviewed in *Crusades* 3 [2004]) book on the Hospitallers, though only for the medieval period.

KARL BORCHARDT
UNIVERSITÄT WÜRZBURG

Piers D. Mitchell, *Medicine in the Crusades. Warfare, Wounds and the Medieval Surgeon*. Cambridge: Cambridge University Press, 2004. Pp. ix, 293. ISBN 0 521 84455 X.

It is only when a book like this appears that one realizes how generations of crusade historians, including myself, have been allowed to pontificate on topics about which we have been quite ignorant. Our only excuse has been that there was not enough hard evidence on which to base more secure argument, but it will be hard for us to fall back on such justifications in future. Dr. Mitchell is not only a medical man, but is also one who has taken the trouble to get to know the archaeologists in Israel. He has had, therefore, an entrée to excavations and to already excavated sites. He has written the fullest treatment so far of aspects of medicine and surgery in relation to the crusades and the Latin settlements in the Levant. He has chosen to concentrate on wounds sustained in battle and their treatment, injuries resulting from torture, medical practitioners, elective surgery, legislation and the influence of the practices of Easterners and Westerners on each other in a region where they came into contact. He promises to cover malnutrition, epidemics, parasites, psychiatric illnesses, attitudes to disease, its spread and the transportation back home of the remains of the deceased in a future book.

Some chapters rely almost entirely on the interpretation of written historical materials. These are useful in drawing together many of the sources, some of them not well known, and Dr. Mitchell makes a very important point in establishing that many more Western practitioners were involved than has been previously supposed. He is not a trained historian, however, and he has been poorly served by the CUP's copy editors, because there are too many inconsistent spellings and tiny historical errors in the text. And he is surely wrong when he maintains that the Hospital of St. John in Jerusalem, the greatest of the crusade hospitals with a huge influence elsewhere, was not engaged in medical care until well into the twelfth century, being at first simply a pilgrim hospice. Arguments from silence are rarely convincing, particularly as we know that the movement establishing proper hospitals was already getting into its stride in western Europe. It is true that the early twelfth-century charters are not very informative, although one issued in Provence before 1119 referred to the hospital's function "ad pauperes recreandos" and another, recording a donation by the count of Barcelona, made a nice rhetorical play on a hospital's role when it referred to penance as "a most excellent medicine for sin." There is also clearer contemporary evidence. Albert of Aachen referred to the hospital functioning in 1101 as one "languidorum ceterorumque inualidorum."

Dr. Mitchell really comes into his own when dealing with archaeological material and on those topics where his medical expertise can be fully displayed. Chapters 3, 5, 6, and 7 are outstanding. Chapter 3, on the archaeological evidence for trauma and surgery, reveals a completely new and potentially fruitful field of study. Chapter 5, on injuries and their treatment, shows the wide variety of measures employed, including some experimentation and much more active interventions on the wounded than has been hitherto supposed. Chapter 6, on the practice of elective surgery and bloodletting, demonstrates that, contrary to established belief, surgical procedures were undertaken, although only relatively safe ones were attempted, including the excision of overgrown gum tissue, cranial surgery and cauterization; there are no examples, for fairly obvious reasons, of procedures which involved cutting deeply into the body. There is evidence for the fairly widespread use of analgesia. In Chapter 7, on the exchange of medical knowledge between Westerners and Easterners, Dr. Mitchell resolutely refuses to follow slavishly the standard convictions that Islamic medicine was superior or that the experiences of crusaders and settlers were brought to bear on European practices, but he also downplays the influence of Salernitan medicine in crusade hospitals, believing that they were more subject to oriental influence than it has been fashionable to suppose. This is an important book, because it opens up a new field of research and does so in an authoritative manner.

JONATHAN RILEY-SMITH
EMMANUEL COLLEGE, CAMBRIDGE

Colin Morris, *The Sepulchre of Christ and the Medieval West. From the Beginning to 1600*. Oxford: Oxford University Press, 2005. Pp. xxii, 427. ISBN 0 19 826928 5

Since the mid-fourth century, pilgrimage to the Holy Land has been a fixed and constant element of Christian devotional life. In a formal sense, pilgrimage has changed relatively little over the centuries. Pilgrims have always tended to visit the same sites associated with the earthly life of Jesus – the places of his birth, baptism, teaching, and above all the sites of his death and burial just outside the walls of first-century Jerusalem. It is easy for medievalists – perhaps especially for crusade historians – to take for granted the phenomenon of pilgrimage to Jerusalem. The burial places of saints and martyrs are a deeply familiar part of the medieval landscape; since people venerated saints' tombs, naturally we should expect them to have paid the same if not more attention to the tomb of Christ. Such an assumption, as Colin Morris's book shows, begs many questions. The first may be how and why Christians first came to identify the tomb of Christ. More interesting questions, and ones that underpin the whole book, are why a religion based on the belief that Jesus physically rose from the tomb should have continued to place such importance on devotion to the empty space occupied by his body between death and resurrection, and how such devotion shaped Christian art, iconography and practice in the West.

The initial discovery of the sepulchre and the associated identification of Calvary only a matter of yards away have usually been attributed to Constantine (or, in hagiographical tradition, to his mother) but Morris suggests that the sepulchre had been known and venerated within the Christian community in Jerusalem since at least the 240s, and quite possibly earlier. Nevertheless, a theology of the holy places developed quickly in the fourth century in the wake of Constantine's adoption of Christianity, and by the 380s a sophisticated liturgy based around the sepulchre was already in place. During the early centuries of pilgrimage to the Holy Land, it is the western Church that seems to have exploited the devotional possibilities of the sepulchre, rather than the eastern. Depictions of the sepulchre – in architecture, in monumental art and in the portable form of ivories, flasks and bottles – indicate the importance of disseminating images throughout the western Church. But these were not simply souvenirs or devotional aids that reminded people of the sepulchre. Reflecting as they do a preoccupation with the narrative of the resurrection rather than with representational accuracy, the images of the sepulchre had a profound effect on the development of the early medieval western liturgy. Thus western worship "turned upon the 'Jerusalem events': solemn entry, passion, resurrection" (p. 119) Morris argues that the holy sepulchre provided a gravitational centre around which the conversion of the Germanic peoples could be based. Jerusalem, rather than Rome, helped to centralize worship, and thus to create a centralizing western Church.

The implications of this argument about the importance of the sepulchre in the early medieval West for historians interested in the roots of crusading should be obvious. Professor Morris's amply documented evidence of western architectural and liturgical familiarity with the sepulchre provides a powerful argument for the view that Pope Urban II was, in 1095, already preaching to the converted rather than proposing something outlandish and exceptional. The holy sepulchre was, by the time of the First Crusade, fixed in the Western consciousness not so much through the steady trickle of pilgrims to the Holy Land as through the enactment of a memorializing liturgy that linked the narrative of salvation firmly to a geographical and historical reality. After the First Crusade, of course, the trickle of pilgrims became a torrent. In the chapter entitled "Christendom Refashioned," Morris shows how the continuing familiarity of the west with the crusader states, through dynastic and political ties, produced new variations on the theme of the representation of the sepulchre in the West. Between 1099 and 1187 the sepulchre was nurtured and celebrated as a reminder of the Christian West's domination over the enemies of Christ, and thus as a symbol of the West as a new Israel. After 1187, as the same celebration turned to longing, the sepulchre symbolized responsibility and ever-present sinfulness.

In the mid-eleventh century, the Burgundian pilgrim Lethbald, whose story is told by Ralph Glaber, yearned to die and be buried in Jerusalem. Four hundred years later, the German Dominican Felix Fabri had no such wish: visiting the holy places was a great spiritual privilege, but Fabri knew where his real home was. In an age when the idea of a national homeland was becoming stronger, what chance did the real sepulchre have in the midst of so many copies and depictions in the West? In fact, western preoccupations with the holy sepulchre changed after 1291, but they did not disappear. Liturgical connections with Jerusalem were maintained through the survival of the communities of canons of the lost shrine churches in the west – for example, the canons of Bethlehem at Clamecy – and through the liturgy of the Carmelite friars. One sign of change is a new critical awareness of the holy sites. Educated Western pilgrims who had seen "the real thing" were concerned to transmit back to the West, through descriptions, drawings and measurements, accurate copies of the sepulchre as well as representations of a spiritual reality. This may have been in part because of the realization that such copies were as close as the West would get to possession of the shrine itself. Yet Morris finds little evidence that changing priorities in crusading in the later Middle Ages meant a commensurate decline in pilgrimage or interest in the sepulchre. Many later medieval pilgrims to the Holy Land were northern Europeans, and as patterns of devotion and worship changed during the Reformation, so pilgrimage became an imaginative exercise that could be internalized with the aid of printed books.

Many of the examples discussed in this book will already be familiar to historians of medieval pilgrimage and crusading alike. *The Sepulchre of Christ and the Medieval West*, however, is more than the sum of individual parts. Generously illustrated and providing detailed case-studies, this is a wide-ranging, authoritative and elegant study of the direction of Western devotion in the Middle Ages.

ANDREW JOTISCHIKY
LANCASTER UNIVERSITY

Robert the Monk's History of the First Crusade: Historia Iherosolimitana, trans. Carol Sweetenham (Crusade Texts in Translation, 11). Aldershot: Ashgate, 2005. Pp. x, 243. ISBN 0 7546 0471 3.

In the medieval period, Robert's *Historia* was the most successful account of the First Crusade by some distance and it is extant today in some hundred manuscripts. Here, Sweetenham is swift to disclaim any idea of a new edition, and presents a translation into English of the nineteenth-century edition in *RHC Oc.* 3. The translation is accompanied by a comprehensive introduction comprising five chapters. The first places Robert in his historiographical context, and includes a discussion of his identity (he was probably *not* the abbot of Saint-Rémi as generally accepted) and of his purpose in writing. A second chapter explores the relationship with the anonymous *Gesta Francorum* (*GF*) and the *GF*'s use by Peter Tudebode, Baudry of Bourgueil, and Guibert of Nogent. This presents little that is new, but the following section is a very useful overview of the ways in which Robert manipulated his main source, including additions and omissions, but also changes in emphasis, especially Robert's "heroes and villains." This leads into a third chapter which considers other sources and discusses in detail the – at times very close – relationship between Robert's *Historia* and the *Historia Vie Hierosolimitane* of Gilo of Paris. Sweetenham, albeit with palpable reluctance, postulates a common "lost source" written in hexameters; she is probably right to reject the idea of Gilo using Robert, but if Grocock and Siberry (1997) are correct in their dating, then it would be possible for Robert to have seen Gilo's work, and we can rule out neither an early redaction by Gilo, nor eclectic borrowings on Robert's part to explain deviations. This chapter concludes with an evaluation of Robert's work, which stresses that the *Historia* is important for historiographical reasons, not as historical evidence for the First Crusade. This is further underlined in chapter 4, an assessment of Robert as author, under the headings Theologian, Historiographer, Literary Craftsman. Finally, a short chapter provides principles of translation.

The translation "aims to steer a middle course between fidelity and elegance," and the translator has largely succeeded in this. Curiosity took me to the Latin text to see what Latin phrases were translated as "talking ... hot air," which occurs twice ("plurima in ventum procederent verba" and "aerem concitas inanibus verbis"). There were other colloquialisms, some of which jarred more than others: a reference to the crusaders' "track record" ("virtus experientiae"); "boring me to death" ("nosque ad fastidium portabis"); "make a quick exit" ("ut cito recederet"); "cut no ice" ("nil proficeret"); "stupid comments" ("verba vana"). However, on the whole the translation is both fluent and accurate, although it does not always make fine historical distinctions. For example, both "Teuthonicus" and "Alemannus" are translated as "German" without comment, and "castle" is used for both "castellum," the watchtower built near the mosque outside Antioch, and "castrum," the old castle requisitioned in the following chapter. Some technical terms are translated unhelpfully: "in a tortoise formation" (for "factam testudinem") does not give a picture of the shield roof; while "threw their shields in front of them" (for "projectis clypeis") gives an equally bizarre impression.

Footnotes cover dates, and names of people and places. They are generally accurate, although "Camela" has been translated as Hamah, when it should be Homs. The identification of biblical borrowings – which are also italicized in the text – is excellent (though note that Psalms are numbered as in the Authorized Version, not the Vulgate). The translator also aims to cover "points of interest or comparison with other texts where this might be helpful." Granted that any measure is subjective, I should have welcomed fewer notes drawing attention to Robert's taste for the macabre or his use of humour (at one point Sweetenham also inserts a "funnily enough" into the text, in case we miss the joke), and more on content. For example, when describing the siege of Nicaea, Robert explains, "Nobody was stationed to the south because there an enormous lake protected the city." Then the Turks attack "because those in the city had sent messengers out to them, telling them to come to the south gate to help them. Meanwhile our men had been besieging that gate in force." The contradiction arises from Robert combining his two sources, and is obviated if the lake is correctly placed beneath the western wall of Nicaea: the topographical error is Gilo's. A similar unfamiliarity with the terrain on his translator's part, if not Robert's, is betrayed at the battle of Antioch, when a section of the Turkish army fights "near the coast": "a parte maris" is better translated "on the side towards the coast" – the Turks are still some miles inland on the plain of Antioch.

The text of the *Historia* is followed by an appendix, "Two letters calling Christians on Crusade." These letters are found in about one-third of the extant manuscripts of Robert, and here translated from Hagenmeyer's *Kreuzzugsbriefe* (1901). They are the (supposed) letter of Alexius Comnenus to Robert of Flanders (Hagenmeyer, no. 1), and the letter of the patriarch of Jerusalem to the West (no. 9). Sweetenham argues that both should be seen as part of Bohemond's recruiting campaign of 1106, which she also maintains is the context in which the *Historia* was produced. She does not satisfactorily explain why, in this case, Robert's heroes are so manifestly (and counterfactually) Godfrey and Hugh. There is a useful bibliography, and a slightly eccentric index: because introduction and text are paginated continuously, it does not distinguish between the two, and while there are subdivisions in entries for the leaders, others are long lists of page numbers.

Sweetenham has made Robert's *Historia* accessible to a wider readership. Hers is a lively translation with a useful commentary. The *Historia* contains many good things, and providing the reader remembers that – despite the title – it is not "history," it will be read with pleasure and profit.

SUSAN B. EDGINGTON
QUEEN MARY, UNIVERSITY OF LONDON

Steven Runciman, *The First Crusade*. Cambridge: Cambridge University Press, 2005. Pp. 201. ISBN 0 521 48739 7 (hardback), 0 521 61148 2 (paperback).

I first read, and was entranced by, Runciman's *History of the Crusades* when I was about sixteen or seventeen. I did not know that it had had a distinctly cool reception in the senior English-speaking academic journals. In *History* Marian Tooley had pointed out that it was "a work of presentation not of interpretation." In *Speculum*, ʿAziz ʿAtiya had written harshly: "This book is a work of compilation where the author handled the fruit of centuries of unremitting labors with more skill than originality." And in the *English Historical Review*, in a brilliant piece in which he foresaw the direction of crusade studies for the next half-century, R. C. Smail had suggested that "this is an odd time to halt and summarize, when there is much new work of fundamental importance long overdue and still to be done." The impotence of academic critics has never been better demonstrated than in this case, because, as everyone knows, the phenomenal success of the *History* with the general public meant that it became – and remained – easily the most admired English account of the crusades. A few copies of the complete work are still being sold fifty years after it had first appeared. There were from the start semi-popular histories which made no use of original material whatever and relied on the evidence provided in Runciman's three volumes, as if he himself was a primary source. Meanwhile he was persuaded to prepare an abridged version of the first volume, covering the course of the First Crusade. This was published in 1980. The present book purports to be a new edition, although it is not apparent that anything other than the packaging has altered.

It is a sign of the changes wrought by time that, rereading Runciman's account, I found myself wondering what it was that had originally inspired me. I had expected the book to be very dated as history, not least because the enormous amount of research published on the First Crusade in the last twenty years, and particularly around its anniversary in the late 1990s, would make any work as old as this obsolete. And Sir Steven's literary style now had an archaic feel about it, which explains why it has proved very hard to get university students to read him. Although an abridgement is necessarily less expansive than an original version, I was struck by the almost total absence of analysis, which had been sacrificed to a bland narrative, lacking any real excitement. There appeared to be no interest whatever in ideas. Problematic issues were either ignored or so drenched in descriptive verbiage that they were invisible. The characterization of men and women, which was much admired at the time, now looks predictable and wooden. And what goes for individuals is even more marked when it comes to groups. Runciman was, typically for his generation, steeped in the romantic novels of Sir Walter Scott, in which the crusaders, colourful and courageous but rough and uneducated, had broken into a more civilized region than their own and had left a trail of wreckage behind them. In Runciman's perception, the Byzantine Greeks, models of toleration and advanced thinking, were faced by semi-barbarous Westerners "on a lower level of civilization," whose "wounded pride," when faced by a sophistication they could not comprehend, "made them obstreperous and rude, like naughty children." Somewhat surprisingly the behaviour of the Muslims – clearly on a higher cultural plane than the Franks, even if less cultivated than the Greeks – was marked by "oriental methods of treachery." A feature of the work, indeed, is such a lack of interest in Islam that Runciman could refer to the Fatimids having "Shia tendencies." His reputation was that of a polyglot, although to be fair to him he never claimed to be able to read Arabic. It is clear from the inconsistency of his transliterations and his reliance on translated sources in the unabridged history that he did not.

For the course of events Runciman relied on Hagenmeyer's *Chronologie*, which guaranteed a certain level of accuracy. Every now and then, however, the blood would flow to his head and he would compose a dramatic set-piece reconstruction – on conditions in Palestine before the arrival of the crusade, on the Council of Clermont, on the destruction of the first wave of crusaders in Asia Minor, on the fall of Antioch and the subsequent battle outside the walls, on the taking of Jerusalem – in which the evidence was sacrificed to imagination and in which a few episodes seem even to have been invented.

Not long before Runciman's death I was asked to interview him for a series which aimed to catch very old and distinguished historians on video before they passed out of sight. The interview did not go well. Although I had known him for over thirty years he was not easy to converse with on camera because he was so unreflective and was really not at all interested in analysis or method. He kept repeating that he was not a historian, but a writer of literature. That he considered himself to be really a literary narrator may explain why academic historians now find him so hard to comprehend. Whether this provides an excuse for the Cambridge University Press to go on issuing a book which is now virtually worthless as history is for others to judge.

JONATHAN RILEY-SMITH
EMMANUEL COLLEGE, CAMBRIDGE

Sylvia Schein, *Gateway to the Heavenly City. Crusader Jerusalem and the Catholic West (1099–1187)* (Church, Faith and Culture in the Medieval West). Aldershot and Burlington, VT, Ashgate, 2005. Pp xvi, 239. ISBN 0 7546 0649 X.

The First Crusade notoriously attracted more historical writing from contemporaries than, perhaps, any previous historical event, and the Latin presence in the Holy Land during the following decades was similarly a matter of great interest to Western writers. As the author says, "Jerusalem looms large in all literary genres of the period, including sermons, theological treatises, chronicles and annals, letters, crusading *excitatoria*, literature and especially poetry." The book was at an advanced stage of preparation at the time of her sudden and unexpected death. A number of colleagues, including Brenda Bolton and Michael Goodich, saw it through publication, and Yvonne Friedman has provided a short but sensitive preface. It has also been equipped with a very good bibliography and an index.

Sylvia Schein has been an important presence in the development of medieval studies, and especially the study of the crusades, during the past two decades. The aim of this work is "to examine the place of Jerusalem in the [Western] Christian spirituality of the twelfth century." Professor Schein's knowledge of the literature of the century is outstanding, covering the abundant crusading chronicles and many other forms of evidence. The chronicler who is least represented in the discussion is Albert of Aachen, and that is a pity, because he seems to stand more firmly than the others in the tradition of earlier thinking. He emphasized strongly the pilgrim character of the First Crusade, and was not as inclined as others to adopt new terminology: the armies are not called *milites Christi*, and his ideas about martyrdom are notably old-fashioned. In her analysis of the wider ranges of Western writing, Professor Schein is both thorough and original. Her insistence on the horror at the pollution of the holy places by the presence of unbelievers is close to the dominant pattern of thought in the West. Pollution, of course, can work both ways: the Muslim description of the Church of the Resurrection (*qiyyama*) as a rubbish-dump (*qumama*) indicated that the other side had the same feelings. The importance of liturgy in shaping the understanding of Jerusalem has emerged from a number of recent studies, and the author is very good on the subject. Innovations included the 15 July procession, the emphasis on *Laetare Jerusalem* Sunday, and the rapid creation of a liturgy *pro deliberatione terrae Jerusalem* immediately after the loss of the city. (Cristina Dondi's important work was not published in time to be used here). There is a particularly good account of responses in the West to the news of Saladin's reconquest of the city, which was to determine the subsequent development of the crusades.

Thinking about Jerusalem was shaped both by Latin spirituality in general and by the striking fact of God's providential deliverance of the city into the hands of believers. The author points us very effectively to many of the changes, but it is a fact that they are extremely difficult to define with confidence. For all the abundance of chronicles and other evidence, there are some nasty holes in the information available. Apart from anything else, as we know from the propaganda of our own era, exhortations to a crusade do not always make for clarity of thinking. Moreover, we have scarcely any twelfth-century crusading sermons, for the few which survive are reconstructions by chroniclers, and the differences among the reports of Urban II's crucial address at Clermont do not exactly fill one with confidence. Writers inevitably echo the Psalms, Jerome and Prudentius, and when they speak of holy places "where his feet have stood," they should not be assumed to be searching for a new theological definition. Pilgrim accounts, although valuable, are relatively few and brief, especially if one thinks of the immense mass of pilgrim literature which survives from the late Middle Ages. For rigorous thought about the crusades, one might turn to the canonists and schoolmen, but twelfth-century canon law had little to say about the crusades. Professor Schein, of course, does mention the way in which it drew upon the "just war" tradition, but as a matter of fact only a few canonists developed this, and they were more interested in warfare among Christians than in the defence or recovery of Jerusalem. Paris theology was primarily speculative for most of the twelfth century: it is only in the last two decades that Peter the Chanter gave political affairs and daily life a central place in the life of the schools. Contemporaries were well aware that God had changed the place of Jerusalem within the Christian dispensation, but only a few of them had the skill to define the new order, and they were not doing so in an identical way.

Inevitably there are some factual details with which a reviewer may disagree. For example, O. Ellger's book (1988) on Abbot Eigil's chapel at Fulda creates serious doubts whether there was a representation of the Holy Sepulchre there; and it seems to me doubtful whether Abbot Wyno was sent to Jerusalem specifically to secure a plan of the edicule for Paderborn (it would not have been a good one, because the building was probably still in ruins). Conversely, Aquileia deserves a mention, as the oldest surviving Western version of the edicule, and one which we know was being used for the *visitatio* ceremony. But such divergences are not surprising in a survey which covers such a range of evidence, on a topic which includes the specialisms of a large number of scholars. This is a book which will be of value to all students of the crusades and those interested in the ideal of Jerusalem. I understand that a further book by Sylvia Schein exists, as least in part, in draft. It is to be hoped that it can be made available, but for the time being at least, *Gateway to the Heavenly City* will form an appropriate memorial to her work.

COLIN MORRIS
UNIVERSITY OF SOUTHAMPTON

Caroline Smith, *Crusading in the Age of Joinville*. Aldershot and Burlington, VT: Ashgate, 2006. Pp. xii, 216. ISBN 0 7546 5363 3.

This book draws on a close reading of Jean de Joinville's *Vie de saint Louis* in order to try to get at laymen's views and experience of crusading in the thirteenth century. Joinville's book is the key text. The author acknowledges that without recourse to it, our knowledge would be impoverished. But Joinville's book also allows one to exploit less explicit and less full sources more fruitfully in that his observations and expressed thoughts allow one to pick up and exploit hints in these other sources that perhaps would otherwise be overlooked. Thus, through and in comparison with the *Vie de saint Louis*, Joinville's other works (his *Credo* and family epitaph) and other sources like sermons, chronicles, songs, and fictional literature (*chansons de geste* and *romances*) yield more abundant information on laymen's views and experiences of crusading than one might have guessed.

A good 25 percent of the study is in fact a description of various sources, their limitations and their possibilities. It is, of course, necessary to offer this description, but the majority of the comments are not surprising. Most scholars are aware that sermons must be treated cautiously as a guide to lay folks' opinions. Most scholars will immediately grasp why preachers trying to drum up recruits did not emphasize the pain and suffering on crusade or the dangers of captivity. And so forth. There is also, it must be said, a great deal of repetition in the book. Together with the amount of "sign posting" (allusions to what has been said in previous chapters or will be said in future ones) this renders the writing clear but somewhat prosaic.

The conclusions also seem predictable or at least not at all astonishing. Some men went on crusade to satisfy family honor where a tradition of crusading had been long established. Others refused to go for fear that their estates would suffer in their absence and, therefore, very instrumentally though not necessarily dishonestly, elevated protection of their families and possessions at home to a virtue equal to that of crusading. It is possible, but how likely will never be known, that the romance theme attracted a few with the idea of the exotic, almost Arthurian, *aventure* of the crusade. One could go on.

The main point is that generalizations about laypeople are not easy. Different situations (age, family considerations, wealth, relation to heresy, and so forth) made some aspects of the crusades attractive in various ways to certain men. Other situations made crusading unattractive. Two intensive case studies of the careers of Jean de Joinville and Olivier de Termes help the author illustrate this point. Jean de Joinville's eagerness to go on crusade in 1248 is contrasted by his refusal in 1270. Youth and not much property explain the first; maturity and a great deal of property explain the second. Olivier de Termes's defense of Languedoc against the northern crusaders in the early thirteenth century and his evolving and increasingly positive relationship with the French monarchy as he grew older, and with crusading to the east, are explained by means of a careful analysis of changing factors that shaped his career more generally.

This book is very restrained in its claims. Yet, its accomplishment is significant in that Smith has endeavored to and succeeded in complicating the rather simple picture of laymen's motivations and experiences in crusading that has hitherto dominated the literature.

WILLIAM CHESTER JORDAN
PRINCETON UNIVERSITY

Damian J. Smith, *Innocent III and the Crown of Aragon. The Limits of Papal Authority.* Aldershot and Burlington, VT: Ashgate, 2004. Pp. xiv, 339. ISBN 0 7546 3492 2.

Although historians may differ in their assessments of the pontificate of Innocent III, virtually all, I believe, would agree that he is the one medieval pope about whom it is possible to know not merely his public acts but also much about his personality. Our sources are not merely abundant, they are very informative. Damian Smith is, therefore, able to present us with a richly detailed picture of Innocent's relations with the crown of Aragon. Still, it is no criticism to say that the picture that emerges is not entirely clear. In fact, it is one of the strengths of this book that Smith resists the temptation to over-interpret his evidence in order to create a more coherent picture. Putting the matter bluntly, much of the mess is part of the overall picture. To clean it up would seriously undermine the result. Smith's cast of characters possess a certain humanity that is not always attractive. This conclusion is true of Peter II, whom the author obviously admires, and Arnau Amalric, whom he apparently does not. Smith is not writing biography, but he does have the ability to present real people in real situations in a convincing manner. His approach is narrative and mostly chronological rather than topical, the main exception being his chapter on the Albigensian Crusade. He focuses narrowly on the Crown of Aragon and its interests, treating relations with other kingdoms and their rulers rather sparingly. To some degree, I believe this decision is defensible, but it does sometimes make for a gap in our understanding. For example, his treatment of relations with Innocent and the young Frederick on the question of the latter's marriage begs for a broader context, especially from the Aragonese point of view. After all, this decision is critical in Aragonese and Italian history into the early modern period. But Smith keeps his eye on the kingdom, ranging from the coronation of Peter II in Rome through the years leading up to the battle of Las Navas de Tolosa.

Given the centrality of the Albigensian Crusade and the issue of heresy in the history of the Crown of Aragon, I believe that this review should devote its limited space to that topic. First, however, I must confess that I feel that this field has too long suffered from a narrow emphasis on heresy, largely based on anti-heretical tracts as sources without sufficient attention being given to other issues, whether dynastic, economic, or ethnic, and studies that will provide a deeper social context for the religious attitudes of the region. We are still at the stage of global assertions, some of which may well offer valuable hypotheses, but do not yet reach the point where we get to know heretics well and know even less about those living in the shadow world of accusation. Whether consciously or not, this lack of certainty informs Smith's treatment of the Albigensian Crusade. Even the pope comes to participate in this uncertainty. The problem is not new to Smith's work. In fact, it has moved to the foreground in many other recent studies of heresy. Moreover, there has been growing recognition of Innocent's hesitation about support for his crusade, but Smith seems to go a bit further and, as a result, alters our picture of the events of the crusade.

Of course, the treatment of the Albigensian Crusade here is narrowly focused, especially on the figure of Peter II. This is both an advantage and a disadvantage. Peter was, after all, peripheral to the crusade, despite his close ties to Languedoc and its great nobles. Smith is quite right, in my opinion, in casting Peter as one whose interests were more feudal and territorial than in the problem of heresy. In any case, there was little of that in the kingdom of Aragon. For Smith, Simon de Montfort is a villain. Smith subscribes to the view that his passion was to carve out a kingdom for himself in the Midi. He was supported by Arnau Amalric and most of the bishops.

Even when Innocent became convinced that the crusade had achieved its objective of stamping out heresy and accepted the arguments presented by Peter II's envoys, they were unwilling to follow the direction set by the pope. Thus the scene was set for the battle of Muret, which cost Peter his life. Smith recognizes that Innocent III's policies were also losers. In the convoluted politics of the period leading up to the Fourth Lateran council, the pope continued to try to rescue the remnants of his policies through negotiations, only to suffer yet further defeat at the Council.

Smith devotes the final chapters of this volume to legal issues and the place of new religious orders in the kingdom. He follows the complicated legal disputes involving Tarragona, Urgell, Lleida, and Huesca in considerable detail. His analysis is useful and will provide additional support for canonists working in this field. His section on reform of religious orders provides insight into the Aragonian aspect of the Trinitarians. He also has a quite interesting discussion of the plight of the Poor Catholics in the kingdom and the difficulties of their position between Catharism and the Waldensians.

Smith has made a worthwhile contribution to our literature on Innocent III. He has also added to our understanding of the problems faced by the emerging kingdom of Aragon during this very difficult period.

JAMES M. POWELL
SYRACUSE UNIVERSITY (EMERITUS)

Kristjan Toomaspoeg, *Les Teutoniques en Sicile (1197–1492)* (Collection de l'École française de Rome, 321). Rome: École française de Rome, 2003. Pp. x, 1011. ISBN 2 7283 0655 9.

Über die Deutschordensballei Sizilien war bisher nur sehr wenig bekannt. Die hier anzuzeigende Arbeit verdanken wir einer besonders glücklichen Überlieferungslage auf der Insel Sizilien, einer Überlieferung, von deren Reichtum die vor rund 40 Jahren durch Kurt Forstreuter zusammengefasste ältere Forschung (K. Forstreuter, *Der Deutsche Orden am Mittelmeer* [1967], S. 110–23) keine Vorstellung hatte. Henri Bresc, der akademische Lehrer des Verfassers, hat sich in der Vergangenheit Teile dieser Archivüberlieferung für seine Studien zur Wirtschaftsgeschichte Siziliens im späteren Mittelalter zunutze gemacht (vgl. Henri Bresc, *Un monde méditerranéen. Économie et société en Sicile, 1300–1450*, 1986). Im Zusammenhang mit diesen Arbeiten entstand zweifellos der Plan, die im Archivio di Stato zu Palermo aufbewahrten Archivalien des Deutschordenshauses zu Palermo, des Haupthauses der Ballei Sizilien, für eine Balleigeschichte vollständig zu erschließen und auszuwerten. K. Toomaspoeg hat sich nicht auf die Ordensüberlieferung beschränkt, sondern zusätzlich eine Reihe weiterer in Palermo erhaltener Quellenbestände herangezogen: die Notariatsregister des Archivio di Stato mit ihren für die Ordensgeschichte relevanten Eintragungen, die Senatsakten im Archivio Storio Comunale und die Notariatsurkunden in der Biblioteca Comunale. Darüber hinaus bezieht er die gesamte außerhalb Siziliens vorhandene Überlieferung mit ein, die von der älteren Forschung nur teilweise genutzt worden ist: die Dokumente aus dem Deutschordenszentralarchiv in Wien (Welschland, Handschriften) und aus dem Geheimen Staatsarchiv Stiftung Preußischer Kulturbesitz in Berlin (Ordensbriefarchiv), Quellen aus dem Archivio di Stato in Neapel, aus dem Vatikanischen Archiv, der Österreichischen Nationalbibliothek Wien und dem Archivo de la Corona de Aragòn (Barcelona) sowie aus verschiedenen kleineren deutschen Archiven. Auf dieser breiten Grundlage wird eine Balleigeschichte erarbeitet, die in zwei große Abteilungen zerfällt. Der erste Hauptteil (S. 21–451) behandelt historisch-politische Zusammenhänge, wirtschaftliche Entwicklungen und sozio-kulturelle Fragen: Zunächst geht es um die Gründe für die Etablierung des Deutschen Ordens auf Sizilien und um die Konsolidierung seines Besitzes; des weiteren zweitens um die Gründe für das Überdauern der Deutschordensniederlassung im Inselkönigreich nach dem Zusammenbruch der Kreuzfahrerstaaten 1291 und drittens. um eine Erklärung für die Beschlagnahmung des Deutschordensbesitzes durch die spanische Krone im Jahre 1492. Entsprechend gliedert sich die Darstellung in drei große Teile, die von den Anfängen und der Konsolidierungsphase in staufischer und angevinischer Zeit (1197–1291) über das schwierige Jahrhundert nach dem Ende der Lateinerherrschaft in Syrien und Palästina, als das Überleben der Ballei nur durch deren Integration in die Gesellschaft Siziliens gesichert werden konnte (1292–1391), bis hin zur Konfiskation des sehr ertragreichen Deutschordensbesitzes durch die spanische

Krone im Jahre 1492 führen, d. h. bis zum Ende einer Phase des Niedergangs, in deren Verlauf die Krone zunächst die Zahlung von Abgaben und Steuern durch den Deutschen Orden durchsetzte und die in der Konfiskation der Ballei im Jahre 1492 durch die spanische Krone kulminierte. Der Verfasser zeigt, dass 1492 nur realisiert wurde, was bereits König Alfons V. der Großmütige von Aragon-Sizilien 1436/37 versucht, aber aus Rücksichtnahme auf Kaiser und Papst am Ende aufgegeben hatte. Der Hinweis auf das Versagen der Ordensleitung in der zweiten Hälfte des 15. Jh., die dem moralischen Verfall und dem Schwinden des Rechtsbewusstseins im Ordenshaus zu Palermo nicht Einhalt gebot, ist berechtigt. Grundsätzlich kann Toomaspoeg aufgrund der ihm zur Verfügung stehenden Materialfülle ein erheblich dichteres Bild der Balleigeschichte zeichnen als es der älteren Forschung möglich war. In Teilen bestätigt er zwar die Einschätzungen der älteren Forschung, doch manche ältere These steht aufgrund seiner Beobachtungen nun zur Disposition. So wird z. B. die Bedeutung Friedrichs II. für die Konsolidierung der Stellung des Deutschen Ordens auf Sizilien künftig neu (positiver) zu bewerten sein, ebenso die Rolle der Ballei (Komturei) Sizilien als Nachschubbasis für den Kreuzzug sowie der Anteil in Sizilien stationierter Deutschordensbrüder an der Verteidigung Akkons im Frühjahr 1291.

Die beiden anderen Leitfragen, die den Aufbau der Darstellung beeinflussen und für jede der drei Epochen in eigenen Kapiteln behandelt werden, sind, wie bereits angedeutet, sozial- und wirtschaftshistorischer Natur. So wird die materielle Grundlage der Ballei Sizilien, die Besitzgeschichte und Wirtschaftsweise der *Magione*, des Haupthauses in Palermo, untersucht. Überzeugend weist Toomaspoeg nach, dass der Deutschordensbesitz auf eine den Traditionen der Insel verhaftete Weise wirtschaftlich genutzt wurde, die sich deutlich von der Praxis im Ordensstaat und im Deutschen Reich unterschied. Die Ausführungen verbessern die bisher sehr lückenhafte Kenntnis der Deutschordensbesitzungen auf Sizilien ganz wesentlich. Hervorzuheben ist, dass er mit dem in Palermo gehobenen Material auf eine zur Bearbeitung wirtschaftshistorischer Fragen besonders ergiebige Überlieferung zurückgreifen kann. Die beigegebenen Karten sowie die Tabellen und Grafiken veranschaulichen seine Befunde.

In den sozialgeschichtlich ausgerichteten Kapiteln der Arbeit befasst sich Toomaspoeg mit der regionalen und sozialen Herkunft der nach Sizilien entsandten deutschen Ordensbrüder und dem in der Balleiverwaltung nachweisbaren Personal. Die Quellen, die sich für diese Fragen auswerten lassen, sind zwar nicht so zahlreich und nehmen erst im 14./15. Jh. an Dichte zu, aber sie geben doch einen gewissen Einblick in die Mobilität der nach Sizilien versetzten Deutschordensbrüder, in ihre Beziehungen zur Heimat und zu dem von ihnen abhängigen Personenkreis auf Sizilien. So wird gezeigt, dass die Übersiedlung des Hochmeisters von Venedig nach Preußen (1309) und die in diesem Zusammenhang erfolgte Unterordnung der am Mittelmeer gelegenen Balleien unter den Deutschmeister Auswirkungen hatte auf die Herkunft der dem Ordenshaus in Palermo zugewiesenen Brüder aus bestimmten Regionen des Deutschen Reiches. Höchst interessant sind die

Beobachtungen, die die Stellung der Deutschordensritter in der spätmittelalterlichen Gesellschaft Siziliens sowie die soziale Stellung und die politischen Verbindungen der in enger Beziehung zum Deutschen Orden stehenden Sizilianer betreffen. An sich nicht weiter überraschend ist die Beobachtung, dass die bürgerlichen und adeligen Gruppen, die enge Beziehungen zur Deutschordensniederlassung in Palermo unterhielten, zu den Gegnern der Herrschaft Karls I. von Anjou auf Sizilien zählten und sich an dem Aufstand des Jahres 1282 beteiligten. Ebenso wenig erstaunt die Tatsache, dass die Vertreter des Deutschen Ordens in Palermo dort mit Vorliebe zu staufisch gesinnten Zuwanderern aus Reichsitalien oder gar zu Deutschen und zu Juden Geschäftsbeziehungen aufnahmen. Toomaspoeg zeigt, dass der Deutsche Orden Beziehungen zu Menschen unterhielt, die ganz unterschiedlicher geographischer und kultureller Herkunft waren. In gewisser Weise liefert er mit diesen Beobachtungen auch einen kleinen Beitrag zur Erforschung der interkulturellen Kommunikation im späten Mittelalter, die auf der Insel Sizilien als einer an der Grenze zwischen islamischer und christlicher Welt gelegenen Drehschreibe im Mittelmeerraum zweifellos ausgeprägter war als in vielen anderen Regionen Europas.

Der zweite große Teil des Buches (S. 453–905) besteht aus verschiedenen Anhängen, in denen ein beträchtlicher Teil der für die Untersuchung grundlegenden Materialien bereitgestellt wird: erstens Namenlisten der auf Sizilien nachweisbaren 261 Deutschordensbrüder und Deutschordenskomture aus der Zeit zwischen 1202 und 1505 (S. 455–84); zweitens ein umfangreicher Quellenanhang (S. 485–905). Hier findet sich neben einer durchdachten Auswahl von insgesamt 20 Dokumenten aus der Zeit zwischen 1215 und 1491 (S. 504–53), die größtenteils aus den Archivbeständen der Deutschordenskommende Palermo (Archivio di Stato Palermo) stammen, eine umfangreiche, chronologisch angelegte Regestensammlung (S. 559–905), die den Inhalt von insgesamt 1103 größtenteils im Staatsarchiv zu Palermo überlieferten Urkunden, Besitzinventaren, Karten und Plänen aus der Zeit zwischen dem frühen 12. und dem Ende des 18. Jh. (1116–1796) erschließt. Hier findet der Benutzer neben teilweise noch ganz unbekannten Privilegien der Ballei Sizilien v. a. Dokumente zur Wirtschaftsführung des Deutschen Ordens und Quellen, die die Herkunft des Deutschordensbesitzes auf Sizilien illustrieren. Diese Quellensammlung macht das Buch zu einem Werk, das auch außerhalb der Deutschordensforschung die verdiente Beachtung finden wird. Ungeduldige Leser werden allerdings das Fehlen eines Sachregisters bemängeln.

MARIE-LUISE FAVREAU-LILIE
FREIE UNIVERSITÄT BERLIN

Annemarie Weyl Carr, *Cyprus and the Devotional Art of Byzantium in the Era of the Crusades* (Variorum Collected Studies Series, 806). Aldershot and Burlington, VT: Ashgate, 2005, Pp. xiv, 378. ISBN 0 86078 936 5.

In 1965, at the end of the Dumbarton Oaks Symposium on "Byzantine Art and the West," Ihor Sevcenko asked the important question, what was the place and significance of Cyprus in the artistic developments of the twelfth and thirteenth centuries in the Mediterranean world? Annemarie Weyl Carr made her first visit to Cyprus a few years later, in 1970, and in effect she began to research and formulate her answers to those questions, work that has occupied her ever since along several lines. In this volume of eleven carefully selected studies she explores the Cypriot artistic world of manuscripts – Section 1: "Cyprus and the 'Decorative Style'" – as well as icons, frescoes, and metalwork – Section 2: "Art in the Kingdom of Cyprus." These are all works of art that are part of the Byzantine tradition, but which, as Dr. Weyl Carr shows us, possess their own Cypriot identity and demonstrate strongly interactive relationships with Crusader, Armenian and other Eastern Christian traditions, Western European developments, especially Italian and French art, as well as Muslim work of the Mamluk period.

The focus of these articles is found in three themes which she usefully directs our attention to in her introduction. One theme is the "decorative style" Byzantine manuscripts, discussed in five articles published between 1980 and 1993; these are manuscripts that she links essentially to Cyprus, but for which she finds relationships elsewhere in the eastern Mediterranean world of Byzantium. Another theme, explored in many of the articles, is the essential function of these manuscripts and other figural arts as works for devotional use. She approaches this theme in terms of "how material evidence speaks of the uses to which artefacts have been put." The third theme is one of cross-cultural encounter. The cultural and artistic interpenetration found in Cypriot works vis-à-vis the other traditions of the eastern Mediterranean poses enormous challenges for analysis and interpretation. Indeed Dr. Weyl Carr's discussion of all three of these themes offers prime examples of the cutting-edge research, penetrating analysis and thoughtful interpretations that she has contributed in becoming the leading expert on medieval Cypriot art in the English-speaking world.

Summary comments on three of the articles can give the reader a sample of her methods and concerns and the important contributions her work makes. In article I, "A Group of Provincial Manuscripts from the Twelfth Century" (1982), Annemarie Weyl Carr has taken the original 13 manuscripts associated by their style, iconography, and palaeography, grouped around the Rockefeller McCormick New Testament in Chicago (MS 965) and identified the "decorative style" in what now numbers over 80 manuscripts. She has associated them with the Byzantine world centered on Cyprus in the twelfth instead of the thirteenth century, but it is a world strongly linked to Palestine as well. Thus her analysis leads us to consider these images as "images on the edge," provincial Byzantine work produced outside of the Constantinopolitan center. By making this substantial argument, she has demonstrated that an important sub-group of the very large ensemble of manuscripts does not relate to the Latin interregnum in Constantinople (1204–61), but is instead a manifestation of twelfth-century Byzantine provincial production for which Cyprus was at the core and Palestine was an important constituent part. The question remains how to integrate the "decorative style" manuscripts into our overall picture of the Byzantine and Crusader East at this time.

Article IX, "A Palaiologan Funerary Icon from Gothic Cyprus" (2001), offers us a rich discussion of how a remarkable icon in a very beautiful multicultural style took shape in the fourteenth-century world of Nicosia. The icon in question is 2.52 m high by 43 cm wide, and the notable features of its production are that the artist has combined an early Byzantine Palaiologan style with a strikingly realistic full-length portrait of the deceased in the manner of Frankish funeral slabs together with its highly elongated Gothic configuration for a funerary purpose. It shows how Constantinopolitan, Cypriot and Gothic cultural and artistic traditions are combined to initiate an important series of funerary icons on Cyprus. This also shows us that Dr. Weyl Carr's scope extends beyond the thirteenth century up into the mid-fourteenth, and deals with the important proposition that understanding the art of Byzantine Cyprus means understanding the period of the Lusignan occupation as well as that of the Byzantine twelfth century

Finally, article VII, "Art in the Court of the Lusignan Kings" (1995), is a particularly sensitive and wide-ranging discussion with an emphasis on the Cypriotness of Cypriot art, particularly that found as commissions for aristocratic members of the Lusignan ruling class. One of the most interesting of the issues addressed is the appearance of Mamluk metalwork as the commission of the king, Hugh IV. The object in question is a magnificent bronze basin, comparable to the *baptistère de St. Louis*, also in the Louvre, and the only *objet* securely linked to the patronage of a Lusignan king other than coinage. It is truly impressive to see how Dr. Weyl Carr assesses the distinctively Cypriot character of this work and what it indicates about the rule of Hugh IV and how his policies "meshed the island into an existing pattern of interchange within the Levant."

In sum, these samples give some indication of what Dr. Weyl Carr has to offer in content. Reading the articles firsthand will introduce you to her remarkable breadth of knowledge and the elegance of her presentation. One importance of Annemarie Weyl Carr's book for scholars today is that she has made major contributions to understanding and responding to the questions cited at the beginning of this review in terms of the figural arts. No other book addresses these issues in such depth. This is a book that every scholar seriously interested in medieval Cyprus and its significance in the Eastern Mediterranean world of Byzantium and the Crusaders, 1100 to 1350, will want to read from cover to cover.

Jaroslav Folda
University of North Carolina

Dorothea Weltecke, *Die "Beschreibung der Zeiten" von Mor Michael dem Großen (1126–1199). Eine Studie zu ihrem historischen und historiographiegeschichtlichen Kontext* (Corpus Scriptorum Christianorum Orientalium, 594; Subsidia, 110). Louvain: Peeters, 2003. Pp. xv, 323. ISBN 90 429 1132 8.

Der syrisch-jakobitische Patriarch Michael, der während des 12. Jahrhunderts lebte, hat, obwohl er zu den bedeutendsten mittelalterlichen Geschichtsschreibern zählt, eigentlich nur bei Spezialisten größere Beachtung gefunden. Allenfalls für die Epoche der Kreuzzüge wird seiner Weltchronik eine gewisse Bedeutung zugesprochen. Hauptgrund dafür ist zweifellos, daß die Chronik in Syrisch geschrieben worden und den meisten Historikern daher nur in der – problematischen – französischen Übersetzung von J. B. Chabot (Paris, 1899–1904) zugänglich ist. Zudem hat Michael sich, wie bei mittelalterlichen Weltchroniken nicht unüblich, vor allem in der Darstellung der früheren Epochen seinerseits auf Vorlagen gestützt, die zu großen Teilen bekannt sind, so daß eine eingehende Analyse seines Werkes nicht notwendig schien. Diese Lücke wird nun durch die vorliegende Arbeit gefüllt, die als Dissertation von C. Colpe angeregt und von C. Elm betreut worden ist, wobei in diesem Fall auch die fachliche Hilfe durch L. van Rompay und H. Kaufhold erwähnt werden sollte. Tatsächlich ist diese Dissertation trotz des Betreuers weniger der Mediävistik zuzuordnen als vielmehr der Wissenschaft des Christlichen Orients.

Nach einer allgemeinen Einleitung widmet W. sich zunächst dem Forschungsstand zu Michael, erörtert anschließend ausführlich die Entwicklung der "syrisch-orthodoxen" Geschichtsschreibung vor der Zeit Michaels, um sich danach auf die Person des Autors und sein Werk zu konzentrieren.

Die Weltchronik Michaels ist zwar im allgemeinen chronologisch geordnet, zeichnet sich aber besonders durch die graphische Darstellung aus, in der das Material organisiert ist: In drei Kolumnen und einem Kanon (einer Art Zeittafel) werden parallel die Profangeschichte, die Kirchengeschichte sowie "Zeichen und Wunder" dargestellt. Hierbei ist die originale Anordnung in den erhaltenen Fassungen durcheinandergebracht worden, da es den späteren Kopisten und Bearbeitern nicht möglich war, die komplizierte graphische Gestaltung der Chronik wort- und bildgetreu wiederzugeben. Weltecke weist überzeugend nach, daß die ursprünglich Anordnung Michaels nicht nur drei Kolumnen, sondern zusätzlich noch den Kanon umfaßt hat, also nicht drei, sondern insgesamt vier Kolumnen, was für das Verständnis der Textordnung von großer Wichtigkeit ist. Eine solche graphische Anordnung begegnet, wie Weltecke zu Recht anmerkt, auch in lateinischen Chroniken des Mittelalters (etwa Martin von Troppau), geht ihnen aber zeitlich voraus. Ein Einfluß Michaels auf diese Chroniken ist allerdings nicht anzunehmen.

Um den originalen Text Michaels und die Absichten des Autors nachvollziehen zu können, müßten eine Edition oder Übersetzung versuchen, die graphische Gestaltung der Chronik nachzuahmen. Auch in der Übersetzung Chabots ist dies nicht der Fall. Im Gegenteil ist die ursprüngliche Fassung hier kaum noch zu erkennen, was leicht zu Fehlern bei der Benutzung führt. Dazu kommt, daß Chabot tatsächliche oder vermutete Lücken in der Chronik Michaels durch die von diesem abhängige Weltgeschichte des Barhebraeus (Abulfaradj) ergänzt, was nur bei genauem Lesen auffällt. Auch wenn Barhebraeus sein Werk anders konzipiert hat, wird ein Vergleich beider Werke daher problematisch.

Wie Weltecke hervorhebt, zeichnet Michaels Werk sich durch eine geradezu "modern" anmutende wissenschaftliche Methode aus, die sich in der Auswahl, Bearbeitung und Diskussion seiner Vorlagen zeigt. Sein Ziel war, die Identität seiner syrischen Kirche und ihrer Anhänger aufzuzeigen in einer Welt, in der seine Glaubensbrüder Untertanen andersgläubiger Herren waren, seien es nun Muslime, lateinische oder griechische Christen. Aus diesem Grund steht die bis zu Christus selbst zurückreichende Tradition der syrischen Kirche im Zentrum der Darstellung. Daneben allerdings steht auch das eigene Erkenntnisinteresse des Autors. Um es mit Welteckes eigenen Worten zu sagen (S. 265): "Michael wollte es wissen. Indem er sammelte, forschte und webte, entstanden vor seinen Augen allmählich seine 'Bilder einer jeden Zeit'."

Welteckes Dissertation, die zurecht auch mit dem Ernst Reuter-Preis der Freien Universität Berlin ausgezeichnet worden ist, geht vor allem der Person Michaels und seinen Absichten beim Schreiben seiner Chronik nach. Alle ihre Ergebnisse können hier nicht im einzelnen ausgeführt werden, aber es steht fest, daß sie die – bisher über Chabot kaum hinausgekommene – Forschung zu Michael auf eine neue Basis gestellt hat. Für jeden, der Michaels Chronik kritisch benutzen will, wird die Lektüre ihres Buches unabdingbar sein, auch wenn dies zugegebenermaßen beim Leser eine hohe Konzentration voraussetzt, denn die Autorin bevorzugt einen auch literarisch anspruchsvollen, aber aufgrund seiner Dichte sehr komplexen Stil, der nicht immer leicht verständlich ist.

Für den Historiker, der sich einen Leitfaden für die Auswertung der Chronik Michaels im konkreten Einzelfall erhofft, ist die Dissertation Welteckes nicht sonderlich ergiebig. In den Teilen, die die früheren Zeiten betreffen, fußt Michael, wie bei Weltchroniken dieser Art ja auch nicht anders zu erwarten, auf anderen Autoren. Zusätzliche Nachrichten, die aus anderen, uns unbekannten oder nicht erhaltenen Quellen stammen, sind selten. Für die eigene Zeit Michaels häufen sich naturgemäß die eigenen Beobachtungen, aber ein Kommentar hierzu war nicht das Ziel der Untersuchung. Weltecke konzentriert sich vor allem auf die Person des Autors, seine Methodik und die von ihm verfolgten Absichten, so daß die Bedeutung ihrer Analyse eher im Bereich der Ideengeschichte und der Historiographie liegt. Dennoch wird das dritte Kapitel, das die Person des Autors und die syrisch-orthodoxe Kirche zu seiner Zeit behandelt (S. 54–126), auch für den "engeren" Kreuzzugshistoriker nützlich sein, da es die religiöse Mischsituation, die während des 11./12. Jahrhunderts im Vorderen Orient geherrscht hat, deutlich herausarbeitet.

RALPH-JOHANNES LILIE
BERLIN-BRANDENBURGISCHE AKADEMIE DER WISSENSCHAFTEN, BERLIN

Short Notices

Chemins d'outre-mer. Études sur la Méditerranée médiévale offerts à Michel Balard, ed. Damien Coulon, Catherine Otten-Froux, Paule Pagès and Dominique Valérian, 2 vols. (Byzantina Sorbonensia, 20). Paris: Publications de la Sorbonne, 2004. Pp. 857. ISBN 2 85944 520 X.

This *Festschrift* presented to Michel Balard contains a preface by Hélène Ahrweiler and a list of Michel Balard's publications as well as the following articles: "Je suis Bertrand de Gibelet" by Gabriella Airaldi, "Les listes de chargement de navires vénetien (xv–début du xvi siècle): un essai de typoligie" by Benjamin Arbel, "Tra Genoa e Chino nel tempo di Cristoforo Colombo" by Laura Balletto, "I Gattilusio tra Genova e Bisanzio. Nuovi documenti d'archivio" by Enrico Basso, "Les territoires de la grâce: l'évêché de Mazara (1430–1450)" by Henri Bresc, "Il pellegrino assente. L'enigma di una mancata partenza per Gerusalemme (Firenze, agosto 1384)" by Franco Cardini, "L'affrontement entre chrétiens et musulmans. Le rôle de la vraie Croix dans les images de croisade (xiiie–xve siècle)" by Fanny Caroff, "Byzance et l'Orient latin: le legs de Manuel Comnène" by Jean-Claude Cheynet, "La dévotion envers les lieux saints dans la Catalogne médiévale" by Pierre-Vincent Claverie, "*Timeas Danaos et dona ferentes*. Remarques à propos d'un épisode méconnu de la troisième croisade" by Franck Collard, "De Chypre à la Prusse et à la Flandre. Les aventures d'un chevalier poitevin: Perceval de Couloigne, seigneur de Pugny, du Breuil-Bernard et de Pierrefitte (133.–141.)" by Philippe Contamine, "Du nouveau sur Emmanuel Piloti et son témoignage à la lumière de documents d'archives occidentaux" by Damien Coulon, "Le voyage d'outre-mer à la fin du xve siècle: essai de définition de l'identité pèlerine occidentale à travers le récit de Nicole Le Huen" by Béatrice Dansette, "De la prise de Thessalonique par les Normands (1185) à la croisade de Frédéric Barberousse (1189–1190): le revirement politicoreligieux des pouvoirs arméniens" by Gérard Dédéyan, "Les couvents des sœurs dominicaines de Nin et de Zadar (xiii–xiv siècle)" by Claudine Delacroix-Besnier, "Le passage des templiers en Orient d'après les dépositions du procès" by Alain Demurger, "*Novus rerum nascitur ordo*: Venise et la fin d'un monde (1495–1511)" by Bernard Doumerc, "Du Levant à Rhodes, Chio, Gallipoli et Palerme: démêlés et connivences entre chrétiens et musulmans à bord d'un vaisseau génois (octobre–décembre 1408–avril 1411)" by Alain Ducellier, "Women and the customs of the High Court of Jerusalem according to John of Ibelin" by Peter Edbury, "La *Chronique Ragusaine* de Junije Rastic et la politique de Venise dans la mémoire collective de Dubrovnik" by Nenad Fejic, "La reina Leonor de Chipre y los Catalanes de su entorno" by Maria Teresa Ferrer i Mallol, "Quelques aspects de la propagande anti-byzantine dans les sources occidentales de la première croisade" by Jean Flori, "The Crusades and military history" by John France, "Autonomie locale et relations avec les Latins à Byzance au xive siècle: Iôannès Limpidarios / Libadarios, Ainos et les Draperio de Péra" by

Thierry Ganchou, "La reforma eclesiástica romana en el desarrollo de formaciones políticas: el caso de los condados catalanes, ca. 1060–ca. 1100" by Luis García-Guijarro, "De la difficulté d'être étranger au royaume de France: les avatars de Colard le Lombard en 1413–1416" by Claude Gauvard, "Qu'allaient-ils faire dans ces galères?" by Jean-Philippe Genet, "Pour une réévaluation des phénomènes de colonisation en Méditerranée occidentale et au Maghreb pendant le Moyen Âge et le début des Temps Modernes" by Philippe Gourdin, "Miradas de viajeros sobre Oriente (siglos xii–xiv)" by Nilda Guglielmi, "Les martyrs franciscains de Jérusalem (1391), entre mémoire et manipulation" by Isabelle Heullant-Donat, "Le consulat vénitien d'Alexandrie d'après un document inédit de 1284" by David Jacoby, "Un patriarche byzantin dans le royaume latin dè Jérusalem: Léontios" by Michel Kaplan, "Les empereurs de Trébizonde, débiteurs des Génois" by Sergej P. Karpov, "Again: Genoa's Golden Inscription and King Baldwin I's Privilege of 1104" by Benjamin Z. Kedar, "Trois documents concernant les marchands vénitiens à Tana au début du xve siècle" by Barisa Krekic, "Monopoly and Privileged Free Trade in the Eastern Mediterranean (8th–14th century)" by Angeliki E. Laiou, "Quelques remarques sur la découverte du sucre par les premiers croisés d'Orient" by Bruno Laurioux, "Un artisan verrier crétois à Venise" by Chryssa Maltézou, "Tissus et costumes dans les relations islamo-byzantines (ix–x siècle)" by Mohamed Tahar Mansouri, "Les croisades dans la Chronique universelle de Bar Hebraeus" by Françoise Micheau, "L'Église arménienne et les chrétientés d'Orient (xii–xiv siècle)" by Claude Mutafian, "Du comté de Champagne aux royaumes d'Orient: sceaux et armoiries des comtes de Brienne" by Marie-Adélaïde Nielen, "Mouvements de populations, migrations et colonisations en Serbie et en Bosnie (xii–xv siècle)" by Marie Nystazopoulou-Pélékidou, "Questioni tra Bizanzio e Genova intorno all'anno 1278" by Sandra Origone, "Les *giorni uziagi*. Hommes de mer vénitiens et jours néfastes" by Gherardo Ortalli, "Contribution à l'étude de la procédure du *sindicamentum* en Méditerranée orientale (xiv–xv siècle)" by Catherine Otten-Froux, "Les Génois et la Horde d'Or: le tournant de 1313" by Serban Papacostea, "Des Lorrains en croisade. La maison de Bar" by Michel Parisse, "Marins et marchands portugais en Méditerranée à la fin du Moyen Âge" by Jacques Paviot, "La celebrazione dei potere: l'apparato funebre per Battista Campofregoso (1442)" by Giovanna Petti Balbi, "Les arsenaux musulmans de la Méditerranée et de l'océan Atlàntique (vii–xv siècle)" by Christophe Picard, "L'Europa dal particolarismo medievale e dall'Impero feudale agli orizzonti aperti" by Geo Pistarino, "Associazionismo e ricerca a Genova, tra tradizione ed evoluzione" by Dino Puncuh, "Lucques, Gênes et le trafic de la soie (v. 1250–v. 1340)" by Pierre Racine, "Zayton, un évêché au bout du monde" by Jean Richard, "Further thoughts on the layout of the Hospital in Acre" by Jonathan Riley-Smith, "L'Apocalypse et le sens des affaires. Les moines de Saint-Jean de Patmos, leurs activités économiques et leurs relations avec les Latins (xiii et xiv siècles)" by Guillaume Saint-Guillain, "Une autre fonction des capitaines de galées du marché vénitiennes: le contrôle des officiers d'outre-mer" by Doris Stöckly, "*De prima origine Sancti Lazari Hierosolymitani*" by François-Olivier Touati, "À propos du commerce vénitien des 'schienali' (schinalia) (première moitié du xv siècle)" by Angéliki Tzavara, "Gênes, l'Afrique et l'Orient: le Maghreb almohade dans la politique génoise en Méditerranée" by Dominique Valérian, "Saint Homebon (†1197), patron des marchands et des artisans drapiers à la fin du Moyen Âge et à l'époque moderne" by André Vauchez, "Les Ornano: des seigneurs feudataires corso-génois (1498–1610)" by Michel Vergé-Franceschi.

The Experience of Crusading. Volume One: Western Approaches, ed. Marcus Bull and Norman Housley. Cambridge: Cambridge University Press, 2003. Pp. xvi, 307. ISBN 0 521 81168 6.
The Experience of Crusading. Volume Two: Defining the Crusader Kingdom, ed. Peter Edbury and Jonathan Phillips. Cambridge: Cambridge University Press, 2003. Pp. xv, 311. ISBN 0 521 78151 5.

These two volumes were published as a *Festschrift* presented to Jonathan Riley-Smith on his sixty-fifth birthday. They contain the following contributions:

Volume 1: "Jonathan Riley-Smith, the crusades and the military orders: an appreciation" by Norman Housley with Marcus Bull, "Views of Muslims and of Jerusalem in miracle stories, c. 1000–c. 1200: reflections on the study of first crusaders' motivations" by Marcus Bull, "A further note on the conquest of Lisbon in 1147" by Giles Constable, "Costing the crusade: budgeting for crusading activity in the fourteenth century" by Norman Housley, "The crusading motivation of the Italian city republics in the Latin East, 1096–1104" by Christopher Marshall, "Odo of Deuil's De profectione Ludovici VII in Orientem as a source for the Second Crusade" by Jonathan Phillips, "Innocent III and Alexius III: a crusade plan that failed" by James M. Powell, "The Venetian fleet for the Fourth Crusade and the diversion of the crusade to Constantinople" by John H. Pryor, "The conquest of Jerusalem: Joachim of Fiore and the Jews" by Anna Sapir Abulafia, "Crusades, clerics and violence: reflections on a canonical theme" by James A. Brundage, "Humbert of Romans and the crusade" by Penny J. Cole, "Christianity and the morality of warfare during the first century of crusading" by H. E. J. Cowdrey, "Holy war and holy men: Erdmann and the lives of the saints" by John France, "The *bible moralisée* and the crusades" by Christoph T. Maier, "The Hospitallers in twelfth-century Constantinople" by Anthony Luttrell, "Serving king and crusade: the military orders in royal service in Ireland, 1220–1400" by Helen Nicholson, "The First Crusade in post-war fiction" by Susan Edgington, "Nineteenth-century perspectives of the First Crusade" by Elizabeth Siberry.

Volume 2: "Jonathan Riley-Smith and the Latin East: an appreciation" by Jonathan Phillips with Peter Edbury, "The 'muddy road' of Odo Arpin from Bourges to La Charitie-sur-Loire" by Jonathan Shepard, "Alice of Antioch: a case study of female power in the twelfth century" by Thomas Asbridge, "Gaufridus abbas Templi

Domini: an underestimated figure in the early history of the kingdom of Jerusalem" by Rudolf Hiestand, "The career of Philip of Nablus in the kingdom of Jerusalem" by Malcolm Barber, "A second incarnation in Frankish Jerusalem" by Benjamin Z. Kedar, "The Old French translation of William of Tyre as an historical source" by Bernard Hamilton, "The Freiburg Leaf: crusader art and *Loca Sancta* around the year 1200" by Jaroslav Folda, "Reading John of Jaffa" by Peter Edbury, "Churches and settlement in crusader Palestine" by Denys Pringle, "King Fulk of Jerusalem as city lord" by Hans Eberhard Mayer, "The adventure of John Gale, Knight of Tyre" by Jean Richard, "Hülegü Khan and the Christians: the making of a myth" by Peter Jackson, "Orientalism and the early development of crusader studies" by Robert Irwin, "Notes on the economic consequences of the crusades" by Michel Balard, "New Venetian evidence on crusader Acre" by David Jacoby, "The role of the Templars and the Hospitallers in the movement of commodities involving Cyprus, 1291–1312" by Nicholas Coureas, "From Tunis to Piombino: piracy and trade in the Tyrrhenian Sea, 1397–1472" by David Abulafia.

SOCIETY FOR THE
STUDY OF THE CRUSADES
AND THE LATIN EAST

BULLETIN No. 27, 2007

Editorial

It is a pleasure for the SSCLE to announce that its new treasurer, **Prof. James D. Ryan, 100 West 94th Street, Apartment 26M, New York NY 10025, U.S.A., james.d.ryan@ verizon.net** has been extremely successful both in re-establishing contact with many members who had not been asked to pay their dues during the past years and in recruiting new members. The three years between 2002 and 2005 without an effective treasurer were difficult indeed. You can read in Professor Ryan's report his warning that a further increase in subscription rates will be needed within the next two years. But it is essentially due to his hard work that the situation is as good as it is, and we should thank him warmly for all his efforts. If you have any queries concerning your subscriptions and payments, please contact him at the above address.

Our journal entitled *Crusades*, now in volume 6 (2007), allows the Society to publish articles and texts; encourages research in neglected subfields; invites authors to deal with a specific problem within a comparative framework; initiates and reports on joint programmes; and offers reviews of books and articles. Editors: Benjamin Z. Kedar and Jonathan Riley-Smith; associate editor: Jonathan Phillips; reviews editor: Christoph Maier; archaeology editor: Denys R. Pringle.

Colleagues may submit papers for consideration to either of the editors. Guidelines for contributors can be found in the back of this Bulletin.

The journal includes a section of book reviews. In order to facilitate the reviews editor's work, could members please ask their publishers to send copies to: **Dr Christoph T. Maier, Reviews editor, *Crusades*, Sommergasse 20, 4056 Basel, Switzerland**. Please note that *Crusades* reviews books concerned with any aspect(s) of the history of the crusades and the crusade movement, the military orders and the Latin settlements in the Eastern Mediterranean, but not books which fall outside this range.

The 2007 cost of the journal to individual members is £22, $41 or €33; the cost to institutions and non-members is £65, $115 or €97. Cheques should be made payable to SSCLE.

Members may opt to receive the Bulletin alone at the current membership price (single £10, $15 or €15; student £6, $9 or €9; joint £15, $23 or €23). Those members who do not subscribe to the journal will receive the Bulletin from the Bulletin editor.

The Bulletin editor would like to remind you that, in order to avoid delays, he needs to have information for the Bulletin each year at an early date, usually in January or February. My address also changs on 1 October 2007: **Prof. Karl Borchardt, c/o Monumenta Germaniae Historica, Postfach 34 02 23, 80099 München, Germany**, for packages: **Ludwigstraße 16, 80539 München**; email: **karl.borchardt@mgh.de** I want to thank all members who provide me with bibliographical data. In order for the Bulletin to be more useful for you, it would be helpful if those members who edit proceedings or essay volumes could let me know not only about their own papers but also the other papers in such volumes.

Dr Zsolt Hunyadi runs our official website: **http://www.sscle.org**. There you can find news about the SSCLE and its publications as well as links to related sites. It is planned to list members' publications recorded in our Bulletins from 1980 onwards, along with additional bibliography related to the crusades, the Latin East and the military orders.

Rothenburg ob der Tauber, June 2007   Karl Borchardt

Message from the President

Our Society is at present preparing the next SSCLE conference which will be held at Avignon in southern France, from the 28th to the 31st of August, 2008. The general theme will be "The Papacy and the Crusades". In this context we also want to commemorate the Albigensian Crusade. But, as usual, anyone who wants to present a paper on a theme dealing with the crusades, the military orders, or the Franks in the East is encouraged to do so. Our secretary, Sophia Menache, will collect the proposals and organize them. At the end of the conference a short trip in the Comtat Venaissin will be offered. For those who want to stay a little longer, and to visit the Albigensian region, another trip will be organized, to be paid for separately. For details of accommodation in Avignon and about the trips, please contact our general secretary, Sophia Menache (menache@research.haifa.ac.il).

You will have noticed the regular publication of our journal "Crusades", for which our editors receive a lot of proposals. This shows the growing importance of our studies. I would like to thank all those who are working for our Society, among them our general secretary, Sophia Menache, our treasurer, Jim Ryan, who has done wonderful work in bringing order to our accounts, and Karl Borchardt, who is responsible for the Bulletin. All members of the SSCLE Bureau held a meeting in Paris last January, and we were happy to collaborate for the benefit of our Society.

Best wishes to all.

Michel Balard

Contents

List of abbreviations 240

1. Recent publications 240

2. Recently completed theses 257

3. Papers read by members of the Society and others 258

4. Forthcoming publications 264

5. Work in progress 274

6. Theses in progress 278

7. Fieldwork planned or undertaken recently 280

8. News of interest to members:

    a) Conferences and seminars 280

    b) Other news 281

9. Members' queries 282

10. Officers of the Society 282

11. Income and expenditure for the SSCLE 282

12. List of members and their addresses 284

List of abbreviations

L'architecture: Nicolas Faucherre, Benjamin Z. Kedar, Jean Mesqui (ed), L'architecture en Terre sainte au temps de Saint Louis, Bulletin Monumental 164 (2006), 3–120.

CEM-Seminar: The Crusades and the Eastern Mediterranean Seminar, Institute of Historical Research and Emmanuel College, Cambridge or London.

DEM: Diplomatics in the Eastern Mediterranean, 1000–1500: Aspects of Cross-Cultural Communication, Proceedings of the Conference, Univ. of Cyprus, Nicosia, 7–9 April 2006, ed. Alexander D. Beihammer, Maria G. Parani, Christopher D. Schabel, The Medieval Mediterranean Series (Leiden: Brill, forthcoming 2008).

DOMMA: Dictionnaire des ordres militaires au Moyen Âge, ed. Nicole Bériou and Philippe Josserand (Paris: Fayard, 2007).

EI: The Encyclopedia of Islam (Leiden: Brill).

EncycCru: The Crusades: An Encyclopedia, 4 vols, ed. Alan V. Murray (Santa Barbara, CA: ABC-CLIO, 2006).

HES: International colloquium on the History of Egypt and Syria in the Fatimid, Ayyubid and Mamluk Eras, Katholieke Universiteit Leuven.

HME: The Hospitallers, the Mediterranean and Europe, *Festschrift* for Anthony Luttrell, ed. Karl Borchardt, Nikolas Jaspert, Helen Nicholson (Aldershot: Ashgate, 2007).

HW: Hospitaller Women in the Middle Ages, ed. Anthony Luttrell, Helen J. Nicholson (Aldershot: Ashgate, 2006), 280pp.

ILH: In Laudem Hierosolymitani: Studies in Crusades and Medieval Culture in Honour of Benjamin Z. Kedar, ed. Iris Shagrir, Ronnie Ellenblum, Jonathan Riley-Smith (Aldershot: Ashgate, 2007).

IMC: International Medieval Congress, Kalamazoo or Leeds.

Knighthoods: Knighthoods of Christ: Essays on the History of the Crusades and the Knights Templar, presented to Malcolm Barber, ed. Norman Housley (Aldershot: Ashgate, 2007), 280pp.

LW: Logistics of Warfare in the Age of the Crusades, ed. John H. Pryor (Aldershot: Ashgate, 2006), 398pp.

MO3: The Military Orders, vol. 3: History and Heritage, ed. Victor Mallia-Milanes (Aldershot: Ashgate, forthcoming, 2008).

MO4: The Military Orders, vol. 4: On Land and by Sea, ed. Judi Upton-Ward (Aldershot: Ashgate, forthcoming, 2008).

MOR: The Military Orders and the Reformation: Choices, State Building and the Weight of Tradition, Papers of the Utrecht Conference, 30 September–2 October 2004, ed. Johannes A. Mol, Klaus Militzer, Helen J. Nicholson (Hilversum: Verloren, 2006), 319pp.

Runciman-Conference: Terceras Jornadas Internacionales: Medio siglo de estudios sobre las Cruzadas y las Órdenes Militares, 1951–2001, A Tribute to Sir Steven Runciman, Universidad de Zaragoza y Ayuntamiento de Teruel, Teruel (Aragon), 19–25 July 2001, ed. Luis García-Guijarro Ramos (Madrid: Castelló d'Impressió SL).

1. Recent publications

AILES, Marianne J., The Admirable Enemy? Saladin and Saphadin in Ambroise's *Estoire de la guerre sainte*, in: Knighthoods 51–64.

ALVIRA CABRER, Martín, Del *Sepulcro* y los *sarracenos meridionales* a los *herejes occidentales*: Apuntes sobre tres "guerras santas" en las fuentes del sur de Francia (siglos XI–XIII), in: Regards croisés sur la guerre sainte: guerre, religion et idéologie dans l'espace méditerranéen latin (XIe–XIIIe siècle), Actes du Colloque international tenu à la Casa de Velázquez (Madrid) du 11 au 13 avril 2005, ed. Daniel Baloup, Philippe Josserand, coll. Méridiennes (FRA.M.ESPA UMR 5136), sér. Études Médiévales Ibériques (Toulouse: CNRS-Université de Toulouse-Le Mirail, 2006), 187–229.

AMITAI, Reuven, The Logistics of the Mongol-Mamlūk War, with Special Reference to the Battle of Wādī 'l-Khaznadār, 1299 C.E., in: LW 25–42.

ANDREA, Alfred J., Conrad of Krosigk; Devastatio Constantinopolitana; Fourth Crusade; Gunther of Pairis; Martin of Pairis; Nivelon of Chérisy; Relics: Constantinople; Schism of East and West, in: EncycCru 1:272; 2:449–457, 549; 3:804, 889; 4:1023–1024, 1078–1081.

ANTAKI, Patricia, Le château Croisé de Beyrouth: étude préliminaire, in: ARAM 13/14 (2001/02), 323–353.

ARAD, Pnina, Thanks to a Neighbour's Bad Reputation: Reconstructing an Area of Thirteenth-Century Acre, in: Crusades 5 (2006), 193–197.

ASBRIDGE, Thomas S., Knowing the Enemy: Latin Relations with Islam at the Time of the First Crusade, in: Knighthoods 17–26.

EL-AZHARI, Taef, The Turkmen Identity Crisis in the Fifteenth Century Middle East, in: Univ. of Szeged, Chronica 5 (2005), 97–107; 13 articles in EncycCru.

BACHRACH, Bernard S., Crusader Logistics: from Victory at Nicaea to Resupply at Dorylaion, in: LW 43–62.

BALARD, Michel, Les Latins en Orient XIe–XVe siècle, coll. Nouvelle Clio (Paris: PUF, 2006), 455pp.; La Méditerranée médiévale: espaces, itinéraires, comptoirs, coll. Les Médiévistes français (Paris: Picard, 2006), 200pp.; L'Italie du Sud et la Quatrième Croisade, in: Bulletin de la Société Nationale des Antiquaires de France (Paris, 2001 [2006]), 254–266; Les relations de Caffa avec son arrière-pays, in: Entre Monts et Rivages: les contacts entre la Provence orientale et les régions voisines au Moyen Age, ed. Philippe Jansen (Antibes, 2006), 265–273; Les actes notariés génois, in: Univers du texte: genèse, fonction et constellation, ed. Shoichi Sato (Nagoya, 2006), 252–264; Il Mediterraneo medievale, crocevia di culture, in: Storie del mare, Quaderni dei Mercoledì Scienza degli amici dell'Acquario di Genova, ed. Lilia Capocaccia Orsini, Silvana Fiorentini Angelini (Genova, 2006), 13–36; Il notaio e l'amministrazione della giustizia nell'Oltremare genovese, in: *Hinc publica fides*: il notaio e l'amministrazione della giustizia, ed. Vito Piergiovanni (Milano: Guiffrè, 2006), 353–369; Il Banco di San Giorgio e le colonie d'Oltremare, in: La casa di San Giorgio: il potere del credito, Atti del Convegno, 11 e 12 novembre 2006, ed. Giovanni Felloni (Genova: Società ligure di storia patria, 2006), 63–73.

BALLETTO, Laura, Il Mar Nero nei notai genovesi: panoramica generale, stato degli studi, progetti di pubblicazione, in: The Black Sea Region Studies, Historical Faculty Moscow State University (St. Petersburg: Aletheia, 2005), 22–42; Uomini dell'Alessandrino nel Vicino Oriente sulla fine del medioevo, in: Alle origini di Alessandria: dal Gonfalone del Comune nella Lega lombarda all'Aquila Imperiale degli Staufen (Alessandria, 2005), 153–167; Les Génois à Phocéee et à Chio du XIIIe au XIVe siècle, in: Byzance et le monde extérieur: contacts, relations, échanges, ed. Michel Balard, Elisabeth Malamut, Jean-Michel Spieser (Paris, 2005), 45–57; L'impresa del genovese Filippo Doria contro Tripoli di Barberia nel 1355, in: Intemelion: Cultura e territorio, Quaderni di Studio dell'Accademia di cultura intemelia 11 (2005), 79–117; Battista di Felizzano e Domenico di Novara fra Genova e il Vicino Oriente a metà del Quattrocento, in: Sociedad y memoria en la Edad Media,

Estudios en homenaje de Nilda Guglielmi, ed. Ariel Guiance, Pablo Ubierra (Buenos Aires, 2005), 35–53; Greci a Genova dopo la conquista turca di Costantinopoli, in: Geschehenes und Geschriebenes, Studien zu Ehren von Günther S. Henrich und Klaus-Peter Matschke, ed. Sebastian Kolditz, Ralf C. Müller (Leipzig, 2005), 351–365; Commerci e rotte commerciali nel Mediterraneo orientale a metà del Quattrocento: l'importanza dell'isola di Chio, in: Memorie della Accademia Lunigianese di Scienze Giovanni Capellini, LXXV, Memorie in onore e ricordo di A. C. Ambrosi (La Spezia, 2005), 191–205; I Genovesi e la conquista turca di Costantinopoli (1453): Note su Tommaso Spinola e la sua famiglia, in: Acta Historica et Archaeologica Mediaevalia 26, Homentage a la Professora Dra. Carme Batlle i Gallart (Barcelona, 2005), 795–833; Tra Genova e l'isola di Cipro nel basso medioevo, in: Genova: Una "porta" del Mediterraneo, ed. Luciano Gallinari (Cagliari – Genova – Torino, 2005), 31–61; Il mondo del commercio nel Codex Cumanicus: alcune riflessioni, in: Il codice cumanico e il suo mondo, ed. Felicitas Schmieder, Peter Schreiner (Roma, 2005), 163–182; Nuovi dati su un'ambasceria cipriota in Occidente durante il regno di Pietro I di Lusignano, in: Επετηρίδα του Κέντρου Επιστημονικών Ερευνών 31 (2005), 91–108; Pera genovese negli atti del notaio Donato di Chiavari (1389–1390), in: Bulgaria Pontica Medii Aevi 4/5 (Sofia, 2006), 115–128; Fonti notarili inedite su Caffa e sul Mar Nero tra XIV e XV secolo, in: ibid. 149–170; I Genovesi entro il Mar Nero nel tardo medioevo: aspetti economici, in: ibid. 331–345; Brevi note su Caffa genovese nel XIV secolo, in: Nuova Rivista Storica 90/2 (2006), 447–474.

BALOUP, Daniel, with Philippe Josserand, ed., Regards croisés sur la guerre sainte: guerre, religion et idéologie dans l'espace méditerranéen latin (XIe–XIIIe siècle), Actes du Colloque international tenu à la Casa de Velázquez (Madrid) du 11 au 13 avril 2005, Méridiennes: Études Médiévales Ibériques (Toulouse: CNRS Univ. de Toulouse-Le Mirail, 2006).

BARBER, Malcolm, The Two Cities: Medieval Europe 1050–1320, 2nd ed. (London: Routledge, 2004), 540pp.; The Trial of the Templars, 2nd ed. (Cambridge: Cambridge UP, 2006), x+398pp.; translations of The New Knighthood. A History of the Order of the Temple, Cambridge, 1994): Die Templer: Geschichte und Mythos, tr. H. Ehrhardt (Düsseldorf, 2005), 360 pp.; Noví Rytíři, tr. J. Kasl (Prague, 2006), 433pp.; Tapinak Şövalyelerinin Tarihi, tr. B. Ülner (Istanbul, 2006), 576pp.; Northern Catharism, in: Heresy and the Persecuting Society in the Middle Ages: Essays on the Work of R. I. Moore, ed. M. Frassetto (Leiden: Brill, 2006), 115–137.

BEECH, George, A Little Known Armenian Historian of the Crusading Period: Gregory the Priest (1136–1162), in: Truth as Gift: Studies in medieval Cistercian history in honour of John R. Sommerfeldt, ed. Marsha Dutton, Daniel Marcel La Corte, Paul Lockey (Kalamazoo, 2004), 119–143.

BOAS, Adrian, L'architecture civile franque à Césarée, Acre et Jérusalem, in: L'architecture 31–44.

BOMBI, Barbara, Innocenzo III e la relazione sulle condizioni del Medio Oriente coevo, in: Fedi a confronto: Ebrei, Cristiani e Musulmani fra X e XIII secolo (Firenze: Edizioni Polistampa, 2006), 231–242.

BORCHARDT, Karl, Jacobus, der Deutsche Orden und Rothenburg, in: Die oberdeutschen Reichsstädte und ihre Heiligenkulte – Traditionen und Ausprägungen zwischen Stadt, Ritterorden und Reich, ed. Klaus Herbers, Jakobus-Studien 16 (Tübingen: Narr, 2005), 25–67; Die Kreuzzüge: Ein Überblick, in: Burgen und Basare der Kreuzfahrerzeit, ed. Hans Altmann, Bernhard Siepen (Petersberg: Imhof, 2005), 8–23; Die Johanniter in Deutschland und die Reformation, in: MOR 101–117; Zentrale und Peripherie: Zum Quellenwert der

Register des Johannitermeisters auf Rhodos im 15. Jahrhundert, in: Vielfalt und Aktualität des Mittelalters, Festschrift für Wolfgang Petke zum 65. Geburtstag, ed. Sabine Arend et al., Veröffentlichungen des Instituts für historische Landesforschung der Universität Göttingen 48 (Bielefeld, 2006), 191–200; Bohemia and Moravia; Hussites, crusades against the; John of Luxembourg (1296–1346); Mergentheim; Ottokar II of Bohemia (d. 1278), in: EncycCru 1:170–175, 2:618–621, 692–694, 3:821–823, 902–903; Die Johanniter: Von der Krankenpflege auf das Schlachtfeld, in: Pax Geschichte 2007, no. 3, 40–47.

BRUNDAGE, James A., The Advocate's Dilemma: What Can You Tell the Client? A Problem in Legal Ethics, in: Medieval Church Law and the Origins of the Western Legal Tradition: A Tribute to Kenneth Pennington, ed. Wolfgang P. Müller, Mary E. Sommar (Washington/DC: Catholic Univ. of America Press, 2006), 201–210; Legal Learning and the Professionalization of Law, in: Law and Learning in the Middle Ages, ed. Helle Vogt, Mia Münster-Swendsen (Copenhagen: DJØF, 2006), 5–27; Latin Christianity, the Crusades, and the Islamic Response, in: Religious Foundations of Western Civilization: Judaism, Christianity, and Islam, ed. Jacob Neusner (Nashville: Abingdon Press, 2006), 627–804.

BURGTORF, Jochen, The Military Orders in the Crusader Principality of Antioch, in: Antioch (969–1268), ed. Michael Metcalf, Krijnie Ciggaar, Victoria van Aalst, Orientalia Lovaniensia Analecta (Leuven: Peeters Press, 2006), 217–246.

BURNETT, Charles, Stephen, the Disciple of Philosophy, and the Exchange of Medical Learning in Antioch, in: Crusades 5 (2006), 113–129.

BURNS, Robert I., "Has this Item Gone in?" The Crusade Against Murçia: Provisioning the Armies of James the Conqueror, 1264–1267, in: Jews, Muslims and Christians Around the Crown of Aragon, Essays in Honour of Professor Elena Lourie (Leiden: Brill, 2004), 35–74; Dogs of War in 13th Century Valencian Crusader Garrisons, in: Journal of Medieval Military History 4 (2006), 164–174; Gegna: Coastal Mooring in Crusader Valencia, in: Technology and Culture 24 (2006), 776–786; Women in Crusader Valencia: A Five-Year Core Sample, 1265–1270, in: Medieval Encounters 12 (2006), 37–47.

CARLSSON, Christer, The Religious Orders of Knighthood in Medieval Scandinavia: Historical and Archaeological Approaches, in: Crusades 5 (2006), 131–142.

CARRAZ, Damien, Ordres militaires, croisades et sentiments politiques chez les troubadours: le cas de la Provence au XIIIe siècle, in: As Ordens Militares e as Ordens de Cavalaria na Construção do Mundo Occidental, Actas do IV Encontro sobre Ordens Militares, Palmela, 30 de Janeiro – 2 de Fevereiro 2002, ed. Isabel Cristina Ferreira Fernandes (Lisbonne: Câmara Municipal de Palmela – Edições Colibri, 2005), 993–1011; L'ordre du Temple dans la basse vallée du Rhône (1124–1312): Ordres militaires, croisades et sociétés méridionales, Collection d'histoire et d'archéologie médiévales 17 (Lyon: Presses Univ. de Lyon, 2005), 662pp.; Le cartulaire du Temple de Saint-Gilles, outil de gestion et instrument de pouvoir, in: Les cartulaires méridionales, Actes du colloque de Béziers, 20–21 septembre 2002, ed. Daniel Le Blevec, Études et rencontres 19 (Paris: Éditions de l'École des chartes, 2006), 145–162; Présences et dévotions autour des commanderies du Bas-Rhône (XIIe–XIIIe siècle), in: Les ordres religieux militaires dans le Midi (XIIe–XIVe siècle), Cahiers de Fanjeaux 41 (2006), 71–99; Mémoire lignangère et archives monastiques: les Bourbouton et la commanderie de Richerenches, in: Propagande et communication XIIe–XIIIe siècles, ed. Martin Aurell, coll. Civilisation médiévale (Poitiers: CESCM, 2007), 461–498.

CASSIDY-WELCH, Megan, Monastic Spaces and their Meanings: Thirteenth-Century English Cistercian Monasteries (Turnhout: Brepols, 2001), 290pp.; Incarceration and Liberation: Prisons in the Cistercian Monastery, in: Viator 32 (2001), 1–25; Testimonies from a

Fourteenth-Century Prison: Rumour, Evidence and Truth in the Midi, in: French History 16/1 (2002), 3–27; Pilgrimage and Embodiment: Captives and the Cult of Saints in Late-Medieval Bavaria, in: Parergon: Journal of the Australian and New Zealand Association for Medieval and Early Modern Studies 20/2 (2003), 47–70; Prisoners of War after Agincourt: Gender, Mourning and Cultures of Captivity in Fifteenth-Century France, in: Lilith: A Feminist History Journal 12 (2003), 9–22.

CERRINI, Simonetta, Festività templari, in: Templari a Piacenza: le tracce di un mito, ed. A. Serena (Piacenza, 1995), 80–83; Nuovi percorsi templari tra i manoscritti latini e francesi della Regola, in: Regione Piemonte, Atti del Convegno I Templari in Piemonte, dalla storia al mito, Torino 20 ottobre 1994, ed. Renato Bordone (Torino, s.d. [1995]), 35–56; La tradition manuscrite de la règle du Temple: études pour une nouvelle édition des versions latine et française, in: Autour de la première croisade: Actes du Colloque de la Society for the Study of the Crusades and the Latin East (Clermont-Ferrand, 22–25 juin 1995), ed. Michel Balard (Paris, 1996), 203–219; Le Sorores Templi, in: Dizionario degli istituti di perfezione 9 (1997), 898–903; A New Edition of the Latin and French Rule of the Temple, in: The Military Orders 2: Welfare and Warfare, ed. Helen Nicholson (Aldershot: Ashgate, 1998), 207–215; Onorio II, antipapa; Urbano II, papa; Celestino II, antipapa; Onorio II, papa; Urbano IV, papa; Martino IV, papa, in: Enciclopedia dei papi (Roma: Istituto dell'Enciclopedia Italiana Treccani, 2000); ed., I Templari, la guerra e la santità (Rimini, 2000); I templari: una vita da fratres, ma una regola anti-ascetica; una vita da cavalieri, ma una regola anti-eroica, in: ibid. 19–48; L'ordine del Tempio: aggiornamento bibliografico, in: ibid. 153–163; Le fondateur de l'Ordre du Temple à ses frères: Hugues de Payns et le Sermo Christi militibus, in: *Dei Gesta per Francos*: Études sur les croisades dédiées à Jean Richard, ed. Michel Balard, Benjamin Z. Kedar, Jonathan Riley-Smith (Aldershot: Ashgate, 2001), 99–110; La Révolution des Templiers: Une histoire perdue du XIIe siècle (Paris: Perrin, 2007).

CHEVALIER, Marie-Anna, La Vision des Ordres Religieux-Militaires par les Chrétiens Orientaux (Arméniens et Syriaques) au Moyen Âge (du début du XIIe siècle au début du XIVe siècle), in: Crusades 5 (2006), 55–84.

CHRISTIE, Niall G. F., ed. with Maya Yazigi, Noble Ideals and Bloody Realities: Warfare in the Middle Ages, History of Warfare 37 (Leiden: Brill, 2006), xx+269pp.; Religious Campaign or War of Conquest? Muslim Views of the Motives of the First Crusade, in: ibid. 57–72; Crusades, in: Medieval Islamic Civilization: An Encyclopedia, ed. Josef Meri, vol. 1 (New York: Routledge, 2006), 184–185, more accurate version, lacking erratum inserted during editing process, available at: <http://www.routledge-ny.com/middleages/islamic/crusades.html>; Abbasids; Arabic Sources; al-Hakim, caliph; al-Isfahani, ʿImad al-Din; al-Sulami, ʿAli ibn Tahir, Caliphate; Homs; Ibn al-Qalanisi; Ibn Shaddad; Ibn Wasil; Kamal al-Din; Nur al-Din; Shiʿites; Sibt ibn al-Jawzi; Sunni Islam; Zangi, in: EncycCru.

CLAVERIE, Pierre-Vincent, L'ordre du Temple en Terre sainte at à Chypre au XIIIe siècle, 3 vols., Sources et Études de l'histoire de Chypre 53 (Nicosie: Cyprus Research Centre, 2005); with Emmanuel and Jean-Pierre Grélois, *Apud Ciprum Nicossiam*: notes sur les relations cyprio-auvergnates au XIIIe siècle, in: Επετηρίδα του Κέντρου Επιστημονικών Ερευνών 31 (2005), 39–71; Un *illustris amicus Venetorum* du début du XIIIᵉ siècle: L'évêque Nivelon de Quierzy et son temps, in: Quarta Crociata: Venezia – Bisanzio – Impero Latino, ed. Gherardo Ortalli, Giorgio Ravegnani, Peter Schreiner, vol. 1 (Venezia: Istituto Veneto di Scienze, Lettere ed Arti, 2006), 485–523.

COBB, Paul M., Usama ibn Munqidh: Warrior-Poet of the Age of the Crusades (Oxford: Oneworld, 2006), 136pp.

COUREAS, Nicholas S., Controlled Contacts: The Papacy, the Latin Church of Cyprus and Mamluk Egypt, in: Egypt and Syria in the Fatimid, Ayyubid and Mamluk Eras 4, Proceedings of the 9th and 10th HES, ed. Urbain Vermeulen (Leuven: Peeters, 2005); The Development of Nicosia as the Judicial Centre of Lusignan Cyprus, in: CRC Annual Review 31 (Nicosia, 2005); Apple of Concord: The Great Powers and Cyprus from 400 AD onwards, in: Kypriakai Spoudai 68 (2003/04 [Nicosia, 2005]); Sinai; Cyprus; Catherine Cornaro; Nicosia; Limassol; Paphos; Kerynia, in: EncycCru; Punishments and Imprecations in the Cypriot Monastic Rules and how they compare with those in other Orthodox Monastic Rules [Greek], in: Epeteris tes Kypriakes Hetaireias Historikon Spoudon (Nicosia, 2006); Medicine in Frankish and Venetian Cyprus [Greek], in: A History of Medicine in Cyprus (Nicosia: Laiki Bank Foundation, 2006).

CRAWFORD, Paul F., Alexandria, capture of; Foulques de Villaret; Poulains; Guillaume de Machaut; St. Thomas, Knights of, in: EncycCru 44–45, 492–493, 548–549, 984, 1181–1182.

CURRY, Anne, Malcolm Barber: an Appreciation, in: Knighthoods xi–xiv.

DEMURGER, Alain, Belchite, le Temple et Montjoie: la couronne d'Aragon et le Temple au XIIe siècle, in: Knighthoods 123–136.

DICKSON, Gary, Boniface VIII; Children's Crusade; Crusade of 1309; Passagium generale; Passagium particulare; Popular Crusades; Shepherds Crusade, First (1251); Shepherds Crusade, Second (1320), in: EncycCru 1:180–181, 242–244, 311–313, 3:934, 934–935, 975–979, 4:1093–1094, 1094–1095.

DIVALL, Richard, Pergolesi – Stabat Mater, MS. Wigancourt Museum, Malta (Melbourne, 2005), 80pp.

DONDI, Cristina, Custodi del canto, in: Jerusalem, special issue of the magazine Amadeus, ed. Giacomo Baroffo (Novara: De Agostini Editore, December 2005), 29–31.

DOTSON, John E., Ship Types and Fleet Composition at Genoa and Venice in the Early Thirteenth Century, in: LW 63–76.

DOUROU-ELIOPOULOU, Maria, The Frankish Principality of Achaea (1204–1432): History, Organization, Society (Thessaloniki: Vanias editions, 2005), 216pp.; The Aragonese and the Catalans in the Eastern Mediterranean in the Thirteenth and Fourteenth Century, in: Κλητόριον in the memory of Nikos Oikonomides (Athens – Thessaloniki, 2005), 73–80; The Albanians in Romania according to Latin Sources of the Thirteenth and Fourteenth Century, in: Interbalcanica: Rapports des Congrès (Athènes, 2006), 127–133; Latin Presence in Romania and its Process of Hellenisation, in: ibid. 221–227; The Angevins and the Lusignans in the Eastern Mediterranean in the Second Half of the Thirteenth Century, in: Epistimoniki Epetirida tis Philosophikis Scholis tou Panepistimiou Athinon 37 (2005/06), 39–45.

ECHEVARRÍA ARSUAGA, Ana, Caballeros en la Frontera: La guardia morisca de los Reyes de Castilla (1410–1467) (Madrid: Uned, 2006); The Queen and the Master: Catalina of Lancaster and the Military Orders, in: Partners in Politics: Queens and Kings in Late Medieval and Early Modern Spain, ed. Theresa Earenfight (London – New York: Ashgate, 2005), 91–108.

EDBURY, Peter W., The Suppression of the Templars in Cyprus, in: St John Historical Society Proceedings (2003 [November 2006]), 24–38; The Old French William of Tyre and the Origins of the Templars, in: Knighthoods 151–164.

EDGINGTON, Susan B., entries for EncyccCru; Antioch. Medieval City of Culture, in: East and West in the Medieval Eastern Mediterranean, ed. Krijnie Ciggaar, Michael Metcalf, vol. 1, Orientalia Lovaniensia Analecta 147 (2006), 247–259; A Female Physician on the Fourth

Crusade? Laurette de Saint-Valéry, in: Knighthoods 77–85; ed. and transl., Albert of Aachen, Historia Ierosolymitana, Oxford Medieval Texts (Oxford, 2007).

EHLERS, Axel, Albrecht von Brandenburg-Ansbach; Anno von Sangershausen; Christburg, treaty; Danzig; Dietrich von Altenburg; Ehrentisch; Heinrich von Plauen; Konrad von Feuchtwangen; Krakow, treaty; Kuchmeister, Michael; Luder von Braunschweig; Ludwig von Erlichshausen; Paul von Rusdorf; Reyse; Siegfried von Feuchtwangen; Ulrich von Jungingen; Werner von Orseln; Woplauken, battle, in: EncycCru.

EKDAHL, Sven, Christianisierung–Siedlung–Litauerreise: Die Christianisierung Litauens als Dilemma des Deutschen Ordens, in: Die Christianisierung Litauens im mitteleuropäischen Kontext: Sammlung von Vorträgen, ed. Vydas Dolinskas, transl. Klaus Berthel, Irma Daugvilaitė, Irena Tumavičiutė (Vilnius: Lietuvos dailės muziejus, 2005), 189–205, in Lithuanian 173–188; three articles for EncycCru.

ELLENBLUM, Ronnie, Crusader Castles and Modern Histories (Cambridge: CUP, 2006).

FAVREAU-LILIE, Marie-Luise, Die Pilgerfahrt nach Santiago de Compostela im Spiegel hansestädtischer Testamente, in: Der Kult des Apostels Jakobus des Älteren in den Hansestädten, Jakobus-Studien 15 (Tübingen: Narr, 2005), 27–48; Die italienischen Handelsniederlassungen in den Kreuzfahrerstaaten (12.–13. Jh.); Landwirtschaft im Orient; Handel in den Kreuzfahrerstaaten, in: Saladin und die Kreuzfahrer: Katalog- und Essayband zur Ausstellung Halle, Landesmuseum für Vorgeschichte, Oldenburg, Landesmuseum für Natur und Mensch, Mannheim, Reiss-Engelhorn-Museen (Mainz: Zabern, 2005), 73–81, 445, 450; Geroldo di Losanna (Valenza), patriarca di Gerusalemme; Gerusalemme, patriarcato Latino, in: Enciclopedia Fridericiana, ed. G. Arnaldi, Arnold Esch, Cosimo Damiano Fonseca, A. Varvaro, P. Zecchino, vol. 1 (Roma: Enciclopedia Italiana Treccani, 2005), 703–707; Caffaro; Embriachi; Genoa and the Crusades; Tyre, in: EncycCru

FOLDA, Jaroslav, Crusader Art in the Holy Land, from the Third Crusade to the Fall of Acre, 1187–1291 (Cambridge UP, 2005) [as in the previous Bulletin], two indices now under http://www.cambridge.org/us/catalogue/catalogue.asp?isbn=0521835836; What is Crusader Art?, Scriptoria and Workshops, Scribes and Painters in Crusader Syria/Palestine in the 13th Century, Introduction, catalogue entries on five manuscripts, London, BL, Egerton MS 1139, Paris, BNF, MS fr. 2628, Dijon, Bibl. Mun., MS 562, Brussels, Bibl. Roy., MS 10175, and Perugia, Bibl. Capit., MS 6, in: Saladin und die Kreuzfahrer, ed. Alfred Wieczorek et al (Mannheim – Mainz, 2005), 176–189, 204–215, 393–394, 404–407; East Meets West: The Art and Architecture of the Crusader States, in: A Companion to Medieval Art: Romanesque and Gothic in Northern Europe, ed. Conrad Rudolph (Oxford: Blackwell, 2006), 488–509; Mounted Warrior Saints in Crusader Icons: Images of the Knighthoods of Christ, in: Knighthoods 87–108.

FOREY, Alan, Desertions and Transfers from Military Orders (Twelfth to Early Fourteenth Centuries), in: Traditio 60 (2005), 143–250; Women and the Military Orders in the Twelfth and Thirteenth Centuries, in: HW 43–70; The Career of a Templar: Peter of St Just, in: Knighthoods 183–194.

FRANCE, John, Two Types of Vision on the First Crusade: Stephen of Valence and Peter Bartholomew, in: Crusades 5 (2006), 1–20; Logistics of the Second Crusade, in: LW 77–94; Byzantium in Western Chronicles before the First Crusade, in: Knighthoods 3–16.

FRIEDMAN, Yvonne, Miracle, Meaning and Narrative in the Latin East, in: Studies in Church History 41 (2005), 123–134; Community Responsibility toward its Members: The Case of Ransom of Captives, in: Holy People, Jewish and Christian Perspectives, ed. Joshua Schwartz, Marcel Poorthuis (Leiden: Brill, 2006), 199–216.

GABRIELE, Matthew, Against the Enemies of Christ: The Role of Count Emicho in the Anti-Jewish Violence of the First Crusade, in: Christian Attitudes toward the Jews in the Middle Ages: A Casebook, ed. Michael Frassetto (New York, 2006), 84–111.

GARCÍA-GUIJARRO RAMOS, Luis, The Aragonese Hospitaller Monastery of Sigena: its Early Stages, 1188–c.1210, in: HW 113–152; The Growth of the Order of the Temple in the Northern Area of the Kingdom of Valencia at the Close of the Thirteenth Century: A Puzzling Development?, in: Knighthoods 165–182.

GERTWAGEN, Ruthy, Harbours and Facilites along the Eastern Mediterranean Sea Lanes to *Outremer*, in: LW 95–118.

GILLINGHAM, John, Stupor mundi: 1204 et un obituaire de Richard Cœur de Lion depuis longtemps tombé dans l'oubli, in: Martin Aurell, Noël-Yves Tonnerre (eds.), Plantagenêts et Capétiens: Confrontations et héritages, Actes du colloque de Poitiers et Fontevraud, May 2004 (Turnhout: Brepols, 2006), 397–411; König Richard I. Löwenherz als Gefangener in Deutschland, in: Beiträge zur Geschichte des Trifels und des Mittelalters 3 (2006), 125–141; Writing the Biography of Roger of Howden, King's Clerk and Chronicler, in: David Bates (ed.), Medieval History and Biography: Essays in Honour of Frank Barlow (Woodbridge: Boydell & Brewer, 2006), 207–220; with Ruth Harvey, Le troubadour Giraut de Borneil et la troisième croisade, in: Rivista di studi testuali 5 (2003 [2006]), 51–72.

GILMOUR-BRYSON, Anne, Italian Templar Trials: Truth or Falsehood?, in: Knighthoods 209–228.

GLASHEEN, Charles R., Provisioning Peter the Hermit: from Cologne to Constantinople, 1096, in: LW 119–130.

GRABINER, Esther, Les vestiges de l'église franque de Séphorie, in: L'architecture 113–120.

GRABOIS, Aryeh, Les pèlerinages du XIe siècle en Terre sainte dans l'historiographie occidentale de l'époque, in: Revue d'histoire ecclésiastique 101 (2006), 531–546; Burchard of Mount Zion; Fidenzio of Padua; Galilee; Haifa; Nablus; Tancred; Tiberias, Lordship, in: EncycCru 1:184, 2:426–427, 495–497, 553–554, 3:863–864, 4:1143–1145, 1183–1184.

HALDON, John, Roads and Communications in the Byzantine Empire: Wagons, Horses, and Supplies, in: LW 131–158.

HAMILTON, Bernard, The Growth of the Latin Church of Antioch and the Recruitment of its Clergy, in: Krijnie Ciggaar, Michael Metcalf (eds.), East and West in the Medieval Eastern Mediterranean, I, Orientalia Lovaniensia Analecta 147 (2006), 171–183.

HAVERKAMP, Eva, Hebräische Berichte über die Judenverfolgungen während des Ersten Kreuzzugs, Hebräische Texte aus dem mittelalterlichen Deutschland, Monumenta Germaniae Historica und Israel Academy of Sciences and Humanities 1 (Hannover, 2005), 1+626pp.

HOCH, Martin, Hattin, battle of (1187), in: EncycCru 2:559–561.

HOLMES, Catherine, Basil II and the Governance of Empire, 976–1025 (Oxford, 2005), 640pp.; Constantinople in the Reign of Basil II, in: Elizabeth Jeffreys (ed.), Byzantine Style, Religion and Civilization: In Honour of Sir Steven Runciman (Cambridge: CUP, 2006), 326–339.

HOSTEN, Jan, De Tempeliers, de Temelorde tijdens de kruistochten en in de Lage Landen (Amsterdam: Pearson Education Benelux, 2006).

HOUSLEY, Norman, ed., Knighthoods; 'The Common Corps of Christendom': Thomas More and the Crusading Cause, in: ibid. 109–121.

HUNT, Lucy-Anne, Art in the Wadi Natrun: An Assessment of the Earliest Wallpaintings of the Church of Abu Makar, Dayr Abu Makar, in: Proceedings of the Wadi Natrun Symposium (February 2002), Coptica 3 (2004), 69–103; For the Salvation of a Woman's Soul: An Icon of St Michael Described within a Medieval Coptic Context, in: Icon and Word: The Power of Images in Byzantium, Studies presented to Robin Cormack, ed. Anthony Eastmond, Liz James (Aldershot – Burlington: Ashgate, 2004), 205–232; Orientalische Christen: Kunst und Kultur zur Zeit der Kreuzfahrer, in: Saladin und die Kreuzfahrer, ed. Alfred Wieczorek, Mamoun Fansa, Harald Meller (Mainz: Zabern, 2005), 191–203; Melisende Psalter; Art of Outremer and Cyprus, in: ÉncycCru; Byzantium – Venice – Manchester: An Early Thirteenth-Century Carved Marble Basin and British Byzantinism at the Turn of the Twentieth Century, in: Elizabeth Jeffreys (ed.), Byzantine Style, Religion and Civilisation, In Honour of Sir Steven Runciman (Cambridge: CUP, 2006), 91–134.

Irwin, Robert, Ibn Zunbul and the Romance of History, in: Julia Bray (ed.), Writing and Representation in Medieval Islam (London: Routledge, 2006), 3–15; Foreword to reissue of Sir Hamilton Gibb, The Life of Saladin (London: al-Saqi, 2006), vii–xviii.

Jacoby, David, Production et commerce de l'alun oriental en Méditerranée, XIe–XVe siècles, in: Philippe Borgard, Jean-Pierre Brun, Maurice Picon (eds.), L'alun de Méditerranée, Collection du Centre Jean Bérard 23 (Naples – Aix-en-Provence, 2005), 219–267; The Venetian Government and Administration in Latin Constantinople, 1204–1261: a State within a State, in: Gherardo Ortalli, Giorgio Ravegnani, Peter Schreiner (eds.), Quarta Crociata: Venezia – Bisanzio – Impero latino (Venezia: Istituto Veneto di Scienze Lettere e Filosophia (Venezia, 2006), 19–79; Christian Pilgrimage to Sinai until the Late Fifteenth Century, in: Holy Space, Hallowed Ground: Icons from Sinai, ed. Robert S. Nelson, Kristen M. Collins, exhibition catalogue (Los Angeles: Getty Publications, 2006), 79–93; Late Byzantium between the Mediterranean and Asia: Trade and Material Culture, in: Sarah T. Brooks (ed.), Byzantium: Faith and Power (1261–1557): Perspectives on Late Byzantine Art and Culture. The Metropolitan Museum of Art Symposia (New York: The Metropolitan Museum of Art – New Haven and London: Yale UP, 2006), 20–41; Marco Polo, His Close Relatives, and His Travel Account: Some New Insights, in: Mediterranean Historical Review 21 (2006), 193–218; The Pisan Commercial Manual of 1278 in the Mediterranean Context, in: Franco Cardini, Maria I. Ceccarelli Lemut (eds.), Quel mar che la terra inghirlanda: Studi mediterranei in ricordo di Marco Tangheroni (Pisa, 2007).

Kasdagli, Anna-Maria, Hospitaller Silver Finds in Rhodes, in: Nomismatika Khronika 11 (Athens 1992), 53–60; Mediaeval Rhodes: Hoards and Rarities, in: MNEME Martin J. Price, Βιβλιοθήκη Ελληνικής Νομισματικής Εταιρίας 5 (Athens, 1996), 319–334; Τρεις ταφόπλακες της Ιπποτοκρατίας στη Ρόδο [Three Hospitaller Inscriptions from Rhodes], in: Archaiologikon Deltion 44/46 (1989–91) [Athens: Meletai, 1996], 191–196 [with English summary]; The Defences of Rhodes and the Tower of St. John, in: Fort 24 (1996), 15–35; The Restoration of the Knights' Hospice of St. Catherine in the Medieval City of Rhodes, in: Proceedings of the 4th International Symposium of the Conservation of Monuments in the Mediterranean, Rhodes 6–11 May 1997 (1997), 483–508; Κατάλογος των θυρεών της Ρόδου [A Rhodian Armorial], Archaiologikon Deltion 48/49 (1994/95) [Athens: Meletai, 1998], 211–246 [with English summary]; The Rhodian Coins at the Museum of the Order of Saint John, Clerkenwell, Monographs of the Hellenic Numismatic Society 3 (Athens, 2002); Νέα στοιχεία για τους τάφους των μεγάλων μαγίστρων του Τάγματος των Ιωαννιτών Ιπποτών στη Ρόδο [New Elements on the Tombs of the Grand Masters of the Order of St. John on Rhodes], in: Athens Annals of Archaeology 35/38 (2002/05), 249–258 [with English summary]; Ο 'θησαυρός' της Παναγίας του Μπούργκου στη Ρόδο [The Hoard of Our Lady of the Borgo in Rhodes (1522)], ΟΒΟΛΟΣ 5 (Athens, 2006), 325–338 [with English summary].

KEDAR, Benjamin Z., The Fourth Crusade's Second Front, in: Urbs Capta: The Fourth Crusade and its Consequences, ed. Angeliki Laiou, Réalités Byzantines 10 (Paris, 2005), 89–110; ed. with Nicolas Faucherre and Jean Mesqui, L'architecture; Les murailles d'Acre franque, in: ibid. 45–52; L'enceinte de la ville franque de Jaffa, in: ibid. 105–107; Some Reflections on Maps, Crusading and Logistics, in: LW 159–183.

KENAAN-KEDAR, Nurith, Les chapiteaux des portes de l'enceinte de Césarée: de la tradition romane à l'art gothique, in: L'architecture 95–98.

KOLIA-DERMITZAKI, Athina, The Ending of the Letters as Means of Detecting Byzantine Perceptions (10th–12th Century), in: Kletorion in Memory of Nikos Oikonomides, ed. Fl. Evangelatou-Notara, Triantafyllitsa Maniati-Kokkini (Athens – Thessaloniki, 2005), 177–220.

KOSTICK, Conor, Women and the First Crusade, in: Studies on Medieval and Early Modern Women, ed. C. Meck, C. Lawless, vol. 3 (Dublin: Four Courts Press, 2005), 57–68; Ireland and the First Crusade, in: History of Ireland, vol. 11 no. 1 (Spring 2003).

LAPINA, Elizabeth, The Paintings of Berzé-la-Ville in the Context of the First Crusade and the *Reconquista*, in: Journal of Medieval History 31 (2005), 309–326.

LEV, Yaacov, Infantry in Muslim Armies during the Crusades, in: LW 185–208.

LICENCE, Tom, The Military Orders as Monastic Orders, in: Crusades 5 (2006), 39–53.

LIGATO, Giuseppe, Cartigli di reliquie di Terra Santa e di altra provenienza presso il convento francescano di S. Maria in Aracoeli a Roma: risultati delle prime ricognizioni, in: Frate Francesco: Rivista di culture francescana 70 (2004), 365–410; Il mosaico pavimentale dell'abbazia di San Colombano e le crociate: il ruolo dei mostri, in: Genova e Bobbio tra storia e cultura, Convegno di studi in occasione di Genova e Lille capitali europee della cultura, Genova, Palazzo Ducale, 3 settembre – Bobbio, Palazzo Vescovile, 4 settembre 2004, ed. Gabriella Airaldi (Genova, 2004), 97–110; La croce in catene: Prigionieri e ostaggi cristiani nelle guerre di Saladino (1169–1193) (Spoleto, 2005); Le profezie della IV crociata, in: La IV crociata: l'osservatorio franco-latino, Atti del convegno dell'Istituto di studi ecumenici, Venezia, 4 novembre 2004, Studi ecumenici 23 (2005), 189–210; Sibilla regina crociata: guerra, amore e diplomazia per il trono di Gerusalemme (Milano, 2005); Bonifacio VIII, la Terra Santa e la crociata, in: Bonifacio VIII: ideologia e azione politica, Atti del convegno Città del Vaticano – Roma, 26–28 april 2004 (Roma, 2006), 241–291; Islam e Cristianità: culture cavalleresche a confronto, in: Fedi a confronto: ebrei, cristiani e musulmani nel Mediterraneo orientale (secoli XI–XIII), Atti del convegno Montaione, 22–24 settembre 2004, ed. Sergio Gensini (Montaione – Firenze, 2006), 35–77.

LOBRICHON, Guy, La Bible au Moyen Âge (Paris: Picard, 2003), 247pp.; Héloïse, l'amour et le savoir, Bibliothèque des Histoires (Paris: Gallimard, 2005), 370pp.; Eloisa, Abelardo, l'amore, il sapere, tr. Alessia Piovanello, Saggi: Storia e scienze sociali (Roma: Donzelli Editore, 2005); with Monique Goullet and Éric Palazzo, Le Pontifical de la Curie romaine au XIIIe siècle, texte latin, trad. et intr. (Paris: Cerf, 2004); with Marie-Hélène Depardou, Monique Goullet et Christiane Veyrard-Cosme, Les Gestes des évêques d'Auxerre, vol. 2, dir. Michel Sot, Classiques de L'Histoire de France au Moyen Âge (Paris: Les Belles Lettres, 2006), 372pp.; with Georges Duby, Histoire de Venise par la peinture (Paris: Citadelles et Mazenod, 2006) [édition revue, corrigée, augmentée d'une première publication en 1991]; Le bibbie ad immagini, secoli XII–XV, in: Forme e modelli della tradizione manoscritta della Bibbia, ed. Paolo Cherubini, pref. Carlo Maria Card. Martini, intr. Alessandro Pratesi (Città del Vaticano: Scuola Vaticana di Paleografia, Diplomatica e Archivistica, 2005), 423–457; Les maîtres francs et l'histoire de la Femme (Apocalypse 12): tentations et résistances mariologiques (VIIIe–XIIe siècles), in: Maria, l'Apocalisse e il Medioevo, Atti del III Convegno Mariologico della Fondazione Ezio Franceschini con la collaborazione della Biblioteca Palatina di Parma, Parma, 11–12 maggio 2002 (Firenze: Edizioni del Galluzzo per la Fondazione Ezio Franceschini, 2006), 43–57; Duby, Georges, in: Dictionnaire des sciences humaines, dir. Sylvie Mesure, Patrick Savidan (Paris: PUF, 2006), 315–316.

Loud, Graham A., Amalfi; Arnold of Lübeck; Conrad III; Frederick Barbaorssa; Gregory VII; Otto of Freising; The Pilgrimage of Henry the Lion; Roger I of Sicily; Sicily and the Crusades; Five letters concerning the Second Crusade; The Lost Autobiographical Chapter of William of Tyre's Chronicle, in: EncycCru 1:58, 96, 270–271, 2:472–475, 544–546, 3:901–902, 963–964, 4:1044–1045, 1104–1107, 1298–1301, 1305–1307.

Lower, Michael, The Barons' Crusade: A Call to Arms and its Consequences (Philadelphia: Univ. of Pennsylvania, 2005), 256pp.; Tunis in 1270: A Case Study of Interfaith Relations in the Late Thirteenth Century, in: International History Review 28 (2006), 504–514.

Luchitskaya, Svetlana, The Crusader's Wife: Perspectives of the History of Everyday Life, in: Wirtschaft – Gesellschaft – Mentalitäten im Mittelalter: Festschrift zum 75. Geburtstag von Rolf Sprandel, ed. Hans-Peter Baum, Rainer Leng, Joachim Schneider, Beiträge zur Wirtschafts- und Sozialgeschichte 107 (Stuttgart: Steiner, 2006), 715–727; L'espace sacre en Terre sainte au cours des croisades: les controversies islamo-chrétiennes relatives aux images, in: Espaces d'échange en Méditerranée: Antiquité et Moyen Âge, ed. François Clément, John V. Tolan, Jérôme Wilgaux (Rennes, 2006), 219–243.

Luttrell, Anthony, Epilog: Die späteren Kreuzzüge, in: Saladin und die Kreuzfahrer, ed. Alfred Wieczorek, Mamoun Fansa, Harald Meller (Mainz, 2005), 127–137; Jaun Fernández de Heredia and the Compilation of the Aragonese Chronicle of the Morea, at www.xoan.net/morea; Conclusioni, in: Gli Archivi per la Storia del Sovrano Militare Ordine di Malta, ed. C. Fonseca, C. D'Angela (Taranto, 2005), 529–534; Les femmes Hospitalières en France méridionale, in: Les Ordres Religieux Militaires dans le Midi (XIIe–XIVe siècle), Cahiers de Fanjeaux 41 (Toulouse, 2006), 101–113; ed. with Helen J. Nicholson, HW; Introduction: a Survey of Hospitaller Women in the Middle Ages, in: ibid. 1–42.

Madden, Thomas F., The New Concise History of the Crusades (Lanham: Rowman and Littlefield, 2005), xiv+261pp.; Food and the Fourth Crusade: A New Approach to the 'Diversion Question', in: LW 209–228; Boniface of Montferrat; Dandolo, Enrico; Fourth Crusade; Michiel, Domenico; Venetian Crusade of 1122; Venice and the Crusades; Venice, treaty of; Zara, in: EncycCru.

Marvin, Laurence W., The Massacre at Béziers July 22, 1209: A Revisionist Look, in: Heresy and the Persecuting Society in the Middle Ages, Essays on the Work of R. I. Moore, ed. Michael Frassetto (Leiden – Boston: Brill, 2006), 195–225.

Menache, Sophia, A Clash of Expectations: Self-Image Versus the Image of the Knights Templar in Medieval Narrative Sources, in: Analecta Torunensia 13 (2005), 47–58; The Birth of Parliaments in the Middle Ages (Tel Aviv: Open Univ., 2006) [Hebrew]; The Catholic Church in the Middle Ages: Ideology and Politics, 4 vols (Tel Aviv: Open Univ., 2006) [Hebrew]; Violence Against Dogs: Religion and Ecology in Medieval Western Christendom, in: Human Beings and other Animals, ed. Benny Arbel et al. (Tel Aviv, 2006), 193–209; The Last Master of the Temple: Jacques de Molay, in: Knighthoods 229–240.

Meschini, Marco, Validità, novità e carattere della decretale «Vergentis in senium» di Innocenzo III (25 marzo 1199), in: Bulletin of Medieval Canon Law 25 (2002/03), 94–113; Innozenz III. und der Kreuzzug als Instrument im Kampf gegen die Häresie, in: Deutsches

Archiv für Erforschung des Mittelalters 61 (2005), 537–583; Battaglie medievali (Milano: Società Europea di Edizioni, 2006); Assedi medievali (ibid.).

MESQUI, Jean, La fortification des croisés au temps de Saint Louis au Proche-Orient, in: L'architecture 5–29; with Nicolas Faucherre, L'enceinte médiévale de Césarée, in: ibid. 83–94.

MILITZER, Klaus, Die Geschichte des Deutschen Ordens (Stuttgart, 2005); Der Wandel in der Begründung der Existenz des Deutschen Ordens und seiner Selbstrechtfertigung vor und nach der Schlacht bei Tannenberg, in: Kancelaria wielkich mistrzów Polska kancelaria królewska w XV wieku, ed. Janusz Trupinda (Malbork, 2006), 179–190; ed. with Johannes A. Mol, Helen J. Nicholson, MOR.

MINERVINI, Laura, La langue française en Chypre, in: Lacrimae Cypriae: les larmes de Chypre ou Recueil des inscriptions lapidaires pour la plupart funéraires de la période franque et vénitienne de l'île de Chypre, dir. Brunhilde Imhaus, vol. 2: Études et commentaires, planches des dessins (Nicosie: Dépt. des Antiquités, 2004 [2005]), 169–174; French language in Outremer; Gestes des Chiprois; Intercultural relations in Outremer; Lingua Franca; Litterature of Outremer and Cyprus; Philip of Novara, in: EncycCru.

MITCHELL, Piers, with Y. Nagar, Ronnie Ellenblum, Weapon Injuries in the 12th Century Crusader Garrison of Vadum Iacob Castle, Galilee, in: International Journal of Osteoarchaeology 16 (2006), 145–155; Child Health in the Crusader Period Inhabitants of Tel Jezreel, Israel, in: Levant 38 (2006), 37–44; The Infirmaries of the Order of the Temple in the Medieval Kingdom of Jerusalem, in: The Medieval Hospital and Medical Practice: Bridging the Evidence, ed. Barbara S. Bowers (Aldershot: Ashgate, 2006), 225–234; The Torture of Military Captives during the Crusades in the Medieval Middle East, in: Noble Ideals and Bloody Realities: Warfare in the Middle Ages, 378–1492, ed. Niall G. F. Christie, Maya Yazigi (Leiden: Brill, 2006), 97–118; Trauma in the Crusader Period City of Caesarea: A Major Port in the Medieval Eastern Mediterranean, in: International Journal of Osteoarchaeology 16 (2006), 493–505.

MOL, Johannes A., The Dutch Presence in the Teutonic Order in Livonia, in: R. Schuddeboom (ed.), Beyond Traditional Borders: Eight Centuries of Latvian-Dutch Relations (Riga: SIA Apgads Zelta gauds, 2006), 19–26; ed. with Klaus Militzer, Helen J. Nicholson, MOR; Trying to Survive: The Military Orders in Utrecht, 1580–1620, in: ibid. 181–208; The Hospitaller Sisters in Frisia, in: HW 179–208.

MOLIN, Kristian, entries on Cypriot rulers and crusader castles in Cyprus and Greece, in: EncycCru.

MURRAY, Alan V., Prosopography, in: Palgrave Advances in the Crusades, ed. Helen J. Nicholson (Basingstoke: Palgrave Macmillan, 2005), 109–129; ed., EncycCru; Adelaide del Vasto; Aimery of Limoges; Alp Arslan ibn Ridwan; Baldwin I of Jerusalem; Baldwin II of Jerusalem; Banyas: Barbarossa Hoard; Bertrand of Tripoli; Captivity; Charles the Good; *Chronicle of Zimmern*; Cono of Montaigu; Conrad IV of Germany; Conradin; Conrad of Mainz; Conrad of Querfurt; Crucesignatus; Crusade of 1267; Dobrin, order; *Domus Godefridi*; Douglas, James; Emicho of Flonheim; Eustace I Granarius; Franks; Frederick I of Austria; Frederick of Laroche; Frederick V of Swabia; Frutolf of Michelsberg; Gervase of Bazoches; Godfrey of Bouillon; Henry of Kalden; *Historia de expeditione Frederici imperatoris*; *Historia Belli Sacri*; Hugh of Fauquembergues; Hugh of Jaffa; Ibelin, battle (1123); John of Würzburg; Joscelin III of Courtenay; *Livonian Rhymed Chronicle*; Leopold V of Austria; Leopold VI of Austria; Mahdia Crusade (1390); Malik Shah I; Malik Shah II; Metellus of Tegernsee; Mont Gisard, battle (1177); Outremer; People's Crusades; Peter of

Blois; Peter of Dampierre; Pons of Tripoli; Rainald III of Toul; Raymond II of Tripoli; Raymond III of Tripoli; Raymond of Poitiers; Saule (battle); Saladin Tithe; Scotland; Sigurd Jorsalfar; al-Sinnabrah; Sultan Shah; Terre de Suete; Tiberias; Transjordan; Tutush II; Walter Mahomet; Walter Sans-Avoir; William VI of Montferrat; William Longsword; William of Puylaurens; William of Tyre; William-Jordan of Cerdagne; Zimmern, Chronicle of; Jerusalem, (Latin) Kingdom of [with Helen Nicholson]; Crusade of Emperor Henry VI [with Janus Møller Jensen], in: EncycCru; Money and Logistics in the Forces of the First Crusade: Coinage, Bullion, Service, and Supply, 1096–1099, in: LW 229–249; Kingship, Identity and Name-giving in the Family of Baldwin of Bourcq, in: Knighthoods 27–38; Baltic Crusades, in: Encarta 2007 Reference Library.

NICHOLSON, Helen J., The Motivations of the Hospitallers and Templars in their Involvement in the Fourth Crusade and its Aftermath, Hill Monastic Manuscript Library Malta Study Center Lecture, 2003, http://www.hmml.org/centers/malta/publications/lecture3.html; The Sisters' House at Minwear, Pembrokeshire: Analysis of the Documentary and Archaeological Evidence, in: Archaeologia Cambrensis 151 (2002 [2005]), 109–138; Echoes of the Past and Present Crusades in *Les Prophecies de Merlin*, in: Romania 122 (2004), 320–340; The Third Crusade, in: Crusades: The Illustrated Histroy, ed. Thomas F. Madden (London: Duncan Baird, 2004), 80–97, 152–153; 'La roine preude femme et bonne dame': Queen Sybil of Jerusalem (1186–1190) in History and Legend, 1186–1300, in: The Haskins Society Journal 15 (2004), 110–124; Knight Templar, Warrior series 91 (Oxford: Osprey, 2004), 64pp.; republished as part of David Nicolle and id., God's Warriors: Crusaders, Saracens and the Battle for Jerusalem (Oxford: Osprey, 2005), 224pp.; The Crusades, Greenwood Guides to Historic Events of the Medieval World (Westport CT: Greenwood, 2004), i+197pp.; *Eracles*; Ernoul; Jerusalem, (Latin) kingdom of [with Alan V. Murray]; Military Orders; Third Crusade; St Maurice, order of; Ralph of Diceto; Richard of Devizes; Rigord, in: EncycCru, 2:405, 407–408, 662–672, 3:808, 825–830, 4:1002–1003, 1035, 1038–1039; ed. with Anthony Luttrell, HW; with Anthony Luttrell, Introduction: a Survey of Hospitaller Women in the Middle Ages, in: ibid. 1–42; Margaret de Lacy and the Hospital of Saint John at Aconbury, Herefordshire, in: ibid. 153–178; ed. with Johannes A. Mol, Klaus Militzer, MOR; Relations between Houses of the Order of the Temple in Britain and their Local Communities, as Indicated during the Trial of the Templars, 1307–12, in: Knighthoods 195–207.

NICOLAOU-KONNARI, Angel, Manuscripts from the Biblioteca Nazionale Marciana in Venice and Cyprus, in: Written Historical Evidence, Catalogue of the exhibition organized at the Leventis Municipal Museum of Nicosia within the framework of the Italian Cultural Month, 2 October–5 November 2006, 29–35; Lusignan Cyprus and Europe, 1192–1489, in: Cyprus Has Always Been Europe, ed. Elena Hadjipaschalis, Polly Lyssiotis, Andreas Lyritsas (Nicosia, 2006), 77–111; L'identité dans la diaspora: travaux et jours de Pierre (avant 1570?–après 1646) et Georges de Nores (1619–1638), in: Identités croisées en un milieu méditerranéen: le cas de Chypre (Antiquité – Moyen Âge), ed. Sabine Fourrier, Gilles Grivaud, Publications des Universités de Rouen et du Havre (Monts, 2006), 329–353; Cyprus during the First Years of the Ottoman Conquest: The Historical Notes on fols 239v–240r of the Codex Ven. Marc. Gr. VII, 16, 1080, in: Επετηρίδα του Κέντρου Επιστημονικών Ερευνών 31 (2005), 193–238 [Greek].

NICOLLE, David, with Chistopher Gravett, The Normans: Warriors Knights and their Castles (Oxford, 2006).

NIELEN, Marie-Adélaïde, Lignages d'Outremer; Assises de Jérusalem, in: EncycCru.

NIELSEN, Torben Kjersgaard, The Missionary Man: Archbishop Anders Sunesen and the Baltic Crusade 1206–1221, in: Crusade and Conversion on the Baltic Frontier 1150–1500, ed. Alan V. Murray (Aldershot: Ashgate, 2001), 95–117; Pope Innocent III and Denmark, Sweden and Norway, in: Analecta Romana Instituti Danici 28 (Rome, 2002), 7–32; with Kurt Villads Jensen, Pope Innocent III and Denmark, in: Innocenzo III – Urbs et Orbis, Atti del Congresso Internazionale, Roma, 9–15 settembre 1998 (Roma, 2003), 1133–1168; Mission and Submission: Societal Change in the Baltic in the Thirteenth Century, in: Medieval History Writing and Crusading Ideology, ed. Kurt Villads Jensen, Toumas Lehtonen (Helsinki, 2005), 216–231.

NOBLE, Peter, ed., Robert de Clari, La Conquête de Constantinople, Société Rencesvals British Branch, British Rencesvals Publications 3 (Edinburgh, 2005), 149pp.; Baldwin of Flanders and Henry of Hainault as Military Commanders in the Latin Empire of Constantinople, in: Knighthoods 65–76.

OMRAN, Mahmoud Said, Egypt under Byzantine Rule: Dar al-Marefa al-Gameeya (Alexandria), 343–347.

PAVIOT, Jacques, La croisade bourguignone au XIVe et XVe siècles: un idéal chevaleresque?, in: Francia 33/1: Mittelalter – Moyen Âge (2006), 33–68.

PEILSTÖCKER, Martin, La ville franque de Jaffa à la lumière des fouilles récentes, in: L'architecture 99–104.

PERRA, Photeine V., with others, The Peloponnesian Towns and the Change in the Configuration of their Population During the Second Venetian Dominion: the Case of Tripolizza, in: Eoa and Hesperia 5 (2001/03), 89–146; Late Medieval Corinth, a Latin Rampart in Southern Greece, in: Historika Themata 41 (Athens, June 2005), 100–115; Latin Domination in the Helladic Lands and in Cyrpus: a Bibliographical Contribution, in: Byzantinos Domos 15 (Thessaloniki, 2006), 421–486; Naupaktos, Methone and Korone between the First Two Venetian-Ottoman Wars (1479–1499), in: ibid. 225–234; Chapt. 9: Latin domination in Helladic lands (1204–1566), chapt. 10: Byzantium and the Western world (11th–15th cent.), in: History of Greeks, 1st ed, vol. 7 (Athens: Domi Publications, 2006), 416–455, 456–489; Chapt. 7: Latin domination in Cyprus (1191–1571), in: ibid. vol. 15, 256–331; ibid., 2nd ed., chapt. 9–10, vol. 8, 520–609, chapt. 7, vol. 19, 310–405 (2006) [Greek].

PETERS, Edward, There and Back Again: Crusaders in Motion, 1096–1291, in: Crusades 5 (2006), 157–171.

PHILLIPS, Jonathan, Armenia, Edessa and the Second Crusade, in: Knighthoods 39–50.

PHILLIPS, Matthew, The Thief's Cross: Crusade and Penance in Alan of Lille's *Sermo de cruce domini*, in: Crusades 5 (2006), 143–156.

PIANA, Mathias, with Hans Curvers, The Castle of Toron (Qalʿat Tibnīn) in South Lebanon: Preliminary Results of the 2000/2003 Campaign, in: Bulletin d'Archéologie et d'Architecture Libanaises 8 (2004), 333–356; The Crusader Castle of Toron: First Results of its Investigation, in: Crusades 5 (2006), 173–191.

PLAGNIEUX, Philippe, Le portail d'Acre transporté au Caire: sources et diffusion des modéles rayonnants en Terre sainte au XIIIe siècle, in: L'architecture 61–66.

POWELL, James M., The Crusades: an Introduction, in: EncycCru xliii–lx; The Crusades, the Kingdom of Sicily, and the Mediterranean (Aldershot: Ashgate, 2007); ed. and tr., The Deeds of Pope Innocent III (Washington/DC: The Catholic Univ. of America Press, 2007 [paperback of 2004 edition])

PROUTEAU, Nicolas, Eudes de Montreuil, maître des œuvres des fortifications de Jaffa, une légende franciscaine?, in: L'architecture 109–112.

PRYOR, John H., The Maritime Republics, in: The New Cambridge Medieval History, ed. David Abulafia, vol. 5: c.1198–1300 (Cambridge: CUP, 1999), 419–446; 'Water, Water Everywhere, Nor Any Drop to Drink': Water Supplies for the Fleets of the First Crusade, in: Dei gesta per Francos: Études sur les croisades dédiées à Jean Richard, ed. Michel Balard et al. (Aldershot: Ashgate, 2001), 21–28; Types of Ships and Their Performance Capabilities, in: Travel in the Byzantine World, Papers from the 34th Spring Symposium of Byzantine Studies, Birmingham, April 2000, ed. Ruth Macrides (Aldershot: Ashgate, 2002), 33–58; The Venetian Fleet for the Fourth Crusade and the Diversion of the Crusade to Constantinople, in: The Experience of Crusading, ed. Marcus Bull, Norman Housley, vol. 1: Western Approaches (Cambridge: CUP, 2003), 103–123; Byzantium and the Sea: Byzantine Fleets and the History of the Empire in the Age of Macedonian Emperors, c.900–1025 CE, in: War at Sea in the Middle Ages and the Renaissance, ed. John B. Hattendorf, Richard W. Unger (Woodbridge: Boydell & Brewer, 2003), 83–104; The Mediterranean Breaks Up, 500–1000, in: The Mediterranean in History, ed. David Abulafia (London: Thames & Hudson, 2003), 155–181; The Stadiodromikon of the De Cerimoniis of Constantine VII, Byzantine Warships, and the Cretan Expedition of 949, in: The Greek Islands and the Sea, ed. Julian Chrysostomides et al. (London: Porphyrogenitus, 2004), 77–108; Geography, Technology and War: Studies in the Maritime History of the Mediterranean, 649–1571 (Cambridge: CUP, 1988) = Akdeniz'de Coğrafya, Teknoloji ve Savaş: Arapalar, Bizanslilar, Batililar ve Türkler, tr. F. & T. Tayanç (Istanbul: Kitapyayinevi, 2004), 259pp.; Marco Polo's Return Voyage from China: its Implications for 'The Marco Polo Debate', in: Travel and Travellers from Bede to Dampier, ed. Geraldine Barnes, Gabrielle Singleton (Newcastle: Cambridge Scholars Press, 2005), 125–157; ed., LW; Introduction: Modelling Bohemond's March to Thessalonikē, in: ibid. 1–24; Digest, in: ibid. 275–292; with Elizabeth M. Jeffreys, The Age of the ΔΡΟΜΩΝ: The Byzantine Navy ca 500–1204 (Leiden: Brill, 2006), lxxviii+754pp.; Naval history, 1096–1099; Naval history, 1100–1249; Ships, in: EncycCru 3:864–869, 869–876, 4:1096–1103.

PURKIS, William J., Elite and Popular Perceptions of imitatio Christi in Twelfth-Century Crusade Spirituality, in: Elite and Popular Religion, ed. Kate Cooper, Jeremy Gregory, Studies in Church History 42 (Woodbridge: Boydell & Brewer, 2006), 54–64.

RICHARD, Jean, Sainte-Croix d'Antioche: un monastère féminin de tradition érémitique au temps des croisades, in: Chronos 13 (2006), 19–35; Le temps des croisades, in: Histoire du Liban des origines au XXe siècle, dir. Boutros Dib (Paris, 2006), 225–263; Les mercenaires francs dans les armées musulmanes au temps des croisades, in: Regards croisés sur le Moyen-Âge arabe, Mélanges Louis Pouzet, Mélanges de l'Université Saint-Joseph 58 (2006), 227–238; La coopération militaire entre Francs et Mongols à l'épreuve: les campagnes de Ghazan en Syrie, in: Florilegia altaistica in honour of Denis Sinor, ed. Elena V. Boikova, Giovanni Stary (Wiesbaden, 2006), 119–128.

RILEY-SMITH, Jonathan, The Military Orders and the East, 1149–1291, in: Knighthoods 137–150.

ROCHE, Jason T., Conrad III and the Second Crusade: Retreat from Dorylaion?, in: Crusades 5 (2006), 85–97.

ROLL, Israel, with Benjamin Arubas, Le château d'Arsur: Forteresse côtière pentagonale du type concentrique du milieu du XIIIe siècle, in: L'architecture 67–81.

SAVAGE-SMITH, Emilie, New Evidence for the Frankish Study of Arabic Medical Texts in the Crusader Period, in: Crusades 5 (2006), 99–112.

SAVVIDES, Alexios G. C., Alexios III Angelos; Alexios IV Angelos; Alexios V Doukas Mourtzouphlos; Ankara, battle of 1402; Chaka bey; Choniates, Niketas; Constantinople, siege of 1453; Crete; Danishmendids; Epiros; Ghazis; Il-Ghazi; Isaac II Angelos; Isaac Komnenos of Cyprus; John VIII Palaiologos; Khitokotia, battle of 1426; Kilij Arslan I; Kilij Arslan II; Seljuks of Rum; Sgouros, Leo; Smyrna, crusade of 1344; Tatikios; Theodore Angelos Doukas Komnenos; Trabizond, Empire; Turcopoles, in: EncycCru; 37 entries, among them: William of Champlitte [collab. Thekla Saksaridou-Hendrickx], Henry VI Holy Roman Emperor [collab. M. Tahar Mansouri], Henri de Valenciennes [collab. B. Hendrickx]) in: Encyclopaedic Prosopographical Lexicon of Byzantine History and Civilization, vols. 5–6 (Athens: Metron-Iolcos, 2006) [Greek]; An ongoing project: the Greek Encyclopaedic Prosopographical Lexicon of Byzantine History and Civilization (EPLBHC) and its forthcoming English edition, in: Proceedings of the 21st International Congress of Byzantine Studies, London 21–26 August 2006, vol. 2: Abstracts of Panel Papers (Aldershot: Ashgate, 2006), 113–115; History of Byzantium with extracts from the sources, vol. III: A.D. 1025–1461, 2nd revised ed. (Athens: Patakes, 2006), 319 pp. [Greek]; with Nikolaos Nikoloudes, The Later Medieval World, 11th–16th cc.: Byzantium – Medieval West – the Orient and Islam – the Balkans and the Slavs (Athens: Herodotos, 2007) [Greek]; Queen Tamara-Thamar of Georgia (Iberia): a medieval 'Semiramis' of the Caucasus, in: Historika Themata 58 (Athens, January 2007), 36–45 [Greek].

SCHABEL, Christopher, with Gilles Grivaud, La ville de Nicosie, in: L'art gothique en Chypre, ed. Jean-Bernard de Vaivre, Philippe Plagnieux (Paris: Académie des Inscriptions, 2006), 89–108; A Tractatus on the Distinction of the Holy Spirit from the Son by a Master of the Val des Écoliers, in: Mediaevalia Philosophica Polonorum 35 (2006), 184–214.

SCHRYVER, James G., Is There ONE Crusader Archaeology?, in: Symposium on Mediterranean Archaeology, Proceedings of the eighth annual meeting of postgraduate researchers, School of Classics, Trinity College Dublin, 20–22 February 2004, ed. Jo Day et al., BAR International Series 1514 (Oxford: Archaeopress, 2006), 155–160; Monuments of Identity: Latin, Greek, French and Cypriot?, in: Identités croisées en un milieu méditerranéen: le cas de Chypre (Antiquité – Moyen Âge), ed. Sabine Fourrier, Gilles Grivaud (Mont-Saint-Aignan Cedex: Publ. des Univ. de Rouen et du Havre, 2006), 385–405.

SCHWARZMAIER, Hansmartin, Kreuzzug und Pilgerfahrt nach Jerusalem: Lebensplanungen und Bußleistungen eines alternden Fürsten in staufischer Zeit [Welf VI.], in: Wirtschaft – Gesellschaft – Mentalitäten im Mittelalter: Festschrift zum 75. Geburtstag von Rolf Sprandel, ed. Hans-Peter Baum, Rainer Leng, Joachim Schneider, Beiträge zur Wirtschafts- und Sozialgeschichte 107 (Stuttgart: Steiner, 2006), 697–714.

STERN, Eliezer, La commanderie de l'Ordre des Hospitaliers à Acre, in: L'architecture 53–60.

STRUCKMEYER, Myra, The Sisters of the Order of Saint John at Mynchin Buckland, in: HW 89–112.

THORAU, Peter, Einige kritische Bemerkungen zum sogenannten »mamlūk phenomenon«, in: Stephan Conermann, Anja Pistor-Hatam (ed.), Die Mamlūken: Studien zu ihrer Geschichte und Kultur, Zum Gedenken an Ulrich Haarmann (1942–1999), Asien und Afrika, Beiträge des Zentrums für Asiatische und Afrikanische Studien der Christian-Albrechts-Universität zu Kiel 7 (Schenefeld, 2003), 367–378; Geschichte der Kreuzzüge (München: Beck, 2004, 2005), 128pp.; Von Karl dem Großen zum Frieden von Tsitva Torok:

Zum Weltherrschaftsanspruch Sultan Mehmeds II. und dem Wiederaufleben des Zweikaiserproblems nach der Eroberung Konstantinopels, in: Historische Zeitschrift 279 (2004), 309–334; »Die fremden Franken« – *al-faranğ al-ğurabāʾ*: Kreuzfahrer und Kreuzzüge aus arabischer Sicht, in: Alfred Wieczorek, Mamoun Fansa, Harald Meller (ed.), Saladin und die Kreuzfahrer, Katalog zur Ausstellung in Halle, Oldenburg und Mannheim (Mainz, 2005), 115–125; Shadschar ad-Durr – Sultanin von Ägypten, in: ibid. 167–169; Sultan Baybars I., in: ibid. 171–173; Fortsetzung der Geschichte von Damskus von Ibn al-Qalanisi mit Beschreibung der Eroberung von Jerusalem, in: ibid. 307–308; »Die Truppen der Türken aber erfasste das Stammesbewusstsein«: Integrations- und Selbstwahrnehmungsprozesse der islamischen Welt in der Auseinandersetzung mit den Kreuzfahrern, in: Heinz Gaube, Benrd Schneidmüller, Stefan Weinfurter (ed.), Konfrontation der Kulturen? Saladin und die Kreuzfahrer, Wissenschaftliches Kolloquium in den Reiss-Engelhorn-Museen Mannheim zur Vorbereitung der Ausstellung »Saladin und die Kreuzfahrer«, 3.–4. November 2004 (Mainz, 2005), 121–135; Wo jedes Sandkorn heiliger Boden ist, Die großen Pilgerziele: Jerusalem, in: Pilgerwege im Mittelalter, ed. with DAMALS – das Magazin für Geschichte und Kultur (Darmstadt, 2005), 27–56; »Turci ante portas«: Der osmanische Angriff auf Unteritalien 1480/81, in: Sabine Penth, Martina Pitz, Christine van Hoof, Ralf Krautkrämer (ed.), Europas Grenzen, Limites 1 (St. Ingbert, 2006), 93–118; Panzerreiter im Pfeilhagel? Anmerkungen zu militärtechnischer Differenz und Annäherung von Orient und Okzident im Zeitalter der Kreuzzüge, in: Militärgeschichtliche Zeitschrift 65 (2006), 63–78.

Throop, Susanna, Vengeance and the Crusades, in: Crusades 5 (2006), 21–38.

Toko, Hirofumi, Byzantium, in: A History of the Mediterranean World (Hiratsuka: Course of Western History, Tokai Univ., 2006), 70–92 [Japanese].

Tolan, John Victor, Esgrimiendo la pluma: polémica y apologética religiosa entre judíos, cristianos y musulmanes (siglos XIII al XV), in: L'esplendor de la Mediterrània medieval (segles XIII–XV) (Barcelona: IMED, 2004), 243–259; Looking East Before 1453: the Saracen in Medieval European Imagination, in: Cultural Encounters between East and West, 1453–1699, ed. Matthew Birchwood, Matthew Dimmock (Newcastle: Cambridge Scholars Press, 2005), 13–28; Affreux vacarme: sons de cloches et voix de muezzins dans la polémique interconfessionnelle en péninsule ibérique, in: Guerre, pouvoirs et idéologies dans l'Espagne chrétienne aux alentours de l'an mil, ed. Thomas Deswarte, Philippe Sénac (Turnhout: Brepols, 2005), 51–64; Las traducciones y la ideologia de reconquista: Marcos de Toledo, in: Musulmanes y cristianos en Hispania durante las conquistas de los siglos XII y XIII, ed. Miquel Barcelo, José Martínez Gazquez (Bellaterra: Universitat Autònoma de Barcelona, 2005), 79–85; *Francisce revertere*: Angelo Clareno, les spirituels, et l'héritage de François d'Assise, in: Le Conflit, ed. Olivier Ménard, Fabienne Le Roy (Paris: L'Harmattan, 2005), 189–197; ed. with François Clément, Jérôme Wilgaux, Espaces d'échanges en Méditerranée: Antiquité et Moyen Âge (Rennes: Presse Univ. de Rennes, 2006).

Tommasi, Francesco, Men and Women of the Hospitaller, Templar and Teutonic Orders: Twelfth to Fourteenth Centuries, in: HW 71–88; The Female Hospitallers of San Bevignate at Perugia: 1325–c.1507, in: ibid. 233–258.

Touati, François-Olivier, La Terre sainte: un laboratoire hospitalier au Moyen Âge?, in: Sozialgeschichte mittelalterlicher Hospitäler, Reichenau: Konstanzer Arbeitskreis für mittelalterliche Geschichte, 19. März 2002, Vorträge und Forschungen 65, ed. Neithard Bulst, Karl-Heinz Spieß (Ostfildern: Thorbecke, 2007), 169–211.

Unger, Richard W., The Northern Crusaders: the Logistics of English and Other Northern Crusader Fleets, in: LW 251–274.

TYERMAN, Christopher, The Crusades: A Very Short Introduction (Oxford: OUP, 2005), 167pp.; tr. Las cruzadas: realidad y mito (Cativa, 2005); God's War: A New History of the Crusades (London – Harvard, 2006), xvi+1024pp.

UPTON-WARD, Judi, Bibliography of Works by Malcolm Barber, in: Knighthoods xv–xx.

URBAN, William, Tyska Orden: Nordens korsriddare, tr. Per Nyquist (Stockholm: Prisma, 2006) [The Teutonic Knights].

DE VAIVRE, Jean-Bernard, ed. with Philippe Plagnieux, L'art gothique en Chypre, Mémoires de l'Académie des inscriptions et belles-lettres (Paris, 2006), 478pp.

VANN, Theresa M., Christian, Muslim, and Jewish Mariners in the Port of Rhodes, 1453–1480, in: Medieval Encounters 13 (2007), 158–173.

VAN WINTER, Johanna Maria, Sugar, Spice of the Crusaders, in: Mediterranean Food: Concepts and Trends, Proceedings of the 15th International Ethnological Food Research Conference, Dubrovnik, 27 September–3 October 2004, ed. Patricia Lysaght, Nives Rittig-Beljak (Zagreb: Biblioteka Nova Etnografija, 2006), 301–309; Godschalk de Kruisvaarder en de Heren van den Bergh, in: Historisch Jaarboek voor Gelderland, Bijdragen en Mededelingen 97 (2006), 141–153.

2. Recently completed theses

ATTA, Zubaida, The Ayyubids of Hamah, M.Ph., 2006.

CARRAZ, Damien, Ordres militaires, croisades et sociétés méridionales: L'Ordre du Temple dans la basse vallée du Rhône (1124–1312), PhD, Univ. Lumière-Lyon 2, 2003, 4 vols.

CARRIER, Marc, L'image des Byzantines et les systèmes de représentation selon les chroniqueurs occidentaux des croisades (1096–1261), PhD, Univ. Paris I, 2006, 500pp., supervised by Michel Balard.

DEMOSTHENOUS, Anthoulles, The Phantasy-Community of Byzantine Cyprus through the Writings of Neophytos the Recluse (1134–c.1214): Social Critique and Class-Differentiation of a Byzantine Saint, PhD, Aegean Univ., Rhodes 2006, supervised by Alexios G. C. Savvides.

EL-FAHAM, Mohammed Khamis, France in the Light of the Chronicle of Suger of St. Denis 1108–1137, PhD, supervised by Mahmoud Said Omran.

GABRIELE, Matthew, Imperator Christianorum: Charlemagne and the East, 814–ca.1100, PhD History, Univ. of California, Berkeley, 2005.

GAT, Shimon, The City of Ramla in the Middle Ages, PhD, Bar-Ilan Univ., 2004, supervised by Yvonne Friedman.

GUTER, Yael, Aspects of Christian Pilgrimage to the Holy Land: The Pilgrims' Experience, PhD, Bar-Ilan Univ., 2005, supervised by Yvonne Friedman.

ISMAIL, Wafaa Ibrahim, Egypt and Syria in the Foreign Travelers during the Byzantine Period, MA, supervised by Mahmoud Said Omran.

KOSTICK, Conor, The Language of ordo in the Early Histories of the First Crusade, PhD, Trinity College Dublin, supervised by Ian S. Robinson and Bernard Hamilton.

MPAIRAKTARES, Georgios, The Greek Verses of Jelal al-Din Rumi and those of his Son, Sultan Veled, PhD, Aegean Univ., Rhodes 2006, supervised by Alexios G. C. Savvides.

NUSSBAUM, Shmuel, Peace Process between Crusaders and Muslims in the Latin East, MA, Bar Ilan Univ., 2003, supervised by Yvonne Friedman.

PHILLIPS, Christopher Matthew, "O magnum crucis misterium": Devotion to the Cross, Crusading, and the Imitation of the Crucified Christ in the High Middle Ages, c.1050–c.1215

RUBIN-RONEN, Jonathan, The Limits of a Vassal's Obedience to his Lord according to the Summa super usibus feudorum of a Crusader Jurist, MA, supervised by Benjamin Z. Kedar.

SCHRYVER, James G., Spheres of Contact and Instances of Interaction in the Art and Archaeology of Frankish Cyprus, 1191–1359, Cornell Univ., May 2005, 301pp.

STRUCKMEYER, Myra, Female Hospitallers in the Twelfth and Thirteenth Centuries.

STUCKEY, Jace, Charlemagne: The Making of an Image 1100–1300, PhD, Univ. of Florida, 2006.

3. Papers read by members of the Society and others

BALARD, Michel, L'empire génois d'outremer, at: Université de Nantes, February 2006; Ricerche recenti sulle Crociate in Francia e in Italia, at: Centro Nazionale delle Ricerche, Roma, 16–17 March 2006.

BALLETTO, Laura, Brevi note su Pera genovese a metà del XIV secolo, at: Mittelalterliches Bulgarien, Byzanz und Europa, Wien, 10–11 November 2006.

BARTOS, Sebastian, The making of a duke in 13th-century Krakow: secular and ecclesiastical perspectives, at: IMC Leeds, July 2006.

BELLOMO, Elena, Diplomazia e crociata nel Mediterraneo di inizio XIV secolo: il francescano savonese Filippo Brusserio, at: Genoa, Columbus and the Mediterranean, 9th Annual International Congress of the Mediterranean Studies Association, Università di Genova, 24–27 May 2006; L'Ordine templare in Italia nord-occidentale: il caso di Testona-Moncalieri, at: Da Moncalieri al Piemonte: Itinerari di storia e cultura del territorio, Moncalieri, 8 June 2006.

BRONSTEIN, Judith, La construcción Hospitalaria en el siglo XIII, at: V Encontro sobre Ordens Militares, Ordens Militares e Ordens de Cavalaria entro o Ocidente e o Oriente, Palmela, Portugal, 15–18 February 2006; The crusaders and other religious groups: the case of Acre, at: Meetings of Populations and Culture in the City of Acre, Past and Present, Acre, 24 March 2006; The Hospitallers' re-organization after Hattin, at: The Middle Ages, Now! Ben Gurion Univ. of the Negev, Israel, 30 March 2006; Financiando la guerra santa: una vision económica en el medioevo, at: Facultad de Ciencias Económicas, Universidad Nacional del Litoral, Santa Fe, Argentina, 28 September 2006.

BRUNDAGE, James A., Full and partial proof in classical canonical procedure, at: Renaissance Society of America, San Francisco, 24 March 2006; My learned friend: professional courtesy in medieval courtrooms, in: IMC Leeds, 13 July 2006; Procedural variations: the impact of professionalization on medieval matrimonial law, at: Regional Variations in Matrimonial Law and Custom in Europe, 1150–1650, Faculty of Law, Univ. of Helsinki, 3 August 2006; Legal ethics: a medieval ghost story, at: International School of Ius Commune, Ettore Majorana Center for Scientific Culture, Erice (Sicily), 6 October 2006, also at: Arizona Center for Medieval and Renaissance Studies, Arizona State Univ., Tempe AZ, 19 October 2006, and at: Harvard Law School, Cambridge MA, 6 November 2006; Violence and war in medieval canon law, at: Center on Religion and Conflict, Arizona State Univ., Tempe AZ, 21 October 2006.

BURGTORF, Jochen, Margat and Valenia in the 12th and 13th centuries, at: International

Castle Research Society, Braubach (Germany), January 2006; Templar and Hospitaller properties in the Principality of Antioch and the County of Tripoli, at: A. A. Bredius Foundation Conference Antioch in the Period from the Byzantine Reconquest in 969 to the Fall of the Crusader Principality in 1268 – Part Two, Kasteel Hernen (The Netherlands), May 2006.

CHRISSIS, Nikolaos, Crusading in Romania: the aftermath of the Fourth Crusade in Byzantine-Western relations, at: Royal Holloway Univ. of London Postgraduate Forum, 1 June 2006; The common cause of Christendom, politics and all that: the interpretation and incorporation of the crusade in Byzantine policy towards the West in the 13th century, at: 21st International Congress of Byzantine Studies, London, 21–26 August 2006.

CHRISTIE, Niall G. F., Reconstructing Mamluk *Fanadiq* (trade hostelries) from 14th-century documents, at: Canadian Society for the Study of Egypt, Vancouver, January 2006; Jerusalem, Eschatology and the *Kitab al-Jihad* of ʿAli ibn Tahir al-Sulami (d. 1106), at: Crusades: Medieval Worlds in Conflict, Saint Louis Univ., Saint Louis, February 2006; Women and warfare in the Muslim literature of the 6th/12th-century Levant, at: 216th Annual Meeting of the American Oriental Society, Seattle, March 2006; Jerusalem in the *Kitab al-Jihad* of ʿAli ibn Tahir al-Sulami (d. 1106), at: The Holy City of Jerusalem: Desire and Conflict – Past and Present, Univ. of British Columbia, Vancouver, March 2006.

CLAVERIE, Pierre-Vincent, Les relations islamo-chrétiennes à l'aune du récit de pèlerinage de Jacques de Vérone (1335), at: 15th HES, 18 May 2006; Les acteurs impliqués dans le commerce des reliques à la fin du Moyen Âge, at: Séminaire de l'Equipe de Recherche sur les échanges dans la Méditerranée Antique et Médiévale, Univ. of Nantes, 16 February 2007.

CONGDON, Eleanor A., What price for this piece of Zambellotto?, at: IMC Leeds.

COUREAS, Nicholas S., Notarial documents from Lusignan Cyprus, at: Univ. of Cyprus Conference on International Diplomatics in the Eastern Mediterranean, April 2006; The reception of Arabic medicine in Lusignan and Venetian Cyprus, at: 15th HES, May 2006; The Greek monastery of St Margaret of Agros in Lusignan Cyprus and its relations with the Latin church and the papacy, at: IMC Kalamazoo, May 2006.

CRAWFORD, Paul F., Agent of the king? Romeus de Brugaria and the Templars, at: IMC Kalamazoo, 4 May 2006.

DICKSON, Gary, The Children's Crusade in England and Scotland, at: Medieval Children 1200–1500, Univ. of Kent, Canterbury, 18 June 2006.

DIVALL, Richard, Naval tactics and the siege of Malta 1565, at: SSCLE Sydney, 2005; The Byzantine and artistic heritage of the Order of Malta, at: SSCLE Sydney 2005; The music of the Order of Malta on Malta, at: Maltese Historical Society, Melbourne, 2005; The artistic heritage of the Order of Malta, at: Carnevale Christi, Melbourne, 2005.

DODD, Erica Cruikshank, Painting in a non-Chalcedonian church: Mar Musa el-Habashi, Syria, at: Ben Gurion Univ. of the Negev, 10 June 2006.

DONDI, Cristina, Liturgies of the military religious orders, at: 11th CIEL Colloquium, Oxford, Merton College, 13–16 September 2006.

DOUROU-ELIOPOULOU, Maria, The evidence of Latin documents of the 13th and 14th century on the Ionian Islands, at: 8th International Panionian Conference, Kythera, 21–25 May 2006; The Angevins of Sicily and the principality of Achaea, at: Greek-Italian Congress, Aigion, 6–9 July 2006; The presence of the Aragonese in Romania in the 14th century based on Aragonese archival documents, at: 21st International Congress of Byzantine Studies "Displaying Byzantium", 20–26 August 2006; Antonio Rubio i Lluch as the historian of the

Catalan domination in Greece, at: Round-table on the Anniversary of the 150 Years of the Birth of Antonio Rubio l Lluch, Athens, 2 November 2006; The Burgundian duchy of Athens (1204–1311), at: The Medieval History of Athens, Athens, 7 November 2006.

EHLERS, Axel, Die Ökonomie der Gnade und der Wert der hohen Zahl: Ablaß-Summarien des Deutschen Ordens im späteren Mittelalter, at: Was zählt: Präsenz und Ordnungsfunktionen von Zahlen im Mittelalter, Internationale Arbeitstagung am Hermann von Helmholtz-Zentrum für Kulturtechnik, Humboldt-Univ. zu Berlin, 16–18 November 2006.

EKDAHL, Sven, Die heilige Birgitta, die Schlacht von Tannenberg und die Gründung des Klosters *Triumphus Mariae* in Lublin, at: Westpreußisches Bildungswerk Berlin-Brandenburg, Berlin.

EVANS, Michael, Explaining or excusing? The crusades, historical objectivity, and the "war on terror", at: Medievalism Conference, Ohio State Univ., 13–14 October 2006.

FOLDA, Jaroslav, Crusader artistic interaction with the Mongols and the Mamluks, at: Crusades: Medieval Worlds in Conflict, Saint Louis Univ., 16 February 2006; Eurasian artistic contacts: crusaders, Mamluks, Mongols, at: IMC Kalamazoo, 4–7 May 2006; The 13th century icon: function, content and ornament, at: Istituto di Studi Umanistici, Univ. of Florence, Palazzo Strozzi, Florence, 13–17 June 2006.

FOREY, Alan J., Aragonse Templars in the Holy Land and Cyprus in the late 13th and early 14th centuries, at: Palmela, February 2006.

FRIEDMAN, Yvonne, "In the name of God and profit": In the wake of pilgrims to the Holy Land, at: Mishkenot Scha'ananim, Jerusalem, 13–14 December 2005; Initiatives of peace in the Latin East: gestures of conciliation, at: Middle Ages Now, Beer Sheva Univ., 30 March 2006; Ransoming captives in Jewish, Christian and Muslim tradition, at: Jews, Christians and Muslims: Cohabitation and Confrontation along the Centuries, The Goren-Goldstein Center for Hebrew Studies, Univ. of Bucharest, 18–19 May 2006; Bowing, presenting gifts and other gestures in negotiations between Christians and Muslims in the Latin East, at: War and Peace, The Historical Society of Israel, Jerusalem, 26–28 June 2006; Gestures of conciliation: nonverbal peacemaking endeavours in the Latin East, at: IMC Leeds, 10–13 July 2006.

GABRIELE, Matthew, The *Descriptio qualiter Karolus Magnus* and the origins of the First Crusade, at: Heeding the Call of the Crusades, Midwest Medieval Conference, Knoxville, 8 October 2004; Charlemagne and Jerusalem: the afterlife of Einhard's *Vita Caroli* and the *Annales regni Francorum* to 1100, at: Charlemagne: History and Legend, IMC Kalamazoo, 8 May 2005; The legend of Charlemagne and the survival of Christendom, at: Univ. of California, Berkeley, 20 January 2006; Some early evidence of Charlemagne's legendary dominion over the East, at: Religious Sameness or Difference Personified, Medieval Academy of America, Boston, 30 March 2006; The legends of Charlemagne and the Last Emperor before the First Crusade: preliminary thoughts, at: IMC Kalamazoo, May 2007.

GAPOSCHKIN, Cecilia, moderator at: The Crusades: Myth and Reality, San Francisco, 23–24 February 2007.

VON GUTTNER-SPORZYNSKI, Darius, Relic or relevant? The Knights of Saint John, at: 15th Biennial Conference of the Australasian Association for European History, Melbourne, 11–15 July 2005, http://eprints.infodiv.unimelb.edu.au/archive/00001943; Recent issues in Polish historiography of the crusades, at: MO4, http://eprints.infodiv.unimelb.edu.au/archive/00001942.

HESLOP, Michael, The search for the defensive system of the knights in southern Rhodes, at: MO4; The search for the medieval defensive systems of southern Rhodes, at: Research

Seminar, History Dept., Royal Holloway, Univ. of London; The search for the Byzantine defensive system in southern Rhodes, at: 21st International Congress of Byzantine Studies, London, 21–26 August 2006.

HOLMES, Catherine, Byzantine historians at the periphery, at: 21st International Congress of Byzantine Studies, London, 21–26 August 2006, see http://www.byzantinecongress.org.uk

HUNT, Lucy-Anne, with Denys Pringle, The artistic programme surrounding the tomb of the Virgin in Jerusalem in the 12th century, at: 21st International Congress of Byzantine Studies, London, 21–26 August 2006.

JOTISCHKY, Andrew, St Sabas, the Holy Land and Greek Orthodox monasticism under crusader rule, at: Anglo-Scandinavian Conference of Church Historians, Lund, September 2005; Pope Eugenius III and the church in the crusader states, at: IMC Leeds, July 2006.

KEDAR, Benjamin Z., *Castellum* and *civitas* in the Latin kingdom of Jerusalem, at: Castles and Towns of the Crusader Period in the Eastern Mediterranean, Marksburg, 27–29 January 2006; with Denys Pringle, The Lord's Temple and the Temple of Solomon under Frankish Rule, at: Sacred Compound – the Temple/al-Haram al-Sharif, Jerusalem, Hebrew Univ. – Al-Quds Univ. – École Biblique française, 28 February–2 March 2006; Religion in catholic-muslim correspondence and treaties, at: DEM.

KOLIA-DERMITZAKI, Athina, Byzantium and the West – the West and Byzantium (9th–12th centuries), at: 21st International Congress of Byzantine Studies, London, 21–26 August 2006.

KOSTICK, Conor, The breakdown of papal authority over the First Crusade, at: IMC Leeds, 14–17 July 2003; The trial by fire of Peter Bartholomew, at: Borderlines VII, Queens Univ., Belfast, 16–18 April 2004; William of Tyre, Livy, and the vocabulary of class applied to the kingdom of Jerusalem 1095–1184, at: IMC Kalamazoo, 6–10 May 2004; The *pauperes* and the fall of Jerusalem 15 July 1099, at: IMC Leeds, 12–15 July 2004; Peter Bartholomew, visions and the First Crusade, at: Ecclesiastical History Society Conference, Liverpool, 21–24 July 2004; Class – the evolution of the term and concept, at: Social History Society Conference, Dublin, 7–9 January 2005; Marxism and the First Crusade, at: London Socialist Historians' Seminar, Institute of Historical Research, London, 13 March 2006; The revival of the *ecclesia primitiva* in the *Historia Hierosolymitana* of Baldric of Dol, at: Ecclesiastical History Society Conference, Cardiff Univ., 20 July 2006.

LAPINE, Elizabeth, La représentation de la bataille d'Antioche (1098) sur les peintures murales de Poncé-sur-le-Loir, at: Strangers, Foreigners and Others, International Medieval Society, Paris, 30 June 2006; References to Maccabees in Guibert of Nogent's *Gesta Dei per Francos* and other sources of the First Crusade, at: Humboldt-Univ., Berlin, 14 May 2007; *Macabruns et Judas*: the uses of the Books of Maccabees in crusading sources, at: Aktuelle Forschungsprobleme des Mittelalters und der Frühen Neuzeit, Univ. Bielefeld, 21 June 2007.

LIGATO, Giuseppe, I crociati e il mare: ericoli, emozioni e impressioni nelle memorie di Giovanni de Joinville, at: Genova, Columbus and the Mediterranean, Congress of the Mediterranean Studies Association, Univ. of Kansas, Genoa, 24–27 May 2006; L'ordine del Santo Sepolcro: il mito delle origine, in: La civiltà cavalleresca e l'Europa, at: Convegno internazionale del Centro Europeo di Studi sulla Civiltà Cavalleresca, S. Gimignano, 3–4 June 2006; Il diario di pellegrinaggio del notaio Nicola de Martoni (fine secolo XIV), in: Il nuovo viaggio in Terra Santa fra basso medioevo e prima età moderna: curiosità inedite, prime suggestioni esotiche, annunci di orientalismo, at: X Seminario organizzato del Centro Internazionale di studi La *Gerusalemme* di San Vivaldo di Montaione, 4–6 July 2006; Memorie storico-epiche della guerra santa e della crociata lungo la Via Francigena fra il Po e il Ticino, at: Epica, storia, arte nelle vicende della Lomellina e di Mortara, tappa della Via Francigena, narrate da Francesco Pezza, Atti della giornata di studio, Mortara, 11 November 2006; Francescani e domenicani animatori del movimento crociato: le origini (sec. XIII), in: San Giacomo della Marca e l'altra Europa: Crociata, martirio e predicazione nel mondo del Mediterraneo Orientale, Monteprandone, 24–25 November 2006.

MADDEN, Thomas F., Remembering the conquest of Constantinople in 1204: then and now, at: Center for Medieval and Renaissance Studies, Ohio State Univ., 4 November 2005; Memory and the crusader conquest of Constantinople in 1204, at: Crusades: Medieval Worlds in Conflict, Saint Louis Univ., 18 Februar 2006, Dept. of History, North Carolina State Univ., 24 March 2006; The crusades: then and now, at: The Center for the Humanities, Univ. of Missouri, 3 April 2006; The crusades in Western eyes: then and today, at: The Institute of Humanities, John Carroll Univ., 27 March 2006.

MARVIN, Laurence W., The logistics of the Albigensian crusade, at: Crusades: Medieval Worlds in Conflict, Saint Louis, 18 February 2006.

MENACHE, Sophia, Historiographical challenges in writing a papal biography at the early Avignon period: Clement V, at: Medieval Academy of America, Boston, 2006; Methodological problems in 14th-century chronicles: between text and context, at: Homo Legens, International Program for Advanced Studies, Paris, 2006.

MITCHELL, Piers, Attitudes to the cause of disease in the crusades, at: Society for the Social History of Medicine, Warwick, 28–30 June 2006; Trauma in the crusader period inhabitants of Caesarea: a port city of the medieval eastern Mediterranean, at: European Conference of the Palaeopathology Association, Santorini, 28–31 August 2006; Combining palaeopathological and historical evidence for the health in the crusades, at: Conference of the British Association for Biological Anthropology and Osteoarchaeology, Birmingham, 15–17 September 2006.

MOLIN, Kristian, The military orders and the chronicle of Morea, at: MO4.

MOURAD, Suleiman Ali, Religious propaganda in the service of a monarch: Ibn ʿAsakir, Nur al-Din, and the Muslim counter-crusade, at: IMC Leeds, 10–13 July 2006.

MURRAY, Alan V., Women behaving badly? Sex and violence in the First Crusade, at: CEM-Seminar, London, 4 December 2006.

NAUS, James, The Third Crusade and the development of European extra-regional identities, at: Crusades: Medieval Worlds in Conflict, Saint Louis Univ., February 2006; Frankish identity in the army of the First Crusade, at: Crusades Studies Forum, Saint Louis Univ., September 2006; Group identity in 12th-century crusade narrative, at: 45th Annual Midwest Medieval History Conference, Evansville, IN, October 2006.

NICHOLSON, Helen J., 'Promisit succurrere Terre Sancte pro posse suo': allusions to the crusades during the trial of the Templars in the British Isles, 1309–11, at: Univ. of Reading Graduate Centre for Medieval Studies Summer Symposium, 29 June 2005.

NICOLAOU-KONNARI, Cypriots of the diaspora: the case of the Nores family in Italy, at: La Serenissima and La Nobilissima: Venice in Cyprus and Cyprus in Venice, Nicosia, 21 October 2006 [Greek].

NIELEN, Marie-Adélaïde, Guillaume de Tibériade: un itinéraire en Orient, at: Séminaire de Christoph Picard, 13 January 2006.

NIELSEN, Torben Kjersgaard, The cartoon controversy – some personal statements, at: The Cartoon Controversy, Aalborg Univ., 28 February 2006; Cultural encounters, categories and typologies, at: Medieval Cultural Encounters in the Baltic Region – Revisiting the Written

Evidence, Aalborg Univ., 8 March 2006; Kaupo the Warrior – a bloody history of crusades and cultural encounters in the 13th century, at: Institute Day, JHIS, Aalborg Univ., 16 June 2006; Henry of Livonia and violence, at: IMC Leeds, 11 July 2006, Daily Life and Violence, Nordic Centre for Medieval Studies, Tampere, 22–23 November 2006; Identities in the making? Crusading writers wrestling with 'the Other', at: Regional and European Identities in the Medieval Baltic Sea Region, Tallinn, 5 August 2006.

OMRAN, Mahmoud Said, The uprising of Damascus against the Mongols in 1260 and its effect on the battle of Ain-Jalud; Al-Muazza, Ayubite king of Damascus, and the Fifth Crusade 1218–1221, both papers at: Damascus in History, Damscus Univ., 20–24 November 2006.

PERRA, Photeine V., The Venetian presence in the Helladic areas (17th–18th centuries): the case of Donato Michiel based on three manuscripts of the Canadian McGill Univ. collection, at: 28th Panhellenic Historical Congress, Thessaloniki, 26–28 May 2006; Relations between Hospitaller Knights of Rhodes and Venice during the first Venetian-Ottoman war 1463–1479, at: 29th Panhellenic Historical Congress.

PIANA, Mathias, Zur Wasserversorgung der Kreuzfahrerburgen, at: Wasserversorgung auf Burgen des Mittelalters, Internationales Frontinus-Symposium, Burg Blankenheim/Eifel, 6–9 October 2005; From Tripoli to Tyre: Urban layout and fortification of the Levantine coastal towns in the Middle Ages, at: Castles and Towns of the Crusader Period in the Eastern Mediterranean, Marksburg/Braubach, 27–29 January 2006; From Montpèlerin to Ṭarābulus al-Mustajaddā – The Frankish-Mamluk Succession in Old Tripoli, at: 15th HES, Leuven, 17–19 May 2006; Frühe Zwinger und Vorbefestigungen an Burgen der Kreuzfahrerzeit, at: Zwinger und Vorbefestigungen, Kolloquium der Deutschen Burgenvereinigung, Schloß Neuenburg bei Freyburg/Unstrut, 10–12 November 2006.

POWELL, James M., Church and crusade: Frederick II and Louis IX, at: American Catholic Historical Association, Atlanta, 2007.

PRYOR, John H., The chain of the Golden Horn, at: SSCLE Istanbul, 5–7 July 2004; The logistics of the siege of Acre, 1189–91, at: IMC Leeds, July 2007.

PURKIS, William J., Pope Calixtus II, the *Historia Turpini*, and the origins of crusading in Spain, at: IMC Kalamazoo, 6 May 2006; Rediscovering reconquest: the impact of crusading ideology on Christian-Muslim relations in Iberia, c.1100–c.1150, at: 75th Anglo-American Conference: Religion and Politics, Institute of Historical Research, London, 6 July 2006; Memories and strategies: inventing a crusading past for 12th-century Spain, at: Collective Memory and the Uses of the Past: An Interdisciplinary Conference, Univ. of East Anglia, Norwich, 7 July 2006.

RACINE, Pierre, Venise et son arrière pays à l'époque de la 4ème croisade, at: SSCLE Istanbul, 5–7 July 2004.

ROCHE, Jason T., Conrad III and the Greek sources for the Second Crusade: errors, omissions and flawed assumptions, at: IMC Leeds, July 2005; "Manganeous Prodromos" as a source for the Second Crusade, at: IMC Leeds, July 2006.

RODRÍGUEZ GARCÍA, José Manuel, Imagen gestos de la Orden Teutónica y las otras órdenes militares en Alemania, at: Curso el Cister y las Órdenes Militares, Fitero (Navarra), August 2006; El arte de la guerra y la Orden del Temple, at: UNED, Segovia, October 2006.

ROLL, Israel, Early Islamic bazaar and crusader castle uncovered at Apollonia-Arsuf, at: Castles and Towns of the Crusader Period in the Eastern Mediterranean, Marksburg/Braubach, 27–29 January 2006;

RUBENSTEIN, Jay, Jerusalem, the First Crusade, and the right of leadership, at: Sewanee Medieval Colloquium, 8 April 2006; Aftermath and disillusionment: When did Europe turn against the First Crusade?, at: Univ. of York, 11 December 2006.

RYAN, James D., moderator at: The Crusades: Myth and Reality, San Francisco, 23–24 February 2007.

RYAN, Vincent, Marian patronage and the Fourth Crusade, at: IMC Kalamazoo, May 2006.

SCHABEL, Christopher, The Ravennica agreement and the Greek clergy in early Frankish Greece, at: DEM.

SCHRYVER, James G., Cyprus at the crossroads: understanding the paths taken in the art and architecture of Frankish Cyprus, at: POCA, Trinity College Dublin, 22 October 2005; The many layers of Hugh IV's brass basin, at: IMC Kalamazoo, 5 May 2006; The relationship of urban center and rural countryside in Frankish Cyprus, at: ASOR Annual Meeting, Washington/DC, 16 December 2006.

SHAGRIR, Iris, The evolution of by-naming in the Latin kingdom of Jerusalem and the Norman kingdom in Italy – an interim report, at: CNRS, Paris, December 2005; Looking through liturgy: ritual, audience and space in the crusader church of the Holy Sepulchre, at: Art, Liturgy, and Religious Cult in Late Antiquity and the Middle Ages, Israel Science Foundation and Dept. of the Arts, Ben Gurion Univ. of the Negev, Beer Sheva, June 2006; The *Visitatio Sepulchri* at the Crusader Holy Sepulchre Church in Jerusalem, at: IMC Leeds, July 2006.

SIDSELRUD, Kaare Seeberg, Ecclesiastical heraldry, at: The Norwegian Heraldry Society.

STRUCKMEYER, Myra, The Hospital of St John and its *cura monialium*, at: CLE-Seminar, Easter term 2006.

THORAU, Peter, Jordanien im Mittelalter: Kreuzfahrer, Ayyubiden und Mamluken, at: Jordanien: Faszination einer 4.000-jährigen Kulturlandschaft, Sonderausstellung Bagdad- und Hedjazbahn, Nürnberg, 11 October 2003; Die islamische Welt am Vorabend der Kreuzzüge, at: Saladin und die Kreuzfahrer, Oldenburg, 27 April 2006.

TOKO, Hirofumi, A spiritual father-son relationship in the Stoudios monastery: Symeon the New Theologian (949–1022), at: 48th Annual Conference of the Society for Near Eastern Studies in Japan, Waseda Univ., Tokyo, 29 October 2006.

4. Forthcoming publications

ALLEN, David Frank, The Hospitaller Castiglione's Catholic Synthesis of Warfare, Learning and Lay Piety on the Eve of the Council of Trent, in: HME.

ATTA, Zubaida, with Taef el-Azhari, The Career of Balak the Artukid, in: Univ. of Szeged, Chronica 7 (2007).

EL-AZHARI, Taef, with Zubaida Atta, The Career of Balak the Artukid, in: Univ. of Szeged, Chronica 7 (2007).

BALARD, Michel, Bilan de la recherche sur les ordres militaires en France, in: As Ordens militares e as Ordens de cavalaria entre o Occidente e o Oriente, Actas do V Encontro sobre Ordens Militares, Palmela, 15 a 18 Fevereiro 2006 (January 2008); Tradition et innovation: l'exemple du notariat médiéval italien, discours inaugural du 131e Congrès des Sociétés savantes (Grenoble, avril 2006); Les relations économiques entre l'Occident et le monde islamique à la fin du Moyen Age: Quelques remarques, in: XXXVIII Settimana di Studi Relazioni economiche tra Europa e mondo islamico. Secc. XIII–XVIII (Prato, mai 2006); La Masseria génoise de Famagouste, in: DEM.

BALIVET, Michel, Elites byzantines, latines et musulmanes: Quelques exemples de diplomatie personnalisée (Xe–XVe siècles), in: DEM.

BALLETTO, Laura, Genova e il Mediterraneo orientale nel tardo medioevo, in: Memorie dell'Accademia Lunigianese di Scienze Giovanni Capellini (La Spezia, 2006).

BARQUERO GOÑI, Carlos, Los Hospitalarios y los últimos reyes de Navarra (1483–1512), in: HME.

BELLOMO, Elena, The Templar Order in North-west Italy (1142–c.1370), "Medieval Mediterranean" (Brill, autumn 2007); New Latin edition and translation into Italian of Caffaro, *Ystoria captionis Almarie et Turtuose, De liberatione civitatum Orientis Liber* and *anonymous Regni Ierosolimitani brevis hystoria*, in Caffaro, *Opere*, in collaboration with Antonio Placanica, Edizione Nazionale dei Testi Mediolatini, Società Internazionale per lo Studio del Medioevo Latino (SISMEL) [winter 2007–2008]; The First Crusade and the Latin East seen from Venice: the Account of the *Translatio sancti Nicolai*, Early Medieval Europe; L'Ordine del Tempio in Italia nord-occidentale (1142–1308): problemi, riflessioni e nuovi indirizzi di ricerca, in: I Templari in Italia, ed. C. Guzzo [2007].

BEREND, Nora, Christianization and the Rise of Christian Monarchy: Central Europe, Scandinavia and Russia, c. 900–c. 1200 (Cambridge UP, October 2007).

BLIZNYUK, Svetlana, Diplomatic Relations between Cyprus and Genoa in the Light of the Genoese Juridical Documents: ASG, Diversorum Communis Ianue, 1375–1480, in: DEM.

BOLTON, Brenda, A Matter of Great Confusion: King Richard I and Syria's *Vetus de Monte*, in: DEM.

BOMBI, Barbara, *Novella plantatio fidei*: missione and crociata nel nord Europa tra XII e XIII secolo, Nuovi studi storici, Istituto Storico Italiano per il Medio Evo, Roma 2007; The *Dialogus miraculorum* of Caesarius of Heisterbach as a Source for the Livonian Crusade, in: Power and Authority, ed. Brenda Bolton and C. M. Meek (Turnhout: Brepols, 2007); An Archival Network: the Teutonic Knights in the 13th and 14th Centuries, in: Proceedings of the Anglo-Scandinavian Conference, Studies in Church History, Subsidies.

BONNEAUD, Pierre, La règle de l'*ancianitas* dans l'ordre de l'hôpital, le prieuré de Catalogne et la *Castellania de Amposta* aux XIVe et XVe siècles, in: HME; articles for DOMMA.

BORCHARDT, Karl, co-ed. with Nikolas Jaspert and Helen Nicholson, HME; Documents from the Hospitaller Registers on Rhodes Concerning Cyprus, 1409–1459: Form and Contents, in: DEM; entries for DOMMA.

BRONSTEIN, Judith, Caring for the Sick or Dying for the Cross? The Granting of Crusade Indulgences to the Hospitallers, in: HME; The Crusades and the Jews: Some Reflections on the Latest Historiography of the 1096 Massacre, in: History Compass (2007); The Decree of 1262: a Glimpse into Economic Decision-Making of the Hospitallers, in: MO3.

BURGTORF, Jochen, A Mediterranean Career in the Late 13th Century: the Hospitaller Grand Commander Boniface of Calamandrana, in: HME.

BURNS, Robert I., Diplomatarium of the Crusader Kingdom of Valencia: The Registered Charters of the Conqueror James I, 1257–1276, vol. 4 (Princeton UP, 2006); no. 5 will be the final volume.

CARR, Annemarie Weyl, Perspectives on Visual Culture in Early Lusignan Cyprus: Balancing Art and Archaeology, in: Archaeology and the Crusades: Proceedings of the Round Table, Nicosia, 1 February 2005, ed. Peter W. Edbury, Sophia Kalopissi-Verti (Athens: Pierides Foundation, 2007).

CARRAZ, Damien, La justice du commandeur (Bas-Rhône, XIIIe siècle), in: Les justices d'Église, Cahiers de Fanjeaux 42 (2007), 241–266; entries for DOMMA; L'ordre du Temple dans la Provence du XIIe siècle: l'ambiguïté d'une nouvelle expérience spirituelle à l'âge des réformes, in: Monachisme et réformes dans la vallée du Rhône (XIe–XIIIe s.), 7e journée d'études du Centre d'Études d'Histoire religieuse Méridionale, Saint-Michel de Frigolet, 18 novembre 2006 (autumn-winter 2007); *Christi fideliter militantium in subsidio Terre Sancte*: Les ordres militaires et la première maison d'Anjou (1246–1342), in: As Ordens Militares e as Ordens de Cavalaria entre o Occidente e o Oriente, Actas do V Encontro sobre Ordens Militares, Palmela, 15 a 18 de fevereiro 2006 (January 2008); *Causa defendende et extollende christianitatis*: la vocation maritime des ordres militaires en Provence (XIIe–XIIIe siècle), in: Les ordres militaires et la mer, 130e Congrès national des sociétés historiques et scientifiques, La Rochelle, 21 avril 2005 (Paris: CTHS); Military Orders and the Town (12th to Early 14th Centuries): the Urban Commanderies Case in the Lower Rhône River Valley, in: Univ. of Szeged, Chronica 6; L'emprise territoriale de la seigneurie monastique: les commanderies provençales du Temple (XIIe–XIIIe siècle), in: Les pouvoirs territoriaux en Italie centrale et dans le Sud de la France: hiérarchies, institutions et languages (12e–14e siècles): études comparées, Actes de la table-ronde de Chambéry, 4 mai 2007, Mélanges de l'École française de Rome – Moyen Âge – Temps modernes.

CASSIDY-WELCH, Megan, Frightful Abodes of Misery: A Cultural History of the Medieval Prison (Pennsylvania UP, under consideration) 300pp.; Practices of Gender in Late Medieval and Early Modern Europe (Turnhout: Brepols, 2007), 250pp.; Grief and Memory from Agincourt to the Treaty of Troyes, 1415–1420, in: Andrew Villalon, Donald Kagay (ed.), New Perspectives on the Hundred Years War (Leiden: Brill, 2007).

CHRISTIE, Niall G. F., Motivating Listeners in the *Kitab al-Jihad* of ʿAli ibn Tahir al-Sulami (d. 1106), in: Crusades 6 (2007); A Rental Document from 8th/14th-Century Egypt, in: Journal of the American Research Center in Egypt.

CLAVERIE, Pierre-Vincent, La perception des musulmans dans l'œuvre d'Héthoum de Korykos, in: HES 5, ed. Urbain Vermeulen (Louvain 2007); Notes sur le mort de saint Louis et les finalités de sa croisade, in: ibid.; Les remembrements épiscopaux dans la Syrie franque, in: L'espace du diocèse à l'époque médiévale, ed. F. Mazel (Rennes: Presses Univ., 2007); L'image de l'islam dans les traductions vernaculaires de Guillaume de Tyr, in: *Festschrift* for Prof. Dr. Urbain Vermeulen: Traditions and Changes in the Realms of Islam, ed. A. van Tongerloo (Louvain: Peeters, 2007).

COBB, Paul M., Islam and the Crusades: The Writings of Usama ibn Munqidh (Penguin Classics, June 2008); Enemies of God: An Islamic History of the Crusades (Oxford: OUP, 2010).

COUREAS, Nicholas, The Migration of Syrians and Cypriots to Hospitaller Rhodes in the 14th and 15th Centuries, in: HME; The Role of Cyprus in Provisioning the Latin Churches of the Holy Land in the 13th and early 14th Centuries, in: HES 5, Proceedings of the 11th, 12th and 13th HES, ed. Urbain Vermeulen and J. van Steenbergen (Leuven: Peeters, 2006); Commercial Relations between Cyprus and Mamluk Egypt and Syria with Special Reference to Famagusta and Nicosia in the 15th and 16th Centuries in: ibid; The Copts in Cyprus during the 15th and 16th Centuries, in: ibid; Commerce between Mamluk Egypt and Hospitaller Rhodes in the mid-15th Century: the Case of Sidi Galip Ripolli, in: ibid, 14th HES, May 2005; A Political History of Nicosia, in: A History of Nicosia, ed D. Michaelides (Nicosia: Mesogeios, 2006); An Ecclesiastical History of Nicosia, in: ibid; Trade between Cyprus and Aragonese Sicily in the late 13th and 14th Centuries in: CRC Annual Review 32 (2006); Mamluks in the Cypriot Chronicle of George Boustronios and their Place within a Wider Context, in: *Festschrift* in honour of Prof. Urbain Vermeulen, Catholic University of Leuven

(Leuven, 2006); Concluding Remarks, in: Archaeology and the Crusades: Proceedings of the Round Table, Nicosia, 1 February 2005, ed. Peter W. Edbury, Sophia Kalopissi-Verti (Athens: Pierides Foundation, 2007); The Structure and Content of the Notarial Deeds of Lamberto di Sambuceto and Giovanni da Rocha, 1296–1310, in: DEM.

CRAWFORD, Paul F., The Trial of the Templars and the University of Paris, in: MO3; Crusades; Hospitallers; Templars; Children's Crusade; Military Religious Orders, in: New Westminster Dictionary of Church History, ed. Christopher Ocker et al. (Westminster: John Knox Press, 2007).

DANSETTE, Béatrice, Ordres religieux militaires et pèlerins occidentaux en Terre Sainte au XIIe siècle, in: DOMMA.

DICKSON, Gary, The Children's Crusade: Medieval History, Modern Mythistory (Palgrave-MacMillan, 2007).

DONDI, Cristina, Liturgy, in: DOMMA; Gerusalemme e gli ordini militari: liturgia e canto, in: Rivista internazionale di musica sacra, ed. Giacomo Baroffo (Lucca: Libreria Musicale Italiana, 2007).

DODD, Erica Cruikshank, Jerusalem: Fons et Origo – Sources in Outremer for the Development of Western Medieval Art, in: Interactions: Artistic Interchange between the Eastern and the Western Worlds in the Medieval Period, ed. Colum Hourihanc, Princeton Index of Christian Art (Princeton NJ).

DOUROU-ELIOPOULOU, Maria, Latin settlement (Franks, Catalans and Italians) in the Byzantine Empire (Romania) after the Fourth Crusade, in: The Mediterranean: History, Culture, Civilization (European Masters in Mediterranean Historical Studies).

DUBA, William O., The Status of the Patriarch of Constantinople in Papal Letters, in: DEM.

EDBURY, Peter W., The Old French William of Tyre, the Templars and the Assassin Envoy, in: HME; The French Translation of William of Tyre's Historia: the Manuscript Tradition, in: Crusades 6 (2007); Crusader Sources from the Near East (1099–1204), in: Byzantium and the Crusades: The Non-Greek Sources (1025–1204), Proceedings of the British Academy 132, 23–38; The Old French William of Tyre and the Origins of the Templars, in: Knighthoods 151–164; A New Text of the Annales de Terre Sainte, in: ILH; ed. with Sophia Kalopissi-Verti, Archaeology and the Crusades: Proceedings of the Round Table, Nicosia, 1 February 2005 (Athens: Pierides Foundation, 2007), xviii+209pp.; The Crusades and their Critics, in: ibid. 179–194; Ramla: the Crusader Town and Lordship (1099–1268), in: Essays on Ramla, ed. Denys Pringle; British Historiography on the Crusades and Military Orders: from Barker and Smail to Contemporary Historians, in: Runciman-Conference; 1191: Conquest, Continuity and Change, in: a collection, ed. Anna Marangou (Athens: Kotinos); Celestine III, the Crusade and the Latin East, in: Essays on Celestine III, ed. Brenda Bolton and Damian Smith; articles for DOMMA.

EDGINGTON, Susan B., with C. Sweetenham, La Chanson d'Antioche, transl. and commentary; see also Bulletin 26 (2006).

EGGER, Christoph, The Problem of Papal Authority as Reflected in Papal Letters, in: DEM.

EHLERS, Axel, Die Ablaßpraxis des Deutschen Ordens im Mittelalter, Quellen und Studien zur Geschichte des Deutschen Ordens im Mittelalter 64 (Marburg: Elwert, 2007).

EKDAHL, Sven, Tannenberg (bataille de), in: DOMMA.

EPSTEIN, Steven, Purity Lost: Transgressing Boundaries in the Eastern Mediterranean, 1000–1400 (Johns Hopkins UP, 2007).

FAVREAU-LILIE, Die Wahrnehmung des Vierten Kreuzzugs außerhalb Venedigs: Perspektiven der Geschichtsschreibung im 13. Jahrhundert, in: The Fourth Crusade Revisited: Papers of the International Conference on the Fourth Crusade, Andros, 27-30 May 2004, ed. E. Chrysos, Otto Kresten, Walter Brandmüller, suppl. vol. of Annuarium Historiae Pontificiae (2007).

FOLDA, Jaroslav, Crusader Art and the East: Eurasian Contacts, in: Cultural Interactions at the Index of Christian Art (Princeton UP).

FOREY, Alan, Judicial Processes in the Military Orders: the Use of Imprisonment and Chaining, in: HME; Henry II's Crusading Penances for Becket's Murder, in: Crusades 7 (2008).

FRIEDMAN, Yvonne, Gestures of Conciliation: Peacemaking Endeavours in the Latin East, in: ILH; Charity Begins at Home? Ransoming Captives in Jewish, Christian and Muslim Tradition, in: Studia Hebraica 6 (2007); Christian-Muslim Peacemaking in the Medieval Latin East, in: Peace, War and Violence, ed. Jost Duellfer, Robert Frank (Berghan Publishers, 2007).

GABRIELE, Matthew, The Legend of Charlemagne and the Origins of the First Crusade: Preliminary Thoughts (under consideration).

GAPOSCHKIN, Cecilia, The Making of Saint Louis (IX): Kingship, Sanctity and Crusade in the later Middle Ages (Cornell UP).

GARCÍA-GUIJARRO RAMOS, Luis, The Valencian Bailiwick of Cervera in Hospitaller and Early Montesian Times, ca. 1230–ca. 1330, in: HME.

GASPARIS, Charalambos, *Catastica Feudorum Crete*: Landownership and Political Changes in Medieval Crete (13th–15th Centuries), in: DEM.

GERVERS, Michael, with Nicole Hamonic, Scribes and Notaries in 12th- and 13th-Century Hospitaller Charters from England, in: HME.

VON GUTTNER-SPORZYNSKI, Darius, The Crusades: Beyond a Definition, in: Proceedings of the Polish Czech Medievalists Forum, Gniezno, 26–29 September 2005 (forthcoming October 2006); The Idea of Crusade and the Piasts during the First and Second Crusades, in: Proceedings of the Conference The Church in the Monarchies of the Premyslids and the Piasts, Gniezno, 21–24 September 2006 (forthcoming 2007); Did Cardinal Hubaldus Preach the Second Crusade in Poland?, in: The Second Crusade in Perspective, II: Eastern Europe and the March towards the Holy Land, ed. Jason T. Roche, Janus Møller Jensen (October 2007); Recent Issues in Polish Historiography of the Crusades, in: MO4; Relic or relevant? The Knights of Saint John, in: Proceedings of the 15th Biennial Conference of the Australasian Association for European History, Melbourne, 11–15 July 2005, Australasian Journal of Politics and History (forthcoming October 2007).

HAMILTON, Bernard, The Templars, the Syrian Assassins and King Amalric of Jerusalem, in: HME.

HERDE, Peter, The Dispute between the Hospitalars and the Bishop of Worcester about the Church of Down Ampney: an Unpublished Letter of Justice of Pope John XXI (1276), in: HME.

HOSTEN, Jan, The Counts of Flanders and their Involvement in the Crusades [book].

HOUBEN, Hubert, Intercultural Communication: The Teutonic Knights in Palestine, Armenia, and Cyprus, in: DEM.

HOUSLEY, Norman, Emmanuele Piloti and Crusading in the Latin East, in: HME.

HUNT, Lucy-Anne, Artistic Interchange in Old Cairo in the 13th–Early 14th Century: The Role of Painted and Carved Icons, in: Colum Hourihane (ed.), Interactions: Artistic Exchange between the Eastern and Western Worlds in the Medieval Period, Proceedings of the Conference Index of Christian Art, Princeton Univ., 8–9 April 2005 (Penn State UP, 2007); Illustrating the Gospels in Arabic: Byzantine and Arab Christian Miniatures in Two Manuscripts of the early Mamluk Period in Cambridge, in: D. Thomas (ed.), The Bible in Arab Christianity, Proceedings of the 5th Woodbrooke-Mingana Symposium on Arab Christianity and Islam 14–17 September 2005 (Leiden: Brill); Eastern Christian Art and Culture in the 13th Century: Cultural Convergence between Jerusalem, Greater Syria and Egypt, in: S. Auld, R. Hillenbrand (ed.), Ayyubid Jeruslaem: The Holy City 1187–1250 (London: Altajir World of Islam Festival Trust); Oriental Orthodox Iconographical and Architectural Traditions, in: K. Parry (ed.), The Companion to Eastern Christianity (Oxford: Blackwell).

HUNYADI, Zsolt, The Military Activity of the Hospitallers in the Medieval Kingdom of Hungary (13th–14th cent.), in: HME.

JACKSON, Peter, The Seventh Crusade 1244–1254: Sources and Documents, Crusade Texts in Translation (Ashgate, 2007).

JACOBY, David, Hospitaller Ships and Transportation across the Mediterranean, in: HME; Medieval Conquest around the Eastern Mediterranean: The Impact upon Administrative and Legal Language, in: DEM.

JASPERT, Nikolas, co-ed. with Karl Borchardt and Helen Nicholson, HME.

JOTISCHKY, Andrew, The Crusades: Critical Concepts in History, 4 vols (London: Routledge, 2008) [reprinted articles and essays with an original introduction].

KALOPISSI-VERTI, Sophia, Relations between East and West in the Lordship of Athens and Thebes after 1204: Archaeological and Artistic Evidence, in: Archaeology and the Crusades: Proceedings of the Round Table, Nicosia, 1 February 2005, ed. Peter W. Edbury and id. (Athens: Pierides Foundation, 2007).

KASDAGLI, Anna-Maria, Heraldry in Medieval Rhodes: Hospitallers and Others, in: MO3; Η νομισματική κυκλοφορία στη μεσαιωνική πόλη της Ρόδου [Coin circulation within the walls of medieval Rhodes], in: 15 Years of Restoration in the Medieval town of Rhodes, Conference Acts, Ministry of Culture, 2007 [with English summary]; Funerary Monuments of Hospitaller Rhodes: an Overview, in: MO4; Ο Προμαχώνας του Αγίου Γεωργίου, το πιο εξελιγμένο οχύρωμα των Ιωαννιτών Ιπποτών στη Ρόδο [The Bastion of St. George, Most Advanced Defence of the Knights Hospitaller in Rhodes], in: Deltion of the Christian Archaeological Society; The Social Context of Gravestones: Two Portraits, in: Crusades 6 (2007); Hospitaller Rhodes: the Epigraphic Evidence (with 12 plates), in: HME; with Angeliki Katsioti and Maria Michailidou, Archaeology on Rhodes and the Knights of Saint John of Jerusalem, in: Archaeology and the Crusades: Proceedings of the Round Table, Nicosia, 1 February 2005, ed. Peter W. Edbury, Sophia Kalopissi-Verti (Athens: Pierides Foundation, 2007).

KEDAR, Benjamin Z., A Note on Jerusalem's Bīmāristān and Jerusalem's Hospital, in: HME; Religion in Catholic-Muslim Correspondence and Treaties, in: DEM; Franks, Muslims and Oriental Christians in the Latin Levant: Studies in Frontier Acculturation (Aldershot: Ashgate, 2007).

KOOL, Robert, Coin Circulation in the *villeneuves* of the Latin Kingdom of Jerusalem: the Cases of *Parva Mahumeria* and *Bethgibelin*, in: Archaeology and the Crusades: Proceedings of the Round Table, Nicosia, 1 February 2005, ed. Peter W. Edbury, Sophia Kalopissi-Verti (Athens: Pierides Foundation, 2007).

KOSTICK, Conor, The Terms *milites*, *equites* and *equestres* in the Early Crusading Histories, in: M. Jones (ed.), Nottingham Medieval Studies (forthcoming 2006).

LAPINA, Elizabeth, La représentation de la bataille d'Antioche (1098) sur les peintures murales de Poncé-sur-le-Loir, in: Cahiers de Civilisation Médiévale; *Nec signis nec testibus creditur*: the Problem of Eyewitnesses in the Chronicles of the First Crusade, in: Viator: Medieval and Renaissance Studies 38 (2007), 1–23.

LIGATO, Giuseppe, La cattura di Guido di Lusignano e della reliquia della Vera Croce ad Hattin (4 luglio 1187) in una miniatura dei "Chronica majora" di Matteo Paris: una combinazione di testo, immagine e propaganda, in: Le reliquie tra storia e attualità, Atti del convegno Venezia, 30 marzo 2006, Studi ecumenici (2007).

LOUD, Graham A., The Latin Church in Norman Italy (Cambridge UP, 2007/08); Varieties of Monastic Discipline in Southern Italy during the 11th and 12th Centuries, in: Studies in Church History 43 (2007).

LOWER, Michael, Conversion and Saint Louis's Last Crusade, in: Journal of Ecclesiastical History (April 2007).

MADDEN, Thomas F., Crusades, in: The Oxford Dictionary of the Middle Ages (Oxford: OUP); Constantinople; Crusades; Venice, in: The Oxford Companion to Exploration (Oxford: OUP).

MAJOR, Balázs, The Rural Site of ʿĀsūr, in: Archaeology and the Crusades: Proceedings of the Round Table, Nicosia, 1 February 2005, ed. Peter W. Edbury, Sophia Kalopissi-Verti (Athens: Pierides Foundation, 2007).

MALLIA-MILANES, Victor, ed. MO3.

MARVIN, Laurence W., The Occitan war: A Military and Political History of the Albigensian Crusade, 1209–1218 (Cambridge: CUP, 2007).

MENACHE, Sophia, Emotions from the Holy Land: The First Crusader Kingdom, in: Runciman-Conference; Iglesia y Monarquía en la Edad Media Tardía: Conflictos y Semejanzas, in: Aragon en la Edad Media 19 (2005), ed. Luis García-Guijarro Ramos; Studium, Regnum and Sacerdotium in the Early Avignon Period: The University of Paris (Minneapolis: Minnesota UP, 2005); Medieval States and Military Orders: The Order of Calatrava in the Late Middle Ages, in: ILH; Elections in the Military Orders in the Late Middle Ages: An Achilles' Heel?, in: Analecta Torunensia 14 (2007); Orality in Chronicles: Texts and Historical Contexts, in: Odysseus: Man in History (2007 [Russian]).

MESCHINI, Marco, Innocenzo III e il «negotium pacis et fidei» in Lingudoca (1198–1215) (Roma: Accademia dei Lincei, 2007); «Pro negotio crucesignatorum»: Innocenzo III e il sostegno della guerra santa, in: Cruce de miradas sobre la guerra santa, Guerra, religion e ideología en el espacio mediterraneo latino (siglos XI–XIII), ed. Daniel Baloup, Philippe Josserand (Madrid); The "Four Crusades" of 1204, in: 6th International Congress of the SSCLE: Around the Fourth Crusade, Before and After.

MILITZER, Klaus, Grundherrschaft und Gerichtsherrschaft des Deutschen Ordens im Reich, in: Ordines militares 14 (2007); Das Problem der zwei Schwerter in der Schlacht bei Tannenberg, in: Festschrift für Hanna Vollrath (Köln, 2007), 377–387; Kreuzfahrer und Ritterorden und deren neue Waffen im Baltikum, in: Fasciculi archaeologicae historicae 18/20 (Łódź, 2008).

MITCHELL, Piers, with Y. Trepper, Intestinal Parasitic Worm Eggs from a Crusader Period Latrine in the City of Acre (Israel), in: Levant; with J. Huntley, E. Stern, Bioarchaeological Analysis of the 13th Century Latrines of the Crusader Hospital of St. John at Acre, Israel, in:

MO3; Disease; War Jnjuries, in: EncycCru; Military Medicine, in: Oxford Dictionary of the Middle Ages, ed. R. E. Bjork (Oxford: OUP); Combining Palaeopathological and Historical Evidence for Health in the Crusades, in: Proceedings of the 8th Conference of the British Association for Biological Anthropology and Osteoarchaeology, ed. M. Smith, M. Brickley (Oxford: Archaeopress); Challenges in the Study of Health and Disease in the Crusades, in: Diachronic Patterns in the Biology and Health Status of Human Populations of the Eastern Mediterranean, ed. M. Faerman (Oxford: Oxbow books); Contrasts in the Standard of Health in Different Communities in the Medieval Kingdom of Jerusalem, in: MO4; The Spread of Disease with the Crusades, in: Between Text and Patient: The Medical Enterprise in Medieval and Early Modern Europe, ed. B. Nance, E. F. Glaze (Leiden: Brill).

MOL, Johannes A., Friesland under the Teutonic Order? A Fantastic Plan from 1517 by Grand Master Albrecht of Brandenburg-Ansbach, in: HME.

MOLIN, Kristian, Castles Belonging to the Teutonic Knights in Cilician Armenia: a Reappraisal, in: MO3.

MOURAD, Suleiman Ali, with James E. Lindsay, Rescuing Syria from the Infidels: the Contribution of Ibn ʿAsakir of Damascus to the Jihad Campaign of Sultan Nur al-Din, in: Crusades 6 (2007).

MURRAY, Alan V., Finance and Logistics of the Crusade of Frederick Barbarossa, in: ILH; The Capture of Jerusalem in Western Narrative Sources of the First Crusade, in: Jerusalem the Golden: The Conquest of the Dream (From the West to the Holy Land), ed. Luis García-Guijarro (forthcoming 2007); The Origin of Money-Fiefs in the Latin Kingdom of Jerusalem, in: Mercenaries and Paid Men, ed. John France (forthcoming).

NICHOLSON, Helen, co-ed. with Karl Borchardt and Nikolas Jaspert, HME; The Testimony of Henry Danet and the Trial of the Templars in Ireland, in: ILH; Aimery de Saint-Maur; amour courtois; Brian le Jay; chasteté; Clontarf; critiques; Dinsley; Eagle; enfant; femme; Garway; Gautier Map; Geoffroy le Templier; Graal; Henri II, roi d'Angleterre; Henri III, roi d'Angleterre; Henri Danet; Irlande; marriage; Matthieu Paris; Osto de Saint-Omer; Pays de Galles; Peter Holt; pouvoir princier; Richard Cœur de Lion; representations; sexe; Slebech; sœur; Stephen de Fulbourn; Walter le Bachelor; Yspytty Ifan, in: DOMMA.

NICOLAOU-KONNARI, ed., Acts of the Conference La Serenissima and La Nobilissima: Venice in Cyprus and Cyprus in Venice, Nicosia, 21 October 2006 (Nicosia, 2007); Pietro and Giorgio de Nores and the Treatise 'Della legittima successione al regno di Cypro', edition with introduction, comments, and appendices (Nicosia: Cyprus Research Centre, 2007); The Use of Documents in the Chronicle of Leontios Makhairas: Diplomatics and Historiography, in: DEM.

NICOLLE, David, Atlas of the Ottoman Empire (Thalamus, 2007), The Scandinavian Baltic Crusades (Osprey 2007); Byzantine, Western European, Islamic and Central Asian Influence in the Field of Arms and Armour from the 7th to 14th century AD, in: Proceedings of the Conference at Cambridge University, 2004 (2007); Crusader Castles in Cyprus, Greece, the Aegean & Black Seas 1191–1522 AD (Osprey 2007); Equipement; Armament; Archers; Banniere; Escadron; Pietons, in: DOMMA; ʿAyn Jalut; al-Mansura 1221; al-Mansura 1250; Armies Muslim; Arms and Armour; Lake Peipus 1242; Siege Warfare; Warfare in Greece; Warfare in Iberia, in: EncycCru; L'équipement militaire des chevaliers, in: Histoire et Images Medievales Hors Series (2007); Warfare in the World of Crusade and Jihad, two vols. (Hambledon, 2007); Late Mamluk & Early Ottoman Military Equipment in the Light of Finds from the Citadel of Damascus (Damascus: Institut Français du Proche Orient, 2007); Archery, in: EI[3].

NIELEN, Marie-Adélaïde, Le Lignage d'Ibelin; Les Sceaux des Ordres militaires, in: DOMMA.

NIELSEN, Torben Kjersgaard, Celestine III and the North, in: Celestine III: The Light of Experience, ed. Damian Smith, Anne Duggan, John Doran (2007); Sterile Monsters? Russians and the Orthodox Church in the Chronicle of Henry of Livonia, in: Clashes of Culture on the Baltic Frontier, ed. Alan V. Murray (Ashgate, 2007).

O'MALLEY, Gregory, British and Irish Visitors to and Residents in Rhodes, 1409–1522, in: HME.

OTTEN-FROUX, Catherine, La curia du capitaine génois de Famagouste au milieu du XVe siècle, in: DEM.

PAHLITZSCH, Johannes, Mamluk Documents from the Archive of the Greek Orthodox Patriarchate of Jerusalem, in: DEM.

PARANI, Maria G., ed. with Alexander Beihammer and Christopher Schabel, DEM; Intercultural Exchange in the Field of Material Culture in the Eastern Mediterranean: The Evidence of Byzantine Legal Documents (11th to 15th Centuries), in: ibid.

PAVIOT, Jacques, Noblesse et croisade à la fin du Moyen Âge, in: Cahiers de Recherches Médiévales (2006); Projets de croisade (v.1290–v.1330), Documents relatifs à l'histoire des croisades publiés par l'Académie des Inscriptions et Belles-Lettres 20 (Paris, 2007); ed. with Philippe Contamine, Philippe de Mézières, Epistre lamentable et consolatoire sur le fait de la desconfiture de Hongrie [Nicopolis] (Paris: Société de l'histoire de France).

PERRA, Photeine V., Caroldo, Gian-Giacomo; Charles I of Anjou; Charles of Valois; Chortatzes House (with A. Savvides); Cornaro Catherine; Cyriacus of Ancona (with Alexios G. C. Savvides); Epirus State; Faber Felix; Falier Marino; Foscari Venetian family; Frederick II of Hohenstaufen; Giustiniani family; Hospitaller Knights; Hugh de Lusignan; Hunyadi Janos; John I Doukas Angelos of Thessaly; John II Doukas Angelos of Thessaly; John of Brienne, in: Encyclopedic Prosopographical Lexicon of Byzantine History and Civilization, vol. 2, 3 (Turnhout:, Brepols); Ζακκαρία γενουατικός οίκος, Ζόρζι Ντολφίν, Ηπείρου αυτόνομο κράτος, Θεόδωρος Κομνηνός Δούκας (Άγγελος), Θεσσαλίας κράτος, Θωμάς Κομνηνός Δούκας, Θωμάς Μοροζίνι, Ιωάννης Κομνηνός Α΄, Ιωάννης Κομνηνός Β΄, Ιωάννης Κομνηνός Γ΄, Ιωάννης Κομνηνός Δ΄ in: ibid., Greek edition, vol. 7 (Athens: Metron/Iolkos Publications); Εφημερίς της Κορίνθου, Κορινθιακή Ηχώ, Κορινθία, Νέα Κόρινθος, Σημαία της Κορινθίας, Τύπος της Αργολιδοκορινθίας, Κωστάρας Βασίλης, Σκουτέρης Χρ. Γεώργιος, in: Encyclopaedia of New Hellenic Press 1784–1996 (Athens, N.R.F.); The Venetian Presence in Helladic Areas (17th–18th cent.): the Case of Donato Michiel based on three Manuscripts of the Canadian McGill University Collection, in: Prakt. 28th Panhellenic Historical Congress, Thessaloniki 26–28 May 2006; A Contribution to Medieval and Postmedieval Corinthian Bibliography (A.D. 324–1715), in: Istorikogeographika 11; The Transition from Hospitaller to Ottoman Rhodes: a Note on the Information by Piri Reis and Ewliya Chelebi, in: Byzantinos Domos 16 (2007).

PHILLIPS, Jonathan, The Second Crusade: Extending the Frontiers of Christianity (Yale UP).

PIANA, Mathias, ed., Burgen und Städte der Kreuzzugszeit im östlichen Mittelmeerraum (Petersberg, 2007); with Adrian Boas, Die Kreuzfahrerstadt Ascalon, in: ibid.; Die Templerburg Chastel Blanc (Burǧ aṣ-Ṣāfītā), in: ibid.; Die Deutschordensburg Montfort (Qalʿat al-Qurʿain), in: ibid.; Die Kreuzfahrerstadt Sidon (Sagette, Ṣaidā), in: ibid.; Die Kreuzfahrerburg Toron (Qalʿat Tibnīn), in: ibid.; Die Kreuzfahrerstadt Tortosa (Ṭarṭūs), in: ibid.; Die Kreuzfahrerstadt Tripoli (Triple, Ṭarābulus), in: ibid.; with Hans Curvers, The castle of Toron (Qalʿat Tibnīn) in South Lebanon: Preliminary Results of the 2004/2006 Campaign, in: Bulletin d'Archéologie et d'Architecture Libanaises 10 (2006 [2007]).

POWELL, James M., St. Francis of Assisi's Way of Peace, in: Medieval Encounters (2007).

PRINGLE, Denys, The Churches of Crusader Acre: Destruction and Detection, in: Archaeology and the Crusades: Proceedings of the Round Table, Nicosia, 1 February 2005, ed. Peter W. Edbury, Sophia Kalopissi-Verti (Athens: Pierides Foundation, 2007).

PRYOR, John H., Soldiers of Fortune in the Fleets of Charles I of Anjou, ca 1266–1285, in: Mercenaries and Paid Men in the Middle Ages and Early Modern Period, Swansea, 7–9 July 2005, ed. John France; Shipping and Seafaring, in: The Oxford Handbook of Byzantine Studies, ed. E. M. Jeffreys, John Haldon; The 'Cargo Manifest' of a Pisan Galley, 1281, in: Festschrift for Andrew Watson, ed. Brian A. Catlos; A View from the Masthead: the First Crusade from the Sea, in: Crusades 7 (2008).

RICHARD, Jean, Aspects du notariat public à Chypre sous les Lusignan, in: DEM.

RILEY-SMITH, Jonathan, Towards a History of Military-Religious Orders, in: HME.

ROCHE, Jason T., Niketas Choniates as a Source for the Second Crusade in Anatolia, in: Festschrift in honour of Prof. Isin Demirkent (February 2007).

RODRÍGUEZ GARÍA, José Manuel, Imagen gestos de la Orden Teutónica en la zona alemana, in: Cistercium 244/45 (2007).

SARNOWSKY, Jürgen, The Convent and the West: Visitations in the Order of the Hospital of St. John in the 15th Century, in: HME.

SAVVIDES, Alexios G. C., Notes on Byzantine-Norman Relations in the Period Prior to the Norman Invasions (till A.D. 1081), in: The Ancient World, Festschrift for John Fossey (Montreal); Byzantino-Normannica: The Norman Capture of Italy (to A.D. 1081) and the First Two Norman Invasions in Byzantium (A.D. 1081–1085 and 1107–1108), Orientalia Lovaniensia Analecta 165 (Leuven: Peeters); The Empire of Trebizond and the Importance of the Study of its History: The Sources and the Diachronical Development of Research, in: Archeion Pontou 52 (Athens, 2006); Georgios Kedrenos, the Undervalued Byzantine Chronicler: a Bibliographical Note, in: Byzantiaka [Greek]; A Note on the 13th-century Byzantine Chronicler Theodore Skoutariotes, in: Byzantina [Greek]; Alexandra Stephanidou (1968–2006): Obituary, in: Byzantinos Domos 15 (2006).

SCHABEL, Christopher, ed. with Alexander Beihammer, Two Small Texts on the Wider Context of the Martyrdom of the Thirteen Monks of Kantara in Cyprus, 1231, in a festschrift; ed. with Alexander Beihammer, Maria Parani, DEM; Antelm the Nasty, First Latin Archbishop of Patras (1205–c.1241), in: ibid.

SCHREINER, Peter, Das vergessene Zypern? Das byzantinische Reich und Zypern unter den Lusignan, in: DEM.

SOLOMIDOU-IERONYMIDOU, Marina, The Crusaders, Sugar Mills and Sugar Production in Medieval Cyprus, in: Archaeology and the Crusades: Proceedings of the Round Table, Nicosia, 1 February 2005, ed. Peter W. Edbury, Sophia Kalopissi-Verti (Athens: Pierides Foundation, 2007).

SMYRLIS, Kostis, The First Ottoman Occupation of Macedonia (ca. 1383–ca. 1403): Some Remarks on Land Ownership, Property Transactions and Justice, in: DEM.

STAHL, Alan M., ed. with Pamela O. Long, David McGee, The Book of Michael of Rhodes, 3 vols. (Cambridge: MIT Press, 2007); The Sterling Abroad, in: The Haskins Society Journal (2006); The Circulation of Medieval Venetian Coinage in the Balkans, in: Coinage in the Balkans, 9th to 14th Centuries, ed. Julian Baker, Ernest Oberländer Târnoveanu (2007);

European Minting and the Balance of Payments with the Islamic World in the Later Middle Ages, in: Relazioni economiche tra Europa e mondo islamico, secc. XIII–XVIII, ed. Simonetta Cavaciocchi, Istituto Francesco Datini, Settimane di studi 37 (2007).

STUCKEY, Jace, ed. with Matthew Gabriele, The Legend of Charlemagne in the Middle Ages: Power, Faith and Crusade (New York: Palgrave Macmillan); "Imagined Crusades": Memory, Propaganda, and the Image of Charlemagne in the Era of the Crusades, in: ibid.

THORAU, Peter, Hārūn ar-Raschīd und das Reich der Abbasiden: Der Kalif aus 1001 Nacht und seine Zeit, in: Mischa Meier (ed.), Sie schufen Europa (München, 2007); Das Testament des mamlūkischen Sultans Qalāwūn und die Nachfolge des Sohnes: Dynastisches Prinzip versus »one generation nobility« in der Entstehungsphase des mamlūkischen Systems, in: Brigitte Kasten (ed.), Herrscher- und Fürstentestamente im westeuropäischen Mittelalter, Norm und Struktur (Köln – Weimar – Wien, 2007).

TOLAN, John Victor, The Vision of Islam in France in the Middle Ages, in: L'Histoire de l'islam et des musulmans en France, ed. Mohammed Arkoun (Paris: Albin Michel, 2006); with Gilles Veinstein, Henri Laurens, L'Europe et le monde musulman (Paris: Armand Colin, 2007); Los Sarracenos: el Islam en el imaginario europeo en la Edad Media (Valencia: Universitat de Valencia, 2007) [tr. Saracens: Islam in the Medieval European Imagination, New York: Columbia UP, 2002]; Saint François et le Sultan: Une recontre vue à travers huit siècles de textes et images (Paris: Le Seuil, 2007) [English version planned for 2008].

TYERMAN, Christopher, The Expansion of Europe and the Crusades, in: A Companion to the Medieval World, ed. C. Laneity, E. English (Oxford: Blackwell).

UPTON-WARD, Judith, ed. MO4.

URBAN, William, Medieval Mercenaries: the Business of War (London: Greenhill, 2006); Bayonets for Hire: the Business of War, 1550–1763 (London: Greenhill, 2007).

VANN, Theresa M., The archives and library of the Sacra Infermeria, Malta, in: The Medieval Hospital and Medical Practice, Avista Studies in the History of Medieval Technology (Aldershot: Ashgate, 2007).

WEBER, Benjamin, Papauté et croisades, XIVe–XVe siècles: bilan historiographique et perspectives de recherches, in: Actes du colloque de Toulouse (Toulouse: Méridiennes, 2007).

ZACHARIADOU, Elizabeth A., Historical Memory in an Aegean Monastery: St. John of Patmos and the Emirate of Menteshe, in: HME.

5. Work in progress

ANDREA, Alfred J., with Andrew Holt, Seven Myths about the Crusades [a popular book of about 200 pages].

ATTA, Zubaida, The History of Sinai across the Ages.

BALARD, Michel, Les épices au Moyen Âge [book].

BARBER, Malcolm, The Crusader States in the Twelfth Century (Yale UP).

BELLOMO, Elena, I sentieri della memoria: crociata e reliquie oltremarine in un'anonima cronaca monferrina medievale; A Neglected Source for the History of the Hospital: The Letter of Master Jobert (1171/72–1177) to the Citizens of Savona; Fulfilling a Mediterranean Vocation: The *Domus Sancte Marie Montis Gaudii de Jerusalem* in Mediaeval Lombardy; Scorci di un orizzonte mediterraneo: Genova e l'Oriente latino nella storiografia italiana (1951–2001); Diplomazia e Crociata nel Mediterraneo di inizio XIV secolo: il Francescano savonese Filippo Brusserio; Da Occidente ad Oriente: il magistero di Barozio, dignitario templare e crociato (1200–1205 circa) [articles].

BIRD, Jessalynn, The "History of the West" (Historia Occidentalis) of Jacques de Vitry, tr. with critical introduction and notes (Liverpool UP); Women and the Crusades (London Books); Christian Society and the Crusades, 1198–1274, a sourcebook in collaboration with Edward Peters and James Powell (Univ. of Pennsylvania Press); articles: Prophecy and the Crusades; Paris Masters and the Development of the Fama-Based Inquisition against Heresy; James of Vitry and Oliver of Paderborn on Eastern Christians.

BOMBI, Barbara, ed. with G. Andenna, Oliviero di Colonia, La quinta Crociata (Milano: Marietti 1820).

BRUNDAGE, James A., The Professionalization of Medieval Canon Lawyers [book]; The Case of the Shrinking Client: A Study in the Vocabulary of the Medieval Legal Profession.

CARRAZ, Damien, Pro servitio maiestatis nostre: ordres militiares et service curial sous Charles Ier et Charles II, in: Diplomatie des États Angevins aux XIIIe et XIVe siècles, colloque de Szeged, 13–16 septembre 2007; Confréries de milites et défense de l'orthodoxie (XIe–XIIIe siècles), in: Noblesse et défense de l'orthodoxie (XIIe–XVIIe siècles), Journée d'études, Univ. de Rennes II, 27 octobre 2007; Les Lengres, entre négoce, fidelité politique et lutte contre l'infidèle: l'opportunisme d'une famille de marchands marseillais au XIVe siécle [paper, 2008].

CARRIER, Marc, The Byzantines as seen by Albert of Aachen [post-doctoral research at McGill Univ.].

CASSIDY-WELCH, Megan, The Aftermath of War: Displacement and Memory after the Albigensian Crusade.

CHRISTIE, Niall G. F., ed. with Deborah Gerish, The Sermons of Urban II and the Kitab al-Jihad of 'Ali ibn Tahir al-Sulami (d. 1106) [book, with edition and translation].

CLAVERIE, Pierre-Vincent, The Oriental Policy of Pope Honorius III (1216–1227) [book].

CONGDON, Eleanor A., Venetian Merchants in the Western Mediterranean, c.1400; Marco Bembo's trade network in the Aegean; Ambrogio Malipiero's network of contacts in Syria in the 1480s: Venetian merchants at work in Ottoman and Mamluk lands.

COUREAS, Nicholas S., The Latin Church in Cyprus 1313–1378 [book]; The Life of Peter Thomas by Philippe de Mézières: A Translation into English [book] (Cyprus Research Centre).

CRAWFORD, Paul F., articles for ABC-Clio's World History Encyclopedia, ed. Alfred Andrea; The Involvement of the University of Paris in the Trial of the Templars [article]; The Templars and the Hospitallers [book].

DIVALL, Richard, ed., The Complete Sacred Music of Nicolo Asoward, Malta 1790–98; Early Maltese Music of the Order of Malta – Wigancourt Museum Malta, 4 vols.

DODD, Erica Cruikshank, The Double-Naved Church in Lebanon; Inscriptions in the Mosque of the Wazir Khan, Lahore; Byzantine Silver Stamps, revised edition, including 75 vessels with stamps discovered since the publication of 1962.

DOUROU-ELIOPOULOU, Maria, with Athina Kolia-Dermitzaki and Triantafyllitsa Maniati-Kokkini, as in Bulletin 22; with Nicoletta Giantsi, The Institutions, the Social Welfare and the Economy in the Mediterranean in the Age of the Crusades (12th to 15th Century) [research program].

EDBURY, Peter W., Philip of Novara: Le Livre de forme de plait [critical edition]; The Third Crusade [book]; with E. Walker, Chronique d'Amadi [translation].

EDGINGTON, Susan B., *Regimen sanitatis* of Guido de Vigevano, edition and commentary.

EHLERS, Axel, The Use of Vow Redemptions by the Military Orders [article].

EPSTEIN, Steven, A Social and Economic History of Later Medieval Europe [book].

FAVREAU-LILIE, Marie-Luise, Die Italiener in den Kreuzfahrerstaaten, Teil 2: 1197–1291 [book]; Die Venezianer im Heiligen Land 12.–13. Jh. [article]; Handel und Religion: Die Beziehungen zwischen italienischen Seestädten und den islamischen Mächten im Vorderen Orient im Zeitalter der Kreuzzüge [article].

FOLDA, Jaroslav, Crusader Art [book]; Ornament in Crusader, Byzantine and Italian Art in the 13th Century.

FOREY, Alan J., The Papacy and the Spanish Reconquest; Western Converts to Islam, 11th to 15th Centuries; Notes on Templar Government and Personnel, c.1300.

FRIEDMAN, Yvonne, Interludes of Peace [a book on peacemaking endeavours in the Latin East].

GABRIELE, Matthew, The Legend of Charlemagne and the Origins of the First Crusade [book].

VON GUTTNER-SPORZYNSKI, Darius, Translation of the Polish Chronicle written by Master Vincentius (so called Kadlubek) in 1190–1208 into English; The Hospitallers and the Templars in the Kingdom of Poland: Early Settlements; Charters of Polish Dukes for the Hospitallers and Templars; The Piast Dynasty and the Crusading Orders; Transmission of the Idea of Crusading to Poland and the Subsequent Polish Experience of Crusading in the 11th and 12th Centuries; Polish Understanding and Response to the Crusading Call; Cardinal Hubaldus' Charter of 1146 for the Canons Regular in Trzemeszno; Henry, Duke of Sandomierz, a Polish Crusader to Jerusalem.

HAMILTON, Bernard, The Crusades and the Wider World (London Books).

HOLMES, Catherine, ed. with J. Herrin and K. Fleet, Unities and Disunities in the Late Medieval Eastern Mediterranean World [papers of a conference held in Oxford in 2005].

HUNT, Lucy-Anne, Christian Painting in Eygpt of the 12th–14th Centuries: A Study in Cultural Interaction [book]; Catalogue of the Illustrated Manuscripts in the Coptic Museum, Old Cairo.

IRWIN, Robert, The History of Orientalism; Circassian Mamluk History; Jerusalem in Late Medieval Muslim Spirituality.

JOTISCHKY, Andrew, The Christians of Jerusalem, the Holy Sepulchre and the Origins of the First Crusade [article]; with Bernard Hamilton, Monasticism in the Crusader States.

KASDAGLI, Anna-Maria, Research in the coinage, inscriptions, heraldry and architecture of Hospitaller Rhodes.

KEDAR, Benjamin Z., A Cultural History of the Kingdom of Jerusalem [book]; Inventio patriarcharum part 2 [article]; The Battle of Arsuf, 1191 [article].

KOLIA-DERMITZAKI, Athina, with Triantafyllitsa Maniati-Kokkini, Relations and Interactions between Byzantium and the Western World in the Political, Social and Economic Fields (11th–15th Centuries) [registration in a data base of relevant information and terminology based on Greek and Latin sources and bibliography sorted by keywords].

LEONARD, Robert D. Jr., Gold coinage of the Latin Kingdom of Jeursalem; "Latin" imitations of Byzantine gold coins.

LIGATO, Giuseppe, Il mito della crociata nel frammento di mosaico pavimentale recuperato dalla basilica di S. Maria Maggiore a Vercelli.

LOUD, Graham A., Roger II and the Making of the Kingdom of Sicily: Translated Sources.

LOWER, Michael, Paying Tribute in the Medieval Mediterranean [article]; Europeans in North Africa Before Colonialism [book].

MAIER, Christoph T., as last Bulletin.

MENACHE, Sophia, Medieval Political Philosophy – A Reinterpretation [Hebrew].

MESCHINI, Marco, Volume di sintesi sulla prima crociata contro gli albigesi (1207–1215).

MITCHELL, Piers, Palaeopathological study of crusader period health at Blanchegarde Castle, Israel; Palaeopathological study of a crusader period cesspool in Acre; Stable isotope analysis of skeletal remains from crusader sites in order to investigate migration and diet.

MOLIN, Kristian, The Chronicle of the Morea: A New Translation, from the Old French Version (Ashgate, forthcoming 2008).

MOURAD, Suleiman Ali, with James E. Lindsay, The Muslim Counter-Crusade: Ibn ʿAsakir and Jihad Ideology in the Crusader Period (Ashgate, forthcoming 2008) [with critical edition and English translation of Ibn ʿAsakir's treatise on jihad].

NICHOLSON, Helen J., The Trial of the Templars in the British Isles, 1308–11 (Ashgate, forthcoming 2008) [edition and translation of the surviving manuscripts recording the testimonies]; The Templars on Trial: The Trial of the Templars in the British Isles, 1308–11 (Sutton); Love in a Hot Climate: Gender Relations in Florent et Octavien, in: Languages of Love and Hate, ed. Matthew Bennet, Susan Edgington, Sarah Lambert.

NICOLAOU-KONNARI, Angel, The Encounter of Greeks and Franks in Cyprus in the Late 12th and 13th Centuries: Phenomena of Acculturation and Ethnic Awareness (Birmingham UP, Ashgate, 2008); ed. with Christopher Schabel, History of Limassol, Medochemie series 2 (2008).

NICOLLE, David, Armies of Medieval Poland, Osprey Men at Arms; The Battle of Poitiers 732, Osprey Campaign; Saracen Citadels, Osprey Fortress; The Teutonic Knights, Osprey Warrior; with Shihab al-Sarraf, Early and Later Medieval Islamic Thinkers, for an Encyclopedia of War and Strategy (2008); Fighting for the Faith: The Many Fronts of Medieval Crusade and Jihad 1000–1500 AD (Pen and Sword 2008).

NOBLE, Peter, Bias in the chronicles of the Fourth Crusade.

PAVIOT, Jacques, The Idea of Crusade in France, end 13th–beginning 16th cent.

PHILLIPS, Christopher Matthew, Preaching the Cross; The Crusade as a Means of Self-Torture.

PHILLIPS, Jonathan, Italy, the Crusades and the Crusader States [a long-term study].

POWELL, James M., Mendicants, the Communes, and the Law [book].

PRYOR, John H., Crusading by Sea: The Maritime History of the Crusades, 1095–1291 [book].

RACINE, Pierre, Frédéric Barberousse: illusions et désillusions d'un souverain médiéval.

RICHARD, Jean, with Christopher Schabel, Bullarium Cyprium (see below).

ROCHE, Jason T., ed. with Janus Møller Jensen, The Second Crusade in Perspective [a collection of articles].

ROLL, Israel, A Sealed Pottery-Complex from the Crusader Castle of Apollonia-Arsuf.

RUBENSTEIN, Jay, Holy War and History: the 12th-Century Historiography of the First Crusade [book].

SCHABEL, Christopher, with Angel Nicolaou-Konnari, A History of Limassol; with Jean

Richard, Bullarium Cyprium: Papal Letters Involving Cyprus 1196–1378, 3 vols., Texts and Studies on the History of Cyprus (Nicosia: Cyprus Research Centre, 2008); with William Duba, Bullarium Hellenicum I: Pope Honorius III's Letters Involving Frankish Greece and Constantinople (Leiden: Brill); with Fritz Saaby Pedersen, Matthew of Aquasparta, OFM, and the Greeks, in a *festschrift*; Serfdom and the Greek Clergy in Lands under Latin Rule.

SHAGRIR, Iris, The Breviary of the Church of the Holy Sepulchre, Jerusalem, ms. of Santo Sepolcro di Barletta; Systèmes de Dénomination: Anthroponymie et Migrations à l'époque médiévale, CNRS international project.

SIDSELRUD, Kaare Seeberg, The Sonnenburg collection of coats-of-arms of members of the Order of St. John – Ballei Brandenburg, spanning the period c.1600–1920, with the hope of publishing the complete collection of 1140 paintings.

STRUCKMEYER, Myra, Women in the Military Orders, 12th to 13th Centuries [book].

THORAU, Peter, Geschichte der Kreuzzüge (München: Beck, ca. 2009); Oriens Latinus Graecus et Arabicus (OLGA): Topographisches Glossar zum Vorderen Orient im Zeitalter der Kreuzzüge, Datenbank und Wörterbuch.

TOLAN, John Victor, with Emmanouela Grypeou, Barbara Roggema, David Thomas, Bibliographical History of Christian-Muslim Relations, 4 vols. (Leiden: Brill, 2009/10); God's Dog: Raymond de Penyafort and the Ordering of Christian Society.

TYERMAN, Christopher, The Crusade and its Secular Structure of Organization [article]; The Irrelevance of Crusading in the Late Medieval Eastern Mediterranean [article]; Crusade Historiography (Manchester UP) [book]; The Crusading Experience (Longman) [book].

6. Theses in progress

ANTAKI, Patricia, La topographie urbaine de la ville de Tyr à l'époque des croisades, PhD, Poitiers Univ., Centre d'Études Supérieures de Civilisation Médiévale.

ARNON, Naama, The People of the Book and the People of the Horses: Relations between the Mongols and the Jews, 1216–1368, MA, Bar-Ilan Univ., supervised by Yvonne Friedman.

BARBÉ, Hervé, Le château de Safed et son territoire durant la période des croisades, PhD, supervised by Nicolas Faucherre and Benjamin Z. Kedar.

BERKOVICH, Ilya, The Battle of La Forbie, 1244, MA, supervised by Benjamin Z. Kedar.

BRIDGER, Heidi, The Conquest and Settlement of Frankish Greece, 1204–61, PhD, Royal Holloway, Univ. of London, supervised by Jonathan Phillips.

CARLSSON, Christer, The Military Orders in Medieval Scandinavia: A Historical and Archaeological Study.

CHRISSIS, Nikolaos, Crusading in Romania: A Study of Byzantine-Western Relations and Attitudes, 1204–c.1282, PhD, Royal Holloway Univ. of London.

COOPER, Barry, The Conceptualisation of the Crusades in the 20th and 21st Centuries, MA, Stirling Univ.

COSGROVE, Walker Reid, The Albigensian Crusade and the Church in Languedoc, PhD, Saint Louis Univ.

DESJARDINS, Robert, Writing and Imagining the Crusade in Fifteenth-Century Burgundy, PhD, Univ. of Alberta, Edmonton.

GOURINARD, Henri, Egypt in Medieval Itineraries, MA, supervised by Martin Aurell and Benjamin Z. Kedar.

VON GUTTNER-SPORZYNSKI, Darius, Crusading in Poland: Its Idea, Reception and the Experience (1102–1194), PhD, Univ. of Melbourne.

JINKS, Alison, Philip Augustus and the Crusades, PhD, Royal Holloway, Univ. of London, supervised by Jonathan Phillips.

KAFFA, Elena, The Church of Cyprus, Achaea and Constantinople during the Frankish Era, PhD, Univ. of Wales, Cardiff, supervised by Peter Edbury.

KARTSEVA, Tatiana, The Latin East in a Dialogue of Medieval Civilizations, PhD, The Russian State Univ. for the Humanities.

LATIF, Osman, Jihad Literature in the Twelfth Century, PhD, Royal Holloway, Univ. of London, supervised by Jonathan Phillips.

MILITANU, Shlomi, The Teutonic Order between East and West, PhD, Bar-Ilan Univ., supervised by Yvonne Friedman.

MILLIMAN, Paul, Disputing Identity, Territoriality, and Sovereignty: The Place of Pomerania in the Social Memory of the Kingdom of Poland and the Teutonic Ordensstaat, PhD, Cornell.

MORTON, Nicholas, The Teutonic Knights in the Holy Land, 1190–1291, PhD, Royal Holloway, Univ. of London, supervised by Jonathan Phillips.

NACHMAN, Julia, Women as Peacemakers, M.A., Bar-Ilan Univ., supervised by Yvonne Friedman.

NUSSBAUM, Shmuel, The Ibelin Family – The Rise and Fall of Frankish Nobility in the Latin East (12th to 14th Century), PhD, Bar-Ilan Univ., supervised by Yvonne Friedman.

O'SULLIVAN, Rhiain, The Principality of Antioch, 1130–1192, M.Phil., Queen Mary, Univ. of London, supervised by Thomas S. Asbridge.

PACKARD, Barbara, Writing the History of the First Crusade, 1099–1291, PhD, Royal Holloway, Univ. of London, supervised by Jonathan Phillips.

PERRA, Photeine V., The Venetian-Ottoman Rivalry for the Conquest of the Helladic Lands (A.D. 1463–1479): The First Venetian-Ottoman War and the World of the Southeastern Mediterranean Area, PhD, Aegean Univ., Dept. of Mediterranean Studies, Rhodes, supervised by Alexios Savvides.

PETRE, James, Crusader Castles of Cyprus: The Fortifications of Cyprus under the Lusignans, 1192–1489, PhD, Cardiff Univ.

PETRO, Theodore D., Returning Crusaders, PhD, Univ. of Cincinnati.

PORRO, Clive, The Order of Christ in 14th Century Portugal, PhD, Queen Mary and Westfield College, Univ. of London.

ROBINSON, Dana C., The Brienne Dynasty and the Crusades, PhD, Royal Holloway, Univ. of London, supervised by Jonathan Phillips.

RYAN, Vincent, The Virgin and the Cross: The Crusaders, Marian Devotion, and the Expansion of the Cult of the Virgin in the Medieval West, PhD, Saint Louis Univ.

WAGNER, Thomas, Krankheiten und Krankenversorgung zur Zeit der Kreuzzüge: Epidemien, Verwundetenpflege, historische Krankheitsbilder, PhD, Univ. of Würzburg.

WEBER, Benjamin, Lutter contre les Turcs: Les formes nouvelles de la croisade pontificale au XVe siècle, PhD, Univ. of Toulouse.

ZELNIK, Yosi, Psychological Warfare in the Latin Kingdom of Jerusalem, PhD, Bar-Ilan Univ., supervised by Yvonne Friedman.

7. Fieldwork planned or undertaken recently

ANDREA, Alfred J., Photographing Moorish sites in Andalucia, 14–29 September 2006.

BALARD, Michel, Une histoire de la Méditerranée au Moyen Âge.

CARLSSON, Christer, AMS-dating of mortar from standing structures in Scandinavian Hospitaller commanderies.

EKDAHL, Sven, with Romuald Odoj, head of the Grunwald Museum, investigation of parts of former poggy terrain in the surroundings of the battlefield of Tannenberg with metal detectors in order to find traces from the fleeing army of the Teutonic Order.

KEDAR, Benjamin Z., is coordinating excavations in Acre's Genoese quarter, 2006–2008.

NICOLLE, David, studies a substantial collection of military equipment and horse harness, probably mid-13th to mid-14th century, found in a tower of the Citadel of Damascus, kept in store in the National Museum of Syria.

PIANA, Mathias, survey and excavations of the castle of Toron / Qalʿat Tibnīn, 4th campaign, April/May 2006.

ROLL, Israel, 18th season of excavations at Apollonia-Arsuf in August 2006, 19th season planned for July 2007.

SCHRYVER, James G., with Tasha Vorderstrasse, re-publishing the PSS Ware from Hama currently stored in Denmark.

SHOTTEN-HALLEL, Vardit, architect in the Conservation Dept. Israel Antiquities Authority, is currently working in Acre's Hospitaller compound.

STAHL, Alan M., visited the Princeton Univ. excavation at Polis, Cyprus, in the summer of 2006, in order to photograph a hoard of Lusignan coins for study and publication.

8. News of interest to members

a) Conferences and seminars

2007 March 22–23 Toulouse, Les croisades tardives: bilan historiographique et état de la recherche, organized by the univ. of Toulouse and the univ. of Prague. Several similar symposia are planned to follow in Prague and Toulouse until 2009 (see below the news by Jacques Paviot).

2007 April 17 The Medieval Centre, Univ. of Southern Denmark, Odense, Medieval Images of the Other in Scandinavia, Western Europe and Byzantium: Stereotypes of Sameness or Multiple Enemy Images?

2007 May 3–6 Kalamazoo and July 9–12 Leeds, IMC, a series of sessions in commemoration of the 700th anniversary of the arrest of the Templars, organized by Helen Nicholson, Jochen Burgtorf and Paul F. Crawford, intended to result in the publication of a volume representing the latest scholarship on the arrests, trials, and suppression of the Order. Filip Hooghe will talk about the arrests of the Templars in Flanders, Bernard Schotte on the participation of Templars and Hospitallers in the Flemish uprising of 1302 against the French.

2007 June 28–July 1, Milwaukee, 16th Annual World History Association Conference, Expanding Horizons, Collapsing Frontiers: The Macro and Micro in World History

2007 September 12–14 Aalborg, Denmark, Crusading at the Periphery of Europe – Crusades in the Iberian Peninsula and the Baltic Region, organized by Iben Fonnesberg Schmidt and Torben Kjersgaard Nielsen.

2008 August 28–31 Avignon: Under the auspices of the University of Avignon, the SSCLE is planning its next conference on "The Papacy and the Crusades". In this context we also want to commemorate the Albigensian Crusade. But as in former conferences, members of the Society will be able to present papers and sessions on the rich spectrum of themes dealing with the crusades and the Latin East. At the end of the conference there will be a short trip in the Comtat Venaissin. And for those who want to stay a little longer and to visit the Albigensian region, another trip will be organized (at additional cost). The academic committee includes: Michel Balard, Helen Nicholson, Norman Housley, Luis García Guijarro, and Sophia Menache. Our secretary, Sophia Menache, will be glad to receive proposals for lectures and sessions (menache@research.haifa.ac.il).

b) Other news

Simonetta CERRINI è stata consigliere scientifico per la pezza di teatro scritta da Gian Piero Alloisio (I Templari: ultimo atto) con Paolo Graziosi, ripresa dalla Televisione Italiana RAI2 al Festival internazionale di Ravello e che porta sulla scena il primo e l'ultimo gran maestro del Tempio con monologhi tratti dalla Lettera Christi militibus di Hugo Peccator.

Jaroslav FOLDA reports that ARTstor is currently negotiating image databases of interest to scholars in Byzantine, Crusader and Islamic art.

Michael HESLOP has been appointed Honorary Research Associate in Byzantine Studies attached to the Hellenic Institute in the History Dept. of Royal Holloway, Univ. of London.

Jan HOSTEN reports that the medieval chapel of the Templar commandery Ter Vlaeght at Ruiselede near Bruges awaits a major restoration. Together with Gilbert Jansseune, who led the excavations of the commandery of Slype (Flanders) in the last decades, the local community of the town of Middelkerke is preparing a museum on military orders in the Low Countries. Jan Hosten himself is trying to create a non-profit organization for the study of the military orders in the Low Countries. He also wants to convert his website www.tempeliers.be into a four-language website on the military orders with more features.

Thomas F. MADDEN: The Saint Louis Univ. Crusades Studies Forum (CSF) is a venue for the presentation of current research, the discussion of recent scholarship, and the exploration of new directions in topics relating to the crusades. Four times each academic year scholars specializing in crusade-related topics are invited to attend the forum and present their own research. During the 2006–7 academic year the CSF Visiting Scholars will be Alfred J. Andrea, Univ. of Vermont, Jessalynn Bird, Northwestern Univ., Paul Crawford, California Univ, and Benjamin Z. Kedar, Hebrew Univ. All are welcome to attend and participate in the forum. For more information see http://www.slu.edu/departments/history/crusades.htm.

Jacques PAVIOT: The Agence Nationale pour la Recherche has accepted a four year project 2007–2010: Les croisades tardives. Les confrontations interconfessionelles et la question des identités en Europe (XIVᵉ–début du XVIᵉ siècles), dir. Daniel Baloup, Benoît Joudiou (Univ. de Toulouse II – Le Mirail et Laboratoire Framespa UMR 5136), Martin Nejedly (Univ. Charles, Prague) [see above: Conferences and seminars].

Alexios SAVVIDES reports that in 2007 volume I (letter A) of the English edition of the Encyclopaedic Prosopographical Lexicon of Byzantine History and Civilization is due to appear by Brepols (Turnhout), with professor Benjamin Hendrickx of Johannesburg University (South Africa) as co-editor and with the editorial assistance of Dr Alicia Simpson, assistant professor at Koc University (Istanbul) and Dr Thekla Sansaridou-Hendrickx, lecturer at Johannesburg University. Volume II of the English edition (letters B, C, D and E) is also scheduled to appear in late 2007, while entries from letter F onwards are expected in 2007 for volume III (letters F, G, H, I and J). Several personages in this collective venture are directly or indirectly connected with the Crusades – especially the first four. Members interested in contributing are cordially invited to contact the editors, Prof. A. Savvides (savvides@rhodes.aegean.gr) and/ or Prof. Benjamin Hendrickx (thekla@telkomsa.net), or the assistant editors, Assistant Prof. Alicia Simpson (asimpson@ku.edu.tr) and Dr Thekla Sansaridou-Hendrickx (thekla@telkomsa.net).

Myra STRUCKMEYER has set up 'Crusades', a new listserv for the scholarly discussion of the crusades, the military orders, and the Latin East. The aim is to create a virtual forum for the exchange of ideas and public notices related to crusading studies through the medium of email, for example, to advertise a conference, to learn about a new resource, or to bring up a historical conundrum. You can subscribe to this listserv by sending an email to listserv@unc.edu and write: subscribe crusades Your Name in the message body. Leave the subject line blank. Once you are accepted (this is a listserv for approved members only), you can send emails to the list, which disperses your message to all members. You, in turn, will receive all emails posted by other members. If you have any questions, please contact Myra Struckmeyer, struckme@gmail.unc.edu

9. Members' queries

Eleanor A. CONGDON would like to know about Venetian merchants' letters in public and private collections, especially concerning Marco Bembo and Ambrogio Malipiero. She would guarantee anonymity for private collectors if they wish this.

John H. PRYOR would be grateful for any references in unpublished archival materials to any matters concerning seafaring and the crusades and crusader states 1095–1291, especially to the maritime activities of the military orders.

Jan HOSTEN asks whether a cooperation between the SSCLE website and tempeliers.be might be possible.

10. Officers of the Society

President: Professor Michel Balard. Honorary Vice-Presidents: Professor Jean Richard, Professor Jonathan Riley-Smith, Professor Benjamin Z. Kedar. Secretary: Professor Sophia Menache. Assistant Secretary: Professor Luis García-Guijarro Ramos. Editor of the Bulletin: Professor Karl Borchardt. Treasurer: Professor James D. Ryan. Website: Dr Zsolt Hunyadi.

Committee of the Society: Professor Antonio Carile (Bologna), Professor Robert Huygens (Leiden), Professor Hans Eberhard Mayer (Kiel).

11. Income and expenditure for the SSCLE from 1 October 2005 to 30 September 2006

Please note that the subscriptions collected during this reporting period were for two year (2005 and 2006) and most of subscriptions were for membership with the journal *Crusades*. Only Volume 4 of the journal was mailed out during the reporting period, however. Because the society is billed only when the journal is published (*Crusades* Vol. 5 was published December 2006), as one reads this report the invoice for Vol. 5 (which arrived in December) and invoices for ordered back issues of the journal ought to be considered as accounts payable totalling £4,340 or $8,246 or €7,233. If that amount, owed but unbilled as of October 1, were included in this report, the "surplus of income over expenditures" would becomes a negative number, and the report would show that in the past year SSCLE assets declined by a total of £1,126 or $2,074 or €1,953.

Income and expenditure for the SSCLE from 1 October 2005 to 30 September 2006

BALANCES CARRIED FORWARD, 1 OCTOBER 2005

INCOME

U.S. Accounts ($)		U.K. Accounts (£)		Euro Accounts (€)	
$12,588.89	Balance brought down	£(1,493.57)	Balance brought down	€1,270.98	Balance brought down
$7,387.06	Subs. etc received	£3,117.75	Subs. etc received	€1,790.59	Subs. etc received
		£9.73	Interest received		
		£383.69	Bank charges refunded		
$20,975.95	Total income	£2,017.60	Total income	€3,061.57	Total income

TRANSFERS BETWEEN ACCOUNTS

$(9,020.00)	transferred from $ account	4,589.83	transferred to £ account		

EXPENDITURES

$370.54	postage, supplies, etc.	£10.90	postage		
$43.36	bank charges	£215.81	interest/bank charges charged	€30.00	bank charges
		£3,500.00	Expenditures for journal		
		£285.90	ICHS dues		
$413.90	Total expenditures	£4,012.60	Total expenditures	€30.00	Total expenditures

SURPLUS OF INCOME OVER EXPENDITURES

$(1,046.84)		£4,088.40		€1,760.59	

BALANCES ON HAND, 30 SEPTEMBER 2006

U.S. Accounts ($)	U.K. Accounts (£)	Euro Accounts (€)
$11,542.05	£2,594.83	€3,031.57

(The report above shows SSCLE funds, held in three currencies, in separate columns, totalling the amount in each currency. The notes that follow refer to the total assets and/or liabilities of the society, and accordingly SSCLE assets are totalled and reported in sterling followed by the equivalent amount in dollars and in euros, in each case rounded to the nearest whole unit.)

Also note that the figures in the columns above show <u>net</u> subscription payments (that is, after bank charges for currency conversion have been subtracted). The bank exacts hefty fees (ranging as high as 10%) when dollars or euros are converted into pounds in small transactions. When larger sums are moved from one account into another the fees are much lower. This is why new accounts in the United States (for dollar deposits) and in France (for euro deposits) have been opened. There will always be bank fees for transfers of money, however, and those fees, added to increases in postage, are major reasons for the dues increase of this year.

You can see that there is still a substantial balance on hand, totaling £10,733 or $20,413 or €16,232. The recent rise in the subscription price for the journal will help prevent erosion of the SSCLE's assets, and many former members have contacted me to renew membership, joining a growing number of new members. During the period covered in this report 37 new or former, long inactive (more than five years) members wrote or emailed me to join or renew membership. During the first few months of 2006–2007 new applicants and members who have been out of touch for several years continue to contact me. In addition, a few members have made modest, but always welcome, contributions to the society, to assist it in its work. **It seems clear, however, that a further increase in subscription rates will be needed within the next two years.** I am closely monitoring the society's funds, to determine the minimum increase needed. For the present the SSCLE is solvent, and I am sanguine concerning its future.

Members should be pleased to learn that additional steps have been taken to make the payment of dues easier, and to reduce charges for bank fees. Three new accounts have been opened. Two of these (those in the United States and in France) are mentioned above. We have also opened a PayPal account, which allows payment over the Internet using a credit card. Despite the slight surcharge to cover PayPal fees to vendors, many members, and particularly those outside the pound, dollar, or euro zones, should find this an easier and less expensive way to transfer money for SSCLE subscription payments.

Once again I express sincere thanks to the members of the SSCLE for their patience as I have taken up the duties of treasurer, and for their forbearance on the not infrequent occasions when I have made mistakes. The members continue to accord me unfailing courtesy, and I am profoundly grateful to them for it.

Respectfully submitted,
James D. Ryan, Treasurer

12. List of members and their addresses

Shawn D. ABBOTT, 924 Greenbriar Road, Muncie IN 47304-3260, U.S.A.; sdbabbott@hotmail.com

Prof. Baudouin van den ABEELE, Rue C. Wolles 3, 1030 Bruxelles, BELGIUM; vandenabeele@mage.ucl.ac.be

Dr David S. H. ABULAFIA, Gonville and Caius College, Cambridge CB2 1TA, ENGLAND, U.K.

Brian ALLISON LEWIS, c/o Sabic, P.O. Box 5101, Riyadh 11422, SAUDI ARABIA

Dr Martín ALVIRA CABRER, C/Marañosa, 2, 4° Izquierda, 28053 Madrid, ESPAÑA; maartinalvira@yahoo.es

Prof. Reuven AMITAI-PREISS, Dept. of Islamic and Middle Eastern Studies, Hebrew Univ., Jerusalem 91905, ISRAEL; amitai@h2.hum.huji.ac.il

Dr Monique AMOUROUX, 2, Avenue de Montchalette, Cassy, 33138 Lanton, FRANCE

Prof. Alfred J. ANDREA, 161 Austin Drive, Apartment 3, Burlington VT 05401, U.S.A.; aandrea@uvm.edu

Patricia ANTAKI, Domaine de Gaillat, 8, Chemin de Lasseguette, 64100 Bayonne, FRANCE; patriciaantaki@yahoo.com

Dr Benjamin ARBEL, School of History, Tel-Aviv Univ., Tel-Aviv 69978, ISRAEL; arbel@ post.tau.ac.il

Dr Marco AROSIO, Università del Sacro Cuore, Milano, ITALY; marco_arosio@tin.it

Dr Thomas S. ASBRIDGE, Dept. of History, Queen Mary and Westfield College, Univ. of London, Mile End Road, London E1 4NS, ENGLAND, U.K.; t_asbridge@qmul.ac.uk

Prof. Zubaida ATTA, 19 Sphinx Building – Sphinx Square, Apartment 85, Muhandessin, Cairo, EGYPT; prof.zatta@yahoo.com

Dr Hussein M. ATTIYA, 20 Ahmed Sidik Street, Sidi Gaber El-Shiek, Alexandria, EGYPT

Prof. Taef K. EL-AZHARI, Faculty of Education and Arts – Shabaka, Safraa P.O. Box 1300, Buraida-Safra, SAUDI ARABIA; taef@tedata.net.eg

Dr Mohammed AZIZ, P.O. Box 135513, Beirut, LEBANON

Dr Bernard S. BACHRACH, Univ. of Minnesota, Dept. of History, 633 Social Sciences Building, Minneapolis MN 55455, U.S.A.; bachr001@tc.umn.edu

Dr Xavier BAECKE, Koningsvarenweg 9, 9031 Gent, BELGIUM; xavierbaecke@hotmail.com

Dr Dan BAHAT, P.O. Box 738, Mevasseret Zion 90805, ISRAEL; danbahat@gmail.com

Archibald BAIN, Dufftown, Banffshire AB55 4AJ, SCOTLAND, U.K.; ArchieBain@ aol.com

Prof. Michel BALARD, 4, rue des Remparts, 94370 Sucy-en-Brie, FRANCE; Michel.Balard@ univ-paris1.fr

Laura BALLETTO, Via Orsini 40/B, 16146 Genova, ITALY; Laura.Balletto@lettere.unige.it

Prof. Malcolm BARBER, Dept. of History, Univ. of Reading, P.O. Box 218, Whiteknights, Reading RG6 6AA, ENGLAND, U.K.; m.c.barber@reading.ac.uk

Dr Michael BARDOT, Dept. Behavioral and Social Sciences, Lincoln Univ., 820 Chestnut Street, Room 310 Founders Hall, Jefferson City MO 65102, U.S.A.; Bardotm@lincolnu.edu

Prof. John W. BARKER, Dept. of History, Univ. of Wisconsin, 3211 Humanities Building, Madison WI 53706, U.S.A.; jwbarker@wisc.edu

Sebastian BARTOS, 319 Oak Center Place, Valdosta GA 31602, U.S.A.; sebartos@ hotmail.com

The Rev. Fr. Robert L. BECERRA, Senior Associate Pastor, St Luke Catholic Church, 2892 South Congress Avenue, Palm Springs FL 33461-2170, U.S.A.; SinaiPantocrator@aol.com

Dr Bruce BEEBE, 1490 Mars Lakewood OH 44107, U.S.A.; lgbeebe@aol.com

Prof. George BEECH, 1745 Hillshine Drive, Kalamazoo MI 49008, U.S.A.; beech@ wmich.edu

Elena BELLOMO, via dei Rospigliosi 1, 20151 Milano, ITALY; elena.bellomo@libero.it

Matthew BENNETT, 58 Mitchell Avenue, Hartley Wintney, Hampshire RG27 8HG, ENGLAND, U.K.; mattbennett@waitrose.com

Dr Nora BEREND, St Catharine's College, Cambridge CB2 1RL, ENGLAND, U.K.; nb213@ cam.ac.uk

Jessalynn BIRD, 1514 Cortland Drive, Naperville IL 60565, U.S.A; jessalynn.bird@ iname.com

Prof. Nancy Bisaha, Dept. of History, Vassar College, P.O. Box 81, 124 Raymond Avenue, Poughkeepsie NY 12604, U.S.A.; nabisaha@vassar.edu

Adam Bishop, 57 Charles Street West, Apt. 1702, Toronto, Ontario MS5 2X1, CANADA; adam.bishop@utoronto.ca

Prof. John R. E. Bliese, Communication Studies Dept., Texas Tech Univ., Lubbock TX 79409, U.S.A.

Dr Adrian J. Boas, Institute of Archaeology, Hebrew Univ. of Jerusalem, Jerusalem 91905, ISRAEL; adianjboas@yahoo.com

Prof. Mark S. Bocija, Columbus State Community College, 550 E. Spring Street, Columbus OH 43216-1609, U.S.A.; mbocija@cscc.edu

Louis Boisset, Université Saint-Joseph de Beyrouth, BP 166 778, Achrafieh, Beirut, LEBANON

Brenda M. Bolton, 8 Watling Street, St Albans AL1 2PT, ENGLAND, U.K.; brenda@bolton.vianw.co.uk

Dr Barbara Bombi, School of History, Rutheford College, Univ. of Kent, Canterbury CT2 7NX, ENGLAND, U.K.; b.bombi@kent.ac.uk

Pierre Bonneaud, Chemin des chênes verts, Pont des Charrettes, 30700 Uzès, FRANCE; pierrebonneaud@yahoo.es

Prof. Karl Borchardt, c/o Monumenta Germaniae Historica, Ludwigstraße 16, 80539 München, for letters: Postfach 34 02 23, 80099 München, GERMANY; karl.borchardt@mgh.de

Prof. Charles R. Bowlus, History Dept., Univ. of Arkansas, 8081 Mabelvale, Little Rock AR 72209-1099, U.S.A.; Haymannstraße 2A, 85764 Oberschleißheim, GERMANY; carolus22000@yahoo.com

Prof. Charles M. Brand, 508 West Montgomery Avenue, Haverford PA 19041, U.S.A.; cmbrand4@earthlink.net

Dr Michael Brett, School of Oriental and African Studies, Univ. of London, Malet Street, London WC1E 7HP, ENGLAND, U.K.

Robert Brodie, 61 St Saviours Wharf, 8 Shad Thames, London SE1 2YP, ENGLAND, U.K.; robert@dbrodie.demon.co.uk

Dr Judith Bronstein, Ilanot 29/2, Haifa 34324, ISRAEL; Judith_bronstein@hotmail.com

Prof. Elizabeth A. R. Brown, 160 West 86th Street PH4, New York NY 10024, U.S.A.; rsbrown160@aol.com

Prof. James A. Brundage, 1102 Sunset Drive, Lawrence KS 66044-4548, U.S.A.; jabrun@ku.edu

Dr Marcus G. Bull, Dept. of Historical Studies, Univ. of Bristol, 13-15 Woodland Road, Clifton, Bristol BS8 1TB, ENGLAND, U.K.; m.g.bull@bris.ac.uk

Dr Jochen Burgtorf, California State Univ., Dept. of History, Fullerton CA 92834-6846, U.S.A.; jburgtorf@fullerton.edu

Olivier Burlotte, Appartment 79, Smolensky Boulvard 6-8, Moscow 119 034, RUSSIA, oburlotte@yahoo.com

Prof. Charles Burnett, Warburg Institute, Woburn Square, London WC1H 0AB, ENGLAND, U.K.; charles.burnett@sas.ac.uk

The Rev. Prof. Robert I. Burns, History Dept., UCLA, Los Angeles CA 90095, U.S.A.; fax (310) 338-3002

Dr Peter BURRIDGE, Harmer Mill, Millington, York YO4 2TX, ENGLAND, U.K.

Ane Lise BYSTED, Dept. of History, Univ. of Southern Denmark, Campusvej 55, 5230 Odense M, DENMARK; bysted@hist.sdu.dk

Dr J. P. CANNING, History Dept. Univ. College of North Wales, Bangor, Gwynedd, WALES, U.K.

Franco CARDINI, P.O. Box 2358, 50123 Firenze Ferrovia, ITALY

Christer CARLSSON, Litsbyvägen 66, 18746 Täby, SWEDEN; cc_arch75@hotmail.com

Dr Annemarie Weyl CARR, Division of Art History, Southern Methodist Univ., P.O. Box 750356, Dallas TX 75275-0356, U.S.A.; during the calendar year 2006: 608 Apple Road, Newark DE 19711, U.S.A.; acarr@mail.smu.edu

Dr Damien CARRAZ, 14, rue François Arago, 84000 Avignon, FRANCE; damien.carraz@wanadoo.fr

Marc CARRIER, 500 Alexandre-Dumas, Granby, Quebec J2J 1B2, CANADA; marctcarrier@yahoo.ca; marc.carrier@mail.mcgill.ca

Dr Megan CASSIDY-WELCH, School of Historical Studies, Univ. of Melbourne, Victoria 3010, AUSTRALIA; mecass@unimelb.edu.au

Prof. Brian A. CATLOS, Dept. of History, Univ. of California Santa Cruz, Stevenson Academic Center, 1156 High Street, Santa Cruz CA 95064, U.S.A.; bcatlos@ucsc.edu

Prof. Fred A. CAZEL Jr., 309 Gurleyville Road, Storrs Mansfield CT 06268-1439, U.S.A.

Dr Simonetta CERRINI[-ALLOISIO], Via Carducci 68A, 15076 Ovada (Alessandria), ITALY; alloisiocerrini@inwind.it

William CHAPMAN, 68 Carisbrooke Gardens, Yeovil, Somerset BA20 1BY, ENGLAND, U.K.; bill-chapman@pilgrim.env.co.uk

Dr Martin CHASIN, 1125 Church Hill Road, Fairfield CT 06432-1371, U.S.A.; mchasin@worldnet.att.net

Nikolaos CHRISSIS, Flat 2C18, International Hall, Lansdowne Terrace, London WC1N 1DJ, ENGLAND, U.K.; nchrissis@yahoo.co.uk

Dr Katherine CHRISTENSEN, CPO 1756 Berea College, Berea KY 40404, U.S.A.; katherine_christensen@berea.edu

Dr Niall G. F. CHRISTIE, Dept. of Classical, Near Eastern and Religious Studies, The Univ. of British Columbia, BUCH C260-1866 Main Hall, Vancouver, BC V6T 1Z1, CANADA; niallchristie@yahoo.com

Ioanna CHRISTOFORAKI, Aristotelous 26, Chalandri, Athens 15234, GREECE; joanna.christoforaki@archaeology.oxford.ac.uk

Dr Julian CHRYSOSTOMIDES, Dept. of History, Egham Hill, Egham, Surrey, ENGLAND, U.K.; j.chysostomides@rhul.ac.uk

Padre Giulio CIPOLLONE, B.S.S.T., Padri Trinitari, Piazza S. Maria alle Fornaci 30, 00165 Roma, ITALY; cipolloneunigre6009@fastwebnet.it

Dr G. H. M. CLAASSENS, Departement Literatuurwetenschap, Katholieke Universiteit Leuven, Blijde Inkomststraat 21, Postbus 33, 3000 Leuven, BELGIUM

Dr Pierre-Vincent CLAVERIE, 9, rue du Bois-Rondel, 35700 Rennes, FRANCE; pvclaverie@minitel.net

David CLOVER, 5460 Ocean View Drive, Oakland CA 94618, U.S.A.; rollsroyreggm24@yahoo.com

Paul M. COBB, Dept. of History, Univ. of Notre Dame, 219 O'Shaughnessy Hall, Notre Dame IN 46556, U.S.A.; pcobb@nd.edu

Dr Penny J. COLE, Trinity College, 6 Hoskin Avenue, Toronto, Ontario M5S 1HB, CANADA; pjcole@trinity.utoronto.ca

Prof. Eleanor A. CONGDON, Dept. of History, Youngstown State Univ., 1 University Plaza, Youngstown OH 44555, U.S.A.; eacongdon@ysu.edu

Prof. Giles CONSTABLE, 506 Quaker Road, Princeton NJ 08540, U.S.A.

Prof. Olivia Remie CONSTABLE, Dept. of History, Univ. of Notre Dame, Notre Dame IN 46556-0368, U.S.A.; constable1@nd.edu

Prof. Robert F. COOK, French Language and General Linguistics Dept., Univ. of Virginia, 302 Cabell Hall, Charlottesville VA 22903, U.S.A.

Barry COOPER, Loretto School, Linkfield Road, Musselburgh, East Lothian EH21 7RE, SCOTLAND, U.K.; bcooper@loretto.com

Prof. Rebecca W. CORRIE, Phillips Professor of Art, Bates College, Lewiston ME 04240, U.S.A.; rcorrie@bates.edu

Walker Reid COSGROVE, History Dept., Saint Louis Univ., 3800 Lindell Boulevard, Saint Louis MO 63108, U.S.A.; cosgrowr@slu.edu

Prof. Ricardo Luiz Silveira da COSTA, Rua Joao Nunes Coelho 264 apto. 203, Ed. Tom Jobim – Bairro Mata da Praia – Vitória – Espíritó Santo (ES), CEP 29.065-490, BRAZIL; riccosta@npd.ufes.br or ricardo@ricardocosta.com

Dr Nicholas S. COUREAS, P.O. Box 26619, Lykarittos, 1640 Nicosia, CYPRUS; ncoureas@moec.gov.cy

The Rev. H. E. J. COWDREY, 19 Church Lane, Old Marston, Oxford 0X3 0NZ, ENGLAND, U.K.; fax (0)1865 279090

Prof. Paul F. CRAWFORD, 5 Mum Drive, Washington PA 15301, U.S.A.; crawford_p@cup.edu or paul.f.crawford@gmail.com

B. Thomas CURTIS, 36 Brockswood Lane, Welwyn Garden City, Herts. AL8 7BG, ENGLAND, U.K.; btcurtis@btinternet.com

Dana CUSHING, P.O. Box 82, Lewiston NY 14092, U.S.A.; dana@antimony.biz

Charles DALLI, Dept. of History, Faculty of Arts, Univ. of Malta, Msida MSD06, MALTA; cdalli@arts.um.edu.mt

Philip Louis DANIEL, Archivist, Equestrian Order of the Holy Sepuchre of Jerusalem, 37 Somerset Road, Meadvale, Redhill, Surrey RH1 6LT, ENGLAND, U.K.; fax 01737-240722

Dr Béatrice DANSETTE, 175, Boulevard Malesherbes, 75017 Paris, FRANCE; beatrice.dansette@laposte.net

Nicole DAWE, 21 New Road, Okehampton, Devon EX20 1JE, ENGLAND, U.K.; ndawe@hotmail.com

Americo DE SANTIS, 88 East Main Street, Box Number 141, Mendham NJ 07945, U.S.A.; ricodesantis@hotmail.com

Julian DEAHL, c/o E. J. Brill, P.O. Box 9000, 2300 PA Leiden, THE NETHERLANDS; deahl@brill.nl

Prof. Bernhard DEMEL O.T., Leiter des Deutschordenszentralarchivs, Singerstraße 7, 1010 Wien, AUSTRIA; tel. 513 70 14

John A. DEMPSEY, 218 Edgehill Road, Milton MA 02186-5310, U.S.A.; milton1@bu.edu

Prof. Alain DEMURGER, 5, rue de l'Abricotier, 95000 Cergy, FRANCE; ademurger@wanadoo.fr

Prof. George T. DENNIS, Loyola Marymount Univ., P.O. Box 45041, Los Angeles CA 90045-0041, U.S.A.; nauarchos@aol.com

Robert DESJARDINS, Dept. of History and Classics, 2-28 HM Tory Building, Univ. of Alberta, Edmonton, AB T6G 2H4, CANADA; robert.desjardins@ccc.ox.ac.uk

Dr M. Gary DICKSON, History, School of History and Classics, Univ. of Edinburgh, Wm. Robertson Building, 50 George Square, Edinburgh EH8 9JY, SCOTLAND, U.K.; garydickson1212@blueyonder.co.uk

Prof. Richard DIVALL, 301 / 228 The Avenue, Parkville, Melbourne 3052, AUSTRALIA; maestro@spin.net.au

Dr Erica Cruikshank DODD, 4208 Wakefield Place, Victoria, BC V8N 6E5, CANADA; edodd@uvic.ca

César DOMÍNGUEZ, Universidad de Santiago de Compostela, Facultad de Filologia, Avda. Castealo s/n, 15704 Santiago (La Coruna), ESPAÑA

Cristina DONDI, 128 Berkeley Court, Glentworth Street, London NW1 5NE, ENGLAND, U.K.; christina.dondi@history.ox.ac.uk

Ara DOSTOURIAN, Box 420, Harmony RI 02829, U.S.A.

Maria DOUROU-ELIOPOULOU, Kephallenias 24, Althea 36 km Sounion Ave., 19400 Attiki, GREECE; meliop@cc.uoa.gr

Mark DUPUY, 119 South Sixth Avenue, Apartment A, Clarion PA 16214, U.S.A.; mdupuy@clarion.edu

John DURANT, 32 Maple Street, P.O. Box 373, West Newbury MA 01985, U.S.A.

Dr Valerie EADS, 308 West 97th Street, New York NY 10025, U.S.A.

Prof. Richard EALES, School of History, Univ. of Kent, Canterbury CT2 7NX, ENGLAND, U.K.; r.eales1@btinternet.com

Ana ECHEVARRÍA ARSUAGA, Facultad de Geografia e Historia, Departimento de Historia Medieval, Av. Conde de Aranda 1, 3° E, 28200 San Lorenzo del Escorial (Madrid), ESPAÑA; anaevjosem@hotmail.com

Prof. Peter W. EDBURY, School of History and Archaeology, Cardiff Univ., Humanities Building, Colum Road, Cardiff CF10 3EU, WALES, U.K.; edbury@cf.ac.uk

Dr Susan B. EDGINGTON, 3 West Street, Huntingdon, Cambs PE29 1WT, ENGLAND, U.K.; s.b.edgington@btinternet.com

Axel EHLERS, Gehägestraße 20 N, 30655 Hannover, GERMANY; aehlers1@gwdg.de

Prof. Sven EKDAHL, Sponholzstraße 38, 12159 Berlin, GERMANY; Sven.Ekdahl@t-online.de

Dr Ronnie ELLENBLUM, 13 Reuven Street, Jerusalem 93510, ISRAEL; msronni@pluto.mscc.huji.ac.il

Prof. Steven A. EPSTEIN, History Dept., Univ. of Kansas, Lawrence KS 66045-7590, U.S.A.; sae@ku.edu

Dr Helen C. EVANS, The Medieval Dept., The Metropolitan Museum of Art, 1000 Fifth Avenue, New York NY 10028, U.S.A.; helenevans@metmuseum.org

Michael EVANS, 6 Marston Ferry Court, Oxford OX2 7XH, ENGLAND, U.K.; m_r_evans@hotmail.com

Prof. Theodore EVERGATES, 146 West Main Street, Westminster MD 21157, U.S.A.

John C. FARQUHARSON, 19 Long Croft Lane, Cheadle Hulme, Cheadle Cheshire SK8 6SE, ENGLAND, U.K.; jc.f@btinternet.com

Prof. Marie-Luise FAVREAU-LILIE, Kaiser-Friedrich-Straße 106, 10585 Berlin, GERMANY; mlfavre@zedat.fu-berlin.de

Jack FERGUSSON, 17 Bethel Crescent, Christchurch 5, NEW ZEALAND; jb.fergusson@ xtra.co.nz

Gordon FITCH, 18 Lincoln Park, Amersham, Buckinghamshire HP7 9EZ, ENGLAND, U.K.

P. J. FLAHERTY, 9 Oak Street, Braintree MA 02184, U.S.A.

Prof. Richard A. FLETCHER, Low Pasture House, Nunnington, York YO62 5XQ, ENGLAND, U.K.; richardfletcher@ukonline.co.uk

Prof. Jean FLORI, Docteur d'État des Lettres et Sciences Humaines, Directeur de Recherche au Centre d'Études Supérieures de Civilisation Médiévale de Poitiers, 69, rue Saint Cornély, 56340 Carnac, FRANCE; flori.jean@wanadoo.fr

Prof. Jaroslav FOLDA, Dept. of Art, Univ. of North Carolina, Chapel Hill NC 27599-3405, U.S.A.; jfolda@email.unc.edu

Dr Michelle FOLTZ, M.D., PMB 33, P.O. Box 1226, Columbus MT 59019, U.S.A.; mfoltz@ imt.net

Dr Iben FONNESBERG SCHMIDT, Dept. of History, Aalborg Univ., Fibgerstraede 5, 9220 Aalborg, DENMARK; imfs@ihis.aau.dk

Harold FORD, P.O. Box 87119, Stone Mountain GA 30087, U.S.A.

Dr Alan J. FOREY, The Bell House, Church Lane, Kirtlington, Oxon. OX5 3HJ, ENGLAND, U.K.

Edith FORMAN, 38 Burnham Hill, Westport CT 06880, U.S.A.

Barbara FRALE, via A. Gramsci 17, 01028 Orte (VT), ITALY; barbara-frale@libero.it

Dr John FRANCE, History Dept., Univ. of Wales, Swansea SA2 7PP, WALES, U.K.; j.france@swansea.ac.uk

Daniel FRANKE, 242 Up Meigs Street, Rochester NY 14607, U.S.A.; dfranke@ mail.rochester.edu

Dr Peter FRANKOPAN, Worcester College, Oxford OX1 2HB, ENGLAND, U.K.; peter.frankopan@worcester.ox.ac.uk

Dr Yvonne FRIEDMAN, 3 Ben Zion, Jerusalem 95423, ISRAEL; yfried@mail.biu.ac.il

Stuart FROST, 44 Ratumore Road Charlton, London SE7 7QW, ENGLAND, U.K.; stuartfrost@fsmail.net

R. FROUMIN, P.O. Box 9713, Hadera 38001, ISRAEL; robin_fr@zahav.net.il

Michael and Neathery FULLER, 13530 Clayton Road, St Louis MO 63141, U.S.A.

Prof. Matthew GABRIELE, Dept. of Interdisciplinary Studies, Virginia Tech, 342 Lane Hall (0227), Blacksburg VA 24061-0227, U.S.A.; mgabriele@vt.edu

Cecilia GAPOSCHKIN, 6201 Wentworth Hall, Dartmouth College, Hanover NH 03655, U.S.A.; M.C.Gaposchkin@Dartmouth.edu

Prof. Luis GARCÍA-GUIJARRO RAMOS, Professor titular de Historia Medieval, Facultad de Huesca, Plaza de la Universidad 3, 22002 Huesca, ESPAÑA; luguijar@posta.unizar.es

Dr Christopher K. GARDNER, Postdoctoral Fellow in History, George Mason Univ., MS: 3G1, Fairfax VA 22030, U.S.A.; cgardner@jhu.edu

Dr Giles E. M. GASPER, History Dept., Univ. of Durham, 43 North Bailey, Durham DH1 3EX, ENGLAND, U.K.; g.e.m.gasper@durham.ac.uk

Sabine GELDSETZER, M.A., Westheide 6, 44892 Bochum, GERMANY; sabine.geldsetzer@ruhr-uni-bochum.de

Prof. Maria GEORGOPOULOU, Dept. of the History of Art, Yale Univ., P.O. Box 208272, New Haven CT 06520-8272, U.S.A.; maria.georgopoulou@yale.edu

Deborah GERISH, Dept. of Social Sciences Box 32, Emporia State Univ., 1200 Commercial, Emporia KS 66801, U.S.A.; dgerish@netscape.net

Dr Ruthy GERTWAGEN, 30 Ranas Street, P.O. Box 117, Qiryat Motzkin 26317, ISRAEL; ruger@macam.ac.il

Prof. John B. GILLINGHAM, 49 Old Shoreham Road, Brighton, Sussex BN1 5DQ, ENGLAND, U.K.; john@jgillingham.wanadoo.co.uk

Prof. Anne GILMOUR-BRYSON, 1935 Westview Drive, North Vancouver, B.C. V7M 3B1, CANADA; annegb@telus.net

Prof. Dorothy F. GLASS, 11 Riverside Drive, Apartment 6-OW, New York NY 10023, U.S.A.; dglass1@att.net

Prof. Aryeh GRABOIS, History Dept., Univ. of Haifa, Mount Carmel, Haifa 31905, ISRAEL; arag@research.haifa.ac.il

Michael GRAYER, 192 York Road, Shrewsburg Shropshire SY1 3QH, England, U.K.; m.grayer@btopenworld.com

Gilles GRIVAUD, 8, rue de Général de Miribel, 69007 Lyon, FRANCE

The Rev. Joseph J. GROSS, Trinitarian History Studies, P.O. Box 42056, Baltimore MD 21284, U.S.A.; jjgross@trinitarianhistory.org

Prof. Klaus GUTH, Greiffenbergstraße 35, 96052 Bamberg, GERMANY; klaus.guth@ggeo.uni-bamberg.de

Darius von GUTTNER SPORZYNSKI, 8 Waters Road, Shepparton, Victoria 3630, AUSTRALIA; d.guttner@unimelb.edu.au

Dr Mark E. HALL, 6826 Walso Avenue, El Cerrito CA 94530, U.S.A.; markhall@gol.com

Adina HAMILTON, 469 Albert Street, Brunswick, West Victoria 3055, AUSTRALIA or History Dept., Univ. of Melbourne, Parkville, Victoria 3052, AUSTRALIA

Prof. Bernard HAMILTON, 7 Lenton Avenue, The Park, Nottingham NG7 IDX, ENGLAND, U.K.

Peter HARITATOS Jr., 1500 North George Street, Rome NY 13440, U.S.A.

Jonathan HARRIS, Dept. of History, Royal Holloway, Univ. of London, Egham, Surrey TW20 0EX, ENGLAND, U.K.; jonathan.harris@rhul.ac.uk

Kathryn D. HARRIS, 6 Gallows Hill, Saffron Walden, Essex CB11 4DA, ENGLAND, U.K.

Dr Alan HARVEY, Dept. of Historical and Critical Studies, Univ. of Northumbria, Newcastle-upon-Tyne NE1 8ST, ENGLAND, U.K.; alan.harvey@unn.ac.uk

Prof. Eva HAVERKAMP, Rice Univ., History Dept. MS 42, for letters P.O. Box 1892, Houston TX 77251-1892 or for packages 6100 Main Street, Houston TX 77005, U.S.A.; haver@rice.edu

David HAY, 164 McCaul Street Apt. 1, Toronto, Ontario M5T 1WA, CANADA

Dr Bodo HECHELHAMMER, Erzbergerstraße 8, 64823 Groß-Umstadt/Heubach, GERMANY;

bodo.hechelhammer@t-online.de or Institut für Geschichte, Residenzschloß, 64283 Darmstadt, GERMANY; bh@polihist.pg.tu-darmstadt.de

Prof. Thérèse de HEMPTINNE, Universiteit Gent, Faculteit van de Letteren, Vakgroep Middeleeuwse Geschiedenis, Blandijnberg 2, 9000 Gent, BELGIUM

Michael HESLOP, The Old Vicarage, 1 Church Street, Lower Sunbury, Middlesex TW16 6RQ, ENGLAND, U.K.; michaelheslop@ntlworld.com

Dr Paul HETHERINGTON, 15 Luttrell Avenue, London SW15 6PD, ENGLAND, U.K.; phetherington@ukonline.co.uk

Dr Avital HEYMAN, 12 Hertzel Street, Ness-Ziona 74084, ISRAEL; avital-h@internet-zahav.net

Prof. Rudolf HIESTAND, Brehmstraße 76, 40239 Düsseldorf, GERMANY

Charles A. HILKEN, P.O. Box 4825, St Mary's College, Moraga CA 94575, U.S.A.; chilken@stmarys-ca.edu

James HILL, 2/4 Cassam Place, Valley Heights, New South Wales 2777, AUSTRALIA

Prof. Carole HILLENBRAND, Dept. of Islamic and Middle Eastern Studies, Univ. of Edinburgh, 7–8 Buccleuch Place, Edinburgh EH8 9LW, SCOTLAND, U.K.

Dr George HINTLIAN, Armenian Patriarchate, P.O. Box, Jerusalem 14001, ISRAEL

Dr Martin HOCH, Konrad-Adenauer-Stiftung, Rathausallee 12, 53757 Sankt Augustin, GERMANY; Lobebaer@web.de

Laura HOLLENGREEN; Univ. of Arizona, School of Architecture, 1040 North Olive, P.O. Box 210075, Tucson AZ 85721-0075, U.S.A.; laurah@u.arizona.edu

Dr Catherine HOLMES, University College, Oxford OX1 4BH, ENGLAND, U.K.; catherine.holmes@univ.ox.ac.uk

Andrew P. HOLT, 6340 N.W. 216th Street, Starke FL 32091, U.S.A.; 904-964-5377; apholt@ufl.edu

Jan HOSTEN, Kaaistraat 12, 8900 Ieper, BELGIUM; jan.hosten@leicon.be

Prof. Hubert HOUBEN, Via Marugi 38, 73100 Lecce, ITALY; houben@sesia.unile.it

Prof. Norman J. HOUSLEY, School of Historical Studies, The Univ. of Leicester, Leicester LE1 7RH, ENGLAND, U.K.; hou@le.ac.uk

Lubos HRADSKY, Svermova 23, 97404 Banska Bystrica, SLOVAK REPUBLIC; lubohradsky@centrum.sk

Prof. Lucy-Anne HUNT, Dept. of History of Art and Design, Righton Building, Cavendish Street, Manchester M15 6BK, ENGLAND, U.K.; l.a.hunt@mmu.ac.uk

Zsolt HUNYADI, 27 Szekeres u., 6725 Szeged, HUNGARY; hunyadiz@hist.u-szeged.hu

Prof. Robert B. C. HUYGENS, Witte Singel 28, 2311 BH Leiden, THE NETHERLANDS

Sheldon IBBOTSON, P.O. Box 258, Rimbey, Alberta T0C 2JO, CANADA; bronwen@telusplanet.net

Robert IRWIN, 39 Harleyford Road, London SE11 5AX, ENGLAND, U.K.; robert@robertirwin.demon.co.uk

John E. ISLES, 10575 Darrel Drive, Hanover MI 49241, U.S.A.; jisles@voyager.net

Prof. Peter JACKSON, School of Humanities – History, Univ. of Keele, Keele, Staffs. ST5 5BG, ENGLAND, U.K.; p.jackson@his.keele.ac.uk

Martin JACOBOWITZ, The Towers of Windsor Park, 3005 Chapel Avenue – 11P, Cherry Hill NJ 08002, U.S.A.

Prof. David Jacoby, Dept. of History, The Hebrew Univ., Jerusalem 91905, ISRAEL; tel./fax 972 (Israel)-2-5860380; jacobgab@mscc.huji.ac.il

Dr Kay Peter Jankrift, Institut für Geschichte der Medizin der Robert Bosch Stiftung, Straußwcg 17, 70184 Stuttgart, GERMANY.

Prof. Nikolas Jaspert, Ruhr-Univ. Bochum, Historisches Institut – Lehrstuhl Mittelalter II, Universitätsstraße 150 (GA 4/31), 44801 Bochum, GERMANY; nikolas.jaspert@ruhr-uni-bochum.de

Prof. Carsten Selch Jensen, Dept. of Church History, Univ. of Copenhagen, Købmagergade 46, POB 2164, 1150 Copenhagen K, DENMARK; csj@teol.ku.dk

Janus Møller Jensen, Institute of History and Civilization, Univ. of Southern Denmark, 5230 Odense M, DENMARK; jamj@hist.sdu.dk

Prof. Kurt Villads Jensen, Dept. of History, Odense Univ., Campusvej 55, 5230 Odense M, DENMARK; kvj@hist.sdu.dk

Prof. William Chester Jordan, Dept. of History, Princeton Univ., Princeton NJ 08544, U.S.A.; wchester@princeton.edu

Philippe Josserand, Dépt. histoire, chemin la Censive du Tertre, BP 81227, 44312 Nantes Cedex 3, FRANCE; philippe.josserand@humana.univ-nantes.fr

Dr Andrew Jotischky, Dept. of History, Lancaster Univ., Lancaster LA1 5PE, ENGLAND, U.K.; a.jotischky@lancaster.ac.uk

Dr Margaret A. Jubb, Dept. of French, Taylor Building, Univ. of Aberdeen, Old Aberdeen, AB24 3UB, SCOTLAND, U.K.; m.jubb@abdn.ac.uk

Elena Kaffa, 2B Thiron Kaimakli, 1026 Nicosia, CYPRUS; niryida@yahoo.com

Sini Kangas, Nuotiote 4P14, 02600 Espoo, FINLAND; shkangas@mappi.helsinki.fi

Dr Fotini Karassava-Tsilingiri, Th. Kairi 14, Nea Smyrni, Athens 17122, GREECE; ptsiling@teiath.gr

Tatiana Kartseva, 73–50 Vavilova Street, Ap. 50, Moscow 117335, RUSSIA; tvkartseva@hotmail.com

Anna-Maria Kasdagli, 59 Stockholmis Street, 85100 Rhodes, GREECE

Prof. Benjamin Z. Kedar, Dept. of History, The Hebrew Univ., Jerusalem 91905, ISRAEL; fax (home) 972-8-970-0802, bzkedar@huji.ac.il

Alexander Kempton, Skøyenveien 30, 0375 Oslo, NORWAY; alexansk@student.hf.uio.no

Prof. Nurith Kenaan-Kedar, Dept. of Art History, Tel-Aviv Univ., Tel-Aviv 69978, ISRAEL; kenaank@post.tau.ac.il

Dr Hugh Kennedy, Medieval History Dept., Univ. of St Andrews, St Andrews, Fife KY16 9AL, SCOTLAND, U.K.

Dr Andreas Kiesewetter, Via La Sila 16/8, 00135 Roma, ITALY; leonidas@ilink.it

Sharon Kinoshita, Associate Professor of Literature, Univ. of California Santa Cruz, Santa Cruz CA 95064, U.S.A.; sakinosh@ucsc.edu

Dr Klaus-Peter Kirstein, Frankenstraße 251, 45134 Essen, GERMANY; k.kirstein@r25.de

Dr Michael A. Koehler, Hertogenlaan 14, 1970 Wezembeek-Oppem, BELGIUM; koehler.family@pandora.be

Prof. Athina Kolia-Dermitzaki, Plateia Kalliga 3, Athens 11253, GREECE; akolia@arch.uoa.gr

Wolf Konrad, 6240 Phillips Road, Mundaring, West Australia 6073, AUSTRALIA; wolf17@telstra.easymail.com.au

Dr Conor Kostick, Dept. of Medieval History, Trinity College, Dublin 2, IRELAND; kosticc@tcd.ie

Prof. Jürgen Krüger, Steinbügelstraße 22, 76228 Karlsruhe, GERMANY; krueger-kunstgeschichte@t-online.de

Hans-Ulrich Kühn, Silcherstraße 9/1, 71254 Ditzingen-Schöckingen, GERMANY; hans-ulrich.kuehn@web.de

Sarah Lambert, 35 Cromer Road, London SW17 9JN, ENGLAND, U.K.; slambert@gold.ac.uk

The Rev. William Lane, Robinites, Charterhouse, Godalming Surrey GU7 2DF, ENGLAND, U.K.; wjl@charterhouse.org.uk

Elizabeth Lapina, 2303 Keyes Avenue, Madison WI 53711, U.S.A.; ealapina@yahoo.com

Dr Robert A. Laures, 1434 West Maplewood Court, Milwaukee WI 53221-4348, U.S.A.; dr001@voyager.net

Stephen Lay, c/o Dept. of History, Monash Univ., Melbourne, AUSTRALIA

Armelle Leclercq, 36, rue de l'Orillen, 75011 Paris, FRANCE; armelle73@yahoo.com

Eric Legg, PSC 98 Box 36, Apo AE 09830, U.S.A.; ericlegg@hotmail.com

Robert D. Leonard Jr., 1065 Spruce Street, Winnetka IL 60093, U.S.A.; rlwinnetka@aol.com

Dr Antony Leopold, 62 Grafton Road, Acton, London W3 6PD, ENGLAND, U.K.

Richard A. Leson, 2720 St Paul Street, Apartment 2FF, Baltimore MD 21218, U.S.A.; ral2@jhunix.hef.jhu.edu

Dr Yaacov Lev, P.O. Box 167, Holon 58101, ISRAEL; yglev@actcom.net.il

Dr Christopher G. Libertini, 27 Lombard Lane, Sudbury MA 01776, U.S.A.; clibertini@aol.com

Laura S. Lieber, Dept. of Religion, Middlebury College, Middlebury VT 05753, U.S.A.; llieber@middlebury.edu

Dr Giuseppe Ligato, Viale San Gimignano 18, 20146 Milano, ITALY; giuseppeligato@virgilio.it

Prof. Ralph-Johannes Lilie, Kaiser-Friedrich-Straße 106, 10585 Berlin, GERMANY; liliefavreau@arcor.de

Dr Ora Limor, The Open Univ. of Israel, 16 Klausner Steet, Tel Aviv 61392, ISRAEL; orali@openu.ac.il

Prof. John Lind, Dept. of History, Univ. of Odense, Campusvej 55, 5230 Odense M, DENMARK; john_lind@hist.ou.dk

Dr Simon D. Lloyd, Dept. of History, Univ. of Newcastle-upon-Tyne, Newcastle Upon Tyne NE1 7RU, ENGLAND, U.K.; s.d.lloyd@ncl.ac.uk

Prof. Guy Lobrichon, 4, Impasse Caillod, 84000 Avignon, FRANCE; guy.lobrichon@univ-avignon.fr or guy.lobrichon@numericable.fr

Prof. Peter W. Lock, 9 Straylands Grove, Stockton Lane, York YO31 1EB, ENGLAND, U.K.; p.lock@venysj.ac.uk

Scott Loney, 4153 Wendell Road, West Bloomfield MI 48323, U.S.A.; scottloney@ameritech.net

Prof. Graham A. Loud, School of History, Univ. of Leeds, Leeds LS2 9JT, ENGLAND, U.K.; g.a.loud@leeds.ac.uk

Prof. Michael Lower, Dept. of History, Univ. of Minnesota, 614 Social Sciences Building, 267 19th Avenue South, Minneapolis MN 55455, U.S.A.; mlower@umn.edu

Zoyd R. Luce, 2441 Creekside Court, Hayward CA 94542, U.S.A.; zluce1@earthlink.net

Dr Svetlana Luchitskaya, Institute of General History, Leninski pr. 89-346, Moscow 119313, RUSSIA; svetlana@mega.ru

Andrew John Luff, Flat 3, The Hermitage, St Dunstans Road, Lower Feltham, Middlesex TW13 4HR, ENGLAND, U.K.; andrew@luffa.freeserve.co.uk

Dr Anthony Luttrell, 20 Richmond Place, Bath BA1 5PZ, ENGLAND, U.K.

Christopher MacEvitt, Dumbarton Oaks, 1703 32nd Street NW, Washington DC 20007, U.S.A.

Merav Mack, Lucy Cavendish College, Cambridge CB3 0BU, ENGLAD, U.K.

Dr Alan D. MacQuarrie, 173 Queen Victoria Drive, Glasgow G14 7BP, SCOTLAND, U.K.

Prof. Thomas F. Madden, Dept. of History, Saint Louis Univ., 3800 Lindell Boulevard, P.O. Box 56907, Saint Louis MO 63108, U.S.A.; maddentf@slu.edu

Ben Mahoney, 131 High Street, Doncaster, Victoria 3181, AUSTRALIA; BMahoney@abl.com.au

Dr Christoph T. Maier, Sommergasse 20, 4056 Basel, SWITZERLAND; ctmaier@hist.unizh.ch

Chryssa Maltezou, Istituto Ellenico di Studi Bizantini e Postbizantini di Venezia, Castello 3412, 30122 Venezia, ITALY; hellenic.inst@gold.ghnet.it or info@istitutoellenico.org

Prof. Lucy Der Manuelian, 10 Garfield Road, Belmont MA 02178-3309, U.S.A.; lucy.manuelian@tufts.edu

Prof. Michael Markowski, Dept. of History, Westminster College, 1840 South 1300 East, Salt Lake City UT 84105, U.S.A.

Dr Christopher J. Marshall, 8 Courtyard Way, Cottenham, Cambridge CB4 8SF, ENGLAND, U.K.

Dr Carlos de Ayala Martinez, Historia Medieval, Ciudad Universitaria de Cantoblanco, Ctra. De Colmenar, 28049 Madrid, ESPAÑA

Prof. Laurence W. Marvin, History Dept., Evans School of Humanities, Berry College, Mount Berry GA 30149-5010, U.S.A.; lmarvin@berry.edu

Kathleen Maxwell, 4016 26th Street, San Francisco CA 94131, U.S.A.; kmaxwell@scu.edu

Prof. Hans Eberhard Mayer, Historisches Seminar der Universität Kiel, 24098 Kiel, GERMANY

Robert Maynard, The Old Dairy, 95 Church Road, Bishopsworth Bristol BS13 8JU, ENGLAND, U.K.; maynard966@btinternet.com

Andreas Mazarakis, Rizou 3, Athens 10434, GREECE; amazarakis@tee.gr

Prof. Rasa Mazeika, 48A Arcadian Circle, Toronto, Ontario M8W 4W2, CANADA

Brian C. Mazur, 718 W. Webster, Royal Oak MI 48073, U.S.A.; bcmazur1066@yahoo.com

Roben McDonald Marlow, 36 Burton Old Road West, Lichfield, Staffordshire WS13 6EN, ENGLAND, U.K.; roben@mac.com

Prof. Sophia MENACHE, Dept. of History, Univ. of Haifa, Haifa 31905, ISRAEL; menache@ research.haifa.ac.il

Marco MESCHINI, Via Fé 15, 21100 Varese, ITALY; marco.meschini@libero.it; marco.meschini@unicatt.it

Margaret MESERVE, Assistant Professor of History, Univ. of Notre Dame, 219 O'Shaughnessy Hall, Notre Dame IN 46556, U.S.A.; margaret.h.meserve.1@nd.edu

Prof. D. Michael METCALF, Ashmolean Museum, Oxford OX1 2PH, ENGLAND, U.K.

Françoise MICHEAU, 8bis, rue du Buisson Saint-Louis, 75011 Paris, FRANCE; fmicheau@ univ-paris1.fr

Prof. Klaus MILITZER, Winckelmannstraße 32, 50825 Köln, GERMANY; klaus.militzer@ uni-koeln.de

Greg MILLER, 105 Valley Street, Burlington Iowa 52601 453, U.S.A.; greg.miller@lpl.com

Jane MILLIKEN, 26 Emmetts Farm Road, Rossmore NSW 2557, AUSTRALIA; janem@ icpmr.wsahs.nsw.gov.au

Paul Richard MILLIMAN, 618 West Willow Street, Apartment 3, Chicago IL 60614, U.S.A.; prm7@cornell.edu

Peter John MILLS, 3 Huxley Road, Leyton, London E10 5QT, ENGLAND, U.K.; petermills@lireone.net

Prof. Laura MINERVINI, Dipartimento di Filologia Moderna, Università di Napoli Federico II, Via Porta Di Massa 1, 80133 Napoli, ITALY; lrminer@unina.it

Dr Piers D. MITCHELL, 84 Huntingdon Road, East Finchley, London N2 9DU, ENGLAND, U.K.; p.mitchell@clara.co.uk

PD Dr Hannes MÖHRING, Wilhelm-Bode-Straße 11, 38104 Braunschweig, GERMANY; hannes_moehring@web.de

Prof. Johannes A. MOL, Grote Dijlakker 29, 8701 KW Bolsward, THE NETHERLANDS; hmol@fa.knaw.nl

Dr Kristian MOLIN, 38 Vessey Terrace, Newcastle-under-Lyme Staffordshire ST5 1LS, ENGLAND, U.K.; kristian.molin@nottingham.ac.uk

Lisa K. MONROE, 7417 Park Terrace Drive, Alexandria VA 22307, U.S.A.; nlmonroe@ earthlink.net

Dauvergne C. MORGAN, 235 Tooronga Road, Glen Iris, Melbourne, Victoria 3142, AUSTRALIA

Dr David O. MORGAN, 302 Orchard Drive, Madison WI 53705, U.S.A.; domorgan@ facstaff.wisc.edu

Jonathan C. MORGAN, 19 Elia Street, Islington, London N1 8DE, ENGLAND, U.K.; jonathan.morgan@whb.co.uk

J. Diana MORGAN, 64 Victoria Avenue, Swanage, Dorset BH19 1AR, ENGLAND, U.K.

Hiroki MORITAKE, Kami-Ono 371, Hiyoshi-mura, Kitauwa-gun, Ehime-ken 798-1503, JAPAN; jerus@hiroshima-u.ac.jp

The Rev. Prof. Colin MORRIS, 12 Bassett Crescent East, Southampton SO16 7PB, ENGLAND, U.K.; cm5@soton.ac.uk

Dr Rosemary MORRIS, Dept. of History, Univ. of York, York YO10 5DD, ENGLAND, U.K.; rm22@york.ac.uk

Cécile MORRISSON, 36, chemin Desvallières, 92410 Ville d'Avray, FRANCE

Nicholas Morton, 139 Bellingdon Road, Chesham Buckinghamshire HP5 2NN, ENGLAND, U.K.; mortonnic@hotmail.com

Suleiman Ali Mourad, Smith College, Wright Hall 114, Northampton MA 01063, U.S.A.; smourad@smith.edu

Roger D. Mulhollen, Center for Study of Ancient Religious History, 13217 W. Serenade Circle, Sun City West AZ 85375-1707, U.S.A.; audrog@aol.com

Prof. M. E. Mullett, Institute of Byzantine Studies, Queen's Univ. of Belfast, Belfast BT7 1NN, NORTHERN IRELAND, U.K.; n.mullett@qub.ac.uk

Dr Alan V. Murray, Institute for Medieval Studies, Univ. of Leeds, Parkinson 103, Leeds LS2 9JT, ENGLAND, U.K.; a.v.murray@leeds.ac.uk

Stephen R. A. Murray, Apartment 351, 176 The Esplanade, Toronto, Ontario M5A 4H2, CANADA; sramurray@hotmail.com

Claude Mutafian, 216, rue Saint-Jacques, 75005 Paris, FRANCE; claude.mutafian@wanadoo.fr

Elizabeth Mylod, 529 Meanwood Road, Leeds LS6 4AW, ENGLAND, U.K.; mesejm@leeds.ac.uk

James Naus, Dept. of History, Saint Louis Univ., 3800 Lindell Boulevard, Saint Louis MO 63108, U.S.A.; nausjl@slu.edu

Alan Neill, 13 Chesham Crescent, Belfast BT6 8GW, NORTHERN IRELAND, U.K.; neilla@rescueteam.com

Prof. Robert S. Nelson, Dept. of Art, Univ. of Chicago, 5540 South Greenwood Avenue, Chicago IL 60637, U.S.A.; olin@midway.uchicago

Michael de Nève, Laubacher Straße 9 SFL, 14197 Berlin, GERMANY or Freie Universität Berlin, FB Geschichts- und Kulturwissenschaften, Koserstraße 20, 14195 Berlin, GERMANY; michaeldeneve@web.de

Dr Helen J. Nicholson, School of History and Archaeology, Cardiff Univ., Humanities Building, Colum Drive, Cardiff CF10 3EU, WALES, U.K.; nicholsonhj@cardiff.ac.uk

Angel Nicolaou-Konnari, 10 Philiou Zannetou Street, 3021 Limassol, CYPRUS; an.konnaris@cytanet.com.cy

Dr David Nicolle, 67 Maplewell Road, Woodhouse Eaves, Leicestershire LE12 8RG, ENGLAND, U.K.; david.c.nicolle@btinternet.com

J. Mark Nicovich, 119 Short Bay Street, Hattiesburg MS 39401, U.S.A.; mark.nicovich@gmail.com

Marie-Adélaïde Nielen, 254, avenue Daumesnil, 75012 Paris, FRANCE; marie-adelaide.nielen@culture.gouv.fr

Prof. Torben Kjersgaard Nielsen, Institute for History, International and Social Studies, Aalborg Univ., Fibigerstraede 5, 9220 Aalborg, DENMARK; tkn@ihis.aau.dk

Yoav Nitzen, 4 H'Adereth Street, Jerusalem 92343, ISRAEL; raem@bezeqint.net

Prof. Peter S. Noble, Dept. of French Studies, Univ. of Reading, Whiteknights, Reading RG6 6AA, ENGLAND, U.K.; lfsnoble@reading.ac.uk

Dr Randall L. Norstrem, 28822 Pacific Highway S., Federal Way WA 98003, U.S.A.; templariidvm@yahoo.com

Shmuel Nussbaum, P.O. Box 2201, Petah-Tiqva 49120, ISRAEL; nshmuel7@netvision.net.il

Dr Gregory O'Malley, 111 Ibstock Road, Ellistown, Leicestershire LE67 1EE, ENGLAND, U.K.; OMalley_Greg_J@cat.com

Prof. Mahmoud Said Omran, History Dept., Faculty of Arts, Univ. of Alexandria, Alexandria, EGYPT; msomran@dataxprs.com.eg

Col. Erhard (Erik) Opsahl, 5303 Dennis Drive, McFarland WI 53558, U.S.A.; epopsahlw@aol.com

Rhiain O'Sullivan, Second Floor Flat, 116-117 Saffron Hill, London EC1N 8QS, ENGLAND, U.K.; rhiainaroundtheworld@hotmail.com

Catherine Otten, 9, rue de Londres, 67000 Strasbourg, FRANCE; otten@umb.u-strasbg.fr.

Robert Ousterhout, School of Architecture, Univ. of Illinois, 611 Taft Drive, Champaign IL 61820-6921, U.S.A.; rgouster@unic.edu

Barbara Packard, 35 Marnham Crecent, Greenford Middlesex UB6 9SW, ENGLAND, U.K.; bcpackard@yahoo.co.uk

Dr Johannes Pahlitzsch, Parallelstraße 12, 12209 Berlin, GERMANY; pahlitz@zedat.fu-berlin.de

Tivadar Palágyi, Tapolcsanyi u. 8, 1022 Budapest, HUNGARY; tivadarp@hotmail.com

Dr Aphrodite Papayianni, 40 Inverness Terrace, London W2 3JB, ENGLAND, U.K.; aphroditepapayianni@hotmail.com

Kenneth S. Parker, 906 South Washington Street, Apartment 107, Alexandria VA 22315, U.S.A.; kscottparker@gmail.com

Dr Peter D. Partner, Murhill Farmhouse, Murhill, Limpley Stoke, Bath BA2 7FH, ENGLAND, U.K.; pdp4@aol.com

Prof. Jacques Paviot, 21, rue de Vouillé, 75015 Paris, FRANCE; paviot.jacques@wanadoo.fr or paviot@univ-paris12.fr

Michael J. Peixoto, 168 East 82nd Street, Apartment 5B, New York NY 10028-2214, U.S.A.

Peter Shlomo Peleg, 2 Mordhai Street, Kiryat Tivon 36023, ISRAEL; fax 972 4 9931 122; ppeleg@netvision.net.il

Photeine V. Perra, Examilia Corinth 20100, GREECE; fperra@hol.gr

David M. Parry, History Dept., Manchester College, 1600 Gravel Avenue, Minneapolis MN 55105, U.S.A.; perr0130@umn.edu

Nicholas J. Perry, P.O. Box 389, La Mesa NM 88044, U.S.A.; nicholasperry@earthlink.net

James Petre, The Old Barn, 8A Church Road, Stevington, Bedfordshire MK43 7QB, ENGLAND, U.K.; jamesp@cipr.co.uk

Theodore D. Petro, New England College, 24 Bridge Street, P.O. Box 74, Henniker NH 03242, U.S.A.; tpetro@nec.edu

Dr Christopher Matthew Phillips, Social Science Dept., Concordia Univ., 800 N. Columbia Avenue, Seward NE 68434-1556, U.S.A.; Matthew.Phillips@cune.edu

Dr Jonathan P. Phillips, Dept. of History, Royal Holloway Univ. of London, Egham, Surrey TW20 0EX, ENGLAND, U.K.; j.p.phillips@rhul.ac.uk

Dr Simon D. Phillips, 21 Perikleous Street, Apt. 101, Strovolos, 2020 Nicosia, CYPRUS; Simon.Phillips@winchester.ac.uk or simphlld@aim.com

Dr Mathias Piana, Benzstraße 9, 86420 Diedorf, GERMANY; mathias.piana@phil.uni-augsburg.de

Clive PORRO, 36 Castle Road, Whitstable, Kent CT5 2DY, ENGLAND, U.K.; clive.porro@btinternet.com

Dr John PORTEOUS, 52 Elgin Crescent, London W11, ENGLAND, U.K.

Jon PORTER, Change and Tradition Program, Butler Univ., 4600 Sunset Avenue, Indianapolis IN 46208, U.S.A.; jporter1@butler.edu

Prof. James M. POWELL, 5100 Highbridge Street, Apartment 18D, Fayetteville NY 13066, U.S.A.; mpowell@dreamscape.com

Jon POWELL, 711 South-East 11th Street, Apartment 43, Portland OR 97214, U.S.A.; jonp@pdx.edu

Dr Karen PRATT, French Dept., King's College London, Strand, London WC2R 2LS, ENGLAND, U.K.

Jennifer Ann PRICE, Dept. of History, Univ. of Washington, P.O. Box 353560, Seattle WA 98195-3560, U.S.A.; japrice@u.washington.edu

Prof. R. Denys PRINGLE, School of History and Archaeology, Cardiff Univ., P.O. Box 909, Cardiff CF10 3XU, WALES, U.K.; pringlerd@cardiff.ac.uk

Dragan PROKIC, M.A., Rubensallee 47, 55127 Mainz, GERMANY; dp.symbulos@t-online.de

Prof. John H. PRYOR, Centre for Medieval Studies, Univ. of Sydney, John Wolley Building A20, Sydney, New South Wales 2006, AUSTRALIA; john.pryor@arts.usyd.edu.au

William J. PURKIS, 46 Fennec Close, Cherry Hinton, Cambridge CB1 9GG, ENGLAND, U.K.; william_purkis@hotmail.com

Ian D. QUELCH, 27 Barn Meadow Lane, Great Bookham, Surrey KT23 3EZ, ENGLAND, U.K.; Ian.Quelch@ntlworld.com

Prof. Pierre RACINE, 8, rue Traversière, 67201 Eckbolsheim, FRANCE; racine.p@evc.net

Yevgeniy / Eugene RASSKAZOV, Worth Avenue Station, P.O. Box 3497, Palm Beach FL 33480-3497, U.S.A.; medievaleurope@apexmail.com

Prof. Geoffrey W. RICE, History Dept., Univ. of Canterbury, Private Bag 4800, Christchurch, NEW ZEALAND; geoff.rice@canterbury.ac.nz

Prof. Jean RICHARD, 12, rue Pelletier de Chambure, 21000 Dijon, FRANCE

Maurice RILEY Esq., 35 Mount Way, Waverton, Chester, Cheshire CH3 7QF, ENGLAND, U.K.; rileymaurice@yahoo.com

Prof. Jonathan S. C. RILEY-SMITH, The Downs, Croxton, St Neots, Cambridgeshire PE19 4SX, ENGLAND, U.K.; jsr22@cam.ac.uk or jonathan.rileysmith@btinternet.com

Rebecca RIST, 50 Roseford Road, Cambridge CB4 2HD, ENGLAND, U.K.; raw2@corn.ac.uk

The Rev. Leonard Stanley RIVETT, 47 Ryecroft Avenue, Woodthorpe, York YO24 2SD, ENGLAND, U.K.

Prof. Louise Buenger ROBBERT, 709 South Skinker Boulevard Apartment 701, St Louis MO 63105, U.S.A.; lrobbert@mindspring.com

Jason T. ROCHE, Seaview, Kings Highway, Largoward, Fife KY9 1HX, SCOTLAND, U.K.; jtr@st-andrews.ac.uk

José Manuel RODRÍGUEZ-GARCÍA, Av. Conde de Aranda 1, 3° E, 28200 San Lorenzo del Escorial (Madrid), ESPAÑA; anaevjosem@hotmail.com

Prof. Israel ROLL, Institut of Archaeology, Tel-Aviv Univ., Ramat Aviv, Tel-Aviv 69978, ISRAEL; rolli@post.tau.ac.il

Prof. Myriam ROSEN-AYALON, Institute of Asian and African Studies, The Hebrew Univ., Jerusalem 91905, ISRAEL

Dvora ROSHAL, P.O. Box 3558, Beer-Sheva 84135, ISRAEL; devorahr@afikim.co.il

Linda ROSS, Dept. of History, Royal Holloway Univ. of London, Egham, Surrey TW20 0EX, ENGLAND, U.K.; linde@lross22.freeserve.co.uk

Prof. John ROSSER, Dept. of History, Boston College, Chestnut Hill MA 02467, U.S.A.; rosserj@bc.edu

Prof. Jay RUBENSTEIN, Dept. of History, Univ. of Tennessee, 6th Floor, Dunford Hall, Knoxville TN 37996-4065, U.S.A.; jrubens1@utk.edu

James RUEL, Ground Floor Flat, 63 Redland Road, Redland, Bristol B56 6AQ, England, U.K.; james-ruel@hotmail.com

Prof. Frederick H. RUSSELL, Dept. of History, Conklin Hall, Rutgers Univ., Newark NJ 07102, U.S.A.; frussell@andromeda.rutgers.edu

Prof. James D. RYAN, 100 West 94th Street, Apartment 26M, New York NY 10025, U.S.A.; james.d.ryan@verizon.net

Vincent RYAN, Dept. of History, Saint Louis Univ., 3800 Lindell Boulevard, Saint Louis MO 63108, U.S.A.; ryanvt@slu.edu

Dr Andrew J. SARGENT, 33 Coborn Street, Bow, London E3 2AB, ENGLAND, U.K.; andrewsargent@dfes.gsi.gov.uk

Prof. Jürgen SARNOWSKY, Historisches Seminar, Universität Hamburg, Von-Melle-Park 6, 20146 Hamburg, GERMANY; juergen.sarnowsky@uni-hamburg.de

Christopher J. SAUNDERS OBE, Watery Hey, Springvale Road, Hayfield, High Peak SK22 2LD, ENGLAND, U.K.; christopher.saunders@savoyim.com

Prof. Alexios G. C. SAVVIDES, Aegean Univ., Dept. of Mediterranean Studies, Rhodes, GREECE; or: 7 Tralleon Street, Nea Smyrne, Athens 17121, GREECE; savvides@rhodes.aegean.gr

Christopher SCHABEL, Dept. of History and Archaeology, Univ. of Cyprus, P.O. Box 20537, 1678 Nicosia, CYPRUS; schabel@ucy.ac.cy

Dr Jochen SCHENK, Emmanuel College, Cambridge CB2 3AP, ENGLAND, U.K.; or Spardorferstraße 7, 91054 Erlangen, GERMANY; jg.schenk@gmail.com

Prof. Paul Gerhard SCHMIDT, Seminar für lateinische Philologie des Mittelalters, Albert-Ludwigs-Universität Freiburg, Werderring 8, 79085 Freiburg i. Br., GERMANY

Dr James G. SCHRYVER, Univ. of Minnesota Morris, HUM 104, 600 East 4th Street, Morris MN 56267, U.S.A.; schryver@morris.umn.edu

William SCHULL, 2707 S. Rutherford Boulevard, Apartment 1004A, Murfreesboro TN 37130, U.S.A.; wschull@gmail.com

Dr Beate SCHUSTER, 19, rue Vauban, 67000 Strasbourg, FRANCE; beaschu@compuserve.com

Prof. Rainer C. SCHWINGES, Historisches Institut der Universität Bern, Unitobler – Länggass-Straße 49, 3000 Bern 9, SWITZERLAND

Per SEESKO, Heden 18, 2., lejl. 10, 5000 Odense C, DENMARK; seesko83@yahoo.com

Iris SHAGRIR, Dept. of History, The Open Univ. of Israel, P.O. Box 808, Raanana 43107, ISRAEL; irissh@openu.ac.il

Prof. Maya SHATZMILLER, Dept. of History, The Univ. of Western Ontario, London, Ontario N6A 5C2, CANADA

Dr Jonathan SHEPARD, 14 Hartley Court, Woodstock Road, Oxford OX2 7PF, ENGLAND, U.K.; nshepard@easynet.co.uk

Vardit SHOTTEN-HALLEL, 12 Dan Street, P.O. Box 1404, Ramat Hasharon 47100, ISRAEL; shotten-hallel@012.net.il

William SHULL, 2707 South Rutherford Boulevard, Apartment 1004A, Murfreesboro TN 37130, U.S.A.; wshull@gmail.com

Dr Elizabeth J. SIBERRY, 28 The Mall, Surbiton, Surrey KT6 4E9, ENGLAND, U.K.; sibersealyham@totalise.couk

Alicia SIMPSON, 8 Karaiskaki Street, Athens 18345, GREECE

Kaare Seeberg SIDSELRUD, Granebakken 9, 1284 Oslo, NORWAY; heraldikk@gmail.com

Raitis SIMSONS, A/k 209, Riga LV 1082, LATVIA; raitiss@btv.lv

Dr Gordon Andreas SINGER, P.O. Box 235, Greenbelt MD 20768-0235, U.S.A.; andysinger@att.net

Dr Corliss K. SLACK, Dept. of History, Apartment 1103, Whitworth College, Spokane WA 99251, U.S.A.; cslack@whitworth.edu

Rima E. SMINE, 25541 Altamont Road, Los Altos Hills CA 94022, U.S.A.

Sheila R. SMITH, 111 Coleshill Road Chapelend, Nuneaton Warwickshire CV10 0PG, ENGLAND, U.K.

Matt SNYDER, 57 Egham Hill, Egham, Surrey TW20 0ER, ENGLAND, U.K.; calidus@gmail.com or m.snyder@rhul.ac.uk

Simon SONNAK, P.O. Box 1206, Windsor, Victoria 3181, AUSTRALIA; heliade@bigpond.com.au

Arnold SPAER, 4 Alharizi Street, Jerusalem 91272, ISRAEL; hui@spaersitton.co.il

Brent SPENCER, 3 9701 89 Street, Fort Saskatchewan, Alberta T8L IJ3, CANADA; ktcrusader@yahoo.com

Dr Alan M. STAHL, 11 Fairview Place, Ossining NY 10562, U.S.A.; amstahl@optonline.net

Prof. Harvey STAHL, Dept. of the History of Art, Univ. of California, Berkeley CA 94720, U.S.A.; hstahl@socrates.berkeley.edu

Eliezer and J. Edna STERN, Israel Antiquities Authority, P.O. Box 1094, Acre 24110, ISRAEL; fax 04-9911682 or 9918074

Alan D. STEVENS, Campbell College, Dept. of History, Belmont Road, Belfast BT4 2ND, NORTHERN IRELAND, U.K.; alan.d.stevens@ntlworld.com

Paula R. STILES, 552 Barstow Road, Shelburne VT 05482, U.S.A.; thesnowleopard@hotmail.com

Dr Myra STRUCKMEYER, 171 North Hamilton Road, Chapel Hill NC 27517, U.S.A.; struckme@alumni.unc.edu

Jace STUCKEY, Louisiana Texh Univ., History Dept., P.O. Box 8548, Ruston LA 71272, U.S.A.; jace@latech.edu or jastuck24@msn.co

Shaul TAMIRI, Hachail-Halmoni, Apartment 8, Rishon le Zion 75255, ISRAEL

Olivier TERLINDEN, Avenue des Ramiers 8, 1950 Kraaïnem, BELGIUM; olivierterlinden@ yahoo.com

Miriam Rita TESSERA, via Moncalvo 16, 20146 Milano, ITALY; monachus_it@yahoo.it

Kenneth J. THOMSON, Edessa, 8 Salterfell Road, Scale Hall, Lancaster LA1 2PX, ENGLAND, U.K.; kenneth@thomsonk91.fsnet.co.uk

Prof. Peter THORAU, Historisches Institut, Univ. des Saarlandes, for letters Postfach 15 11 50, 66041 Saarbrücken, for packages Im Stadtwald, 66123 Saarbrücken, GERMANY; p.thorau@mx.uni-saarland.de

Dr. Steve TIBBLE, Copsewood, Deadhearn Lane, Chalfont St Giles, Buckinghamshire HP8 4HG, ENGLAND, U.K.; steve.tibble@btinternet.com

Prof. Hirofumi TOKO, 605-3 Kogasaka, Machida, Tokyo 194-0014, JAPAN; ttokou@ toyonet.toyo.ac.jp

Prof. John Victor TOLAN, Département d'Histoire, Université de Nantes, B.P. 81227, 44312 Nantes, FRANCE, or: 2, rue de la Chevalerie, 44300 Nantes, FRANCE; john.tolan@ univ-nantes.fr or John.Tolan.2@numericable.fr

Prof. François-Olivier TOUATI, La Croix Saint-Jérôme, 11, allée Emile Bouchut, 77123 Noisy-sur-Ecole, FRANCE; FrancoisTouati@aol.com

Catherine B. TURNER, Flat 3, 1055 Christchurch Road, Boscombe East, Bournemouth BH7 6BE, ENGLAND, U.K.

Dr. Christopher J. TYERMAN, Hertford College, Oxford, Catte Street, Oxford OX1 3BW, ENGLAND, U.K.; christopher.tyerman@hertford.ox.ac.uk

Dr Judith M. UPTON-WARD, 6 Haywood Court, Reading RG1 3QF, ENGLAND, U.K.; juptonward@btopenworld.com

Prof. William L. URBAN, 1062 East 2nd Avenue, Monmouth IL 61462, U.S.A.; urban@ monm.edu

Theresa M. VANN, Hill Monastic Manuscript Library, St John's Univ., Collegeville MN 56321, U.S.A.; tvann@csbsju.edu

Fiona Weir WALMSLEY, 41 Broomley Street, Kangaroo Point, Queensland 4169, AUSTRALIA; f.walmsley@optusnet.com.au

Dr Marie-Louise von WARTBURG MAIER, Paphosprojekt der Universität Zürich, Rämistraße 71, 8006 Zürich, SWITZERLAND; paphos@hist.unizh.ch

Benjamin WEBER, 24, rue du Tour, 31000 Toulouse, FRANCE; benji.tigrou@gmail.com

Dr Daniel WEISS, History of Art Dept., Johns Hopkins Univ., 3400 North Charles Street, Baltimore MD 21218, U.S.A.; dweiss@jho.edu

Dr Mark WHITTOW, St Peter's College, Oxford OX1 2DL, ENGLAND, U.K.; mark.whittow@st-peters.oxford.ac.uk

Timothy WILKES, A. H. Baldwin & Sons Ltd., 11 Adelphi Terrace, London WC2N 6BJ, ENGLAND, U.K.; timwilkes@baldwin.sh

The Rev. Dr John D. WILKINSON, 7 Tenniel Close, London W2 3LE, ENGLAND, U.K.

Dr Ann WILLIAMS, 40 Greenwich South Street, London SE10 8UN, ENGLAND, U.K.; ann.williams@talk21.com

Prof. Steven James WILLIAMS, Dept. of History, New Mexico Highlands Univ., P.O. Box 9000, Las Vegas NM 87701, U.S.A.; stevenjameswilliams@yahoo.com

Gayle A. WILSON, P.O. Box 712, Diamond Springs CA 95619, U.S.A.; gayle@inforum.net

Peter van WINDEKENS, Kleine Ganzendries 38, 3212 Pellenberg, BELGIUM; Peter.VanWindekens@vlm.be

Prof. Johanna Maria van WINTER, Brigittenstraat 20, 3512 KM Utrecht, THE NETHERLANDS; j.m.vanwinter@let.uu.nl

Prof. Kenneth B. WOLF, Dept. of History, Pomona College, Pearsons Hall, 551 North College Avenue, Claremont CA 91711-6337, U.S.A.

Dr Noah WOLFSON, 13 Avuqa Street, Tel-Aviv 69086, ISRAEL; noah@meteo-tech.co.il

Peter WOODHEAD, Tarry Cottage, Church Lane, Daglingworth near Cirencester, Gloucestershire GL7 7AG, ENGLAND, U.K.

Dr John WREGLESWORTH, Fountain Cottage, 98 West Town Road, Backwell, North Somerset BS48 3BE, ENGLAND, U.K.; john@wreg.freeserve.co.uk

Prof. Shunji YATSUZUKA, 10-22 Matsumoto 2 chome, Otsu-shi, Shiga 520, JAPAN

William G. ZAJAC, 9 Station Terrace, Pen-y-rheal, Caerphilly CF83 2RH, WALES, U.K.

Prof. Ossama Zaki ZEID, 189 Abd al-Salam Aref Tharwat, Alexandria, EGYPT; ossama_zeid@hotmail.com

Joseph ZELNIK, 25 Wingate Street, Raanana 43587, ISRAEL; jzelnik@017.net.il

Prof. Monique ZERNER, Villa Stella, Chemin des Pins, 06000 Nice, FRANCE; zernerm@unice.fr

Institutions subscribing to the SSCLE

Brepols Publishers, Begijnhof 67, 2300 Turnhout, BELGIUM

Bibliothécaire Guy Cobolet, Le Bibliothécaire, École Française d'Athènes, 6, Didotou 10680 Athènes, GREECE

Centre de Recherches d'histoire et civilisation de Byzance et du Proche-Orient Chétien, Université de Paris 1, 17, rue de la Sorbonne, 75231 Paris Cedex, FRANCE

Centre for Byzantine, Ottoman and Modern Greek Studies, Univ. of Birmingham, Edgbaston, Birmingham B15 2TT, ENGLAND, U.K.

Couvent des Dominicains, École Biblique et Archéologique Français, 6 Nablus Road, Jerusalem 91190, ISRAEL

Deutsches Historisches Institut in Rom, Via Aurelia Antica 391, 00165 Roma, ITALY

Deutschordenszentralarchiv (DOZA), Singerstraße 7, 1010 Wien, AUSTRIA

Dumbarton Oaks Research Library, 1703 32nd Street North West, Washington D.C. 20007, U.S.A.

Europäisches Burgeninstitut, Schlossstraße 5, 56338 Braubach, GERMANY; ebi@deutsche-burgen.org

Germanisches Nationalmuseum, Bibliothek, Kornmarkt 1, 90402 Nürnberg, GERMANY

History Department, Campbell College, Belfast BT4 2 ND, NORTHERN IRELAND, U.K.

The Jewish National and University Library, P.O. Box 34165, Jerusalem 91341, ISRAEL

The Library, The Priory of Scotland of the Most Venerable Order of St John, 21 St John Street, Edinburgh EH8 8DG, SCOTLAND, U.K.

The Stephen Chan Library, Institute of Fine Arts, New York Univ., 1 East 78th Street, New York NY 10021, U.S.A.

Metropolitan Museum of Art, Thomas J. Watson Library, Serials Dept., 5th Avenue at 82nd Street, New York NY 10028, U.S.A.

Museum and Library of the Order of St John, St John's Gate, Clerkenwell, London EC1M 4DA, ENGLAND, U.K.

Order of the Christian Knights of the Rose, Brent R. Spencer, Grand Master, P.O. Box 3423, Fort Saskatchewan, Alberta T8L 2T4, CANADA

Order of the Temple of Jerusalem and the Industrial Temple, Grand Priory of Knights Templar in England and Wales, Treasurer, 14 Goldthorne Avenue, Sheldon, Birmingham B26 3JY, ENGLAND, U.K.

Serials Department, 11717 Young Research Library, Univ. of California, Box 951575, Los Angeles CA 90095-1575, U.S.A.

Sourasky Library, Tel-Aviv Univ., Periodical Dept., P.O. Box 39038, Tel-Aviv, ISRAEL

Teutonic Order Bailiwick of Utrecht, Dr John J. Quarles van Ufford, Secretary of the Bailliwick, Springweg 25, 3511 VJ Utrecht, THE NETHERLANDS

Türk Tarih Kurumu [Turkish Historical Society], Kizilay Sokak No. 1, Sihhiye 06100 Ankara, TURKEY

The Warburg Institute, Univ. of London, Woburn Square, London WC1H 0AB, ENGLAND, U.K. [John Perkins, Deputy Librarian, jperkins@a1.sas.ac.uk]

Eberhard-Karls-Universität Tübingen, Orientalisches Seminar, Münzgasse 30, 72072 Tübingen, GERMANY

University of California Los Angeles Serials Dept. / YRL, 11717 Young Research Library, Box 951575, Los Angeles CA 90095-1575, U.S.A.

University of London Library, Periodicals Section, Senate House, Malet Street, London WC1E 7HU, ENGLAND, U.K.

University of North Carolina, Davis Library CB 3938, Periodicals and Serials Dept., Chapel Hill NC 27514-8890, U.S.A.

Universitätsbibliothek Tübingen, Wilhelmstraße 32, Postfach 26 20, 72016 Tübingen, GERMANY

University of Reading, Graduate Centre for Medieval Studies, Whiteknights, P.O. Box 218, Reading, Berks. RG6 6AA, ENGLAND, U.K.

University of Washington, Libraries, Serials Division, P.O. Box 352900, Seattle WA 98195, U.S.A.

University of Western Ontario Library, Acquisitions Dept., Room M1, D. B. Weldon Library, London, Ontario N6A 3K7, CANADA

W. F. Albright Institute of Archaeological Research, 26 Salah ed-Din Street, P.O. Box 19096, Jerusalem 91190, ISRAEL

Guidelines for the Submission of Papers

The editors ask contributors to adhere to the following guidelines. Failure to do so will result in the article being returned to the author for amendment, or may result in its having to be excluded from the volume.

1. Submissions. Submissions should be made on 3.5 inch, high-density IBM compatible disks or on CDs. Please send these to one of the editors. Remember to include your name and address on your paper.

2. Length. Normally, the maximum length of articles should not exceed 6,000 words, not including notes. The editors reserve the right to edit papers that exceed these limits.

3. Notes. Normally, notes should be REFERENCE ONLY and placed at the end of the paper. Number continuously.

4. Style sheet. Please use the most recent *Speculum* style sheet (currently *Speculum* 75 (2000), 547–52). This sets out the format to be used for notes. Please note that this is not necessarily the same format as has been used by other edited volumes on the crusades and/or the Military Orders. Failure to follow the *Speculum* format will result in accepted articles being returned to the author for amendment. In the main body of the paper you may adhere to either British or American spelling, but it must be consistent throughout the article.

5. Language. Papers will be published in English, French, German, Italian and Spanish.

6. Abbreviations. Please use the abbreviation list on pp. ix–xi of this journal.

7. Diagrams and Maps should be referred to as figures and photographs as plates. Please keep illustrations to the essential minimum, since it will be possible to include only a limited number. All illustrations must be supplied by the contributor in camera-ready copy, and free from all copyright restrictions.

8. Italics. Words to be printed as italics should be italicised if possible. Failing this they should be underlined.

9. Capitals. Please take every care to ensure consistency in your use of capitals and lower case letters. Use initial capitals to distinguish the general from the specific (for example, "the count of Flanders" but "Count Philip of Flanders").

Editors

Professor Benjamin Z. Kedar
Department of History
The Hebrew University
Jerusalem 91905, Israel

Professor Jonathan S. C. Riley-Smith
Emmanuel College
Cambridge CB2 3AP
U.K.

SOCIETY FOR THE STUDY OF THE CRUSADES AND THE LATIN EAST
MEMBERSHIP INFORMATION

The primary function of the Society for the Study of the Crusades and the Latin East is to enable members to learn about current work being done in the field of crusading history, and to contact members who share research interests through the information in the Society's Bulletin. There are currently 420 members of the SSCLE from 30 countries. The Society also organizes a major international conference every four years, as well as sections on crusading history at other conferences where appropriate.

The committee of the SSCLE consists of:
Prof. Michel Balard, *President*
Prof. Jean Richard, Prof. Jonathan Riley-Smith and Prof. Benjamin Z. Kedar, *Honorary Vice-presidents*
Prof. Sophia Menache and Luis Garcìa-Guijarro Ramos, *Secretary and Assistant Secretary*
Prof. James D. Ryan, *Treasurer*
Prof. Karl Borchardt, *Bulletin Editor*
Dr Zsolt Hunyadi, *Website*.

Current subscription fees are as follows:
• Membership and Bulletin of the Society: Single £10, $15 or €15;
• Student £6, $9 or €9;
• Joint membership £15, $23 or €23;
• Membership and the journal *Crusades*, including the Bulletin: £22, $41 or €33.